Lysenko and the Tragedy of Soviet Science

Lysenko and the Tragedy of Soviet Science

Valery N. Soyfer

Translated from the Russian by
Leo Gruliow and Rebecca Gruliow

Rutgers University Press
New Brunswick, New Jersey

Library of Congress Cataloging-in-Publication Data

Soyfer, Valery.
    Lysenko and the tragedy of Soviet science / Valery N. Soyfer ;
translated from the Russian by Leo Gruliow and Rebecca Gruliow.
        p.   cm.
    Includes bibliographical references and index.
    ISBN 0-8135-2087-8
    1. Science and state—Russia (Federation)—History. 2. Political
purge—Russia (Federation)—(History. 3. Genetics—Russia
(Federation)—History. 4. Lysenko, Trofim Denisovich, 1898–1976.
5. Geneticists—Russia (Federation) I. Title.
Q127.R9S65   1994
575.1'0947—dc20   93-39566
                                                              CIP

British Cataloging-in-Publication information available

To the blessed memory of my father,
Nikolai Ilyich Soyfer, I dedicate this book

Contents

A Note on Transliteration

The transliteration system used here is essentially the same as that employed by the *Current Digest of the Soviet Press*:

а	a		к	k		х	kh
б	b		л	l		ц	ts
в	v		м	m		ч	ch
г	g		н	n		ш	sh
д	d		о	o		щ	shch
е	e[1]		п	p		ъ	(omit)[4]
ё	yo[2]		р	r		ы	y
ж	zh		с	s		ь	(omit)[4]
з	z		т	t		э	e
и	i		у	u		ю	yu[5]
й	ï[3]		ф	f		я	ya[6]

1. е = ye when initial and after ь. ъ, and all vowels except ы, or when preceded by vowel-consonant combinations as in Slavyan*ye*.
2. ё = o after ж and ш.
3. Combinations уй and ий = y.
4. ь and ъ before vowels = y.
5. ю after ы = iu.
6. я after ы = ia; after и = a, as in Izves*tia*.

Abbreviations

AG	*Agricultural Gazette* (Selskokhozyaistvennaya gazeta)
AN SSSR	Akademia nauk Soyuza sovetskikh sotsialisticheskikh respublik (Academy of Sciences of the USSR)
BVASKhNIL	*Bulletin of the All-Union Lenin Academy of Agricultural Sciences* (Byulleten Vsesoyuznoi akademii selskokhozyaist vennykh nauk imeni Lenina)
BJ	*Botanical Journal* (Botanichesky zhurnal)
BV	*Bulletin of Vernalization* (Byulleten yarovizatsii; founded in 1932; name changed to *Vernalization* in 1935)
EG	*Economic Gazette* (Ekonomicheskaya gazeta)
LSUH	*Leningrad State University Herald* (Vestnik Leningradskogo gosudarstvennogo universiteta)
NW	*New World* (Novy mir)
SA	*Socialist Agriculture* (Sotsialisticheskoye zemledeliye)
SB	*Soviet Botany* (Sovetskaya botanika)
SRA	*Socialist Reconstruction of Agriculture* (Sotsialistichaya rekonstruktsia selskogo khozyaistva)
UBM	*Under the Banner of Marxism* (Pod znamenem marksizma)
VASKhNIL	Vsesoyuznaya Akademia selskokhozyaistvennykh nauk imeni Lenina (Lenin All-Union Academy of Agricultural Sciences)
Vern.	*Vernalization* (Yarovizatsia; formerly *Bulletin of Vernalization*)
VIR	Vsesoyuzny institut rasteniyevodstva (All-Union Institute of the Plant Industry (originally a division of the Commissariat of Agriculture; converted in 1925 to the All-Union Institute of Applied Botany and New Crops)

Preface to the Russian Edition

How can one re-create not simply events that are long past, but the atmosphere of those times? Without conveying that atmosphere, can one truthfully recount the lives of people of those years, lives that were bright and distinguished and at the same time terrible and bloody?

When I started work on this account of the Lysenko years, it was not these thoughts that possessed me. The outcome of what had happened in the USSR and the pattern of events that had led up to it were clear to me, and my main goal was to search out the factual details. In addition to the usual kinds of library research, I was able to speak to many of the participants. Their gray heads sometimes trembled, but their eyes shone, burning with rage. Many thirsted for revenge, both among those who had been humiliated and among those who had been the agents of humiliation but had now lost power.

Gradually, the atmosphere of those times began to materialize and the dramatis personae of the story to move like real-life characters: Nikolai Vavilov, handsome, broad-shouldered, with the velvety bass of a Paul Robeson, and Trofim Lysenko, dry as a stick, stoop-shouldered, with his strong, strident tenor. They interrupted one another and created rival choruses; the clash of passions overshadowed the facts, and the scholar's quest for specifics gave way to the desire to create a chronicle of the times, to describe the characters and the atmosphere in which they lived.

But I realized then that I did not have the right to deprive my readers of the opportunity to draw the picture for themselves. If I did not provide the specifics, the actual words spoken and written, I would risk losing the readers' confidence. And so it is in that form that I present my work, hoping my readers will be patient with this approach to setting forth the history of Lysenko's rampage through Soviet biology.

I gathered the material for the book over many years, beginning in 1954. As often as possible, I read parts to friends, both those who were biologists and those who were not, and sought to correct the shortcomings they noted. The historian E. Pechuro gave tremendous help; her constructive advice on structure, the conceptual scheme, the evaluation of social processes, and style was very important to me. The late Andrei D. Sakharov read the early chapters, and both they and the later ones benefited from his advice. The counsel of writers S. I. Lipkin, I. L. Lisnyanskaya, Ye. G. Makarova, G. N. Vladimov, and Yu. A. Karabchiyevsky, as well as chess-grandmaster B. F. Gulko, who read all the chapters, was useful. I am sincerely grateful to them. I am also deeply grateful to many of my colleagues, particularly V. Ya. Aleksandrov, V. P. Efroimson, D. V. Lebedev, V. S. Kirpichnikov, L. I. Korochkin, V. V. Borisov, V. I. Ivanov, Yu. B. Vakhtin, T. N. Scherbinovskaya, S. I. Maletsky, I. M. Yaglom, Ya. Ye. Gluzman, M. D. Golubovsky, M. D. Frank-Kamenetskii, and M. G. Petrenko-Podyapolsky, who aided in the search for material, provided some of the illustrations, and gave valuable advice. My wife, N. I. Yakovleva-Soyfer, provided incalculable assistance by virtue of her critical attitude, and she also helped in the typing and proofreading.

Moscow, October 1987

Preface to the
American Edition

All my life I have had the good fortune to meet interesting people and to enjoy their friendship. Those friendships allowed me a unique perspective on one of the saddest episodes in the history of science and in the history of the twentieth century: the triumph of Lysenko and Lysenkoism in the Soviet Union. Those friendships have also given me both the motive and sources for writing this book about Lysenko.

In the late 1930s, under the merciless regime of repression established by Lenin and Stalin, people in the Soviet Union were forced to lead schizoid lives. To survive at all, they had to dissemble their beliefs and deepest feelings. The very word "truth," pravda, became meaningless: the incessant, often crude lies in the country's largest newspaper, as if in mockery of its name, *Pravda*, made the word suspect. However, after the death of Stalin (March 1953), people began to shed their fear of repression, at first cautiously and then, after Khrushchev's exposure of "the Stalin cult," openly. The writer Ilya Ehrenburg aptly named this period in the mid-1950s "the thaw." It was during this unshackling of public and private mentality that I was lucky enough to grow up. Among my own generation, in particular, many people no longer felt intimidated, thanks not only to their own strength of character, but also to the marked change in the social climate. Although we still held sacrosanct the notions of communism, still subscribed to the condemnation of capitalism, and accepted the image of America as Public Enemy Number One, we were already starting to think more freely. So I was open to meeting with persons with whom I might once have feared to be associated.

The most important influence upon my future development came about through acquaintance with Sergei Sergeyevich Chetverikov, one of the founders of Russian genetics. Chetverikov had been arrested on a political charge in 1929, and, after serving a sentence of exile in the Urals, was forbidden to return to Moscow. He came to Gorky (Nizhni-Novgorod) where he found employment at the university. I met him in 1955, one year after I had graduated from a Gorky secondary school and had entered the Timiryazev Agricultural Academy in Moscow, the Timiryazevka, as we affectionately nicknamed it. One summer vacation, when I came home to Gorky to see my mother, Pyotr Andreyevich Suvorov, a professor at Gorky University, took me to meet Chetverikov. After that, on my frequent visits home from Moscow, I would rush off to Chetverikov's apartment. We spent days and evenings together and became fast friends.

Chetverikov was then leading the lonely existence of a pariah. In 1948 the charlatan agronomist Lysenko had persuaded Stalin to outlaw genetics on the grounds that it was a "bourgeois science" alien to the principles of socialism. As a convinced geneticist, Chetverikov was dismissed from his job at Gorky University. His misfortune was compounded by the loss of his eyesight.

Chetverikov was a descendant of one of Russia's most distinguished noble families (the great theatrical reformer Konstantin Sergeyevich Stanislavsky also came from this family). His strength of character left a deep impression upon me. Even as a youth, this son of a millionaire had displayed a mind of his own. Rather than yield to his father's insistence that he study engineering, Chetverikov renounced his family's wealth and went off to pursue research in biology. He harbored socialist ideas until life itself caused him to reject them. When the arrest came, students, associates, and friends turned their backs on the millionaire's son. He experienced poverty and unwarranted exile.

My acquaintance with Chetverikov enabled me, little by little, to get to know many of the leading geneticists in Moscow as well. For them, too, I think, contact with young people was precious, for genetics remained a forbidden field in the mid-fifties. I was bursting with energy, and I drew all my student friends into this circle of defiant outcasts.

Inevitably, without consciously trying to elicit their stories, I absorbed their firsthand accounts of the crushing of genetics, information that contributed so much to this book when I came to write it. I became familiar with the geneticists and all those around them. The picture of their struggle for genuine science, as opposed to party pseudo-science, opened up before me.

These people knew how much Lysenko's errors had cost the Soviet Union. Lysenko, a practical agronomist with little education, had proposed one agricultural innovation after another to the party leaders. All his proposals were hastily concocted, untested, and one after another they failed—and yet Stalin and, later, Khrushchev took him at his word, while spurning all who criticized him. The critics were expelled from their positions. Many were jailed. Lysenko, operating with impunity, was emboldened to go on to ever greater knavery, while meantime agriculture was being devastated, the land was being laid waste, and young people were taught scientific nonsense.

Stalin and other Communists had seized upon a slogan coined by Ivan Michurin, an amateur gardener, "We cannot await nature's favors. Our task is to grasp them from her." The slogan resounded from every rostrum and loudspeaker, and the press emblazoned it time and again in those years. The Kremlin ordained a gigantic "Stalinist plan for the transformation of nature." Huge electric power dams changed the flow of the Volga and the mighty Siberian rivers, and the first atomic power plant arose at Obninsk.

The notion that nature could be reshaped at will to suit communism was an easy corollary from Lysenko's claim that there was no such science as genetics. His endlessly repeated assertion that the laws of genetics were a hoax perpetrated by bourgeois enemies had other appalling consequences. The geneticists, who had worked so hard to improve the lot of the people, lost everything: their jobs, their self-respect as scientists, and, often, their lives. Hearing all this from those who lived through the purges instigated by Lysenko, I could not fail to appreciate the noble spirit that imbued their efforts.

As I talked to the geneticists, I also began to discover their opponents, Lysenko and his adherents. My book describes my encounters as a Timiryazevka student in 1954–1957 with Lysenko and the lengthy discussions I had with him in those years. I found him an unattractive but interesting personality. He spoke like a simple peasant and reasoned with a logic based on superficial comparison of objects and phenomena, in sharp contrast to the scientific logic of my teachers of genetics and physics. At the same time, he had a masterly command of every twist and turn of Bolshevist politics, the weak spot of many scientists.

After the Timiryazevka, I transferred to biophysics in the physics department of Moscow State University in 1957. In those years physics enjoyed high esteem in the USSR. Under Stalin some politicians had demanded that relativity theory and other branches of physics be outlawed, but the physicists escaped the fate of the geneticists and cyberneticists. Since the state's might clearly depended upon nuclear weapons, atomic energy, and semiconductors, the physicists were spared. And the physicists of that period sought to revive genetics. Future Nobel Prize winners Igor Ye. Tamm, Andrei D. Sakharov, Nikolai N. Semyonov, and Piotr L. Kapitsa actively supported the geneticists. It was at this time that I met Igor Yevgenyevich Tamm, and it was upon his advice that I enrolled in the physics department of Moscow University and later undertook postgraduate study in the Atomic Energy Institute. Ultimately, though, I found my way into the study of molecular biology and genetics and made that my life's work in science. As a molecular geneticist I studied the induction of mutations in bacteriophages with high doses of X-rays, then investigated the combined action of chemical and radiation mutagens, and later described repair processes in higher plants. American geneticists had hitherto been unable to find these important reactions in plants, and the evidence of existence of repair was met by the scientific community with interest.

At another point in my life, I came to know the Lysenko camp at close quarters. In 1970 the Lenin Academy of Agricultural Sciences invited me to help set up a new institute of applied molecular biology and genetics. This academy, which had been Lysenko's fiefdom for almost three decades, consisted almost entirely of his adherents. My years of work at the academy had brought me into personal contact with many of his followers and the apparatchiki who were his supporters in the highest party and government bodies.

That is how I became personally acquainted with individuals who appear in these pages. To supplement their testimony, I have drawn on heaps of documents and records. Until very recently, these were largely inaccessible to scholars in either the Soviet Union or the West, and they are still hard to find. How I came to make use of these records in this chronicle deserves some comment.

A distinctive feature of modern American society is the involvement of lawyers at every turn, whereas the Soviet way of life required one to rely solely upon oneself for protecting one's interests (except, of course, when hauled before a court). Consequently, almost everyone preserved every letter, document, record, or paper of personal concern, and in the course of a lifetime each person accumulated a large dossier, containing often unique information. (This practice continues today in Russian society even after the dissolution of the Soviet Union.) In this way I amassed a variety of documents, at first concerning myself, and then began to fill a shelf in the closet with documents about everything relating to the history of genetics. Beginning in 1961, I began to publish articles and finally books about this history, and this, in turn, entailed a wider search for old documents. I was able to obtain some from official archives, but I got access to most of them thanks to the help of colleagues.

Since I knew many of the older generation of geneticists, I often questioned them about one event or another, and almost invariably succeeded in finding someone whose home files contained the minutes of meetings of learned councils, stenographic transcripts of conference proceedings and speeches, the text of resolutions adopted, the directives and orders issued by institute directors, etc. In this way, without recourse to state archives, I managed to secure extensive, and in some cases exhaustive, materials about many of the events described in this book. I also obtained documents from archives, primarily the archives of the Lenin Academy of Agricultural Sciences and the former Ministry of Agriculture. In addition, I had access to the archive of Gorky State University, which was important in researching the story of Chetverikov's life. My files bulged, but the time had not yet come for the great design of a history of Soviet genetics.

That time came unexpectedly. From the moment I took part in establishing a new institute at the Lenin Agricultural Academy in 1971 and particularly after I became scientific director of the institute in March 1974, I experienced pressure on two scores. The party apparatchiki with whom I had to deal in the science department and agriculture department of the party Central Committee took to pressing me to join the Communist Party, which I would not do. At the same time, the party organization of my institute, taking advantage of the fact that I was not a party member, conducted an offensive against me, allegedly for hiring too many Jewish scientists. By 1976 the pressure assumed a new form: I was accused of turning into a dissident. At a meeting of the party organization of the institute, attended by a representative of the Central Committee of the CPSU, Emma L. Nikitenko, I was accused of political unreliability; the next meeting revoked my right to travel abroad to scientific conferences. Soon I was forbidden to submit articles to international journals. When I ignored this ruling and continued to send out papers about my laboratory's research in molecular genetics and radiobiology, a KGB representative threatened me with dismissal.

They were closing in, and at the end of 1978 my wife and I applied to leave for the West. The institute immediately removed me from scientific research. My wife, who had worked with me since 1970, was dismissed outright. Then, in 1980, after we both publicly supported protests against the exiling of Andrei D. Sakharov to Gorky, I too found myself out on the street.

Now my time was my own, and I decided to set about writing a full-scale book about Lysenko. The KGB, of course, knew what I was up to. I discovered that its operatives had bugged my apartment and installed recording devices in my neighbors' apartments. The KGB opened all my mail and summoned me to interrogations, at which they threatened me and my family. Thus forewarned, I took precautions. Several friends agreed to hide my most precious source material in their homes. KGB operatives stood watch at the entrance to our nine-story apartment house all day. Late at night, when they went home to bed, I emerged, alone or with my wife, carrying what I had written during the day. The friends who stored my source materials in cartons behind their doors had given us keys to their apartments. We silently opened an apartment door, left a package containing the latest addition to my manuscript, and removed the papers I needed for the next chapter. I finished the first draft of the book in 1983 and succeeded in sending it abroad.

I could breathe more easily now, and I showed the manuscript to some of my colleagues. I began to get valuable feedback. A number of scientists, particularly biologists of the older generation—Vladimir P. Efroimson, Iosif A. Rapoport, Vladimir Ya. Aleksandrov, Daniil V. Lebedev, and others—called my attention to errors or oversights and provided a mass of additional material. I set to work on a second draft, and then, as more and more material piled up, a third, a fourth, and finally a fifth revision. I had no computer, so each fresh version had to be completely retyped, and each time I had to find someone who would take it abroad. In 1983 Stephen R. Burant, then a graduate student at the University of Wisconsin, took one of the drafts with him and presented it to the university library in 1983. In 1986 Peter Day, a leading figure in the Genetics Society of America, took a later version of the manuscript to Rutgers University Press.

During those years I became more and more active in the human rights movement, gathering information about the Soviet persecution of scientists and Jewish refuseniks, and seeking to transmit this information to the West. I participated in Amnesty International and frequently met with Western government officials, members of parliaments, and correspondents of the press, radio, and television. The KGB and the Communist leaders were thoroughly aware of these activities of mine and tried in every way to block me.

I often asked myself why the authorities, constantly trying to intimidate and stop me, did not simply arrest me. After all, many of my friends were behind bars for doing exactly what I was doing. I see only one explanation. During the years when I was officially a scientist in good standing, and even more after I was expelled from the institute for political reasons, I made every effort to maintain contacts with the free world, with all who were prepared to be on friendly terms with me. I accepted invitations to receptions at the embassies of the United States, West Germany, Great Britain, and the Netherlands. We kept up a friendship with many fine Western representatives then stationed in Moscow, such as British cultural attaché John Gordon, U.S. ambassador Arthur Hartman, Malta ambassador Guzeppi Schembri, the Canadian embassy first secretary John Di Gangi, West German cultural attaché Klaus Schramayer, and others. I think this played a decisive role; I remained at liberty thanks to the growing interest in me in the West. Because correspondents of the *New York Times*, the *Los Angeles Times*, the *Baltimore Sun*, the *Boston Globe*, the *Chicago Tribune*, *U.S. News & World Report*, and the *Washington Post* were frequent visitors in our home; because Peter Arnett made CNN broadcasts from our apartment; because Jack Kemp, Patricia Schroeder, Howard Metzenbaum, Alfonse D'Amato, Paul Sarbanes, Dennis DeConcini, and other senators and members of Congress visited me whenever they came to the USSR; because the authorities knew of our talks with George P. Schultz and his deputies Richard Schifter and Paul Wolfowitz or the hours-long discussions with Edward Kennedy or Barbara Mikulski—because of all this the authorities feared to do themselves more harm by making a martyr out of me. I am deeply moved when I recall the hours spent with us by American and European scientists visiting Moscow or the telephone calls from Nobel Prize winners, inviting me to their lectures at Moscow institutes. In these circumstances the institute directors could not prevent me from attending, and following the lectures I was able to talk with people from the free world to which we wanted to belong. At the same time, it was crystal clear to the Soviet authorities that I was doing nothing inimical to my country and violating no laws by my actions, my articles, or my books, including those published in the West.

A section of the book, together with the letter my wife and I signed in defense of Sakharov, appeared in a samizdat collection marking Andrei Dmitriyevich Sakharov's sixtieth birthday in 1980. This collection was reprinted later in many languages, including English ("Andrei Sakharov and the Fate of Biological Science in the USSR," *On Sakharov*, New York: Knopf, 1982, 172–180.) In effect, this publication was one of the reasons seized upon for expelling me from the institute. The Russian-language magazine *Kontinent* in Paris printed a long article, excerpted from the book, in 1987. That same year G. Ya. Baklanov, editor of *Znamya*, a Moscow monthly, signed a contract to serialize a magazine version of the book, but the KGB forbade it, and Baklanov gave in. However, *Ogonyok*, the most widely read magazine in the country with a weekly circulation of 2.7 million, carried a long article about Lysenko, incorporating portions of the book. The *Ogonyok* article infuriated party Central Committee ideologist Yegor K. Ligachev. At this point we finally obtained a favorable response to the twice-repeated appeal from President Ronald Reagan to Gorbachev to allow our family to leave. We were even being pressed to hasten our departure to the West.

Then a strange thing happened. Vitaly Korotich, the editor in chief of *Ogonyok*, conveyed a request from Mikhail Gorbachev that we send him a letter asking to be permitted to retain Soviet citizenship in our existence abroad. I did so immediately, but it appeared that Ligachev disagreed, and he prevailed. No sooner had we been granted permission to leave with Soviet passports—as Gorbachev wished—than the decision was reversed on Ligachev's orders, our Soviet citizenship was revoked, and we left for the United States as political refugees in 1988. To the best of my knowledge, this was the last instance of deprivation of citizenship of dissidents in the USSR.

Ligachev was not content with this. At his demand, an issue of *Ogonyok* had to carry a set of readers' letters attacking my book. By that time my wife, our son, and I were living in Columbus, Ohio. The nineteenth party conference, conceived by Gorbachev as a congress intended to reform the party, convened in Moscow in July of that same year. Boris Volodin, a member of the party Central Committee, delivered a speech about me, calling me a traitor to the country who had run away from the battle for perestroika. Every Soviet newspaper, from *Pravda* on down, carried his speech.

In 1989 the London journal *Nature* published a long article that drew on the material for this book. The Munich Russian-language magazine, *Strana i Mir*, carried another section from the book. When the Moscow popular science magazine *Priroda* (which, like the title of the British journal, means "nature") devoted an issue at the end of 1992 to the best articles that had appeared in the London magazine during the past 175 years, it chose among them my article on Lysenko. The book was used during the hearings of the Constitution Court, the highest judiciary body of the Russian State, when the legality of the Communist Party was questioned (see *Rossiishaya Gazeta*, July 29, p. 2).

In 1989 Hermitage Publishers issued the complete Russian text of the book in the United States under the title *Power and Science: History of the Crash of Soviet Genetics* (Vlast' i Nauka). In 1993 it was reprinted by the publishing house Lazur of Moscow. One of America's best journalists and translators, Leo Gruliow, and his daughter, Rebecca Gruliow, translated the Russian for Rutgers University Press. I am grateful to them for their excellent translation. Rutgers University Press further edited and abridged the translation (to half the book's original length) to make it more accessible to English-speaking readers.

I am exceedingly grateful to George Soros and the Education Foundation of America for underwriting the English translation and to Rutgers University Press's science editor, Dr. Karen Reeds, for her assistance in the work on the English edition of the book. I received important critical suggestions from Professors Mark Adams (University of Pennsylvania), Loren R. Graham (Massachusetts Institute of Technology), Douglas R. Weiner (University of Arizona), Robert Hoffman (Smithsonian Institution), and my wife, Dr. Nina Soyfer. All my life I shall remain deeply thankful to Professor Peter Day, who drew the publisher's attention to my book.

In conclusion I wish to emphasize that Lysenkoism remains deeply entrenched in Russian science, despite perestroika and glasnost and the end of the USSR. Many of those who were raised in the Lysenko tradition still occupy key positions in Russia's science administration. Lysenkoism left a baneful legacy in the form of these followers of Lysenko who continue to teach and work in many universities and institutes. They may conceal their bias, but it cannot fail to affect the level of education and training of new biologists. We know that the hardest thing is to change people's thinking. Hence, I believe that books such as mine will not only contribute to preserving the historical record but will help people today to dispel the incubus of the recent past. That is essential in today's Russia as it turns toward democracy and the ideals that the rulers of that great country trampled underfoot for so many decades.

Valery N. Soyfer
Oakton, Virginia, May 1993
Clarence J. Robinson Professor of Biology and the History of
Science and Director of Molecular Genetics Laboratory,
George Mason University; Foreign Member of the Russian
Academy of Natural Sciences, Member of the New York
Academy of Science.

Lysenko and the
Tragedy of
Soviet Science

Introduction

"What will history say of you?" the innocent yet condemned man asked Governor Dmitry Bibikov. "Rest assured, it will know nothing of my deeds," came the answer.

—N. Eidelman, *Lunin*

What do you mean, "Why bring it to mind"? If I suffered an evil illness and was cured and cleansed of it, I will always remember it happily. I won't remember only when I am suffering just as before or even worse and want to deceive myself. If we remember the past and look it straight in the eye, our new, present coercion will also be revealed.

—L. Tolstoy, *Conversations with Tolstoy*

Thanks to the efforts of Soviet propaganda, the name of Trofim Lysenko disappeared for a time from the Soviet press and was effaced from the memory of Soviet people. The young in the Soviet Union generally have not known who Lysenko was; perhaps they confuse him—the central character of this book—with the Ukrainian composer of the same name. In the West, on the other hand, Lysenko's name has become synonymous with fraud, demagogy, and the use of political dictates to crush scientific dissent. As the American historian Loren Graham has observed, "If one mentions Marxism and biology to a West European or American of even modest education, he or she thinks of Lysenko."[1]

But in the past few years, Lysenko's name has begun to be mentioned again in Russia, along with the pejorative term *Lysenkovshchina*. [The Russian suffix *-shchina* carries a strong implication of fear and contempt.—Trans.] Whereas "Lysenkoism" would identify without aspersion the ideas and practices associated with his name, Lysenkovshchina connotes not merely the doctrines but also everything negative about them, all the tyrannical means he employed to foist his ideas and practices upon the country and exert his power over the scientific community. Yet, by hanging a negative flag on Lysenko's name, the term of disparagement may seem to dismiss the Lysenko phenomenon out of hand, with no suggestion that it deserves serious analysis. Indeed, despite the recent references to Lysenko and the Lysenkovshchina, the Soviet media have not adequately described his personality, what he did, or its significance.

Lysenko appeared on the scientific horizon in 1928. Soon after, he was taking off like a rocket into the firmament of Stalin's empire, at the very

time when an age-old way of life was being overthrown by Stalin's collectivization of Soviet agriculture and industrialization of the economy. Millions
of Lysenko's fellow peasants were dying of starvation or being herded into
jolting cattle cars on their way to Siberia. Several prominent scientists saw
him as an original, rough-hewn talent and were quick to support him. But
the chief factor in his breathtaking career was something else: his recognition by the circle of leaders of the Soviet Union. It was thanks to this that
he attained high positions on the national level, as a deputy of the USSR
Supreme Soviet and, for more than ten years, vice-chairman of one of the
two chambers of the Soviet parliament. He became an academician, or
full member, of three scientific academies—the Ukrainian Academy of
Sciences, the Lenin All-Union Academy of Agricultural Sciences
(VASKhNIL), and the USSR Academy of Sciences—and was later appointed
president of VASKhNIL and director of the Breeding and Genetics Institute in Odessa and the Genetics Institute of the USSR Academy of Sciences
(AN SSSR) in Moscow. He was thrice awarded the Stalin Prize (first degree), was named a Hero of Socialist Labor, and received the country's
highest honor, the Order of Lenin, eight times. For over a quarter of a
century, in his own name or through figureheads, Lysenko controlled
many governmental or public agencies dealing with agriculture, biology,
and medicine. He participated in the leadership of Soviet peace organizations.

After gaining power, Lysenko turned to open and merciless struggle
against all who did not accept his innovations or who tried to follow an
independent line in science. Although the Communist Party dictated
thought in the social sciences beginning early in the 1920s, the natural
sciences enjoyed one more decade of relative freedom. Biology then became the first to experience the full weight of ideological control. Today,
even the Soviet press has finally acknowledged what scientists have known
for decades: that the person who, in the name of the Party, conducted a
wholesale slaughter in biology and agronomy was Trofim Lysenko. Research and teaching about hormones, neurophysiology, cell theory, genetics, and other biological disciplines were senselessly and fiercely crushed.

Physics, chemistry, mathematics, and other natural sciences largely escaped what happened in biology. These sciences were already far advanced,
their laws and results were applied in practice everywhere; and without
them, progress in technology (especially in military technology) would
have been impossible. Consequently, although there was an attempt to
introduce an inquisition like the one in biology (for example, some Marxist philosophers and Party officials tried to condemn Einstein's theory of
relativity), it misfired. However, cybernetics, a new discipline that had not
yet acquired its technology, was declared a bourgeois heresy and was suppressed with the same means and the same rhetoric as genetics. Other
branches of science had their own versions of Lysenkoism—a process that
has not ended.

Lysenko's meager education did not prevent him from presenting himself as the great reformer of all biology. In place of a strict experimental approach, he introduced what he called a "science of the kolkhoz and sovkhoz system." This "science" relied on the assembly of data (with no attempt to check their accuracy) from thousands of questionnaires that Lysenko and his staff distributed to kolkhozes and sovkhozes. These "data" from the collective farms and state-owned farms were made the basis for claims of tremendous results from the "experiments" conducted by the people. By such deception, Lysenko was able to persuade Stalin and other Party leaders that his innovations and proposals would surely benefit the country. At the same time, critics of Lysenko were accused of opposing scientific progress and the socialist reorganization of the countryside and of being "idealists" or, worse, outright saboteurs, accomplices of the international bourgeoisie. They were dismissed, imprisoned, exiled.

Lysenko and his entourage caused the country great moral and political harm. A generation of scientists, technicians, and bureaucrats raised in his image took charge of Soviet science in the years that followed. Lysenkoism showed how a forcibly instilled illusion, repeated over and over at meetings and in the media, takes on an existence of its own in people's minds, despite all realities. Indeed, it vividly revealed the nature of the Soviet system. In addition, Lysenkoism wrought incalculable material damage upon the Soviet economy. It cannot be compared with the harm caused by collectivization, which ruined the agriculture of the USSR, but Lysenko did contribute immensely to the process of rural destruction. For decades, his pseudoscientific recommendations promised the people and the Party leadership fine new varieties of crops, harvests of unprecedented size, and unlimited milk and meat. But the promises never materialized; agriculture fell short of its goals more and more each year.

The history of Lysenkoism has been the object of intensive study in the West,[2] and it has received attention in the Soviet Union as well.[3] Nevertheless, a systematic description of Lysenko's scientific and public activity does not exist, and in consequence one often encounters errors in Western literature; for example, there is a widespread misconception that at the start of his career Lysenko was still quite a decent researcher, a capable plant physiologist, and only later became corrupted.[4] Therefore, I saw it as my first task to investigate thoroughly Lysenko's works, and to do so on the basis of primary sources, in order to avoid falling into the established patterns. It was also necessary to deal with the science-related social currents that facilitated Lysenko's progress, and that was a second aim of this book.

The facts of Lysenko's scientific activity, however, constitute merely the outline, the background, against which a phenomenon unfolded that was independent in its genesis and in the forces involved. This phenomenon is the political dictatorship over all aspects of life in totalitarian countries. It has attracted great attention, unrelated to Lysenko, from scholars belonging to various schools of thought.[5] Lysenkoism, in my opinion, offers a unique opportunity both for an analysis of this phenomenon in its application to science and for a description of its characteristic features on the basis of concrete material. Such an analysis and description constituted the third chief aim of my book. I hope I have succeeded in eradicating some misconceptions concerning the nature of Lysenkoism as a political trend, particularly Zhores Medvedev's view, which he expressed in his essential and otherwise factual book, that Lysenkoism is a specific product of Stalin's perversion of morality, that it arose from the absence of effective control by society over its own development in the conditions of the "cult of personality."

On the contrary, I have tried to show that Lysenko's rise was a logical outcome of Party dictation over science, the only possible outcome given the political barriers to pluralism, the suppression of any dissent, the belief that the proletariat and the peasantry should exercise control over scientists and over the intelligentsia as a whole, and many other reasons rooted in political, not scientific, factors. I have argued that Lysenkoism was by no means a result of the erroneous, unscientific views of one individual, supported by the leaders of the official ideology and the machinery of state, but *a social phenomenon* in conditions ostensibly of planned science but actually of harsh and unceasing Party dictatorship over the scientists. The distortion of morality wrought by this dictatorship led to the uncontrolled power of demagogues, charlatans, and timeservers, zealously carrying out the orders of the Party and simultaneously feeding empty promises to the leaders at the top, suppressing scientific opposition, and often turning scientific organizations, generously subsidized by the state, into springboards for their own elevation and enrichment. I contend that the ideological foundations of Lysenkoism had been laid when the intelligentsia was proclaimed a "nonproletarian" stratum of society and when Lenin called for the formation of a new intelligentsia, recruited from the working class and the working peasantry and free of "the imprint of the exploiters."

Mythmaking is a characteristic aspect of totalitarian society. Lysenko, a protégé of the Communist Party though never a Party member, used his wits and became first among the biologists to grasp what was wanted and expected of them: timely and grandiose schemes promising rivers of milk and honey. When his schemes failed, he cast the blame upon those who carried out the plans or, more often, on scientific adversaries, whom he accused of adopting anti-Marxist or vitalist or simply wrong scientific positions.

Early on, Lysenko adopted the strategy of all the most successful politicians in Soviet science: while aiming criticism at "ideological enemies," one must always blow a new soap bubble, directing attention to its iridescence, and when it, too, bursts, again accuse the genuine scientists whom you have slandered, even those who may have been ardently serving the cause of building socialism in the USSR. In Lysenko's case, it was actually his benefactor, Nikolai I. Vavilov, who was the target of this injustice. Lysenko found proof of his own rightness both in quotations from the classics of Marxism-Leninism and in the falsified reports of results that his subordinates provided. At the same time, he remained alert to the possibility of a shift in the Party winds. By these means, Lysenko kept his hold over Soviet science both during the years of the Stalin personality cult and in the years of struggle against the cult in Khrushchev's regime. He was not the only one to conform to this standard of behavior in Soviet science and in Soviet society as a whole, but he gave it unprecedented scope.

It has also seemed to me important to deal with one more problem: the scientists' resistance to Lysenko's pseudoinnovations. All his life, Lysenko felt that he carried little weight with his scientific colleagues and that they did not take his ideas seriously. His method of dealing with this situation was to pour invective upon his critics, brand them with political stigmata, and discredit their ideas. Yet he never succeeded in completely crushing the opposition. There were always bold souls, even in the years of the bloodiest Stalinist terror. I have taken the obligation upon myself to report in detail the struggle of those who fell in the battles. The pages and chapters devoted to those heroes are but a small tribute of respect from a person of a later generation, a tribute all the more necessary because their names are fading into oblivion. After expending their energy and spirit in combat with Lysenko, these scientists often could not realize their full creative potential, but their names deserve honor in the history of the struggle for freedom in science.

This aspect of the story of Lysenkoism is important also because it demonstrates how scientists in extreme situations divide into fighters, appeasers, and traitors. These categories have heuristic significance, but even greater moral significance: The Lysenko story shows that any short-term gains (such as acquiring high positions in the governance of science) achieved by betrayal turn into ineradicable shame over the long term. Potential lovers of an easy life should be quite clear about this.

I believe, finally, that the common belief in "the downfall of Lysenkoism" in the USSR must be reconsidered. In the judgment of the majority of investigators of Lysenkoism, symbolized in the title of the American edition of Medvedev's book, *The Rise and Fall of T. D. Lysenko*, the Lysenko forces lost their power in Soviet biology after the Party Central Committee condemned Khrushchev in 1964 for his mistakes in governing the country and specifically criticized his support of Lysenko. After that, genetics began to revive in the USSR and the propaganda of Lysenkoism ceased. The impression spread that Lysenkoism had indeed fallen, died, and disappeared from Soviet science. But although Lysenko's genetics institute was closed down, all the other scientific institutions, large and small, where Lysenkoists had been in charge remained untouched, with all his people in place. Therefore, it would be naive to believe that Lysenkoism is finished. There has been a certain amount of camouflage, but the roots of

Lysenkoism remain, and not only in biology. The methods of "doing science" that arose during the development of Lysenkoism continue to be employed. The leaders of science still indulge the penchant for grandiose schemes, manipulation, and bluff in the attempt to retain power. Can one say, then, that Lysenkoism died with the discrediting of Lysenko?

In fact, Lysenko himself was not dethroned, and his crimes against science and the people have still not been acknowledged by the authorities, let alone made the object of courtroom trial. At the time of his death in 1976, he was still an academician of three academies and a Hero of Socialist Labor, still entitled to retain all the accompanying material benefits—the salary of an academician, honoraria, royalties, a country cottage, a limousine with a personal driver, special medical benefits, special supplies of foods, and so on. A staff of almost 150 was still working under his direction at the Lenin Hills Agricultural Experiment Station of the USSR Academy of Sciences.

What is more, it seems to me that even Lysenko himself might have averted his "downfall." In the 1970s, the Party had begun to recognize the practical benefits socialism could gain from molecular biology and genetics, but for the first time in his career, Lysenko failed to notice that a change was taking place. He lost his hold on power by rebelling against molecular genetics and failing to recruit supporters among those who were eager to become leaders of this new discipline. Perhaps his incredible scientific ignorance, perhaps age (he was then in his seventies), but most likely the fact that he could count no competent biochemists among his cohorts led him to attack where it would have been advantageous to keep his peace. He might have gone on happily, he could have continued to flourish, had he preserved flexibility, had he thought up a new scheme of genetic engineering with a Marxist-Leninist flourish to raise the yield of wheat or potatoes. But, with his bulldozer temperament, he fought this innovation as he had all others—and lost. Thus, Lysenko's "downfall" was a personal drama and had nothing to do with the fate of Lysenkoism as a social phenomenon. The latter flourishes to this day in Russian science, as is suggested by the cases of Rem V. Petrov and Irina N. Blokhina. Petrov, in his doctoral dissertation submitted in 1954, claimed to have demonstrated the formation of abdominal typhoid bacteria and dysentery bacilli from unstructured "living matter," in accordance with the supposed discovery of Olga B. Lepeshinskaya (see chapter 12); in 1988, he became a vice president of the USSR Academy of Sciences (AN SSSR), and he remains so in 1993. Blokhina had declared that she confirmed that Lepeshinskaya generated cells of abdominal typhus from *nonliving* matter; today, she is a full member of the Academy of Medical Sciences and director of a large research institute.

It may be said that what I discuss in the book was inherent in all science in the USSR and that the term Lysenkoism is therefore too narrow and does not show that similar phenomena were characteristic of Soviet science as a whole, not merely of biology and agronomy. The social, professional, and practical disasters brought on by Party dictatorship do mark many other branches of science. However, since I am dealing specifically with the situation in the framework of biology, it does not seem reasonable to replace the term "Lysenkoism" with another of wider scope, such as socialism. Lysenkoism remains a striking, concrete expression of the general phenomenon.

If the leaders of Russia are truly eager (as they often declare) to have science flourish, they must draw lessons from the history of Lysenkoism. Where demagogy and ideology reign, creativity cannot thrive. But where the only measures of scientists' value are their own abilities and achievements, science will prosper. The leaders must stop dictating the direction of science and restore the democratic traditions in which Russian science once gloried. I would like to be an optimist and believe these changes have already taken place. But to indulge myself in that way would run the risk of being taken as a wild-eyed dreamer.

1

"We All Came from the People"

They went out from us, but they were not of us; for if they had been of us they would have continued with us; but they went out, that it might be made plain that they all are not of us.

—1 John, 2:19

Our strength lies in the fact that our Bolshevik Party and our dear socialist motherland nurtured us. Our strength lies in the fact that we have been guided in our work by Darwinism and that we are guided by the great theory of Marx-Engels-Lenin-Stalin. If all this is taken from us, we become powerless.

—T. D. Lysenko, "My Path into Science"

A Peasant's Son

A boy was born to the Ukrainian peasant family of Denis and Oksana Lysenko in the village of Karlovka, Poltava province, on December 30, 1898. They named him Trofim. Later, Oksana bore two more sons and a daughter.

The children worked in the fields and around the house, but the greater part of the work and considerable responsibility fell to the lot of the eldest son. Thus, although he was bright and industrious, he received no formal education for a long time. He learned to read and write only when he entered the two-year village school at the age of thirteen. He completed that school in 1913, and then studied for a little more than two years in the elementary horticultural school in the city of Poltava.[1]

Those who completed this school could expect a better life than ordinary peasants; they usually went to work as gardeners for the wealthy landowners in the area, but Trofim had higher aspirations. From his lessons and conversations with his teachers, he learned that in Uman, halfway between Odessa and Kiev and less than two hundred miles from Poltava, lay the Vocational School of Agriculture and Horticulture, which had been founded on the famous estate of Count Potocki in 1796, when Uman was still a part of Poland, and which was now the most distinguished school of its kind in Russia.[2] In the autumn of 1916, while still a student in Poltava, he took the entrance examinations for Uman, but though he did well in most subjects, he failed the examination in Scripture.[3] He determined to try again, and he was able to win admission a year later. Although Lysenko's reading and writing skills and his general cultural background may have been weak, he had a keen memory and an ability to grasp phrases, figures, and dates quickly.

However, war interfered with his education. The town of Uman was caught between armies first in World War I and then in the Russian Civil War that followed the Bolshevik Revolution. Uman fell to the Reds and then to the Whites, by turns; only in 1920 did the Reds take permanent possession. Consequently, the teaching was so irregular that the graduates had to take makeup classes. To that end, Lysenko was sent to Kiev for several months in 1921 to take courses organized by the Chief Administration of the Sugar Industry. He then served an internship at a small selection station in the town of Verkhnyachka, near Cherkassy. The tasks of these selection stations, which were organized and operated by the government, were to test and produce new varieties of economically important plants, to distribute seeds and cuttings, and to provide instruction to local farmers in their cultivation. A few of the stations also conducted scientific research on problems of agriculture.

After two months in Verkhnyachka, Lysenko moved to the sugar trust's selection station in Belaya Tserkov, fifty miles south of Kiev. Here he received his first official title, "beet selection specialist," though actually his duties had little to do with beet selection but involved routine work with "kitchen-garden plants and spring crops." He is reported, however, to have tried, without success, to develop a new variety of tomatoes. He also became familiar with the method, known to specialists, of grafting shoots as well as buds in order to obtain a greater number of seeds.[4]

In 1923, Lysenko published two short articles (one of them coauthored) about his work.[5] Though the content of the articles was insignificant, the fact of their publication suggests that Lysenko did want to make a name in scientific circles. Nevertheless, he showed no sign of the drives that ordinarily inspire scientists—the love of knowledge for its own sake and the desire to report the discovery of a new law, to describe a new fact, or to challenge an accepted scientific opinion.

But his desire to obtain a higher educational degree—a prerequisite to the realization of his ambitions—was very strong. During those years, the Bolshevik leaders were striving to enlarge the contingent of students from the proletarian and peasant classes. Lysenko seized this opportunity, and in 1922, without leaving his work in Belaya Tserkov, he entered the Kiev Agricultural Institute as a correspondence student in agronomy, completing the course in 1925 and receiving a certificate as an agronomist. Yet, having examined pages written in Lysenko's own hand, I can affirm that the inadequacies of his education remained obvious throughout his life. It is not too much to say that the world of books was alien to him. Moreover, he did not know any foreign language, and so he never became familiar with science outside the Soviet Union. In 1956, during one of several lengthy discussions I had with him when I was a student at the Timiryazev Agricultural Academy in Moscow, Lysenko boasted that his translators reviewed literature in eighteen languages—but, he added, "There's no point in scanning the works of these *busurmany* [a derogatory word for "foreigners"—transl.]. You must draw your own conclusions and not rely on authorities, especially from the West. You never can tell when they may mislead you." Throughout his life, he never took any of the standard scientific examinations and he was unable to complete either a master's or a doctoral dissertation. Instead, he found a different way to the top, appealing to the sentiment expressed in a popular song, "We all came from the people." He easily found a place in the system that promoted people from the plow and the workbench—"the cook's children," in Lenin's words, "the shock workers, the vanguard who inspire a labor upsurge," in Stalin's.

The Move to Gandzha and First Success

Lysenko remained in Belaya Tserkov for about four years. During that time, he became involved in a relationship with a married woman, and when her husband objected, he felt compelled to leave.[6] In 1925, he was appointed a junior specialist at the Ordzhonikidze Central Plant-Breeding Experiment Station, which had been founded two years previously in the city of Gandzha (later Kirovobad), Azerbaidzhan. His job was to study the "selection of leguminous, fodder-grain, and green-manure plants."[7]

He arrived at a propitious moment. The Gandzha station, like many others, had recently become affiliated with the All-Union Institute of Applied Botany and New Crops. This institute, which was headquartered in Leningrad, had itself been founded only a few months before. Its creation was announced at a special meeting in the Kremlin, and the government clearly attributed great significance to it. It later became the All-Union Institute of Plant Industry (VIR). VIR grew into a huge center of basic and applied research on plants and agronomy, independent of the AN SSSR, with several thousand employees working in many branches, subdivisions, and experiment stations all over the country and even abroad. Its director was the distinguished botanist Professor Nikolai I. Vavilov.

Vavilov's enthusiasm suffused all of the institute's activities, and the Gandzha station shared in the sense of excitement. Vavilov was collecting and testing new varieties on a massive scale from many countries, and Gandzha had a prominent part in these efforts. Research fellows and eminent scientists came to visit frequently. The station's director, Nikolai F. Derevitsky, was one of the country's leading specialists in the application of mathematical models to agronomy. The task he assigned to Lysenko was selected in such a way that the young specialist would be equal to it: investigation of the possibilities of growing leguminous crops in the area. At the time, such crops were not commonly grown in Azerbaidzhan. Despite the relatively warm autumns and winters in the region (Lysenko later noted that "the average daily temperature rarely dropped below 0° C."),[8] by springtime there was a shortage of feed for the livestock. Derevitsky—possibly at Vavilov's prompting, since this was very much his kind of idea—wanted to try to introduce leguminous plants that were grown in more northerly latitudes, in the hope that they would survive the winter, thus providing green fodder and, when the remaining shoots were plowed under before spring planting, enriching the soil as well. Lysenko's assignment did not hold any experimental complexities or call for complicated technology. It could just as well have been entrusted to a laboratory assistant with minimal education.

In the first year, Lysenko made only one sowing, of peas. The winter of 1925–1926 was a mild one; the plants survived and by springtime had produced healthy shoots. It was a promising beginning, but of course a single experiment was not decisive. The results had to be corroborated by repeated plantings. Other events, however, intervened.

The first of these events was a visit to the Gandzha station by a prominent journalist, Vitaly Fyodorovich, who wrote for *Pravda*. Perhaps because Derevitsky placed high hopes on the experiments with peas, or perhaps because Fyodorovich was looking for a prototype for the role of hero from a "proletarian" background, he was introduced to Lysenko, who told him about the work with peas and showed him the fields and the crops. The result was a long and adulatory article in *Pravda*, "The Winter Fields."[9]

In keeping with the spirit of the times, the correspondent acclaimed the fact that his hero did not have much education: "He did not attend a university. . . . He didn't study the hairy legs of flies, but went to the root of things." Fyodorovich recounted that, during the two days Lysenko led him through the fields, he appeared to be ascetic, serious and quiet, tight-lipped, speaking excitedly only about plants exotic to the USSR, like peanuts. The entire time, he smiled only once, when he recalled his mother's Ukrainian cherry dumplings. "If one were to judge from first impressions, Lysenko has the look of someone with a toothache; poor fellow, he has a despondent appearance. He is sparing with words, and his face is undistinguished. One recalls only his gloomy eyes, searching the ground with the expression of one contemplating murder, at the very least."

Of Lysenko's work with peas, Fyodorovich wrote:

Lysenko is solving (and has solved!) the problem of enriching the soil without animal or mineral fertilizers, by planting winter crops in the barren fields in the Transcaucasus winter, so that the livestock need not perish for want of fodder, and the Turkic peasant can live through the winter without trembling at thought of the morrow. . . .

The barefoot professor Lysenko now has followers, pupils, an experimental field; and the luminaries of agronomy visit in the winter, stand before the station's green fields, and gratefully shake his hand.

Although Lysenko must have known that the correspondent had greatly exaggerated when he proclaimed that the problem had been solved, such praise would make anyone giddy. In all innocence, Lysenko may have painted himself and the project in an overly attractive light, but it is hard to understand why an urbane journalist would be taken in. Perhaps he was simply behaving cynically. If the authorities wanted to promote people from the plow and the workbench, why not stretch a point and conjure up a solution to an acute problem that had been achieved by the heroic endeavors of a "barefoot professor"? In any case, Fyodorovich's superficial approach and his contempt for true scientists stimulated Lysenko's craving for easy success. Even the sneer at those who studied "the hairy legs of flies" had its effect: For the rest of his life, Lysenko hated those fruit flies, *Drosophila*, the favorite object of geneticists' study.

Vernalization: Was It a Discovery?

After the *Pravda* article appeared, Lysenko turned to a different subject. At the same time, the Gandzha station underwent several changes. Derevitsky was dismissed as director, while Lysenko's affairs prospered. He was given three student aides, one of whom, Aleksandra A. Baskova, soon became his wife. Donat A. Dolgushin, his future long-term collaborator, also began to work with him.

From the autumn of 1926 through the spring of 1927, this team devoted itself to a study of the influence of low temperatures on plants, and this was the second event marking a turn in Lysenko's career. His assistants kept records of the dates of sowing, germination, flowering, and maturation of crops of wheat, cotton, rye, oats, and barley planted on experimental plots, and they also made observations of temperature—simple data, routinely collected to check on the development of plants. These were assembled into lengthy tables, annotated by Lysenko in a rather elementary way, and they were published in 1928 in a monograph under the imprint of the Gandzha station, with Lysenko as author.[10] Of the 169 pages in this monograph, 110 consisted of the tables of data—observations that usually belonged in laboratory notebooks, not in scientific papers and books.

In this work, Lysenko made the only attempt in his life to use formulas. They were three simple formulas for calculating the average temperatures needed to complete individual phases of development. One of them, for example, was $A + Bn = \sum t°$, where A is the quantity of heat needed for the transfer of a plant to the next phase of development, B is the temperature at which this phase can be initiated, n is the number of days of duration of the phase, and $t°$ is the sum of temperatures in a given period of time. In the preface, Lysenko thanked Derevitsky and Igor Yu. Staroselsky for their help with the formulas. Thereafter he never used any sort of mathematics in his articles, and in the 1950s he declared that physics and mathematics were of no use to biologists.

Lysenko set forth nine clearly formulated conclusions in the monograph. They amounted essentially to the idea that completion of the first phases of development requires amounts of heat energy specific to the plant. Spring varieties of grains, for example, need a higher sum of temperatures during the early stages of germination than do winter varieties. On that basis, he argued that, by altering the temperature during those early phases, it would be possible to turn "one and the same variety, under some thermal conditions, ... into a spring variety and ... under other conditions into a winter one."[11] The monograph presented sums of temperatures necessary for the transition from the phase of simple vegetative growth to the generative phase. Despite its defects—the presence of irrelevant material, inadequate treatment of data, disregard of the works of other authors, and the absence of a bibliography—the study showed that Lysenko was aspiring to solid scientific research. The work did not contain practical suggestions; the data were insufficient for that.

In both Soviet and non-Soviet literature, the opinion is widespread that this was a pioneering and original study, the logical outgrowth of Lysenko's work on peas. Roll-Hansen, for instance, has pointed out that "even Lysenko's severest critics among the geneticists rated several of his physiological works highly."[12] It is doubly important, therefore, to consider whether Lysenko's work was independent of earlier investigations and why he suddenly abandoned the promising pea crops and switched to a new subject. The explanation that Derevitsky's dismissal as station director made it unnecessary to continue projects begun under him can hardly be taken seriously. It is just as untenable to try, as those investigating Lysenko's works have sometimes done, to present his study of "development by stages" as a logical outgrowth of his work on peas. His first primitive research project and the emergence of a new theory of development were unrelated in concept and method; the one did not derive from the other.

The role of temperature (as well as of other factors) in the transition from one phase to another in the development of plants had been studied in Germany and the United States in the first decades of the twentieth century.[13] The subject had been studied in Russia even earlier,[14] and it continued to be studied in the Soviet Union.[15] Indeed, the specific phenomenon of the formation of spikes on winter grain crops after exposure of the germinating plants to cold was known to plant physiologists as early as 1858.[16] Even more specifically, the term "vernalization" (from "vernal," of or relating to spring), had been used to label the phenomenon. Those contemporaries who studied it considered the scientific problem to be to understand its causes, its scientific peculiarities, and the biochemistry of the process, and then to find the means of controlling it in order to put it to practical use. But there was nothing new in Lysenko's findings.[17] It might still be argued that he was unaware of the previous studies and that he can thus be credited with an independent establishment of the principle. Yet even this does not appear to be the case.

It must be said, first of all, that Lysenko's study of vernalization had no relationship to his earlier work on peas. It is not clear why Lysenko turned to this new subject. Most likely, he heard of the possibility of transforming winter forms into spring forms from the staff members of the VIR who visited Gandzha each summer. These people probably knew of the earlier work; in fact, Nikolai A. Maksimov, who had done some of that work himself, was head of a laboratory at VIR. However that may be, it can be shown that, at a very early point in his experiments, Lysenko knew what the results would be and how to interpret them.

In 1926, Gavriil S. Zaitsev, a well-known specialist who had studied the behavior of cotton and other plants in Central Asia after their exposure to various environmental factors, published a book in which he not only posed the problem of the temperature sums but also presented the solution.[18] Lysenko, in the introduction to his 1928 monograph, mentioned Zaitsev's method of "isophases," and he wrote: "The intervals between the sowing of seeds and the appearance of the shoots he [Zaitsev] considered as two independent isophases. The further appearance of each leaf is an isolated isophase . . . and so on. The duration of each isophase expressed in days is inversely correlated with the sum of temperatures."[19] Later on in the monograph, Lysenko cited this scientist's work three more times, as if comparing their respective conclusions.[20] However, the comparisons are so vague as to suggest not that they were made after Lysenko had completed his own research but that Lysenko simply borrowed Zaitsev's ideas, as well as his methods, without crediting him.

An article by V. T. Batyrenko affords another indication of the attention being paid in those years to the role of low temperatures on sprouts. The article reported that in 1929 one D. Moskalev was able to accelerate the maturation of spring wheat, rye, and barley by two to two and a half weeks by chilling the germinating seeds.[21] In 1936, I. Vasilyev flatly denied the assumption that Lysenko had blazed a trail in the investigation of vernalization; he cited several Russian and German authorities.[22]

Further evidence for this conclusion was found in the main agricultural newspaper—which is itself an interesting fact, because Lysenko's career was founded on articles in the popular press rather than in scientific journals. The Russian agronomist Nikolai M. Tulaikov wrote, in an article published on November 13, 1929: "I had occasion to have a lengthy conversation with Lysenko at the Gandzha experimental station at the beginning of 1927 [i.e., when Lysenko's work on vernalization was just beginning]. . . . We discussed the application to various local plants of the laws established by Professor G. S. Zaitsev about the sums of temperature necessary for the cotton plant to pass through different phases of development."[23] Tulaikov's recollection of this conversation was still fresh, though two years had passed, and he spoke quite definitely of application to various plants of an already discovered law. It thus becomes clear why Lysenko referred to Zaitsev four times in his 1928 monograph, compared his conclusions with Zaitsev's, and reiterated each time how similar they were.

Indeed, it should be emphasized that it was in this conversation with Tulaikov that Lysenko obtained clarification of the details of Zaitsev's experiments. It is also worth noting that Tulaikov did not reject Lysenko's results; he merely called for caution in their interpretation. Nevertheless, that caution and the very fact that Tulaikov recalled Lysenko's awareness of Zaitsev's laws left a deep mark in the mind of the would-be innovator. Lysenko never referred to Zaitsev again. Rather, he later came to insist that it was he, Lysenko, who had discovered the principles of vernalization.[24]

Tulaikov's article raises another question, that of Lysenko's moral character. I have searched diligently in the articles and books of the period for any indications of a gradual change from a young Lysenko striving to become an independent-minded agronomist to an automaton responsive to the very tone of commands from above, but I have found none. On the contrary, I was struck by the consistency of his behavior from the very outset. He seemed to have stepped directly into his role, without even the need for rehearsals. Another might have fretted and felt doubts and fears; Lysenko stepped boldly onto center stage and played his part without hesitation.

The Report at the Genetics Congress

In December 1928, at a national conference of the Sugar Trust in Kiev, Lysenko presented a paper on the effect of temperature on plant development and its potential application to a program of research on sugar beets.[25] (It is interesting that Lysenko never referred to this program again and never did conduct any serious studies of the vernalization of beets.) Three weeks later, Lysenko delivered another report, this time in Leningrad and to a more significant audience: the First All-Union Congress on Genetics, Plant Breeding, Seed Production, and the Raising of Pedigreed Livestock. Among those attending was Sergei M. Kirov, the Communist Party leader in Leningrad, as well as geneticists from all over the world.

Two circumstances account for the appearance of Lysenko among so eminent a group. Vavilov had planned the conference not only as a review of the achievements of Soviet biology in the years since the Revolution but also as a showcase for the researchers of his VIR, including both those from the experiment stations and those from the principal laboratories. Secondly, Vavilov had taken a liking to Lysenko from their very first meeting and was trying to help him. A few days before Lysenko made his presentation, Vavilov had praised his work in an interview that was published in the Leningrad youth newspaper after the conference ended.[26]

Lysenko's paper, coauthored with Dolgushin, said that it was merely an exposition of the data presented in his 1928 monograph, but actually it was a fundamentally different kind of work. The monograph had been dry and academic in style. The paper at the Leningrad congress struck a bolder note, proclaiming loudly that behind the seemingly dull exposition lay a revolutionary idea that would make possible a sweeping change in agriculture: the sowing of winter grains in the spring, like ordinary spring crops.

Normally, winter wheat is sown in the fall, germinates before the onset of cold weather, resumes growing when winter is over, and is harvested the following summer. This practice is subject to several risks: In winters with little snow and hard frosts, the crop may be killed; if ice forms, the crop may be "suffocated" beneath the crust; and if the spring is too wet, the crop may rot before it can be harvested. What Lysenko and Dolgushin claimed in their paper at the Leningrad congress was that, if newly sprouted seeds of winter wheat were merely exposed to cold but not sown, the seedlings would go on to produce ears of grain when planted in the spring. This would avoid the risks of fall sowing and, they asserted, would increase the crop yield as well, since winter wheat normally gives a greater yield than spring wheat. The generally accepted belief that winter varieties of wheat would not grow spikes if planted in the spring was declared to be false. The paper stated that "there are no calendar limits dividing winter from spring forms; each variety behaves quite individually."[27] (By the end of 1929, Lysenko had gone much further: he was denying the very existence of different varieties. "In our present view," he asserted, "there are neither winter nor spring varieties; there are only grains and grasses with varying degrees of 'winterism' . . . and we can artificially overcome 'winterism.'")[28]

The paper by Lysenko and Dolgushin did not create any great stir. Later the same day, in the same section of the congress, Maksimov presented a report on the influence of cold on plants, a topic on which he was regarded as an authority. He and his collaborators had obtained data through extensive experiments, but he offered no "revolutionary" conclusions or implications for immediate practice. Indeed, at the end of the congress, during a discussion of the papers, Maksimov criticized the paper by Lysenko and Dolgushin, in particular challenging the suggestion that their conclusions could already be put into practice.[29] Although Maksimov was mild and polite in his comments, Lysenko, as we will see in a later chapter, never forgave Maksimov for this "offense."

Lysenko and Dolgushin may have been saved from further unpleasantness at the congress. The program included a paper by Zaitsev, "The Effect of Changing the Duration of Daylight on the Cotton Plant." Zaitsev had gone beyond both Lysenko and Maksimov, studying the effect on plant development not only of temperature but of other environmental factors as well. However, en route to the conference, Zaitsev was stricken with peritonitis and died; his paper was never read.[30]

When the newspaper *Leningrad Pravda* reported on the congress, under the headline, "Winter Cereals Can Be Turned into Spring Cereals," it did not even mention the names of Lysenko and Dolgushin. It referred only to Maksimov's presentation, and it expressly criticized attempts at hasty practical application of his findings under field conditions.[31]

Father and Son Declare Their "Discovery" of Vernalized Winter Wheat

Lysenko was not content to let matters rest there. The success of the 1927 *Pravda* article had taught him how to gain the spotlight. He discovered how little it took to capture the imagination of journalists in search of a sensation. In the summer and fall of 1929, several of the nationally circulated newspapers reported that in the previous spring, Lysenko's father, Denis, a member of the Bolshevik Labor kolkhoz in the village of Karlovka, had conducted an "experiment" with vernalized winter wheat. One of the stories, which appeared in *Pravda* in July, mentioned the Fyodorovich article of nearly two years earlier, and went on to describe what had now happened:

> The agronomist Lysenko . . . has continued his experiments . . . in Azerbaidzhan. There Lysenko . . . prepared a first small batch of the Ukrainka variety of winter wheat for spring sowing and sent it . . . 3,000 kilometers north to his father, a leading middle peasant [*peredovoi krestyanin-serednyak*] in the village of Karlovka. . . . The elder Lysenko sowed . . . the wheat in the normal manner on his own field in the spring of 1929, following his son's instructions.
>
> A week ago, at Lysenko's invitation to the Commissariat of Agriculture of the Ukraine, a specially appointed commission visited his field. . . . Harvesting can begin about July 20–25. . . . According to the determination of the commission, the harvest . . . should come to nearly three [metric] tons per hectare, as compared with an average yield of one ton for all other spring wheat in the district.[32]

It is striking, and revealing, that another article, also published in *Pravda* but about ten weeks later, described the events quite differently. This article was by Aleksandr G. Shlikhter, the commissar of agriculture for the Ukraine (see biographical sketches). Shlikhter's position was not an easy one at that time. The harsh winters of 1927 and 1928, together with the destructive consequences of the collectivization campaign that began in 1928, had left the Ukraine stripped of grain, so the promise of greatly increased yields in the future must have been very appealing. Shlikhter began by alluding to the congress on selection and genetics that had taken place in Leningrad (though, curiously, he said it had been held in August and September of "last year," instead of in January of that same year), and he observed that the paper by Lysenko and Dolgushin had gone "almost unnoticed." He continued:

> On his way to the congress, Comrade Lysenko visited his peasant father and told him about his experiments and the paper he planned to present at the congress. The father decided to test his son's discovery in practice and risked sowing a

winter variety in the spring. . . . For three years, he had planted Ukrainka seeds
during the winter, but . . . now . . . he soaked nearly 50 kilograms in warm water
in his peasant cottage. . . . The seeds began to sprout. . . . He placed them in two
sacks so that they lay in an even layer approximately 15 centimeters deep,
covered the bags with snow . . . [left them] until springtime . . . and planted
them on May 1, 1929. . . . The neighbors, upon learning that old man Lysenko
had sown winter wheat in May, decided that he had gone out of his mind. . . .

On July 10 of this year, the peasant Lysenko came to the Ukrainian Commissariat of Agriculture with excellent samples of ripened winter wheat spikes. . . .
On July 12–13, a commission of the Commissariat of Agriculture verified on site
the remarkable results of the peasant Lysenko's experiment and brought samples
of the wheat spikes to Kharkov [which was then the capital of the Ukrainian
republic]. The commission established the following facts by inspecting the
crop in the field and interrogating local people, agronomists, and Lysenko
himself. . . . The winter wheat had grown absolutely normally and had produced
a crop of over two and a half tons per hectare, but spring wheat sown at the same
time and side by side with the winter wheat was flattened by the June rains and
yielded half as much.[33]

Thus, in one version, Trofim himself prepared the experimental batch
of seeds in Azerbaidzhan; in the other, it was his father who soaked the
seeds, and they were his own. The first article referred to "a small batch"
of seeds; in the second, the small batch had grown to "nearly 50 kilograms." (Some biologists have suggested that perhaps, when grain was
being expropriated from the peasants during the collectivization campaign, Lysenko's father concealed two sacks of seeds in the snow; the
seeds became wet from the snow and sprouted; and, in the following
spring, he planted them on the off chance that they would grow and
mature.) According to the first article, Lysenko invited the Ukrainian
Commissariat of Agriculture to visit the "experimental" fields, whereas the
second article says his father brought samples of the wheat to the commissariat, after which the commissariat sent a commission to Karlovka.[34] Furthermore, in the July *Pravda* article, the vernalized seed had been sown on
a plot of one and a half hectares; in an article that appeared in two
different publications in 1932, Lysenko wrote that the sowing had been on
a half-hectare plot.[35]

There are also discrepancies in the figures for the yield obtained from
this "experimental" sowing. In July, before the crop had been harvested,
the commissariat's commission estimated the yield of spring-sown winter
wheat at "nearly three metric tons per hectare." Shlikhter reported it, after
the harvest, as having been "over two and a half tons per hectare." In later
articles, Trofim Lysenko spoke of 24 centners, or 2.4 metric tons[36]—which
would still be three and a half times the national average for spring wheat
at that time.[37] In the biography of Lysenko published in 1953, the figure
of 140 poods (22.4 centners) was cited.[38]

In 1935, Lysenko soberly stated that, in the preceding year, "the average
increase in yield due to vernalization was 1.14 centners [0.114 metric

tons] per hectare on the 1,060 kolkhozes that reported harvest data."[39] That would be an increase of only about 15 percent over the 1928–1929 average. In the same year, Lysenko *père* spoke of increases of 3 centners per hectare in 1933, declining to 1.75 in 1934 and to 1.2 in 1935.[40] This is no more than what might be expected. Consequently, we must regard the reports of a large harvest from vernalized winter wheat as false.

Even if vernalization per se could increase yields, there are countervailing factors to be considered. First, mold develops on moist grain. Second, in order to subject the sprouted seeds to cold and at the same time prevent overheating, the mass of seeds must be constantly turned, which inevitably would break many of the small, tender sprouts. As a result, there were fewer shoots to be germinated in the field, so that more seeds had to be sown. Moreover, it was impossible to achieve uniform treatment of all the seeds, particularly in the agricultural conditions of the time. Finally, although the plants grown from vernalized seeds may bear heavier ears than plants grown from seeds sown in the normal way, there are fewer of them.

What all of this indicates is that there were no trustworthy data about the results of the "experiment." Indeed, it would not qualify as an experiment at all by the ordinary criteria of science. There were no comparisons between experimental and control samples, there was no repetition of the work, and there was no rigorous description in a scientific publication. (Indeed, all the descriptions of the work appeared either in newspapers or in Lysenko's own journal, *Vernalization*.)

Heedless of such considerations, the two *Pravda* articles had in common a conclusion of unrestrained enthusiasm: in July, "The prospects opened up by this extraordinary discovery of agronomist Lysenko, corroborated by such outstanding experimental data, are so great that they are beyond immediate calculation"; and in October, Shlikhter exclaimed, "The agronomist Lysenko has completely overthrown the definition of winter forms prevailing hitherto. . . . Agronomist Lysenko's discovery will lead our agriculture onto a high road of vast possibilities and extraordinary achievements and greatly increase the tempo of our socialist construction." One cannot exclude the possibility that the commissar of agriculture and his deputy—who were Party functionaries, not agronomists—did not understand a thing about farming, but how could the commission of the commissariat, which did include specialists, fail to see the discrepancies in the accounts of father and son? It was strange that the leaders of agriculture of the Ukraine and indeed of the whole country foresaw no difficulties and failed to check possible miscalculations. It was as though all at once they believed in the power of a miracle and decided that they had the firebird in their hands. Indeed, it was no accident that they were seduced by myths promising to solve all problems at one stroke, rather than facing the real and serious work of putting agriculture on a sound foundation. All Soviet life was permeated by myths, by expectations of the imminent approach of communism, a bright future just ahead. The notion of ordinary working people achieving miracles, shock workers "born to make fairy tales come true" (in the words of a popular song of the time), perfectly matched the mood.

As the years passed, the Lysenkoist literature established the legend that the spring sowing of winter wheat had come about not by chance, but by scientific planning—ostensibly an ordinary, normal scientific experiment. Lysenko himself asserted more than once that in the summer of 1929 his father had conducted a deliberate experiment and the results obtained represented "conformities with the law of the newly discovered theory of plant development by stages."[41]

Lysenko profited from the Soviet press's glorification of his work. Although no scientist had corroborated his "discovery" or the effectiveness of the new method, he was handed a handsome gift at the end of 1929. By special decree of the Ukrainian Commissariat of Agriculture, a large laboratory was created for him in the Odessa Institute of Plant Breeding and Genetics, one of the country's leading scientific institutions of its kind, directed by the prominent scientist Andrei A. Sapegin. From a junior specialist at a small experimental station in Azerbaidzhan, Lysenko was transformed into the head of a laboratory of an institute of the Ukrainian Academy of Agricultural Sciences. He used the opportunity not to embark on systematic verification of the idea of turning winter varieties into spring varieties, but to increase his public renown.

2

The Unrecognized Threat

Possessor of Rasputin's gift
  Of mesmerizing people's minds
With lunatic ideas. . . .

—I. I. Puzanov, *Shattering the Idols*

Repulsive means for good ends make the ends themselves repulsive.
—Anton Chekhov

A New Scientific Method: Publicity

On November 13, 1929, the *Agricultural Gazette*, official organ of the USSR Commissariat of Agriculture, devoted nearly an entire page to a discussion of the vernalization of winter varieties of wheat. (Note that the discussion dealt with *winter* varieties. Half a year later, Lysenko would realize that his method of vernalizing winter wheat offered no advantages,[1] and he would then switch to advocating cold treatment of soaked seeds of *spring* varieties instead. The vernalization of spring varieties would not change them into some other variety: They simply remained spring varieties. Lysenko ignored the significance of the switch for his claims about heredity and environment; he merely chalked it up as another major discovery.) The newspaper had invited four well-known scientists to consider the advantages of vernalizing winter wheat: Sapegin, Tulaikov, M. Prik, and P. I. Lisitsyn. All four spoke of Lysenko's work with respect, though without great enthusiasm, and they agreed that the concept of vernalization should be tested further, though they all considered it premature to apply the idea in practice on a wide scale.[2] It probably never occurred to any of them that there had been no true experiment at all on the transformation of winter into spring wheat. They simply assumed that, if the newspapers hailed "Lysenko's experiments" and "agronomist Lysenko's discovery," such experiments must have taken place, and as responsible scientists, they believed that the results should be studied further.

A few days after that discussion was published, the *Agricultural Gazette* printed another set of articles on the subject, under the headline, "Vernalization of Winter Varieties: A New Achievement in the Fight for the Harvest." Accompanying them was the editor's comment, in large, bold type: "The Institute of Applied Botany and New Crops has long employed cold germination to transform winter into spring varieties. Vernalization of winter varieties is, thus, not a new departure, but agronomist Lysenko's work carries great importance because it introduces the cold germination method into large-scale use in the fields. Vernalization of winter varieties promises to increase the yield in many regions." No mention was made of the previous discussion. The only concession made to testing was that it would help "to perfect the Lysenko method for possibly wide practical use." The comment continued, still in boldface type: "Comrade Lysenko's experiments lead us straight to a solution of one of the most serious problems of the day—the grain problem. The use of vernalized winter sowing material will guarantee the grain against freezing."[3] The processes of scientific discovery and verification were being moved out of the laboratories and onto the newspaper pages. For the first time, commissariat officials were openly using the press to pressure scientists.

It is important to note here the role that newspapers played in Soviet society. Daily and weekly papers like *Socialist Agriculture*, *Agricultural Gazette*, and *Sovkhoz Gazette* were run by the Party, not to provide objective agricultural information, comment, or news, but to articulate the Party line to farmers, villagers, and others involved in agriculture. Other fields also had their own newspapers and magazines, serving the same end. Over and over again, we shall see how the newspapers signaled to their readers—sometimes subtly, often blatantly—just who was in favor and who was fated for disgrace and perhaps death.

It may seem irresponsible for reputable scientists to have agreed to be drawn into a discussion of an unverified project, but the grain supply had been so imperiled by two successive cold and snowless winters that it was urgent to seek any avenue that promised improvement. Specialists at all levels were ready to do anything they could to meet the crisis. The scientists, moreover, probably did not realize where the authorities were leading them, and their statements that the proposition was not without interest, although there was a long way to go before practical application, could have sounded differently to different audiences. Most of the public and the agriculture officials dismissed the professors' reservations as academic quibbling and hedging, whereas the scientists may have assumed that soon, as sensible people do, somebody would actually set about studying, checking, and weighing the proposition, determining whether there was a rational kernel in the idea, and, if so, whether it merited taking up on a large scale.

A week later, the discussion was brought to a resounding conclusion in an article by Lysenko himself. Its very publication in this context was an announcement that, in the eyes of the administrative and Party leadership, Lysenko stood above the specialists of the old school. In the article, Lysenko insisted that he had made an original discovery. In order to set himself apart from Gassner, Maksimov, and others who had called the preliminary chilling of seeds the "cold germination method," Lysenko called his method "winterizing" (*ozimost*), and he laid claim to having devised a "hypothesis of winterizing." He then asserted that he had discovered a new natural phenomenon, "vernalization," that transformed any winter variety into a spring crop. He declared:

> "Winterizing" opens up truly vast prospects for agriculture in many areas of our [Soviet] Union. It is necessary here, however, to be clear and precise, since some, even prominent, scientists confuse Gassner's "cold germination" method with the method of "winterizing" plants proposed by me. . . .
>
> *The hypothesis of "winterizing" plants opens up broad prospects, by comparison with which the experimental sowing of winter varieties in the spring will be only a small part of all the practical possibilities this method can offer agriculture.* . . . It uncovers genuine, broad possibilities of finding spring varieties that develop earlier and with higher yields than the poor-grade spring wheat that now produces too small a harvest in many areas of the USSR. . . . The Ukrainian Genetics Institute and the Azerbaidzhan Agricultural Experimental Station are already working energetically on these questions, and their positive results are likely to become the common heritage in the near future.[4]

This article indicated that Lysenko had tried to introduce himself as an influential scientific figure and foreshadowed his dictatorial rule over Soviet biology.

Kolkhoz Science by Questionnaire

One of Lysenko's first actions as head of the new laboratory at the Odessa institute was to send circulars to kolkhozes and sovkhozes all over the country, recommending that they make maximum use of the vernalization of winter wheat and report the results to the Odessa institute. To facilitate the tabulation of these results, three questionnaires were distributed, each containing columns for entering certain data: amount of vernalized seed sown, size of sown area, and date when shoots appeared (form No. 1), dates of start and finish of formation of ears (form No. 2), and date of maturation and information on threshing and size of harvest (form No. 3).

There was nothing wrong with the idea of questionnaires as such. The data Lysenko sought could answer many questions. But this was not what Lysenko should have been doing. The scientific method required data of another sort altogether. Inasmuch as the "Lysenko experiment" was as yet nonexistent, proclamations in the press notwithstanding, he was under an obligation to actually conduct the experiment and obtain the necessary results, even if retroactively, and only then propose the introduction of whatever procedures had been shown to be effective.

But Lysenko knew virtually nothing about the principles of scientific research. He may have sincerely believed that the questionnaires were a practical and genuine way to "carry on science" on a massive scale.[5] He did not understand that the questionnaire method was no substitute for the comparison of results of repeated experiments conducted under identical conditions (identical soils, identical treatment of the soil, identical plantings, identical climatic conditions, and so on). Consequently, it was futile to collect and summarize data from however many kolkhozes and sovkhozes, for that did not allow a judgment to be made about the advantages and shortcomings of vernalization.

Furthermore, the staff distributed the questionnaires during the chaotic period of collectivization. In the organizational confusion of the times, vernalization could at best be realized only on paper. Yet Lysenko and his collaborators later maintained that, by the spring of 1930, "hundreds of kolkhoz experimenters" were engaged in the vernalization work. But the data from the questionnaires were never published. Indeed, it is not even known how many of the questionnaires were returned.[6] Nevertheless, citing their existence, Lysenko proceeded to bombard officials in Kharkov and Moscow with proposals for decrees to require the kolkhozes and sovkhozes to adopt vernalization, holding out the promise that great increases in harvests would follow. Newspapers and leaflets propagandized for the new agricultural method, and the authorities threatened dire punishment for those who were negligent about vernalization. Headlines like "Enemies at Work in the Granary" and "We'll Teach Anti-Vernalizers a Lesson" appeared over stories in the press. Meanwhile, nothing about the negative aspects of vernalization was printed in the mass media.[7] It can be expected that these indications of official attitudes would themselves affect the responses to the questionnaires, rendering them altogether worthless for scientific purposes.

In the provinces, as might be expected, people filled the questionnaires with exaggerated figures for which no one felt responsibility; these were mere scraps of paper, such as flooded the kolkhoz and sovkhoz offices to collect desired responses. A poor showing invited grave peril, and since no one checked the figures and no one answered for their accuracy, every kolkhoz clerk, team leader, or bookkeeper understood what was called for and knew just how to adjust the figures. Thus, even an honest tally of the data would have been useless. Later, when the government introduced vernalization quotas for each province, it became unsafe to fill in the reports even with figures showing small increases. The bluff snowballed.

Later, Lysenko himself acknowledged the ineffectiveness of questionnaires: It seemed that even in 1932 (data for the preceding years were never disclosed) "not all the experimental points sent all three questionnaire forms by August 27. Form No. 3 (harvest and yield) was especially poorly represented. . . . Only 59 questionnaires were received from all the provinces."[8]

Nevertheless, Lysenko's method aroused no objection from the agricultural leaders either in the Ukraine or in Moscow. On the contrary, the USSR commissar of agriculture, Yakov A. Yakovlev (see biographical sketches), eagerly accepted each new claim that Lysenko made. Stalin himself set an example for the selective use of statistically based methods of planning and evaluating economic activity. In a speech delivered at a plenary session of the Party Central Committee and Central Control Commission in 1929, he said:

> Rykov tried to frighten the Party by claiming that sown acreage in the USSR showed a tendency toward systematic decrease. He implicated the Party, hinting that Party policy was to blame for the reduction in the sown area. . . .
>
> Is it true that the sown area shows a tendency toward systematic decrease? No, it is not true. Rykov used average figures for the sown areas throughout the country. But average numbers, without correcting the data by districts, cannot be considered a scientific method.
>
> At some point Rykov must have read Lenin's *The Development of Capitalism in Russia.* If he did, he must recall that Lenin severely criticized bourgeois economists who used average figures for growth of sown areas but ignored the data by districts. It is strange that Rykov now repeats the mistakes of the bourgeois economists.[9]

The implication was clear: statistics were acceptable only if they gave the results the leadership wanted.

First Defeat for the Geneticists

Early in 1930—even though vernalization had produced no results as yet—Lysenko was honored by an invitation to present a paper before Soviet agriculture's highest advisory body, the collegium of the USSR Commissariat of Agriculture. The collegium consisted of the commissar of agriculture, his deputies and department heads, and the president and vice-presidents of the prestigious VASKhNIL; its recommendations on the most vital agricultural matters carried the force of orders. It was one of the keys to Lysenko's success that, despite his peasant origin and his relative lack of education, he was not intimidated in the presence either of eminent scholars or of Party bosses. He understood that what was important was to repeat that vernalization increased yields and to make alluring promises of even greater achievements in the future.

The paper that Lysenko delivered at this meeting was well received. Yakovlev praised him highly for his contribution to the solution of the problems of food production, and the commissariat adopted a resolution approving vernalization. Thereafter, Lysenko read a paper almost every year at meetings of the collegium, and he received frequent invitations to other meetings and conferences as well, where he appeared together with the country's leading scientists. With each speech, he grew bolder in his presentation of numerical data. He came to realize that no one was going to check his figures and that, in any event, he could count on the new ideology, his class origin, and the political winds sweeping the country to protect him.

In February 1931, Lysenko read a paper at a meeting of the presidium of VASKhNIL. Afterward, the presidium adopted a resolution, signed by Vavilov, announcing that vernalization had already "justified itself." The resolution stated:

The presidium of the Lenin Agricultural Academy . . . recognizes these experiments to be deserving of special attention, and a whole set of institutes (the Institute of Plant Industry, of the Protection of Plants, and others) have been mobilized to help Comrade Lysenko . . . [and] instructed to place in his charge specialists, a first-class collection of wheat varieties, and so forth. . . . The author of the method . . . has been given a substantial monetary prize.[10]

The next day, under blaring headlines, the national press printed a report of the meeting and the resolution of the academy's presidium. A few months later, the commissariat's collegium issued a directive that vernalized seeds of winter wheat were to be sown on 10,000 hectares in the Russian Republic and on 100,000 hectares in the Ukraine.[11] This was followed by a grant of 150,000 rubles a year to Lysenko's laboratory to conduct research, publish a journal, the *Bulletin of Vernalization*, and provide other support.[12]

By 1932, Lysenko was insisting on large-scale vernalization not only of wheat but also of crops on which he had not yet conducted any research at all: potatoes, corn, millet, sorghum, Sudan grass (*Sorghum halepense*), and soybeans. In 1933, he added cotton, and in 1934, fruit trees.[13] This kind of juggling of proposals and expansion of demands, without any basis in evidence, became a characteristic Lysenko tactic.

Meanwhile, in September 1931, Lysenko once more displayed his skill at stealing the spotlight. The occasion was a conference under the title, "The Problem of the Struggle for a Large and Stable Harvest," organized by the Commissariat of Agriculture and chaired by Commissar Yakovlev. Following introductory remarks by the commissar and presentations by such prominent scientists as Tulaikov, Academician Dmitry N. Pryanishnikov (Vavilov's teacher and an outstanding agrochemist), and the well-known selection specialist Georgy K. Meister, Vavilov reported on recent advances in plant genetics and selection, paying special attention to the work of two amateur horticulturists, the American Luther Burbank and the Russian Ivan Michurin (see chapter 5), and to the achievements of two geneticists, Herman Muller of the United States and Georgy D. Karpechenko of the Soviet Union. In 1927, Muller had discovered the mutagenic action of X-rays on *Drosophila*. (The first application of Muller's discovery to produce mutant forms of plants was made by Sapegin.) Karpechenko, who was present at the conference, had succeeded in producing something that does not occur in nature and that most scientists had believed was impossible to produce artificially: a fertile hybrid of two different genera. By using a technique that doubled the chromosome sets of the egg and pollen cells of a radish plant and a cabbage plant, Karpechenko had managed to produce fertile hybrid offspring. The work had won for him the International Rockefeller Prize and worldwide renown.

Nonetheless, Vavilov singled out Lysenko and vernalization for special praise:

Of particular interest . . . is the work of Lysenko, who has concretely approached the practical transformation of late-ripening varieties into early-ripening ones, changing winter into spring varieties. The facts he has discovered are indisputable and deeply interesting. . . . *Lysenko's experiment has shown that late Mediterranean varieties of wheat can be turned into early-sowing forms in our conditions by special treatment before sowing.* Many of these varieties surpass our ordinary varieties both in quality and yield . . . Immediate, sustained, collective organizational work is needed in order to realize the highly interesting facts established by Lysenko.[14]

Lysenko's speech was the most businesslike one of the conference; by now, he took for granted praise like that given by Vavilov. He began with a "vehement protest" against "the overly simplified conception of his work as an attempt to achieve spring planting of winter-spring crops." This interpretation of his "theory"—as he persisted in calling it—had "already begun to 'become obsolete.'" He said he was calling for cold treatment of other plants beside wheat, and he dwelt on the need to search for varieties that would best respond to cold germination. He also touched on the distinction between the processes of growth and of development. And then he stunned the audience: He said that by changing one single factor, temperature, he had managed to immediately increase the crop yield of Azerbaidzhan wheat, sown in Odessa, by 40 percent! He cited no other figures in the report, a shrewd bit of psychology. One startling figure said more than a hundred could.

He dwelt upon one other matter that hardly attracted anyone's notice but bears directly upon our further narrative: He assured those present that he intended nothing more than a simple clarification of one particular question of plant physiology, and that—while it was unquestionably because of this change that the yield of wheat had been raised and there was also the hope that yields of other crops could also be raised—still, he was not trying to shake the foundations of science or subject them to revision. "One could get the sort of impression that I constantly have to fight against: that the vernalization method is in opposition to that of plant breeding. One cannot accept such thinking. There is no opposition. *On the contrary, there could be no vernalization without genetics and plant breeding. . . . Vernalization gives us the ability to use genes, and in this lies its fundamental significance.*"[15]

As we shall see, Lysenko soon changed his stance toward genes and genetics; a year later, he was to declare that genes did not exist and that geneticists were enemies of socialism. But to those attending the conference, and particularly Yakovlev, the most important point in his speech was the dramatic announcement of a very large increase in the crop yield.

From our point of view, the most noteworthy aspect of the conference was that not one of the scientists questioned Lysenko's claim—not even Vavilov or Meister, who surely understood that Lysenko's assertion was groundless. For the first time, eminent scientists, in the presence of agricultural officials, failed to offer a challenge on a vital point. Perhaps they did not realize that their silence served to corroborate a false claim. It was a decisive moment in the fate of biological science in the Soviet Union.

With Lysenko's hypnotic "40 percent" still ringing in their ears, the conference participants took up the question of reducing the time necessary for developing new plant varieties. This discussion arose from a purely arbitrary decree that had been adopted a month before, without consulting the scientists, by the joint presidium of the Party Central Control Commission and the Commissariat of Workers' and Peasants' Inspection, two of the most influential and powerful organs in the Soviet Union. The decree "ordered" that selection be speeded up to the point where it would take only one-third or one-fourth as long to produce new varieties as it had been taking. In the discussion, Meister, one of the most successful of the country's selection specialists, who had developed varieties that covered tens of millions of hectares, tried to make the commissariat officials understand that the idea of such an acceleration in the development of new varieties was scientifically absurd: "You see, if it takes ten to twelve years to develop a variety in present conditions, to 'steal' three or four years from nature would require an incredible feat in itself. But to speak of shortening the time for growing a new variety to five, four, or three years is impossible."[16]

Judging from the newspaper account of the conference, Yakovlev did not respond, but when the next speaker repeated that new varieties could be developed "only in ten years" at best, the commissar stopped him with the curt retort: "We do not have ten years to wait."[17]

On the following day, Yakovlev's impatience with scientific foot-dragging boiled over in an exchange with Karpechenko. The latter's paper at the conference was a brilliant but recondite account of the theoretical basis for crossing plants of different genera. To the practical commissar, Karpechenko's work—for all its international fame—seemed useless. Yakovlev began to prod the young geneticist, at first gently, then more and more insistently, to answer a specific question.

Yakovlev: What would you say if you were asked what can be done in the next few years to create a drought-resistant variety of wheat?
Karpechenko: We must change the nature of the plant by studying the characteristics I have mentioned. We need a technical base.
Yakovlev: We will give you the base. I agree to your every request in advance. Now tell me how we can raise the yield of our crops, how we can launch a counteroffensive against dry spells.
Karpechenko: We need to "marry," first, a huge collection of plants with, second, geneticists, plant breeders, physiologists, and climatologists. I think this ought to be done by the closest coordination of our existing laboratories.
Yakovlev: What goal should we set them?
Karpechenko: It seems to me we ought to put our botany in order and choose the greatest possible number of varieties. Then we geneticists will consult with other

scientists. We can undertake the genetic research, but the specialists in plant breeding will have to add their input in all that follows. The problem is very complicated, but if we work systematically on a very large scale with a great number of plants, we will achieve definite successes. I repeat, *this problem is very complicated*; if we want to obtain hybrid drought-resistant forms, we must go about it by turning out a first generation. *We are conducting this kind of work right now, but we do not yet have concrete results. This is a very difficult task.*[18]

Karpechenko's responses were serious, responsible, and honest, but not politically astute, especially coming on the heels of Lysenko's speech. He could have said that one cannot shut one's eyes to real problems, and he could have challenged Lysenko by saying that he would not follow the example of those who manipulated figures irresponsibly, promising the unattainable. He might still have gained in the eyes of the commissar and at the same time put Lysenko in his place. Instead, Karpechenko spoke vaguely of future prospects, and it was apparent to all that he had no practical program and that his talk of conferring with other scientists on abstract matters would not produce a kilogram of additional grain that day or the next. His statements about the "difficulties" of the problem would have irritated any commissar looking for concrete results—the more so when another young man stood by who, though not anointed with a foreign prize, was doing what the country needed.

So, without a fight, without even realizing that they should have fought, Karpechenko and Vavilov, Meister and Tulaikov lost their best chance to challenge Lysenko. Misled by Lysenko's air of respect toward genes and genetics, the biologists let him gain ascendancy over them. They took no precautions; they even joined in the praise for the newcomer. Of course, they could not have known that he was simply biding his time, waiting for the right moment to announce that genes did not exist, that genetics was a lot of nonsense, a bourgeois distortion, and that the geneticists were the enemies of socialism. Yet they should have known that even the slightest slackening of requirements for scientific proof would lead to harmful consequences, for the history of science is replete with examples.

Yakovlev's position was understandable. He was under pressure, too, from the Party leadership—Stalin above all—to produce immediate, decisive results in agriculture comparable to those that had been achieved in industry. Taking the floor after Karpechenko, he declared:

Imagine that we have come to you as entrepreneur-landowners and told you that incredibly low harvests are draining the strength from our best grain-producing regions, such as our Volga granary and southwestern Siberia. The Soviet "landowner" asks: What can be done to help in this situation? Our standards are rising, greater possibilities are opening up, the peasants have joined kolkhozes. How can science help them? . . . Our sovkhozes astound the Americans who visit us; visiting Germans assure us they never dreamed of anything like it. Huge lines form to see our exhibition in Königsberg. Surely all this indicates that we have immense possibilities! So how can Soviet science help our agriculture, given these immeasurable possibilities?[19]

Without mincing words, Yakovlev made it clear that things had to change. The Party and the government were demanding immediate, concrete, even heroic, efforts by the scientists to obtain practical results. When Maksimov, who spoke next, tried to give an evasive scientific answer to a question put to him by Yakovlev, the commissar cut him off rudely with remarks about "the inadmissibility of games in science" and about the need to turn from theory to practice. He also said, in a sentence that was printed in boldface type in the published account of the proceedings: "The agricultural sector expects the agroscientists to address precisely the needs of socialist agriculture."[20] With such "expectations" as a background, it is not surprising that in October 1931, at the Ukrainian Congress on Selection, Lysenko was greeted with an ovation.[21]

Triumph at the Drought Management Conference

The All-Union Conference on Drought Management, held in Moscow at the end of October and the beginning of November 1931, marked another step upward for Lysenko. The importance of this conference to the Soviet government is indicated by the fact that it was addressed by both Mikhail I. Kalinin, chairman of the Central Executive Committee and thus the titular head of state, and Vyacheslav M. Molotov, chairman of the Council of People's Commissars, or prime minister in western terminology. Lysenko was included among the scientists who spoke at the conference, a sign of the eminence he had already achieved. He declared again that wide use of vernalization would make it possible to combat drought, long a scourge of Russian agriculture. He now felt freer to argue with those who gave a more cautious evaluation of the prospects for vernalization, especially Maksimov, in view of Yakovlev's recent criticism of him. "Professor Maksimov and his research associate Comrade Razumov," he said, "have quite glibly explained [contradictory data] by stating that there is antagonism between the vegetative and reproductive stages of development. There is no such antagonism."[22]

Lysenko's rejection of other scientists' conclusions was not based on any new data of his own. He himself said that he did not yet have information on the results of vernalization and could speak only of preliminary data. Referring to "1,260 pure lines, chiefly of hard wheat, . . . taken from various districts of Soviet Azerbaidzhan, which are under investigation," he said that "the total weight of the harvest was not calculated, but in weight per grain and from the weight of 1,000 grains . . . it is evident that we obtained grain incomparably better than our Ukrainian wheat."[23]

It was simply irresponsible for Lysenko to say that one method of treating seeds was superior to another on the basis of the weight of 1,000 grains collected from an unspecified source, instead of actually weighing the harvest or at least systematic samples of it. But this did not deter the political leaders from giving Lysenko their complete support. *Pravda* reported that, at the conference, "Comrade Yakovlev placed special emphasis on the importance of agronomist Lysenko's work," and *Izvestia* said:

> Comrade Yakovlev stressed that particular attention must be given to the question of Comrade LYSENKO'S work. Comrade Lysenko himself still does not realize the ENORMOUS significance of his own work. . . . It is our task . . . to apply Comrade Lysenko's method on a MASS scale, a scale at the least of hundreds of thousands of hectares, as early as the spring of 1933. Only when this is done will the matter be placed on a scientific, a truly revolutionary, footing.[24]

Furthermore, Molotov spoke highly of Lysenko's speech in the lobby,[25] and Yakovlev thereafter became even more admiring of Lysenko. A resolution adopted at the conference cited "the necessity of working to establish ways of treating seeds of other types of plants [besides grains] before planting."[26]

The roots of this willingness to accept untested nostrums lay in two factors. One was a widespread infatuation with all sorts of wild projects, an infatuation born of a belief that the time was not far off when nature, people, and society would be transformed. The other factor was the concentration of power in the hands of persons who may have been knowledgeable about revolutionary tactics but were unqualified to make critical evaluations in the realm of science and technology.

The conference on drought management clearly illustrated both these factors. Vernalization was not the only project greeted with enthusiasm. An engineer by the name of Avdeyev (or Avava—it was given both ways in the press) proposed the construction of a dam thirty-seven meters high and four kilometers long across the Volga River, the longest river in Europe, to divert its flow away from the Caspian Sea toward the Aral Sea in order to irrigate millions of hectares of the arid trans-Volga steppe. He took no account of the effects on the Caspian Sea, or on the Volga, never mind the possible global environmental changes. He simply promised that the dam would eliminate drought over an enormous territory.

Another engineer, B. Kazhinsky, urged that balloons and airplanes be sent up to ionize the atmosphere and induce rainfall, paying no attention to calculations of cloud moisture in the areas of concern or to the effectiveness of the ionization methods then available. Nevertheless, both these proposals were described enthusiastically in the press, giving readers the impression that the problem of drought was about to be solved.[27] Yet today, more than half a century later, the struggle to deal with the vagaries of climate and weather is still continuing.

The outcome of all of those discussions was exceptional, even for those times. Though not a soul had yet been fed with bread from vernalized wheat, in December 1931 Lysenko received his first government decoration: the Order of the Red Banner of Labor, "for work on vernalization."[28]

3

Bluff after Bluff

Such a virtuous and sorrowful anecdote:
Now the old nags are putting the people out to pasture!
—Vladimir Solovyov, 1885

Our young agricultural science actually is already overtaking
bourgeois science and already has surpassed it in some spheres.
   Comrades, you know that task of the old science: to help the
bourgeois, the kulaks, and any and all exploiters. The aim of our
science, on the other hand, is to serve the cause of kolkhoz development. . . .
   Of course, it is not for us to pity the bourgeois scientists. But,
seriously, we are sorry for them simply as people. The fate of the
bourgeois scientists is not a happy one.
—T. D. Lysenko, February 15, 1935

More Orders to Agricultural Science

In order to impress Party and government leaders with their achievements, Lysenko and his assistants would from time to time add up the
higher yields reported by some kolkhozes and attributed to vernalization,
and they would then multiply the total by the country's sown area and
thus extrapolate enormous estimates of the size of the harvest.[1] These
vastly inflated estimates looked all the more attractive against the backdrop
of agricultural catastrophe. Between 1928 and 1932, the USSR endured
the terrible consequences of a disastrous drought and of three of Stalin's
programs: collectivization of the farms; the arrest and exile (mainly to
Siberia) of nearly ten million so-called kulaks—the richest and most successful farmers—and their families; and the requisition of all grain, including food grain, animal feed, and seed stocks, by the army and special
teams of factory workers. Widespread starvation ensued in Russia and the
Ukraine. In 1929, crops were left standing in the fields in some places and
had to be harvested by the army in others, because whole villages had
been wiped out by the arrests or by starvation.

"The years of the height of agricultural reorganization, 1931 and 1932,
were years of the greatest decline in the grain harvest," Stalin himself was
obliged to admit at the Seventeenth Party Congress in 1934.[2] According to
Molotov's report to the congress, the average grain yield for 1928–1932
was only seven and a half metric centners per hectare, far below the plan
target.[3] Matters were even worse for livestock. Instead of the large growth

in the herd that Stalin had expected before collectivization began, live-stock numbers fell. Molotov's figures showed that during collectivization (1928–1932), the country lost more than 40 percent of its cattle (down from 70.5 million to 40.7 million), over 40 percent of its horses (from 33.5 million to 19.6), almost 65 percent of sheep and goats (from 146.7 million to 52.1) and approximately 55 percent of its pigs (25.9 million to 11.6).[4] Appalling as these numbers were, Molotov deliberately understated them. The actual drop in the number of cattle, sheep, goats, and pigs was greater. Yet neither Stalin nor his colleagues in the Party leadership could admit that collectivization was a disaster, renounce it, and offer any real program to improve agriculture.

In order to "improve" management of the newly collectivized farms, twenty-five thousand "representatives of the proletariat" were sent from the cities to head up the kolkhozes.[5] These city folk did not know the vital difference between food grain and seed stock, so they failed to object (and sometimes even assisted) when the army requisitioned seed stock along with all the rest of the grain. The peasants were left to sow with whatever they could find. As a result, seeds of almost all the most valuable established varieties disappeared. Even Stalin admitted in 1934 that "the seed situation in grain and cotton is such a mess that it will take years to straighten it out."[6]

Many of the long-established Russian wheat varieties were of good quality: high in protein and resistant to disease, drought, and cold, although not always high in yield. They provided dependable, if not maximum, harvests, even in years of bad weather. A scientifically based system of developing and testing new varieties could have led to further improvements, and the science of genetics that had emerged at the turn of the century provided the knowledge to make that possible. Indeed, many of the old Russian varieties became progenitors of the modern American and Canadian varieties. Soviet efforts along these lines were based upon the decree, "On Seed Production," drafted by Lisitsyn and signed by Lenin in 1921. The decree required that seed testing and production be performed in specially designated scientific units.[7]

Upon the establishment of VASKhNIL in 1929, Vavilov, its founder and first president, recruited a staff of leading agricultural scientists and set about organizing a network of research institutes and experiment stations. He improved upon the already existing systems for the development, testing, and quality control of new varieties of plants, and he insisted on determining the climatic zones that best suited these varieties. The Soviet press reported in 1933 that a British organization had declared that, in the preceding years, the VIR had conducted "the greatest experiments the world has ever seen."[8]

The question of new varieties and of the principles of seed production arose repeatedly at conferences at various levels. The government initially took a favorable view of Vavilov's proposals. On his recommendation, the

Council of Labor and Defense adopted a resolution in July 1929 recognizing "the necessity for a further expansion of the area sown to improved, pure-varietal seeds."[9] Meanwhile, Aleksei I. Rykov, who was then (until 1930) chairman of the Council of People's Commissars, was making speeches calling for a complete transition to pure-varietal seed within two to three years. Realizing that the process could not be speeded up simply by faster discovery of new varieties, the scientists sought to increase the total volume of work in selection, by creating more selection stations and trying out many varieties simultaneously.

But the Party and government were impatient. On August 2, 1931, the presidium of the Central Control Commission and the collegium of the Workers' and Peasants' Inspection adopted a sweeping resolution, "On Selection and Seed Production," which ordered the Commissariat of Agriculture, VASKhNIL, and VIR

> to set as a prime task in wheat selection the attainment within three to four years of the following: high yield, . . . uniformity of seed (vitreousness), adaptation to mechanized farming . . . , resistance to cold and drought, improved milling and baking qualities, resistance to pests and diseases, and qualities necessary for forcing the northward and eastward spread of the crop . . .
> to complete, basically by 1933, the entire replacement of ordinary seed with tested and pure-varietal seed, . . .
> to base the work of selection stations on new foreign technology, using the latest improved selection methods (grounded in genetics) . . . , thus reducing the time needed to obtain new varieties (to 4–5 years instead of 10–12)."[10]

The authorities essentially were ordering that new, improved varieties be created in a single season, despite the anarchy prevailing in the wake of collectivization, and that high-quality seeds be propagated in such numbers as to be the only seeds sown two years later. It was an impossible goal. The combination of desired qualities in wheat has not been achieved to this day. It was the height of wishful thinking to demand that the specialists produce new, improved varieties within four to five years, rather than ten to twelve. The reference to genetics was ironic, for it was the laws of genetics and plant growth which themselves precluded such speed. They required a process of selection and hybridization, testing in various soils and climates, and finally propagation that would normally take fourteen or fifteen years, not ten or twelve, let alone four or five. Even though Lenin's decree in 1921 had fully recognized these time-consuming requirements of science, the Party bureaucrats in 1931 chose to ignore them.

Lysenko Opens Fire on Genetics

Lysenko at this time was on the staff of the Odessa Institute of Genetics and Plant Breeding. At the end of 1932, he announced that he was undertaking to develop a variety in the time frame set in the August 1931 resolution. Academician Sapegin, the institute's director, had been making great efforts to place the work of plant breeding on the firm foundation of genetics. (Sapegin was among the first scientists in the world to employ X-rays to obtain new forms.)[11] He insisted that all crossing be done on the basis of pure lines, to facilitate the task of tracing characteristics, and he understood the necessity of mathematical calculations. He required that the members of his staff master the theory of genetics and the international scientific literature about it, but also that they spend time in the fields, making careful examinations of what might appear to be identical plants. This meticulousness was alien to Lysenko and his crew of "vernalizers" and led to frequent conflicts.

Sapegin's widow has related that the last straw was an incident in the autumn of 1930 or 1931. After the harvest of the experimental plots and before the sowing for the next season, Sapegin chanced to notice that some sheaves of wheat had been left unthreshed. At first, he thought that some lazy or forgetful assistant on Lysenko's team was to blame, but on closer inspection of all the plots, he discovered the truth: The sheaves had been left standing on purpose, and only on the control plots. By systematically "forgetting" to weigh these sheaves in the yield of the control plots, Lysenko's staff had exaggerated the relative yield of the experimental crop. Furious at this discovery of scientific fraud, the director insisted that Lysenko go out to the fields with him.[12]

Some time afterward (sources differ as to the exact date), Sapegin was arrested as a "wrecker." According to I. Ye. Glushchenko—one of Lysenko's first special graduate students, later his biographer and close collaborator(see biographical sketches)—Commissar Yakovlev, during his visit to the Ukrainian capital, Kharkov town, had been told that a variety developed by Sapegin had turned out badly, and Yakovlev had then publicly proceeded to criticize the Odessa institute director severely. The local authorities reacted—or perhaps overreacted—and arrested him. He was imprisoned for about two years, and then was not allowed to return to Odessa; however, Vavilov found a place for him in his Moscow genetics institute.

There is no documentary evidence that Sapegin's removal was the work of Lysenko, but whether it was or not, Lysenko long afterward bore a grudge against the place where he had been so humiliated. In 1937, when the struggle for the position of president of VASKhNIL was reaching its climax, he wrote in *Pravda*: "The institute to which I transferred in 1930 worked in the old-fashioned way, cut off from the broad masses like monks in their cells. What was worse, ties with practical workers were considered shameful for a scientist."[13]

After Sapegin's arrest, Lysenko devoted himself completely to wheat selection. Dolgushin later described the atmosphere at the institute in these words:

Modern Morganist genetics . . . had not justified itself in the least. . . . And so, when the revolutionary idea of a new approach to selection knocked loudly on closed doors, the noise alarmed [this] science, immersed as it was in theory, and it gathered its forces to fall upon Academician Lysenko for disturbing its exalted peace. . . . Amid the din of this fierce battle, the small, closely knit team of researchers working under T. D. Lysenko's direct leadership in the Odessa Institute of Genetics and Plant Breeding, a group inspired by a single idea and firm faith in victory, overcame all obstacles, carefully circumvented the pitfalls, and marched confidently and perseveringly on to the designated goal: a variety to be created in two and a half years.[14]

Lysenko's strategy was to revise a basic principle of plant breeding to read, "The parent plants should be chosen for the smallest number of negative qualities rather than for the largest number of favorable ones."[15] Presenting this as the latest word in science, he took two varieties, each of which, in his opinion, had only a single drawback: Girka 0274, a local Odessa variety developed by Sapegin, resistant to several diseases but late-ripening; and the pure line Erythrospermum 534/1, developed by V. P. Gromachevsky in Azerbaidzhan, which was early-ripening but low in yield. By crossing them, Lysenko hoped to obtain a wheat that would be early-ripening, like Erythrospermum, and disease-resistant, like Girka. He and his supporters never considered the possibility of the opposite outcome: a cross that retained the *bad* characteristics of each parent. They declared quite seriously that "by crossing these two varieties, we are bound to get a spring wheat free of the parents' defects."[16] Any beginning genetics student would have known that the probability of getting the desirable genes in offspring depended on the positions of those genes relative to each other on the chromosomes. To determine their relative positions would have required a whole series of crosses and the calculation of the number of crosses and generations that would have to be studied, as well as taking account of many other considerations that even an elementary knowledge of genetics would suggest.

But Lysenko and his pupils did not bother with calculations. They spent a mere "several days" to draw up a simple theory, of which, they declared, "There could be only one proof: the creation of a new spring wheat that would be earlier-ripening and higher-yielding."[17] Then the tailors set about weaving the emperor's new clothes.

Fifty seeds of the two parent varieties were planted in ordinary clay pots in a greenhouse in December 1932, and the resulting fifty plants were crossed in January and February 1933. A mere thirty seeds were obtained, whereas the crossing of fifty parent plants should have yielded several thousand. Such a failure meant either that there had been a mistake in the procedure or, worse, that the varieties were genetically incompatible. But Lysenko's team was not going to draw any untoward conclusions. In April, they planted the thirty "precious" first-generation seeds in the greenhouse. The result again was not propitious: Fewer than half the plants formed ears—i.e., the plants were evidently partially sterile. Never-theless, every grain that could be gathered was sown in July. All the seed was jumbled up together, violating a rule of plant breeding that is particu-larly important in working with partially sterile plants.

Dolgushin's chronicle of the experiment now reported a fresh failure: "The seeds did not sprout for a long time . . . some did not sprout at all."[18] Failure recurred, generation after generation. They should have thrown away all the material and started over again, but they could not stop, even though Dolgushin confessed that, "truth to tell, we later regretted that we did not properly appreciate the danger that the seed would not sprout."[19]

By the fourth generation, they finally had a yield of several thousand seeds. Rather than sowing all of these seeds and carefully tracking the progeny of each, Lysenko and his assistants "selected" twenty seeds that seemed to them to fit their expectations. They divided these twenty seeds into four groups that they called "families" or "varieties." But again, the plants that grew from the twenty seeds were weak and semisterile.

> What a pity so few people saw those twenty spindly plants in our greenhouse, the plants that held all our hopes, desires, and thoughts. Some of our geneticists—who recommended, from their standpoint, crossing well-nigh all the seed material the globe possessed and then scouring the hectares of the hybrid fields by candlelight for unknown "suitable" plant forms—may have laughed sincerely then. We knew from the beginning that among the twenty plants we selected there had to be several forms completely meeting our requirements, because most of them, except for possibly "false" early-ripening forms, lacked the only characteristic defects of the two parents—the requirements of a "long" stage for vernalization and for the length of the light stage. . . . This was the guiding thread that gave us confidence in victory.[20]

Only eight months remained of the two-and-a-half-year period set by Lysenko himself at the end of 1932, and those months fell in late 1934 and the winter of 1935. To keep his promise, Lysenko needed to have by the spring of 1935 several hundred kilograms of seeds, from varieties that had been proven through at least three generations of testing in state plots. Yet, with less than a year remaining, all he had to show for his efforts was a mere handful of seeds from each of the four "families." Failure loomed before him.

Lysenko solved his problem by juggling figures. He gave each of the four paltry batches of seeds a four-digit number—1055, 1160, 1163, 1165—to give the impression that these four "hybrids" were the best of over a thousand lines. He planted these seeds in July 1934, not in the field, though it was summer, but in "40 boxes, 48 seeds in each." As Dolgushin described the results:

> After several days sprouts appeared, but very unevenly. . . . Even after ten days some did not germinate at all. In this respect our 1160 hybrid behaved somewhat better—

on the tenth day approximately 50% germinated. The others produced only a few shoots; characteristically, they developed extremely slowly and abnormally. It was also noted that the offspring of one and the same family behaved variously. Some sprouted well, others were late, and some gave forth no shoots at all. Lysenko returned from an absence on August 1. It was decided to lower the temperature at any cost. Our first thought was to send the boxes, at least those containing our basic hybrids, to the Odessa seaport refrigerator. Our second idea, on which we settled . . . was to bring in eighty kilograms of ice that evening. Women workers hastened to place ice in the boxes and cover them with paper and straw.[21]

Even these heroic efforts yielded minimal results; the plants sprouted a bit more, but by no means evenly. No plant breeder in the world would have worked with such material, but the Lysenkoists were not embarrassed. At the beginning of October, they moved the forty boxes into the greenhouse, gathered all the seeds indiscriminately, and by November 25 they sowed again, "to obtain approximately a kilogram of seeds of each of the four hybrids to plant in seed-testing plots in the spring of 1935."[22] Yet a hundred kilograms was hardly enough to allow for a serious test.

One night the following January, Odessa's southern clime sprang a surprise. The temperature suddenly dropped to –26° C. (–15° F.). The greenhouse began to freeze. Pot-bellied iron stoves were brought in, and Lysenko's team "'robbed' someone's apartment of another stove and pipe. For lack of firewood, we took lumber and boards 'illegally' and chopped the wood then and there in the hothouse. . . . People flitted . . . from one stove to another to keep the fires and the draft going, to avert accidents and to repair the damage when accidents occurred. Despite all efforts, by morning the temperature in some parts of the hothouse was –3° C. [27° F.]. In those places the soil in the boxes froze."[23] Moreover, smut beset some of the plants during the ripening period. The plants had failed to retain Girka's strong feature, resistance to disease.

By the spring of 1935, they had only a half kilogram of seeds of 1163, slightly more of 1055, and one and a half kilograms each of the two other "hybrids." They sowed these in the field and supposedly showed these plantings to participants in the June circuit session of VASKhNIL. There is some question as to whether Lysenko displayed the actual varieties he had grown, or something else that would have looked good to the specialists. Anyone familiar with wheat varieties could have seen that Lysenko's varieties were semisterile. Indeed, Dolgushin's own account makes it clear that the plantings were nothing to boast about.

The entire sixth generation suffered uneven sprouting and poor setting power. By now, it was clear that the "experiment" had not confirmed the theory and that Lysenko had failed to make good on his pledge. But he was untroubled by doubts. On July 25, 1935, he sent a lengthy telegram to Party and government officials in the area of agriculture:

With your support, we have fulfilled our promise to develop within two and a half years, by means of crossing, a spring wheat variety for the Odessa region that is earlier-ripening and higher-yielding than the [standard] regional variety, Lutescens 062. Four new varieties have been obtained.

We consider beardless 1163 and 1055 to be the best varieties. We attribute the smaller increase in the harvest of variety 1163 as compared with the other new varieties to a great sparsity of sowing of this variety because of insufficient seed in the spring. We already have fifty to eighty kilograms of seed of each new variety. The two varieties 1163 and 1055 have been sown again in the fields to propagate the seed.[24]

Lysenko went on to give the strong impression that his four varieties were indeed true varieties, carefully tested—"thrice repeated," he said—and yielding 1,200 and 1,400 kilograms per hectare, far more than the standard variety. Like his labels for the four "varieties," his data were clearly faked. "Thrice repeated" meant that he had sown three plots in the same year, not that he had repeated the tests for three successive generations, as the varietal testing regulations required. And his figures for yields did not even agree from one part of the telegram to another. The impressive yields of 1,200 and 1,400 kilograms claimed toward the end of the telegram had simply been extrapolated from the best yields of the tiny plots at Odessa—the 50–80 kilograms in hand that he had mentioned at the beginning.

Another page of the telegram was even bolder. It proclaimed a wholly new fundamental theory of plant breeding and seed production, without explaining what the theory was all about. The development of four first-class varieties in record time was presented as a trifling by-product, compared to what could be accomplished with this epochal new theory. This was a tactic that Lysenko afterward used more than once: He would first trumpet a forthcoming achievement, and then, when it failed, he would bring another new project out of his hat, meanwhile blaming his scientific adversaries, "wreckers," or negligent collective farmers for the failure of the previous effort, charging all of them with being enemies of socialism.

The telegram concluded on a characteristic note of optimism combined with an emphasis on the need for continued support:

> Our theoretical premises (not yet proved in practice) give us grounds to hope for tremendous practical effect from the renewal of seeds of self-fertilizing varieties. If our experiments bear out our assumptions in 1936, the kolkhozes and sovkhozes would have elite seeds of the basic regional varieties by 1937, and the bulk of the farm acreage would be sown to renewed seed in 1939.
>
> We hope to enjoy your continued leadership and great support of our further projects.[25]

Nevertheless, the Lysenkoists themselves were obliged to discard three of the "varieties" as unsuitable, and 1163, the one Lysenko particularly counted on and urgently ordered propagated, was criticized by plant breeders the following year.[26] But by then, Lysenko had won the confidence of the supreme leadership.

Summer Planting of Potatoes

Within a single year, starting late in 1932, Lysenko's chief postulate took form: the science of genetics was not viable. From that it followed naturally that geneticists were just not capable of seeing that, in the coming golden age, those new social structures—the kolkhozes and sovkhozes—would span countless expanses. The "laws" of genetics had perhaps been justified and demonstrated once upon a time, but only for a different, a bourgeois society. In the golden age, any need for them would vanish. Proceeding from these postulates, he later proclaimed a whole series of "discoveries." In doing so, he moved along several lines. He learned to falsify, to count on faked data for support, to ignore any results that did not confirm his artificial constructs and predictions. He developed his own phraseology and drew upon ringing stock phrases, and he learned how to keep abreast of political changes at the highest levels.

Following his foray into wheat varieties, he next used these methods to attack the problem of increasing the potato yield in the south. Without conducting any experiments, he decided that when a potato tuber is left in warm soil for a couple of months, the "breed" (*poroda*—the peasant term that Lysenko used to refer to hereditary characteristics) deteriorates. Conversely, if the tuber is planted in cool soil (closer to the autumn, for instance, when temperatures would be lower), the "breed" would improve in one or two seasons. The way to increase the potato harvest was thus clear.

Lysenko's suggestion for the summer planting of potatoes could hardly be considered original. For centuries, farmers of the Mediterranean area, coastal areas of the United States, and other regions with a warm, damp autumn have employed the practice of planting potatoes in midsummer rather than in late spring to avoid drought at the critical moment of ripening, but no one has ever suggested that this practice changed the potato's hereditary properties or had anything to do with deterioration or improvement of the "breed."

Following Lysenko's instructions, Yevgenia P. Melnik planted tubers of the Ella variety of potatoes on a quarter-hectare plot at the Odessa institute on July 6, 1933. According to Lysenko's later account, they did yield a crop, because that summer was an unusually rainy one. "That was why we were able to obtain potatoes on a plot where one crop had already been raised—something that could not be achieved without irrigation in ordinary years in the south."[27] However, the "breed" did not improve, and Lysenko, comparing the summer planting with the usual plantings, admitted that the results "seemed not to confirm the thesis that summer planting would stop degeneration of the seed material."[28] Nevertheless, this did not deter him from continuing to advocate the method. In the summer of 1934, nearby kolkhozes were ordered by the government to sow one or two hectares with potatoes that the Lysenkoists sent from Odessa.

Lysenko claimed that in late autumn the farms reported a fine crop. He said the size of the individual potatoes gathered after summer planting was especially impressive: 300 to 500 grams, and even some that were one and a half or two kilograms.[29] He declared that the new theory about the reasons for the "degeneration of potatoes in the south" had been proven, listed it among major achievements of the new biology, and assured the Party leaders that the potato crop in the south would increase rapidly, thanks to this latest contribution to science.[30]

He then put into operation his accustomed method. A salvo of articles lauding the summer planting of potatoes appeared in the newspapers—at least eleven such articles between March and November 1935.[31] He pushed decrees through the All-Union and the Ukrainian commissariats of agriculture making summer planting compulsory. At the 1935 session of VASKhNIL, Lysenko declared that, thanks to summer planting, "the entire south [of the European part of the USSR] will be assured of 200 percent of sowing potatoes in 1937."[32] In one article, he spoke of the verification of summer plantings on three hundred hectares of twenty-five kolkhozes; in another, the figures had increased twentyfold.[33]

Inevitably, he touched on the political implications of his innovations. Why had these innovations never been taken up by the practical capitalists of the despised West? "To admit that the nature of the potato cultivated in the south has been changed is to recognize that the heredity of organisms changes with the conditions of life. It is to the disadvantage of the bourgeois science of hereditability, however, to recognize this dependence. It does not recognize it to this day."[34]

Lysenko's zeal went beyond a willingness to undertake any assignment set from above. He announced his own "counterplan," as the practice came to be known in the mid-thirties, to exceed the goal and shorten the time frame. This tactic of accepting a task from on high and turning it into a supertask became a Lysenko characteristic.

A dictatorship strives to instill obedience, so that the citizens of the country follow orders unquestioningly, even eagerly. Slogans, repeated thousands of times, accompany one's every step and become an integral part of one's thinking and existence, until the individual will and personal aspirations cease to exist, and there is only the ardent desire to fulfill directives. This process of subjugating people's will, thought, and energies to the dictator's demands encounters particular resistance among people whom the dictator needs most: the creative, innovative members of the intelligentsia and especially the scientists, whose calling requires that they test all ideas carefully. To the authorities, this situation presents a dilemma. On the one hand, creativity, and therefore technological advancement, appears to be impossible without this skeptical underpinning; on the other hand, it can easily turn into criticism and fault-finding, and thence to political dissent. In a totalitarian environment, dissent imperils the foundations of the social structure. The tendency is to exaggerate the peril and consequently to reject the benefits of criticism. Accordingly, in the Soviet Union the leaders made clear that they appreciated only those scientists who could be handled as easily as ordinary workers and peasants, who were ready and eager to scale scientific heights upon command.

The supertask was more than mere submissiveness; it was the transformation of an order into an inner, personal need to exceed a goal set from on high. The fact that a member of the intelligentsia had taken on a "managed imperative" and had begun energetically to carry it out was an important development in the eyes of the leaders. Lysenko had grasped this fact; he defined his task and supertask, and he played his cards brilliantly, at a time when the great majority of scientists were not yet aware of the stakes.

4

Vavilov and Lysenko

Here's food for thought:
A genius is born to elevate the lowly,
and the lowly are born to scoff at genius.
— Inna Lisnyanskaya, "Rains and Mirrors"

In our country, it is easy to become a scientist if one has the aptitude
and the desire. Soviet life itself forces one to become a scientist to
some degree. It is very difficult, even impossible, for us to maintain a
sharp, impenetrable division between scientist and nonscientist.
Every intelligent participant in the kolkhoz and sovkhoz system is to
some extent a representative of agronomical science. This is the
strength of Soviet science and each Soviet scientist, and this is why
the path that led me into science is ordinary and accessible to any
Soviet citizen.
— T. D. Lysenko, "My Path into Science"

The Vavilov Family

Like Lysenko, Nikolai Vavilov came of peasant stock, on both his father's
and his mother's side, but one generation removed. His father, Ivan, was
the child of serfs who lived about sixty miles from Moscow.[1] Ivan was musi-
cally gifted and had a strong voice, so that he stood out among the children in the local church choir. His parents, upon the advice of the local
priest, sent him to Moscow to study singing.

After some time as a member of the choir of the Novo-Vagankovo
Church, Ivan decided to quit his studies and work as a "boy" (*malchik*—the
actual title of an occupation) for the merchant Saprynin. Later, he went to
work in a store run by the owners of the Prokhorov textile mill. There he
quickly attracted notice by his striking organizational and commercial ca-
pabilities. He soon became manager, first of the store, then of a division
of the Prokhorov firm, and then was appointed co-director of the company, responsible for foreign sales. At the beginning of the 1890s, he
founded his own commercial enterprise and became a prominent and
wealthy businessman. He attained the highest rank in the merchants' guild
and was elected a Moscow city councilor.

Vavilov's wife, Alexandra Postnikova, like him, had only an elementary education. The couple had seven children, three of whom died in childhood. While
the father dedicated himself completely to his business and public duties, the
mother devoted all her energies to the family. Their youngest son, Sergei, said

of his parents: Father . . . was intelligent, completely self-taught, but read and wrote a great deal and was undoubtedly cultured. Apparently he was an excellent organizer; his affairs were always in order. He was very bold, not fearing new undertakings. He was a socially active person, a liberal, a true patriot. . . . He was loved and esteemed. . . . Mother was wonderful, had high moral standards. . . . She had no personal interests of her own, she always lived for others. . . . I have seen few such women in the world.[2]

After the Bolshevik Revolution, Ivan Vavilov, by then a millionaire, emigrated to Bulgaria; his family remained in Russia. In 1921, Nikolai Vavilov, while on a mission abroad, managed to see his father in Berlin and tried to persuade him to return to Russia. However, he did not return until 1928, only to die two weeks after he had returned.

All of the surviving Vavilov children became scientists. Sergei became a physicist, discovered the so-called Cherenkov rays, and ultimately became president of the Academy of Sciences. Daughter Aleksandra was a physician and bacteriologist, and Lydia a microbiologist. Nikolai became world-famous as a biologist, traveler, and geographer.

Vavilov's Early Career

Nikolai Vavilov was born on November 25, 1887. At his father's insistence, he attended a commercial vocational school rather than a classical gymnasium, which meant that he was precluded from entering a university. After completing this school, Nikolai entered the Moscow Agricultural Institute (later named Timiryazev Agricultural Academy), located on the outskirts of Moscow. This was not an unimportant institution; several first-rate professors taught there. Vavilov soon gained attention by his industry and intelligence. His master's degree thesis, "Slugs (Snails) Damaging the Fields and Gardens of Moscow Province," earned him the Moscow Polytechnical Museum prize in 1910.

At the recommendation of one of his favorite teachers, the founder of Russian agrochemistry, Dmitry Nikolayevich Pryanishnikov, Nikolai Vavilov was kept on at the institute to prepare for a professorship. Shortly afterward, however, he changed his field of specialization and left to go to work for Professor D. L. Rudzinsky, who in 1903 had organized the first plant-breeding station in Russia. In 1912, Vavilov was sent abroad. He planned to spend two years traveling and studying in England, Germany, Austria, France, and the United States, but this program was disrupted by the outbreak of World War I. He did manage to obtain good training in England, in the Cambridge laboratory of William Bateson, one of the founders of genetics, and he continued his investigations of plant immunity to disease, a problem that had interested him since student days.

On his return to Russia in 1914, he got his first teaching position, at the Golitsyn Women's Higher Agricultural Courses. He also taught summer courses at the Moscow Institute of Agriculture. This early teaching experience left him dissatisfied, because it allowed him little time to pursue his own research.

In 1916, Vavilov traveled to Persia on an expedition that was partly military and partly scientific. Russia was at war with Turkey, and Vavilov was instructed to determine why the Russian forces were suffering from a mysterious illness: As soon as the soldiers had eaten even a small amount of bread made of the local flour, they fell into a state resembling drunkenness. Vavilov's earlier botanical studies helped him to establish quickly that the bread became "inebriating" from the presence in the flour of *Fusarium* mold spores and the seeds of an intoxicating weed, darnel ryegrass (*Lolium temulentum L.*).[3]

This trip was in many respects pivotal for Vavilov. It sparked his interest in the question that was later to become central to his scientific work: Where had cultivated plants first become domesticated?

The following year, Vavilov took a new teaching position, at Saratov University. His first lecture, delivered in September 1917 and entitled "Contemporary Problems in Agricultural Plant Cultivation," was widely praised.[4] Soon his lectures were attracting not only students but also his colleagues, the members of other departments at the university. After only a month in Saratov, he was invited to become assistant to the founder and director of the Department of Applied Botany and Plant Breeding of the Ministry of Agriculture. The director, Robert E. Regel, a prominent botanist, had a staff of fourteen assistant directors; they and their chief were required, in addition to their other duties, to attend the meetings of the ministry's scientific committee, whose members included some of Russia's outstanding scientists. Regel wanted Vavilov to be a consultant to the ministry on all questions of agricultural science, to carry out his own research, and to manage a network of experiment stations, departments, and bureaus throughout the country. Vavilov said he would accept the invitation only with the conditions that he keep his position in Saratov and that he turn his experimental field there into one of the department's bases. These conditions were accepted. The date of his appointment was the very day the Bolshevik Revolution broke out (October 25 [old style], 1917). Vavilov, as we shall see, was an ardent supporter of the Revolution.

Making use of his new position, Vavilov obtained funds to expand Saratov University, and his resourcefulness brought his colleagues' consent that the courses he taught be open to anyone associated with the university's agronomical faculty. As a result, young research agronomists began to gather around Vavilov, and he became friendly with many Saratov selection specialists, a number of whom later developed important plant varieties. Meanwhile, however, the burden of organizational and administrative duties consumed all of his energies, again leaving him little time for his scientific work. But Vavilov did have a trait shared by many of the greats of human history: He needed very little sleep, only four or five hours a night.

Thus, he was able to follow world literature on a wide range of questions and to consider many theoretical problems. Such determination soon produced brilliant results.

In 1920, a group of botanists and other scientists, at Vavilov's suggestion, organized an All-Russian Conference of Plant Breeders in Saratov. On the first day of the conference, June 4, an event occurred that would stand out in the history of Russian science. During the month before the conference, Vavilov had formulated a hypothesis. He had collected extensive information on which characteristics of different species, genera, and families of plants are subject to hereditary variation—i.e., mutation. His attention was attracted to the phenomenon of parallelism: When a particular kind of variation occurred in a structure of one group of plants (e.g., a change in the color, form, size, or other characteristic of ears of wheat), a similar variation was often observed in closely related groups (e.g., a similar change of characteristic in the ears of other grains). On the basis of the recurrence or periodicity of characteristics, Vavilov formulated a law of homology in hereditary variability.[5] In much the same way that one could predict the properties of still undiscovered elements on the basis of the Mendeleyev periodic table of elements, Vavilov used his law to predict the presence in nature of several subspecies of plants that were unknown at that time. Thus, the law would have some practical significance in helping to direct the search for varieties needed for plant breeding. In addition, it provided Vavilov with a means for uniting data from genetics with descriptive data from plant morphology, anatomy, and taxonomy.

Vavilov read a paper on this hypothesis at the opening session of the conference. Entitled "The Law of Homologous Series in Hereditary Variation," it was received enthusiastically.[6] The Saratov botanist Vyacheslav R. Zalensky made a statement that became famous: "This conference has become a historic event. The biologists congratulate their Mendeleyev." Vavilov's presentation also impressed Tulaikov, who participated in the meeting on behalf of the Experimental Division of the Commissariat of Agriculture and who headed all the country's research in agronomy. Reporting on the conference to his division, Tulaikov emphasized Vavilov's outstanding work and called him "the pride of Soviet science." He nominated Vavilov to be director of a State Institute of Agronomy that was being planned for Soviet Russia. But before that appointment could materialize, Regel died, in Petrograd, and Vavilov was named as his successor.

Vavilov's new duties confronted him with the difficult conditions of the postrevolutionary period. On November 5, 1920, he wrote to his collaborator Ye. I. Barulina (soon to become his second wife):

> I am sitting in the office at the desk of the late Robert Eduardovich Regel, and one sad thought follows another. Life here is difficult; people are going hungry; new life needs to be breathed into everything, as there is almost no life left here; it is as if things were, if not dead, then seriously ill, paralyzed. Everything needs to be rebuilt. Only the books and good traditions remain undying.

It is cold and uncomfortable in my room. For several hours I listened to a report on the burdens of life: cold, hunger, a hard life, and deprivation. There are up to 40 people on staff here. Many of them are good and excellent workers. Several are getting ready to leave because of the deprivations. They have been waiting for changes for the better on my arrival.

Dear friend, I fear that I will not be able to cope with everything. It doesn't depend on one person. Rations, firewood, salaries, clothes. I am not afraid of anything, and difficulties long ago became a challenge. But I fear not for myself, but for the institution and fellow researchers. It's not just a matter of organizing work productively, which I can do, but of putting the personal lives of many in order. It is all more difficult than it appeared from afar.[7]

In 1925, after months of discussions between Vavilov, teachers in science and agronomy, and Soviet government officials, Vavilov's department was converted into the Institute of Applied Botany and New Crops, with all the prestige and resources that this new status commanded. The chairman of the institute's scientific council was Nikolai P. Gorbunov, executive secretary of the Soviet Council of Commissars and formerly Lenin's personal secretary (see biographical sketches). The institute, said Gorbunov at the opening ceremonies, was to be "the first link in the creation of a national academy of agricultural sciences bearing the name of V. I. Lenin."[8] It was described as having "six basic experiment stations, six . . . experiment institutions, five laboratories, fifty-five research stations located in different geographical locations, and an office in New York." Its "central task" was "to increase the productivity of all species of agricultural plants and forests in the Soviet Union," for which purpose the government had appropriated four million rubles for the import of "first-class" seed material and three million "for the expansion of seed-growing." The expectation was that "by autumn this should produce a million poods [1 pood = 16.38 kilograms] of native seeds of exceptional quality, surpassing the best foreign models." Gorbunov, in a speech at the meeting, invoked Lenin's will as the inspiration for the institute, and he referred to Vavilov as a "world-class scientist."[9]

Vavilov's Travels

Vavilov had long been aware that there was much to learn about botany and plant materials in distant places. In 1916, he had traveled through the Pamir Mountains on foot and on horseback; in 1921, he had visited the United States and Europe, and in 1924 he had traveled through Afghanistan. He now decided to expand significantly the scale of his foreign expeditions and also to undertake a series of expeditions to all corners of the Soviet Union. Thus, in 1926–1927 he traveled through the Mediterranean countries. In 1927, he again went to the Far East. In 1932, he visited North and South America. He became familiar with the details of Danish and Swedish agriculture.

The main goal of these expeditions was precisely formulated: to gather samples of wild and cultivated plants and seeds that could be put to maximum use in the conditions of the Soviet Union. Gradually, the gathering of a collection of seeds became the fundamental task of the Institute of Applied Botany and New Crops. Everywhere he went, Vavilov searched for rare forms, reconstructed ancient selection methods, and interpreted them in the light of the latest scientific literature. In the course of this work, the idea crystallized in Vavilov's mind that the earth had had several basic centers of origin of cultivated plants, mainly places where civilization was actively developed and where humans adapted wild plants to their needs, unconsciously carrying out a spontaneous sort of selection of future varieties.

In 1924 Vavilov wrote from Afghanistan to his friend and Saratov colleague, the psychiatrist Pyotr P. Podyapolsky: "I have scoured all of Afghanistan, penetrated to India and Baluchistan and the Hindu Kush Mountains. Near India, we found date and rye progenitors and saw watermelons, muskmelons, hemp, barley, and carrots. We crossed the Hindu Kush four times, once along the route of Alexander the Great . . . I collected innumerable medicinal plants."[10]

In order to identify the sources of cultivated plants, Vavilov read ancient books, studied the Talmud, and visited the sites of archaeological excavations in the Sahara Desert and on the island of Crete. He was astounded by the high level of culture that had been reached by the ancient peoples who had settled what are now the Arab lands but had since lost sight of their achievements. He spent nearly two months in Palestine and what was then Transjordan, devoting much of the time to reading ancient Jewish religious texts "in order to reconstruct a picture of agriculture in biblical times."[11] From Jerusalem in 1926, he wrote to his wife: "I spent two days in the Arabian Desert. I found the cucumber of the prophets. I went south; from here I will go as far as the Sinai Desert, then to Jerusalem, Transjordan, the Dead Sea, then to Samaria, Galilee, in short, the whole of Scripture. I love this country. It is wonderful, with its mountains, olives, seas, varied landscapes, endless ruins, and long history."[12]

In another letter, he told his wife of reading in a Russian newspaper that he had been awarded one of the government's highest honors, the Lenin Prize (he was one of its first recipients). His response, characteristically, was: "In and of itself, it doesn't interest me. We are all equally [poor] proletarians. But I am touched by the attention. We'll keep trying.[13] With a knowledge of twenty-two languages and dialects,[14] he won over everyone with his openness and with a manner at once masculine and refined; he found a common language with the Negus of Abyssinia, with the stiff-mannered Vilmorins (a world-famous family of French plant breeders), and with native guides in the Sahara Desert.

Vavilov's Scientific Achievements

Vavilov gradually became the leading organizer of Soviet biology, its recognized and respected leader. In 1923, he was elected a corresponding member of the USSR Academy of Sciences. In 1925, the same year in which he received the Lenin Prize, he became a member of the USSR Central Executive Committee (a small body that was later replaced by the Supreme Soviet, the national legislature), and a year later, of the Central Executive Committee of the Russian Republic. Both the Russian Geographical Society and the Italian Geographical Society awarded him medals. In 1929, he was unanimously elected an academician, or full member, of the USSR Academy of Sciences—at 42, the youngest person to be so honored.[15] (Elected at the same time were Vladimir S. Gulevich, a biochemist; Pyotr P. Maslov, an agrarian economist and Social Democrat who had severely criticized Lenin more than once; Mikhail A. Menzbir, a zoologist; Georgy A Nadson, a microbiologist and one of the first to investigate mutation; Mikhail N. Pokrovsky, a historian and prominent Party representative; Dmitry N. Pryanishnikov, an agrochemist and Vavilov's teacher; Gleb M. Krzhizhanovsky, a power engineer and Party activist; and Nikolai I. Bukharin, a Party leader.) In 1931, Vavilov was elected president of the Soviet Geographical Society.[16] The academies of many countries elected him a foreign member.

In 1929 Vavilov was named president of VASKhNIL. As he rose to the top of the Soviet scientific elite, he increased the number of institutes under his direction and created new centers where he "planted" his scientists. These included separate institutes for pomology, vegetable production, subtropical crops, forage crops, corn, potatoes, cotton, flax, oil-producing crops, hemp, soybeans, grape and tea plants, and the grain industry of the southeast. He himself headed both VIR and the Genetics Institute, both of them in Leningrad; and even when the latter was moved to Moscow, Vavilov retained the directorship of both and as a result had to divide himself between Leningrad and Moscow.

As one might imagine, it was not possible to find first-class researchers to fill the positions at so many newly formed institutions. Thus, many of the institutes that sprang up at Vavilov's initiative were staffed with second-rate people, some of whom later sought Lysenko's backing. However, Vavilov visited these institutes systematically, critically examining the work of his protégés, pointing out their errors, and suggesting new directions for their research. His strategy was to grant them initiative while at the same time setting certain requirements for their work and pulling and prodding them forward.

This organizational work consumed more and more of Vavilov's energy, so that he no longer had time to carry out his own experimentation. Academician Pyotr L. Kapitsa, the physicist, who was also an academician as well as a winner of the Nobel Prize, has commented:

> Only when you are working in a laboratory with your own hands . . . can you achieve real results in science. You can't do good work using someone else's hands. The person who gives several score minutes to the supervision of scientific work cannot be a great scientist. . . . I am convinced that, as soon as even

the greatest scientist ceases to work himself in the laboratory, he not only stops growing but stops being a scientist altogether.[17]

This assertion is hardly an immutable law, but it does point to a difficulty in Vavilov's life as scientist and administrator. Nevertheless, thanks to his fantastic capacity for work and to his love of books and of the printed word in general, Vavilov painstakingly followed every nuance of theoretical thinking in biology and agronomy.

He had an amazing memory. Not infrequently, upon appearing at an experiment station in some provincial place, he would resume a conversation with someone he had seen perhaps once before in his life and then only in passing, picking up the thread of their discussion just where it had been left at their previous meeting: "You know, last time we were talking about Baur's work. Just last week, I read an article on the same topic in the *Journal of Agronomy*." Academician Nikolai V. Turbin, who was an apprentice at VIR, has told me of the following incident:

> We were leaving the VIR late one evening and overtook Nikolai Ivanovich on the stairs. We went together to the cloakroom. The middle-aged cloakroom attendant—I don't recall her name at the moment, and couldn't if I saw her— came out from behind the barrier with Nikolai Ivanovich's coat ready for him and helped him put it on. He took leave of her and us and walked to the door, engrossed in his own thoughts.
>
> Suddenly he stopped at the door for a second, slapped himself, and opened his briefcase, searching for something. He returned to the cloakroom and, turning to the woman, addressed her by first name and patronymic, apologizing: "Why, it's your daughter's birthday today! Her twentieth. I remembered in the morning and got a little gift, but became preoccupied and forgot about it. Forgive me. Congratulations to you and your daughter. Please give her this from me."
>
> With these words, he kissed her. No one else could have done it like that, and no one loved so sincerely and selflessly.

It appeared there was no limit to the energy of this man. Among his other achievements, he edited the great three-volume encyclopedia, *Theoretical Foundations of Plant Breeding*,[18] and he founded many Soviet agricultural journals. He wrote books and articles, gave lectures and presented papers, corresponded with hundreds of scientists, befriended writers and actors, and frequently attended the theater. His door was always open; he never came home without two or three guests for dinner. He had a warm heart for fellow researchers, both male and female, and was never snobbish. And meanwhile, he directed an academy and two institutes in Moscow and Leningrad and traveled to the most remote corners of the world to gather an extraordinarily valuable collection of seeds, which eventually came to number nearly 250,000 samples.

Vavilov the Soviet Patriot

Vavilov was not only a dedicated scientist but also an ardent patriot. He approved of the revolution and placed himself at the service of the new regime by directing his main efforts toward developing every possible practical application of his scientific knowledge. His conscious carrying out of programs predetermined from above could not but be combined, of course, with an instinctive tendency toward the wider and wider development of his own firmly established work. Vavilov did not passively accept all the mechanisms of the new regime's consolidation, but he unwittingly reproduced these mechanisms in his own realm, in the creation of his own school.

There was another side of his activity, which followed from his staunch devotion to the ideals of the Revolution. He invariably and in his own passionate way stressed that the Revolution was leading to the creation in the Soviet Union of the finest social system. He viewed the collectivization of agriculture enthusiastically and argued with family and friends who doubted the rightness of the transition to complete and unyielding absorption of the peasants in collective farming.

In 1929, Vavilov and Tulaikov spoke at the Sixteenth Party Conference. Both speakers hailed the social changes in the country, particularly collectivization. The two scientists said they spoke for all their colleagues in accepting the establishment of cooperative farming and the new tasks that collectivization posed for the biological and agricultural sciences. Vavilov said, "We do have agronomical science, but the enormous tasks put forth by the Party and by life demand exceptional attention to *the organization and reorganization of agronomical science itself.*" Tulaikov added, "Our country's social structure opens up full freedom of scientific creativity and the adoption of scientific truths by the great mass of individual peasants and by cooperative and large-scale collective and Soviet agriculture."[19]

At home and abroad, Vavilov did not cease to propagandize the achievements of the Revolution and to support the initiatives of the Soviet regime. Even in the most intimate conversations with trusted friends, when no one could overhear, he remained just as enthusiastic a supporter of the Soviet way of life, believing in the ultimate triumph of high ideals. A vivid example of this faith was a conversation Vavilov had with Theodosius Dobzhansky, who disclosed it after Vavilov's arrest. Dobzhansky, who became a leading geneticist, was born in Russia and had been a student of Yury A. Filipchenko's at Leningrad State University. After a three-year professional training assignment in the United States, he decided in 1927 not to return to the Soviet Union. During one of Vavilov's visits to the United States, they happened to be alone in the woods, and Dobzhansky bluntly asked Vavilov how he was getting on. Vavilov's reply was an impassioned monologue, maintaining that nowhere else could one apply one's abilities as widely as in Soviet Russia. Dobzhansky recalled:

Vavilov was a passionate Russian patriot. Outside Russia he was considered a Communist, which he was not. But he accepted the revolution wholeheartedly because he thought it would open greater possibilities . . . for Russia's people. . . . In October 1930, during a trip to the Sequoia National Forest with the author of these lines (there was no one near us), Vavilov said with great enthusiasm and conviction that in his opinion the possibilities for satisfying human needs in the U.S.S.R. were so great and so inspiring that for their sake alone one could excuse the cruelty of the regime. He asserted that nowhere else in the world is the work of the scientist valued as highly as in the U.S.S.R.[20]

Mark Popovsky, Vavilov's first biographer, has written:

Abroad, Nikolai Ivanovich spoke with inspiration of "the scientific strength of the Soviets." In his opinion, it was the direct duty of a visiting scientist from Red Russia to refute enemy slander, to assert the truth about the young Soviet biology and agronomy. Toward this end he did not begrudge time or effort. . . . This Russian scientist's impassioned speeches, full of facts, made many skeptics reconsider the potential of Russian science.[21]

Another illustration of Vavilov's attitude comes from his letters. On November 7, 1932, the fifteenth anniversary of the Revolution, he wrote from Cuzco, Peru, to Nikolai V. Kovalev, vice director of the VIR:

I am taking everything that I can. It will prove useful. The Soviet Union needs everything. It must know everything in order to put itself and the world on the road. We will find the road!

What we are doing is even clearer from afar. . . . We are stirring up the world. And we will get through to the heart of the matter. The institute's work is of great national and worldwide importance. . . .

From a distance our work looms even larger. . . . We will continue the revolution that has started in the plant industry.[22]

Three years later, in an article for *Pravda*, he wrote:

Our country's socialist agriculture shows a powerful potential for unprecedented possibilities. The kolkhozes and sovkhozes have become a lever for monumental changes in agriculture.[23]

Admittedly, he could have written such things from abroad because of the possibility of surveillance of his correspondence by state agents, and the phrases in the newspaper might have been intended to satisfy the requirements of the official ideology, which had already taken shape. But it is no less likely that he said these things in utter sincerity.

Over the years, Vavilov strengthened his position of leadership in Soviet biology. But each of his actions, seemingly logical and progressive, pushed him closer to the edge of an abyss that ultimately would swallow him. The higher he rose, the more his work became a barrier to a movement that was born in the same corridors of power in which Vavilov felt he belonged—a movement that, as it gathered force, took a different direction, corresponding more closely to the ideals of the system.

How Vavilov Helped Lysenko's Advancement

The seed collection of the VIR was an extremely valuable resource for plant breeders. Thousands of people were involved in its study, sowing the seeds and recording their growth, seeking new forms that could be put to use in Soviet agriculture. But a difficulty soon appeared. Many of the seeds, taken from plants that had grown in climatic conditions different from those in Russia—different lengths of day and different seasonal changes of weather—either failed to germinate or, if they did germinate and grow, bore fruit unevenly. Thus, the hope that these plants could be used for plant breeding, especially for crossing and intercrossing with existing Russian varieties, began to evaporate.

Vavilov felt that the method of vernalization could open a way out of this situation. If even winter varieties, subjected to the proper thermal treatment, began to bear in the spring period, then the difficulty might be overcome. If the varieties from the institute's seed collection could be "synchronized," so that they flowered simultaneously with local varieties, it would be possible to cross-pollinate the flowers of any two varieties and to obtain hybrid descendants. Moreover, according to Lysenko, vernalization would increase the energy of germination, propagation, and flowering, thus overcoming the problem of feeble growth. This would be a giant step for the country's selection program, providing an immense diversity of plant material. Vavilov began actively to help Lysenko, who himself may not yet have sensed the possibilities that Vavilov recognized.

Vavilov's ready acceptance of Lysenko's speculative and unproven hypothesis is understandable. Personally cut off from experimentation, immersed in a mass of organizational affairs, and believing the words of others as he would his own, Vavilov succumbed to the Lysenkoist fantasies. He did not realize how imperfect the hypothesis itself was, nor how far it was from experimental verification. Like many other scientists, he failed to notice that Lysenko had strewn about more promises than he had kept.

Another factor was that Maksimov, who was close to Vavilov, already had a favorable view of Lysenko. Vavilov trusted Maksimov, who had written in 1929 that Lysenko's idea should be put into practice (see chapter 1). Thus it was that, from the first steps of his scientific career, Lysenko found a powerful supporter in Vavilov.

Some biologists of the older generation believe that Lysenko had won Vavilov to his side before Lysenko spoke at the Congress on Genetics in January 1929.[24] It has been said that their first meeting took place in Gandzha and that the young agronomist received a personal invitation from Vavilov on that occasion to submit a paper to the congress.[25] Documentary proof of this opinion is lacking, but there is one suggestive piece of evidence. The congress opened on January 10; Lysenko's paper was scheduled for the last working session, on January 15; but on January 11, a Leningrad newspaper published this conclusion of Vavilov's about Lysenko's work: "Considering this characteristic [the effect of low temperatures], we can earmark our varieties and cultures better for particular zones."[26]

Historians of the Lysenko years disagree about the importance of Vavilov's sponsorship in Lysenko's early career. On the one hand, Popovsky argues that Vavilov rendered invaluable help to Lysenko with his enthusiastic descriptions of the latter's work.[27] Zhores Medvedev, on the other hand, strongly opposes this view, contending that the excerpts cited by Popovsky from Vavilov's letters and speeches should be interpreted merely as the lapses of a busy administrator; Vavilov may well have signed papers submitted to him by assistants without scrutinizing their contents.[28] In a later work, Popovsky quoted passages from several of Vavilov's speeches to rebut Medvedev's position and reinforce his own by showing that Vavilov spoke for himself and said what he thought.[29]

My own research indicates that Vavilov's support did indeed play a decisive part in Lysenko's career, by promoting the belief that Lysenko was a talented agronomist, geneticist, and plant physiologist. One piece of evidence has already been mentioned: the praise lavished on Lysenko in a resolution of the presidium of VASKhNIL, signed by Vavilov, its president, following Lysenko's presentation of a paper before the presidium early in 1931 (see chapter 1). Later that year, another resolution, also signed by Vavilov, appropriated thirty thousand rubles for "the development and expansion of Comrade Lysenko's work in reducing the length of the vegetative period of cereals, cotton, corn, soybeans, vegetable crops, etc."[30] In November 1931, Vavilov wrote to Iogan G. Eikhfeld, an agronomist who was working at the Polar Station of the VIR: "What Lysenko has done and is doing is of exceptional interest and the Polar Division should develop this work."[31]

In the spring of 1932, the members of the Soviet delegation were being chosen for the Sixth International Genetics Congress, which was to be held in Ithaca, New York, in August 1932. Vavilov, as head of the Soviet national committee for the congress, tried—though unsuccessfully—to have Lysenko included, playing upon the fact that the makeup of Soviet delegations to international scientific conferences was based not on an evaluation of scientific contributions but on one's biographical and political record. Vavilov even sent Lysenko a letter in which he told him it would be useful for him to travel to the United States, since "there would be much of interest for a geneticist" there.[32]

Perhaps most remarkable of all, in May 1932, Vavilov traveled to Odessa, was quite inspired by the idea of vernalization, and wrote from there to Kovalev that "Lysenko's work is wonderful. It obliges us to view much in a new way. The world collection needs to be worked on through vernalization."[33] Thus, Vavilov showed again that he valued Lysenko's work so highly that he was ready to filter his special creation, the world seed collection, "through the sieve of vernalization" (as he put it on many occasions). From geneticists who had worked with Vavilov for years, I heard often that Vavilov made it clear to everyone that he regarded Lysenko as a highly talented, self-made scientist. Lysenko interpreted this to mean something more: that Vavilov saw him as a real geneticist and maybe even as someone capable of criticizing the geneticists. Vavilov's misplaced admiration of Lysenko was to have disastrous consequences.

When Vavilov spoke at the Sixth International Genetics Congress, and in lectures he delivered afterward in the United States and France, he praised "the marvelous discovery recently made by T. D. Lysenko in Odessa."[34] It is clear from Vavilov's descriptions of Lysenko's method— that "the essence consists of influencing the seeds by individual combinations of darkness, temperature, and moisture"[35]—that he had gone far beyond Lysenko in thinking through the factors that might be involved in vernalization. After his return, Vavilov published an extensive account of his trip in *Izvestia* on March 29, 1933, in which he said that "neither in Canada nor in the . . . United States did we see any fundamentally new discoveries . . . equaling the work of Lysenko."[36]

Yet another sign of Vavilov's attitude was his nomination of Lysenko in 1932 for membership in the Ukrainian Academy of Sciences.[37] Once again, though, his effort foundered, because of the objections of colleagues." In December 1933, the Party newspaper *Socialist Agriculture* reported that Vavilov and Lysenko had visited a district in the North Caucasus the summer before, where they had inspected the sowing of cotton using vernalized seeds. The story claimed that vernalization had doubled the yield of cotton, and in boldface type the newspaper called for "the immediate promotion of vernalization on the cotton fields of the kolkhozes and sovkhozes."[38]

This purported success with cotton was important on another plane. Stalin personally had set the goal of expanding the acreage sown to cotton, in order to end the country's reliance upon imports of this raw material. Therefore, both the agricultural and the Party agencies were intent on improving cotton production. Such an achievement, apparently validated by the country's leading expert in cultivated plants, Academician Vavilov, the president of VASKhNIL, could hardly pass unnoticed.

Vavilov also manifested his admiration for Lysenko's work during a meeting of the board of the USSR Commissariat of Agriculture in December 1933. A story about the meeting described the scene as Lysenko made a report:

> On the table lay a row of sheaves of wheat. The sheaves were arranged in pairs. One stalk in each pair was long, the ears heavy, with fully developed grains. The other stalks were stunted, the ears half-empty, the grains puny. . . . The sheaves

with stout heads came from vernalized plants. . . . The sheaves . . . of Comrade Lysenko demonstrated more clearly than diagrams, more convincingly than figures, what a powerful weapon vernalization is in the fight against drought and hot, dry winds.[39]

Lysenko capped this display of fat ears and lean ones by citing figures for remarkable yields and predicting still better ones:

On some kolkhozes [in the North Caucasus], vernalization . . . provided approximately 6–8 centners of additional grain per hectare [i.e., on top of the average yield of 11–14 centners]. . . . I reckon we can obtain a DOUBLING of the harvest in certain instances. . . . And if this hasn't been done up to now, to a significant degree this is the fault of the farm agencies.[40]

A careful observer, however, on taking a closer look at these sheaves and hearing these predictions, would have had reason to be skeptical. Indeed, Lysenko himself failed to use these figures again. Instead, he later claimed only that the additional yield from vernalized plants was not greater than 10 to 15 percent even under the best of conditions. But if that figure— itself likely to be an exaggeration—was accurate, then any difference in the mass of the ears of vernalized and control plants would have been undetectable to the naked eye. Hence, we must assume that Lysenko was deliberately magnifying the benefits of vernalization by picking out the best-looking ears in the vernalized field and the worst from the controls for his demonstration.

If Vavilov had any doubts about Lysenko's claims, he did not voice them at this meeting. On the contrary, he pointed out a new application for vernalization: the acceleration of breeding new varieties.

Up to now, specialists in plant breeding have worked with chance combinations. Now the work of Comrade Lysenko opens up completely new, unforeseen possibilities for plant breeding, because we can and must work with a purposefulness previously unthinkable in plant-breeding work.
Plant breeding work must be sharply changed and reorganized in light of Comrade Lysenko's experiments.[41]

Because Lysenko had already been testing his powers along these lines for a year, Vavilov's support was psychologically very valuable. But, regretfully, it must be said that Vavilov's support was based on his failure to understand just how primitive Lysenko's experiments were and to distinguish between a fraud and real proof. Perhaps this was a result of his own limited experimental background. In any case, it is a fact that Vavilov was incapable of evaluating Lysenko's work properly.

Vavilov continued to accept Lysenko's work without question and to emphasize its value in the utilization of his own collection of cultivated plants from around the world. In 1934, he told a conference on plans for work in genetics and plant breeding:

There is perhaps no other branch of plant physiology in which such serious breakthroughs have occurred as in this field [the control of vegetative period]. We consider the work of T. D. Lysenko in this respect to be outstanding. . . .

The relatively simple method of vernalization, and the possibility of its broad application, open up wide horizons. Study of the effect of vernalization on the world collection of wheat and other crops has disclosed facts of exceptional significance. Under the influence of the simple procedure of vernalization, the world assortment of wheat has yielded completely altered varieties.[42]

This passage is striking for its false drama. In fact, there had been no "completely altered varieties." Although Vavilov had himself tried to carry out vernalization on wheat, the exaggerated claim came from Lysenko. Vavilov had given orders for wheat seed of the VIR to be vernalized and planted near Leningrad and in Odessa. Some of the plants of varieties that ordinarily do not develop ears in the Odessa region happened to produce mature seeds, and Lysenko published these results as proof that now all varieties could be planted outside their usual zones.[43] Without waiting to see if the method led to real practical results, Vavilov and his students enthusiastically proclaimed his overly eager assessment of its significance.[44]

Vavilov recorded in his notebook that, when reporting on the work of VASKhNIL to the Council of People's Commissars in May 1934, he had once more emphasized Lysenko's services.[45] He also included a number of articles about Lysenko's work in his 1935 book *Theoretical Foundations of Plant Breeding*, and on June 17, 1935, he told the VASKhNIL presidium that "Lysenko is a cautious researcher, extremely talented; his experiments are irreproachable."[46]

Meanwhile, Vavilov had also been working in other directions to promote Lysenko's status in the scientific world. In March 1933, he recommended that Lysenko be awarded a Lenin Prize. "Lysenko's work on the so-called vernalization of plants," he wrote, "is undoubtedly the most outstanding achievement of the past decade in the field of plant physiology and related disciplines. Lysenko's discovery is exceptionally interesting, both theoretically and practically, and we should consider Comrade Lysenko a leading candidate to receive the prize."[47] Lysenko did not receive the prize, but Vavilov's support remained unshakeable. In 1934 he nominated Lysenko to be a corresponding member of the USSR Academy of Sciences, saying that, "although he has published comparatively little, his latest work represents an immense contribution to world science."[48]

Other scientists, however, were not so convinced that Lysenko deserved such recognition; his work had, after all, not been rigorously reviewed before publication nor validated by repetition in other laboratories. Moreover, some scientists were perturbed, as Vavilov should have been, by Lysenko's openly contemptuous attitude toward serious science. For example, in Vavilov's presence at a meeting of VASKhNIL in February 1934, Lysenko had said, "It is better to know less, but to know just what is necessary for practical work today and in the immediate future."[49] So Vavilov's efforts to win these high honors for Lysenko failed for the time being.[50]

Lysenko Becomes an Academician

Outside scientific circles, however, Lysenko's strength was growing. In a speech before Stalin and other Party leaders at the Seventeenth Party Congress in 1934, Commissar Yakovlev characterized Lysenko as the best representative of the new system of training and promoting workers in agricultural science:

> We have established a system whereby young specialists graduating from higher educational institutions—and they are socially far closer to us than the previous generation of specialists—are all assigned to work exclusively in the district headquarters and the machine and tractor stations. We have . . . such people as agronomist Lysenko, a practical worker whose vernalization of plants has opened a new chapter in agricultural science, who is now heeded by the entire agricultural world, not only here, but abroad as well . . .
>
> These are the people . . . who will be the backbone of the real Bolshevik apparatus, the creation of which is demanded by the Party, by Comrade Stalin.[51]

Lysenko made the most of his support from Vavilov and the higher powers as an innovator. He traveled from conference to conference and published one newspaper article after another. The *Bulletin of Vernalization*, though nominally a publication of the Institute of Plant Breeding and Genetics of the Ukrainian Commissariat of Agriculture,[52] became in effect a medium for publicizing his own work. Indeed, a note in each issue of the journal said that it would "widely report the scientific research achievements of Comrade T. D. Lysenko's laboratory on problems of regulating the vegetative period of crop plants." In 1932 and 1933, it published ten articles by him (one of which was coauthored with Dolgushin). None of these articles could be called scientific. They presented rudimentary tables of data from kolkhozes and practical instructions on how to carry out vernalization of wheat, potatoes, and other crops. But because they appeared in this journal, Lysenko arrogated the right to present them as the latest word in science.

In addition to these articles, Lysenko published, at about the same time, a small brochure, *Vernalization of Agricultural Plants* (originally in Ukrainian, later translated into Russian and other languages); *Vernalization and the Budding of Potatoes*, a sixteen-page pamphlet written jointly with his wife; together with Dolgushin, instructions for collective farmers on the vernalization of wheat and cotton; a magazine article on the possible role of vernalization in plant breeding; and his first four speeches, which had been delivered some time earlier.[53] In a single year, he had transformed himself from a promising practical worker into a renowned scientist, with forty-eight publications to his name (sixty-five if newspaper articles are included).

After this, the road to scientific "respectability" was smooth. On May 27, 1934, his election as a full member—not just a corresponding member, but all the way to academician—of the Ukrainian Academy of Sciences was announced.

One of the national propaganda journals in the field of agriculture promptly devoted sixteen pages, with more than forty photographs, to the work of Lysenko's institute in Odessa. Under the previous director, Sapegin, this institute had been a center of research in plant genetics, and the article included a photograph of Sapegin's innovative X-ray apparatus for inducing mutations in plants, but the main emphasis was placed on Lysenko's efforts:

> The principal achievement of the selection institute is the wonderful work of agronomist T. D. Lysenko in plant development physiology. T. D. Lysenko, a peasant from Poltava province, elected a member of the Ukrainian Academy of Sciences for his work, created the theory of development by stages . . . the theory provides the possibility of deliberately establishing new varieties of agricultural plants, with foreknowledge of the results.
>
> Application of T. D. Lysenko's discovery permits us to expect confidently that in the next two to three years the plant-breeding institute will provide new varieties of spring wheat, barley, potatoes, cotton, castor-oil plant, sesame, and other crops, guaranteeing large and dependable harvests in the Ukrainian steppe.[54]

The reference to Lysenko's social origins was, of course, a reflection of Party policy.

The journal's predictions of imminent successes could have come only from Lysenko or his colleagues. They must be regarded as deliberate lies or naive hopes, for there was no possibility of obtaining new crop varieties so quickly; for some of the crops mentioned, the preliminary work had not even begun. But the fact remains that Lysenko had become an academician of the Ukrainian Academy. With the license of this title, he could act more freely and speak with the air of an outstanding scientist enjoying the confidence of his fellow professionals. For Lysenko's purposes, it was probably a more meaningful title than the one Vavilov had failed to obtain for him. "Academician" certainly sounded better than mere "corresponding member," even if the Ukrainian Academy did not have the prestige of the USSR Academy of Sciences.

In the same year, 1934, Lysenko was named research supervisor of the Ukrainian Institute of Plant Breeding and Genetics, becoming in effect the institute's head. He would take over the position of director two years later.

5

1935: The Year of Triumph

So now the flea was richly dressed
In velvet and in silk,
With stars and crosses on his chest,
Like others of his ilk.
The king he made him minister,
And soon, as I've heard tell,
His cousins at the court they were
All ministers as well.

—Goethe, *Faust*, Part One

Dogmatic thinking, uncontrollable desire to impose regularity, overt
passion for rituals and reiterations per se are exactly characteristic of
eccentrics and children. Increased experience and maturity are
more likely to create a cautious and critical attitude than dogmatism.
—K. Popper, *Logic and the Growth of Scientific Knowledge*

Stalin: "Bravo, Comrade Lysenko, Bravo!"

The year 1935 was a special one for Lysenko. It was the year in which
Stalin praised him—indeed, hailed him enthusiastically.

In February of that year, a conference of shock workers of agriculture
was held in the Kremlin. It was attended by prominent scientists, such as
Vavilov and Pryanishnikov, as well as Party and government leaders, including Stalin himself. But it was Lysenko who was greeted with the most
enthusiastic reception.

I heard Lysenko speak many times during the 1950s, when his speeches
were perhaps not as passionate as they had been earlier, but even then he
produced a magical effect upon his listeners. He had a gift for virtually
hypnotizing them, creating an atmosphere that made them forget everything else and take whatever he uttered as a revelation. Lysenko could
hardly have mesmerized Stalin, who himself knew how to play on the
moods of the crowd, but Stalin would have recognized how useful this
charismatic quality could be for his own ends.

Lysenko began his speech at this conference by invoking the tens of
thousands of kolkhozes involved in the "practical science" of vernalization.
"But, comrades, have we done everything here that could be done?" he
asked, and then answered himself: "No, not everything, not by far. As a
matter of fact, even though the kolkhozes employing vernalization have
raised 3–5 million more [poods] of grain this year ... these 3–5 million

poods are a trifle . . . Our task is to increase the productivity of all the kolkhoz and sovkhoz fields."

He went on to praise summer planting of potatoes and called for working "in such a way that by 1936 all the potato seed of the Odessa region would be 100 percent productive. This would be a real accomplishment, true science. This would not be difficult, but it should be done properly." But, he observed, these ideas were still not warmly received in many places: "It would be good if this year at least the southern provinces, at least the Odessa kolkhozes, really got to work on this, under the direction of the farm agencies. Unfortunately, some local officials of the regions and districts still greatly underrate this task."

Up to this point, the speech, though delivered with fervor, would hardly have elicited any feelings in Stalin beyond condescending approval. But Lysenko's next maneuver was bound to win Stalin over, to make him attend to Lysenko: He accused all his critics of sabotage.

You see, comrades, saboteur-kulaks are found not only in your kolkhoz life. . . . They are no less dangerous, no less accursed, in science. A great deal of mortification has had to be endured in defending vernalization in all kinds of battles with so-called scientists. . . . Comrades, was there—and is there—really no class struggle on the vernalization front? . . .

Indeed there was . . . Instead of helping the collective farmers, they sabotaged things. Both within the scientific world and outside it, a class enemy is always an enemy, even if a scientist.

So, comrades, that is how we carried out this work. The kolkhoz system pulled it through. The kolkhozes have pulled it through and are pulling it through on the basis of the sole scientific methodology, the one and only scientific guiding principle, which Comrade Stalin teaches us daily.

This denunciation of his colleagues called forth a storm of rapturous applause. Everything else had automatically been greeted with enthusiasm, but the highlight of the speech was contained in those words. Lysenko's calculations were on target. Stalin was so moved at this point that he jumped up, clapping, and shouted, "Bravo, Comrade Lysenko, bravo!" The hall broke out in wild applause.[1]

Such praise from Stalin was extraordinarily important; in the conditions of the time, it meant more than the opinion of all the academicians combined. It immediately raised Lysenko above all other scientists.

Pravda's detailed account of Lysenko's speech, complete with his portrait, and including Stalin's memorable interruption, was quickly picked up and reprinted by other Party newspapers and magazines. However, neither *Pravda* nor the majority of the others published the part of Lysenko's speech that came after Stalin's exclamation and that contained this very revealing passage:

In our Soviet Union, comrades, *people* are not born. Human organisms are born, but *people* are created from organisms in our country—tractor drivers, motorists, mechanics, academicians, scientists, and so on. And I am one of the people created in this way. I was not *born* as a human being, I was *made* as a human being. And to feel myself such, comrades, in such a position—it is to be more than happy.

Putting aside Lysenko's obligatory humility, we see in these words the clearest statement of his combined ideological and personal motives for rejecting the science of heredity.[2]

The Contribution of Isaak Prezent

Lysenko's speech owed at least some of its success to rhetorical flourishes that he had picked up during the previous year from a colleague, Isaak I. Prezent (who was generally known as Isai). Some Soviet and Western historians of science have said that it was Prezent who supplied Lysenko with Marxist phraseology, translating his agronomical discourse into the terms of ideological struggle.[3] That clearly was not the case: as we have seen, Lysenko had assimilated the jargon quite well on his own. Nevertheless, it seems likely that Prezent's skills lent a special brilliance to this side of Lysenko's activity.

Prezent was born in 1902 and was graduated in 1926 from the three-year program of the department of social sciences of Bubnov Leningrad University.[4] Soon after, he came to Vavilov's attention and was appointed to the VIR. But he left the institute only a year later, bearing a lifelong enmity for Vavilov. (Many people believe that Vavilov fired him.) His next position was as a specialist in dialectical materialism at the Herzen Pedagogical Institute, also in Leningrad. In 1930, he was mentioned among the officials of the Leningrad branch of the Communist Academy.[5] In the same year, he became chairman of the Leningrad Society of Materialist Biologists and the next year head of the department of the dialectics of nature and evolutionary studies at Leningrad University, while remaining a docent at the pedagogical institute and a scientific associate of the first rank at the Institute of Philosophy of the Leningrad branch of the Communist Academy. At that time and shortly afterward, Prezent published several works.[6]

At the beginning of the 1930s, Prezent took part in a purge in the field of botany, and he was a principal figure in the campaign against the nature conservationists, which led to the arrest of Vladimir V. Stanchinsky, one of the founders of community ecology in the Soviet Union.[7] Prezent also denounced the prominent scientist and educator Boris Ye. Raikov, by declaring, in a paper before Leningrad education officials:

Raikov is nothing other than . . . a class enemy . . . an agent of that very bourgeoisie . . . one of the weights that lies on the scales of the bourgeoisie and wants to make the bourgeoisie victorious; if you will realize that this enemy wants to destroy all the achievements, all the gains that the proletariat has made with its blood, then such a Raikov can rouse nothing but loathing, disgust, and hate in every upright comrade who has cast his lot with the workers' soviets.[8]

Although completely innocent, Raikov was arrested, tried, and exiled to the north. (He was able to return in 1945 and was subsequently elected a member of the Academy of Pedagogical Sciences.)

After Raikov's arrest, Prezent's co-workers began to fear and despise him. In his search for somewhere else to work, he decided to attach himself to Lysenko. The two men had first met in 1929, when Lysenko spoke at the First All-Union Congress of Geneticists and Breeders. After the speech, Prezent suggested to Lysenko that it would be good to link vernalization with Darwinism. Those who heard the conversation noted that Lysenko apparently did not know whom Prezent was talking about, and later, he asked Prezent who this Darwin was and where he could meet him![9] Toward the end of 1935, when Lysenko appeared a second time before Stalin, he acknowledged his earlier ignorance: "I often read Darwin, Timiryazev, and Michurin. A colleague in our laboratory, I. I. Prezent, has helped me with this. He showed me that Darwin laid the foundations for the work that I am doing. And frankly, comrades, I have to admit here before Iosif Vissarionovich that, to my shame, I have really not studied Darwin."[10]

The bond between Prezent and Lysenko was renewed when they made a trip together to Askania-Nova in the summer of 1933. Previously, Prezent had been paying his respects to genetics and its contribution to dialectical materialism.[11] Now, he began to condemn genetics and, in general, mathematical and statistical approaches to biological laws. Moreover, in his speeches, Prezent began to extol Lysenko, mentioning his "outstanding achievements" at every opportunity.[12]

Short, fidgety, waving his arms one moment, breaking into a dance the next, Prezent added color to Lysenko's otherwise lusterless entourage. "The professor" (as he styled himself after moving to Odessa) introduced into Lysenkoist rhetoric a sharp tone, laced with quotations from sources as diverse as Marxist-Leninist classics, popular writers, and Scriptures.

He did one other very important thing for Lysenko. While claiming to be the founder of an entire doctrine, Lysenko was unable to find a suitable label for it. "Lysenkoist biology" went too far, perhaps dangerously so. Prezent hit on a brilliant solution. To Lysenko's mixture of Marxist-Leninist philosophy, Darwinist biology, and the Stalinist doctrine of the intensification of the class struggle in direct proportion to the strengthening of socialism, he gave the name "Michurinist biology."

Ivan V. Michurin (1855–1935), the son of a landowner of Ryazan Province, had developed many varieties of fruits and berries, becoming famous for this in Russia and even abroad. He also perfected a series of technical methods of crossing varieties, including vegetative grafting. Having been expelled from secondary school for impertinence, he had acquired his knowledge by self-education, resulting in the formation of a confused and primitive, yet original, view of the laws of biology. He did not claim to be a geneticist; indeed, in his articles and notes he repeatedly indicated the need for future researchers to check his deductions. But he did like to debate and speculate. He sent articles and letters about horticulture to all sorts of journals, entering into arguments on a wide range of topics with authoritative scientists. Most of his postulates lacked a sound scientific basis and were discarded over the years as incorrect.

Before the Revolution, Michurin had called on the gentry to rally around the throne.[13] However, he changed his allegiance when the Bolsheviks came to power. He initiated friendly contacts with Vavilov and, with Vavilov's help, became acquainted with the highest leaders of the country. Lenin instructed the officials of Tambov province to improve Michurin's material conditions. Kalinin visited Michurin in 1922 and again in 1930, and Michurin was the recipient of a laudatory telegram from Stalin.[14] During his lifetime, the town of Kozlov, where the fruit-grower's nursery was located, was renamed Michurinsk in his honor. A film about him, *South in Tambov*, was made (also while he was still alive), depicting Michurin as a Soviet Luther Burbank, and he was awarded the Order of Lenin and the Order of the Red Banner of Labor. The popularity of this simple amateur who had allegedly achieved unprecedented results was enormous.

When Michurin died in 1935, Prezent, who had boasted of his acquaintance with Michurin, saw an opportunity. The term "Michurinists" had been applied by the newspapers a few years earlier to amateur horticulturists, but Prezent now decided to use "Michurinist biology" as a catchall name for all of Lysenko's theories and proposals. With a careful selection of quotations from Michurin's contradictory writings, Prezent and Lysenko were able to present him as an inveterate opponent of Mendel and other geneticists. At an early stage of his work, Michurin had indeed opposed what he called "Mendel's notorious laws about peas," but later he came to understand the significance of what Mendel had done and wrote diametrically opposite statements about it, which the Lysenkoists of course failed to mention.

Prezent moved to Odessa in the fall of 1934 and immediately became Lysenko's close collaborator, working with him on many projects. In 1935, Prezent became coeditor of *Vernalization*, the journal that had replaced the *Bulletin of Vernalization*. One curious incident reveals something about both Prezent and his relationship with Lysenko. In 1937, Prezent was arrested for seducing a minor. At about that time, Lysenko received a visit from Pavel A. Baranov (who later became director of the Komarov Botanical Institute of the AN SSSR). At Lysenko's home, the two men drank heavily, and Lysenko, weeping, asked for Baranov's help: "Poo-oo-r me, wha-a-at shall I do? They've a-a-arrested m-m-my Isai! Isai mu-u-ust be rescued! What wi-i-ll I do without hi-i-im?"[15] Under the circumstances, Baranov was unable to help, but Lysenko managed to find friends who persuaded higher-ups in the NKVD that Prezent was not a saboteur but a convinced Bolshevik and that his human weakness therefore ought to be excused. The case was settled amicably, and Prezent was released.

"Marriage of Love"

At about the time that Prezent arrived in Odessa, Lysenko became fascinated by a new idea. He decided that all varieties of plants deteriorated from year to year but that this damage could be arrested if they were cross-pollinated, intravarietally or intervarietally. In this way, he said, the yield not merely of a single crop but of all crops throughout the country would be increased. Lysenko used a vivid term—coined by Prezent—to describe such indiscriminate cross-pollination: "marriage of love."

This notion flew in the face of all the canons of genetics and of centuries-old practice. Indeed, propagation of varieties had always been carried out so as to prevent the chance pollination of flowers of one variety with pollen of another variety. To ensure this, farms that cultivated seed grain deliberately planted each variety far from any other; and not infrequently, a farm specialized in only one variety. But Lysenko declared that this exacting and painstaking work was useless, even harmful, that the methods being used were incorrect, and that on the contrary seed-growers should deliberately cross-pollinate varieties in order to raise their productivity.

In keeping with this idea, Lysenko proposed that plants of different varieties that had hitherto been carefully protected from contamination with "alien" pollen now be subjected to this cross-pollinating procedure: While the plants in different plots were in flower, a long string held at both ends should be dragged through them in order to bring about massive cross-pollination. With plants that were strictly self-pollinating by nature, this procedure would not work, so he suggested that the petals or husks enclosing the flowers be torn off and pollen transferred with a brush from flower to flower.

Lysenko offered no evidence to support his new theory but simply presented it as a truth that did not need corroboration. Furthermore, he insisted that any objections arising from the laws of genetics must be false. Whereas earlier he had denied individual laws of genetics, he now rejected the entire science. But this time he not only failed to win a sympathetic reception among biologists for his novel doctrine; he aroused general indignation. For the first time, Vavilov sharply opposed him. In a conference at the Commissariat of Agriculture in 1934, at a meeting of the Seed-Growing Association that same year, and at a session of the presidium of VASKhNIL in the spring of 1935, Vavilov criticized Lysenko's idea, although he did so politely and within the framework of a purely scientific discussion.

Soon afterward, Stalin's attitude toward Vavilov abruptly changed. For many years, Stalin had looked kindly on Vavilov. He met with the biologist frequently and brought him into the Central Executive Committees of both the USSR and the Russian Republic. But in the middle of 1935, a rupture occurred between them. Anna I. Revenkova, who once worked

with Vavilov and published a biography of him after his posthumous rehabilitation, has described this encounter:

> Stalin sent for Vavilov... inviting Vavilov to visit him late at night. Vavilov
> answered that at that hour he slept but he could come to Stalin any time during
> the day. Stalin received Vavilov the next day.... A disagreement arose between
> them concerning the role of the VIR.... They parted, telling each other that
> their "paths had separated." Soon afterward, N. I. Vavilov was removed from the
> position of president of the Lenin Academy [of Agricultural Sciences] and
> dropped from membership in the All-Union Central Executive Committee.[16]

(Details of Revenkova's account are open to doubt.) Vavilov's dismissal
from the post of president of VASKhNIL took place on June 4, 1935.[17] His
successor was an old Party member, Aleksandr I. Muralov. Vavilov remained
a vice-president of the academy, together with Georgy K. Meister and
Mikhail M. Zavadovsky. We cannot say that Vavilov's dismissal was directly
connected with his hostility toward Lysenko. Nevertheless, it is striking
that on the very day that Vavilov was demoted, Lysenko was appointed
(not elected) a full member of VASKhNIL by a special decree of the
Council of People's Commissars. His new rank as academician marked his
move from the provincial to the national scene. He was now a member of
the Soviet scientific elite. Even though the decree was not immediately
made public, it was a matter of general knowledge.

The New Academician

Lysenko's first opportunity to take advantage of his new status came within
the month. On June 25, 1935, the country's leading grain specialists gathered in Odessa to consider Lysenko's proposals. Lysenko himself presented the main paper. Once again, he spoke of vernalization (earlier that
year, the Council of People's Commissars had decreed that 600,000 hectares
be planted with vernalized spring wheat), summer planting of potatoes,
and his rejection of the theoretical principles of selection and seed-growing.
His greatest emphasis, however, was on the forced cross-pollination of self-
pollinating varieties. He enthusiastically described the crude technique of
collecting pollen from individual flowers with a brush and transferring it
to other flowers:

> And then the stigma [of the flower] can take whichever gamete [i.e., pollen
> cell] it wants. Having done this, we can comfortably leave the field. We have
> done our share. We have given the ovule the possibility of selecting what it
> wanted. Comrade Prezent quite aptly called this kind of [cross-]pollination a
> "marriage of love." On the other hand, self-pollination is a forced marriage, not
> a marriage of love. No matter how much the given ovule wants to "marry" that
> "fellow" growing next to her, she cannot because her pellicle is closed and won't
> let foreign pollen in.[18]

Lysenko's ideas, presented in these naively anthropomorphic terms, were criticized by all the specialists present. Vavilov spoke categorically against the "marriage of love." In addition to expressing fears that these proposed practices would destroy established varieties, the scientists cited Lysenko's gross errors in the use of elementary terms. For example, under no circumstances could the material obtained after cross-pollination be called "pure varietal material," and the word "elite" when applied to the impure material sounded like mockery. They also pointed out that many varieties had not degenerated during a hundred years of self-pollination, so that the very premise of "degeneration" was invalid.

The resolution passed at the end of the meeting made note "first and foremost of the work being carried out under the direction of Comrade Lysenko on questions concerning the study of development by stages," but it cast doubt on all of Lysenko's other hypotheses (except summer planting of potatoes, which, apparently, continued to appeal to Vavilov), saying merely that it was "deemed expedient to conduct discussions" of them.[19]

But now that Lysenko had attained the rank of academician, it was more difficult to oppose him. He could simply describe any sort of criticism as "hindering," "harming," or "putting spokes in the wheels." A year after the conference, *Vernalization* reported:

> Academician Lysenko's statement [about the necessity of intravarietal crossing] was greeted with a storm of objections from a number of scientific workers. In 1936, collective farmers answered these unfounded objections by deeds. About two thousand kolkhozes in twelve regions and territories of the Ukraine and the Russian Republic set to work energetically.... According to data obtained from 752 kolkhozes on August 20 of this year, in these kolkhozes alone, 2,498,090 plants of winter and spring wheat and other crops were castrated [*sic*] and cross-pollinated.... Therefore, all in all approximately eight millions [*sic*] plants in 2,000 kolkhozes were castrated and cross-pollinated. All the selection stations of the world have not crossed as many self-pollinating plants in the half-century of their existence as did two thousand kolkhozes in one year.[20]

The comparison with "all the selection stations of the world" was of course absurd, since nowhere else in the world was there any intention to practice cross-pollination.

The VASKhNIL Meeting of October 1935

Not long after the dismissal of Vavilov as president of VASKhNIL, the decision was made to change the nature of its annual meetings: to hold them more often, and to undertake wide public discussion of the problems raised at the sessions. The October 1935 session of the academy was to be the model. Well before the meeting, the newspapers began to print articles by scientists, explaining the ideas that they would present at the sessions, and by farmers and journalists, evaluating the proposals coming from the ivory tower. The articles pointed out, among other things, that the improved food situation in the country had led to the lifting of food rationing (on October 2, 1935, seven years after it had been imposed during the drive for collectivization), and they contrasted this triumph of socialist agriculture with food shortages in fascist Germany.[21]

Lysenko's rising star was abundantly evident in these articles. Several of them were by Lysenko and his fellow researchers. Another included praise from the commissar of agriculture of the Ukraine. *Pravda* published a front-page photograph of Lysenko and a Stakhanovite agricultural worker inspecting Lysenko's spring wheat, and an editorial praising Lysenko's example. Before and during the conference, interviews with Vavilov, Muralov, and Meister, among others, appeared, all mentioning Lysenko with respect. Vavilov's constantly repeated words of esteem for Lysenko created the impression—which Vavilov may not have intended and which did him no good in the end—that he was enthusiastically in favor of everything Lysenko stood for.

These encomiums for Lysenko were matched by criticism of the geneticists. In particular, the mistakes of the VASKhNIL specialist in animal genetics, Aleksandr S. Serebrovsky, came under fire. In a series of articles over the course of the year, Serebrovsky had proposed a major restructuring of animal breeding on the basis of classical genetics. However, as a pure theorist, he was ignorant of the fine points of practical livestock breeding, and so he laid himself open to the critical comments of farmers and experts in animal husbandry.

The stage was set for another Lysenko triumph. At the opening of the meeting, Muralov, the academy's new president, declared that "Lysenko's doctrine of the stage-dependent nature of plants" had already played a tremendous role, whereas "genetics has given no guidance whatsoever concerning the choice of parental pairs for crossing. . . . Some geneticists still have not emancipated themselves completely from the fetters of the prejudices and traditions of bourgeois science."[22] Evidently, other members of the academy objected to these words—perhaps privately, for there was nothing about it in the press. At any rate, on the last day of the meeting Muralov returned to this question and attempted to gloss over the problem: "I want genetics, as a science, to serve socialist farming right now, forthwith," he said. "Therefore I stand for a policy in science that will bring genetics and breeding programs closer together."[23] Muralov, who owed his position to his Party credentials rather than to any scientific competence, could hardly be expected to know that genetics and breeding were "together" every day, but that immediate results were impossible. Nevertheless, his words conformed to Lysenkoist phraseology, and he thereby lent his stature to the support of Lysenko's ideas.

Lysenko's own speech at the meeting wholly ignored the criticisms that had been made earlier. "Where is the management of development in ontogenesis worked out better?" he asked, and the new academician answered himself, "Nowhere in the world, and it is hardly likely to be mastered soon anywhere as well as we have developed it here." He continued in the same vein:

> Where else in the world has the selection of parental pairs for crossing been so clearly and precisely worked out and so brilliantly assimilated? One can travel to Odessa and satisfy oneself that a new variety of wheat has been grown by crossing within two years and five months. Where else in the world are such facts recorded?
>
> Where abroad has a theory been developed on the basis of which a peasant— or, in our country, a collective farmer—can in one year carry out colossal work in plant breeding to increase the stability of wheat during the winter? We have this theory worked out. You can hear about it and discuss it in Odessa.
>
> Where in the world has the question of the fight with degeneration of early varieties of potatoes in southern regions been cardinally and conclusively resolved? This disease occurs worldwide. Only in our country has this question been resolved, and not in any institutes devoted to viral diseases. In Odessa, on the fields of the institute, there are crops of potatoes without any signs of degeneration. Not far from Odessa, on 25 kolkhozes, there are 300 hectares of such crops. In 1936, an area of 5,000 hectares is assured. For 1937, the entire south will be provided with 200 percent of seed potatoes of early varieties (not imported). Where in the world has such a phenomenon been recorded?[24]

Beginning with this speech, Lysenko dropped any pretense of answering his scientific critics in scientific terms. He now had the standing he needed to change his rhetoric. When he was not using straight denunciation, he adopted a chiding, didactic tone. He frequently invoked, for example, "the science of kolkhoz and sovkhoz fields" as a countervailing force against "bourgeois biological science, [which was] incapable by the very nature of capitalist agriculture of testing the veracity of its conclusions."[25] At the October meeting of VASKhNIL, he instructed the assembled academicians:

> We are taught that the sole reliable criterion of the veracity of all scientific deductions is practice.... Explanations that fail to show the laws of existing phenomena and do not offer a guiding principle for action are unscientific, even if they are provided by academicians.... Everyone is familiar with the subjects of physiology, agrochemistry, plant breeding, genetics; these subjects are absolutely detached from one another. However, within this scientific heritage, one subject is missing: kolkhoz and sovkhoz horticulture....
>
> Now, comrades, our first task is to master the very rich scientific legacy of I. V. Michurin, one of the greatest geneticists. We must above all master the legacy of Michurin and Timiryazev and demand of ourselves, of academicians in the first place, and of students, graduate students, and specialists, a thorough knowledge of the works of these two great people. But [instead] we are interested only in how many foreign books someone has read.[26]

The attention to Lysenko and the attack on the geneticists and specialists in plant breeding did not end with the close of the conference. Three days later, *Socialist Agriculture* devoted three of its four pages to an article by Lysenko's colleague, Dolgushin, in which genetics was presented as a feeble and harmful science and geneticists as confused people who wandered through the fields, "candle in hand," searching for unknown "suitable forms" of plants.[27] The allusion to candles was especially malicious, surely intended to imply that geneticists were religious believers and attended church, for where else do people walk with candles in their hands?

Molotov Criticizes Vavilov

Although Vavilov had been removed as president of VASKhNIL, he remained as its vice-president and as director of VIR and the Genetics Institute. He was also mentioned in *Pravda* on October 5, 1935, as being on the editorial board of a new edition of the agricultural encyclopedia. In December 1935, however, he suffered a real humiliation, at a meeting of leaders of VASKhNIL with Molotov, who was then the chairman of the Council of People's Commissars and thus the formal head of government.

At the meeting, Molotov was presented with VASKhNIL's research plan. As he scrutinized the list of topics, he came upon one entitled "A Study of the Domestication of the Fox." "And what is the aim of this?" he asked. The subject had been put into the plan by the animal breeders, and Academician Serebrovsky was supposed to supervise it, but for some reason he had not been invited to the meeting. However, a decade or so earlier, Vavilov had supported the idea of the acclimatization and hybridization of animals, including wild animals, with the goal of domesticating them, and so he rose to defend the topic. His explanation infuriated Molotov, who turned from foxes to the work of the VIR and, raising his voice, accused Vavilov of squandering money on a collection of seeds that was of no use to anyone and then letting the seeds rot, anyway. This latter part of Molotov's harangue was not immediately published, but the reference to foxes was:

> Comrade Molotov pointed out that . . . it is necessary to guard and carefully help the work of every truly knowledgeable agricultural scientist, which not only does not exclude but presupposes a critical attitude toward scientists who shut themselves off from the interests of the state, wasting time on the study of "problems" of the domestication of the fox and such things.[28]

Nine days later, the rest of Molotov's attack did appear in the press. "Practical farming has not been made easier because this [world seed] collection is stored in the institute's cupboards," the article said, and that was followed by a paean to the "brilliant works of Academician T. D. Lysenko, an outstanding innovator and revolutionary of agricultural science, working with methods of the very opposite sort, i.e., relying on the vital connection with the vast kolkhoz masses," and then by a question: "Isn't it strange that a number of scientists still have not found it essential to show Lysenko ... active support?"[29] There was no need to mention Vavilov by name: To every knowledgeable reader, it would have been immediately clear that he was the object of Molotov's anger. This was the first time that the names of Lysenko and Vavilov had been juxtaposed as antipodes in science.

The December 1935 Meeting with the Participation of Stalin

The contrast between the fortunes of Lysenko and Vavilov became even clearer at the end of 1935, at a meeting of outstanding farm workers with Party and government officials, attended by Stalin and other leaders and by several prominent scientists, including Vavilov. By this time, Vavilov had ample reason to reconsider his protégé. Yet in public and in print, he maintained his stance of judicious approval for Lysenko. Thus, in his editor's foreword to the first volume of *Theoretical Foundations of Plant Breeding*, Vavilov wrote that "particular attention has been given to the methodology of plant breeding for immunity to diseases, for physiological characteristics of resistance to drought and winter hardiness, and for chemical composition and the problem of the vegetative period, on which new light has been shed in recent years by the works of Academician T. D. Lysenko."[30] His own opening chapter asserted that vernalization played an important role in plant breeding.[31] Another article that he contributed contained a section entitled "The Vernalization Method and Its Significance in the Utilization of World Plant Resources," in which he wrote:

> Lysenko's teaching about stage-dependent phenomena opens up exceptional possibilities for the utilization of the world collection [of seeds gathered by Vavilov and his co-workers]. ...
> The method of vernalization established by T. D. Lysenko has uncovered vast possibilities of putting to use the world's stock of herbaceous crops. All our varieties, old and new, like the entire world collection itself, henceforth must be studied by vernalization, for ... vernalization can give striking results, literally altering varieties, transforming them from varieties unsuited to a given region under ordinary conditions into productive, high-quality forms. ...
> Undoubtedly we are on the eve of a revision of the entire world's stock of cultivated plants ... The vernalization method is a powerful resource for breeding.[32]

At the meeting of farm workers at the end of 1935, Vavilov's support for Lysenko appeared to be stronger than ever. It is worth quoting at length from his speech to demonstrate this:

> I must mention the brilliant work being carried out under Academician Lysenko's direction. Here one can say with complete assurance that his doctrine of development by stages is a major world achievement in horticulture. [*Applause.*] ...
> I ... have been almost fanatically occupied in recent years with collecting, with gathering from the entire world, anything valuable among all crops. ...

Only Comrade Lysenko understood that it is frequently possible to obtain valuable varieties from two dissimilar, geographically distant, seemingly not very suitable varieties; their combination gives exactly what we need. . . .

Stakhanovites of agriculture . . . already are appearing among us. This movement is just starting. Perhaps we need to throw away some ballast. To rise into the stratosphere, as we know, . . . it is sometimes necessary to throw out what seems to be relatively valuable ballast. . . .

On my own behalf and on behalf of the collective under my management at the Institute of the Plant Industry and our entire Lenin All-Union Academy of Agricultural Sciences, I would like to say that we find it a great happiness to work together with you, to march in step with you, to learn from you. [*Stormy applause.*] We want to learn from you and teach you. [*Applause.*] . . .

Moving toward one definite goal—the creation of a new, supreme socialist culture, under the leadership of the great Stalin, under the leadership of the Communist Party—we hope that we will honorably fulfill the task Comrade Stalin has set us. [*Applause.*][33]

If this was an effort by Vavilov to restore good relations with Stalin, Vavilov's speech it did not produce the desired effect.[34] As soon as Vavilov began to speak, Stalin ostentatiously rose and left the hall. Perhaps Vavilov also hoped for some reciprocating words from Lysenko, who, after all, at the meeting in February 1935, also in Stalin's presence, had said, "Academician Nikolai Ivanovich Vavilov has collected twenty-eight thousand varieties of wheat from all over the world. Academician Nikolai Ivanovich Vavilov has done a tremendous and useful thing."[35] But Lysenko was now silent; he no longer had anything to gain from returning Vavilov's praise.

On the other hand, none of the speakers at the meeting was received as enthusiastically as was Lysenko himself. "The conference greeted Comrade Lysenko with loud applause; everyone rose," the newspapers reported. Even Stalin stood and clapped. In his speech, Lysenko tried, as he had done in Stalin's presence back in February, to show how independent his work was from all previous science and especially from that of contemporary scientists. He asserted that the majority of scientists worked "to no purpose." "In research work in agriculture the norms and tasks are basically still not established, not made specific, and in the majority of cases a researcher does not know whether he has fulfilled his assignment or not" and thus at best, after many years, they discover—and even then, only the honorable specialists—that they had eaten the people's bread in vain, since "all those years they had generally not been doing what needed to be done." He went on to tell of his difficulties in relations with scientists: the great effort required to put vernalization into practice, "battling scientists who did not believe in it."[36]

After he had made several references to "the workers of science who argue about the incorrectness of [his] methods," Yakovlev, then head of the agricultural department of the Central Committee, asked from the presidium, "And who exactly? Why not name them?" Lysenko replied:

I could name names, although here it is not the names that are important, but rather the theoretical stand. Professor Karpechenko, Professor Lepin, Professor Zhebrak [all closely linked to Vavilov], and generally the majority of geneticists disagree with our position. In the recently published work, *Theoretical Principles of Wheat Breeding*, Nikolai Ivanovich Vavilov, while agreeing with a number of theses advanced by us, also disagrees with our basic principle of rejecting defects during the selection process.[37]

Lysenko concluded his speech on, so to speak, an upbeat note. He assured Stalin and the other Party and government leaders of the impending and inevitable victory of his supporters:

Among the workers of agricultural science in our [Soviet] Union are now many of the new generation, and many of the best representatives of the old specialists, to emulate.... And I, comrades, am quite certain that now, when the Stakhanovite movement, headed by the great leader of the world proletariat, Comrade Stalin, has spread with unprecedented vigor through all sectors, through all regions, through the entire territory of our mighty Soviet Union, agricultural science will not remain an untouched island in this movement. Long live the great leader and guide of the world proletariat, organizer of kolkhoz and sovkhoz victories, Comrade Stalin![38]

Stalin did not deliver a speech at the meeting, but Yakovlev, in a summation on behalf of the Party leadership, referred to Lysenko in glowing terms: "Here spoke the young academician Lysenko, who created the theory of vernalization and discovered a means of speeding up by three to four times the development of new varieties, and who solved the problem of developing healthy potato seed that would not degenerate in the south."[39] His appraisal was echoed by the commissar of agriculture, Mikhail A. Chernov, who called on others to "follow more boldly the path of which Comrade Lysenko spoke, the path of vernalization of our crops." Rejoicing in the prospect of easily achieved increases in yield, as promised by Lysenko, the commissar asked: "Is this task really difficult? Do you need to build factories for this? To build mills? No, for vernalization of seeds you need to have a good granary or barn, the most ordinary thermometer, and an agronomist... eager to support this effort. All this is within our powers. And therefore planting of vernalized seeds must grow at a swift pace."[40]

The day after the meeting ended, *Pravda* announced the award of honors to the "Stakhanovites of agriculture." Lysenko (as well as Meister) received the highest award of the Soviet Union, the Order of Lenin. Underscoring the award to Lysenko, *Pravda* added this human-interest item:

"COULD WE EVER HAVE DREAMED OF SUCH A GREAT HONOR?"
Letter from Academician T. D. Lysenko's
Parents to Comrade Stalin
Our beloved, dear Stalin! The day we learned that our Trofim was awarded the Order of Lenin was the most joyous day of our lives. How could we ever

have dreamed of such a great honor, we, poor peasants from the village of Karlovka in Kharkov province?

It was hard for our son Trofim to get an education before the Revolution. He was not admitted—a peasant boy, a muzhik's son—into the agronomy school, even though he received only the highest grades in school. Trofim had to become a gardener in Poltava. He would have remained a gardener for life had it not been for the Soviet regime. Not only the older Trofim, but his younger [brothers and sister] went to study at institutes. . . . The high road to knowledge was opened up to the muzhik's son. . . . Is there any other country in the world where the son of a poor peasant could become an academician? No! . . .

We do not know how to show you our gratitude, dear Comrade Stalin, for this great happiness, the conferring of the highest award upon our eldest son. I, Denis Lysenko, have worked hard during my 64 years; nevertheless, I am not quitting working in my own Bolshevist Labor kolkhoz, for work is enjoyable now, for life has become better and more cheerful [a phrase often used by Stalin]. I work on the kolkhoz as an experimenter, gardener, beekeeper, and horticulturist. After studying courses in plant breeding here, from my son, I taught four collective farmers to cross plants. I myself crossed 13 plants and conducted experiments in vernalization of beets, as a result of which I get double the harvests. Recently I thought up a special machine for applying liquid fertilizer to beets and commissioned the kolkhoz blacksmith to make it. It is by these works, to the extent of my powers as an old man, that I show my gratitude to you, Comrade Stalin, and the Communist Party and Soviet system that you direct.

With kolkhoz greetings!
Denis Nikanorovich Lysenko (father of Academician
Lysenko), Oksana Fominichna Lysenko (mother).
Odessa, January 2.[41]

6

Confrontation with the Geneticists

It already seemed to him:
He was all-powerful.
—Semyon Lipkin, *A Nomadic Fire*

Knowledge of a particular truth may not be altogether comfortable
at a given moment, but once that moment has passed, that same
truth becomes useful for all times and for all peoples.
—Claude-Adrien Helvetius, *On the Mind*

The Failure of Vernalization of Wheat

Lysenko's first practical proposal had been vernalization of winter wheat.
However, it soon became clear that, rather than raising the yield, this
method led to substantial losses. So, after only a year, his calls for cold
treatment of winter wheat ceased, and instead Lysenko began to propagandize vernalization of spring wheat. But he did not refer to the failure
of the earlier idea; he acted as if nothing exceptional had occurred, simply
that science had taken a step forward and now spring rather than winter
crops needed to be germinated in the cold.

However, things did not go well with the vernalization of spring varieties, either. Lysenko held forth in the newspapers, at conferences, and at
meetings about the millions of poods of additional grain bestowed upon
the nation by vernalization.[1] Meanwhile, however, disturbing data were accumulating about what was really happening with vernalization.[2] There was
no way that Lysenko could have sown with vernalized seeds the entire area
that had been planned for these crops. In 1932, for example, instead of
the 110,000 hectares planned for vernalized crops, only 19,277 hectares
were said to have been sown.[3] Even this figure is doubtful; it was calculated by Lysenko's assistants, purportedly on the basis of questionnaires
about the actual harvest that came from only 59 kolkhozes and covered an
area of only 300 hectares. So no one could say with any assurance just how
much grain had been gathered or from how large an area.[4]

Nevertheless, Lysenko displayed such unique propaganda skills and so
stunned everyone with the speed with which vernalization was introduced
that no one managed to weigh properly either his new ideas or their
applicability. Before anyone realized quite what was going on, orders were

flying from the center about thousands of hectares, then about tens of thousands, and finally about millions of hectares of cultivated fields that were supposed to be covered with vernalized wheat.

Gradually, however, both the theoretical and the practical sides of this method were subjected to serious examination. One after another, the specialists noted that there was nothing original in Lysenko's proposals. Furthermore, they found that any benefit that vernalization manifested did not exceed that offered by the usual selection work with varieties.[5] While Lysenko claimed to have carried out rigorous tests of vernalization, the only truly scientific trials were being performed by experimental field stations under VASKhNIL's auspices. By 1935, plant breeders at thirty-five experimental stations, scattered across the whole country, had accumulated four to five years worth of results from careful, controlled tests with at least thirty-five varieties of spring wheat. Plots of the standard varieties and their vernalized equivalents had been grown side by side, with identical soil, cultivation, fertilization, and irrigation. All conditions of growth were held the same. Studying so many varieties allowed the breeders to check with precision and accuracy the merits and disadvantages of vernalized spring wheat. This trial was performed under the leadership of Professor Peter N. Konstantinov of Timiryazev Academy, an expert in the methodology of agricultural experimentation and a full member of VASKhNIL. Konstantinov was an outstanding breeder whose varieties were planted over millions of hectares and, as a result, his conclusion was especially meaningful. He summarized the results of the studies: "On the average, both decreases and increases [in yield] from vernalization were observed over the years, but vernalization produced almost no increment in the five-year average."[6]

But not only had vernalization failed to justify itself; it had in fact wrought great harm. For weeks every year, the energies of collective farmers had been deflected into turning over the heaps of sprouting plants, wetting them, fighting mold, and so forth. Because so many of the seeds were damaged from the repeated shoveling, the quantity of seeds required for sowing a given field had to be more than doubled.[7] During planting, a significant number of the sprouts were broken, and so beginning in 1933, Lysenko frequently warned that plantings had to be more dense than usual[8]—and this at a time when the country was suffering from acute shortages of seed as of all other grain.

As soon as reliable data were assembled and checked, scientists began to object to the forcible introduction of vernalization. At first, they spoke out at scientific conferences, and then they wrote articles for the newspapers. They did not reject vernalization as such, but cautioned against its indiscriminate use.

> The universal use of this method, without regard to variety, region, the nature of the year, and the weather at time of sowing, is mistaken. . . . Research staffs at

[Lysenko's] institute are inclined to measure the effects of vernalization by the number of days by which plant development was accelerated. Such an interpretation is incorrect, since the harvest and its quality is the function of a complex interaction of a multitude of factors (social, technical, and natural) that are quite variable over time and in space. . . . The fastest-ripening plants often have turned out to be those with the lowest yield and sometimes lower quality, especially in rainy years.

Thus, they went on, vernalization should "be used in given areas only on an experimental basis." They chided Lysenko for his violation of scientific principles: "Often, negative results are discarded. . . . Even the objective data of experimental institutions are not always accepted at the institute, merely because they do not show large effects or show negative results." Finally, as if foreseeing the storm of indignation that their calm, serious comment would provoke, the authors concluded their article with the following words: "The above observations have as their sole aim the elucidation of the truth. Unfortunately, the polemical methods of Academician Lysenko himself and his individual fellow researchers by no means promote intelligent discussion and hence the elucidation of the truth."[9]

Nonetheless, the central authorities issued orders year after year to double and triple sowings with vernalized seeds. But these plans were never fulfilled; even the "paper figures" in the reports were far short of what had been called for. In the Odessa region, where Lysenko's institute was located, vernalized seed was supposed to be used for all wheat production by 1936. (The area of this region was larger than that of Belgium, and 80 percent of it was devoted to agriculture.) Yet in that year the Central Committee of the Communist Party of the Ukraine declared in a resolution that, in fact, only 11.9 percent of the early spring crops had been sown with vernalized seed.[10]

Failures in the Rapid Development of Wheat Varieties

An equally unpleasant picture was unfolding with Lysenko's other much-advertised "success," his pledge to develop four varieties of spring wheat simultaneously within a little over two years. At the Kremlin conference held to honor outstanding achievers in agriculture at the end of December 1935 (see chapter 5), Lysenko stunned Stalin and all present with his pledge that "from the 500 grains . . . that we had at the beginning of 1934, we will obtain 800 times that amount by the autumn of 1935" and that this rate would be maintained both in 1936 and 1937.[11] But by the spring of 1936, the quantity of seeds was at best one-tenth the amount promised, although the exact amount was never made clear. In one speech, Lysenko reported 120 kilograms of each variety, in another 130 kilograms, and in a third 1.5 centners, or 150 kilograms.[12]

These were the years of "socialist competition" and "labor heroism," when Stalin held up the record-breaking accomplishments of the coalminer Stakhanov as a model for every worker. The productivity statistics and norms were meaningless under the prevailing conditions. Although most goods were technologically simple to produce, they were still not available in sufficient quantities, and buyers snatched up even low-quality products. The authorities at all levels reacted to the demand by urging workers to become "Stakhanovites": to work faster and overfulfill their quotas. Many workers responded accordingly, but others simply pretended to be exemplary.

In any case, while such labor heroism may work for industry or agriculture, it is fundamentally inapplicable to science. Slapdash experiments, without appropriate controls and replication, and hasty application bring so many surprises and undesirable consequences that the speedup becomes counterproductive. Lysenko, however, joined in the Stakhanovite movement, eliciting pledges from the staff of the Odessa institute and transmitting them to the newspapers. The institute pledged to develop four new varieties of spring wheat and to obtain fifty tons of seed of each variety.[13]

When November 1935 came around, all that the Lysenkoists could report was about fifteen tons (156 centners) instead of fifty.[14] Lysenko later acknowledged this fact but tried to present it as if it were an indisputable success:

> Since the growing of the aforesaid varieties (1163, 1160, and 1055) had the essential aim of testing in practice the correctness of the stage theory of development as the basis of plant-breeding work, the fact that varieties of spring wheat were grown on this basis for the Odessa region means that the pledge that the institute undertook has been fulfilled.[15]

Indeed, he proceeded to hold out an even more glittering prospect: the creation of a new variety of wheat in *one* year.[16] At the end of 1935, Lysenko made it sound as though the testing stage were already past.[17] Yet later, apparently inadvertently, he blurted out that no "variety" or "varieties" had undergone either production or government testing.[18] Lysenko did sometimes admit that he was gripped with fears:

> I personally ... was worried by the question of whether these varieties would hold up, whether they would deteriorate from what I observed on the plots for testing of varieties in 1935. ... All the time I was tormented by the thought: Would this happen with our new varieties of spring wheat? After all, everyone knows instances in which many varieties behave wonderfully on the [test] plots but then for some unknown reasons turn out to be no good when introduced in field production.[19]

Actually, such cases rarely occur in the work of plant breeders who use a multistage process of testing varieties on successively larger fields precisely in order to exclude the possibility that unstable seed material would be distributed for field planting. Lysenko was preparing the ground for the failure of his "varieties"—laying down a smokescreen, confusing the issue by emphasizing the rapidity of their development while ignoring their true value.

Perhaps Stalin could not have known, on hearing Lysenko in December 1935, just how many half-truths, untested promises, and deliberate deceptions ran through his speech. Those who, like myself, heard Lysenko speak on many occasions, however, could not help but notice how often he contradicted himself. First he spoke of one variety, then of three varieties, then of four, and so on. This could not have been the result of a faulty memory. On the contrary, during several lengthy conversations that I had with Lysenko in the 1950s I was impressed time and again by his remarkable memory, his ability to quote from memory long sections from his writings. Eventually his listeners must have realized that the "varieties" of which he spoke existed only in his imagination.

But Lysenko had only scorn for colleagues who pointed out discrepancies in his figures; he was convinced that these "bookworms" could do him no harm. For he had grasped the psychology of the leaders of the new society and had realized that putting "false currency" into circulation was not merely tolerated but even welcomed. Therefore, he made use of any means that would impress the authorities with his supposed achievements. The chemist Yakob M. Varshavsky has given a vivid example of this sort of conduct:

In 1937, after the arrest of N. P. Gorbunov, the executive secretary of the USSR Academy of Sciences, his duties were temporarily turned over to my friend, the chemist Vladimir Ivanovich Veselovsky . . . On one of his first days in this new capacity, he was called to the Kremlin for a meeting with Stalin on the urgent question of the breakdown in Moscow's vegetable supply. Lysenko was summoned from Odessa to attend this meeting.

As was customary, the scientists (among them Professor Lorkh, creator of one of the best varieties of potato) reported on the measures they were taking or intended to take. Suddenly, Stalin called upon Lysenko to explain the Moscow potato situation. Lysenko stepped forward, pulled several small potatoes from one pocket, spread them out on the table before Stalin, and said that on the previous day he had taken the initiative of inspecting the field of the Potato Farming Institute where Lorkh worked and had dug up the first potato plant that he saw, and this was the kind of small potatoes that grew in the institute's fields. Then he put his hand in his other pocket and brought out three big potatoes, which he also placed before Stalin, and said that this was the kind of potato that grew beneath practically any plant on his field in Odessa.

The effect of this trick, which had nothing to do with science, exceeded all expectations. Stalin began to reprimand the scientists, demanding that they immediately mend their ways and follow Lysenko's methods.[20]

For several more years, up to the start of World War II, Lysenko continued to speak of varieties of spring wheat, identified by four-digit numbers, that supposedly were being reproduced but had not reached the field stage. Gradually, however, his speeches began to refer only to "variety no. 1163," and the remaining varieties were not mentioned. Even this "variety" was deficient, as specialists pointed out:

> The grain of wheat 1163 is too farinaceous and, according to Academician Lysenko, makes poor-quality bread. . . . In addition, the variety is subject to smut damage. But, if one considers that this variety has not fully gone through the selection process, that is, it is not ready for and, moreover, has not undergone governmental variety testing, then the question arises of its own accord, what is the need for this variety—unready and unapproved—to be reproduced at such a pace? It would be hard to straighten out the country's seed growing if we were to rush undeveloped varieties, lacking even the right to be called varieties, into the fields in such an anarchic manner.[21]

Thus, Lysenko's "variety" was a total failure: It did not prove that new varieties could be developed in a shorter period of time, and it was of low quality. All that can be said for it is that, unlike vernalized winter wheat, it did no direct harm, for it was never sown on any large scale. But it did do damage of another sort, in that it fostered a tendency to present fake results under the slogan of a struggle for progressive Soviet science.

Lysenko was not fazed by this failure. At the Kremlin meeting in December 1935, he had promised to produce a remarkable new variety of cotton within two years. A few months later, he renewed the pledge before a group of Ukrainian agricultural "labor heroes" and leaders of the Ukrainian Communist Party, and he added: "If I do not obtain 40 kilograms of seeds of the new variety [of cotton] by springtime, then by the summer I would not be able to provide five tons, which would mean that I could not fulfill the promise given in the Kremlin to Comrade Stalin. . . . if I do not fulfill this task, what right will I have to call myself a scientist?"[22]

Failure in the Summer Planting of Potatoes

At the same meeting in December 1935, Lysenko declared: "I will fight with all my strength to deserve the right to report to Comrade Stalin next year that all 16,000 kolkhozes of the southern Ukraine have already solved the problem of overcoming the degeneration of the potato."[23] But the potato harvests turned out to be small, and it became impossible to conceal this further. Lysenko's explanation was that the fields had been "planted with any old seed gathered from the harvest from the summer planting of the previous year," and this had been done because "on many kolkhozes" the seed material "was squandered and not saved . . . simply because someone wanted the kolkhozes not to have planting material and hence, of course, a good harvest."[24] Yet earlier he had proclaimed that any potato would be healthy and produce a high yield provided only that it had undergone his new procedure of summer planting, which would even improve its hereditary nature. Nor did he miss the opportunity to cast a stone at the scientists who did not accept his innovation unconditionally, including those academicians and employees on the staff of VASKhNIL "whose duty it was to know that this task was their responsibility (whose side they were on is another matter)."[25]

The Council of People's Commissars, however, rejected all doubts. In 1937, it adopted a resolution declaring that "the Council of Commissars of the Ukrainian Republic, beginning in 1938, is obliged to cease planting potatoes using degenerated seed material in the southern part of the Ukrainian Republic and to switch completely to planting potatoes using nondegenerated seeds."[26] Later, Lysenko often cited this resolution as showing that his method—regardless of what happened in the fields—was affirmed by the government and hence had to be irreproachable. But this resolution was not fulfilled, either, as Lysenko admitted in 1938: "To implement this decree, summer planting in the Ukraine was planned for 53,000 hectares in 1937. In fact, 13,333 hectares, which is 25% of the government assignment, were planted."[27] In 1938, the plan for summer planting of potatoes with "nondegenerated seed" was reduced to 49,800 hectares.[28]

Yet this plan, too, remained unfulfilled. After the Second World War, Lysenko acknowledged that as late as 1940, according to his own (probably inflated) data, the country had in all 7,300 hectares of summer-planted potatoes.[29] In any case, it turned out that the summer plantings had failed utterly to improve the health of the crops or to prevent rot. Meanwhile, other, more promising methods of potato cultivation were being neglected, so that the true loss went far beyond what had happened on those few hectares.

Lysenko, of course, continued to maintain that summer planting of potatoes was "a shining achievement of Soviet agronomy."[30] He even attempted to revive the idea a decade later at a plenary session of the Party Central Committee in February 1947. The resolution he proposed there was duly passed, but it was ignored by practitioners. The absurdity of this agronomical "miracle" had become obvious.[31]

The VASKhNIL Discussion in 1936

Given his ascent up the administrative ladder, Lysenko became increasingly insolent, crude, and prickly. Having donned the mantle of a Stakhanovite,[32] he knew he had the support of the authorities. The danger to his critics was clear from the title of a *Pravda* editorial: "People Who Do Not Help Stakhanovites Are Not Our People."[33]

For some time, the geneticists and the plant-breeding specialists kept their tempers, addressing their suggestions to Lysenko in a polite way, whether out of fear or out of common courtesy. Fear would have been justified: Stalin's words, "Bravo, Comrade Lysenko, bravo!" carried enormous weight. Nevertheless, there was a limit to their endurance. In 1936, a number of leading specialists demanded that a discussion be held on genetics and plant breeding within the framework of VASKhNIL, and it took place in Omsk in August of that year. Just before the meeting, Lysenko and Vavilov had what has been described as a "peaceable and friendly" conversation when they inspected the fields of the Lysenkoist Nikolai Tsitsin in Omsk.[34]

However, as soon as the meeting began, all Lysenko's friendliness evaporated. In response to Vavilov's comments and his references to the international scientific literature, Lysenko, in a fury, accused him of deliberately distorting the truth:

> We would be misleading the audience . . . if we were to cite the sort of examples Vavilov often cites, "refuting" the pattern of development of hybrid plants that we have elucidated. . . . Take his example of flax . . . the whole trouble is that this phenomenon, in my view, did not occur, although Vavilov maintains that it was his own experiment and he himself saw it with his own eyes.

Moreover, Lysenko made this astonishing declaration: "Until the past few days, Academician N. I. Vavilov, Professor Karpechenko, and a number of others have nakedly and in an unprincipled manner spurned the fundamental pattern of development of hybrids that has been revealed to us [Lysenko and Prezent]."[35]

Lysenko had apparently come to believe in his own infallibility. He could not see why scientists insisted on trying to repeat his work or why, when they could not reproduce his results, they rejected his methods, data, and theories. He took upon himself the role of a mentor, preaching to Vavilov and "the majority of academicians and specialists," who, he acknowledged, shared Vavilov's point of view. Because he was unable to oppose the geneticists with scientific arguments or to dispute with them as an equal, he had only one recourse: to declare that all of genetics was false and only hampered progress in the present stage, the stage of the formation of kolkhoz and sovkhoz science.

That was indeed the line he took at the fourth plenary session of VASKhNIL in December 1936. This session became the arena of a real battle. Even before it began, both Lysenko's adherents and his opponents published articles that gave warning of the heated debates that could be expected.[36] At the session itself, over the course of a week and a half, Vavilov, N. K. Koltsov, Serebrovsky, Lisitsyn, Konstantinov, Muller, Anton R. Zhebrak, and others spoke against Lysenkoism. One of their main objections was to the uncritical diffusion of vernalization. Lisitsyn, who had originally approved of Lysenko's desire to speed up the maturation of grains, now ridiculed the vernalizers' boasting:

> At present we do not have an exact notion of what vernalization has to offer. Academician Lysenko says that it provides tens of millions of poods added to the yield. A story from Roman history comes to my mind. A seafarer, before setting out on his journey, decided to offer a sacrifice to the gods to assure his safe return. He searched for a long time for the best temple for his sacrifice,

and everywhere he found plaques with the names of those who had offered sacrifices and been saved. "But where are the plaques of those who offered sacrifices but were not saved?" the sailor asked the priests. "I would like to compare the mercy of different gods."

I also would like to ask Academician Lysenko: You cite harvests of tens of millions of poods. But where are the losses that vernalization has caused?[37]

Konstantinov reviewed the data from the tests of vernalization over several years. His figures were so striking that even *Pravda* had to acknowledge them in its report on the session: "The number of instances in which harvests have been reduced as a result of vernalization is not so small that we can disregard them."[38] Konstantinov spoke calmly, explaining why Lysenko's methods could not be applied in practice and why the attacks on the method of crossing closely related plants (the inbreeding method) were wrong. He said:

If Academician Lysenko were to give greater attention to the principles of modern genetics, it would facilitate his work in many respects. Many of the phenomena over which Academician Lysenko is racking his brains as he thinks up various theories to explain them ("marriage of love," "torture," "the gene demand," etc.) have already been scientifically explained by modern genetics. While rejecting genetics and the genetic foundations of selection, Academician Lysenko has not given genetics anything theoretically new in exchange.[39]

Meister, who served as session chairman, used even harsher words. He rejected the proposition put forth by Lysenko and Prezent that the practical work of building socialism demanded the replacement of the "old," bourgeois sciences with their new sciences. "The position taken by Comrades Prezent and Lysenko toward modern science is utterly incomprehensible and out of keeping with the philosophy of the proletariat," Meister said, though adding, "This does not mean that we intend to belittle the significance of Lysenko's discoveries, of course." He singled out genetics as the indispensable. theoretical basis of plant breeding and repudiated Lysenko's censure of the field. He argued that Lysenko's failures in developing new varieties and in the work on inbreeding stemmed from his failure to study genetics: "At the Odessa station, inbreeding doesn't give any results. But this is no great misfortune. The causes of failure should be looked into. After all, there are things to be learned from the geneticists and the plant breeders." The concluding sentences of Meister's speech were especially severe:

In the article "Revival of Varieties," Lysenko tries to ridicule all of contemporary experimental work with chromosomes. However, it is those lines that are really ridiculous, not as concerns genetics, but because of the shallow attitude toward science, manifested, moreover, without inhibition. . . . Why should you treat your failures as principles and undermine the plant-breeding specialists, the most experienced of whom will disagree with you all the same? . . . It is impossible, of course, to forbid Lysenko and Prezent to write whatever and however they want, since such articles are published. But it is completely incomprehensible how an official organ of the Commissariat of Agriculture of the Soviet Union can run articles that disrupt plant breeding and seed production.

It is time to stop the disruption of seed production. It is time that the farm agencies put into practice the decrees and regulations established for seed production. Then degeneration of varieties will disappear, unprincipled demagogy will be ended, and, through breeding programs, our fields will be covered with the best varieties, as was true in the past in some of our territories and provinces.[40]

Academician Mikhail M. Zavadovsky, an expert in embryology and individual development and vice-president of VASKhNIL, pointed to the "low level of Lysenko's and Prezent's attacks" and said, "The Shchedrinesque language to which Prezent resorts should be used when one needs to *crush*, not when one wants to *correct*." (This was a very courageous thing to say, for Stalin frequently quoted Saltykov-Shchedrin and used the same contemptuously sarcastic tone.) Zavadovsky also criticized the casual attitude of many geneticists toward Lysenko's mistakes, which they saw as the immaterial and harmless idiosyncrasies of an ignorant agronomist. Zavadovsky urged geneticists to make a careful analysis of those mistakes, to critique them in detail, to debunk them publicly and not just in private conversation, as was frequently done. A geneticist, he said, "can ill afford to be indulgent" when "he sees a jumble of nonsense in his opponents' speeches."[41]

Vavilov, in his report, also pointed out the Lysenkoists' failure to understand the fundamentals of science. He cited examples of the tremendous contribution of science to practical work, and in particular of genetics to the development of plant breeding. Counting on Lysenko and his adherents to be sensible, he concluded with a call for "greater attention to one another's work, more respect for one another."[42]

Some specialists apparently felt that, in the circumstances, it was unsafe to refrain from publicly accepting Lysenko's basic propositions. This was particularly manifest in the speech by M. M. Zavadovsky's brother, Boris, who was also a member of VASKhNIL:

> Above all, I must express my admiration for the force with which Academician T. D. Lysenko has raised a number of cardinal questions. . . . I also consider it imperative to destroy the myth of "vandals" who do not know the value of genetics and allegedly have set out to destroy it. It is necessary categorically to repulse all attempts . . . to depict Comrade Lysenko's attack on some of the canons of classic genetics as a manifestation of "ignorance, lack of knowledge of the principles of this science."[43]

In keeping with this statement, B. M. Zavadovsky did not hold back from attacking Vavilov, Serebrovsky, Muller, his own brother, and others who had spoken before him.

Nikolai P. Dubinin took a different tack. He called Lysenko's mistakes "delusions" and affected to believe that they were temporary and accidental, springing from excessive confidence in Prezent, who was deemed responsible for all the mistakes of his chief. Dubinin reproached his scientific colleagues (chiefly his teachers, Koltsov and Serebrovsky) for "most crude, reactionary mistakes . . . at times discrediting science," and he claimed to have found errors in Vavilov's law of homologous series.[44]

This position of Dubinin's was no "sin of youth." More than thirty years later, he published a memoir, *Perpetual Motion* (Vechnoye dvizheniye), whose undisguised purpose of humiliating his former teachers and glorifying himself provoked several parodies that circulated in samizdat form; one of them was called *Perpetual Promotion* (Vechnoye vydvizheniye). In his memoir, Dubinin discussed the 1936 VASKhNIL session and again eulogized Lysenko and severely criticized the speeches of the geneticists:

> The reports by N. I. Vavilov, A. S. Serebrovsky, and H. J. Muller . . . did not contain any new ideas, either theoretical or practical, and did not indicate ways for quickly and directly applying science to production. These leaders' speeches relied on genetics' past.
>
> T. D. Lysenko's report bore a different character. . . . He attacked his opponents from new positions, advanced several fundamentally new ideas in the light of his own theory of plant development by stages, pointed out the necessity of reconsidering the scientific principles of plant breeding, and dealt extensively with the relation between science and production.
>
> It is obvious that in these circumstances the social significance of T. D. Lysenko's position was to be preferred. Hopes for success from the application of science in agriculture began to be linked with his proposals. The discussion greatly weakened the positions of N. I. Vavilov and A. S. Serebrovsky.[45]

Dubinin found particularly negative Koltsov's concluding speech, which appealed to both the Lysenkoists and their opponents to investigate more thoroughly the tasks before them and to strive toward an understanding of the truth, rather than to juggle words. According to Dubinin, Koltsov should have criticized Vavilov in the following way:

> I ask Nikolai Ivanovich Vavilov, do you know genetics as you should? No, you do not. . . . You don't read our *Biological Journal* articles carefully, of course. You hardly studied *Drosophila*, and if you were given the ordinary student laboratory task of determining where a particular mutation lies on a chromosome, you would very likely not solve it immediately, since you did not take the student course in genetics in your time.[46]

In their speeches, the Lysenkoists—Prezent, Dolgushin, and Sergei S. Perov—declared in no uncertain terms that genetics was a harmful science, in fact not a science at all but a bourgeois distortion of scientific thought. They urged not only that the geneticists be put in their place but also that genetics be completely prohibited in the Soviet Union, as a science of saboteurs. Prezent asserted: "Socialism and the dictatorship of the proletariat cannot fail to produce creative discussion. Our discussion has nothing in common with the discussions that take place in the West and in America." Furthermore, he said, "the banner of *Drosophila*, which decorates the chest of many a scientist, we leave to those geneticists for whom *Drosophila* has become an idol, blinding them all to the remarkable satisfaction of building a renewed Soviet science, a science of socialism." He also devoted much time to browbeating Vavilov and discrediting his scientific leadership.[47] Dolgushin, too, called upon the geneticists "to forget Mendel, his followers, and Morgan, crossing-over . . . and the rest of genetic wisdom."[48]

Of course, the session participants impatiently awaited Lysenko's speech. So much well-founded criticism had been directed at him that it seemed impossible to refute it without facts and appropriate explanations. But Lysenko demonstrated a different attitude toward criticism. "Several of those engaging in the discussion in the journals took a lofty tone," he began. "With what seem to me to be frequent exaggerations and with the aim of juggling the facts in their favor, I cannot accept this." Again he ridiculed the assertions that varieties grown according to the laws of genetics were stable and that the products of intravarietal cross-pollination were not. And again, rather than attempting to substantiate his scientific views, he accused Vavilov of intentionally distorting the truth. Any facts that contradicted his theories he simply declared unnecessary:

> N. I. Vavilov maintained in his report that intravarietal crossing should not be conducted and is useless. . . . Vavilov pointed out that there are many examples indicating that varieties of wheat, barley, and other self-pollinating crops have lasted 100 years and longer. . . . Even if the number of self-pollinating crops that have existed for centuries were many times greater than cited by N. I. Vavilov in his report, these facts nowadays are no longer needed.

He took issue with a number of scientific propositions, including the one with which Vavilov was identified:

> What I have set forth . . . of course also radically contradicts the "law" of homologous or parallel series of mutability of N. I. Vavilov. This "law" is fundamentally based on the genetic combination of corpuscles of the "substance of heredity" that are immutable throughout a long line of generations. I do not feel that I have the strength, knowledge, and ability to properly destroy this "law," which does not correspond to the reality of the evolutionary process. But in my own work I constantly encounter the unacceptability of this "law": The work itself says that it is impossible to become reconciled to this "law" if you are struggling for effective, purposeful mastering of the evolution of plant forms.[49]

Getting more and more worked up, Lysenko accused Konstantinov of malicious deception and Meister of failing to understand (even refusing to understand) the sources and scope of his work.[50] He accused

Karpechenko, Sapegin, Serebrovsky, Muller, and others of deliberately distorting his statements, misquoting him, and concealing his successes. He intimated that his critics, above all Vavilov, were causing harm to the building of socialism. "To acknowledge the law of homologous series means to give up on the problem of managing the nature of plants," he said.[51] Such a definitive rejection of Vavilov's hypothesis was a corollary of Lysenko's views. According to the law of homologous series, mutations in closely related species and genera of plants must arise predominantly in homologous sections of the chromosomes. Vavilov's law thereby rigidly defined the limits of mutability and excluded the possibility of easy manipulation of heredity. Lysenko considered the environment's direct and rapid influence on plants indisputable: It was easy to change the nature of plants, there were no genes, and so there was no reason to reinforce conservatism over mythical hereditary structures.

Lysenko announced his immediate plans to the session—in particular, his intention quickly to transform all winter grains into spring grains, not by vernalization, as he had wanted to earlier, but by effecting a complete hereditary change, turning winter forms permanently into spring varieties. Lysenko said that Vavilov and a collaborator by the name of Kuznetsova, studying the genetic nature of winter and spring forms, had tried to determine which and how many genes controlled these properties. In Lysenko's opinion, by adopting this approach, "they let a good project slip from their hands." His prescription was simple: If they would relinquish the notion of genes,

> they would easily come to the conclusion that winter plants at certain moments in their life, under certain conditions, can be transformed, can change their hereditary nature into a spring type, and vice versa—which we are quite successfully doing experimentally now. By taking our point of view, N. I. Vavilov, too, will be able to refashion winter plants into spring ones. Moreover, any winter variety, in any quantity, can be made into a spring one.[52]

At this, Vavilov challenged Lysenko from the floor: "You can refashion heredity?" to which Lysenko responded with complete self-confidence, "Yes, heredity!" And he continued: "Unfortunately, the concept of genetics, with its immutable genes in a long line of generations, with its nonacknowledgment of natural and artificial selection, nevertheless holds sway in the minds of many scientists."[53] It was an unjust statement: of course, no geneticist rejected natural or artificial selection.

This session of VASKhNIL was apparently very important to Vavilov on a personal level. Up to then, he had believed that Lysenko was a good practical worker who simply didn't understand theory and was surrounded by brazen intriguers like Prezent, and that if one were to explain everything to him properly, to set forth the scientifically established facts of genetics, then Lysenko would understand and gladly accept them. Consequently, Vavilov instructed Muller, who was then working in Vavilov's institute, and another researcher, Aleksandra A. Prokofyeva-Belgovskaya, to prepare microscope slides illustrating various stages of chromosomes, as well as color diagrams on paper with written explanations. Vavilov believed that anyone who viewed the chromosomes through the microscope and then studied the diagrams and explanatory text could check with his own eyes that it all corresponded perfectly with the representations of the geneticists.

The slides and explanations were set up in the foyer of the presidium of VASKhNIL, on the first floor. Vavilov examined them and exclaimed, "Well, here at last everything is perfectly clear. Now with these we will be able to explain it all!" It would have been awkward for Vavilov to tell Lysenko—who was, after all, an academician and an institute director—that this entire "campaign" had been arranged especially for him. Instead, when Lysenko and Prezent arrived, Vavilov, after exchanging greetings, announced tactfully that his colleagues had prepared some interesting chromosome slides and explanations, and he invited Lysenko to examine them. Lysenko and Prezent bent over the microscopes, cast a cursory glance at the explanatory illustrations, and quickly went on to the next microscopes. The entire examination took less than five minutes, and they left the foyer without comment.[54]

Vavilov and Serebrovsky were anxious to show that genetics did have applications to domesticated plants and animals, that, despite its profoundly theoretical nature, genetics already had given much to practice and would become a veritable gold mine in the future. But they soberly acknowledged that much work stood between the discovery of fundamental laws and their practical application. The Lysenko camp seized upon this. They declared that the geneticists promised only future progress; they were not offering anything today or even the day after. And the country could not wait. As Tsitsin said, "T. D. Lysenko proves that genetics, in its present state of development, lags several years behind the rapidly growing socialist reality."[55]

The Lysenkoists found it especially convenient and safe to attack Muller, as a representative of an alien country as well as an alien science. His explanations of what mutations were, how often they occurred, and how to affect the rate of occurrence were treated with sarcasm by Lysenko in his closing speech:

I am grateful to Professor Muller for his brilliant report. Today his concluding remarks were no less brilliant. Muller definitively dotted his i's. He said precisely and clearly that genes mutate only after tens and hundred of thousands of generations. Phenotype has no effect on genotype. . . .

In sum, it seems that the chicken develops from the egg, but the egg develops not from the chicken, but directly from a former egg. We can see what Professor Muller is saying, we understand. He has disclosed his position. . . .

The geneticists' fundamental mistake is that they accept the immutability of genes over a long line of generations. True, they acknowledge the gene's mutability after tens and hundreds of thousands of generations, but thank you for such mutability!

We, recognizing mutability of the genotype in the process of ontogenetic development of plants . . . can already, by our methods of raising, change the nature of plants in a controlled manner in each generation.

I am convinced that this sphere of work in the Soviet Union will expand rapidly in the near future. . . . This is the task of our Soviet science.[56]

In his concluding remarks, Lysenko rejected all the criticisms made of him and accused the geneticists of "having turned out in many instances to be illiterate about biological phenomena."[57]

Meister, as vice-president of VASKhNIL, closed the session. However, his speech now diverged radically from his earlier cogent criticisms of Lysenko. He began by declaring that the academy leadership did not consider genetics to be a pseudoscience, as the Lysenkoists would have liked, and he called upon the geneticists not to be too worried. Then, in an attempt to reconcile the opposing views, he made remarks that were mutually exclusive. On the one hand, he said:

Our young Soviet scientist N. P. Dubinin, who has won praise abroad, spoke here in defense of genetics, but under the influence of the panic gripping him he quite unexpectedly began to demonstrate to us that genetics is free of formalism and strictly materialistic. I would like to point out to N. P. Dubinin that this panic is groundless. The Lenin Academy of Agricultural Sciences is in no way threatening genetics as a science in the USSR.

But there his defense of genetics stopped, and he turned to criticizing both the field and the specialists working in it. The geneticists, he alleged, greatly exaggerated the stability of genes; on the whole, they were removed from practical work and had even lost touch with it, and instead of helping agriculture they at times undertook the introduction of unneeded and even harmful methods, such as artificial insemination of animals. Vavilov, in particular, said Meister, "instead of taking a critical attitude toward his own mistakes, including mistakes of methodology, has become carried away with an enumeration of the endless achievements of the Institute of Plant Industry. Moreover, he declared, without any basis, that the law of homologous series was "anti-Darwinist" in nature. Meister's remarks condemning Vavilov and the geneticists appeared in *Pravda* and thus acquired the air of a final verdict.[58]

The discussion had taken on such political significance that it was reported on *daily* in the central party press. But the reports were selective: The views of Lysenko's critics were stated so sparingly that it was impossible to understand them, while Lysenko's speech, with its attacks on genetics and geneticists, was published in its entirety in *Izvestia* and in two Party newspapers in the field of agriculture.[59]

Yet Vavilov still believed one could reason with Lysenko and that the main obstacle was the latter's weak methodological preparation and lack of depth. Evidence of this came to light many years later, after Vavilov's posthumous rehabilitation. Not long after this session of the academy, Georgy A. Mashtaller, had written an article for the Russian popular-science magazine *Nature* (*Priroda*—not to be confused with the well-known international science journal, *Nature*, published in England), describing the discussion and presenting it as a complete victory of Lysenko over his opponents. The editors sent the article to Vavilov for review, and his response demonstrated once more that he did not consider all Lysenko's activity incorrect and dangerous to science, but saw in it only isolated erroneous aspects:

> The author has interpreted the discussion very much in his own way. The sharpness of the discussion arose from the fact that many of Academician Lysenko's experimental conclusions elicited and elicit profound doubts. An experiment is conclusive only when you can repeat it and obtain definite results. Many of the experimental conclusions advanced by Academician Lysenko's school, unfortunately, require further precise proofs on the basis of all the vast experience of modern genetics. If these proofs will be obtained, this will significantly diminish the sharpness of the discussion.[60]

Of course, it is equally possible to see in this statement a reluctance on Vavilov's part to express his thoughts openly, instead playing the political game demanded by the existing political circumstances and stating only a minor doubt. However, many who knew Vavilov are inclined to believe that he wrote just what he thought. After receiving Vavilov's review, *Nature* did not publish Mashtaller's article. In academic circles, Vavilov's word still carried weight.

7

Agricultural Science
by Terror

To unleash unplumbed, slumbering impulses is easy; to control
them is harder.

—Maximilian Voloshin, *Magic*

The Russian intelligentsia had for over a century been the traditional repository of the ideas of resistance to despotism and above all
to thought control. It was natural that the Purge struck at it with
particular force.

—Robert Conquest, *The Great Terror*

The Peasant Scientists

By 1937, Lysenko had risen to the highest rank of Soviet science. However,
the scientists who had joined him were only a tiny group, though an
influential one. Prudence, ideology, and the memory of his own peasant
origins demanded that Lysenko recruit the masses to his side.

Press reports of Lysenko's activities in these years presented him as
ceaselessly working for the good of the country. He traveled to famous
institutions throughout the USSR, participated in prestigious meetings,
and appeared before the nation's leaders. Meanwhile, his students were
visiting kolkhozes, gathering questionnaires, and soliciting the ideas of
farmers. Conversely, the Odessa institute frequently invited peasants from
all over the Ukraine to meetings and short courses on vernalization, summer planting of potatoes, and Lysenko's other theories and plans.

One group of graduate students at the institute especially boosted the
sense of public participation in Lysenko's activities. In 1933, in reaction to
the rapid growth—more than twentyfold—in the number of agricultural
specialists (a growth fostered by Vavilov as he sought to staff the nearly
twenty new institutes set up under the auspices of VASKhNIL) and to
supposed defects in their training, the Party Central Committee made
some changes. The number of students was reduced, and forty places were
reserved for "special graduate students," to be chosen from among staff
members of Party organs, the press, and the Komsomol, and other politically active people.[1] Seven of these vacancies were given to Lysenko to fill,
allowing him to recruit valuable new supporters.

These special graduate students had a great impact on the Odessa institute. In particular, their resourcefulness, honed by their experience of the world (at least the Communist world) beyond the institute, made them stand out. For example, one of them, Ivan Ye. Glushchenko, told me in 1976 the story of how he, after joining Lysenko, wrote to the U.S. Department of Agriculture, asking for an account of the characteristics of Russian wheat used in developing American varieties. An employee left over from Sapegin's time at the institute composed the letter for him and translated it into English. The Americans promptly responded, the same employee translated the answer into Russian, and Glushchenko used the translation verbatim as a chapter of his dissertation. Glushchenko went to read this chapter to Lysenko, who was spending the summer at the seashore in a dacha so spartanly furnished that he and his guest, Prezent, had to use their heavy peasant coats for bedding. Glushchenko sat down on a stool and read "his" work. His two listeners were surprised at the depth of his knowledge. "When did you become so smart?" Lysenko asked. When Glushchenko explained how he had gotten the chapter, Lysenko's sole response was to praise him for his resourcefulness.

Lysenko often talked to those attending the courses at his institute. Rustic in appearance, dressed like any ordinary collective farmer and using the same blunt and simple language, always appearing at these courses in the company of ordinary people, Lysenko won the sympathy of his audiences. Toward the same end, Lysenko surrounded himself with plain folks, peasants occupied in sowing or repairing the farm machinery or preparing the seed. In their boots and their padded jackets, spattered with earth and soiled with machine oil, they sought his advice.

A photograph of the Lysenkoist "corps" of those years shows them obviously just returned from the fields. Their boots still muddy, they posed for the picture without ceremony: eight of them seated on a bench, nine ranged behind them along the wall of a building. The one woman, A. I. Gapeyeva, wore mittens, while the others tucked their hands in the sleeves or pockets of their coats or padded jackets. Only two or three wore ties; the others wore traditional Russian blouses or dark shirts. It is impossible to distinguish the usually dapper Dolgushin from the unsophisticated Glushchenko, A. D. Rodionov from F. G. Lutsenko, S. A. Pogosyan from G. A. Babadzhanyan, or any of them from Lysenko, seated in the center, his hand thrust into his coat pocket, his legs crossed. If one did not know his face, one would not say that this was an academician and the director of an institute. It was easy to accept him as "one of ours."

Lysenko appealed particularly to those who were seeking to enter into the mysteries of science. To become a scientist without traversing the long, difficult path of grammar school, high school, and university or institute—many thirsted for this. It was not surprising that Lysenko's example, appeals, and promises got an enthusiastic response from hundreds of peasants, burning with the dream of being transformed, as if in some Russian fairy tale, into scientists.

At that time, the nation's leaders sought to use collective farmers as major arbiters in a scientific dispute. The weight given to the "opinion of the masses," even if it was organized from above, has to be seen in the context of the extraordinary spirit of optimism that was felt in Soviet society from the beginning of the 1920s and continuing, although somewhat abated, into the mid-1930s. It is difficult for us now to realize that those years gave the world amazing examples of inspired labor and the sublime poetry and prose of Mandelshtam, Babel, Pasternak, and Bulgakov, even though it also gave rise to Lysenko and Beria and lifted them to the summit of the society. Perhaps we can no longer feel what it meant for millions of people to have the good fortune to learn to read and write, to hold a book in their hands for the first time, to listen to the radio for the first time, watch a film for the first time, for the first time . . . for the first time . . . for the first time. . . . Liberated people, newly literate, writing— for the first time in their lives—fingers shaking with the effort, "We are not slaves. Slaves we are not."

Lysenko took advantage of this yearning for equality, education, and a better life by encouraging the aspirations of would-be peasant scientists. He himself would often lead discussions with them in the short courses at the Odessa institute. He would describe in simple language and stories how plants grow and develop, how the Lysenkoists sought to increase yields with the help of the farmers' invaluable scientific observations, and how, on the other hand, the scientists spurned their efforts and thwarted their hopes.

His journal, *Vernalization,* was filled with letters from peasants singing the praises of the "hero of the people" and contrasting him to the "laboratory scientists" and the "bourgeois time-servers." In turn, the journal celebrated the accomplishments of "the people's academicians." It devoted a special column to photographs of these peasant-scientists in their "cottage-laboratories" (as the cottages used for holding meetings, displaying brochures, and storing any equipment more complex than rakes and shovels were designated): one thoughtfully scrutinizing a thermometer, another explaining something from a book open before him to "a fellow academician." In an editorial for a special issue marking the twentieth anniversary of Soviet rule in 1937, *Vernalization* proclaimed:

> Boldness in posing and solving problems and a constant sense of responsibility to the socialist motherland . . . research work by the masses, the participation of thousands of kolkhoz experimenters . . . the audacious advancement of talented researchers from among the masses of kolkhoz experimenters . . . —these are the remarkable features of Soviet agrobiology.[2]

Lysenko insisted that agrobiology learned as much from the collective farmers as they learned from it. As one example, he said that, thanks to the "experiments" by collective farmers with intravarietal crossing, he had learned to his surprise and delight that the protein content of wheat had gone up and that this led to a more palatable and nutritious bread. "I did not know this until I received the samples from the kolkhozes."[3] He neglected to say—possibly he did not know— that the link between palatability, nutritive value, and protein content had been noted by scientists decades before.

A People's Academician

The head of the cottage-laboratory at the Legacy of Ilyich kolkhoz in the village of Maltsevo, in the Chelyabinsk (now Kurgan) region, became the model peasant-scientist. His name was Terenty S. Maltsev, and in October 1937 he attended a seminar at the Odessa institute, where he gave a long speech. "Maltsev does not have a formal education," commented *Vernalization*, "but in cast of mind, powers of observation, and ability to investigate, analyze, and generalize, he is a real man of science."[4] In his speech, Maltsev said:

> Only in 1919, upon returning from captivity under the Germans, I chanced to read through a number of antireligious, popular-science, and political brochures, after which my thinking underwent a change from superstition to knowledge. And dialectical materialism, which I started studying only two years ago, really opened my eyes to nature. It was hard, but I got to the core of it and the fruit was sweet. Earlier, whatever I read about nature in the scientists' books seemed correct to me; now, I have begun to understand the literature, and now I simply cannot leave science alone. Some inner force draws me deeper and deeper into discerning all of life's small secrets, exploring all the chance phenomena and recognizing them as necessities, so as to be able with ease to use the laws and phenomena of nature for the good of my socialist motherland.[5]

Like other peasant-scientists, Maltsev was uninhibited by any lack of knowledge. He spoke calmly and even challengingly about his scanty education but quite confidently about his ability to surpass the geneticists and avoid their mistakes.

> Experimenters like us must be systematically kept posted in popular form on events on the forefront of science. We experimenters too want to know about all the new gains science makes. Only we must be told about all this in more understandable language, but without simplifying the content, without emasculating what is "sweetest." I will say for myself that I really very much would like to get to know about the life of plants and learn at least a little how to control them in order somehow to be of service in the conquest of nature for the benefit of the free men of our country. But it is very difficult for me to cope with this and to understand all this properly. After all, I didn't study anywhere; I didn't even spend a day in the village school, but I've been attaining knowledge all my life step by step by my own efforts, as a self-taught person. And there are many like me in our country, to whom the revolution and Soviet rule opened up a path to science. The scientific specialists must help us kolkhoz experimenters to enter deeper and deeper into science, and this will give us the most

abundant harvest in the form of our own kind of conscious and diligent kolkhoz scientific cadres.[6]

He also gave unqualified endorsement to Lysenko's ideas:

I frequently ask myself: What would become of genetics and the geneticists if people like T. D. Lysenko did not prod them? Would the geneticists find a way out of the dead end into which they have been led by the hypothesis of the independence of genes? Although, I repeat, I am still little versed in genetics, yet I have understood that there cannot be any kind of hereditary substance independent of the soma . . . and I cannot by any means understand the geneticists who believe that the reproductive cells simply reside "in the homes of the somatic cells" without acquiring any "habits" or "skills" from their hosts, the somatic tissues. Anyone will say it is absurd that they don't. Genetics maintains that every trait or group of traits is a "gene" or group of "genes." But I ask, how many traits can an organism, moreover a multicellular one, have? I think it would hardly be possible to assemble enough digits to express the number of characteristics absorbed in the human mind. . . . And when you ponder such questions, involuntarily you become amazed at the fantasy of the geneticists, who, you see, must assume that the chromosomes have such a number of genes as would exceed the bounds of any sort of fantasy. . . . My mind cannot accept the geneticists' doctrine of the immutability of genes, either. . . . When I read the geneticists' speeches, then as far as I can see, the geneticists are pervaded by metaphysics, and somehow the paths of further development of their doctrine cannot be seen, or, rather, they come up against a wall. . . .

In my opinion, Lysenko is a thousand times right in that by his new methods of work and by constructing his new, revolutionary theory, he has systematically thrown down challenge after challenge to the representatives of the old genetics, like rocks thrown into stagnant water.[7]

The published account of the meeting commented that Maltsev's speech "would do honor to any professor of genetics if the latter rightly understood genetics."[8] And of course Maltsev frequently spoke out in the press and on the radio in glorification of Stalin, saying things like, "The Stalinist epoch has opened up vast horizons before the working people of our country and created all the conditions for a successful and joyous life for them," and "It is a joy to realize that . . . our wise leader and teacher Iosif Vissarionovich Stalin is concerned about each one of us."[9]

To do Maltsev justice, he did not seek high positions; he lived out his entire life in his village. But his zeal was well rewarded. He was named a corresponding member, and later honorary member, of VASKhNIL and a deputy to the USSR Supreme Soviet. He won a Stalin Prize and was twice awarded the title of Hero of Socialist Labor. On November 13, 1985, he was shown on Soviet television receiving his sixth Order of Lenin, on the occasion of his ninetieth birthday.

Tulaikov's Arrest and Death

Maltsev's name was associated with a technique that was supposed to protect the soil in the arid conditions that typify much of the farmland of the USSR. The Soviet Union often suffered severely from droughts and from dust storms that carried away the fertile soil from millions of hectares. Maltsev proposed shallow plowing that would not destroy the precious topsoil and planting late to avoid the worst weather. He was praised successively by Khrushchev, Brezhnev, and Gorbachev. During one dustbowl crisis, Brezhnev even traveled to the village of Maltsevo to seek Maltsev's advice on when and how to plow. In 1987, Gorbachev consulted with Maltsev, rather than with scientists and agronomists, when trying to understand shortcomings in Siberian industry and agriculture.

Maltsev may have gotten his ideas, in part, from Canadian and American experience, which had been described many times in popular-science publications, and he may himself have guessed shrewdly how to farm in areas where drought is common. However, his methods, even in their details, closely resemble those proposed by Nikolai Tulaikov, whom we have met before (see chapter 1). Tulaikov was a renowned agricultural scientist, an academician, and director of the Saratov Institute of Grain Farming. His main field of research was agriculture in arid regions. He had written the country's most authoritative treatises on the subject, in which he took a rational, flexible approach to the problems of coping with the weather in the Soviet Union's zones of "risky agriculture."[10] For many years, his proposals were supported by the top Soviet agricultural leaders. He headed the scientific committee of the Commissariat of Agriculture after the Revolution; he was awarded a Lenin Prize in 1929; and in 1932, he was elected a full member of the AN SSSR. The nation's newspapers frequently published his articles and asked him to comment on events in the scientific life of the country.[11] However, neither his scientific stature nor his membership in the Party could prevail over Stalin's need for scapegoats for the failure of collectivization.

At the joint plenary session of the Party Central Committee and the Party Central Control Commission in January 1933, when gnawing hunger was mowing people down like the plague, Stalin spoke in lofty phrases of the unprecedented rise in our agriculture, and in March of the same year, by resolution of the board of the OGPU [the secret police], 35 officials of the USSR Commissariat of Agriculture were shot without trial for "subversion" and "use of an official position to create starvation in the country."

Opposed to Tulaikov's ideas were those of the agronomist Vasily R. Williams (see biographical sketch). Although the social origins of Williams and Lysenko were different (Williams having been trained as a professor under the old system), there are marked parallels between their careers. Lysenko regarded Williams as one of his heroes, and the two enthusiastically supported each other's "theories." Williams claimed that his complex system of rotating crops, tilling, and, above all, planting perennial grasses over much of the land would preserve the moisture-retaining structure of the soil. On behalf of his ideas, he joined in the Stalinist repressions that made the thirties a decade of terror for millions of Soviet citizens. Between 1930 and 1933, Williams's accusations of sabotage led to the arrest, imprisonment, or exile of a large group of agronomists and agrochemists associated with Tulaikov, Pryanishnikov, and Vavilov: Tsintsadze, Doyarenko, Chayanov, and Krutikhovsky, to name only a handful of the thousands of agricultural-science workers who were arrested in the first wave of repressions.

Lysenko demonstrated his cooperation with Williams by making the first overt move. In April 1937, in an article aimed chiefly at Konstantinov, Lysenko declared that certain proposals for the methods of cultivation in arid regions amounted to sabotage.[12] Although he did not name Tulaikov, any reader knowledgeable about agronomy would have known whom he was alluding to. A week later, an explicit attack on Tulaikov was made by a follower of Lysenko's, Vsevolod N. Stoletov.[13] He charged that Tulaikov had acted in collusion with enemies of the people and conducted sabotage that was aimed at disrupting the kolkhozes. Simultaneously with the publication of this article, three of Tulaikov's collaborators—Samarin, Voitovich, and Gava—were arrested.

Three days later, the scientific staffs of Tulaikov's institute and of the experiment station directed by Meister gathered at a hastily called meeting. For reasons that are not known, Tulaikov was not present. On the following day, the newspaper of the regional and city Party committees of Saratov announced the unanimous condemnation of Tulaikov by his students and colleagues; and two days later, the same newspaper gave a lengthy account of the meeting. The article asked, "Are the erroneous opinions of N. M. Tulaikov accidental?" and it answered:

No. Everyone knows his earlier "theories" about the advantage of shallow plowing, monocultures, the limits of the harvest, the ineffectiveness of fertilization in the conditions of the Lower Volga area, and so forth. These "theories," as Professor Smirnov, Professor Gulyayev, Professor Zakharin, and Professor Levoshkin correctly pointed out at the meeting, were used and are used now by enemies of the people, saboteurs of agriculture, Trotskyites, and their right-wing confederates. . . . Where are the roots and what is the reason for the appearance of the alien, harvest-limiting "theories" of Academician N. M. Tulaikov? The "theories" of Academician N. M. Tulaikov came from his lack of faith in the cause of socialist restructuring of agriculture in the USSR, his admiration for bourgeois theories. . . . One of the fundamental errors of Academician Tulaikov is conservatism, fear that the institute will be penetrated by such revolutionary theories in agronomy as, for example, the theory of Academician Lysenko. . . . [Tulaikov] juggled figures and facts (Comrade Vyalov spoke brilliantly about this) and incorrectly managed the work of the institute he headed.

Apparently, only two people attempted to defend Tulaikov at all. One of them, a Comrade Vostokov, said that "Academician Tulaikov only swung from one theory to another, but these theories did not have any intrinsic connection." Comrade Yakovlev responded that "Academician Tulaikov has one position, one line, one 'theory,' directed at harming socialist agriculture." Yakovlev was echoed by Delinikaitis, Popov, Plachek, Sus, N. G. Meister, and others.[14]

Those present at the meeting went on to criticize friends, students, and followers of the disgraced academician. They condemned, among others, Academician Rudolf E. David, one of the founders of agricultural meteorology in the USSR, who had expressed, both orally and in a letter, his disagreement with the accusations against Tulaikov.

When a report about the meeting was published in the official organ of VASKhNIL, the initiative for the attack on Tulaikov was ascribed to the "masses." According to this account, the salvos of criticism were launched not by Stoletov and Lysenko but by Tulaikov's colleagues at the institute.[15] Not long afterward, the main publications carried articles condemning Tulaikov for his "sabotaging" activity.[16] By the end of the year, Tulaikov's name was being frequently reviled in the Soviet press.

Some time afterward, Tulaikov was arrested, and on January 20, 1938, he was shot. At the beginning of the 1940s, a circular was distributed to the country's libraries instructing them to "remove and pulp the works of N. M. Tulaikov."[17] Meanwhile, Stoletov became an associate of Lysenko's and was later appointed deputy director of the Institute of Genetics.

After Khrushchev exposed Stalin's "cult of personality," Tulaikov's name was restored to honor and his works were again brought into the light of day. Indeed, Khrushchev told the Party Central Committee that Tulaikov had been an innocent victim. Yet the rehabilitation still distorted the facts. Khrushchev presented Lysenko and Maltsev as all but the true heirs of Tulaikov's work:

> Trofim Denisovich Lysenko has suggested planting on stubble. Or take plowing with the drill plow, used in steppe conditions, specifically in the southern Ukraine. It is true that there was a time when this method of plowing was condemned. Professor Tulaikov advocated this method of cultivating the soil. He was later severely criticized for this; they even invented [the term] "Tulaikovism." But now what Comrade Maltsev is doing bears some similarity to Tulaikov's methods.[18]

And Khrushchev's words glossed over Tulaikov's fate.

The farmers of the United States and Canada applied Tulaikov's ideas, but his compatriots did not. The dust storms that carried off fertile layers of soil from millions of hectares in Kazakhstan, the Ukraine, and the Altai and Volga regions were the cost of turning a deaf ear to Tulaikov's warnings and of blind faith in the nostrums of Williams, Stoletov, and their followers. The soil-protecting systems of farming proposed by Maltsev and then once again "discovered" by the Siberian farmer Aleksandr Barayev (who was awarded a Lenin Prize in 1972 for this "discovery") had long before been put forth and scientifically substantiated by Tulaikov.

Tulaikov's idea about the necessity of amelioration of the soil in arid regions of the Volga steppe began to be carried out nearly forty years later—but then it was attributed to Leonid Brezhnev. Then, as Brezhnev's name faded into oblivion, Gorbachev advocated the idea of soil amelioration. Unfortunately, even then, the work was not conducted at all in the way Tulaikov had proposed. Today, Yeltsin doesn't have enough resources to speak about such high-cost programs.

The effects of the terror wrought by Williams and Lysenko on G. K. Meister's grain selection group at Saratov has been revealed vividly in the contrasting recollections of staff members before and after the destruction of their colleagues. V. N. Mamontova, a former student of Meister's, described the earlier times: "We were friends, visited each other; Meister danced in high spirits at New Year's, Tulaikov played the flute splendidly, Doyarenko sang romances he himself had composed." A young colleague, hearing this account, was filled with envy and was left aghast at how times had changed. An old employee whom the others knew simply as Auntie Lusha, testified to the fear that surrounded the most commonplace activities of life at the institute after the purges began. As she recalled sadly, Meister and one of his colleagues, Aleksei P. Shekhurdin,

> would get together, dearie, in the evening to drink tea. And they would sit opposite one another and stir with their spoons, and nary a word. . . . It was an evil time. You'd scarcely say anything, and right away they'd inform on you. But these two were bosom friends. And so they would sit all evening. And only at parting [would they say]: "It's been so pleasant visiting, Aleksei Pavlovich!" "Excellent, Georgy Karlovich!"[19]

Lysenko As a Governmental Figure

In addition to being a theorist, experimentalist, teacher, and propagandist, Lysenko now began to take part in the government. It was a predictable development. The press had made him into a hero of the Soviet establishment, his name figured on posters and in newspapers and magazines, and his plain face with its high cheekbones had become familiar to all. When there was nothing to say about Lysenko, they wrote about his father, reporting such trivia as that Denis Lysenko had been "accepted as a participant in the nationwide agricultural exhibition."[20]

In 1936, Lysenko participated in the work of the Extraordinary Eighth Congress of Soviets and was a member of the editorial commission that drafted the final text of the so-called "Stalin Constitution."[21] In 1937, he became a member of the USSR Supreme Soviet,[22] and in the following year, he was appointed vice-chairman of one of its two chambers, the Council of the Union.[23] Thus, Lysenko held nominal rank higher than Stalin himself, for Stalin was a member only of the executive body, the presidium of the Supreme Soviet, which had no legislative power. When the Supreme Soviet met in the Great Kremlin Palace, there were three levels of platforms: On the lowest were seated the Party and government leaders, including Stalin; the rostrum for speakers was positioned a little higher; and at the very summit were the chairmen and vice-chairmen of the two legislative chambers. Thus, Lysenko for many years sat in the Kremlin above Stalin. As vice-chairman of the Council of the Union, Lysenko presided at meetings that had nothing to do with science or agriculture but did extend Soviet repression in other directions. He was there, for example, on August 2 and 3, 1940, when the Supreme Soviet "unanimously approved" the annexation of Lithuania, Latvia, Estonia, Northern Bukovina, and the Khotin, Akkerman, and Izmail provinces of Bessarabia.[24] In the steady stream of front-page photographs of the Supreme Soviet, every citizen of the country could see Lysenko—seated, standing, applauding, but always towering above Stalin, Molotov, Beria, Voroshilov, Khrushchev, or Vyshinsky. There was no higher place of honor.

Lysenko also took an active part in meetings of the Party Central Committee and at Party congresses, even though he was not a Party member. He frequently delivered reports and patriotic speeches at these meetings. The fact that he was not a Party member perhaps impressed many people, for not joining the Party meant preserving one's self-respect. This, however, was done deliberately; to demonstrate the unity of Party and people, individuals who were not formally Party members were presented to the public as enthusiastically supporting the undertakings of the leadership.

Meanwhile, the list of awards given to Lysenko grew longer and longer. Late in 1935, he received his first Order of Lenin, "for growing high-yield varieties of agricultural plants."[25] Over the years, he received seven more Orders of Lenin, the title of Hero of Socialist Labor, the Stalin Prize (in 1941, 1943, and 1949), and other orders and medals.

Thus, by 1937 the organizational and political structure of Lysenkoism was completed, just as its pseudoscientific methodology had crystallized. The discussion of whether genetics benefited agricultural science, and its place among the disciplines allowed in Soviet society, went on for two more years. Not only scientific articles and books but also popular essays about the field and the people in it continued to be published. For example, the writer Konstantin Fedin told of the enthusiasm shown by the students of genetics:

I conducted a questionnaire in several Leningrad higher educational institutions.... Here is the answer of a 26-year-old female student from a working-class background: "I am a geneticist. Questions of heredity interested me even before entering higher education. My future should be one of the happiest: First of all, I dream of becoming a professor. In Leningrad, a great palace will be built in which they will work out the problems of genetics. There, thousands of students and a mass of scientific workers will learn. To study and to transmit my own knowledge to the masses is a great joy.[26]

However, the romanticism of such dreams for the future had already been replaced by the ruthlessness of the present. Other mansions awaited those who still dreamt of "palaces of genetics." For disagreeing with the dogma of the agrobiologists, for not knowing how to throw out "unsuccessful" results, for a chance word misconstrued, for malice unwittingly incurred, tens of thousands of people suffered. They lost their jobs, the right to teach, their human dignity, their lives. I remember as a boy overhearing a conversation between my mother and my father, who worked as an editor between 1947 and 1950 for the Gorky State University newspaper, *For Stalinist Science*. An old teacher of foreign languages had been fired from the university because she had students translate a text that was "inappropriate," since it mentioned the name of someone who had fallen into disfavor; someone informed on her, and a respected teacher was lost. My parents spoke softly, in whispers, and horror could be read on their faces.

8

Lysenko Singles Out
Vavilov and Koltsov

Ringed with a rabble of scrawny chieftains,
Servile dwarfs, eager to please—
  Pawns to use in his intrigues.

—O. Mandelshtam, *Collected Works*

His associates' ignorance, his opponents' weakness and insignificance, his open lies and his self-assured narrow-mindedness raised
him to the very summit. . . . There was no evil act, no petty deception
he could perpetrate that his entourage described as other than a
great deed.

—L. N. Tolstoy, *War and Peace*

Vavilov under the Fire of Party Criticism

For Trofim Lysenko, reaching a position of command in the world of
science was only the first objective. Having obtained power, he had to find
ways to hold on to it. Normally, prestige and advancement in science
come with scientific achievements, but Lysenko had no hope of competing on that ground. Instead, he systematically made his career by cultivating
the favor of politicians, the press, and plain folk, by discrediting leading
scientists—his secretary kept a card file to help him keep track of any
scientist who held "inappropriate" opinions or who might challenge his
sway[1]—and by filling vacancies with his protégés. Their qualifications lay
in their loyalty to him and in their lack of professional knowledge, creativity, and talent. Like Lysenko himself, they were the products of the socialist
system as it had manifested itself within the scientific sphere. They had
neither a commitment to scientific truth nor, thanks to the "abolition of
religion," any fear of God to keep their moral weaknesses in check.

Lysenko's methods reproduced those of his master. In Leninist circles,
Stalin had been regarded as a mediocrity, ill-educated and uncultured. As
a youth in the criminal underworld, he had learned the brutal tricks of
power that enabled him to eliminate his rivals in the Communist Party
and replace them with submissive nonentities. The disregard of ethics and
traditional morality, the defamation of opponents, the evasion of personal
responsibility for repressions, the use of the secret police (first called the
Cheka, later the NKVD, reorganized in 1922 as OGPU, yet again as NKVD

in 1934, and finally as KGB in 1954)—all these became part of Lysenko's repertoire as well.

From the first, Lysenko displayed a genius for claiming and keeping a monopoly of power over his field. His promises were on a grand scale, and he acted vigorously, played to perfection the part of a self-taught man of the people, observed all the outward forms, and "seduced" many prominent scientists (although in all probability most of them simply compromised with their consciences). With their help, he managed his next crucial step in the consolidation of power: taking his dispute with Vavilov out of the scientific and agricultural arena and onto the battleground of political orthodoxy.

On January 5, 1937, Yakovlev, then head of the Party Central Committee's agricultural section, delivered a speech to the staff of Selkhozgiz, the Agricultural Publishing House. He departed from a routine review of the press's plans in order to strike out at genetics and the geneticists. By defending the immutability of genes, the geneticists were, he said, reactionaries and even saboteurs. "It is no mere happenstance that 'by oversight' the name of Charles Darwin has vanished from textbooks. This was their doing." (He was deliberately distorting the facts: Darwin's name had not disappeared.) Taking his cue from Stalin's *Anarchism or Socialism* (originally published in 1906 and reprinted many times later), where the terms "neo-Darwinists" and "neo-Lamarckians" were used in describing how evolution prepared the way for revolution, Yakovlev coined the parallel term "neo-Mendelism" (which Lysenko promptly adopted) to brand the geneticists, and, he said ominously, "The success of . . . neo-Mendelism is due less to its scientific than to its political nature."[2]

Yakovlev's remarks signaled a sharp change in the fate of classical genetics in the USSR. At one stroke, this important Party official, with close ties to Stalin, dismissed genetics from the ranks of the "progressive," "materialistic," and "proletarian" sciences and relegated it to the category of ideologically pernicious studies, adding it to the scrap heap of "bourgeois," "negative," and "idealistic" disciplines (as they had been called since Lenin's time[3]), which already included psychoanalysis and several branches of economics and pedagogy.

In his speech, Yakovlev made quite clear exactly whom he considered to be the chief proponent of politically erroneous views. Though he was attacking genetics, he singled out not a geneticist, but the botanist Vavilov: "The so-called theory of homologous series does not follow Darwinism." He went on to expound a connection between genetics and fascist doctrine, explaining in popular terms that genetics "forms the basis for the theory, popular in some countries, of the superiority of a particular race, allegedly possessing the best genetic stock, or of the wealthy classes, ostensibly possessing a monopoly of especially precious genes." He went so far as to proclaim that genetics was a new variant of religious doctrine. In his words, "genetics . . . counterpoises the genotype to the phenotype, just as religions everywhere counterpoise body and soul. . . . The concepts of immortal soul and mortal body that figure in most religions, Weismann's immortal germ-plasma and mortal somatic cells, the immortal genotype of plants, humans, and animals encased within the mortal phenotype . . . despite diversity of outward form, are not all these theories expressions of one and the same clerical superstition?" Finally, Yakovlev demanded "that the further development of genetics proceed from the point of view of the theory of development . . . rather than be turned into the handmaiden of Goebbels' ministry [i.e., the Nazi propaganda ministry]."[4] This was an allusion to Lysenko's and Prezent's division of genetics into two schools: the idealistic, formal, classical Mendelian genetics, and their own materialist, Michurinist genetics, the "biology of development."

Lysenko's journal *Vernalization* immediately printed Yakovlev's speech and followed it up in the next issue with an article by Prezent in the same tenor. (As if to underscore their points, the same issue also carried the text of a speech by Stalin in which he called for "every Bolshevik . . . to recognize the enemies of the people, no matter how well disguised.") Prezent wrote that opponents of "creative Soviet Darwinism"—i.e., Lysenkoist doctrine—should realize that they stood in the way of the advance of "the Soviet scientific community, in the person of Lysenko and Michurin." As a clear warning of the fate that could await geneticists, he listed those already arrested:

> the Trotskyite Uranovsky, an enemy of the people who, operating as a "methodologist" of the Academy of Sciences, sold out our scientific interests wholesale and retail . . . the geneticist Agol, another Trotskyite bandit, who worked hard to poison the minds of our readers with the metaphysics of Weismannism . . . the anthropogeneticist Levit, who also earned a kiss just as "honestly" from our inveterate scientific foes by placing at the disposal of those who hate humankind a great deal of "material" about an allegedly fatal "hereditary predisposition."

To drive home the political associations between the geneticists and Stalin's foes, Prezent coupled this list of scientists with the name of Nikolai Bukharin, a Party leader who had been purged by Stalin.

> It is noteworthy that Bukharin, friend of the Trotskyites and enemy of the people, . . . in speaking of Darwinism and the modern age in his article "Darwinism and Marxism" . . . fully accepted the metaphysical aspect of genetics and proclaimed "the further development of Darwinism" to lie in "the doctrine of combinational variability on the basis of Mendel's laws, Johannsen's 'pure lines,' and the generalizations of the American school headed by Morgan."

And, he added, while Bukharin scorned Timiryazev and Michurin, "he liked very much Vavilov's 'law of homologous series.'"[5] The threat to Vavilov was plain to every reader.

The Attack on Koltsov

For the time being, however, the Party focused its censure on Nikolai Koltsov, a cell biologist and a pupil of the outstanding Russian zoologist N. A. Menzbir. Koltsov had graduated from the Moscow Imperial University in 1894, had done graduate research in some of Europe's finest laboratories, and had quickly become one of the world's leading biologists. Shortly before the Bolshevik Revolution, he organized the Moscow Institute of Experimental Biology, which became the central research institution for study of the cells, their structure, physiology, and biochemistry, and of genetics, at the level both of cellular biology and of populations.

In 1928, Koltsov advanced the idea that hereditary traits were inscribed in special molecules; his hypothesis about the double helical structure of the hereditary molecules anticipated scientific discoveries of the structure and biosynthesis of DNA and proteins by a quarter of a century.[6] Koltsov's research, which came to be regarded as classic, concerned many aspects of the life and structure of living organisms. He continued his experimental work to the end of his life. Each day, usually in the afternoon, he mounted the stairs from his ground-floor apartment in the Institute of Experimental Biology to spend several hours in intensive analysis of the experimental data obtained by his research staff. Since the staff was by choice small, he was able not only to train the researchers himself but also to direct their efforts personally.

Another of Koltsov's contributions to Russian science was his work, first as associate editor (from 1912), then as editor in chief (until 1930), of the magazine *Nature* (*Priroda*). Koltsov got the best scientists of Russia to write for the journal and made it the leading journal of information for intellectuals on the successes of natural science. In addition, Koltsov was involved in social and humanitarian activities. He did a great deal for the education of women in Russia. In 1903, he joined the group of professors who organized the Moscow Higher Courses for Women, and he taught the course in biology there until 1918.[7] His opposition to injustice had cost him temporary deprivation of the right to teach in Moscow University in 1909; and in 1911, he resigned in protest against the decision of Minister of Education Kasso to dismiss sixty faculty members. Koltsov frequently defended Russian scientists who had been unjustly accused, and he did not change his principles after the Revolution. When his colleague Sergei S. Chetverikov, the founder of the field of population genetics, was accused of a political misstep in 1928, Koltsov dropped everything else and went to Chetverikov's defense in various state agencies. He managed to have the charges against Chetverikov reduced, but Chetverikov was nevertheless sentenced to exile (by administrative order, without a court trial). His colleagues gave him an extraordinary send-off with champagne and flowers at the railroad station.[8]

Koltsov also joined with those who were disillusioned with the way the

ideals of the Revolution were being carried out and set up an underground "National Center." We know too little about the organization to
say anything definite about what it tried to do, but in 1920 Koltsov and
twenty-seven other persons were tried for participation in it. Koltsov was
accused of hiding the organization's funds and granting the use of his
apartment for meetings of its leadership. He spent a short time in detention, was given a suspended sentence of five years, and suffered no further
punishment. The writer Maxim Gorky, a close friend of his, was influential
in securing his release.[9]

One basis for the political attacks on Koltsov was his scientific interest in
eugenics. He gathered information on the inheritance of intellectual abilities and planned to establish a section on human genetics at his institute.
In 1920, he was elected chairman of the Russian Eugenics Society, a position he held until the society disbanded in 1929. Beginning in 1922, he
was editor (after 1924, associate editor) of the *Russian Journal of Eugenics*,
which published his speeches and writings on the subject.[10]

But Koltsov's greatest recognition, both in the USSR and abroad, comes
from his studies of the physico-chemical processes in cells. His leadership
of genetics in the country was also extremely significant. The genetics
laboratory in his institute continued its high level of work even after
Chetverikov was arrested, and such scientists as Dubinin, Iosif A. Rapoport,
Boris L. Astaurov, and Dmitry D. Romashov worked under his guidance.
Koltsov became the undisputed leader of experimental biology in the
Soviet Union, and this did not escape the notice of those who set out to
attack both genetics and biology as a whole.

Koltsov had taken a firm stand against the Lysenko forces during the
discussion of genetics and selection at the fourth session of VASKhNIL in
December 1936 (see chapter 6). Realizing perhaps more fully and clearly
than his colleagues where the organizers of the discussion were headed,
he addressed a letter to Muralov, who was the president of VASKhNIL at
the time, declaring that such a discussion and the support given to liars
and demagogues could benefit neither science nor the country. He showed
this letter to many participants in the session, including Vavilov, apparently in order to get them to join in his condemnation of the proceedings.
Most of them, including Vavilov, concurred in his judgment, but did not
speak out.[11]

Koltsov's opposition to Lysenkoism led to attacks upon him. Yakovlev
had set the example in his speech at Selkhozgiz, in which he described
Koltsov as "an obscurantist promoting fascism [and] trying to turn genetics into a tool of reactionary political struggle." The denunciation rose in
intensity at a meeting hastily called by the Party *aktiv* of the VASKhNIL
presidium on April 1, 1937, following the arrests of many presidium personnel and several heads of VASKhNIL institutes. As soon as the meeting
began, Muralov launched an attack on Koltsov. Speaking of ideological
errors of omission, he declared:

We have not drawn all the conclusions that we, as officials of agricultural science, should have drawn, conclusions stemming from the capitalist encirclement of the USSR and the need to intensify vigilance to the utmost. Academician Koltsov's letter to the president of the academy after the discussion, saying that the discussion brought no benefit, only harm, serves as a clear example of this.[12]

The composition of this meeting was unusual: Outsiders with no relation to the presidium, such as Prezent (whom Lysenko brought with him), were invited, but only five academicians were on hand. Normally, a meeting of this kind would have been open to all members of the presidium, whether Party members or not, and would have been well-attended by the academicians. It is conceivable that they did not take this meeting seriously, but they may equally well have stayed away out of fear, hoping that by their absence they would avoid attention and escape attack. But Koltsov (who had never joined the Party) was unafraid. He did attend, asked for the floor, and answered the attacks without hesitation.[13] He said that the newspapers had reported the proceedings of the December 1936 session inaccurately. "Their accounts did not provide a clear impression of what was said. The result was to place geneticists under a cloud. It became difficult to teach genetics." To accuse the Soviet press in this manner was extraordinary in those times. The printed word possessed almost mystical force, and it took considerable courage to speak out as Koltsov did.

As for his letter to Muralov, Koltsov said he continued to consider it correct and his colleagues' behavior wrong, especially the resolution they had adopted. "One of the vice-presidents of the academy said that two-thirds of the participants in the discussion would have put their names to my letter," he declared. At these words, Muralov interrupted him:

Muralov. That same vice-president voted for our resolution.
Koltsov. That could be. The speeches by Zavadovsky and Vavilov [who were then vice-presidents of VASKhNIL] perplexed those who heard them. No sooner had these two expressed their views than they turned around and voted for the resolution.

The minutes of the meeting go on to say that "Koltsov would not retract a single word of his letter, which he regarded as justifiable criticism." "I do not recant what I wrote," he concluded.

After this exchange, the attack on Koltsov shifted to a different issue. Pointing to the fact that Koltsov had founded the Russian Eugenics Society—and ignoring the society's disbanding in 1929—Lev S. Margolin, executive secretary of VASKhNIL and editor of its *Bulletin,* declared that Koltsov "has zealously advocated fascist, racist conceptions" (although there had never been the slightest hint of this in Koltsov's works). Prezent picked up this theme: "Academician Koltsov said here that he does not retract a single word of his fascist ravings." Prezent concluded on a high note of demagoguery: "Soviet science is not the science of a country or geographical region, it is the science of a social class. Our academy should pay heed to the social-class line in science; then we would have a really Bolshevik academy that would not make the mistakes it now commits." G. Ye. Yermakov, director of the All-Union Institute of Animal Husbandry, virtually called for Koltsov's arrest: "Is 'tolerance' appropriate when Academician Koltsov takes the floor and defends his fascist ravings? Aren't we obliged to call it just plain counterrevolution?" In the minutes of the meeting, the recording secretary wrote that "subsequent speakers and the resolution adopted by the meeting fully reflected the participants' indignation at Academician Koltsov's remarks, in which he tried to defend the reactionary, fascist positions set forth in his notorious brochure."[14] The minutes quoted the resolution: "The meeting considers it quite intolerable that Academician Koltsov spoke in defense of his plainly fascist eugenic doctrines, and demands that he make a thoroughly clear appraisal of his harmful teachings."

Vavilov was among the last to speak. He did not utter a word in support of Koltsov; he even distanced himself from Koltsov with bombastic phrases about the urgent need to correct mistakes and to be vigilant at a time when enemies were at work everywhere. In short, his remarks did not at all differ from the speeches of Muralov, Margolin, and Prezent. At the end of his remarks, he went even further. In the face of his own convictions and his frequently repeated statements about the practical impossibility of trying to improve lines by intravarietal crossing, he decided to lend his support to Lysenko's importunings. In the words of the minutes of the meeting: "Vavilov considered it advisable for the president and a group of academy members to go to Odessa and to submit to the Commissariat of Agriculture a series of proposals concerning Academician Lysenko's work." We will return later (chapter 9) to this seeming retreat by Vavilov on so basic an issue.

On April 3, *Socialist Agriculture* carried a report of the meeting that had been written by Aleksandr A. Nurinov, who had been given the job of one of the arrested institute directors, Vladimir V. Stanchinsky. Its title, "On an Excessively Tolerant Note," emphasized that even the sharp tone of condemnation at the meeting had been too magnanimous. The fact that several officers of VASKhNIL's presidium and directors of its institutes had been arrested, wrote Nurinov, cast a shadow on the VASKhNIL's leaders for their carelessness regarding the academy's personnel. Nurinov declared that the VASKhNIL leadership had not taken the wave of arrests seriously and was not waging the necessary struggle against saboteurs. "Comrades Muralov and Margolin treated irresponsibly the organization of this extremely important meeting," he wrote. "Comrade Muralov did not bring to light the political roots of harmful theories. He overlooked the criminal, subversive activity of some now-exposed members of academy sections." Nevertheless, he explained, Muralov and Margolin had retained their positions. Judging from the way Nurinov spoke of Muralov and Margolin, someone wanted to very much to remove them from those positions (even though they had just attacked Koltsov and supported Lysenko); Nurinov, after all, was only a low-ranking figure from the provinces, but he seemed to be well primed about his subject.

By contrast, Nurinov said, Lysenko and Prezent had taken an active part in the meeting. "In a thoroughgoing speech, Lysenko showed that the academy presidium gave him little help. 'As a result, I had to go over the academy's head,' Lysenko said," according to Nurinov, who did not explain—and perhaps did not need to explain—to whom Lysenko turned when he went over the scientists' heads.[15]

Later, an article of Yakovlev's in which he repeated the accusations he had made in his speech to the Selkhozgiz staff was printed in both *Pravda* and *Socialist Agriculture*. The article retained the section accusing the geneticists of "a fascist application of the 'laws' of this science [genetics] for their own political purposes," after which Yakovlev asked rhetorically, "Who is it that openly opposes Darwinism?" and he answered, "No one except arrant obscurantists and ignoramuses." Among the latter he included Koltsov and a close associate of Vavilov's, Professor Konstantin I. Pangalo.[16]

At the same time, *Socialist Agriculture* published an article by Prezent and Nurinov, also attacking genetics and quoting Yakovlev. Their article took on a sinister tone:

> In the epoch of the Stalin Constitution, in the age of *genuine democracy* of the working people . . . we must *demand* clear and unambiguous answers from scientists to the questions about whose side they are on and *which ideology guides them*. . . . None of our scientists has the right to forget that wreckers, saboteurs, and the Trotskyite agents of international fascism will try to take advantage of any chink, any manifestation of *our* carelessness in any sphere, including, by no means last, the sphere of science.

They accused Koltsov of having harbored fascist inclinations even before the rise of fascist doctrines. As evidence, they took individual statements about eugenics from old articles and quoted them out of context. They did not refrain even from crude vilification: "In Biblical times, Balaam's ass spoke with human voice, and in our times Prophet Koltsov has shown that the process can be reversed."[17]

The accusations were repeated in the central newspapers in subsequent days. Finally, in July 1937, in an article in the main official agricultural magazine, Koltsov was explicitly called a fascist accomplice. Previously, he had been accused of sympathizing with fascist distortions; now this was turned around. The authors of the article asked whether the Nazi outlook had not been based on Koltsov's views "and those of his associates at the *Russian Journal of Eugenics*."[18]

To Koltsov's honor, he showed great courage, refusing to retreat from his views. It was this that most infuriated his adversaries. In their eyes, his refusal to recant any of the statements he had made demonstrated the case against him.

Vavilov Makes Concessions

Vavilov, on the other hand, reached for a strategic compromise. He could hardly have been thinking of his personal safety; his later actions showed how bold and courageous he was. The more likely explanation is that he did not realize the noose was tightening and hoped that in time those in power at the summit would appraise Lysenko's "innovations" soberly and realize the importance of authentic science to agriculture. Therefore, he probably reasoned, he had to gain time, particularly in order to protect his co-workers who put their faith in him. Eighteen of them had been arrested between 1934 and 1939 in the VIR alone. From the reminiscences of his friends, we know that he was anguished by the arrests.[19] Hence, he apparently decided that it would be prudent to accept publicly some of Lysenko's propositions that he had previously rejected. This step indicated that Vavilov believed that Lysenko was the greatest threat and that compromise with him might save Vavilov's two institutes, the VIR and the Institute of Genetics.

Thus, on April 28, 1937, an unexpected document appeared in the press. In it, Vavilov was reported to have abandoned his objections to open intravarietal crosses. Under a large headline in the center of the front page of *Socialist Agriculture*, an article said that Muralov, Vavilov, and Meister had visited Odessa "at the invitation of Academician T. D. Lysenko to learn about the results of intravarietal cross-fertilization of wheat" and that "the presidium [of VASKhNIL] had determined that *the method* of experiments on intravarietal cross-fertilization carried out by *T. D. Lysenko was acceptable to Academicians Vavilov and Meister*." Accompanying the article was an order from Commissar of Agriculture Chernov declaring that, since intravarietal crossing had fully justified itself, agricultural administrations were to apply this method widely on kolkhozes and sovkhozes.[20] It is clear that, at least on Vavilov's part, this was a mere maneuver. A few days after this article appeared, he wrote a letter to Muller in Madrid, where the American geneticist had gone to join the communists in the Spanish civil war. "Professor Meister and I visited Odessa recently to verify Lysenko's work on plant-breeding," he said. "I must say that there is too little convincing evidence. I had expected more."[21] The day after publication of the report of VASKhNIL's decision and the commissar's directive, *Socialist Agriculture* carried an editorial gloating over the fact that the leading biologists had changed their stand. "It is known that the majority of geneticists and plant-breeding specialists fought this proposal. The supporters of formal genetics proclaimed the method . . . to be unscientific." The editorial named Konstantinov, Lisitsyn, and Kostov among them, and noted with satisfaction that the top men of science, Vavilov and Meister, now accepted

Lysenko's method, thanks to which the Commissariat of Agriculture had ordered intravarietal crossing to be carried out on 12,000 kolkhozes.[22]

Lysenko and his followers hastened to make the most of the breakthrough. On May 4, *Socialist Agriculture* published a letter from Lysenko urging "more use of intravarietal crossing," and on May 21 it devoted the entire second and third of its four pages to a spread in praise of the method, with an article by Lysenko.[23] In the center of one page was a photograph with the caption, "Academician T. D. Lysenko shows N. I. Vavilov and G. K. Meister the results of intravarietal crossing." Two humble pupils seemed to be heeding a proud teacher. Only their morose expressions gave away their true feelings.

The Arrest of Muralov and Meister

If Vavilov had hoped to salvage matters by a meek admission of Lysenko's claims, the hope was futile. In July 1937, the magazine of the Commissariat of Agriculture printed two long articles concerning agriculture in the third Five-Year Plan, one by Williams and the other by Vavilov. It all seemed quite normal—leading scientists discussing the problems raised by the Party leadership at the Central Committee session—except for one detail: In an introductory statement, the magazine disclaimed Vavilov's article:

> The editors ... consider that Academician Vavilov ... has ignored the most important questions of selection, seed production, and the work of the State Seed Bank under the VIR, for which he is among those responsible. Academician Vavilov has not disclosed the reasons for the muddle in the seed bank's testing of varieties or why the seed bank removed high-yield varieties from production. The public considers strange Academician Vavilov's prolonged silence on the questions raised in [Yakovlev's] *Pravda* article on Darwinism and some anti-Darwinists. Vavilov's article is published below for purposes of discussion.[24]

In the 1930s, "published for purposes of discussion" meant that an article was being repudiated and that its author was to be condemned.

Arrests followed within the month: first, a group of officials of the Commissariat of Agriculture, notably the economist Aron I. Gaister (see biographical sketches), and then officials of VASKhNIL, including Aleksandr S. Bondarenko, Margolin, and its president, Muralov. Muralov had been the first of the academy leaders to give in to Lysenko on intravarietal crossing, but it made no difference to his fate. He perished on October 30, 1937, apparently executed by a firing squad.[25]

However, Lysenko did not succeed to the position of president of VASKhNIL. Meister was appointed president pro tem, and Vavilov remained vice-president. The Lysenko camp was not satisfied, and the struggle continued, especially as it concerned the institutes with which Vavilov was associated. It reached its height at the end of November 1937, when *Socialist*

Agriculture began to carry abusive articles nearly every day. The Flax Institute was severely criticized. Sabotage was reported in the Institute of Mechanization and Electrification of Agriculture and the Institute of Hydrotechnology and Soil Amelioration, where it appeared that the new director, Aleksei N. Kostyakov, was as much a saboteur as the old one, Abol, who had been arrested earlier.[26] The failures of the Cotton Institute were condemned; it had been established with Vavilov's participation, and the article singled Vavilov out as the perpetrator of the failures:

> Academician N. I. Vavilov also bears responsibility for the literary and scientific "works" [of the institute]. Last June, he left a laudatory entry ... in the institute guest book. ... Academician Vavilov ought to explain the motives behind such inappropriate praise of the institute. Did he really not notice what was going on at the institute, at its research bases and on its experimental fields? Many of the saboteurs and enemies of the people who operated insidiously in the institute have been exposed. The consequences of the sabotage must be completely eradicated.[27]

The hint was transparent; readers could hardly fail to draw the conclusion that Vavilov himself was guilty. Surely the experienced Vavilov must have been aware of sabotage in the institute, yet he shielded enemies. He had to have an ulterior motive for doing so, and hence the "eradication" of the "consequences of the sabotage" could not leave an accomplice of saboteurs untouched.

A group of wreckers was also "unmasked" in the Institute of Potato Farming. A well-known authority in potato selection, Aleksandr G. Lorkh, was purported to have given damaging instructions to potato growers, and he was arrested soon afterward.[28] The aim of these attacks was to seize control of VASKhNIL by riding the wave of repression spreading throughout the country. Vavilov, of course, was not the only target—and, at this stage, perhaps not yet the main target—of the attacks, but he had to be isolated and neutralized. Meanwhile, to eliminate the possibility of criticism from above, the attackers had given first priority to control of the academy.

Meister did not hold out as president of VASKhNIL for even a year. Late in 1937 or early in 1938, he was arrested as an enemy of the people. Meister had directed the Saratov Selection Station, and only a year before his arrest its twenty-fifth anniversary had been celebrated with pomp. It had been noted that varieties bred under Meister's direction were sown on more than 7,241,000 hectares, and that in the person of Academician Meister, we have a "true Bolshevik scientist, an energetic fighter for large harvests, a bold experimenter who seeks to master nature and strives for wide application of his scientific discoveries for the benefit of our great motherland."[29] In prison, Meister went mad and later was shot.[30]

Under OGPU Surveillance

Unknown to Vavilov, he had been under surveillance by the secret police as early as 1931. Even while he was traveling abroad, speaking in defense of the Soviet system, somewhere in the depths of the OGPU case No. 268615, with his name on it, was being compiled.[31] This case number is in itself awesome. It meant that more than a quarter of a million people were objects of the intense interest of OGPU agents in the Moscow central office alone. And it wasn't just one or two eager informers and agents who "toiled" at compiling each such case, following the suspect's every step, recording each word and gesture, distorting acts and surmising intentions. How many of these voluntary or coerced assistants of the executioners were there in the country? Millions? Tens of millions? This at a time when the "period of mass arrests" had not yet even begun![32]

The atmosphere of mass terror that gradually embraced every sphere of life and all levels of Soviet society reached the realm of biology and agriculture early in the 1930s. Soil scientists and agrochemists, especially those from Pryanishnikov's school, were the first to suffer, thanks to their opposition to Williams's unscientific proposals. The struggle against Williams's pet theories of crop rotation and fertilizers cost many lives. Among the biologists and agricultural scientists who had been arrested by 1932 were the agricultural chemists Alexei G. Doyarenko and V. K. Krutikhovsky, the prominent Darwinist Professor Boris Ye. Raikov, agronomists Socrat K. Chayanov and V. V. Talanov, the former director of the Odessa selection station Andrei A. Sapegin. . . . It goes without saying that agronomists and selection specialists of lower rank were arrested and sentenced by the hundreds.

The first blow at Vavilov had been struck at the same time, in March 1932, when a large group of leading personnel of the VIR was arrested and sent into exile: N. A. Maksimov, its deputy director; the selection specialist Viktor Ye. Pisarev; the cytologist Georgy A. Levitsky (who was released, but only temporarily); the botanists M. G. Popov and Kuleshov; N. P. Avdulov, the author of an important monograph on grain; K. M. Chingo-Chingas, director of the institute's flour-milling division; and others. Without doubt, all these arrests and deportations added material to the case against Vavilov.

There were also a number of denunciations of Vavilov himself. After Vavilov's posthumous rehabilitation, the government established a commission under the Academy of Sciences to study his legacy, and a member of the commission, the writer Mark A. Popovsky, was given access to the OGPU-NKVD-KGB file on him. It was known that Vavilov had written several important studies while in prison, and Popovsky was asked to review the records in order to find out whether they included any of the manuscripts of these studies. Later, he revealed what he had learned in a series of public lectures in Moscow, Leningrad, and Novosibirsk, and in several publications.[33] From these materials, the names of Vavilov's betrayers have become known. Among them were scientists who had been well respected.

First and foremost was Academician Ivan V. Yakushkin of VASKhNIL. Yakushkin had known Vavilov since student days; his sister Olga had studied with Vavilov in the Moscow Agricultural Institute and had then worked with him for fifteen years. According to Popovsky, Yakushkin, "being at odds with Soviet rule, fled the Crimea with the remnants of General Wrangel's retreating White army. . . . in 1930 he was seized in the 'first wave' of mass arrests." He was held in prison nearly a year, but was freed after he agreed to serve as a secret collaborator (*seksot*). In June 1955, at hearings held by the military prosecutor's office, Yakushkin confessed, among other things, that in September 1931 he turned in a ten-page report saying the VIR was a nest of anti-Soviet activity in genetics and plant breeding and that Vavilov was the organizer of a gang of enemies of the people.[34]

Another name that came up in the Vavilov file was that of Aleksandr K. Kol, a research fellow in Vavilov's institute. Kol was arrested in 1931 and, says Popovsky, "at the first interrogation signed a statement that a counter-revolutionary group led by Vavilov was at work in the institute. The Yakushkin pattern was being repeated."[35] However, this case may not be so simple as extraction of false testimony under duress. In 1929, Kol had published an article leveling accusations against the VIR:

> Work . . . on the centers of origin of plants has now replaced V. I. Lenin's revolutionary task of invigorating the Soviet farmland with new plants. Under cover of the name of Lenin, an institute that has no relation to Lenin's ideas or aims, but is alien to them in a class sense and hostile to them, has grown powerful and is trying to win hegemony over our agricultural science.[36]

Such an article could not have been printed merely because of Kol's personal antipathy toward Vavilov. Someone wanted it published, and it could well have been the same people who had in 1931 issued the government resolution to reduce the period for developing varieties to four years. They may have been taking advantage of Kol's spiteful energies for their own purposes. It seems hardly coincidental that it was in 1931 that the OGPU began its secret file on Vavilov. Without orders from the highest level, it would have been impossible to open a case against a man who was a member of the Central Executive Committee of the USSR and the Russian Republic.

Kol, who was older than Vavilov, had worked for six years in the United States, in the laboratory of Professor Niels E. Hansen (4 January 1866–5 October 1950) in South Dakota (State College in Brookings), and on his return home Vavilov appointed him head of the laboratory for the introduction of plant species in the VIR. But the relationship between them was never smooth. Kol aspired to higher status, disdained his everyday responsibilities, and frequently accused Vavilov of mistakes. He behaved this way both before his imprisonment and after. Indeed, it is possible that his arrest, which was very brief, was simply a cover for him.

In any event, Kol persisted in attacking Vavilov. In 1936, he accused the institute director of having his expeditions "collect samples principally at markets," of "endless delays in introducing into field production the material obtained," and of failing to turn over to "Michurinist experimenters" plants that were important to the agriculture of the Soviet Union, such as sugar cane from western Afghanistan and the date-like *unabi* from western China. He drew parallels between Vavilov's theory of plant evolution and fascist race theory, and he declared:

> The large staff of the VIR did not see, or did not want to see, valuable genes right under its nose and would have allowed them to disappear from the face of the earth if some collective farmer had not saved them, hiding the seeds in his bosom and cultivating them in his kitchen garden. . . . The fruitlessness of the theories of Vavilov and his school and the enormous practical and scientific successes of Academician Lysenko show where true science lies.[37]

Grigory N. Shlykov was another informer on Vavilov's staff. He came to the VIR as a graduate student and received the degree of candidate of agricultural sciences (equal to the Ph.D. in the West) in 1935. Shortly afterward, he was appointed head of the institute's subtropical department. In 1936, he attacked Vavilov in an article and in a book,[38] and in a scathing speech he delivered at the fourth session of VASKhNIL. We now know that he did not limit himself to this open assault upon his director, but was also secretly charging him with sabotage.

The Attacks on Vavilov Intensify

It is difficult to believe that Vavilov, experienced administrator that he was, did not surmise what these staff members really were. Perhaps it was precisely because he did guess their true role that he refrained so long from responding to them, or perhaps he did not deign to lower himself to their level. But finally, in December 1936, he struck back. In an article in *Socialist Reconstruction of Agriculture*, he described Kol's and Shlykov's writings as distortions, "a crooked mirror twisting reality." He charged that they ignored the practical varieties he had introduced and instead wanted him to introduce cacti, amaranth, *Physalis* (ground-cherries or strawberry tomatoes), *Echballium* (squirting cucumber), and other exotica. As in Krylov's fable, he said, "they can see everything but the elephant." Vavilov also gave a withering description of Shlykov's book as being filled with mistakes, irresponsible statements, and outright falsehoods.[39]

Kol transferred, or was transferred, to the Institute of Northern Grain Farming and Leguminous Grain Crops, but he kept up his attacks on Vavilov and on the VIR. In Lysenko's journal, he repeated his claim that the work of the VIR was incompatible with the tasks of the socialist reconstruction of plant-breeding. Despite a staff of 700 and expenditures of fourteen million rubles a year, he wrote, the institute "has given our collective farming nothing of substance . . . in twelve years."[40] Pryanishnikov, who had already seen the arrests of many colleagues and students, spoke up unhesitatingly for his former pupil; after the journal *Socialist Reconstruction of Agriculture* published one of Kol's articles, Pryanishnikov sent the journal and the VASKhNIL presidium a letter demanding that the editor be reprimanded.[41]

Vavilov and his institute were increasingly hemmed in. New staff members who spent the lion's share of their time on intrigue and informing were appointed to the institute by orders from above, against the director's will. Among them was Stepan N. Shundenko, who was assigned to do graduate research under Mikhail I. Khadzhinov, a pupil of Vavilov's who had become a leading geneticist and plant-breeding specialist. Shundenko was simply incompetent and was unable to produce a dissertation. As his mentor, Khadzhinov was taken to task for Shundenko's failure to make progress on his dissertation. Like Vavilov, Khadzhinov was not a Party member and was kept in the dark about such matters as the real reason for Shundenko's appointment. Khadzhinov, a gentle, shy person, hit upon what he thought was a simple solution: He wrote the dissertation for his student.[42] In this way, Shundenko received the degree of candidate of science, and he then went on to become the instigator of sentiment against Vavilov in the institute.

Once Shundenko had his degree, Lysenko, either on his own initiative or on instructions from the secret police, began to press for a leading role for him in the institute. At the start of 1938, he issued an order promoting Shundenko, over Vavilov's written protest, to the post of deputy director for scientific research.

The botanist Yevgenia N. Sinskaya has given this description of Shundenko: "One felt something sinister in this frail, nervous figure with dark, penetrating, and constantly darting eyes. He quickly hit it off with another such repulsive person, the graduate student Shlykov. Together they set about disrupting the life of the institute." Sinskaya recalls an indecent jingle that went the rounds of the institute, describing Shundenko as a "puny little devil," Shlykov as a "would-be Napoleon," and both of them as "shit."[43]

The system of informers took advantage of human weakness, pushing over the brink people who in other circumstances would have remained normal and decent individuals. The corruption of Helma K. Emme, a cytogeneticist, is a case in point. For many years, she was friendly with the Vavilov family, but the secret police decided to turn her into an informer. The NKVD began to summon her late at night and to intimidate her. Finally, threatened with the arrest of her son Andrei, she signed false reports against Vavilov. Only on her deathbed, during the siege of

Leningrad, did she confess to her son what she had done. In the 1950s, he joined the ranks of the Lysenko adversaries, wrote a serious study of the harm that Lysenkoism had done, and sent it to the Party Central Committee. As a staff member of the popular-science magazine *Technology for Young People* (Tekhnika molodyozhi), he fought to publish anti-Lysenko articles. It was from him that Popovsky learned the tragic story of his mother.[44]

Another case that helps us understand the mores of that era is that of Fyodor F. Sidorov, who held one of the forty places in VASKhNIL institutes that were reserved by Party decree for "special graduate students." Sidorov worked in the branch of the VIR in Pushkin, a suburb of Leningrad. He was supposed to see to the propagation of the seed material that had been gathered by institute expeditions from all over the world. In 1937, when he occupied the position of senior scientific staff member, he was so careless and ignorant that he ruined some unique seed material. Upon learning of this, Vavilov immediately ordered Sidorov dismissed. On the day the dismissal order was posted, Sidorov presented himself to the NKVD chief in Pushkin and made an accusation: "I hereby report sabotage by the heads of the All-Union Institute of the Plant Industry, Vavilov and [his deputy, A. B.] Aleksandrov, which has caused disruption of the work of developing stable varieties and the infection of seeds with disease and pests."[45] Aleksandrov, who had been deputy director of the institute since 1935, was promptly arrested; he perished in prison. Sidorov was reinstated, and after Vavilov's arrest he was promoted to the position that Aleksandrov had held.[46]

Even all of this was only part of the humiliation that Vavilov had to suffer. At a meeting of the trade union of the VIR staff on May 8, 1937, several minor staff members accused Vavilov of scientific errors. The agronomist Kuprianov denounced the law of homologous series and all the other discoveries of Vavilov's, which, in his ignorance, he lumped together as "the Vavilov theory." "This harmful theory must be burned out with a hot iron," he proclaimed, "for the working class has coped with its tasks without benefit of the bourgeoisie, has taken over the reins of government, and has achieved definite successes. . . . Vavilov will have to change, because Stalin has said one must work like Lysenko, not like Vavilov."[47] A graduate student, Donskoi, demanded that the director resign: Lysenko was absolutely right about everything and there was no further place for Vavilov in science.[48]

In addition to what Popovsky has revealed, friends of Vavilov's have given me two other documents that tell a great deal about Shlykov's activities. The first of these is a letter he sent to the science section of the Party Central Committee early in 1938. The text, though somewhat incoherent, is worth quoting in its entirety:

> I enclose the annual report of the work of the Department of New Cultures of the Institute of the Plant Industry and request your aid in the further work of its existence.

Its dissolution will lead to the undivided sway of standardized theoretical thought [a favorite phrase of Lysenko's describing Vavilov's views] in the system of the Institute of the Plant Industry, since the difficult role of theoretical opposition to N. I. Vavilov has befallen me, as head of the division—difficult because, in view of the weakness of the local Party cadres of specialists and the insignificant stratum of non-Party specialists who take their cue from them, and in view of the system of penetration of N. I. Vavilov's entourage by careerists and enemies of the people, an initiative of a critical [attitude] toward the local theoretical and working traditions is doomed to complete failure without outside help. I have experienced this myself and experience it every day.

Comrade Shundenko, appointed deputy to N. I. Vavilov, and, I believe, any other deputy to such a willful, cunning, and bullheaded character, is an isolated case, in my opinion, from which it would be overly optimistic to expect real prospects of genuine theoretical and practical restructuring of the institute. But that same Shundenko, freed of N. I. Vavilov's constant and very artful suppression of initiative, and entrusted and called upon to exert full responsibility for the institute, i.e., appointed not deputy but director, would carry out faster, fuller, and better restructuring of the institute toward practically strict, purposeful selection work and genuine (agronomical and biological) and rapid identification of seeds for plant breeding. N. I. Vavilov might be better used as a specialist in that case. The institute would cease to be a sinecure of one person such as is N. I. Vavilov, who, though a very, very great specialist, is muddleheaded in matters of theory and unquestionably not sincerely working for our [Soviet] system. I do not wish to be a prophet, but I know we shall have to come to that sooner or later. The swamp that is the institute cannot be drained by N. I. Vavilov, and the role of his deputies in this respect is frightfully difficult, given their very modest possibilities in the matter of the selection and assignment of personnel, a prerogative that Vavilov always retains for himself.

In this letter, Shlykov implied that Vavilov was a saboteur but stopped short of saying so outright, since a letter to the Central Committee might not be kept secret. In a denunciation of Vavilov addressed to the NKVD shortly afterward, however, Shlykov dispensed with hints and bluntly charged sabotage. By then, the roster of those arrested included—in addition to Muralov and Gaister—Yakovlev (the very Yakovlev who had himself attacked Vavilov earlier in the 1930s), Commissar of Agriculture Chernov, and Karl Ya. Bauman, head of the Party Central Committee's department of science, inventions, and discoveries. Shlykov now set out to portray Vavilov as the same kind of "enemy" and "wrecker" as the arrested men and as maintaining direct ties with them. Certain that nothing in the possession of the NKVD would be disclosed, he felt free to drawn monstrous conclusions from trifling facts:

To Comrade Malinin, NKVD: Enclosed is a copy of my letter to Comrade [R. I.] Eikhe [the new commissar of agriculture], accompanying the annual report of the Department of New Cultures.

I have already sent you this report, calling particular attention to the introduction and the conclusion; although I am confident that Comrade Eikhe will give it appropriate distribution, I decided nevertheless to send you a copy, and here is why.

Before the bandits Chernov, Yakovlev, and Bauman are exterminated, an investigation should be conducted into what they did by way of sabotaging the organization of agricultural research, the experimental stations, and the testing and development of new varieties. I am more and more convinced that here there may have been a division of labor with Vavilov, as the virtual head of the country's plant-breeding research throughout the whole period since the October Revolution. Wasn't their outwardly negative attitude toward him (and at one time also toward their puppet, A. I. Muralov) simply a cover for the actual relationship of accomplices? There are no bounds to their villainy and cunning. It is simply hard to believe that the restorers of capitalism overlooked such a figure of authority in wide circles of agronomy as Vavilov, and especially an old-time figure. Was he not associated with their overall organization, as a person they well knew to hold rightist convictions, one who came out of a milieu of millionaires? From Bukharin's writing, I judge that the right wing knew him well.

In this connection, wasn't the fuss raised by the foreign press at the end of 1936 over the "persecution" of Vavilov and its publication of false obituaries of him a provocation that they themselves instigated and organized with his knowledge and sanction? After all, it was not mere happenstance that materials illuminating the situation in the Institute of the Plant Industry, of which you have copies in part, and which were sent to these people as Party and government representatives, failed to bring about favorable results. There is little doubt also that they could have warned Vavilov of these materials.

In particular, when the book *Controversial Questions of Genetics and Plant Breeding* was being published in 1937, somebody in the presidium of VASKhNIL required that the part of my speech at the fourth session of the academy in which I spoke about the fascist content of Vavilov's conceptions be deleted from the stenographic transcript. When I received the text in the mail from the academy for a final check before publication and discovered the deletion of the most essential part, I returned the text with a written protest against the deletion, but in vain. So I drew the conclusion that these people—the book was printed after Muralov, Bauman, and Yakovlev read all the articles—were not interested in genuine exposure of Vavilov and his theories. This was not a minor matter. I well know that the transcript of my report was asked for urgently at the Party Central Committee that same day. The request was made by one of Yakovlev's assistants (I don't remember the name—a Georgian name) who also turned out to be an enemy of the people. He said he wanted it for Bauman and Yakovlev. Isn't it symptomatic that no one considered it necessary to talk with me and look into the circumstances that led me to those categorical conclusions concerning Vavilov and the Institute of the Plant Industry? In that report, with facts in hand, I did indeed expose the twaddle of Vavilov's theories and the harm of his practice.

Therefore, I apply through you to your entire system to take measures to investigate the above-mentioned circumstances and get to the bottom of the sabotage in the organization of agricultural science, which means also to free ourselves quickly from the consequences of the wrecking. The interrogation of Chernov did not expose his practical wrecking policy in agricultural science. I consider that an omission. By exposing this kind of sabotage, we could addition-ally speed the process of uniting the truly Soviet scientists in the system of VASKhNIL.

This letter—preserved by a miracle—is, of course, not unique. As testi-mony to the epoch of repression, it hardly differs from thousands, per-haps millions, of other informers' denunciations, penned by petty souls in search of power and rewards. However, it did not bring immediate action. Vavilov was still not arrested or dismissed from his positions. But the Shundenkos and Shlykovs, the Prezents and Yakushkins, did not rest, nor did their manipulator Trofim Lysenko.

Lysenko Becomes President of VASKhNIL

On January 11, 1938, *Socialist Agriculture* carried an editorial charging widespread sabotage in VASKhNIL and blaming Vavilov, Zavadovsky, and Konstantinov for hostility to Lysenko's ideas in the institutes.[49] Less than two months later, on February 28, 1938, Lysenko finally became president of the academy. He now had a free hand to deal with his opponents.

The new president indicated his plans in an article in *Pravda* on April 9. Instead of calling for wider scientific research, he proposed cutting the scientific staff by half or even two-thirds; academicians, he said, "should follow the example of the Stakhanovites." Most importantly, Lysenko pro-claimed a fundamental change in direction: henceforth, he declared, aca-demicians "were obliged to draw the deepest generalizations and conclusions from kolkhoz and sovkhoz practice"—that is, they were now to follow Party policy rather than exercise scientific leadership.[50]

The first step was Vavilov's removal from the post of academy vice-president. The next was an event that struck at all of genetics, not just at Vavilov. The Seventh International Congress of Genetics had been sched-uled to be held in Moscow in February 1937. This plan was approved by the Soviet government in 1932, but the date had then been moved to August 1938. The congress program was ready; notices had appeared in Soviet scientific journals and in biology journals all over the world; 1,700 scientists were ready to come. Then, suddenly, Molotov ordered all prepa-rations stopped. The geneticists did not assemble until a year later, in 1939, and in Edinburgh, at that. The congress chairman's seat remained vacant; it was reserved for the absent Vavilov.

The NKVD went on building up a case against Vavilov. Each newspaper and magazine article was added to his file, along with transcripts of the geneticists' discussions with Lysenko, the secret reports from Kol, Yakushkin, Shundenko, and others, and the records of interrogations of the arrested agricultural chiefs.[51]

Those who were arrested conducted themselves variously. Academician David, arrested soon after he publicly defended Tulaikov, testified after torture that "a large nucleus of prominent [agricultural] academy members, headed by Vavilov, Koltsov, Meister, Konstantinov, Lisitsyn, and Serebrovsky, actively opposed Lysenko's revolutionary theory of vernalization and intravarietal crossing." Tulaikov, after hours of interrogation and torture, testified against Vavilov and other academy officials. But Gorbunov would not say anything ill of Vavilov, and Yakovlev, who had publicly criticized Vavilov while at liberty, staunchly refused to testify against him in jail. Meister "several times called Vavilov a traitor, but repudiated his testimony just as many times. Subsequently, Vice-President Bondarenko repudiated his testimony during his trial, and was later shot."[52]

Vavilov evidently remained unaware of the swelling NKVD file, and there were no outward signs of Lysenko's part in it. His henchmen operated in secrecy. Lysenko himself, however, engaged openly in efforts along a different line. He took his attack on Vavilov to the Kremlin.

Vavilov Is Officially Rebuked

In May 1938, the Council of People's Commissars convened a meeting to review the research plans of the AN SSSR. Outwardly, it would have appeared to be a routine occasion on which to brief the government leaders about the scientists' program of work for the year and to allow the commissars to review the scientific priorities. Only two people who could be called scientists were present: Lysenko and electrical engineer Gleb M. Krzhizhanovsky. The others who attended the meeting were Molotov and Lazar M. Kaganovich, members of the Politburo as well as of the Council of People's Commissars; S. V. Kaftanov, commissar of higher education; and Nikolai A. Voznesensky chairman of the State Planning Commission.

The report of the meeting said that the Council of People's Commissars had rejected the research plans submitted by the AN SSSR because "pseudo-science has found a haven in some institutes, and the representatives of this pseudo-science are not being fittingly rebuffed." The plans were sent back to the academy for revision, with orders that "the roster of the academy be replenished with new, including young, scientific forces."[53] The effect of this decision was to extend to the natural sciences the dictatorship that had existed for a decade in the humanities and the social sciences.

The report did not specify the institutes in which "pseudo-science" had found a "haven," but the leaders of the academy knew what was meant. They formed a commission to investigate the work of the Genetics Institute and appointed Academician Boris A. Keller to head it. Keller had been director of the Botanical Institute but had lost that post two years before. He then became director of the Soil Institute, but within a year and a half lost this position also, and was put in charge of the academy's small Moscow Botanical Garden. (The huge present-day Botanical Garden did not yet exist.) Keller was familiar with genetics, and in an article published in December 1936 he had written that "the abstract concept of the gene was taking on material reality, thanks to advances in genetic research . . . Individual genes on their chromosomes were almost becoming visible with the aid of microphotography under ultraviolet light."[54] By April 1938, however, a month before he was assigned to investigate Vavilov's institute, he was accusing people at the Botanical and Zoological institutes of being divorced from the practical needs of socialist construction, and advising them to follow Lysenko's approach.[55] From conversations with surviving staff members of Vavilov's institute, I have learned that Keller was consulting with Lysenko on everything at this time.

Matters were moving swiftly. In a speech to the personnel of higher educational institutions on May 17, 1938, Stalin commanded his audience to fight "the high priests of science" "who had "retired into their shells," and "to smash old traditions, norms, and viewpoints" that had become "a brake on progress."[56] On May 25, the presidium of the AN SSSR called a special meeting to discuss the institutes criticized by the Council of People's Commissars. The account of the meeting published the next morning indicated that the worst situation was in two institutes, those of genetics and geology. Summing up the presidium session, a *Pravda* editorial declared: "The example of yesterday's meeting of the presidium of the Academy of Sciences demonstrates clearly that the restructuring of the work of its institutions has not begun in earnest. The leaders of the academy risk coming unprepared to the general meeting of the academy only two days hence."[57]

By now the tattoo of newspaper reports had told millions of readers about the fall from grace of the once leading figure in biology and agrobiology. One can imagine the impact that the crescendo of attacks had upon the officers of the president of the AN SSSR was Vladimir L. Komarov. A botanist, born and raised in Petersburg and for many years a professor in the university there, he had assumed the presidency in 1936, at the age of 67. He had no obvious animus against Vavilov, but long experience had taught him caution and conformity, and of course he understood full well what lay behind *Pravda*'s clamor about the academy. Accordingly, another meeting of the presidium was summoned on May 27, and now, instead of generalities about shortcomings in scientific institutions, attention was directed specifically to Vavilov's work as director of the Genetics Institute.

Again the party intervened in this supposedly scientific matter to lend ominous and broad significance to the consideration of Academician Vavilov's sins. Next day, *Pravda*'s report of this meeting disclosed Lysenko's personal participation in the vilification of Vavilov:

> Yesterday's meeting of the presidium of the USSR Academy of Sciences discussed the work of the Genetics Institute. After Academician N. I. Vavilov submitted a report, Academician B. A. Keller spoke on behalf of the commission investigating the institute.
>
> "The Genetics Institute," Academician Keller said, "not only does not combat

hostile-class viewpoints on the biology front, but its mistakes provide grist to the mills of antiscientific 'theories.' Research is only poorly and haphazardly linked to practice. The institute refuses to acknowledge T. D. Lysenko's scientific works." "The institute has produced some valuable research but has no general plan based on the demands that the Soviet country makes of science."

Pravda specifically mentioned that "the presidium agreed with the conclusions of the commission, which introduce considerable changes in the institute's research program. The [academy's] Division of Mathematics and Natural Sciences has been directed to conduct a broad scientific discussion of the problems of genetics, with the participation of officials of the Philosophy Institute." In what *Pravda* described as "a stirring speech," Lysenko himself told the meeting:

> The institute does not develop genuine guiding theory, the basis of all research. Therefore the individual successes that the institute has had in many years of work have been isolated and fragmentary. The ideas of Michurin are not reflected at all. The development of the Michurinist heritage in the country proceeds without the institute's assistance or participation. On the contrary, anti-Michurinist and anti-Darwinist views are widespread in the institute.[58]

The resolution adopted at the meeting declared that "the academy must smash and eradicate obsolete traditions and forsake servility toward them once and for all. Nevertheless, some institutes have continued to worship antiscientific fetishes."[59] But the resolution named only one institute, the Genetics Institute, and it laid the responsibility for the bad work of the academy as a whole at the feet of one person. In the circumstances, Vavilov had no choice but to make a public confession of "mistakes" and promise to correct them, which he did at a meeting in the Genetics Institute.[60] His repentance did no good. The presidium of the AN SSSR continued to attack him. It declared that "conditions are lacking at the institute for the correct methodological training of young scientists and for theoretical assistance to senior scientists," and it went on to resolve:

> These shortcomings are associated in large measure with the direction given the work by Academician N. I. Vavilov, whose law of homologous series is based on the concept that the organism is a mosaic of genes. That view, with certain corrections, is still put forward. . . . On the whole, a narrowly chromosomal approach to the phenomena of heredity, characteristic of formal genetics, prevails in the institute."

The presidium resolution hailed "the agreement of Academician T. D. Lysenko's to organize research in the Genetics Institute on the basis of the theoretical constructs and methods which he has developed."[61]

Thus, with one stroke Lysenko had accomplished two tasks: he had pilloried Vavilov, and he had penetrated the AN SSSR and its Genetics Institute. In Vavilov's own institute, he set up his own section and quickly brought in a number of his closest associates, including Glushchenko, A. A. Avakyan, and G. A. Babadzhanyan.

Nevertheless, when the presidium of the AN SSSR submitted a new research plan for 1938 to the Council of People's Commissars, the *Pravda* story on July 27, 1938, indicated the Party's view of the plan by putting the word "new" in quotation marks. The Council of Commissars predictably rejected the plan on the grounds that it "repeated the shortcomings of the old one."[62] A quarter-century later, the rejected lines of work were to be praised to the skies as research in which the Soviet Union had made great strides, only to fall behind after the government's interference. But at the time, as a *Pravda* editorial on July 29, 1938, "Place Science in the Service of the Country," underscored, only Lysenko's research plans would win the approval of the academy and the Council of People's Commissars. The Party newspaper again hailed the "son of a peasant" who had become "a leading world scientist . . . in an incredibly short time" and whose "brilliant work" in vernalization, intravarietal crossing, and summer planting of potatoes had brought "an abundant harvest."

Rapid promotion of young, new scientists to membership in the academy now began, in accordance with orders from above. The academy elections held in January 1939 ended in another victory for Lysenko and his supporters: Tsitsin was elected a full member, and after a slight hitch—Lysenko was short of votes in the first round, but the academy leaders demanded a second vote—so was Lysenko himself. He was now a member of three Soviet academies.

At the same time, Molotov and Andrei Ya. Vyshinsky, the prosecutor at the purge trials (see biographical sketches), were also elected full members, and Stalin was elected an honorary member.

Koltsov's Dismissal as Institute Director

Although the 1937 meeting at VASKhNIL had condemned Koltsov's views on eugenics, and although Prezent, Nurinov, and others used this opportunity to launch savage attacks on Koltsov in the press,[63] one circumstance stood in the way of further action against him: the Institute of Experimental Biology, which he founded and directed, belonged not to the AN SSSR or to VASKhNIL, but to the Commissariat of Public Health, which apparently held Koltsov in high regard and supported him. His foes found a way around this obstacle. In January 1938, the institute was transferred to the AN SSSR.

Koltsov accepted this move and submitted a report to the academy, outlining the institute's aims and structure. He contended that, to maintain its worldwide reputation in cell research, the institute had to preserve its three major departments: cell biology, the cytological foundations of heredity and mutation, and the cytological foundations of developmental physiology. Koltsov concluded the report with an expression of confidence that "the institute will of course retain the name . . . under which it has functioned for 21 years and which emphasizes its experimental nature and the duality of its theme: the unification of evolutionary theory with the study of the cell."[64] But not one of Koltsov's recommendations was accepted; the AN SSSR proved to be a wicked stepmother to its adopted child. It changed the name immediately to the Institute of Cytology, Histology, and Embryology, and soon set about changing the institute's structure, while the director began to experience treatment that he had previously been lucky to escape.

In January 1939, when candidates were being nominated for election to the AN SSSR, *Pravda* published an article entitled "Pseudo-Scientists Do Not Belong in the Academy of Sciences of the USSR," signed by Aleksandr N. Bakh, Khachatur S. Koshtoyants, Nikolai I. Nuzhdin, and others. Chief among those who they felt had no place in the academy were Koltsov and Lev S. Berg, an outstanding zoo geographer, evolutionist, and explorer.[65] In the aftermath of this article, Berg failed to be elected a member of the academy (he was elected in 1946) and the academy presidium appointed a special commission, headed by Bakh, to investigate Koltsov's institute. Among the commission members were Lysenko, Prezent, Sapegin, the surgeon Nikolai I. Burdenko, and two corresponding members of the academy, Koshtoyants and N. I. Grashchenko.[66]

Commission members interviewed institute staff members, gathered material, and then called a general meeting of the institute staff, at which the commission planned to set forth its impressions, present a resolution, and hear from the staff.

Such meetings often brought to the fore spiteful malcontents who seized the opportunity to make accusations against their superiors. But Koltsov's institute was notably lacking in disaffected staff members. Only two people— Dubinin, who was then head of the institute's genetics department, and the outsider Koshtoyants, both of whom probably had ambitions of becoming director of the institute—voiced criticism at this meeting, and they found nothing more to condemn than Koltsov's old views on eugenics, which they themselves described as having been temporary delusions, long forgotten and of no influence upon the director's present work. Even these two confirmed that Koltsov was an outstanding scientist and an honorable man.[67]

Koltsov was deeply offended by Dubinin's behavior. He had helped Dubinin more than once. He had hired Dubinin when the latter had been dismissed from the Communist Academy for quarrels with and accusations against Serebrovsky, and he had petitioned to grant Dubinin a doctoral degree in biological sciences without the need to write a dissertation and had made sure the degree was awarded. He had praised Dubinin several times in his articles.[68] He could not forgive Dubinin's betrayal of him, and he never spoke to Dubinin again.

Koltsov addressed the meeting in calm, firm tones, saying things that few in such a position dared voice in those times. He rejected all accusations, refused to accept any blame, and made it quite clear that he despised those who denounced him for "misdemeanors," past or present. "I erred twice in my life," he said. "Once, in my youth and inexperience I identified a spider incorrectly. Another time, I did the same thing with another invertebrate. Until I was 14, I believed in God, then I came to understand that there was no God and began to treat religious superstitions as any educated biologist would. But can I maintain that until age 14 I was wrong? This was my life, my way, and I will not renounce myself."[69]

Although the commission's resolution included references to Koltsov's ideological mistakes, the mistakes were out of the distant past, and the commission could find nothing to accuse him of in the present, and it refrained from calling him a saboteur.

The presidium of the AN SSSR met on April 16, 1939, to consider the commission's report. Despite the press attacks and the efforts of several commission members to inflame the situation, the commission refrained nonetheless—in a decision that was unusual for those years—from calling Koltsov a saboteur and enemy of the regime and adopting a report that would justify his arrest. It removed him as director of the institute, but left allowed him to remain in the institute and even retained a laboratory for him. It replaced him as director neither by Dubinin nor by Koshtoyants but by a Lysenko follower, Georgy K. Khrushchev.

Koltsov had assembled a staff of devoted and decent personnel in the institute and had established a remarkably creative atmosphere; despite its modest size, it was one of the most productive institutes. An act of one of its research fellows, Valentin S. Kirpichnikov, indicates the spirit that prevailed there. In late 1939, Kirpichnikov, convinced that Lysenko had misinformed Stalin about genetics, wrote Stalin a letter, citing clear and striking examples of that science's importance to agriculture and rebutting the charges of the fascist nature of eugenics. He sought the aid of Commissar of Light and Food Industries Polina S. Zhemchuzhina to obtain an audience with Stalin concerning the matter. (Zhemchuzhina was Molotov's wife. Later, she was accused of sabotage and, without objection from Molotov, was arrested as an enemy of the people.) Uncertain whether he would be able to see her, he had prepared a bold appeal addressed to her:

Academician Lysenko, known to the entire country for his work on vernalization and summer planting of potatoes, has declared the very fundamentals of genetics to be unscientific. Thanks to his authority and the backing of the press . . . Lysenko's position is accepted as the Party line by many inside and outside the Party and is considered part of Marxist theory. As a result, genetics is being banished from the schools, from higher education, and from various institutes; even institutes of the Academy of Sciences are planning to dismiss those who do not agree to change their convictions overnight or who dare to criticize Lysenko. It is painful to see a science that has contributed greatly to practical results, . . . a science in which the Soviet Union has achieved a leading world rank, proclaimed a false, anti-Darwinist, bourgeois science. It hurts to see prominent Soviet scientists being discredited and many persons, with greater regard for their own situation than for the fate of science, turning to double-dealing and renouncing their own views, though they understand perfectly well what is happening. It hurts to see the enemies of genetics trying to link it with eugenics, even though we know fascist racist "science" has nothing in common with real science. . . . Finally, the Soviet Union is losing many friends among the leftist intelligentsia of the capitalist countries."[70]

As it turned out, Kirpichnikov was admitted promptly to see Zhemchuzhina. She heard him out attentively and promised to give Stalin his letter. That was the last he heard of it. However, within a year the institute's new director contrived to drive him out of the institute, despite his respectable research on the genetics of fish, and even tried to bring him to trial—with falsified records—for purported absence from work. Remarkably, the court dismissed the case.

Prezent, incensed that the attempt to destroy Koltsov had failed, renewed the attack in an article on Koltsov's "pseudo-scientific views," published in *Under the Banner of Marxism* (Pod znamenem Marksizma), the Party journal devoted to the discussion of Marxist-Leninist theory. He voiced scorn for Koltsov's critics, especially Dubinin, as having been insufficiently militant, and he assailed the institute staff for defending the director. "But Koltsov," he wrote, "did not consider it necessary to reconsider and renounce his opinions, adding that everything he had written was 'historically correct.'"[71]

It was probably Koltsov's defiant and uncompromising stand that enabled him to preserve his beloved institute. Today, the Koltsov Developmental Biology Institute of the Russian Academy of Sciences, bearing his name and continuing the traditions established by its founder, is one of the best biological institutes of the Soviet Union.

Lysenko Presses the Attack on Vavilov

The day after Lysenko had been elected to the AN SSSR, *Socialist Agriculture* carried an article by Vavilov that was a firm defense of genetics against the Lysenkoists. "We Soviet scientists cannot turn our backs on modern genetics," he wrote. "We must reject the suggestions sometimes heard that there is a crisis in world genetics and a need to create some sort of original genetics in disregard of world science. To those who propose the elimination of modern genetics we say: First offer a substitute of equivalent value. Let chromosomal theory be replaced by a new theory, but not a theory that sets us back seventy years."[72]

A furious response by Lysenko appeared in the same issue. Vavilov knows, he wrote, that "Mendelism cannot be defended before Soviet readers by describing it and expounding its fundamentals." It was now, he explained, "especially impossible" to fool the millions of Soviet readers with this "reactionary . . . idealistic . . . absurd falsification of science," when they possessed "such an all-powerful weapon as *The Short Course of the History of the*

Communist Party. The reader who masters Bolshevism cannot sympathize with metaphysics or Mendelism, because that is exactly what Mendelism is: veritable, undisguised metaphysics."[73]

Afterward, a number of geneticists wrote to protest the newspaper's consistent advocacy of Lysenko's position. Among them were Anton R. Zhebrak and two young research fellows at Moscow State University, Nikolai I. Shapiro and Mikhail E. Neigauz.[74] (At the start of the Nazi invasion, Neigauz volunteered to go to the front and died in action early in the war.)[75] None of the letters was published. Instead, a member of the editorial staff concocted a "survey of letters to the editor." The majority of readers, he claimed, opposed genetics. Students of the Timiryazev Agricultural Academy, he said, had been obliged to listen to a lecture by Zhebrak, a "Morganist," but had rejected genetics and objected "to turning their academy into a breeding ground for Mendelism-Morganism and foisting such professors as Zhebrak upon them."[76]

Kirpichnikov, who had become a senior lecturer at the Moscow Institute of Fisheries and the Fishing Industry, then wrote a letter to *Socialist Agriculture*. In this letter, which was co-signed by several other young geneticists and copies of which were sent to the agriculture department of the Party Central Committee and to Leningrad Party secretary and Politburo member Andrei A. Zhdanov as well, Kirpichnikov condemned the practice of acquainting Lysenko's followers with the geneticists' letters beforehand and the newspaper's substitution of abuse for genuine criticism. He wrote:

> We young Soviet scientists, graduates of Soviet institutions of higher learning, openly defend Mendelism and Morganism from all the often spiteful or illiterate attacks. We consider modern "chromosomal" genetics the strongest support for Darwinist doctrine and cannot comprehend how a Soviet newspaper can allow such methods of discussion. . . . The newspaper has been slandering so-called "formal" genetics for a long time. . . . We ask you, comrade editor, what aims is the newspaper pursuing in trying to deceive readers and discrediting itself and Soviet science in the eyes of our scientists, as well as scientists friendly to the USSR in capitalist countries?[77]

The letter ended up in the editor's wastebasket.

Earlier in 1939, the Commissariat of Agriculture had called a nationwide conference, from February 27 to March 4, on plant breeding and seed production. It became the occasion for another move against Vavilov and the geneticists. The conference opened with two papers, one by Lysenko, the other by A. Ya. Frenkel, head of the division of selection stations of the Central Varietal Administration, both depicting the geneticists' stand as invalid and harmful. During the discussion session, Iogan G. Eikhfeld of the Northern Station of the VIR, Anatoly V. Pukhalsky of the Shatilov Selection Station, Pyotr P. Lukyanenko of the Krasnodar Selection Station (see biographical sketches), and many others, all of them using the same words, expressed their support for Lysenko's and Frenkel's views.[78]

Vavilov, however, charged that Lysenko's supporters "were discarding the experience of world science without any basis . . . while world science follows the path laid down by Mendel, Johannsen, and Morgan."[79] Zhebrak spoke in the same vein, after which Lysenko and Prezent categorically rejected all their arguments out of hand. Vavilov's pronouncements at the meeting, Lysenko said, were "so unclear, so scientifically vague, that one can only conclude from them that 'varieties fall from the sky.'" He managed to imply that Vavilov's views were linked with fascism: "Vavilov kept referring to the scientist Roemer, who wrote his book in Germany in fascist times. I am prejudiced against present-day German science, which propounds the permanency and immutability of race."[80]

Commissar of Agriculture Ivan A. Benediktov summed up the meeting. He was completely on Lysenko's side. "The USSR Commissariat of Agriculture," he said, "supports Academician Lysenko in his practical work and theoretical views and recommends that selection stations employ his methods in seed production and plant breeding."[81] The guidelines that the meeting set for selection stations endorsed this recommendation.

Vavilov's Last Year of Freedom

The NKVD had filled more than five folders of its Vavilov file when, on December 13, 1938, it opened a new one, case No. 300669. The first folder in this new file bore the heading "Genetics" in large, bold lettering across the cover. Among the first documents in this new file was a memorandum entitled "Struggle Waged by Reactionary Scientists against Academician T. D. Lysenko." It reviewed the many years of surveillance and investigation of Vavilov; described Vavilov's acts as reactionary and hostile to Soviet rule; claimed that Vavilov and Pryanishnikov were "using every effort to discredit Lysenko as a scientist"; and called for the arrest of Vavilov. It was written and signed by B. Z. Kobulov, the deputy commissar of internal affairs (i.e., the deputy to Beria, the head of the NKVD), who was an alternate member of the Party Central Committee.[82]

The arrest did not follow, but Vavilov undoubtedly knew that the web being spun around him was much more than a minor intrigue. Two years before, when Western newspapers had reported him arrested, he had been asked to deny it in print and had been glad to avail himself of the opportunity. His statement in the press, in the form of a letter to the editor of one of the central newspapers, might have been summed up in Mark Twain's famous words, "The reports of my death are greatly exaggerated." In the intervening two years, however, Vavilov's chances had not improved in the slightest, as he well knew.

On November 27, 1987, Maria G. Zaitsev delivered a talk about memories of her father, the scientist whose deductions had led Lysenko to study the effect of low temperatures upon plants (see chapter 1). Her father had been a friend of Vavilov's, and the daughter described a visit to the Vavilov home, where she enjoyed the companionship of Vavilov's son

Oleg. "The clouds were gathering. . . . Nikolai Ivanovich [Vavilov] remarked bitterly that whenever he took the train in Leningrad he wondered whether he would reach Moscow. He warned us children to watch our tongues. He tore off a strip of paper and wrote several lines in English, to the effect that "if you don't want to blurt out anything damaging, consider first of whom you are speaking, with whom you are speaking, and where and when.'"[83]

Outside the family circle, however, Vavilov remained as confident, calm, and poised as ever. He continued to direct the VIR and the Genetics Institute, though Lysenko and his chorus let no opportunity go by to denigrate Vavilov's work.

Vavilov delivered a report as director of the VIR at a meeting of the presidium of VASKhNIL on May 23, 1939. Academy President Lysenko and Acting Vice-President Pavel P. Lukyanenko chaired the meeting. Instead of listening to Vavilov, the new leaders of the academy repeatedly interrupted and badgered him. Vavilov referred to the many outstanding specialists trained in the institute and then began to describe its current work, with brief mention of the scientific principles of selection "wholly based on Darwin's evolutionary teaching," when Lysenko and Lukyanenko started to bombard him with questions:

Lukyanenko: Why do you speak of Darwin? Why don't you choose examples from Marx and Engels?
Vavilov: Darwin worked on questions of the evolution of species earlier. Engels and Marx held Darwin in high regard. Darwin isn't everything, but he is the greatest of biologists, the man who proved the evolution of organisms.
Lukyanenko: You seem to think that humans originated in one place. I don't believe that it was in one place.
Vavilov: I said not that it was in one place, but that it was in the Old World. Modern biological science, Darwinian science, says that humans appeared in the Old World and that they appeared only 20–25,000 years ago in the Old World. There were no humans in America before that period, and although this may be curious, it is well known.
Lukyanenko: Is that related to your view of domesticated plants?
Vavilov: Briefly, my conception of the evolution of domesticated plants, my basic idea underlying the study of plant materials, is that the center of origin of plant species is a law that one and the same species does not arise independently in a variety of places, but spreads through the continents from some one region.
Lukyanenko: They say the potato was brought from America. I don't believe it. Do you know what Lenin said?
Vavilov: The facts and historical documents attest to it. I would be happy to tell you about it in detail.
Lukyanenko: I asked you a basic question and it turns out that if potatoes appeared in a single place we must recognize that . . .
Lysenko: It is a fact that potatoes were brought to old Russia. You can't argue with facts. But that isn't the point. The point is something else. Comrade Lukyanenko is right. The point is that if the potato originated in America, does

this mean it could not arise in Moscow, Kiev, or Kharkov, from an ancestral species, until the Second Coming? Can new varieties of wheat arise in Moscow, Leningrad, or any other place? I think they can. How, then, are we to view your idea about the centers of origin? That is the point.

Vavilov. . . . When I studied with Bateson, a very great scientist . . .

Lukyanenko: An anti-Darwinist.

Vavilov: Oh, no. Some day I'll tell you about Bateson, a most fascinating, most interesting person.

Lukyanenko: Couldn't you learn from Marx? Maybe you hurried through his works, satisfied yourself with broad generalities, but "a word is not a sparrow on the wing."

Vavilov: A book by [J.B.S.] Haldane came out recently. He is a very interesting figure, a member of the British Communist Party, a prominent geneticist, biochemist, and philosopher. This Haldane has written an interesting book entitled *Marxism and Science*, in which he tried . . .

Lukyanenko: He was criticized.

Vavilov: The bourgeois press criticized him, of course, but he is so talented that he was admired even while being criticized. He showed that the dialectic has to be used skillfully. He says Marxism is applicable in the study of evolution, in history, wherever many sciences intersect; when we deal with complex matters, Marxism can be prescient, as when Engels foresaw by fifty years many of today's discoveries. I must say that I am a great devotee of Marxist literature, not only ours, but foreign as well. There, too, attempts are being made at applying Marxism.

Lukyanenko: Marxism is the only science. Darwinism is, after all, only a part; Marx, Engels, and Lenin gave us the real theory of cognition. And so when I hear Darwinism mentioned without Marxism, it may seem correct, on the one hand, but it turns out to be quite otherwise.

Vavilov: I studied Marx four or five times, and I am prepared to go on studying him. Let me conclude by saying that the staff of the institute consists basically of highly qualified specialists, productive workers; and we ask the academy and you, Comrade Lukyanenko, to help our collective create conditions for good work. As for these tiresome labels, we ought to get rid of them.

Lysenko concluded by saying that he agreed it was "difficult" for Vavilov to carry on his work and that he was "sincerely sorry" for Vavilov, but that Vavilov was "insubordinate" toward him and hence the VIR was also insubordinate. "We cannot go on in this way . . . . "We shall have to depend on others, take another line, a line of administrative subordination."[84]

The upshot of the meeting was an unprecedented resolution, moved by Lysenko and adopted by the presidium, to declare the work of the VIR unsatisfactory.[85] That autumn, Lysenko took advantage of Vavilov's absence on a brief trip to issue an order to dissolve the entire scientific council of the institute. The order removed the institute's leading scientists who were close to Vavilov: Karpechenko, Levitsky, M. A. Rozanova, Ye. F. Vulf, L. I. Govorov, K. I. Pangalo, N. A. Bazilevskaya, Ye. A. Stoletova, F. Kh. Bakhteyev, N. R. Ivanov, N. V. Kovalev, and I. V. Kozhukhov.

Vavilov had met Beria several times in the latter's summer home during visits to Georgia, but the friendly relationship meant nothing in the face of Lysenko's strength. Beria had become head of the NKVD. In July 1939, Beria sent a letter to Molotov that in effect requested authorization to arrest Vavilov, on the ground that "according to information on hand, since Academician T. D. Lysenko's appointment as president of the agricultural academy, Vavilov and the bourgeois school of so-called formal geneticists which he heads has been conducting a systematic campaign to discredit Academician Lysenko as a scientist."[86] The authorization was not forthcoming, perhaps because Vavilov's work was still needed in agriculture, perhaps because of Vavilov's prominence abroad. The hesitation is surprising, in view of the fact that there was no compunction about arresting other eminent scientists, scholars, and artists. Whatever the reason, Vavilov remained at liberty. But Lysenko did not give up.

The Party Journal Stages a Discussion of Genetics

There had been repeated talk, in various organizations and at various levels, of the need for a philosophical discussion of the problems of genetics. The final impetus for holding such a discussion may have been provided by a letter addressed to Zhdanov in the spring of 1939 from a group of ten leading Leningrad scientists, including Karpechenko, Levitsky, Rozanova, Yury I. Polyansky, Yuliy M. Olenov, and Mikhail Ye. Lobashev. A young graduate student of Karpechenko's, the research fellow Daniil V. Lebedev, participated in the drafting of the letter, but to protect him the signers forbade him to add his signature. "It's too soon for you! Preserve yourself!" Karpechenko told him. It was from Lebedev that I learned of the existence and content of this letter.

The letter, calm in tone but blunt, spoke of the critical, even tragic, situation in biology, and it pointed out that the rejection of genetics could lead to terrible practical failures. Apparently, it made a strong impression on Zhdanov. The word went around that the letter had reached the highest level and was being studied in the Kremlin. And indeed, while articles attacking Vavilov continued to appear,[87] the Party Central Committee did sanction an open discussion between the opposed camps. All of the twelve who had signed the Leningrad letter were invited, suggesting strongly that their letter had brought on the debate.

The conduct of the discussion was entrusted to the editorial board of *Under the Banner of Marxism.* These auspices immediately gave the discussion a political character. Academician Mark B. Mitin was appointed chairman. Mitin, a member of the Central Committee, had graduated from the Party's Institute of Red Professors and had become director of the Philosophy Institute of the AN SSSR. Later he became chairman of the Society for the Dissemination of Political and Scientific Knowledge and editor in chief of the journal *Problems of Philosophy.* Above all, he was a coeditor of Stalin's publications and was received by Stalin many times. The participants who spoke for genetics did not and could not know what Lysenko and his followers undoubtedly knew: that Mitin, a supporter of Lysenko, had been summoned to Central Committee headquarters on the eve of the discussion to receive instructions concerning its conduct.[88]

The week-long discussion began on October 7, 1939. From the start, the Lysenko forces showed that they were confident of the outcome. When some participants spoke of a division of biologists into practical workers insufficiently versed in theory and theoreticians who did not fully recognize the needs of practice, V. K. Milovanov, director of VASKhNIL's Animal Husbandry Institute, replied that "we do not have two disputing groups. . . . Specifically, there is no Lysenko group, there is only a moribund group of geneticists, divorced from practical life, that has utterly discredited itself in the practice of agriculture."[89] Keller added that "formal genetics has emasculated Darwinism,"[90] a grave charge, since Darwinism was considered an inalienable part of Communist doctrine.

Some speakers who well understood genetics nevertheless followed the Lysenko line. B. M. Zavadovsky said that formal genetics "has failed to justify itself and therefore has no right to exist."[91] His brother, M. M. Zavadovsky, defended genetics, provoking the editorial comment that "M. M. Zavadovsky did not show a desire to engage in self-criticism and did not even try to explain why disputes among geneticists have arisen and have continued for so long."[92] Sos I. Alikhanyan, trying at once to dissociate himself from Lysenko's criticism of Mendel's statistical principles of inheritance and yet remain in Lysenko's good graces, found nothing better to say than that "no geneticist has explained biological phenomena by mathematical laws."[93] (For more on Alikhanyan, see chapter 9.)

On the other hand, Yuly Y. Kerkis, a young researcher in Vavilov's institute, defended the Mendelian laws. He had conducted a series of experiments that confirmed them and disproved the claims of Lysenko and Glushchenko concerning vegetative hybridization (the transmission of characteristics acquired through grafting). Kerkis's report of the results of his experiments greatly displeased Lysenko, who shouted from his seat, "Hands are needed, as well as a brain." Kerkis replied by reminding the audience that Lysenko had once said that "to obtain a definite result, one must want to obtain just that result, and if you want to get a specific result you will get it," and he cited Lysenko's principle of selecting researchers: "I want only people who will get the results I want." Seemingly not the least embarrassed, Lysenko called out, "That's right!"[94]

Vavilov spoke like a new man, putting behind him all attempts at compromise with Lysenko. "Lysenko's position not only runs counter to the group of Soviet geneticists, it runs counter to all of modern biology . . . ," he said. "In the guise of advanced science, we are advised to turn back essentially to scientifically obsolete views out of the first half or the middle of the nineteenth century. . . . What we are defending is the result of tremendous creative work, of precise experiments, of Soviet and foreign practice."[95]

Lysenko was no less categorical:

> I do not recognize Mendelism . . . I do not consider formal Mendelian-Morganist genetics a science. . . . We Michurinists object . . . to rubbish and falsehood in science, we cast overboard the hidebound, formal tenets of Mendelism-Morganism. . . . And now N. I. Vavilov and A. S. Serebrovsky . . . stand in the way of objectively and correctly getting down to the essence of Mendelism, exposing the false and contrived nature of the Mendel-Morgan doctrine and ending the teaching of it in higher educational institutions as a positive science.[96]

As an example of what he considered Vavilov's deception of the Soviet people, Lysenko cited Vavilov's calls for the development of hybrid corn to raise the grain yields as it had raised them in the United States. "To the Mendelians who point to America, I want to say . . . where is there even a single variety developed by this method?"[97] Vavilov, of course, had spoken of the crossing of two inbred lines to obtain a higher yield from the first infertile hybrid generation—a very different thing from a new variety. But Lysenko was demanding to be shown a new variety. This difference was surely obvious to most of the specialists present. Lysenko denounced Vavilov's work as director of the VIR and charged him with insubordination to the leadership of VASKhNIL,[98] and he accused Vavilov of hostility to the Michurinist heritage—an ironic charge, since it was Vavilov who had drawn attention to Michurin when the latter was almost unknown.[99]

As was to be expected, the philosophers in charge of the conference supported the Lysenko forces. In his introductory remarks, Mitin called upon the geneticists to turn to the positions of the "Michurinists." His treatment of the subject of hybrid corn was typical of his tactics. Noting that Vavilov had cited American experience and had displayed American books and quoted data from them, Mitin commented:

> Academician Vavilov has spoken . . . of world genetics. . . . But what is characteristic of his presentation? . . . I would say, admiration of the thick volumes that he showed us without the slightest attempt at analysis of their contents. Can it be that everything in these volumes is right, these very thick, very solid-seeming volumes, printed on high-grade American paper and looking so respectable—can it be that nothing in these volumes requires a critical approach? Pardon my candor, Nikolai Ivanovich [Vavilov], but when we listened to you, we got the impression that you do not want to question theoretically many of these so-called world authorities with whom perhaps we ought to quarrel and fight![100]

Mitin heaped scorn upon Serebrovsky as well for having demonstrated a butterfly he had developed that did not fly. "That is very good," he said. "This butterfly doubtless has some practical value. Fine. But you will agree that that is very little to show for eight years of work by a person commanding the arsenal of science."[101]

Another philosopher, Pavel F. Yudin (see biographical sketches), strove to represent genetics as the science of an alien class, and the geneticists as harmful bearers of the views of this alien class, persons who could not be accepted in Soviet science or in Soviet society generally. Accordingly, he said, "the teaching of genetics must be eliminated from secondary schools, while retaining it in higher educational institutions as a footnote to the teaching of Darwinism in order that the students may know that there actually have been such people and such a doctrine." He said to the geneticists: "You could bring great benefit . . . to the cause of socialism . . . if you renounced the rubbish and dross that have piled up in your science."[102]

The conference thus amounted to an ideological condemnation of genetics as a science and of the specialists in the field. Because *Pravda* reported the conference at length, and because a rather complete transcript of the proceedings, with commentary by the editors, was published in *Under the Banner of Marxism*, the denunciation of the geneticists was taken to be a Party directive and had the repercussions of any such directive.

Vavilov's Last Meeting with Stalin

One month after the conference, on November 20, 1939, Stalin sent for Vavilov. When Vavilov entered the room—as he later recounted the meeting to a friend—Stalin was pacing back and forth, head down, pipe clutched in his hand. He did not respond to Vavilov's greeting nor even look up. Vavilov waited. Then, realizing that it was useless to stand aimlessly silent, Vavilov began to report on the work of the institute. Stalin went on pacing from corner to corner like a caged tiger, saying nothing. When about five minutes had passed in this manner, Stalin went to his desk, sat down, and, without a word of greeting, interrupted Vavilov in mid-sentence:

"Well, citizen Vavilov, how long are you going to go on fooling with flowers and other nonsense? When will you start raising crop yields?"

Vavilov tried to explain the role of science, including the study of flowers, in establishing a solid basis for agriculture, and thus in increasing crop yields. Stalin listened briefly, then said curtly: "You may go."[103]

One can imagine Vavilov's depression as he left the dictator's office in the Kremlin. Nevertheless, he tried to maintain his capacity for work and to keep up his spirits, although his once iron health was weakening. At about this time, he wrote to his friend Pangalo, who had been exiled to the Karaganda region in 1932: "As always, two drives are at work here, the creative and the destructive. They will always operate, as long as the world exists. There are no terribly menacing circumstances, so go on working confidently; draw up the projects as soon as you can. Regardless of obstacles, we continue to pursue our policy as a comprehensive plant-breeding institute."[104]

The chilling interview with Stalin did not frighten Vavilov back to his earlier conciliatory tone toward Lysenko. As if prophetically, he had declared in the previous spring, at a session of the Leningrad Regional Bureau of the Section of Scientific Workers:

We shall go to the pyre, we shall burn, but we shall not retreat from our convictions. I tell you, in all frankness, that I believed and still believe and insist on what I think is right, and not only believe—because taking things on faith in science is nonsense—but also say what I know on the basis of wide experience. This is a fact, and to retreat from it simply because some occupying high posts desire it, is impossible.[105]

Even after the interview, at the beginning of 1940, he wrote to Commissar of Agriculture Benediktov: "Lysenko's high administrative position, his intolerance, and his low level of culture lead to a peculiar introduction of ideas that are close to outmoded scientific views (Lamarckism), and which are regarded as exceedingly dubious by the majority of those acquainted with the field. Using his position, Lysenko has actually begun reprisals against his ideological opponents."[106] Lysenko was surely fully informed of the correspondence.

Vavilov would have had to be blind to remain unaware of the realities of those times. At the meeting held in 1983 by the N. I. Vavilov Society of Geneticists and Breeders to honor Vavilov's memory, Aleksandra A. Prokofyeva-Belgovskaya described the drastic change that took place in his attitude:

Until the end of 1936, he treated Lysenko's ideas with great interest. He constantly set the tone for us by saying our opponents were poorly educated and we ought to help them. . . . His benevolent attitude toward Lysenko amazed us. To the very end, he believed in being honorable. "They don't quite understand," he often told us. . . .

But then came the hard years. Nikolai Ivanovich [Vavilov] began to lose his cheerfulness and vitality . . . although he still hoped everything would turn out well and truth would conquer. I remember him quoting Darwin: "The stubborn distortion of truth is powerful, but happily its power does not last." Today we can say it lasted 25 years and we still feel its aftereffects. . . .

I saw him for the last time in the spring of 1940. I was working at the microscope in the laboratory late in the evening. The overhead lights were turned off, the room was quiet and dark. Suddenly the door opened and in walked Nikolai Ivanovich. I had never seen him look like that. Tired and silent, he sat down without removing his coat or hat, leaned his walking stick on the arm of the chair, and sat silent for a long, long time. I rose quietly, heated the tea kettle, made tea, and offered him a glass without a word. He drank the tea and went on sitting in silence. His face reflected agony. . . .

Finally he rose, walked to the door, turned in the doorway, and quoted Shakespeare's line, "Ophelia, there is no truth on earth."

That was the evening, I later learned, after his last meeting with Molotov. That was when he finally saw everything clearly.[107]

Vavilov had been meeting with Molotov almost every week in connection with preparations for the International Genetics Congress. On this last occasion, Vavilov had been left to sit outside Molotov's office for hours.

Igor K. Fortunatov, son of a close friend of Vavilov's, has also recalled a conversation with Vavilov that took place during that time. He and Vavilov had gone for a long walk around town in May 1940. Vavilov did not want to return to his small office in the VASKhNIL building on Bolshoi Kharitonievsky Lane. He complained that "the bureaucracy" was tormenting him. He complained also of ill health; for two years, he said, he had suffered from aching joints, and his heart was giving him trouble. He couldn't take the time for medical treatment, he said, "and it would be pointless. It's time to bring my life to an end. I've suffered enough in this life."[108]

Yet, no matter how depressed Vavilov felt at times in that last year, he found the strength to defy Lysenko. In the summer of 1940, he signed an appeal drawn up by Khadzhinov and Kozhukhov to the Party Central Committee (copies were sent to Commissar of Agriculture Benediktov and to Deputy Commissar V. S. Chuyenkov), setting forth Lysenko's mistakes on hybrid corn. The letter noted that in 1938 alone the United States had increased its corn harvest by 100,000,000 poods by using hybrids of inbred lines, and pointed out that the Soviet planned economy could attain a greater rise in its harvest were it not for Lysenko's persecution of hybrid corn projects and outright deception of Soviet society with his claims that the method was without promise. The letter, Vavilov's copy of which is in my possession, went on to denounce Prezent and Boris P. Sokolov, a plant-breeding specialist at the Dnepropetrovsk Experimental Station, for obstructing hybridization and distorting the facts.

In the two years before his arrest, Vavilov assembled and helped to edit a collection of articles by his students and colleagues. It was to be a book, entitled *A Critical Review of the Fundamentals of Genetics*—a thorough survey of all that was new in world genetics and a solid response to the attacks that had been leveled at the geneticists.[109] Among the articles to be included were M. S. Navashin and A. A. Prokofyeva-Belgovskaya, "The Role of the Nucleus in Heredity and Chromosomal Theory"; V. L. Ryzhkov, "The Role of Cytoplasm in Heredity"; M. I. Kamshilov, "Heredity and Development"; Kh. F. Kushner, "Modificational Mutability and Its Role in Evolution and Selection"; M. L. Belgovsky, "The Problem of the Gene"; N. P. Dubinin, "Darwinism and Genetics" and "Heredity and Mutability in the Works of I. V. Michurin"; and V. V. Khvostova, "The Contemporary Condition of the Teaching of Vegetative Hybridization." Vavilov himself had also written a lengthy article for the book; it was posthumously printed in the fifth volume of his collected works.

Publication of this collection might have shaken Lysenkoism's credibility and undermined the critics of genetics, and so, not surprisingly, great efforts were made to prevent publication. At a meeting of the presidium of the AN SSSR in 1940, Yudin, Keller, and Emilian Yaroslavsky criticized the very idea of such a work. When the meeting was over, the troubled Vavilov telephoned one of the co-editors of the collection. Describing his attackers, he quoted Vladimir Solovyov's lines, "In the sky the candelabras glow / but darkness reigns here down below."[110]

Work on the book continued until Vavilov's arrest. On October 1, 1940, when Vavilov was under detention, Yudin sent Komarov, the president of the AN SSSR, and Vice-President Otto Yu. Shmidt an official report reviewing the manuscript of the book and objecting sharply to its publication. Yudin called the geneticists "representatives of an anti-Marxist ideology" and wrote that the collection "belittles in every way Michurin's significance, portrays his path as a series of errors by a narrow empiricist, and . . . completely denies vegetative hybridization, which it places within ironic quotation marks." Yudin concluded that the essays, taken as a whole, disregarded the results of the discussion of genetics and selection conducted by *Under the Banner of Marxism*, failed to reconsider the basic premises of formal genetics, and did not follow the "Darwin-Michurin theory," as demanded by the presidium of the academy. The collection was never published.

9

Koltsov and Vavilov Perish

Land of searches, torture and prisons dreaded,
Russia, the land where Thought is beheaded.
> —Konstantin Balmont, "To Alexander Herzen"

Then there is the one who does not succeed in life: the poisonous
worm devours his heart.
> —Friedrich Nietzsche, *Thus Spake Zarathustra*

Vavilov's Arrest

On March 31, 1940, soon after the Soviet Union gained Finnish territory as a result of the 1939–1940 "winter war," the Commissariat of Agriculture sent an expedition consisting of Lysenko followers to assess this newly gained territory and make recommendations for how it was to be farmed. However, the expedition's recommendations proved so absurd that, when the USSR acquired the Transcarpathian Ukraine a few months later, the commissariat sent an expedition headed by Vavilov instead. One can imagine how Lysenko took this rebuff. On top of this, Lysenko and Vavilov met by chance a few days before the start of Vavilov's expedition, and according to friends of Vavilov, he told Lysenko in no uncertain terms what he thought of him.[1] For Lysenko this was probably the last straw.

From August 1 to 7, 1940, the Supreme Soviet met to hear Molotov's foreign-policy report and to incorporate the Baltic states and the Transcarpathian Ukraine into the Soviet Union. Newspaper photographs of the session show Lysenko seated in the row of dignitaries directly behind the leaders of the Party and government. He thus had abundant opportunities to talk privately with them and overcome any lingering resistance to Vavilov's arrest. This may have been where Vavilov's fate was decided.

Vavilov left Moscow for the Transcarpathian Ukraine in late July. The newspaper *Leningrad Pravda* reported his departure, but, as was common in such cases, misled readers as to the route. It announced that the expedition was going to study pasture and grazing land in the Caucasus, hundreds of miles from Vavilov's true destination.[2]

To carry out the expedition's goals of collecting plants, inspecting local fields, and consulting local scientific workers in the western Ukraine,

Vavilov's team split into three groups. Vavilov and two aides, Vadim S. Lekhnovich and Fatikh Kh. Bakhteyev, used a student dormitory at Chernovitsy as their base. On August 6, with a group of local scientists, Vavilov set off by car for the Carpathian Mountains. Lekhnovich and Bakhteyev had to return early, and on their way back they were stopped by four men in a black car. The four men asked where they could find Vavilov; they said they had come to retrieve some urgently needed documents that he had accidentally taken from Moscow. The black car went off in pursuit of Vavilov as the two aides made their way to the dormitory.

The old waiter at the dormitory told them that, after dark, "Professor Vavilov returned and wanted to go to his room, but a black car arrived just then and the people in it wanted him to go back with them to Moscow for urgent negotiations. The professor left his case and asked me to tell his comrades that he would be back soon." Lekhnovich and Bakhteyev waited in their moonlit room. They were not worried; Vavilov was often sought on urgent state business. Near midnight, there was a knock at their door; two young men said that Vavilov was waiting at the airport, and they gave Lekhnovich a note:

Dear Vadim Stepanovich:
In view of my abrupt summons to Moscow, give the bearer all my belongings.
    N. Vavilov
    23:15, 6/VIII/40.[3]

Bakhteyev collected Vavilov's things; to the aides' surprise, the messenger politely but firmly insisted on packing every piece of Vavilov's luggage himself, down to the last scrap of paper. Lekhnovich and Bakhteyev wanted to go to the airport, but the luggage left room for only one more person in the car. The messenger's companion in the car told them rudely that there was no reason for either of them to come. Bakhteyev nonetheless tried to open the door and get in. "The man in the car hit me so hard that I fell down," he recalled. "Then he ordered the driver, 'Get going!' The door slammed and the car disappeared."[4] At last he and Lekhnovich understood that something terrible had happened to Vavilov.

In his letter to Pangalo (see chapter 8), Vavilov had remarked that two opposed camps were at odds over his fate. Now there was striking evidence of this. The NKVD had made the arrest in secret, in the remote Transcarpathian region, far from prying eyes. In Leningrad and at the Commissariat of Agriculture in Moscow, everyone thought Vavilov was simply away on an important mission. So, while the NKVD held Vavilov in a Lubyanka cell, the agricultural authorities, all unwitting, proceeded to award him the Great Gold Medal of the All-Union Agricultural Exhibition. Stalin had dreamed up this exhibition as a showcase of collective farming, displaying agricultural bounty in elaborate pavilions surrounded by statuary and gilded fountains. (Khrushchev later turned it into the Exhibition of National Economic Achievements.) The awards bearing the exhibition's name were to be among the highest honors the government bestowed. On August 21, 1940, *Leningrad Pravda* reported that Vavilov—who had never before received so much as a routine certificate of merit—was now given a gold medal and a cash award of 3,000 rubles. The report described Vavilov as "now working at the VIR."[5] Vavilov's colleagues at the institute were overjoyed.

Lysenko was pleased, too, though of course for other reasons. The order for Vavilov's arrest declared:

> It has been established that for purposes of disproving new theories advanced by the Soviet scientists Lysenko and Michurin in the fields of vernalization and genetics, Vavilov directed many departments of the VIR to conduct special research to discredit the theories put forth by Lysenko and Michurin. . . . While promoting deliberately hostile theories, Vavilov has been conducting a struggle against the theories and research of Lysenko, Tsitsin, and Michurin that possess decisive importance for the agriculture of the USSR.[6]

That Lysenko did not conceal his satisfaction is indicated by an incident recounted in Glushchenko's memoirs. Lysenko had brought Glushchenko from Odessa in 1939 and placed him in Vavilov's Genetics Institute in Moscow. Glushchenko was inspecting the harvest on the institute's tomato plot when a car drove up and Lysenko emerged. "Do you know where your director is?" Lysenko asked. "How would I know? I don't keep tabs on him. He's probably in Leningrad," Glushchenko replied. "He is not in Leningrad. He is under arrest," Lysenko said, obviously gloating, and returned to his automobile.[7] When Prezent was asked, at a meeting in Leningrad, where Vavilov was, he answered, apparently without a trace of irony, "Am I my brother's keeper?"—the words of Cain after he slew his brother and the Lord asked him where Abel was.[8]

Shortly after Vavilov's arrest, Professor Nina A. Bazilevskaya of the VIR encountered Shundenko in a cafe in the center of Moscow, near the headquarters of the NKVD. Shundenko, who had disappeared from Leningrad, was wearing a new uniform of an NKVD officer. Bazilevskaya did not even nod to him, but he looked her straight in the eye and smiled. Years later, it came to light that he had been brought into the institute to carry out "an important government assignment" as the NKVD officer in charge of the Vavilov case.[9]

Vavilov's arrest gave Lysenko a free hand. With redoubled energy, he set about destroying the institutes Vavilov had established. First, he made himself director of the Genetics Institute and soon forced out all the geneticists who had been Vavilov's pupils and colleagues, except for three: Prokofyeva-Belgovskaya, her husband Mark L. Belgovsky, and Tenis K. Lepin. At the ceremonies in 1988 marking her eightieth birthday, Prokofyeva-Belgovskaya speculated about Lysenko's reasons for retaining these three. "Lepin," she said, "was an unexcelled wheat specialist, and Lysenko simply needed him. Mark Belgovsky directed work with the *Drosophila*, the organism which Lysenko hated and scorned, although at the same time he was always fearful of displaying his ignorance of it; accordingly, he allowed Belgovsky to remain, saddling him with the strictest orders to see to it that 'not a single fly perished'—which was of course an absurd injunction." "As for myself," she continued, "I never did understand why Lysenko kept me on the staff. It may have been because I had worked with Muller during his stay in the Soviet Union, and Lysenko feared Muller's influence on Western opinion." There may also have been a personal reason: She told a close friend that Lysenko felt a platonic infatuation with her. He would not have been alone in this. Her striking beauty had captivated Muller and many others.

As geneticists were dismissed, one after another, the work of the Genetics Institute came to bear less and less relation to its name. The case of Yuly Kerkis is illustrative. Kerkis undoubtedly incurred Lysenko's hostility by undertaking to check the validity of experiments conducted by Lysenko's followers on the possibility of vegetative hybridization and then by a series of experiments demonstrating the Mendelian laws of heredity. Lysenko had dismissed many institute researchers on the grounds that they were dealing with "irrelevant themes," but he could hardly oust Kerkis on these grounds: Lysenko himself had made vegetative hybridization the institute's central subject. So Lysenko's men turned to harassing him, denying him space in the greenhouses and the experimental fields and even bringing criminal charges against him. On October 31, 1940, Kerkis obtained permission to leave the institute fifty minutes before closing time in order to discuss the mathematics of his experiments with two leading Soviet mathematicians, A. N. Kolmogorov and A. A. Lyapunov. A decree of June 26, 1940, had extended working hours and made absence from work a high crime. Lysenko's assistant director charged Kerkis with violating this decree. The court heard testimony but on November 5 it dismissed the case. However, conditions at the institute became so intolerable for Kerkis that he finally submitted his resignation. This incident came to light only years later, after Kerkis's death, when records of the trial were found among his papers.[10]

Lysenko had a harder time purging the VIR. It had almost a thousand employees, several dozen experimental stations, and laboratories and support sectors throughout the country. Scholars of world renown headed the laboratories and departments. Lysenko had to find ways of condemning their work with at least some semblance of objective charges. What followed was "a witch hunt," Ye. N. Sinskaya has recalled.

Staff and party meetings became unbearable. Every one of us was in genuine danger of a heart attack. . . . N. N. Ivanov, the elderly professor who headed the biochemical department of the institute, became one of the first victims of the terror. He became agitated at one of the scientific council meetings, then became involved in an argument at the office that they wanted to take away from him, and he went home and said: "I can't go on living like this." He lay down, and an hour later he was found dead.[11]

A commission appointed by Lysenko and endowed with sweeping powers came to Leningrad to eradicate the Vavilov spirit from the institute. Karpechenko, Levitsky, Govorov, and Konstantin A. Flyaksberger, head of the wheat department, were still there, and their presence inspired some small hope among their colleagues that the institute might yet survive the worst ravages. At one meeting, after several staff members had joined in denouncing their arrested director, Yefrem S. Yakushevsky rose and put them to shame, saying that it was impossible to forget Vavilov's tremendous accomplishments, that to their dying day they would be indebted to him for their own successes, and that he, Yakushevsky, would never believe in Vavilov's guilt; the arrest was obviously a mistake, and it was inconceivable that it would not be corrected.

Lysenko's men kept up the offensive. *Leningrad Pravda* carried an article on August 28, 1940, charging the biology department of Leningrad University with hostility toward Darwinism and the Michurin doctrine and accusing Professors Karpechenko and Levitsky of being "conservatives."[12] In those times, however, such articles became so common that they were not considered especially menacing. Lysenko had to crush the remaining resistance.

He finally determined to go to Leningrad to carry through the purge of the institute himself. On the eve of his arrival, the council—whose members he had appointed a year earlier (see chapter 8)—prepared a special welcoming gift: it voted almost unanimously (24 ayes, 1 abstention) to place the "kolkhoz academician" in nomination for a Stalin Prize in science.[13] The next day, October 13, Lysenko arrived at the institute where, eleven years earlier, Vavilov had launched him upon his career by inviting him to a genetics conference.

On October 15, the newspaper of Leningrad University carried an article by Yury I. Polyansky, a professor of genetics, lauding Lysenko's "brilliant achievements" and "the tremendous theoretical and practical significance of his work." The article attacked classical genetics, with its "many profound anti-Darwinist distortions that required Soviet biologists to subject the metaphysical principles of this science to sharp criticism."[14]

That afternoon, students at the university assembled to hear a lecture by Lysenko. He called upon them to reject everything they had been told over the years by Filipchenko, Vavilov, Karpechenko, and other geneticists. "The trouble is that some facts only seem to be facts," he said. Weismann, he declared, had cut off the tails of mice, but their offspring continued to be born with tails, hence the conclusion was drawn that the maiming was not transmitted by heredity. The Michurinists did not dispute this, but why? "Everyone knows that the tail is not involved in the formation and development of progeny; the tail is affected only very, very remotely in the hereditary relationship of parent and offspring."[15]

Subsequently, Karpechenko became the object of harsh attacks. The university newspaper proclaimed that "the genetics department remains a stronghold of reactionary doctrines. The university administration should draw a suitable conclusion from this fact." Prezent's wife, Potashnikova, who was a lecturer and a Party official at the university, warned everyone that Karpechenko was "doomed." At the end of the year, he was dismissed from the VIR and soon thereafter from the university. He was arrested February 15, 1941.[16] Govorov was arrested at the same time. Levitsky, Flyaksberger, Kovalev, and Maltsev were arrested on June 28, 1941. All were falsely accused, sentenced to be shot, and rehabilitated after Stalin's death. [Added in proof: For new information about these arrests, see p. 357.]

The commission investigating the VIR delivered its report at a meeting of the presidium of VASKhNIL in November. The agronomist Eikhfeld chaired the commission; the other members were Shlykov; Ivan A. Sizov; Mosolov, vice-president of VASKhNIL; and the agronomists Teterev and Zubarev, the latter a member of the collegium of the Commissariat of Agriculture. After hearing the report, the presidium adopted a resolution, signed by Lysenko, declaring that "the institute has not coped with the tasks assigned to it"; that it was "now difficult to determine the scientific and practical value of the samples" in the institute's seed collections; that "study of the collections was incorrectly organized and has not yielded conclusions useful to farming and science" and that "careless storage of the collections caused the loss of samples"; and that the institute "has done too little to introduce promising varieties into agriculture." The resolution ordered most of the institute's activities and collections to be transferred to other institutions, and many of its departments and laboratories to be shut down. Eikhfeld was appointed the new director.[17] The nation's (and perhaps the world's) finest scientific institution in the field of agronomy was thus destroyed. The directors and leading researchers of a number of other institutes were arrested at the same time.

One long-standing target of Lysenko's attacks escaped arrest, but must still be accounted a victim of these repressions: In December 1940, Koltsov died suddenly. His death was surely hastened by his summons to be a witness in Vavilov's case and by repeated interrogations by the NKVD. One of the world's greatest scientists had died, and no one was allowed to honor his memory.

Vavilov in Detention

Lysenko had eliminated Vavilov as a scientist and a leader of science, and he had destroyed Vavilov's institutes, but Vavilov remained alive. However, the NKVD was putting its own form of pressure on him. On August 24, 1940, after less than two weeks in a Lubyanka cell, but following twelve hours of continuous interrogation, Vavilov gave in and, like many others in the same situation—whether because they could no longer bear the beatings and torture or because they believed that false admissions would save their lives—he signed a confession: "I admit to being guilty of having participated since 1930 in an Anti-Soviet Delegation of Rightists in the system of the USSR Commissariat of Agriculture."[18] He may have been instructed to date his conspiratorial activity from 1930 in view of the fact that the NKVD file of secret agents' reports on him started in 1931.

Although the interrogation let up when Vavilov wrote this confession, he was still required to concoct a statement about "sabotage" in the VIR when it had been under his direction. According to Popovsky, who found the statement in the NKVD archives, Vavilov described as sabotage "such 'malign' acts as enlarging the sown areas, establishing narrowly specialized institutes, and raising corn—acts approved by Party agencies and included in state plans signed by the same persons who sanctioned his arrest."[19]

In his statement, Vavilov named Yakovlev, Chernov, Eikhe, Muralov, Gaister, Gorbunov, Volf, Chernykh (vice-president of VASKhNIL), Tulaikov, and Meister as fellow-plotters. It was a strange list: a commissar, two deputy commissars, Lenin's secretary and the chief scientific secretary of the AN SSSR, and presidents and vice-presidents of VASKhNIL. Did he put these names down because he knew that all of them had been shot or had died in prison and were beyond further harm? If his interrogators had dictated the list, it had to be on orders from above. Who else would want to lump together the whole past agrarian leadership of the country? If it was Stalin himself—in an effort to deflect blame for the country's agricultural troubles—then he may have been planning to charge the "delegation of rightists" in a show trial like the trials of Trotskyites and Bukharinites. That might explain why the investigation dragged on so long, by the standards of those times: Almost a year passed between the "confession" of August 24, 1940, and the sentencing of Vavilov on July 9, 1941.

There is another possible explanation: that during the two weeks of interrogation, Vavilov resolved to cook up such an absurd story that it would reach the highest ears, cause delay, and perhaps enable him to prove his innocence. This seems unlikely, since Vavilov was taunted sadistically during the investigation and would have wanted to get it over with quickly. Popovsky relates that the following exchange took place at the beginning of each interrogation session: His interrogator, Khvat, asked, "Who are you?" "I am Academician Vavilov." "You're a bag of shit, not an academician."[20] Moreover, to associate his name with such an organization as "a delegation of rightists" was a sure way to mount the scaffold, and we know that Vavilov wanted to live: He wrote appeals begging to be sent to the front, to serve in a penal battalion such as was given suicidal missions in battle.

We do not know which, if any, of these speculations is correct. We know only that the investigation continued. At some point—whether before or after the confession is not clear—Vavilov addressed a letter to Beria, then head of the NKVD, declaring, "I never betrayed my motherland either in thought or deeds, I never participated in any form of espionage for foreign states, I never engaged in counterrevolutionary activity, but devoted myself entirely to scientific research."[21]

When the case came to trial in July 1941, it had taken on a somewhat different character. The fact that war had been declared with Germany less than a month before, on June 21, 1941, may have influenced this change of strategy on the part of the NKVD. Instead of a "rightist delegation" network involving the entire agrarian leadership, only a small group of Vavilov's scientific colleagues—no commissars or Party chiefs—was charged, and the crimes they were alleged to have committed were commonplace ones for those times. Accused with Vavilov were Karpechenko and Govorov, former heads of laboratories of Vavilov's institute; Anton K. Zaporozhets, director of the Institute of Fertilizers and Soil Science, who was not closely associated with Vavilov; and Boris A. Panshin, director of the Sugar Beet Institute (whom Vavilov even disliked). The investigation now moved quickly.

To provide expertise regarding Vavilov's scientific activity, a commission was formed consisting of Deputy Commissar of Agriculture Chuyenkov; Mosolov and Zubarev, who had been members of the Eikhfeld commission; Academician Yakushkin of VASKhNIL; and D. Vodkov, a plant breeder from the Kamennaya Steppe Experimental Station. The list of members was approved by Lysenko,[22] and the commission worked under the supervision of NKVD Major Shundenko.

During the 1955 hearings preceding Vavilov's rehabilitation, Zubarev gave the following testimony about how this commission provided its "expertise":

> Major Shundenko summoned me and Chuyenkov to headquarters and told us we had to provide expert judgment for the Vavilov case. I don't recall the details. . . . I remember, however, that our commission never met as a whole and conducted no inquiry . . . but when we were presented with a prepared text—I don't know who wrote it—we signed it. I had to sign. Not to do so would have been difficult, given the circumstances.[23]

For his part, Yakushkin told the hearings:

> Apparently I was chosen because, as a secret collaborator of the NKVD, I could be counted on to provide the desired conclusions in the Vavilov case. . . . Commission members Vodkov, Chuyenkov, Mosolov, and Zubarev were hostile toward Vavilov. Vodkov simply hated him. Chuyenkov was under Lysenko's strong influence and a natural enemy of Vavilov. Zubarev was in Lysenko's employ and strongly influenced by him, and Mosolov, one of Lysenko's aides, was another Vavilov enemy.[24]

Many years later, when I was a student at the Timiryazev Agricultural

Academy, I saw Academician Yakushkin often. He had short hair and a goatee and always wore a tightly buttoned khaki military tunic and riding breeches, like Stalin. Pinned to his blouse were medal ribbons from which hung several gold medals bearing Stalin's silhouette and palm leaves, the emblems of a Stalin Prize winner. The impression he gave was that of a distant, aloof maestro, with an air of importance, majesty, and wisdom. His lectures were elaborately staged, with many colorful charts and with demonstrators and aides scurrying to and fro. However, at the end of 1955 his hauteur abruptly disappeared, and he became absent-minded and forgetful. Students often saw him walking late at night. Sometimes he appeared plunged in thought, at other times incomprehensibly agitated. He continued to wear the military tunic with the Stalin Prize medals—but sometimes with only underpants below this tunic. People said he was losing his mind. We know now that the prosecutor's office had begun to summon him to explain the secret false accusations he had sent the NKVD in the past, and that Vavilov was one of his victims. He was tormented by fear of possible retribution, and the torment deprived him of sleep and memory. He did not survive long.[25]

But Vavilov's chief persecutor, Trofim Lysenko, was not summoned to explain. He had not done the dirty work personally. The Yakushkins, Shundenkos, Chuyenkovs, and Khvatses had done it at his direction.

All the circles of hell through which Vavilov had passed prior to his trial were as nothing compared to what awaited him now. He was allowed to see the charges against him only the day before the tribunal met. They included not only sabotage but also treason, espionage, and counterrevolution. Vavilov immediately wrote a denial of the accusations, saying they were based on slander and falsehood and were entirely unconfirmed by the investigation.[26] His protest was ignored. The tribunal ruled that all the points in the indictment had been proved, and it condemned him to execution by firing squad. The trial took five minutes.[27]

Vavilov wrote a plea for mercy. Beria petitioned the presidium of the Supreme Soviet to reduce the sentence to a long term of imprisonment, and the petition was apparently granted, but a new obstacle arose. Vavilov was transferred to a Saratov jail, whence he wrote to Beria on April 25, 1942:

On August 1, 1941, three weeks after sentencing, your representative in the Butyrka prison [in Moscow] told me that you had applied to the presidium of the USSR Supreme Soviet to reduce the sentence and give me the gift of life. On your instructions, I was transferred from the Butyrka jail to the inner prison of the NKVD on October 4, 1941, and on October 5 and 15 I had talks with your representative about my attitude toward the war and fascism and about using me as a scientist of wide experience. On October 15, I was told I would be granted every opportunity for scientific work as an academician, and that this would be finally arranged within two or three days. But three hours after this talk, on that same day, October 15, 1941, I was moved to Prison No. 1 in Saratov in connection with an evacuation, and there, for lack of accompanying documentation about the rescinding of the sentence and your institution of proceedings for its amendment, I was again placed on death row, where I remain to this day.[28]

Vavilov had no way of knowing what this "evacuation" was about; he may have believed that his transfer to Saratov had to do with a clash over his personal fate. But it was instead the fate of Moscow and perhaps of all Russia that was at stake that night. For on the evening of October 14, 1941, Stalin had received the news that the Germans were at the gates of Moscow. Government offices began to burn their records; the subway was ordered shut and the escalators removed. Panic set in. In the courtyard of the Scientists' Club, long lines formed for travel permits that were being issued to certain scientists, granting them space in a train leaving Moscow. Prokofyeva-Belgovskaya and a fellow biologist, Miliya N. Engelgardt-Lyubimova, were assigned to distribute the permits. Prokofyeva-Belgovskaya has recalled that night:

We wrote out a pile of travel orders on ordinary slips of paper, stamped them with the rubber stamp of the AN [SSSR], and went on handing them out for several hours.

I went home, exhausted. I dropped on the sofa without removing my coat. The steady ringing of the telephone woke me. I was dazed. I lifted the receiver and heard my brother, a colonel in the Stalin Military Academy of Mechanization and Motorization, saying: "Go to the Kursk railway station immediately. I'll wait for you at the main entrance."

A crush of women, children, and old people filled the square in front of the railroad station. The cold was piercing. Children were weeping, the hubbub was indescribable, but people stood patiently. The submissiveness of those thousands amazed me. Between one hundred and two hundred soldiers formed a chain blocking the entrance to the station. I made my way to the front, where my brother took me through into the station. Here quiet reigned, the lights glowed brightly, and high officials and their wives stood about in clusters. Here and there I heard laughter, probably someone telling a joke. On the platform, well-dressed women, some in furs, stood around the doors of a waiting train. Large containers were labeled "Handle with care—crystalware," "Handle with care—paintings—this side up." Some soldiers carefully wheeled a piano along the platform. . . .

I have often thought about who are the people and who are the elite, and felt that the gap between them led to no good. To this day, the slavish patience of the people amazes me. That night they could have forced their way into the station and filled the half-empty trains that were laden with paintings and crystal chandeliers.[29]

Many government offices were evacuated from Moscow that night. Automobiles bearing those who could claim space in them filled the road to Gorky. I remember the day of October 16 vividly. It was my fifth birthday. We lived in Gorky, in a gloomy, gray, six-story building in a complex called the Communism Houses, behind the drama theater in the center of town. The small square between our building and the theater was packed bumper to bumper with the cars that brought evacuees from Moscow. Uninvited guests appeared in our apartment. Early in the morning, an officer came to tell my mother that we had to "double up." The wife of Party Central Committee Secretary A. S. Shcherbakov and their son took one of our two rooms. The government of the Latvian Republic occupied a single room off the landing on our floor of the building.

When the Moscow officialdom took flight on that fateful night, all important prisoners were removed from the Lubyanka. That was the circumstance that prevented Vavilov from benefiting from Beria's "clemency." Vavilov's appeal to the NKVD chief continued:

Despite my considerable physical stamina, I have developed scurvy in the difficult conditions of death row (no exercise, no receipt of packages, no commissary for purchases, no soap, usually no reading matter, etc.). The Saratov prison chief tells me that my situation and indeed my fate depend entirely on the central authorities.

It is my intention to go on, as befits a Soviet scientist, to complete much unfinished work for the benefit of the Soviet people and my motherland. When I was allowed pencil and paper in the inner NKVD prison [in Moscow] during the investigation of the case, I wrote a big book, *A History of the Development of World Agriculture (World Agricultural Resources and Their Utilization)*, with chief attention to the USSR. Before my arrest, I had completed a work of many years, *Combating Plant Disease by the Introduction of Resistant Varieties*. Other works remain uncompleted: *Field Crops of the USSR; World Resources of Grain Varieties and Their Use in the Soviet Breeding Program; Plant-Breeding in the Caucasus (Its Past, Present, and Future)*, and a major study, *Origins of Agriculture on Five Continents*, incorporating the results of 25 years of travels in Asia, Europe, Africa, and North and South America.

I am 54 years old. I have a good deal of experience and knowledge, particularly in the field of plant cultivation; I am fluent in the leading European languages, and I would be happy to dedicate myself entirely to my motherland, to die doing work that benefits my country. I am sufficiently strong, both physically and morally, and in this difficult time for my motherland I would be glad to be put to use for the defense of the country in my specialty as a plant biologist working to increase food and industrially important crops.

I ask you, I beg you, to ease my lot, to clarify my fate, to let me know my destiny, to grant me work at my specialty, at least in modest fashion (as a researcher and teacher), and to allow me contact in one form or another with my family (my wife, two sons—one a Komsomol, probably in military service—and my brother, an academician and physicist), of whom I have had no word in more than a year and a half. I beg you earnestly to hasten the decision on my case.

N. Vavilov[30]

On June 23, 1942, Vavilov's death sentence was commuted to twenty years of "deprivation of freedom." But the reprieve came too late. He was dying of emaciation. In January 1943, he began to suffer from dystrophic diarrhea. He was moved from his cell to a hospital. Death came on January 23. His body was dumped in a common grave.[31]

One detail remains to be added. Even before Vavilov's rehabilitation, Lysenko continued to mention him publicly. When Lysenko's works were reissued in the early 1950s, he did not excise Vavilov's name from them, as he did with the names of others who had been arrested, such as that of Yakovlev, who had been his patron.

To many, this seemed strange. During the period of the Stalin "cult of personality," it was standard practice to condemn to oblivion anyone who had been arrested or executed. The name was simply excised, obliterated, never to be mentioned in public or cited in print, even in works of the past that had originally referred to him or her and were being republished. The individual simply disappeared from view, as if he or she had never existed, even if the person were still living. The only exceptions were Stalin's chief adversaries, whose names could be used by way of collective denunciations—Trotskyites, Zinovievites, Bukharinites, and the like. Hence, it was remarkable that Lysenko retained the references to Vavilov and never ceased to mention him. I think this was because for him Vavilov remained Enemy No. 1, a person whom he could never forget, and he continued to ascribe special significance to the disputes with him, even after hunger and torments brought Vavilov's life to an end in the Saratov prison in 1943.

Fighters, Appeasers, and Traitors

Vavilov's arrest gave the Lysenko forces fresh impetus in the struggle for power and enabled them to attack genetics and the geneticists more openly. This showed clearly during the discussion of the research program of the AN SSSR for 1941. A draft plan had been drawn up with Vavilov's participation and included a research program he had proposed as director of the Genetics Institute. The debate on the draft plan took place three months after his arrest.

A few days before the debate, the academy's Party bureau hastily summoned a caucus of the secretaries of the Party units in the academy's Moscow institutes and the academicians and institute heads who were Party members. The invitations, signed by Vice-President Shmidt, spoke of an "urgent meeting." How urgent may be gauged from the fact that the invitations were hand-delivered on the morning of October 30, 1940, for a meeting called for six o'clock that same evening. The outcome of the meeting was a resolution demanding research plans that would be "closer to practical needs." For the Lysenko forces, this meant dropping all research in "formal genetics" and replacing it with work along "Michurinist" lines.

At the general meeting of the academy a few days later, Shmidt delivered the report on the academy's research plans, following the guidelines laid down by the Party caucus. The next speaker, Vyshinsky, Stalin's henchman, who had just been elected to the academy, was much more threatening. Ranting and scolding, he picked the plan to pieces and demanded the elimination of everything connected with "criminal genetics." So great was the fear Vyshinsky inspired that Shmidt, a prominent Party member since 1918, a scientist noted for his work in geography and cosmogony, hero of the conquest of the Arctic Seas and a Hero of the Soviet Union, fainted.[32]

Even in these extremely difficult conditions, not everyone abandoned the struggle against Lysenkoism or accepted the role of appeaser or of traitor to scientific principles. One who continued the struggle was Vavilov's old friend and teacher, Academician Pryanishnikov. Pryanishnikov's contribution to science as a founder of agrochemistry had earned him great respect, even though it brought him neither many government awards nor lofty administrative positions. His daughter, V. D. Fedorovskaya, noted in her diary: "Father cannot stand falsehood in science. Strictly logical and absolutely precise in his research, he is merciless in exposing charlatans, careerists, and the unscrupulous."[33] Instead of quaking with fear when colleagues were arrested, he defended them publicly—for example, when Professor A. G. Doyarenko was arrested, and again in the mid-thirties when Tulaikov and the chemist Sh. R. Tsintsadze were arrested, and upon the arrest of twelve members, including Director Zaporozhets, of the Institute of Fertilizers and Soil Science, which Pryanishnikov had founded.[34] At about the same time, the assistant director, Sergei S. Sigarkin, and Professor Dikusar, both of whom were close to Pryanishnikov, were also arrested. Everyone naturally assumed that it would be Pryanishnikov's turn next. In an article carried by *Pravda* on September 4, 1937, a certain Ye. Lyashenko, an undistinguished staff member of the Institute of Fertilizers and Soil Science, denounced a project, the compilation of agrochemical maps, on which Pryanishnikov's department was working. The maps were an innovation, showing where, when, how much, and which fertilizers were needed. Today, one cannot imagine proper agrochemical service without such maps, but they aroused only suspicion in the minds of kolkhoz and sovkhoz officials. Lyashenko described them as "the fruit of sabotage," costing tens of millions of rubles and produced, without supervision by VASKhNIL or the Commissariat of Agriculture, by enemies of the people who yearned for restoration of the kulaks. He charged that the agricultural authorities had failed to "crush this enemy nest."[35] Two weeks later, *Socialist Agriculture* echoed the charge.[36]

The epicenter of the Stalin purges was shifting from Party and economic circles to biology and agronomy. The earlier purges had been the consequence of a struggle for power. The new focus on biology and agronomy stemmed from the gross failures in agriculture and the desire to blame them on ritual scapegoats, specialists from an "alien class."

"Activists" demanded the convening of a plenary session of VASKhNIL's section on agrochemistry and soil science. When the session opened, on the morning of November 14, 1937, the participants found copies of *Socialist Agriculture* awaiting them on their chairs, containing another article by Lyashenko. He cited his earlier *Pravda* article as if it had been a Party directive to do away with soil maps, which he claimed were calculated to obtain minimal harvests and which he said were entirely beyond the comprehension of collective farmers. Besides, they represented servile kowtowing to foreign agrochemistry.[37] In the following days, each issue of *Socialist Agriculture* carried reports assailing Pryanishnikov in a rising crescendo. One of several reports signed only "S. B." referred to speeches by "kolkhoz-farmer-academicians."[38]

Pryanishnikov was not frightened or silenced. When speakers talked of "enemies of the people," Pryanishnikov demanded that they confine their remarks to scientific questions. When the four-day session had ended, *Socialist Agriculture* reported that the meeting's plenum had "condemned Academician Pryanishnikov's remarks and his behavior at the session as unworthy of a Soviet scientist."[39]

A while later, the paper accused Pryanishnikov of opposing the elimination of saboteurs; the headline on the story read, "Mercilessly Root Out Enemies and Their Rabble from Scientific Institutions."[40] This could hardly be seen as anything other than an incitement to arrest him.

Yet Pryanishnikov continued to fight the unequal battle. After Vavilov had been arrested, Pryanishnikov fought for his former student's release. He plagued President Komarov of the AN SSSR, a cautious, temporizing person, to appeal to Molotov, Beria, and others on Vavilov's behalf. Together with Vavilov's brother, Sergei, he visited Beria and Molotov to seek a review of the charges against Vavilov and his rehabilitation. When they turned him down, he went back to Molotov with a request to lighten the prison regime so that Vavilov might continue his scientific research there. The request went unanswered.[41] He was then bold enough to submit Vavilov's works in 1941 for a Stalin Prize.[42]

He continued to voice sharp and repeated criticisms of Lysenko and Lysenko's followers. In the spring of 1941, for example, he wrote a letter to Beria, saying that Lysenko, as president of VASKhNIL, had "disorganized the academy's work. The academy essentially has ceased to exist. There is only the president-commander and a staff subservient to him. Meetings are never held to discuss scientific questions, there are no elections of academicians. . . . The president says, 'Why do I need new academicians, when I don't even know what to do with those we have?'"[43] In 1943, upon publication of Lysenko's article "Heredity and Its Variability,"[44] Pryanishnikov sent a telegram to the president of the AN SSSR demanding that the academy consider the question of expelling the author of that uniquely illiterate work.[45] And on September 18, 1944, at a time when Lysenko was unrivaled in his domination over biology, Pryanishnikov sent the academy a long memorandum, demolishing, point by point, Lysenko's draft annual report of the academy's biology division. It is worth quoting at length both because it is a vivid example of Pryanishnikov's courage and because it was an important step in the destruction of the myth of Lysenko's "great contributions" to science and agriculture:

> I find many errors in the genetics section of the draft report that was sent to me for review. They must be eliminated, I believe, if the reputation of the USSR Academy of Sciences is to be maintained.... Pages 51–52 present abstract, metaphysical reasoning suggestive of a return almost to the epoch of phlogiston, including many anonymous, inaccurate statements to which the division and the academy as a whole cannot subscribe. One such is the confused thesis that heredity is "the quality of a living body that demands definite conditions for its development and life." This has nothing to do with heredity.
>
> The assertion that "Academician Lysenko represents the Michurin school in genetics" is also wrong. Lysenko has nothing in common with Michurin. The latter was primarily a hybridizer, and it was quite logical for him to speak of the training of an individual specimen (a long-lived tree), but Lysenko speaks of "training" annual plants as creating new forms that pass on their characteristics to future generations.... The fundamental point is that Lysenko does not and cannot represent a new direction in genetics because *he is not a geneticist at all*.... [He] is not conducting a single bit of genetic research in the Genetics Institute.... The research there consists of elementary agrotechnology work or primitive questions of physiology (such as the release from dormancy)....
>
> [His] book *Heredity and Its Variability* contains no new ideas or findings and amazes one by its abstractions, such as "winding and unwinding" [the concept that the organism develops through the unwinding of an inner spring wound up by past generations and itself winds up the spring for future generations]; it is filled with errors of elementary natural science....
>
> In his latest speeches, such as at the Commissariat of the Food Industry, Academician Lysenko himself no longer calls himself a geneticist, but an agrobiologist, i.e., a representative of elementary, undifferentiated experimentation employing *no scientific method*, not even a correct method of field experiment, since the absence of repetition deprives a field experiment of proof....
>
> The appearance abroad of such a book as *Heredity and Variability* would undermine the reputation of Soviet science. Measures should therefore be taken to prevent this book from getting abroad, and in future the works of its author, claiming innovations in genetics, should undergo a competent scientific review.
>
> In addition, I consider it necessary to call attention to the heading on page 53, "Vegetative Hybridization of Plants." To me, the term is as much an oxymoron as "hot ice" or "dry water." No claim that the term is "generally accepted" can be convincing ... and no citation of authorities will help, since an error of logic should not be passed over in silence, regardless of who introduced the error. The Academy of Sciences should not place its seal on inaccurate terminology.[46]

Pryanishnikov's biographer, Oleg N. Pisarzhevsky (himself one of the first journalists to write against Lysenkoism in the 1950s), concluded that this uncompromising courage and outspokenness is what saved Pryanishnikov's life. The fate, by contrast, of another leading agricultural expert, Dr. Pyotr G. Shitt, who faced similar assaults, suggests that outspokenness was the best defense: Shitt failed to defend himself, remained silent, and was arrested.

The stands taken by Pryanishnikov, Konstantinov, Koltsov, Lisitsyn, and other biologists undoubtedly laid the groundwork for the exposure, a quarter of a century later, of the proponents of unscientific views. But even in those earlier times, many were put on guard by the discrepancy between speeches about innovations that would shower blessings upon Soviet agriculture and the reality of agriculture's miserable condition. In a once bountiful land, with the world's largest sown area and pasturage, the shortages of the most basic foodstuffs grew worse and worse. It was not just Lysenko's fault, of course, but was also a result of the socialization and mismanagement of agriculture, yet he contributed in no small measure.

Others who refused to yield to the dictates of the Lysenkoists showed their courage in different ways. V. P. Efroimson went to prison for an open defense of his views. Ya. L. Glembotsky, N. N. Sokolov, and B. N. Sidorov left Moscow for Yakutia, in Siberia, where they managed to go on with their scientific research. M. I. Kamshilov moved to an Arctic outpost on the Kola Peninsula in the Barents Sea; Ye. N. Vasin and B. N. Vasin went to Sakhalin, and R. B. Khesin to Kaunas, in Lithuania. Yu. Ya. Kerkis became chairman of a sheep-herding kolkhoz in Central Asia. S. S. Chetverikov preferred to retire as a pensioner, and S. N. Ardashnikov, V. V. Sakharov, and others simply gave up scientific research altogether.

However, the great majority of biologists, not to mention the lower-level personnel of agricultural science, were appeasers. Some did not see or did not want to see the unscientific nature of Lysenko's proposals. For those who lacked serious scientific grounding, following Lysenko was a protection against criticism by real scientists. Most of these specialists, trained under the abbreviated teaching programs and with the Michurinist textbooks introduced by the Lysenko forces, did not know enough science to distinguish truth from falsehood in Lysenko's arguments and terminology. It was they who constituted the bulwark of support for Lysenkoism.

Finally, there were the knowledgeable ones who understood Lysenko's tactics quite well but nevertheless chose to join his camp, partly out of fear, partly out of a desire for their own advancement, and partly out of a desire for public recognition. They were the ones who believed "Paris is worth a mass."

Academician Boris M. Zavadovsky of VASKhNIL was one such. In contrast to his brother, M. M. Zavadovsky (see chapter 8), he praised Lysenko personally, particularly at the 1936 academy session at which the geneticists first rose to challenge Lysenko's ideas. "The geneticists cannot explain Lysenko's great scientific achievements," he said, "they cannot define the place of his doctrines in the system of the biological sciences."[47] He spoke in this vein until the August 1948 session of the academy, when he performed an about-face and finally came out openly and boldly against

Lysenko's errors. He then called him dictatorial, opposed the views of Lysenko to those of Darwin, and protested against the administrative persecution of geneticists. "We should criticize Sakharov, Navashin, and Zhebrak when they commit scientific errors, but when I heard a summons here to crush the Mendelist-Morganists and forbid them the opportunity to work, the harm that such acts would cause the national economy became entirely clear to me."[48]

But other equally good scientists never admitted to seeing the harm Lysenko did. For example, N. I. Nuzhdin had studied under Vavilov and worked with him. He conducted research for a doctoral dissertation in classical genetics, but reshaped it to fit the Lysenkoist mold and went on to serve Lysenko the rest of his life, earning by way of payment the rank of corresponding member of the AN SSSR (though Lysenko's and Khrushchev's efforts to raise him to the rank of academician were blocked by the courageous stand taken by Academicians I. Ye. Tamm, Andrei D. Sakharov, and V. A. Engelgardt).

Mikhail Ye. Lobashev, despite his training as a geneticist, produced a monograph that purported to show that Russian livestock breeding had proceeded independently of Western animal husbandry and had surpassed it in every respect. "An original Russian theory of selection arose long before Darwin," he asserted. Although he had devoted many years to the study of gene mutation, trying (unsuccessfully) to discover induced mutagenesis, he proceeded to disavow the field: "The theory of Morganism-Weismannism has proved impracticable [and] impotent." "To underestimate scientific discoveries and consign them to oblivion is characteristic of bourgeois science, divorced from the people," he wrote. "Only Soviet Michurinist biology undertook to study the rich experience of the people . . . and applied it to socialist animal husbandry."[49]

Abba O. Gaisinovich, who considered himself a student of Serebrovsky's, translated chapters of the American genetics textbook of Sinnott and Dunn into Russian.[50] When such ventures became awkward, however, he switched to the "safe" sphere of the history of science and provided a commentary on the works of the famous Russian scientist Ilya I. Mechnikov, who had worked on immunology in Paris from 1887 until his death in 1916 and had been vice-director of the Pasteur Institute. Gaisinovich's observations were of the following sort:

> Not in the least embarrassed to differ with Darwin himself on natural selection, Mechnikov provided talented and independent further development of this question. Mechnikov's depth and profundity stand out sharply if one compares his conclusions with the mutation theory that arose a quarter of a century later and led to the most anti-Darwinist and metaphysical conclusions. . . . The narrowness of the Darwinist concept of mutability as a gradual and continuous process of the appearance of small changes was obvious to Mechnikov. . . . As is well known, Academician T. D. Lysenko today ascribes central significance in species formation to sudden changes. . . . It is important to note that Mechnikov

took a position close to the Michurinist teaching on the causes of hereditary mutability. . . .

Mechnikov's views on questions of hereditary mutability took shape before Weismann began to propound his fantastic and idealistic "germ plasma theory," but even after that, Mechnikov was hostile . . . to the new "nuclear theory of heredity" and criticized it.[51]

Aleksandr S. Krivisky was another geneticist who betrayed the training he had received. Krivisky had been a student in the laboratory of Academician Georgy A. Nadson (who perished in prison), he read English and German and was well informed about progress in world science, yet he made such pronouncements as, "Contrary to the opinion of many foreign Morganist microbiologists, the external environment can . . . change the hereditary qualities of cells," and "Michurinist biology has definitely established that hereditary qualities are not transmitted through reduplication of hypothetical hereditary units, but by the assimilation of formative substances, particularly clearly manifested in the processes of vegetative hybridization."[52] Elsewhere, Krivisky maintained that "vegetative hybridization" goes on in the world of microbes, that what he called "the notorious 'genes'" did not exist in nature, that the postulates of Lysenkoism had been firmly established, and that, "contrary to Morganist fabrications, the organism is never in a state of complete rest"—although he surely knew that geneticists had never voiced such nonsense and although he himself had studied gene mutation. Indeed, he had seen his colleagues in Nadson's laboratory demonstrate, for the first time ever, the mutability of genes under both radiation and chemical influence.[53] He also wrote that "after the historic session of VASKhNIL which utterly demolished Weismannism-Morganism, Soviet microbiology completely rid itself of those false doctrines"; that the unproved assertion of Sergei N. Muromtsev (see chapter 12) that some microorganisms change into others was correct; and that "T. D. Lysenko's well-known statement that the formation of new species proceeds through a noncellular state is completely applicable to microorganisms."[54]

Many of the appeasers later made a 180° turn when Lysenko lost power. Lobashev produced a genetics textbook for higher educational institutions, Gaisinovich tossed off articles on the history of genetics, and Krivisky headed the biology abstracts journal. A particularly striking example of this cynical maneuvering was Sos Alikhanyan. Early in his career, he had been the director of a small club, but he developed an interest in the philosophy of natural science and then—without obtaining an education in biology—he participated in the genetics discussions in the late 1930s on the side of the geneticists. He was appointed to the biology department of Moscow State University, where he gave popular lectures on genetic theory and was an activist in the Party organization. But he had to confess to errors (see chapter 10), casting the blame on his teachers, after which he turned to ardent preaching of the Michurinist doctrine. He declared he had discovered no less than vegetative hybridization in microorganisms. With the support of the Lysenkoists, he defended a doctoral dissertation on vegetative hybridization and repeatedly sought—in vain—to become a corresponding member of, first, the Armenian Academy of Sciences and then the USSR Academy of Sciences. But unexpectedly the winds shifted and, when the Lysenko forces had suffered setbacks, Alikhanyan sounded the retreat just as loudly as he had sounded the charge. At a conference in 1965 at Moscow State University, attended by several hundred persons (including myself), he declared that there had been a mistake: It seems he had discovered not vegetative hybridization at all, but something else, the process of exchange of genetic information among microbes, a process also described in the West by Joshua Lederberg, who won a Nobel Prize for that discovery, but, of course, *after* Alikhanyan had made the discovery. Faina M. Kuperman, a professor at the university and a supporter of Lysenko, shouted to Alikhanyan from the front row, loud enough for the whole auditorium to hear: "So when were you lying—before or now?" Alikhanyan became a prominent figure among the organizers of the new genetics in the USSR and was named director of the Research Institute on the Genetics and Selection of Industrial Microorganisms as well as a professor in the department of genetics and selection of Moscow State University (see also chapter 14).

Perhaps the most egregious case of the chameleon-like character of the appeasers is that of Grigory Shlykov, one of the most vicious calumniators of Vavilov. After World War II, Shlykov was tried and sentenced to several years in a labor camp.[55] He was freed after Stalin's death, and in 1962 he submitted a dissertation to the Georgian Agricultural Institute for the degree of doctor of agricultural sciences.[56] In it, he refers repeatedly to Vavilov as virtually a personal friend—no longer an enemy of the motherland, but a patriot. Vavilov, he writes, gave unprecedented scope to the work of utilizing new plant varieties, and he dwells upon the wealth of sources tapped by the VIR in China, India, Korea, Vietnam, Indonesia, and the Americas, and upon the institute's "broad and purposeful" role in introducing new plants and new varieties. He even had the effrontery to write:

> Here, in working contact with N. I. Vavilov, we gave birth to the idea of the need to work out the introduction of plants as a system of experiment and knowledge, a new plant-breeding discipline. In 1931, Vavilov entrusted to the author of this dissertation and P. M. Zhukovsky the task of organizing and heading the system of experimental points for the testing of new cultures in various zones of the USSR.

Yet Shlykov also lists among his own works his book *The Introduction of Plants*, which Vavilov had said was "unsurpassed as a distorting mirror," and his articles of the 1930s in which he called Vavilov an enemy of the state and described his activities as sabotage. He probably assumed that young scientists would not be inclined to dig out old journals; and as for the archives of the NKVD, they were sealed.

The conclusion of the dissertation is the greatest stroke of virtuosity of all. The author takes issue with the international rules of plant nomenclature and declares his intention of capitalizing the designations of plants named in honor of individual scientists, because his moral principles would not allow him to demean great scientists by using lower case. He gives only a single example: Vavilov wheat, *Triticum Vavilovi.* "We . . . deliberately write it [not *T. vavilovi* but] *T. Vavilovi.*"[57]

What about Lysenko himself? Could one do greater harm to one's country than he did? And did he realize what he had done? Was it ignorance that lay behind his gloomy exterior? Boundless ambition? Blind adaptation of all his actions to the ideology of the leaders? Surely Lysenko and his ilk knew that the leaders' "miracle" of the transformation of history, like Lysenko's own "miracle" of the transformation of nature, was a chimera. Knowing that the promised miracles were bound to fail, did they decide that only terror and hysterical alarms over "internal and foreign enemies" could force the majority to obey submissively? Or were the Lysenkos programmed to act like automatons, like drivers who automatically obey road signs?

I do not believe that Lysenko was simply Stalin's blind tool. Lysenko's attraction to miracles and his faith in them was born of the wider faith in a shining future that underlay all the dreams of the "transformation of nature." Faith in miracles took the place of science, just as faith in social transformations moved the leaders of the new society. That is why those leaders eagerly welcomed every prophecy of Lysenko's. Like addicts who realize the harm of their addiction yet still pursue the narcotic, these leaders recognized the deception yet wanted to be deceived. When the promised miracles failed, the Lysenkoists did not turn back to science; instead, they drew up even more unreal plans, issued even more glowing reports, and so it went in a dizzying spiral.

10

Lysenko's Support Falters

Many people went to the meeting,
  Made plans, gathered their stuff, making
    ready to get things moving.
  But as personalities, they were blanks,
    mere marionettes.

—Boris Pasternak, "Spektorsky,"

Obviously we had no intention of turning off from the Leninist
path. . . . True, we had to beat up some of the comrades. But there's
no helping that. I must admit I had a hand in it. (Stormy applause,
shouts of "Hurrah!")

—J. V. Stalin, May 6, 1935

Lysenko at the Farm at Lenin Hills

Upon becoming president of VASKhNIL in 1938, Lysenko sought a base
in Moscow, one that had fields with good soil and with water for irrigation,
close to the capital and easy of access. He found the ideal spot in a
picturesque, well-appointed old estate, about twenty miles southeast of
Moscow, known as Lenin's Hills.[1] It included a complex of attractive, elegantly furnished buildings erected in the eighteenth century on the banks
of the Pakhra River. The estate had a fine road from Moscow and a direct
telephone line to government offices. When the capital was transferred
from Petrograd to Moscow, following the revolution in 1918, Lenin chose
this estate as his country residence, keeping the furnishings as they were.
He went there almost daily, traveling in two armor-plated Rolls-Royces.
Kalinin, the chairman of the Central Executive Committee and thus the
official—but powerless—president of the country, also found a country
seat for himself near Gorki. The Council of Commissars established a farm
nearby to provide for the needs of both these government-owned retreats.
The farm was large, about 1,500 hectares (3,700 acres), and naturally it
was very well maintained, with fine barns, electric power, and good roads.

After Lenin's death in 1924, the estate was renamed Lenin Hills. It
remained in the possession of the Council of Commissars until 1938 and
was used to raise food for the tables of the Kremlin leaders. This farm
suited Lysenko's purposes. The residences on the estate, plus a small park,
became a Lenin museum, but the farm was turned over to Lysenko in
1938. Frequent mention of it in the press conveniently linked his name
with Lenin's.

Lysenko secured all kinds of privileges for his farm. He was granted exemption from obligatory delivery of the crop to the state at the official low prices; instead, the farm was permitted to sell its produce at open-market retail prices. He obtained the best farm machinery, fertilizers, and plenty of farm labor. Ordinarily, farmers might wait as long as six months before being paid for their work (and as a result they were constantly in debt to the village store), but at Lenin Hills the earnings and the bonuses for plan fulfillment were paid on time. Not surprisingly, the fields were always well tended, and the harvests were ample. For the rest of his life, Lysenko based his recommendations on the results obtained at this farm.

But holding up Lenin Hills as a standard for the country's kolkhozes amounted to yet another deception. The mechanisms of the deception became clear in a report submitted in 1965 by a commission of the AN SSSR that had been appointed to investigate the farm. In the first place, there was the chicanery of Lysenko's assistants, who loaded the soil with manure and fertilizers, then sprinkled it the following year with a "patent mixture" utterly lacking in nutritive value, and proceeded to declare this mixture miraculous; or they fattened the cattle on high-grade feed while assuring everyone that the cattle were getting the same diet as on an ordinary kolkhoz. Even more important, farming conditions here were utterly unlike those of other farms. As the report pointed out, its land was better cultivated; it had "ten tractors (15.5 in conventional tractor units), eleven trucks, two bulldozers, two excavators, and two combines, more than meeting the farm's needs"; its "basic assets" per unit of cultivated land were "nine times the average for sovkhozes of the Moscow region, its working assets triple, and its power capacity almost 2.5 times the average"; and "almost the entire grain output" of the farm remained with it "for its own needs, chiefly as feed."[2]

Lysenko began work at Lenin Hills in 1939. He brought his favorite collaborators there: Prezent, Dolgushin, Avakyan, and Mikhail A. Olshansky. The first year was occupied with settling down in the new place. Lysenko spent most of his time on the paperwork that he condemned so strongly in others.

The year 1938 passed in this manner, and 1939 as well. The debates with the geneticists required considerable preparation. He had to fight hard. As 1940 went on, the struggle against the geneticists intensified. Reorganizing the Genetics Institute after Vavilov's arrest was yet another claim on his time. He had to expel the people left behind by the previous director, assemble new personnel, and maneuver among his own followers to keep the reins in his own hands. When the Nazi invasion was launched in June 1941, no noteworthy research had yet been started at Lenin Hills.

The War Years

In the very first year of the war, the Nazis' seizure of vast territory comprising some of the best farm land made the already grave agricultural situation critical. Theoretical disputes were thrust aside; the scientists had to turn to practical tasks. Here, Lysenko made a contribution. In order to meet the crisis, land was turned over to individuals and families for garden plots. Most of these plots were planted to potatoes. Lysenko urged revival of the old practice of planting potato eyes while using the remainder of the potato for food. Many newspapers carried his directions on how to slice off peels containing the eyes and how to store them through the winter and spring. His advice helped to stave off famine—and spread his popularity among the people.

As the Wehrmacht advanced, factories, plants, and institutes were evacuated beyond the Urals. The institutes of the AN SSSR found themselves in Tashkent, Alma-Ata, Sverdlovsk (now Yekaterinburg), and other remote cities. Some laboratories of the Genetics Institute moved from Odessa to Frunze, in Central Asia (now Bishkek, or Pishpak); others operated in the Siberian Grain Research Institute in Omsk. At the latter, Lysenko often occupied a room next to the office of the director, Gavriil Ya. Petrenko, and he tried to effect a reorganization of that institute's work along his own lines.[3]

The autumn of 1941 was a cold one in Siberia and the Far East. As Lysenko traveled across Siberia and Kazakhstan, he realized that much of the grain could be lost to snow and frost, so he ordered that it be harvested even before it had ripened, in order to get whatever had managed to grow. No doubt, much grain was saved by this advice. Characteristically, though, he made exaggerated claims for the results: "I know of no instance in which the wheat harvest, when reaped according to our instructions, declined in yield or quality," he said in 1942.[4]

He engaged in other practical work: determining the germinating capacity of wheat stored in earthen mounds, and studying the possibility of shipping northern potatoes south for immediate planting. These were important questions in that difficult time, and although—or because—they required no scientific analysis, he dealt with them effectively. However, he could not refrain from promoting untested recommendations. He urged extensive summer planting of sugar beets in Uzbekistan, for example; because of the arid climate, the beets withered in their early stages.

Just before the outbreak of the war, Lysenko had once again promised to produce new winter-resistant grain varieties for Siberia in two to three years.[5] Having again failed, he then proposed a new method for planting local Siberian varieties: instead of plowing, to sow directly on the stubble left after cutting the spring grain, thereby saving tractor wear and tear, fuel, and labor. In addition, he claimed, the root system of the stubble would protect the newly planted seed against frost.[6] The idea of sowing directly on the stubble was borrowed from Tulaikov—as Khrushchev himself was later to acknowledge—but, being ignorant of the principles behind it, he garbled it. Neither the physical concept of the stubble's heat conductivity nor the mechanism for acquiring physiological resistance to cold was properly worked out. Despite the awe Lysenko had inspired in the provinces, the proposal met criticism from Siberian scientists, including institute director Petrenko, with whom Lysenko thereafter ceased to be on speaking terms. Lysenko appealed the issue to the USSR Commissariat of Agriculture, which ordered the method employed throughout Siberia. For fifteen years, it brought heavy losses, until in 1956 a Party journal admitted that the method was harmful; that Lysenko and his supporters, "ignoring obvious facts, . . . made unwarranted claims and branded as scientific conservatives those conscientious agricultural specialists who looked the facts in the face"; and that, "as a result, in the Omsk region alone, tens of thousands of hectares sown on stubble never yielded even so much as the seed that was planted." The journal neglected to mention that Party circles had backed Lysenko.[7]

Postwar Challenges to Lysenko

The war left agriculture in ruins all across the European USSR, and the inefficient kolkhoz system could not cope with the difficulties. Moreover, a severe drought struck all the farm regions, including not only the European USSR but Siberia and Kazakhstan as well, in 1946. The famine of 1947 is remembered as no less drastic and in some places more so than that of the war years. Lysenko, now the unchallenged master of Soviet agronomy and biology, was expected to produce scientifically based directions to alleviate the crisis, but he offered only recommendations that seemed futile and primitive even to lay observers and that evoked skepticism among some of the country's leaders.

There may have been another reason for a growing distrust of Lysenko. His brother, a metallurgical scientist living in Kharkov, had enjoyed Trofim's reflected glory. He was arrogant, conceited, and given to reporting people he disliked to the secret police.[8] When the Nazis occupied Kharkov, he placed himself in their service and was appointed mayor. When the Nazis were temporarily driven out of Kharkov, they took him with them and, upon regaining the city, reinstated him as mayor.[9] Lysenko may well have been worried about retribution for his brother's behavior. After all, being a "relative of an enemy of the people" was a crime under Stalinist-era law.

In 1945, the American journal *Science* carried an article by Zhebrak, describing the achievements of Soviet science but also presenting a candid, accurate, and unflattering criticism of Lysenko, saying that "many Soviet geneticists in no way support his attempt to reexamine and discard a number of the fundamental postulates of our science."[10] Politburo member Voznesensky had commissioned the article, and Shcherbakov, head of the Soviet Information Bureau and also a Politburo member, had specifically authorized its publication in the United States.[11] Its appearance abroad reflected the lack of enthusiasm toward Lysenko at this time.

There were other signs as well. In 1946, the AN SSSR began to set up an

institute to conduct research in cytology and genetics; among the supporters of this project were Vavilov's brother, Sergei, who had been elected
president of the academy in July 1945, and Zhebrak and Dubinin. Dubinin
himself was elected a corresponding member of the AN SSSR in the face
of fierce opposition from Lysenko.[12] A 1946 article by USSR Agriculture
Minister Benediktov said not a word about Lysenko or the Michurinists.[13]
And in February 1947, a resolution of the Party Central Committee expressed disapproval of some of Lysenko's ideas—accelerated selection
methods, the taboo on hybrid corn, and the replacement of winter wheat
with spring wheat in the Ukraine. The resolution noted the lack of good
winter wheat varieties for Siberian regions, despite Lysenko's claim that
such varieties had been developed under his direction, and it called for a
sharp improvement in plant breeding.[14] Another suggestive event was the
translation and publication in the Soviet Union of *What Is Life? The Physical Aspects of the Living Cell,* by Erwin Schrödinger, the Austrian physicist,
Nobel Prize winner, and one of the founders of quantum mechanics, who
had become interested in genetics. Finally, Lysenko's claims that Soviet
biology surpassed the "bourgeois" biology of the Western nations were no
longer as persuasive as they had been. Many people now had access to
information about the great progress in biology in the capitalist countries
and about the profits earned from hybrid corn alone. Lysenko himself was
forced to admit, at least orally, the benefit of inbred lines.[15]

Nevertheless, Lysenko retained his positions as president of VASKhNIL,
director of two institutes, and member of the Supreme Soviet. The question naturally arises: Why did the country's political and scientific leaders
not take steps to curtail his role and give agriculture a chance to emerge
from chaos? One reason may be that, in the conditions of political control
of science and the totalitarian management of the economy, Lysenko's
activities as a whole satisfied the system's requirements and were viewed as
an entity, regardless of individual mistakes. The failures were seen not as
logical consequences of the invalid theory underlying Lysenko's ideology,
but as isolated instances, atypical of the innovator. It is not by chance that
Lenin's adage, "The only person who makes no mistakes is the one who
does nothing," was a popular one in the USSR.

Another reason for the toleration of Lysenko was the fear of change,
the inevitable homeostasis of a totalitarian society. To make an abrupt
change in the leadership of an already weak agriculture could lead to even
worse consequences, and so the conclusion was drawn that it was better to
leave matters as they were. Finally, many, including people who stood near
the top of the hierarchy, knew how dangerous it was to challenge a Stalin
favorite, especially one who had proven his capacity to defame his critics
and to emerge unscathed from any situation.

Nonetheless, Lysenko had to defend himself, and he did so by once
again cloaking his political accusations in the language of scientific debate. He proceeded to take on the most fundamental propositions of

Darwinism. On November 5, 1945, he brought the staffs of the selection stations together in Moscow and delivered a long lecture to them, in which he proposed to save Darwinism from Darwin. The creator of the theory of evolution, he said, had uncritically accepted Malthus's idea of overpopulation: "If one studies nature carefully, it is not hard to perceive that such overpopulation as would arouse intraspecies competition does not occur." Indeed, "Species and varieties never reach the point of over-population; on the contrary, underpopulation is the invariable rule." Therefore, organisms of the same species do not compete for "a place in the sun" but instead help their species to flourish, often at the cost of their own lives.[16]

The biologists greeted Lysenko's new theory with scornful dismissal.[17] Lysenko tried to demonstrate the error of Darwin's central thesis by com-plicated arithmetical calculations. To the biologists, this brought to mind an earlier incident, when a graduate student of Lysenko's, N. I. Yermolayeva, had published the results of an experiment undertaken to demonstrate that the Mendelian laws of inheritance were wrong. To test the Mendelian ratio of 3:1 in the distribution of a clearly inherited characteristic, she repeated plants Mendel's experiment. In each of the families of hybrid plants, the outcome differed from the Mendelian prediction.[18] Geneticists pointed out, however, that, when data from all the families were com-bined, the ratio was close to 3:1 (2.8:1 and 2.7:1 in various experiments), but Lysenko took Yermolayeva's data as a decisive refutation of Mendelian genetics. "Mechanical" pooling of data from different families was, he insisted, irrational and was irrelevant to biology; if the rule was not borne out within families taken separately, the biological meaning of the Mende-lian law disappeared.[19]

A short while later, the preeminent Soviet mathematician A. N. Kolmogorov, in an analysis of Yermolayeva's data, drew two curves: the ideal, as predicted by theory, and the actual, using Yermolayeva's data. The curves coincided so strikingly that one might have suspected the data to have been contrived to create the closest correspondence with Mendel's law. Kolmogorov entitled his article "On a New Confirmation of Mendel's Laws."[20]

Nevertheless, beginning early in 1946, Lysenko—now styling himself the "heir" to Darwin's work—published a series of articles under the title "Natural Selection and Intraspecies Competition."[21] Piotr M. Zhukovsky, an academician of VASKhNIL, wrote a critical response.[22] Lysenko used two tactics to meet Zhukovsky's challenge. First, to create an impression of universal support of his new theory, he began to reprint his article "Natu-ral Selection and Intraspecies Struggle" over and over in various publica-tions.[23] This device also served to give the theory an appearance of exceptional significance in the eyes of lay people. If one and the same article was reprinted everywhere, it must be important. Then he struck a blow directly at Zhukovsky by publishing in *Pravda*, on June 28, 1948, an article in which he declared that Zhukovsky "thoroughly demonstrated his ignorance of the theory of Darwinism, as well as his great capacity for distorting the sense of the quotation of others whom he cited. . . . . My article denied intraspecies struggle and recognized interspecies struggle. Zhukovsky understood nothing of this because he has no comprehension of the elementary principles of Darwinian theory, yet nevertheless he chose to raise any and all objections."[24]

The article failed to intimidate the scientists. Lysenko began to hear rumors from one source after another that biologists—no longer just the geneticists—were preparing to challenge him. The combination of Kremlin dissatisfaction and scientific opposition could be disastrous.

Zhebrak Faces a Court of Honor

However, the political climate was changing in a way that gave Lysenko a fresh chance. Stalin, true to his doctrine that the class struggle grew sharper as the construction of socialism advanced, had been revising the forms of ideological pressure. By the end of the war, he realized the danger inherent in the fact that hundreds of thousands of soldiers had seen how people lived in capitalist countries and had become aware of the contrast with Soviet life. To counter it, the Kremlin propaganda machine began to ring all the variations on the themes of the ideological and technological backwardness of the West, the cunning of the imperialists, and the alien nature of the Western way of life. In August 1946, Zhdanov delivered the first of several "pogrom" speeches, about the "erroneous" stand of the literary magazines *Star* (Zvezda) and *Leningrad*. In the language of the day, a "pogrom" speech was one that incited an attack (not necessarily directed at Jews) against anyone who held ideologically incorrect views.[25] Speeches followed assailing composers, cinematographers, philosophers, and historians—even classicists who interpreted the slave uprisings in ancient Rome "incorrectly."

The millstones began to grind down the "chameleons" and "cosmopolites" who cherished the approval of Western colleagues more than the honor of their motherland. One ludicrous form of this newly appeared chauvinism was the flood of magazine and newspaper articles reminding readers that the steamboat, the locomotive, the telephone, the radio, and the airplane were all Russian inventions. "Yes, and Russia is the birthplace of the elephant" was the ironic whispered response of the skeptics. But it was no joking matter when the trials began, charging anyone suspected of Western sympathies as traitors and spies and imposing harsh sentences for those crimes.

Because of these political changes, Zhebrak's 1945 *Science* article—perceived at the time as a signal of official disapproval of Lysenko—could by 1947 be used as a club against its author. The Lysenkoists seized upon it as grounds for accusing the geneticist of nothing less than betrayal of the motherland. In an article published on March 6, 1947, in *Leningrad Pravda*,

Prezent declared, "The latest decisions of the Party Central Committee on ideological questions . . . require us to root out any remnants whatsoever of groveling before foreign trends and to boldly expose decaying and decadent bourgeois culture." Turning specifically to genetics, he said, "At the imperialist stage of its development, festering capitalism has brought forth a stillborn mongrel of biology, the thoroughly metaphysical, antihistorical doctrine of formal genetics." Quoting a similarly vitriolic passage from Stalin's *Problems of Leninism,* Prezent went on to denounce not foreign geneticists, but Soviet. He declared that the American journal *Science* was published by "one of the profascist obscurantists, Karl Sax . . . a malevolent foe of Marxism," and that Zhebrak was "singing the same tune as" Sax. "That is exactly what Timiryazev Academy Professor A. R. Zhebrak has done. In an article published abroad about a Sax speech, he has essentially aligned himself with the profascist Sax in appraising the theoretical achievements of our progressive Soviet school of biologists, the Michurinist school headed by Academician Lysenko." Actually, Zhebrak's article had criticized Sax, who, he said, had given "an incorrect estimate of the general position of biology in the USSR."[26] In spite of this, Prezent demanded that Zhebrak be "exposed and removed."[27]

When this article failed to achieve its purpose, other means were employed for the same end. On August 30, 1947, a letter signed by the writers Aleksei Surkov and Aleksandr T. Tvardovsky and the publicist Gennady Fish appeared in the *Literary Gazette,* saying, "We cannot overlook Zhebrak's malicious, slanderous statement that Lysenko's work essentially harms Soviet science and the claim that only the tireless efforts of Zhebrak and his fellow-thinkers will save science."[28] Three days later, *Pravda* carried an article by a little-known economist, Ivan D. Laptev (who signed himself "professor"), accusing Zhebrak of "betraying the interests of the motherland" and of "adopting the enemy camp's position." Many passages in Laptev's article repeated those of the writers' letter, indicating orchestration behind the scenes. His concluding words recalled the repressions of 1937: "Let us haul before the court of society those who stand in the way . . . of surpassing foreign scientific achievements in the shortest possible time . . . and whose antipatriotic acts disgrace our progressive Soviet science."[29]

A newly created institution was ideally suited to carrying out Laptev's demands. On March 2, 1947, at the suggestion of Zhdanov, the Party Central Committee had established "courts of honor" at the central ministries and administrative bodies.[30] When a criminal trial was deemed inappropriate, a group of colleagues trusted by the Party would be gathered to condemn the alleged misdeeds and to uphold the "honor" of the organization. Zhebrak held two positions: as a faculty member at Timiryazev Academy in Moscow and as president of the Belorussian Academy of Sciences in Minsk. As head of the department of genetics and plant breeding in the Timiryazev Academy, Zhebrak fell under the jurisdiction of the

Ministry of Higher Education. Its head, Kaftanov, a friend of Lysenko's, ordered such a court of honor to rule on the charges against Zhebrak.

The trial took place before a large audience. It was presided over by I. G. Kochergin, a surgeon who headed a branch of the Ministry of Higher Education. (Before the trial began, M. A. Suslov, a secretary of the Party Central Committee had given Kochergin instructions for conducting it.) Dubinin and N. V. Turbin, a doctor of science who enjoyed Lysenko's trust at the time (see chapter 4), addressed the court—although Turbin turned out to be less an accuser than a witness for the defense. Zhebrak defended himself calmly and skillfully, and the verdict was mild. The court reprimanded Zhebrak for having made "unpatriotic" remarks to an American audience, but it did not reproach him for his criticism of Lysenko or for describing him as an agronomist rather than as a geneticist.[31]

Nevertheless, Zhebrak was removed as president of the Belorussian Academy of Sciences soon afterward. State security police raided his apartment in Minsk with an order for his arrest, but he had hidden with friends. The Belorussian minister of state security, G. Tsanava, demanded that Zhebrak return to Minsk, apparently to face detention, but Zhebrak defied the order and escaped arrest.[32]

The general reaction among scientists was that Zhebrak had gotten off lightly, and that emboldened them to criticize Lysenko publicly. At the beginning of November 1947, a special conference was convened at Moscow State University to examine Lysenko's theories. It was held in the university's largest hall and drew an overflow audience of more than a thousand.[33] Academician Ivan I. Shmalgauzen and Professors Aleksandr N. Formozov and Dmitry A. Sabinin made objective presentations of the fallacies of Lysenkoism. According to those who were present, the chairman several times invited Lysenko's supporters in the auditorium to respond to the criticism, but they were silent. The Moscow State University Press also issued a collection of articles refuting the Lysenkoist viewpoint. A long article by the scientists who had spoken at the conference was published for a general audience, but it was accompanied by a reply by Lysenko's supporters. Branding the opponents of Lysenko "Malthusians" (and hence foes of Marxism), the Lysenkoists said of the Moscow State University "ignoramuses" that "theirs is not merely a political sally, but an attempt to pit the Soviet public against the Darwinist Lysenko."[34]

Two weeks after the conference, on November 18, 1947, the *Literary Gazette* carried a flattering interview with Lysenko, in which he tried to explain why bourgeois Western scientists and their Soviet supporters (particularly Zhukovsky) denied the truth of his revision of Darwinism.[35] The newspaper followed this up with comments by Lysenko's supporters, including one by Turbin, who declared flatly: "Lysenko's views are correct. Intraspecies competition does not exist. His critics' opinions are utterly unjustified and distort the true state of affairs."[36] Toward the end of the year, the newspaper printed a roundup of letters from readers, an excerpt from the proceedings of a meeting of the philosophy department of Moscow State University, and a summation of the entire discussion by M. B. Mitin, then head of the paper's science department. Mitin slung together phrases about "dogmas . . . to which . . . scientific conservatives cling" and excerpts form readers' letters, including many claiming to be from "Soviet scientists filled with wrath and indignation . . . who reject the slander" of Lysenko. The newspaper proclaimed Lysenko and his supporters the victors in the debate.[37]

All the same, the Lysenkoist forces had suffered a setback. Probably for the first time since the end of the war, Lysenko's views had come under serious, thoughtful, and sharp public criticism. Meanwhile, more and more facts were accumulating to show how detrimental Lysenko's proposals had been, including the success of hybrid corn—a purely genetic accomplishment—and the use of genetic methods in the United States to yield relatively inexpensive antibiotics. So the geneticists continued to cherish the hope that they could convince the Party leaders that Lysenkoism as a whole was wrong. Another conference was convened at Moscow State University from February 3 to 6, 1948, at which Academicians Shmalgauzen and M. M. Zavadovsky and Professor Ilya M. Polyakov showed that the Lysenkoist idea of direct adaptation of living organisms to the environment contradicted both scientific facts and the modern understanding of mutability and evolution. Two biologists, Aleksandr A. Lyubishchev and Vladimir P. Efroimson, sent the Party Central Committee manuscripts of their books, each more than a hundred typewritten pages, containing detailed analyses of Lysenko's mistakes and the damage they had wrought.[38] Copies of these manuscripts were also passed from hand to hand among scientists, and by the end of the 1950s the basic facts in them had become widely known. Members of the staffs of the laboratories of Serebrovsky and Koltsov persuaded several officials of the Party Central Committee to review the geneticists' proofs of the "notorious Mendelian laws."

The Zhdanovs, Father and Son, Criticize Lysenko

The geneticists' hopes of reaching top Party officials were finally realized through Yury Zhdanov, the son of Politburo member Andrei A. Zhdanov. Yury had been a student in organic chemistry at Moscow State University, where he had a brief internship in genetics under V. V. Sakharov and had become convinced of the validity of Mendel's laws. After completing the university, he did graduate work in Marxist philosophy under Bonifaty M. Kedrov at the Institute of Philosophy of the AN SSSR, defended his dissertation (which discussed issues in organic chemistry) for a candidate's degree, and began rapidly moving up the career ladder. In about 1947, he was appointed head of the science department of the Party Central Committee. In 1949, he married Stalin's daughter, Svetlana Alliluyeva. (They separated in 1953.) His acquaintance with genetics thus came to play an important part in the political climate around Lysenko.

Stories that Andrei and Yury Zhdanov criticized Lysenko frequently at Party meetings in the postwar years have long been widespread in the literature. Zhores Medvedev has said that in the spring of 1948, the elder Zhdanov "raised the question of strengthening the leadership" of VASKhNIL, which would have meant replacing Lysenko as president.[39] Alliluyeva later wrote that Yury's opposition to Lysenko even aroused Stalin's anger.[40] Nevertheless, the high rank of Andrei Zhdanov and Yury's position as head of the Central Committee's science department allowed the son a limited degree of freedom. According to V. V. Sakharov, Yury met frequently with classical geneticists from the time he received his Central Committee appointment and gradually came to understand what Lysenko stood for and the end results of his many years of promises.

The elder Zhdanov, too, evidently regarded Lysenko coolly. In his many speeches between 1946 and 1948 denouncing Soviet cultural figures and scientists, he did not once take up the seemingly useful topic of the role that Lysenko, a peasant's son, was playing in strengthening the Marxist-Leninist position in biology. Loren Graham argues that Andrei Zhdanov was rather skeptical of Lysenko, which appears more logical than the arguments of other Western scholars, who are inclined to see Zhdanov as a patron of Lysenko, if only because their methods had much in common.[41] At the same time, there is no doubt that Stalin's sympathy for Lysenko was quite in keeping with the leader's political ideals and remained constant until almost the end of Stalin's life. This sympathy was well known throughout the country and could not be ignored in the Central Committee's science department, even though this department did not supervise agricultural science.

At any rate, it is reliably known that at the end of 1947 and the beginning of 1948, the science department gathered a considerable body of data about Lysenko. Many geneticists visited Yury Zhdanov's department in the gloomy gray Central Committee building on Staraya Ploshchad, across from the Polytechnical Museum, presenting memoranda and reports on various aspects of the Lysenkoists' activity. As Graham points out, unless and until the Central Committee archives are opened, it will be hard to know exactly what the relationships between Lysenko and the Party leaders were in those years.[42] On the whole, however, we can be confident that the Party apparatchiks in the country's highest organ were well informed about the struggle with Lysenko and that many sympathized with the geneticists, even though, possessing no power except to carry out decisions, they could only follow Stalin's orders.

Hence, it may cause surprise that Yury Zhdanov, as head of the science department, suddenly attacked Lysenko very sharply and did so, moreover, at an important Party meeting in the spring of 1948. Yet such an event does not seem to me exceptional, and not just as a matter of the young Zhdanov's bold personal convictions. More likely, his boldness had to do with his father's stance. He also counted on his future father-in-law's regard, as well as the traditional antagonism between the science department and the farm-science sector of the Central Committee's agriculture department. Even the sharp form in which he couched his remarks evokes no surprise. Soviet Party history contains plenty of instances of sharp, unexpected attacks upon highly placed persons for alleged errors of theory or practice that previously had been entirely ignored. A passage in a speech or report by someone in the top party apparatus usually provided the signal to open fire—often a digression unrelated to anything else in the speech and perhaps criticizing a Party comrade who had sat next to the speaker in the presidium only the day before, the two chatting amiably before a large audience.

Among the ways of informing the local Party officialdom about changes of intraparty policy or personalities were seminars for lecturers of the regional Party committees. As a rule, copies of reports, often in the form of "theses," were prepared (for limited distribution) for these seminars, so that the lecturers, on returning home, could spread the desired information as a guide to action. One such seminar was held at the Polytechnical Museum in Moscow on April 10, 1948. Yury Zhdanov delivered a lecture on the state of affairs in biology. In effect, he devoted his report to a criticism of Lysenko for his monopolizing of science, his repeated promises of great practical successes, and his unscientific theories. Zhdanov echoed the habitual clichés about the value of Lysenko's innovative idea of vernalization and mentioned more than once that Lysenko had contributed a great deal to Soviet biology. It was not these standard tributes that caught the attention of Zhdanov's audience, however, but the negative judgments that he voiced. After opening the lecture with a discussion of problems of Darwinism, Zhdanov disagreed with Lysenko's novel views, criticized the role and position adopted by the *Literary Gazette* and the philosophers who "intervened in the [biologists'] debate and not only did not facilitate its resolution, but further confused the issue." Then Zhdanov described Lysenko's work as follows:

To a great extent, Trofim Lysenko is battling ghosts of the past.

Lysenko's conception largely reflects the first stage of knowledge, the stage of general contemplation of plant and animal organisms.

Academician Lysenko adamantly opposed colchicine. Speaking of the scientists working with colchicine, he wrote: "Colchicine is one of the strongest poisons; it . . . deforms plants. Cells cease to divide normally, and something like a cancerous tumor develops." . . . So we have "one of the strongest poisons," "cancerous tumor," "abnormal development"—a bouquet of epithets that is far from appropriate for encouraging a new task. It is strange to hear an innovator say that a new plant form is abnormal. But I tell you: We don't give a damn about normal or abnormal, the important thing is to get bigger crops, a higher harvest! (*Applause.*)

In 1935, Trofim Denisovich Lysenko, acting out of his limited conception, held us back from introducing a new form of corn. I believe that here we were

1. Lysenko, after being elected as an Active Member (Academician) of the All-Ukrainian Academy of Sciences in 1934. From *Na Stroike MTS i Sovkhozov*. Photo by Shaikhet.

2. The 1930 meeting of the VASKhNIL, where Lysenko made his mark. First row: *second from left*, Nikolai Vavilov; *third from left*, Nikolai Tulaikov; *fourth from left*, T. D. Lysenko.

3. The Lysenko Guards in the Odessa institute, 1936. *Left to Right: standing*, S. A. Pogosyan, I. K. Shimansky, M. Lyubchenko, F. G. Kirichenko, Kotov, I. D. Kashpersky, D. A. Dolgushin, A. M. Favorov, I. E. Glushchenko; *seated*, G. A. Babadzhanyan, Deputy Director for administration D. G. Korniakov, T. D. Lysenko, F. G. Lutsenko, A. I. Gapeyeva, V. F. Khitrinsky, A. D. Rodionov.

4. Before his departure from Odessa, T. D. Lysenko, newly nominated as president of VASKhNIL, posed for a ceremonial photo with his "guards." Note the Lenin Prize decoration and symbol of Deputy of Supreme Soviet on Lysenko's lapel. *Left to right: first row*, Isaac Prezent, T. D. Lysenko, Evelyna Pavlovna Dolgushina (Dolgushin's wife); *second row*, Berta Abramovna Glushchenko (Glushchenko's wife), Ivan Evdokimovich Glushchenko, Aleksei Danilovich Rodionov (*standing*), Aleksandra Alekseyevna Baskova (Lysenko's wife), Donat Aleksandrovich Dolgushin. 1938. Courtesy of I. E. Glushchenko.

5. On a highly publicized visit to Donetsk to promote vernalization, Lysenko (*second from right*) advises peasants and party leaders on methods of sowing vernalized potatoes. *On the right*, Aleksei D. Rodionov, the scientist (promoted from simple worker despite his lack of education) responsible for the vernalization program. *In the center*, Deputy Chairman of the Agricultural Department of the Donetsk Party Obkom, A. L. Rapoport (in white shirt) and Secretary of the Party Committee of the Mine named in honor of Lazar Kaganovich. From *Vernalization*, 1935, no. 2:101. Retouching was done for the original publication.

6. Isaac Prezent visits Ivan Michurin, ca. 1934. The photo shows signs of retouching.

7. Stalin, Andrei A. Andreyev, Anastas I. Mikoyan, and S. V. Kosior listen to Lysenko. At a meeting of party and government leaders in the Kremlin, honoring the top tractor operators, machinists, and workers bringing in the best harvests, December 29, 1935. From *Pravda*, January 3, 1936, no. 3 (6609): 1. Photo by N. Kalashnikov and N. Kuleshov.

8. Tsitsin shows samples of seeds to Stalin. *At right,* Yakovlev. From *Pravda* 1935.

9. Lysenko demonstrates the results of intravarietal crossing to Academicians N. I. Vavilov (*left*) and G. K. Meister (*center*) during their visit to Odessa. From *Socialist Agriculture*, May 21, 1937, no. 114 (2502): 3.

10. T. D. Lysenko's father, Denis Nikanorovich Lysenko, shows off a stalk of branched wheat he had grown to a representative of the kolkhoz *Bolshevik Labor.* The caption to this photograph, published in 1937 in *Socialist Agriculture*, claimed: "Each spike of the wheat yields more than 100 grains." The photo demonstrates that Lysenko knew about the qualities of branched wheat in 1937, well before he promised Stalin to develop the miracle variety he proposed to name "Stalin's branched."

11. Members of the session of the Supreme Soviet of the USSR greet the report of Vyacheslav M. Molotov, Chairman of the Sovnarkom and Narkom of Foreign Affairs of the USSR, on the "voluntary entry into the USSR of the Baltic countries, Western Ukraine, Bukovina, and Western Byelorussia" with a storm of applause. *From left*: Timoshenko, Budionniy, Khrushchev, Badaev, Kalinin, Malenkov, Babaev-Khivali, Zhdanov, Stalin, Molotov (at rostrum), Mikoyan, Ligachev, Kaganovich, Voroshilov, Pervukhin, Beria, Bulganin, and Vyshinsky. *Top*, at the raised desk of the Chairmen of the Supreme Soviet: Lysenko, Yusupov, Andreyev, Schvernik, Aslanova, and Kulagin. From *Pravda*, August 2, 1940, no. 213 (8259): 1.

12. Ivan Vyacheslavovich Yakushkin, scientist and KGB agent. 1950s.

13. Lysenko with a loaf of wheat bread, presented to him by the Government Commission on Testing of Grain Crops. From *Ogonyok*, October 10, 1948, no. 41: 9. Photo by A. Gostev.

14. T. D. Lysenko with branched wheat. 1949. From *Ogonyok*.

15. A smiling Trofim Denisovich and giggling kolkhoz girls admire branched wheat. From *Molodoy Kolkhoznik* 16, no. 1 (1949): 21.

16. In the greenhouse of the Institute of Genetics of the USSR Academy of Sciences. *At left*, Lysenko's secretary, Faina Feinbron; Glushchenko; and others. Lysenko is in front on the right. 1946, Moscow. Courtesy of I. E. Glushchenko.

17. At the August 1948 session of VASKhNIL, Lysenko holds up pressed plant samples, stating that these were products of the transformation of rye into wheat. Photo by Dm. Baltermants.

18. Olga Borisovna Lepeshinskaya. 1952. From *Priroda*.

19. Cartoons by popular political satirist Boris Efimov for an article "Fly-lovers and Man-haters," by Aleksandr N. Studitsky: a gleeful geneticist with his marching partners, a brutal police officer and a Klansman; and a capitalist admiring fruitflies, while the gallows loom behind him. From *Ogonyok*, 1949, reproduced without comment in the American journal *Heredity*.

20. War veteran Joseph A. Rapoport opens the annual conference of geneticists and plant breeders at the Institute of Chemical Physics in Moscow. February 1980. Photo by V. Soyfer.

21. Vladimir P. Efroimson, early 1930s (*left*) and soon after his release from a second prison term, early 1956.

22. The opening ceremony of the Second Congress of Geneticists and Plant Breeders of the USSR, where the All-Union Society of Geneticists and Plant Breeders named in honor of Nikolai Vavilov was organized. Moscow, Main Hall of Main Botanic Garden of the USSR Academy of Sciences, May 30, 1966. *First row,* N. V. Timofeyev-Ressovsky; *second row,* Vladimir P. Zosimovich (*left*) and Pyotr F. Rokitsky.

23. Daniil Vladimirovich Lebedev and Vladimir Yakovlevich Aleksandrov in Leningrad. December, 1986. Photo by V. Soyfer.

24. Sergei Sergeyevich Chetverikov, ten years after he was dismissed from his position at Gorky State University, blind and forgotten by his students and colleagues. Winter 1958. Photo by V. Soyfer.

25. Lysenko in the greenhouse of the Institute of Genetics of the USSR Academy of Sciences. Moscow, late 1950s.

26. Lysenko at Khrushchev's side, after the presentation of the Medal for Labor Prowess by K. E. Voroshilov, Chairman of the Presidium of the USSR Supreme Soviet. *From left: first row,* A. B. Aristov, K. E. Voroshilov, Nikita Khrushchev, T. D. Lysenko, B. I. Edelshtein, N. G. Ignatov; *second row,* G. A. Denisov, M. P. Georgadze, A. S. Shevchenko, G. I. Vorobev, D. S. Polyansky, V. V. Matskevich, N. T. Efremov, P. N. Demichev, V. I. Konotop. 1963. From *Ogonyok.*

27. In 1957, the Lysenkoists invited the eminent French plant breeder, Roger de Vilmorin, for a lecture, as a way to demonstrate they were au courant with international science. This photo shows the Lysenkoists trying to hide their discomfiture after hearing de Vilmorin's praise of the success of classical genetics and the enthusiastic applause of the students and scientists in the audience. In the Tsar's Hall of the Yusupov Palace (current home of the Presidium of VASKhNIL). *Left to right: seated,* I. V. Yakushkin, T. D. Lysenko, R. de Vilmorin, P. P. Lobanov, D. D. Brezhnev, N. V. Tsitsin, K. I. Skryabin; *standing,* unidentified, A. G. Utekhin, unidentified, I. I. Prezent, A. Yablokov, I. I. Sinyagin, unidentified, Askochensky, N. S. Sherbinovsky, unidentified. Photo courtesy of T. N. Sherbinovsky.

28. French plant breeder Roger de Vilmorin meets the students of the Moscow Timiryazev Agricultural Academy on November 29, 1957. *From left:* Roger de Vilmorin, Professor Nikolai A. Maisuryan, unknown, students V. Soyfer and M. Lapshin. Photo by A. Kuvaldin.

29. Lysenko, Khrushchev (*second from right*), M. A. Suslov, and Fedor Vasilievich Kallistratov, director of Lenin Hills, chest-high in wheat at Lysenko's farm and experiment station. 1955.

30. A heated discussion during a visit of foreign scholars to the Institute of Genetics of the USSR Academy of Sciences. *From left to right*: A. T. Trukhinova, A. K. Fedorov, unidentified foreign guest, B. L. Izvekova, T. D. Lysenko, unidentified foreign guest, Yu. L. Guzhov, N. I. Nuzhdin (*front*). Late 1950s.

seeing theoretical narrowness causing material damage, and we must appraise critically anything new that comes from the Lysenko school.[43]

Zhdanov described as "undesirable, sensationalist publicity" "Lysenko's promise to 'find' new plant varieties in literally two to three years. Such was the pledge he made before the war to develop within two to three years a frost-resistant winter wheat for Siberia that would rival the stability of local varieties."

In conclusion, Zhdanov said that "the attempt to suppress other trends, to defame scientists who use other methods, has nothing in common with [true] innovation," and he added: "We must liquidate attempts to establish monopolies in one or another scientific sector, for any monopoly leads to stagnation. . . . Trofim Denisovich has accomplished a great deal, and we say to him: Trofim Denisovich, there is much you have not yet done, and you have closed your eyes, moreover, to a whole series of plant forms and methods of taming nature."

Nevertheless, Zhdanov was by no means an absolute defender of genetics and geneticists. Rather, the outlook he expressed in his lecture was eclectic, since he spoke of the materialist foundations of the geneticists' conclusions and criticized the "Lysenko school" for "underestimating the importance of analysis, underestimating the study of chemical, physical, and biochemical processes, the patient study of cell structures"; and although he mentioned "the discrete nature of heredity, the modern theory of organizers and genes," he asserted at the same time that "when some scientists say there is a substance conveying hereditary characteristics, this is nonsense." He also condemned the geneticists for "being overly preoccupied with *Drosophila*, diverting them from very important practical goals." Like Lysenko (and Stalin), he placed the accent on the absolute aim of transforming nature. "We Communists," he said, "are in accord with the doctrine that affirms the possibility of transforming and reorganizing the organic world, rather than sudden, unexplained, and accidental changes of a mysterious hereditary plasma. It is this aspect of the neo-Lamarckian doctrine that Comrade Stalin stressed and appraised in his work *Anarchism or Socialism?*"

Finally, Yury Zhdanov rejected Lysenko's basic premise: that the dispute with the geneticists was a political struggle in which the sides were divided into supporters of bourgeois and socialist outlook. "It is untrue," he said, "that a struggle is going on among us between two biological schools, one representing the Soviet viewpoint and the other representing bourgeois Darwinism. I think we should reject this formula, because the dispute is between scientific schools within Soviet biology, and neither side in the dispute can be called bourgeois." Under the ideological conditions of the time, it was a bold stand for a Party official.

The speaker had made no secret beforehand of the kind of lecture he would deliver, and rumors about it had reached Lysenko, who decided to listen to it in a somewhat unusual way. M. B. Mitin, besides being head of the science department of the *Literary Gazette*, was deputy chairman of the Society for Dissemination of Political and Scientific Knowledge, the public lecture agency, which had its headquarters in the Polytechnical Museum where Zhdanov spoke. Lysenko sat in Mitin's office, where a loudspeaker was set up to carry the sound from the auditorium. he could follow the proceedings in private.

This behavior told much. Lysenko had not previously resorted to such subterfuges. He was used to challenging others in open battle. One can imagine the powerful impression that his appearance in the hall might have made upon audience and speaker alike. But now his situation apparently had deteriorated to the point where he and his supporters could neither prevent the lecture by intrigues nor confront the speaker.

Instead, Lysenko sat in an office separated from the auditorium by only a short corridor and listened to a Party leader speak for the first time in many years about his, Lysenko's, mistakes. There was something tragic in this scene: the fifty-year-old president of VASKhNIL, the most famous scientist in the nation, sitting behind a closed door, obliged to listen to the young Zhdanov casting him down from the pedestal. He did not muster the courage to take the dozen steps down the hallway and enter the auditorium to confront Zhdanov. The two men left the building without facing each other, and it was Lysenko who hid from his accuser.[44]

Lysenko Writes a Letter to Stalin

Soon after the lecture, Lysenko resolved on a desperate step. In an attempt to salvage his shaky situation even at the risk of abdicating his scientific throne, he wrote to Stalin and the elder Zhdanov, submitting his resignation as president of VASKhNIL. It was unprecedented for so highly placed a bureaucrat to renounce a post that the Party had assigned to him. The text of this letter is worth presenting in full.

The academy presidency ranked with the post of a deputy minister of agriculture, and Lysenko held several honorary offices also. No such highly placed bureaucrat had ever resorted to so risky an experiment as resigning. It just wasn't done. Gestures of bravado, attempts to play upon your indispensability by renouncing a post assigned to you, were not tolerated. The Party put you there, and the Party would decide whether and when to dismiss you or promote you—such was the inviolable rule for functionaries before, during, or after Stalin. Yet Lysenko had the temerity to violate the rule and to write to Stalin. To the best of my knowledge, neither that fact nor the text of this long letter was known until recently, and so I present the letter in full.[45]

To CHAIRMAN OF THE U.S.S.R. COUNCIL OF MINISTERS
Comrade Josef Vissarionovich STALIN
To SECRETARY OF THE PARTY CENTRAL COMMITTEE
Comrade Andrei Aleksandrovich ZHDANOV
From Academician T. D. Lysenko

It has become very difficult for me to function as president of the V. I. Lenin Academy of Agricultural Sciences and even as a scientist. Therefore, I have determined to appeal to you for help. An extremely abnormal situation has arisen in agrobiology.

It is commonly known, and I consider it normal, that a struggle has been and is being waged between the old metaphysical trend in this science and the new Michurinist trend.

For understandable reasons, the Weismannists and the neo-Darwinists, have embarked on a new maneuver. While changing literally nothing in their scientific premises, they have proclaimed themselves supporters of Michurin and charge that we who share and develop the Michurinist doctrine allegedly are narrowing and distorting the Michurinist doctrine. It is likewise understandable why the Weismannists and the neo-Darwinists direct their entire assault against me personally.

In these circumstances, it is extremely difficult for me to function as head of the academy.

But all this was to a certain extent normal and I understand it. The criterion by which we judge the veracity of trends and methods in scientific research is the degree to which they foster socialist agriculture. This has been the principle from which I, as a head [of an academy], have drawn the strength to develop the Michurinist doctrine and to give ever greater support to practical agriculture. It has also been the best way to combat metaphysical views in biology.

Despite the lack of scientific objectivity and the often outright calumny to which the adversaries of the Michurinist trend have resorted—and although it has been difficult for me—nevertheless, relying on the practical work of kolkhozes and sovkhozes, I have found the strength to withstand their assault and to go on developing theory and practice.

But now something has happened that indeed makes me throw up my hands.

At a seminar of lecturers of regional Party committees on April 10 of this year, Comrade Yury Andreyevich Zhdanov, head of the science department of the Party Central Committee's propaganda administration, delivered a report on "Controversial Questions of Modern Contemporary Darwinism."

In this report, the speaker repeated personally, in his own name, the anti-Michurinist enemies' calumnies of me.

I realize that the large audience of regional Party committee lecturers, hearing these anti-Michurinists' slanders from a speaker who heads the science department of the Party Central Committee's propaganda administration, took them to be true. Consequently, the falsehoods of the anti-Michurinist neo-Darwinists will have much greater effect in the regions, both among scientific personnel and among agronomists and officials of practical farming, thereby strongly hindering the scientists under my direction from applying their results in practical farming. It is also a great blow that is hard for me to suffer.

I turn to you, therefore, with a request that is very important to me: to help, if you consider it desirable to do so, in this matter that seems to me very serious for our agricultural science and biology.

The assertion that I cannot take criticism is wrong, so wrong that I shall not answer it in detail in this instance. I have always submitted any of my work, whether in the realm of theory or practice, to criticism, from which I have learned to benefit for the cause and for science. My whole life in science has proceeded under the control of criticism, and that is good.

The speaker did not call upon me and never spoke with me, although his report essentially directed all its criticism against me. I was refused an invitation to the seminar and listened to it carefully not in the auditorium, but by loudspeaker in another room, the office of Comrade Mitin, deputy chairman of the Society for the Dissemination of Political and Scientific Knowledge.

One can judge what I understood to be the burden of the report if only from my quite fragmentary notes of its concluding portion. I enclose some of these notes.

The accusation was repeatedly made that, in the interests of the Michurinist trend in science that I share, I have suppressed the opposite school by administrative action. In fact, for reasons independent of myself, this is unfortunately far from so. The direction that I share, the Michurinist, is the one suppressed.

I believe I would not be exaggerating if I said that I personally, as a scientist but not as president of the Agricultural Academy, have contributed no little to the growth and development of the Michurinist doctrine through my scientific and practical work.

The fundamental misfortune and difficulty in my work as president has been that I have been presented with what I am deeply convinced are improper demands to ensure the development of diverse scientific trends (not diverse branches of science, but diverse schools).

I cannot accept this demand. But I also could not suppress the contrary scientific trend—first, because in science these matters are not decided by administrative decree, and, secondly, I could not do it because the defense of neo-Darwinism is so extensive.

In effect, I have been not the president of the agricultural academy, but the defender and leader of only the Michurinist trend, and it is still completely the minority in higher scientific circles.

The difficulty also lies in the fact that as president of the academy I had to present the scientific and practical work of representatives of the Michurinist school (a clear minority in the academy) as the work of the whole academy, while the anti-Michurinists engaged less in creative endeavor than in pedantic criticism and calumnies.

I can promote the development of the most diverse branches of agricultural science, but only of the Michurinist school, the school of science that recognizes that living nature changes with the conditions of life and that recognizes the inheritance of acquired characteristics.

I have long accepted, and I share and am developing, the Williams teaching on farming and soil development and the Michurinist doctrine of the development of organisms. Both are doctrines of a single scientific trend.

I would be pleased if you found it possible to grant me the opportunity to work only on this basis, where I feel my strength lies and where my work could benefit our Soviet science, the Ministry of Agriculture, and the practice of our collective and state farming in various of its aspects.

Please excuse the clumsy wording of this letter, due largely to my present state of mind.

The letter was unquestionably a masterpiece. Lysenko struck just the right note; humble, apologetic, even downcast in manner, while unbendingly stern and intolerant in substance. He realized the full complexity of this momentous phase and found the precise words for it.

When he had spoken before Stalin for the first time in 1935, he had gloried in his achievements. Here, he sought to portray himself, on the contrary, as an unfortunate lamb for whom the reactionary geneticist wolves were sharpening their teeth. He refrained from attacking Zhdanov, confining criticism of him to an implication of excessive credulity, as if to say that in his youthful innocence Zhdanov had trusted the old wolves, but it was they who were the slanderers. The air of humility, conveying Lysenko's obedience and readiness to carry out any orders unquestioningly, was calculated to obtain carte blanche to punish enemies, real or potential, who had been able to foist a lot of lies upon even Yury Zhdanov.

It is important to point out that Lysenko did not conceal his desire to punish his scientific opponents. He complained, on the one hand, of the accusation "repeatedly made ... that I have administratively suppressed the opposite school" and, on the other hand, that "for reasons independent of myself, this is *unfortunately* far from so." The implication is that he was not being *allowed* to conduct an effective purge of his opponents. His characterization of his side as "a clear minority" seems to be a hint that this restriction should be lifted. And his assertion that he had been presented with "improper demands to ensure the development of diverse scientific trends" was an appeal to the deep impulses of a leader who had long been engaged in the eradication of all ideas and schools of thought other than his own. His conclusion amounted to a promise that, once he was freed of the necessity of fighting scientific opponents, he would perform wonders to "benefit our Soviet science ... and our collective and state farming."

The enclosed notes that Lysenko referred to consisted of a brief summary of his interpretation of Zhdanov's speech. They are also very interesting, for they allow us to understand how Lysenko responded to the criticism contained in Zhdanov's lecture and how he pursued his goals.

1. Lysenko raises barriers to the development of science (rejection of hormones, vitamins, etc.).
2. Lysenko champions only a certain part of the necessary scientific research, namely biological, but rejects physics and chemistry in biology.
3. It is disgraceful that there are people who, out of narrow interests, slander others' work. Andreyev, one of the Lysenko school, writing in the magazine *Selection and Seed Growing,* spoke against growth substances. (Speaker quoted.)

4. Lysenko denies the existence of hormones.

5. Lysenko has set back our introduction of hybrid corn by 13 years.

6. A critical attitude is not taken toward Lysenko, although he has made mistakes. Example: his pledge to develop a frost-resistant variety for Siberia. Nothing came of it. In an article in *Izvestia* he has already given up on this but nowhere has he said he erred.

7. Lysenko tries to slander and suppress much that is new in science. This is different from the innovator that Lysenko used to be, and what Andrei Aleksandrovich Zhdanov said in his speech about pseudo-innovators (he quoted it) applies to you, Trofim Denisovich Lysenko.[46]

Although young Zhdanov's speech created a stir, Lysenko suffered no immediate unpleasantness. But neither did his letter to Stalin and the elder Zhdanov bring any quick response. He thereupon took another step. Having obtained a stenographic transcript of Yury Zhdanov's speech from Minister of Agriculture Benediktov, he returned it to Benediktov on May 11, 1948, together with a statement containing a definite request to be relieved of his position as president of VASKhNIL:

To USSR Minister of Agriculture
Comrade Ivan Aleksandrovich Benediktov

I am returning the transcript of "Controversial Questions of Darwinism."

I consider it my duty to state that in both the report and the revised transcript (which in many places has been slightly softened, compared with what I thought I heard), the speaker presented in his own name old slanders of me by the anti-Michurinist-Morganist-neo-Darwinists.

This kind of criticism was voiced in secret from me, so that I would be unable to object and refute it, either in person or in print.

As an indication of the level of scientific criticism of my work, I append an extract from page 30 of the transcript, where one of my propositions is analyzed. Please compare this passage with my article on the question. The relevant page from my article is clipped to the extract. All the rest of the criticism is on the same level.

The edited transcript does not give the titles and pages of my works from which passages were quoted. The reader has no opportunity to compare the speaker's statements with mine. I have already repeatedly declared that I cannot go on working as president of the All-Union V. I. Lenin Academy of Agricultural Sciences [VASKhNIL] in the conditions in which I have been placed.

For the good of agricultural science and practice, I ask you to take up the question of relieving me of the post of president and enabling me to conduct scientific research. In that way, I could be of much greater use to both our farming practice and the development of biology of the Michurin school in various areas, including the training of scientific personnel.

Academician T. D. Lysenko

This document suggests that Lysenko already knew Stalin's reaction to his earlier letter, because the tone of this letter is quite different from the tone of the previous one. Gone is the humility. Here, Lysenko goes on the offensive, accusing Yury Zhdanov of scientific incompetence and dishonest scholarship, and he insists that he was an innocent victim of secret criticism, even though Zhdanov's speech was far from secret.

A "Branched Wheat" Variety Named "Stalinskaya"

What Yury Zhdanov's audience probably found most convincing was the record of Lysenko's failures to deliver on his many promises. On paper, Lysenko and his assistants were always able to present confirmation of his ideas; the results of their tests always seemed to coincide with their chief's predictions.[47]

But words are one thing, and a real harvest on real fields is another. That was what the head of the Party Central Committee's science department was saying. Zhdanov did not, however, speak of Lysenko's latest enthusiasm, still untested but already sparking hopes on the part of Stalin himself.

The possibility had arisen a decade earlier that a variety of "branched" wheat could be developed that would yield five to ten times as much grain as ordinary wheat. As Yury A. Zhdanov told me in 1987 in my home at Moscow, he knew of this idea, on which Stalin and other leaders set great store. In conversation with Stalin, Lysenko had already pledged to achieve a success in this project greater than anything world selection had ever known. The project was still being worked out and tested, and it was premature to mention it publicly. Zhdanov had already asked the geneticists, including Zhebrak, to assemble information about branched wheat, but, because he did not tell them why he wanted it, Zhebrak and the others did not treat the request as urgent.

The great attention suddenly paid to a new wheat and Stalin's personal interest in it were typical of those times. The prospect of a cheap and simple solution to a complicated and pressing problem held great allure.

In 1938, a kolkhoz worker in Central Asia, a woman named Muslima Begiyeva, apparently had obtained a huge harvest by growing wheat that produced branched ears. There were several times as many grains of wheat in these ears as in ordinary varieties, and Begiyeva expected the yield to be record-setting. The press spread word of this achievement and named the wheat "Muslinka."[48] Sheaves of the branched wheat were despatched to the All-Union Agricultural Exhibition in Moscow. Peasants from all over the country were brought to the exhibition, and thus it happened that two young Georgians from the Kakhetia region, impressed by those sheaves, tore off a few of the ears and sowed the seeds the next year on their kolkhoz. But the men were then drafted into the army, and branched wheat was forgotten until after the war. In 1946, a sheaf of the branched wheat from Kakhetia was sent to Moscow. Without further ado, the sample was entered in the State Variety Register under the name of Kakhetian Branched.[49] The reason for this haste was that the seeds and sheaf had been shown to Stalin, who was pleased by his fellow Georgians' success with the wheat, especially since things had gone poorly with the original seed. Begiyeva's seed had ceased to produce branching ears, and she had been unable to restore its branching, no matter how she tried.[50]

In 1946 Stalin summoned Lysenko and gave him the task of developing the Georgian collective farmers' wheat and introducing it throughout the country as soon as possible.[51] Lysenko accepted the 210-gram packet of precious seed from Stalin's hands, assured the "leader of all peoples and all nations" that he would accomplish the mission, and left, elated, for Lenin Hills.

This moment is extremely significant in any appraisal of Lysenko's character. Lysenko was being confronted with a task that a scientist of principle would have thought twice before accepting. But to have Stalin show this confidence in him, just when other Party leaders seemed to be turning away from him, made this a significant moment in Lysenko's life.

There was nothing reprehensible in Stalin's interest in branched wheat—after all, he knew little about science or plants. On the contrary, it bespoke the assiduous manager. Lysenko's enthusiastic response seemed just as natural. If the leader ordered, how could he refuse? However, it was natural only on first sight and only to someone ignorant of the truth of the matter. *But Lysenko did know the truth about branched wheat: he undoubtedly had experimented with it himself more than once and discovered that it was a snare and a delusion.*

Russian scientific literature had dealt with branched wheat for more than a hundred years.[52] Lysenko himself had long known of its existence: witness a photograph published by *Socialist Agriculture* in 1937 of none other than Lysenko's father holding ears of this type of wheat. The caption read:

> Denis Nikanorovich Lysenko, father of Academician Lysenko and director of the cottage laboratory of the Bolshevik Labor Collective Farm, Karlovka District, Kharkov Province, has planted many varieties of grain and vegetables on 60 experimental plots. Lysenko, at left in photo, is showing the collective farm chairman a new wheat. Each ear of this wheat contains more than 100 grains. Photo by Ya. Sapozhnikov (Sovfoto).[53]

There is further evidence that Lysenko knew about branched wheat. In 1940, an article entitled "Branched Forms of Winter Wheat, Rye, and Barley" had been published in Lysenko's own journal, *Vernalization*, describing the conditions in which these forms arose.[54] Even if he read nothing else, Lysenko surely at least glanced at his own magazine. In any event, the question of branched wheat had been discussed so often in Russian and world scientific literature back into the previous century and its failure had been so thoroughly analyzed that Lysenko could not have failed to be aware of the facts, even if he did not follow scientific publications carefully but merely had worked at his own wheat selection in the 1930s.[55]

Therefore, were he a scientist of integrity, even just ordinarily honest, he would have refused the task then and there. He knew very well that in accepting the packet of seeds from Stalin he was engaging in deceit. But it was getting so hot for him, that even a bare hint of Stalin's interest would have made him do whatever Stalin asked. And so he chose to say nothing bad to Stalin about branched wheat.

Back at Lenin Hills, he assigned his most docile assistants, Avakyan, Dolgushin, and Ivan D. Kolesnik, to work on the problem. He demanded that they multiply the variety quickly, study it, improve it, and introduce it onto the fields of the country's kolkhozes. His most knowledgeable aides, Prezent and Glushchenko, remained aloof from the project; it seems likely they did remember the evidence of earlier failures with branched wheat and suspected that Stalin's order could not be fulfilled. They did not sign articles on the subject and did not give interviews to the press or pose for photos about it.

With Lysenko predicting fantastic yields from branched wheat of 50, 75, 100 and more centners per hectare—"a harvest of a hundred centners should become average for it in the near future!"[56]—his disciples went to work at full speed. In the first year, Avakyan and Lysenko's father planted the seed thinly, as old practices dictated. Kolesnik took the resultant seed to his native Ukraine "to humor the seeds." By the spring of 1948, the newspapers were reporting amazing results with the new wheat.[57] Meanwhile, Dolgushin set himself to "changing" spring branched wheat into winter wheat by the "marriage-of-love" method.

These successes were reported to Stalin, and it is reliably known that when the elder Zhdanov once more criticized Lysenko before Stalin, the latter retorted that Comrade Lysenko was engaged in work of high importance to the country, and even if he was carried away when he promised to increase the wheat yield fivefold throughout the country and would succeed only in increasing it 50 percent, that would be quite enough; therefore, we must wait and see what comes of it.[58] No one else in Stalin's entourage dared to dispel his optimism, and Stalin probably did not want to be disabused. Zhebrak told Yury Zhdanov that some wheat branched, but only when so thinly planted that "one ear was too far from the next to hear its rustling" (*kolos ot kolosa nye slyshit golosa*) and thus the wheat never produced a bigger crop than ordinary varieties did. Evidently, however, Zhdanov lacked the evidence and power to expose the deception. So Stalin's intoxication with branched wheat enabled Lysenko to escape unscathed from the tight spot he was in—"to go through the water without getting wet," in the Russian expression—and even to drown all his critics.[59]

Lysenko Appeals to the Top

In May 1948, members of the Politburo and the heads of several Central Committee departments were summoned to a special meeting. Dmitry T. Shepilov, who was head of the propaganda and agitation department of the Central Committee of the Bolshevik party, recounted the story of this meeting to me in January 1988. Shepilov had earned a doctorate in economics before the war and had been offered the post of director of the Institute of Economics, but he had gone off to the front as an ordinary soldier, had risen to the rank of general, and subsequently had been transferred to the Central Committee apparatus. It was he who had scheduled Yury Zhdanov's lecture, knowing full well what young Zhdanov was going to say. "Perhaps I felt a bit less constrained than other officials of Central Committee departments," he explained, "because I knew I could always work as an economist if I were dismissed from the Central Committee staff." Approval for the lecture had been given by Suslov, the secretary of the Central Committee of the Party with responsibility for propaganda and agitation. Shepilov was brought to this special meeting, held in Stalin's office, by Andrei Zhdanov. Here is his description of what transpired:

> Stalin opened the meeting as soon as the elder Zhdanov and I arrived, and abruptly turned to the subject of Yury Zhdanov's undeserved insult to Comrade Lysenko. Pipe in hand and puffing on it frequently, Stalin paced the room from end to end, repeating practically the same phrases over and over: "How did anyone dare insult Comrade Lysenko?" "Who dared raise his hand to vilify Comrade Lysenko?" "To defame such a person!" At last he paused and asked: "Who authorized it?" There was the silence of the grave. Everyone remained quiet and looked down. Then Stalin halted beside Suslov [chief of agitation and propaganda] and asked: "Who is our agitprop?" Suslov hung his head and did not answer.
>
> To this day I don't know why—perhaps out of the wartime habit of accepting responsibility—I rose and replied loudly, like a saluting soldier: "The decision was mine, Comrade Stalin." They all stared at me as if I were out of my mind. Stalin approached and looked into my eyes. I did not avert my gaze. I can honestly say I never saw such a look as he gave me. His eyes seemed to possess some incredible force. Their yellow pupils transfixed me like the eyes of a cobra coiled to strike. He did not blink once as he stared into my eyes for what seemed an eternity. Then he asked softly, "Why did you do it?" I began to speak agitatedly about the tremendous harm Lysenko was doing to the country, about how he tried to suppress all his scientific opponents, about the inordinate exaggeration of his scientific services and the insignificant results that came of all his promises. Stalin went on pacing the room, then stopped and interrupted me in midsentence. "So," he said. "I see. We'll set up a committee to clarify all the facts." He began to list the committee members: Molotov, I think, Voroshilov, someone else, and then me—a weight lifted from my heart—and then he paused, looked long at Suslov, and at last added: "Suslov," and again fell silent, while I wondered why he had not included either of the Zhdanovs. Did it spell an end to their careers? After long thought, Stalin uttered: "And Zhdanov," fell silent once more, and added: "senior."[60]

Persons close to Lysenko all agree that Stalin sent for him in July 1948. In the course of their conversation, Lysenko sensed that Stalin's attitude toward him was not at all bad, and he seized the opportunity. He promised to correct the situation in agriculture quickly, but he set one condition: that he not be badgered or defamed, that he not be bothered by those faultfinders who constantly looked to the West, and that instead he be given a little help. Lysenko emphasized over and over that the country would suffer tremendous harm if biological research were to continue to be based on the foreign formal genetics of Weismann, Morgan, and Mendel instead of on the Michurinist doctrine. If, on the other hand, formal genetics were rejected, as an idealistic, bourgeois science, extremely harmful to the cause of socialism, the Michurinists would be encouraged to raise the yields of all crops. For example, the national harvest could be increased fivefold, even tenfold, with the help of branched wheat, to which Comrade Stalin himself had directed their attention and which they had already developed practically to the stage of a variety. Lysenko asked that the variety be named 'Stalinskaya' branched wheat. Stalin accepted Lysenko's approach.[61] Not only had Lysenko averted his downfall; he had been given the right to wreak vengeance upon his scientific adversaries.

One obstacle stood in the way. Any discussion of basic questions at academy meetings, not to mention sessions of the scientific councils of institutes or universities, invariably led to opposition from those who disagreed with him. Lysenko now wanted not a discussion, but a crushing blow to his foes, all of them, beginning at the highest level. The best setting would be a session of VASKhNIL, under his leadership as president. A resolution of the academy, supported in the press, would serve as a directive, binding upon everyone. But Lysenko feared, not without reason, that he was about to lose control over the academy. Not long before Lysenko's meeting with Stalin, elections had been scheduled to fill vacancies caused by the arrest, execution, and natural death of many members of the academy. Lists of nominees already had been posted, and it appeared that the Lysenkoist candidates had little chance of being elected. If the elections followed the usual democratic procedure, Lysenko would find that a majority in the academy opposed him.

At this critical juncture, Stalin came to his rescue, by calling off the scheduled elections and decreeing the appointment of the academicians whom Lysenko needed to assure control of the academy. On July 28, 1948, *Pravda* announced that, "in accordance with the charter" of VASKhNIL, thirty-five new members had been appointed.[62] Many of them were close associates of Lysenko—Avakyan, Dolgushin, Kolesnik, Olshansky, Prezent, and I. S. Varuntsyan—or were devoted followers, such as N. G. Belenky and P. P. Lukyanenko, or had been closely linked to Williams, such as V. P. Bushinsky.[63] Laptev, the economist who had led the attack on Zhebrak, was rewarded with an appointment. So was the NKVD officer S. N. Muromtsev, who for several years had been commandant of a *sharashka*, a jail in which scientists and engineers worked as prisoners and where a bacteriological weapon was under development. Muromtsev had personally participated in the beating of two members of the Academy of Sciences, P. F. Zdrodovsky and L. A. Zilber, while they were in his custody.[64] The announcement concluded with the statement that the academy's "regular July session . . . will be devoted to the discussion of a report by Academician T. D. Lysenko, 'On the Situation in Soviet Biological Science.'"[65] If the choice of new members of VASKhNIL implied that Lysenko had regained his influence at the top, the rescheduled session of the academy was to prove it to all.

11

The Defeat of
the Geneticists

The August 1948 VASKhNIL Session

The session of VASKhNIL that began on July 31 and continued until
August 7 is known as the August 1948 session. At the beginning, the
geneticists and biologists generally could not have known that this session
was to be qualitatively different from earlier scientific gatherings. Stalin
had not simply given Lysenko the go-ahead to crush his opponents, he
also placed great political importance upon crushing them. Yet, there
were signs that this session was going to be different from previous ones.
Some generally accepted rules of procedure had been violated: As we have
seen, it was not announced until three days before it was to begin; and
admission was by invitation only—and the overwhelming majority of invitations went to Lysenko supporters. Of course, there was almost no one
left to speak for the geneticists, anyway. Vavilov, Koltsov, and Lisitsyn were
dead, and Serebrovsky had just died on July 26. Nevertheless, some of the
leading scientists were not sent invitations. Although Dubinin, a corresponding member of the AN SSSR since 1946 and the most prominent
geneticist still active, knew the session was to be held and was invited to
participate, he chose, as Sergei M. Gershenzon put it to me in 1970, to
"hide in the bushes": he suddenly went hunting in the Urals.

Another omen was Lysenko's presence as the speaker on the opening
day, despite Yury Zhdanov's strong criticisms only four months before.
Lysenko's report (which, according to Glushchenko, was written by him,
Prezent, Vsevolod Stoletov, Avakyan, I. Khalifman, I. Varuntsyan, and Noy
Feiginson) had been personally reviewed by Stalin beforehand and bore

his handwritten comments in the margins.[1] It was an unyielding indictment of genetics and biology:

> In the epoch of the struggle between two worlds, there have emerged two antithetical, opposed trends, running through the warp and woof of almost all the biological disciplines... the sickly, metaphysical Morganist "science"... [and] our efficacious Michurinist agrobiology.[2]

The central part of Lysenko's report bore the heading, "Two Worlds [i.e., socialist and capitalist]—Two Ideologies in Biology."

To drive home the successes of Lysenko's work, the participants and the press were taken by bus the next day, August 1, to Lenin Hills, where

> they saw a wall of standing wheat, wheat unfamiliar to farmers, with clusters of branched ears on each stalk. Each ear held five grams of grain. A paper bagful of seed had produced six sacks of grain. That meant a hundred, perhaps even a hundred and fifty, centners per hectare. Alongside ran the Pakhra, an ordinary Moscow river, and nearby gleamed the building where Lenin died 24 years ago.[3]

When the meeting resumed the next day, the discussion of Lysenko's report began. *Pravda* devoted a full two or three of its four pages each day to the speeches. Behind the scenes, the Kremlin monitored everything that went on. V. N. Stoletov served as a messenger between Lysenko and the Politburo. At the close of each day's meeting, he reported to Malenkov, Stalin's second in command, what had gone on; and each morning, he coordinated the list of speakers with Lysenko and brought P. P. Lobanov, the deputy minister of agriculture who was chairing the meeting (and who was among those appointed members of the academy in the decree of July 28), a short list of those who were to be called upon.[4]

The daily meetings were dominated by Lysenko's followers. Yakushkin, who had been the chief witness against Vavilov, asserted that hybrid corn in the United States was just "hocus-pocus, tricks, and games that American seed companies play."[5] Neo G. Belenky declared that "no special heredity-bearing substance exists, any more than phlogiston, the fire-bearing substance, or the caloric, the heat-substance."[6] Sergei S. Perov, an old Party functionary famous chiefly because Molotov had once stayed in his house, exclaimed, "Only a scientist determined to commit scientific suicide could conceive of the gene as an organ, a gland, with a developed morphology and a very specific structure. To imagine that the gene, part of a chromosome, possesses the capacity to emit unknown and undiscovered substances... is to indulge in metaphysical, nonexperimental speculation, which spells death to experimental science."[7] "Mendelism-Morganism... is the carrier of idealistic agnosticism in biology (*applause*), affirming that biological laws are unfathomable," said G. A. Babadzhanyan, a former Lysenko graduate student who had become director of the Genetics Institute of the Armenian Academy of Sciences.[8]

There were outright calls for police action. Ye. I. Ushakova protested vehemently that higher educational institutions continued to teach the Mendelian laws: "How could we have come to this? Isn't it time someone answered for it, and answered for it seriously?"[9] The NKVD officer Muromtsev threatened: "Have no doubt that, if the representatives of the Mendel-Morganist school do not recognize the need for a creative approach to the tasks confronting biology and do not recognize their responsibility to [aid] practical work, they will find themselves cast out both from socialist science and from the practical work of socialist construction in our country."[10] Turbin, who had become head of the Leningrad University department of genetics and plant breeding, told the session: "Under cover of their academic titles, fanatical adherents of Morganism-Mendelism commonly engage in essentially empty blather. We must cleanse . . . the institutes . . . of their dominance."[11]

It seemed as if no arguments could be voiced against a clampdown on science. It is important to point out, however, that several scientists—including Zhebrak (who was repeatedly interrupted by insulting shouts from the floor), Boris M. Zavadovsky, and Zhukovsky—presented bold defenses of science. Two others, Alikhanyan and Polyakov, criticized individual details in Lysenko's report.

A particularly noteworthy statement was that of Iosif A. Rapoport. A pupil of Koltsov's, he had been at the front throughout World War II and had lost an eye in battle. He asked for the floor as soon as Lysenko finished speaking, but was given a turn only in the middle of the evening session on August 2. He spoke rapidly, passionately, with fierce conviction. (The strongest parts of his speech did not appear in the published transcript.)[12]

Rapoport began by enumerating the achievements of genetics: the discovery of the nature of the gene and mutation, of the ways of speeding the mutation process, and of the nature of viruses, the development of hybrid corn and polyploid plants, and so on. He said it was a disgrace not to make practical use of genetics for the benefit of the socialist motherland:

One cannot agree with those comrades who demand that the course in genetics be removed from the programs of higher educational institutions and that we reject the principles on the basis of which we have created and are now creating valuable varieties and strains.

We should not simply ape everything done abroad, but we are obliged to master everything created abroad—to master it critically and creatively, as Lenin taught us. We must grasp each new development and foster it, so that new cadres grow that will be able to advance science.

Only by truthfulness and criticism of our own mistakes can we attain the great future successes that our motherland expects of us.[13]

As the transcript of the session shows, he was not once interrupted; indeed, he was applauded at the conclusion of his remarks.

The next speaker, however, was Babadzhanyan, and he launched an attack against Rapoport. He denied that any use had come from the study of chromosomes, he reviled mutagenesis (the aspect of genetics with which Rapoport was especially associated), and he proclaimed that all mutations are invariably harmful and that "organisms thus obtained are nothing but defects and monsters!"

> After all, Rapoport could not demonstrate here that newly obtained mutants were fundamentally different in any way from the innumerable [useless] mutations obtained previously. On the contrary, there is every reason to believe they are of the same strain. Finally, if we grant that a small number of nonharmful, nonlethal mutations have indeed been obtained, who needs them? Who needs *Drosophila* that are inherently useless?[14]

Rapoport began to protest from his seat. Babadzhanyan turned to insults, stooping so low as to say that Rapoport was unable to see the rotten nature of formal genetics because he was missing one eye. There followed this exchange:

> *I. A. Rapoport.* But there are useful mutations, many of them. Why do you close both eyes to them?
> *G. A. Babadzhanyan.* In the first place, they are useful mutations in a useless object. (*Applause.*)
> *I. A. Rapoport.* We have methods for combating tuberculosis and other diseases.
> *G. A. Babadzhanyan.* Just promises.
> *I. A. Rapoport.* Whereas you promise to develop a variety in two years, but neither keep your promises nor admit your mistakes!
> *G. A. Babadzhanyan.* "We carry our theory into practice," Rapoport says. What theory are you carrying into practice? By its very nature, your theory is aimed against practice. Your "theory" doesn't just relate to practice indifferently or neutrally. . . . The Mendelians are opponents not only of established and proven achievements, but also potential opponents of all future achievements. (*Applause.*)[15]

Ivan I. Shmalgauzen, a prominent specialist in evolution, came under attack day after day. He was even mocked for the fact that he was ill and unable to participate in the session. He came and tried to bear himself calmly under the accusations, but it was evident that he was very frightened; the chief thing he sought to convey to the audience was a wish to dissociate himself from the views of Weismann and Morgan and demonstrate that there were no serious differences between his own position and Lysenko's assertions.

By contrast, another of the courageous speakers was Vasily S. Nemchinov, an economist and statistician and a member of both the AN SSSR and the Belorussian Academy of Sciences and also of VASKhNIL. Nemchinov had been director of the Timiryazev Agricultural Academy since 1940, and in that capacity had made it possible for many of the best scientists and opponents of Lysenko—Pryanishnikov, Konstantinov, Zhebrak, and the noted evolutionist Aleksandr A. Paramonov, among others—to continue their work. At the same time, however, Nemchinov gave freedom of action to the Lysenkoists at the academy, seeking only to assure that the competition of ideas was restricted to the laboratories and fields and did not turn into political struggle.

When Nemchinov rose to speak on the last day of the discussion of Lysenko's report, the session had essentially ended in complete triumph of the Lysenkoists, and the victory of obscurantism over science was assured. The session awaited only speeches by two of the most authoritative Lysenkoists, Stoletov and Prezent, before hearing Lysenko's concluding remarks and a letter of greetings from the participants to Stalin. Yet at that moment the Lysenkoists heard something they never expected. Before them stood a mountain that, in the words of an old song, they could neither obscure from view nor get around.

"I see that our scientists are divided on some questions," Nemchinov began. "Personally, as director of the Timiryazev Academy, I see nothing bad in this. . . . They say there is no Michurinist line at the Timiryazev Agricultural Academy, that our personnel, the professors and so on, are anti-Michurinists. That is untrue," and he proceeded to list those who related their work to the Michurinist line.[16]

He then went on to talk about his relationship with Zhebrak. Earlier in the session, Nemchinov had been accused of facilitating Zhebrak's work and approving everything Zhebrak did. Nemchinov responded by reaffirming his respect for Zhebrak as a scientist, while pointing out that, if Zhebrak had erred, personal regard would not keep Nemchinov from saying so. Those who claim otherwise know the truth full well, yet "consider it necessary for some reason to mislead the Soviet public."[17] Someone in the audience shouted, "They're right!" From that moment onward, Nemchinov was constantly interrupted by shouting and insults. Yet he refused to retreat. Here is what the transcript of the proceedings shows:

Voice from the audience: Does the chromosome theory belong in the golden treasury?

V. S. Nemchinov: Yes, I repeat, yes, I hold that the chromosome theory of heredity has entered the golden treasury of humankind and I continue to maintain that position.

A Voice: You are no biologist, how can you judge?

V. S. Nemchinov: I am not a biologist, but I am able to test this theory from the viewpoint of the science in which I conduct research, statistics. (*Stir in the hall.*) It also corresponds to my own understanding. But that is not the point. (*Stir in the hall.*)

A Voice: What do you mean, it's not the point?

V. S. Nemchinov: All right, it is the point, if you wish. Then I must say that I cannot share the viewpoint of those comrades who declare that chromosomes bear no relation to the mechanisms of heredity. (*Stir in the hall.*)

A Voice: There are no mechanisms.

V. S. Nemchinov: You just think there are no mechanisms. This mechanism can not only see, it can color and determine. (*Stir in the hall.*)

A Voice: Colors! And statistics!

V. S. Nemchinov: I disagree with the viewpoint expressed by the chairman that the chromosome theory of heredity and specifically some of Mendel's laws represent some sort of idealistic viewpoint or some sort of reactionary theory. Personally, I consider that wrong. That is my point of view. (*Stir in the hall, laughter.*)

A Voice: It's interesting to hear that from the director of the Timiryazev Academy!

V. S. Nemchinov: Then let me state my view. I do not consider it right to stop all A. R. Zhebrak's work on amphidiploids even if he committed an unpatriotic misdeed that has been deservedly condemned.

A Voice: You ought to resign.

V. S. Nemchinov: Perhaps I should. I don't cling to my job. (*Stir in the hall.*)

A Voice: That's bad.

V. S. Nemchinov: But I believe my viewpoint is right and I consider the aggressive nature of the speeches and acts aimed at forbidding A. R. Zhebrak's work to be wrong . . .

A Voice: Tell us how you feel about the points made in [Lysenko's] report.

V. S. Nemchinov: My attitude toward T. D. Lysenko's report is this: I believe that its basic theses are right and so are the basic ideas it contains—that agrobiology should be mobilized to serve the needs of collective farming and that its methods of work should be carried over to all the farm fields.

A Voice: Theoretically.

V. S. Nemchinov: In the realm of theory I consider Trofim Denisovich wrong about the chromosome theory of heredity.

At this the Lysenkoists began to interrupt even more furiously, but Nemchinov stood fast. He finished his remarks with these words:

I bear the moral and political responsibility for the policy of the Timiryazev Academy. I am morally and politically responsible for the policy I pursue; I consider that policy correct, and I will continue to pursue it. If this policy proves wrong, I shall be told so, or the hopes and expectations voiced here for my departure form the post will be fulfilled. It would be intolerable, in my view, to put a stop to Professor Zhebrak's work at the Timiryazev Academy.

At this point, Prezent shouted, "Morgan-type work, right?" To which Nemchinov repeated, "I bear the moral and political responsibility and I shall bear it as long as it is mine," and with those words he left the rostrum.[18]

By any standard, Nemchinov's behavior was heroic, and for him—as earlier for Konstantinov, Koltsov, Pryanishnikov, and Rapoport—so forthright a stand may have provided him with protection. He lost his position as director of the Timiryazev Academy, but he remained an active scientist until his death in 1964, training his students and surrounded by respectful attention.[19]

Some of those who spoke in defense of genetics seemed prepared to resign themselves to defeat—e.g., Shmalgauzen and Polyakov. But most of those who might have spoken in opposition to the Michurinists had been kept out of the meeting, and some who were admitted were intimidated. Aleksandr A. Malinovsky, for instance, asked for and was granted the floor, but when the chairman announced his turn to speak, Malinovsky withdrew his name; later, he explained to me that some of his friends, knowing his excitability, had advised him against taking the platform. Avakyan's complaint that the geneticists were reluctant to join in debate can only be construed as hypocritical.[20]

When Prezent spoke, he dropped all inhibitions and jeered at his opponents, stooping even to punning on their names. "There now remain only a few open and declared Morganists in our country; perhaps one must really be a blockhead [*dubina*—clearly, a reference to Dubinin] to remain one (*applause*)." He also directly addressed several of his adversaries. To Polyakov, for example, he said, "Darwinism nowadays is not what it was in Darwin's time. . . . The Darwinist doctrine did not know today's selection level, could not know it, but you, Professor Polyakov, are obliged to know it. After all, you should be wiser than Darwin, if only because the bird perched on the sage's head sees farther than the sage. (*Laughter.*)"[21]

Yet many of the geneticists, particularly in the first days of the session, did not grasp what was happening. After all, it had been only a short time since Lysenko was suffering defeat after defeat. The day after *Pravda* announced the appointment of new members to VASKhNIL and the calling of the academy session, Efroimson, who was expecting to hear the Party Central Committee's reactions to the long critique of Lysenkoism which he had prepared so hopefully the year before, telephoned the Central Committee's science department and told V. Vasilyeva, a member of the department staff, "I just don't understand what is going on, but remember that everything I wrote is God's truth." "Surely you don't think for one moment that I doubt it?" she replied.[22] Word of this answer spread swiftly among the geneticists, supporting their confidence that truth would triumph. Their hope was that the Lysenko forces were staking everything on a gamble—and would lose.

On the final day of the session, an event occurred that opened everyone's eyes. That morning, *Pravda* printed a repentant letter to Stalin from Yury Zhdanov, retracting his views and trying to draw a line between the personal views of Yury Zhdanov the chemist-philosopher and Yury Zhdanov the head of a department of the Central Committee. Although Zhdanov still voiced criticism of Lysenko, in trying to reconcile these contradictions within himself, he referred to the requirement Lenin set his adherents, to disregard actually observed phenomena that might lead them to sink into "objectivism." Party discipline proved stronger than scientific truth.

I give Zhdanov's letter in full because it so vividly delineates the moral environment of totalitarian rule.

TO COMRADE J. V. STALIN, CENTRAL COMMITTEE OF THE COMMUNIST PARTY

In addressing a lecturers' seminar with a report on controversial questions of modern Darwinism, I unquestionably committed a whole series of grave mistakes.

1. The very organization of the report was wrong. I obviously failed to take into account my new position as an official of the Central Committee apparatus, underestimated my responsibility, and did not realize that my presentation would be taken as the official stand of the Central Committee. This was a result of a "university habit" of expressing my personal viewpoint in any scientific debate, without pausing for reflection. Consequently, when I was invited to deliver a report at the lecturers' seminar, I decided then and there to speak my own thoughts, qualifying them as "my personal point of view" so that my remarks bound no one in any way. This was surely a "professorial" attitude (in the bad sense), not a Party position.

2. The fundamental mistake in the report itself was that it sought to reconcile warring schools in biology.

From the very first day of my work in the science department, representatives of formal genetics have been coming to me with complaints that useful plant varieties they have developed (buckwheat, kok-sagyz [Russian dandelion], geraniums, flax, citrus fruits), possessing improved qualities, were not being introduced in farming and were being resisted by Academician Lysenko's adherents. These unquestionably useful plant forms were obtained by direct chemical or physical influence on the germ cell. The Michurinist doctrine does not deny the possibility and desirability of such action, while recognizing the existence of many other, more important ways of changing the organism. Formal genetics considers its methods (strong shocks to the organism by Roentgen rays [X-rays], ultraviolet light, colchicine, acenaphthene) to be the only possible methods. I am aware that the mechanism of these agents' effects upon the organism can and should be explained by Michurinist and not by formal genetics.

My mistake was that in deciding to defend these practical results, which are "gifts of the Greeks," I did not mercilessly criticize the fundamental methodological flaws of Mendel-Morganist genetics. I admit that this is a narrowly pragmatic approach to practice, it is pursuit of the kopek.

The struggle among different schools in biology often takes the ugly form of squabbles and rows. And it seemed to me that this was all just such squabbling and quarreling. Consequently, I underestimated the matter of principle involved, treated the question carelessly, and did not analyze its profound causes and roots.

All this combined to create a desire to "reconcile" the disputing sides, to eradicate the disagreements and to emphasize what united, not what divided, the adversaries. But in science, as in politics, principles are not reconciled, they triumph; the struggle is waged not by suppressing but by disclosing contradictions. The attempt to reconcile principles on the basis of pragmatism and narrow practical concerns, the underestimation of the theoretical aspect of the conflict, led to eclecticism, to which I plead guilty.

3. My sharp and public criticism of Academician Lysenko was wrong. Academician Lysenko is now the recognized leader of the Michurinist school in biology, he has defended Michurin and his doctrine from attacks by bourgeois geneticists, and he has himself done much for science and our farming practice.

In view of this, criticism of Lysenko, of his individual shortcomings, should be so conducted as not to weaken but to strengthen the position of the Michurinists.

I disagree with some of Academician Lysenko's theoretical propositions (the denial of intraspecies struggle and mutual aid, underestimation of the internal specific character of the organism); I believe he still makes poor use of the treasure-trove of the Michurinist doctrine (which is why Lysenko has failed to develop any substantial agricultural plant varieties), and I consider that he gives our agricultural science weak leadership. VASKhNIL, which he heads, functions at far from full capacity. It conducts no work at all in animal husbandry and the economics and organization of farming, and research in agrochemistry is weak. But all these shortcomings should not be criticized as I did in my report. My criticism of Lysenko made the formal geneticists "third-party beneficiaries."

Being wholeheartedly devoted to the Michurinist doctrine, I criticized Lysenko not for being a Michurinist, but for insufficiently developing the Michurinist doctrine. Objectively, therefore, the Michurinists lost by such criticism, and the Mendelist-Morganists gained.

4. Lenin pointed out repeatedly that recognition of the necessity of one or another phenomenon holds the danger of succumbing to objectivism. To some extent, I did not escape this danger.

In large measure, I characterized the place of Weismannism and of Mendelism-Morganism (I do not differentiate between them) in the manner of Pimen [the medieval scribe]: that is, viewing good and evil with indifference. I mistakenly set myself the task of "recognizing their place in the development of biological theory" and finding the "rational core" in them, instead of sharply attacking their scientific positions (represented among us by Shmalgauzen and his school), which constitute, in the realm of theory, a veiled form of clericalism, a theological concept that species originate from individual acts of creation, and which in practice lead to "limitation," to rejection of man's ability to transform the nature of animals and plants. As a result, my criticism of Weismannism proved weak, objectivist, and essentially superficial.

The upshot was that the chief blow fell upon Academician Lysenko, but it ricocheted against the Michurinist school.

Such were my mistakes, as I see them.

I consider it my duty to assure you, Comrade Stalin, and in your person the Communist Party Central Committee, that I have been and remain a convinced Michurinist. My errors were due to insufficient understanding of the history of the question and a misreading of where the lines are drawn in the battle for the Michurinist teaching. All this because of inexperience and immaturity. I will correct my mistakes by deeds.

Yury Zhdanov[23]

Publication of this letter on the day the VASKhNIL session closed was an ominous sign. If Zhdanov had been forced to recant, what could less influential individuals expect? Some of the participants in the session learned on the evening of August 6 that the letter would appear in *Pravda* the next day. Zhukovsky and Alikhanyan, two who had defended genetics at the session—not as strongly as Rapoport or Nemchinov, but nevertheless quite definitely—took fright and decided they had better renounce their stand publicly. Realizing that if they waited until the next day, after the letter had appeared in print, the sincerity of their repentance would not sound very convincing, they immediately telephoned Lobanov to tell him they were recanting and to beg him to pardon them and allow them to submit statements at the closing meeting. (Polyakov followed them with a similar recantation.)

In their speeches—which paralleled each other point for point—Zhukovsky and Alikhanyan took care to point out that what they were about to say had no connection with the Zhdanov letter. Zhukovsky declared that the speech he had delivered two days before "was unworthy of a Communist Party member and a Soviet scientist. . . . I believe I have a moral obligation to be an honest Michurinite, an honest Soviet biologist. . . . May the past that divided us from T. D. Lysenko (not always, it is true) disappear into oblivion. Believe me that today I take a Party step and speak as a true Party member—that is to say, sincerely."[24] And Alikhanyan:

> As a Communist, I cannot and ought not . . . stubbornly oppose my personal views and outlook to the entire steady advance of the development of biology. . . .
> Beginning tomorrow, not only will I free my own scientific work of the old, reactionary Weismannist-Morganist views, but I will also reform all my pupils and comrades and change them. . . .
> I declare categorically to my comrades that henceforth I shall fight against those who thought as I did yesterday . . . I will not only criticize what has been fallacious and Weismannist-Morganist in my work, but I will also take an active part in this forward movement of Michurinist science.[25]

Alikhanyan was prepared even to take on the function of hangman of his own former colleagues who rejected the compromise with conscience that he himself had just made; Alikhanyan promised he would "reform" them. This was one of the most revelatory public examples of spiritual suicide under dictatorial pressure. Even Zhdanov, a nonspecialist, had spoken about Lysenko's mistakes, but neither Zhukovsky nor Alikhanyan found the strength to do so. Instead, they repudiated all their previous scientific activity, anathematized everything they had previously held sacred, and fawned upon the Lysenkoists for having put them on "the true path."

Lysenko administered the final blow in his concluding remarks. "One of the notes handed up to me asks how the Party Central Committee views my report," he said. "My answer is that the Party Central Committee has considered my report and approved it." At this point, the transcript notes: "*Stormy applause, turning into an ovation. All rise.*"[26] Five years later, a few days after Stalin's death, Lysenko declared that "Stalin . . . personally edited the draft of the report 'On the Situation in Biological Science,' explained his corrections to me in detail, and instructed me on how to phrase individual parts of the report. Comrade Stalin attentively followed the results of the work of the August session of VASKhNIL."[27]

The Purge in Soviet Biology

The decision of the Party Central Committee, that thenceforth only one school of thought would be tolerated in biology, opened the way for squaring accounts with all scientists at every level. All those whom the Lysenkoists had marked as open or potential adversaries were now branded "Weismannist-Mendelist-Morganists." Throughout the country, the Party began to summon the most knowledgeable and creative specialists in every field of biology to appear before Party committees to repent their "mistakes" and renounce their beliefs. Those who yielded to the pressure were then placed on display at open meetings where they were called enemies of science and forced to beat their breasts in self-reproach. Any who held out against this humiliation were driven out of the scientific institutions; indeed, many were expelled even after their recantations.

The harassment was meted out on a rising scale according to rank. Minor staff members got off with a light scare, but heads of scientific institutions got rough treatment. The halt, the lame, the sick, the elderly, the war heroes—none were spared. In the provinces the scale of torments increased in proportion to distance from the capital. As but a single example, a conference for the Ukrainian republic was held in Kiev from August 30 to September 2. Glushchenko and Olshansky came from Moscow and presented introductory reports. Then the geneticists were led on stage, one by one, to confess their mistakes, under the crossfire of interrogators. The entire Lysenkoist fraternity came from Odessa, their supporters arrived from other cities, and they incited one another to a high pitch.

Sergei M. Gershenzon, a former student of the great population geneticist Chetverikov, not only denounced his teachers as well as Koltsov, Serebrovsky, Dubinin, and Vavilov; he also diligently reviled himself:

> In my research, I adopted untrue, antiscientific, formal-genetics positions that were rightly denounced in Academician Lysenko's report . . . and I proceeded from entirely wrong assumptions. . . .
> I always highly valued Michurin's and Lysenko's work, yet at the same time . . . I distorted the very core of the Michurinist teaching. . . .
> I had too superficial a knowledge of Marxist methodology, I had insufficiently studied the classics of Marxism—Marx, Engels, Lenin, and Stalin—and insufficiently studied the works of Michurin and Lysenko. That is why my research manifested one of the worst forms of kowtowing to bourgeois culture: acceptance and support of the reactionary ideas exported to us from the West in the form of Mendelism-Morganism.[28]

Gershenzon and many of his colleagues may have thought that Lysenkoism was now firmly established in Soviet science and hence they vowed never to turn back to genetics as long as they lived. Not for one moment can one believe that they did this sincerely. In fact, they all reverted to normal genetic research less than two decades later. Meantime, however, Gershenzon pronounced these words:

....I declare my complete renunciation of formal genetics, of the Mendelist-Morganist outlook, and switch entirely to the standpoint of Michurinist science. I realize that a mere verbal declaration is not enough. In the course of my further work, I shall dedicate all my strength and knowledge to exposing the pseudoscientific and reactionary nature of Morganism-Mendelism and to wholeheartedly serving Soviet agrobiology.[29]

Even after that, Olshansky went right on hectoring Gershenzon, denying that his work had represented a "jumble of various views," as Gershenzon claimed, and accusing him of "consistent Weismannism."[30]

Party members, of course, were in an especially difficult position. The Party demanded absolute recantation and a renunciation of past views on pain of expulsion. Beyond that loomed the prospect of possible imprisonment and sentence to a labor camp. The overwhelming majority took the path of abject admission of errors. For example, a week after the session ended, *Pravda* printed a letter from Zhebrak, dated August 9, in which he said: "As long as our Party recognized both trends in Soviet genetics . . . I firmly defended my views, which differed from those of Academician Lysenko on various points. But now . . . as a Party member, I do not consider it possible to go on holding views that our Party Central Committee has declared erroneous." Even that was apparently not enough. Beneath the letter, *Pravda* printed an "Editors' Note," declaring that Zhebrak was mistaken in saying that the Party had recognized two trends in genetics; the Party had recognized and recognizes only the Michurinist doctrine. The editors concluded with the warning that "Professor A. R. Zhebrak's further work will show whether his statement is sincere."[31]

Rapoport was also a Party member, but, as he told me personally on two occasions, he chose to act differently. After a Party meeting voted to expel him, he refused to fight to keep his membership. He went to the district Party committee and turned in his Party membership card.[32]

Two weeks after the end of the August 1948 session, the Ministry of Higher Education removed Nemchinov as director of the Timiryazev Agricultural Academy and replaced him with Stoletov, Lysenko's messenger during the session.[33] Zhebrak was also dismissed and his laboratory was closed down.[34] Konstantinov was also dismissed as head of Timiryazev's department of crop breeding and seed production. Lysenko seized this chair and the nation's oldest and most respected higher educational institution in the field of agriculture was now completely in Lysenko's hands. A wave of dismissals followed, in which about three thousand biologists lost the jobs they had held in institutions of research and higher education.[35] The universities affected included those in Moscow, Leningrad, Gorky, Kharkov, Kiev, Voronezh, Saratov, Tbilisi, and many other towns. Some of the people who were dismissed were also arrested. Efroimson, who had been arrested in 1932 and freed in 1935, was rearrested in May 1949, as a "socially dangerous element."[36] A particularly tragic case was that of Dmitry A. Sabinin, a plant physiologist. A consistent critic of Lysenko (see chapter 10), he was expelled from the faculty of Moscow State University; though he found work as a biologist in the Crimea, he could not endure the continuing persecution and shot himself on April 22, 1951.[37]

In order to underscore the new situation, the presidium of the AN SSSR scheduled a meeting for August 24, to which the heads of several ministries were invited. The academy's president, Sergei Vavilov, in his opening speech, said that "it is not a matter of discussion ... It is necessary to eradicate servility and kowtowing to things foreign in the biological sector, as well as everywhere else"; that it was "the duty of the presidium to strengthen the work of the leadership of the biology division and to create favorable conditions for development of the Genetics Institute headed by Academician Lysenko"; and that it was "necessary to reorganize the work of the Institute of Evolutionary Morphology and the Institute of Cytology, Histology, and Embryology" (Koltsov's old institute).[38]

Academician Leon A. Orbeli, a leading physiologist and secretary of the academy's biology division, followed with a report. Orbeli's fate was already decided. Everyone, including Orbeli himself, realized full well that the president's words about the need to strengthen the leadership of the biology division were not idle talk. Nevertheless, the division secretary managed to deliver a calm, balanced report on the situation in the academy's biological institutions.[39]

This merely poured oil on the flames of polemical fervor. The tone of the subsequent discussion was set not by scientists, but by the ministers who had come to the meeting. Minister of Sovkhozes N. A. Skvortsov proclaimed that "our scientists ... are obliged, as Comrade [A. A.] Zhdanov put it in his report on the magazines *Zvezda* and *Leningrad*, not merely to 'answer blow for blow' in fighting these rotten slanders and attacks on our Soviet culture and socialism, but to take the offensive and scourge bourgeois culture, which is in a state of decay and corruption."[40] Minister of Higher Education Kaftanov excoriated the geneticists as lackeys of the bourgeoisie and particularly of American imperialism:

Such inveterate enemies of our motherland as the White émigrés Dobzhansky, Timofeyev-Ressovsky, and others, who out do themselves in serving the American bosses, have raised their heads from under the cellar door of American imperialism to slander the USSR and Michurinist biology. ... To our regret, such troubadours of Mendelism-Morganism as Zhebrak, Dubinin, Navashin, Shmalgauzen, and others echo them, while the USSR Academy of Sciences, which is the headquarters of Soviet science, and its biology division have given them full opportunity to use the platform of the academy's institutes and journals to pour filth upon Academician Lysenko and his pupils and to revile progressive, advanced Michurinist biological science. ... We should not merely speak, but scream about the intolerable shortcomings in the work of many biological institutions of the Academy of Sciences.[41]

The top officials of the Stalinist state and Lysenko's immediate entourage ascribed only the basest motives to the geneticists' interests and employed only the vocabulary of party clichés. Nuzhdin, who was to become Lysenko's deputy director of the USSR Academy of Science's Genetics Institute, set the tone:

> Lenin wrote: "The *social* position of professors in bourgeois society is such that only those who sell science into the service of capital are allowed to become professors, only those who agree to speak the most incredible antisocialist nonsense, the most unconscionable absurdities and rubbish. The bourgeoisie forgives the professors all this, just so they engage in 'annihilating socialism' " This is why Mendelism-Morganism remains widespread abroad in spite of its lack of practical results.[42]

On the other hand, Lysenko's collaborators claimed the moral high ground for themselves. Koshtoyants said that, "above all, the Soviet scientist must proceed on the basis of state morality, public morality. From this standpoint, which is basic to us, I must say that no small, chance benefit can atone for the harm wrought by Weismannism-Morganism."[43] Norair M. Sisakyan, then the deputy director of the Biochemistry Institute of the AN SSSR (see biographical sketches), expounded: "Today, it is obvious to all that the Michurinists' goals are . . . noble and correspond completely to the spirit and aspirations of the great scientists of our people . . . whereas the strivings of the anti-Michurinists are diametrically opposite and coincide with the aspirations of the most reactionary representatives of foreign biology."[44]

Orbeli took the floor once more on the final day of the session. He asked to be relieved of the duties of academician-secretary of the biology division, saying, however, that "my leaving should not be regarded as any kind of protest against the turn of events now taking place. On the contrary, I am in complete sympathy with this change."[45]

In concluding the session, Sergei Vavilov reiterated the ideological basis for assessing the situation in biology: the division of experimental science into bourgeois and proletarian science, the "Party nature" of science, and the emphasis upon practice as primary.

> Of course, Soviet natural science employs many laws and methods that have entered into and will enter into bourgeois natural science, but our science, the science of a socialist country advancing toward communism, is separated from bourgeois science by the chasm of an entirely different ideology, the chasm of an entirely different task confronting us—the task of serving the people in every way, serving its demands, its practice, and its needs."

Sergei Vavilov closed with these words:

> Comrades! As we part after these important discussions and decisions, we cannot fail to recall the man whose genius and sharp eye correct our mistakes on all paths—in politics, economics, and science. I am speaking, comrades, of Iosif

Vissarionovich Stalin. (*Stormy applause. All rise.*) . . . Hail Comrade Stalin! (*Stormy, prolonged applause, turning into an ovation for Comrade Stalin.*)[46]

It is hard to imagine how Nikolai Vavilov's brother, a physicist who shared (so today's Soviet historiographers assure us) his brother's point of view about the validity and value of genetics,[47] could have brought himself to say these things, except from fear of sharing his brother's fate.

The resolution adopted at the end of the session put the final touch to the rout of the geneticists.

Resolved:
   1. To relieve Academician L. A. Orbeli of the duties of academic secretary of the biology division. . . . To make Academician T. D. Lysenko a member of the division's bureau.
   2. To relieve Academician I. I. Shmalgauzen of the duties of director of the A. N. Severtsov Institute of Animal Evolutionary Morphology.
   3. To abolish the laboratory of cytogenetics headed by Corresponding Member of the Academy Dubinin in the Institute of Cytology, Histology, and Embryology. . . . To close the laboratory of botanical cytology in the above institute.[48]

And so the list went on.

From the agricultural and biological sciences, the persecutions spread to the medical sciences. In September, the presidium of the USSR Academy of Medical Sciences held a special meeting, at which Lysenko was the guest of honor. For two days, the denunciations and recantations rolled on, reported in great detail in a special issue of the Party newspaper *Medical Worker* (Meditsinsky rabotnik) on September 15.[49] Some members seized the opportunity to avenge the slights of past years. Olga B. Lepeshinskaya, an Old Bolshevik turned cell biologist, denounced the "Morganists" who had "hindered and belittled" her claims to have shown "the transformation of living matter into cells" (see chapter 12). M. M. Nevyadomsky complained: "For thirty years I tried to show that the cancer cell is a parasitic microorganism that develops by evolution from the body of a virus, but the circles controlling medical science are concealing this remarkable fact." N. A. Semashko, who had been the first commissar of health in Lenin's government, argued that anyone who believed in genes perforce believed in eugenics and that such "biological predestination" made medicine pointless; the conclusion to which "Weismannism" led is that "we ought to close the maternity homes and the public health network, because they help and support the weak who 'dilute' the race." Some, such as L. Ya. Blyakher and S. N. Davidenkov, made speeches of repentance.

Only a few refused to recant and defended scientific principles: Georgy F. Gauze, who headed the antibiotic production program, and Dmitry N. Nasonov, who specifically rejected Lepeshinskaya's theory.

The participants adopted a letter of greetings to Stalin, in which they said: "Our science is obligated to you, dear Iosif Vissarionovich, for all its best achievements, for its entire progress. . . . We promise you, our dear leader, that we shall promptly correct the mistakes we have committed. . . . We will fight for the Bolshevik Party spirit in medicine and public health, eradicating hostile bourgeois ideology and servility to things foreign in our midst." The newspaper *Medical Worker* itself appealed to the personnel of medical establishments to "thoroughly cleanse the Soviet medical-science field of idealistic and metaphysical weeds so as to advance in seven-league boots and speed the attainment of the task set by the great Stalin—not merely to overtake the achievements of foreign science but to overtake them in the immediate future." In fact, the "weeds" were already being pulled. The presidium resolved to close the laboratories where "Weismannism-Morganism easily found a place for itself," to "review the structure and direction of the scientific work" in others, and to dismiss the heads of several (including not only the uncompromising Gauze but also the repentant Blyakher).[50]

So it went in all spheres of science having even the slightest relationship to biology—in the schools, technical colleges, and higher educational institutions, in libraries and publishing houses, and in administration. It was forbidden to use old textbooks; works on genetics were removed from libraries; plantings of mutant plants were torn up (including valuable lines, whose loss inflicted tangible harm upon the country); even collections of the *Drosophila* with which the geneticists had worked for so many years were destroyed.

Lysenko followers and opportunists promptly filled the vacancies. Honest scientists, incapable of being turncoats, and those who were slow to trim their sails to the wind, found themselves shut out of the scientific institutions.

To mark Lysenko's fiftieth birthday, the presidium of the USSR Supreme Soviet awarded him another Order of Lenin on September 29, 1948, "for outstanding services in the cause of developing advanced science and great, fruitful practical activity in agriculture." Forgotten were Yury Zhdanov's continuing criticisms of Lysenko's ineffective practical activities, which had been contained in the letter of repentance to Stalin and published in *Pravda* not two months earlier (see above). The Odessa Plant Breeding and Genetics Institute was named after Lysenko.[51]

The Lysenko "doctrine" had become omnipotent in agriculture, biology, and medicine, and soon representatives of other sciences began to call for similar measures in their fields. A group of physicists and philosophers proclaimed the necessity of immediately exposing bourgeois distortions in Einstein's theory of relativity. In the December 1948 issue of the *Herald of the U.S.S.R. Academy of Sciences,* Academician Yevgeny A. Chudakov, a member of the academy's presidium, demanded the urgent reorganization of "the technical sciences in the light of the decisions at the session of

VASKhNIL,"[52] and in a book about the structure of the stellar system, a prominent astronomer asserted that he had "sought to take into account the outcome of the . . . session of VASKhNIL on the situation in biology."[53]

Lysenko's triumph lost the USSR a good friend in the United States. Herman Muller had maintained his political support for the Soviet Union despite the cancellation of the International Genetics Congress in 1938, despite his friend Vavilov's death, and despite the incessant Lysenkoist attacks on him personally. But at the end of 1948, he resigned in protest as a foreign member of the AN SSSR. To the Lysenkoists, it was another victory and the occasion for another propaganda campaign against the enemies of Soviet science:

> Muller declares that in its decision on questions of biology the Academy of Sciences pursued political aims and that science in the USSR is subordinated to politics.
>
> We Soviet scientists are convinced that nowhere in the world is there or can there be science that is divorced from politics. . . .
>
> In speaking against the Soviet Union and its sciences, Muller has earned the delighted approval and recognition of all the reactionary forces of the United States.
>
> The USSR Academy of Sciences parts with its former member without regret. He has betrayed the interests of true science and openly joined the camp of the enemies of progress, science, peace, and democracy.[54]

The political importance that the Kremlin leaders ascribed to Lysenko's victory was also reflected in Molotov's speech on the thirty-first anniversary of the Bolshevik Revolution. Referring to the August session of VASKhNIL, he said:

> The discussion on questions of heredity raised great questions of principle concerning the struggle of genuine science, based on the principles of materialism, against reactionary, idealistic survivals in scientific work, such as the Weismannist doctrine of unalterable heredity, which denies that acquired characteristics can be transmitted to later generations. The discussion emphasized the creative significance of materialist principles for all branches of science. . . . We should remember the task set . . . by Comrade Stalin: "Not only to overtake the achievements of foreign science, but to surpass them in the immediate future." The discussion of questions of biology also had great practical importance, particularly for further successes in socialist agriculture. Not in vain has this struggle been headed by Academician Lysenko, whose services in our common struggle for an upsurge in socialist agriculture are well known to all. . . .
>
> *The scientific discussion of questions of biology was conducted under the guiding influence of our Party.* Here, too, Comrade Stalin's guiding ideas played a decisive role, opening up broad perspectives in scientific and practical work.[55]

Was Stalin Predisposed toward Lysenkoism?

A question that has arisen repeatedly in the studies of the history of Soviet biology is: Why did Stalin take to Lysenkoism so ardently? Why did Lysenko's naive and superficial ideas about the direct influence of the external environment upon heredity, his fervent approval of the principle of the inheritance of acquired characteristics—views that were, in general, quite easily disproved by experiment—find a ready response in Stalin?

Medvedev and Graham deny that there is a connection between Lysenko's assertions and Stalin's own ideas. They contend that, although Stalin's support was very important in Lysenko's rise, it is difficult to find evidence of sympathy for the Lysenkoist view in Stalin's writings on theory. They note that Oparin and other Lysenkoists, citing Stalin's 1906 work, *Anarchism or Socialism?*, held that Stalin was long predisposed toward neo-Lamarckism; but they say, that these claims were based on a single sentence in that work related to biology, and that it was, in Medvedev's words, a "casual, meaningless statement."[56] The sentence is one in which Stalin, following a reference to the Mendeleyev periodic table of elements and to "the great significance of qualitative and quantitative changes in the history of nature," wrote: "The theory of neo-Lamarckism, to which neo-Darwinism is giving way, testifies to the same thing in biology."[57]

However, *Anarchism or Socialism?* contained much more that related to biology. It included a discussion of Darwinism and Lamarckism as ways of explaining evolutionary development and a consideration of Cuvier's theory of catastrophes as one way of explaining revolutionary transformations. These reflections occupied a central place in the first part of the work, "The Dialectical Method." Stalin arbitrarily applied biologists' observations about changes in organisms to the solution of problems of societal development; he saw in the biological data an illustration of the dialectical unity of quantitative and qualitative changes "as progressive elements carry on their everyday work spontaneously [i.e., by evolution] and make small, quantitative changes in the old order." Ultimately, the small changes cause a revolutionary situation to arise, in which, in Stalin's words, "those same elements unite, imbued with a single idea, and swoop down upon the enemy camp in order to wipe out the old order and introduce *qualitative changes* in life, establishing a new order." Stalin's reference to "qualitative and quantitative changes" has to be understood as shorthand for his personal philosophy of science (if anything so primitive deserves to be so called). From the start, Stalin had always looked for simple, easily grasped schemata. He regarded the transformation of quantity into quality as one of the chief forms of the movement of matter (or, as he put it, "the transition of quantitative relations into qualitative relations"). For him, it had the status of a law of nature, and, more broadly, it was the chief philosophical law of dialectical materialism. Thus, the close coupling of neo-Lamarckism to Stalin's cherished "law" must be taken as a sign that, in Stalin's mind, the two were congruent.

Stalin went on to assert that "evolution prepares revolution and creates the soil for it, but revolution crowns evolution and facilitates its further work." Completing the discussion of the transition of quantitative changes into qualitative, and the corresponding relationship of evolutionary and revolutionary transitions, he wrote: "Just such processes occur in nature also. . . . Everything in nature should be regarded from the standpoint of the movement of development." And it is at this point he mentioned Mendeleyev's periodic table and the sentence quoted by Medvedev and Graham about neo-Lamarckism occurs.[58]

But that was not all. Stalin then went on to invoke Lamarck and Darwin in his efforts to refute the anarchists. Seeking to demonstrate that the dialectical method was correct, he said that "Lamarck and Darwin also were not revolutionaries, but their evolutionary method placed biological science on its feet." He put Lamarck before Darwin not for chronological but for ideological reasons; he was confident that neo-Lamarckism would prevail. He disclosed even greater support for the superficial explanations of development that are peculiar to neo-Lamarckism when he considered the positive and negative sides in development and in movement: "Any phenomenon of life has two tendencies as soon as life changes and is in movement: a positive and a negative tendency. We must defend the former and reject the latter."[59]

This division of life processes into only two polar tendencies exemplifies Stalin's failure to conceive of a far wider spectrum of tendencies in developmental processes and their interdependence. In the years of the flowering of the Stalinist dictatorship, this attitude of his toward nature and natural resources, under the banner of Michurin's slogan, "We cannot await nature's favors, our task is to seize them from her," led to ecological disaster.

Then, in opposition to the anarchists who, in his words, supposed that "Marxism rests on Darwinism and regards it uncritically," Stalin made another very important comment: "Darwinism rejects not only Cuvier's cataclysms but also dialectically understood development, including revolution, since—from the standpoint of the dialectical method—evolution and revolution, quantitative and qualitative change, are two necessary forms of one and the same movement."

This statement is factually wrong in itself, unproven, and far from Darwin's own views; nevertheless it demonstrates quite characteristically the roots of Stalin's negative attitude toward Darwinism, an attitude that took shape back in those years, long before Lysenko emerged on the path of struggle against genetics.

Finally, *Anarchism or Socialism?* showed that Stalin had assimilated Lamarck's idea of the inheritance of acquired characteristics and the consequent explanation of evolution through the slow adaptation of organisms to a changing external environment. In exaggerated and simplified form, this idea enabled Stalin to explain the forward march of evolution, on the one hand, and the supremacy of matter over mind, on the other:

> There were not yet any living beings, but so-called "nonliving" nature already existed. The first living being did not possess consciousness, it possessed the quality of *irritation* and the rudiments of *sensation*. Then animals gradually developed the capacity to *sense*, which slowly turned into *consciousness* as the structure of their organism and nervous system developed. If the ape always walked on all fours, if it had not straightened its spine, its descendant—man—could not have used his lungs and vocal cords freely and thus could not have possessed the power of speech, thereby radically retarding the development of his consciousness. Or, further: If the ape had not risen to its feet, its descendant, man, would have been obliged to walk on all fours forever, to look down and obtain his impressions from the ground; he would have been unable to look up and around, and consequently would not have been able to supply more impressions to the brain than a four-legged animal. All this would have fundamentally retarded the development of human consciousness. . . .
>
> It turns out that the development of the material aspect, the development of the external conditions, *precedes* the development of the ideal aspect, the development of consciousness. First the external conditions change, first the material aspect changes, and afterwards consciousness, the ideal side, changes accordingly.[60]

These comments of Stalin are also notable for showing that, even at the dawn of his political career, he was willing to deal with questions requiring specialized knowledge that he lacked. His ignorance was not a hindrance then, nor was it later, when he turned, with equal self-assurance, to expounding philosophical categories, propounding economic "laws" of the development of socialism, and deciding that Lysenkoist doctrine should be the basis of agricultural policy.

Thus, in my opinion, it seems clear that Lysenkoism not only suited Stalin's interests but was in full accord with his views. The two men shared the same pattern of thought. They derived their conceptions from the same roots: a little learning, the reduction of complex matters to a primitive level, and goals that invited monopolization of power in their respective spheres.

Of course, it would be equally erroneous to ascribe the entrenchment of Lysenkoism solely to Stalin's personal views. Lysenkoism was also the logical outcome of Leninism and of the Bolshevik attitude toward the intelligentsia and the primacy given to practice. In sum, the chief cause of Lysenkoism's vitality was totalitarianism.

Nevertheless, it must be added that the political mantle that Lysenko and his followers wrapped around themselves and their constant invocation of the words of Marx, Engels, Lenin, and Stalin doubtless contributed to Stalin's benevolent regard for Lysenko. Besides, the organizational stratagems Lysenko used and his preaching of the importance of testing proposals on the kolkhoz and sovkhoz fields instead of in the quiet of the laboratory surely impressed Stalin, too. The bold gestures, such as the telegrams to "Comrade Stalin, the Kremlin, Moscow," were in the spirit of the times; almost daily the Soviet press featured such telegrams, reporting achievements of the sender's institution or voicing loyal support of the latest Party or government measure, with elaborate tributes to Stalin.

Still another element was Lysenko's constant pretense of the simple life, exemplified by his wrinkled jacket with curling lapels, his peasant blouse, and his old-fashioned rawhide belt, grease-stained and twisted, which he continued to wear even after his pupils presented him with a new and stylish belt.

Among persons who knew Lysenko even relatively well, a legend prevailed that he disdained wealth and lived very simply. Only a handful of individuals knew that his simplicity was a pretense—and, as the Russian saying puts it, worse than thievery—and during his lifetime those individuals preferred to maintain silence about it. Actually, Lysenko was a very wealthy man. His salary exceeded the earnings of the most famous scientists, and in addition he received honoraria for serving on various commissions and on the presidium of the AN SSSR.[61] From Stalin, he received the gift of a country home—it resembled a plantation estate—in the picturesque hamlet of Mozzhinka, near Zvenigorod, not far from Moscow. He was given awards, decorations, and orders that carried substantial monthly stipends; he was awarded the 200,000-ruble first-degree Stalin Prize three times; newspaper and magazine articles brought him large fees, and he received royalties for the numerous editions of his books. Over a period of many years, moreover, he received substantial compensation for the "improvement" of plant varieties by intravarietal crosses. In June 1937, the Council of Commissars ordered that a payment of four kopeks per hectare be made for all plantings of an improved variety, half to go to the selection station from which it had come and half to the selection specialists who had developed it ("up to a maximum of 50,000 rubles a year," the decree stated).[62] Medvedev colorfully compared the hopes of obtaining a bigger crop from such intravarietal crosses to attempts to increase the volume of water in a bottle by shaking it. This did not prevent the authorities from paying fantastic sums, by the standards of those times, for plantings of "renewed and improved" seed on millions of hectares.

Meanwhile, Russia was losing the leading position that it had once held in genetics. Five years after the August 1948 session, Watson and Crick discovered the double helix of DNA, the discovery that opened the era of molecular genetics. Yet in Soviet Russia twenty years earlier, Koltsov had predicted that the molecules of heredity would have a double structure. But Koltsov was persecuted, called a fascist and obscurantist, and removed from his position as director of an institute.

Similarly, it was in Soviet Russia that Chetverikov had laid the foundations of a whole science, population genetics, whose significance to present-day ecology is almost impossible to exaggerate. But Chetverikov was driven out, humiliated, and insulted following the August 1948 session. He died in Gorky, helpless and forgotten in his own country at a time when gold plaques were being struck in his honor in the West. It was in Soviet Russia that Nadson and Grigory S. Filippov discovered radiation mutagenesis; Nadson was arrested, and he perished in prison. It was in the Soviet Union that Solomon G. Levit established the world's first institute for the study of human genetics; Levit was shot in prison, and his institute was closed down. Levit's extremely talented student, Solomon N. Ardashnikov, was one of the thousands dismissed in the wake of the August 1948 session; he lived from hand to mouth for several years and never resumed work in his own specialty. Rapoport was first in the world to experiment extensively with chemical mutagenesis, but even the book containing his pioneer article was ordered burned in 1948.

In place of this scientific distinction, the country now faced backwardness in genetics, plant selection, treatment of hereditary ailments, and the production of antibiotics and other aspects of biotechnology. The Soviet Union was left stranded at the side of the road while other countries that had never dared dream of competing with Russia in genetics rushed on ahead.

12

The Period of Great Agronomical Deceptions

There is nothing more dangerous than blind passion in science. This is a direct path to unjustified self-confidence, to loss of self-critical-ness, to scientific fanaticism, to false science. Given support from someone in power, it can lead to suppression of true science and, since science is now a matter of state importance, to inflicting great injury on the country.
　　　　—N. N. Semyonov, "Science Does Not Tolerate Subjectivism"

It feels as though a sticky, slimy, oozing stupidity were continually being produced in the depths of our life. It accumulates and then begins to squeeze out and to fill every pore of our society. And there is nothing you can do about it, for this stupidity is the natural product of our own activities.
　　　　—A. A. Zinovyev, *A Bright Future*

The Stalin Plan for the Transformation of Nature

On October 20, 1948, two and a half months after the close of the August 1948 session of VASKhNIL, all the country's newspapers announced the launching of a grandiose project, whose scope was beyond compare with anything in history. The Party Central Committee and the USSR Council of Ministers had resolved, and Stalin had signed into effect, the "Plan for Erosion-Control Forest Planting, Introduction of Grassland Crop Rotation, and Building of Ponds and Reservoirs to Guarantee Large and Dependable Harvests in the Steppe and Forest-Steppe Regions of the European USSR."

Over an area of 120,000,000 hectares—that is, an area equal to that of Britain, France, Italy, Belgium, and the Netherlands combined—belts of forest were to be planted to block the hot dry winds (the so-called "black storms"), alter the climate, and thus guarantee a food supply to the Soviet people for centuries to come. Maps accompanying the announcement showed that the area stretched from ancient Izmail in the west to the Urals in the east and from Tula in the north to the Crimea in the south, and that it included the Bashkirian and Volga steppes and a large part of the Ukrainian grain region. The principal share of the crops of hard wheat, sugar beets, and sunflowers (the main vegetable-oil crop in the Soviet Union) were grown in these lands, and nearly half of all animal products came from them. This vast territory was to be transected by broad north-south belts of future forests, from which networks of narrower belts extended, and within the cells of this network was to be a spider web of forested fields among the kolkhozes. The plan was to involve 80,000 kolkhozes, 2,000 sovkhozes, more than 3,000 machine and tractor stations (22,000 tractors and a great deal of other machinery were allocated for the work), and tens of millions of people. The overall scheme was called the "Stalin Plan for the Transformation of Nature."

The imagination of the ordinary Soviet citizen, starved during the failed harvests of the war and postwar years, was tantalized by the claims made for this unprecedented project. The droughts would be conquered and harvests would become stable, since the path of the dry winds would be blocked by tens of billions of saplings, primarily oak, planted in the steppe. It was said that, if all the forest belts, thirty meters in width, were laid end to end, they would encircle the equator more than fifty times. The Stalin plan envisaged allotting up to 15 percent of the forest stand to fruit trees and bushes; now all Soviet children would eat fruits and berries to their hearts' content! The surfaces of 44,000 ponds and reservoirs would glisten among the trees. Throughout the country, in shop windows, offices, and movie theaters, colorful posters were put up showing Stalin as a *bogatyr*, a legendary medieval Russian knight, with the inscription "We will conquer drought, too!"—implying that the war against Nature would be waged as successfully as the war against Germany had been.

A Chief Administration of Erosion-Control Forestation, with the status of a ministry, was formed under the USSR Council of Ministers, and a protégé of Lysenko's, Yevgeny M. Chekmenev, was installed at its head. Chekmenev had been deputy minister of sovkhozes; at the August 1948 session of VASKhNIL, he was one of those who had railed against Rapoport and Serebrovsky, asserting, "There is no nonparty science. This was demonstrated long ago. Michurinist biology is a principled, Party science and will not tolerate compromise [with bourgeois science]."[1] Now, having moved up in the Stalinist hierarchy, Chekmenev promised the Soviet people mountains of food:

> The gullies, the destructive bane of the steppes, will disappear. The menacing black storms will be extinguished. Drought will fade away; the climate will become milder, moister, and the life of the people in the steppe will be incomparably more comfortable, easier, finer, and richer. The kolkhozes and the sovkhozes will gather dependable, progressively larger harvests of grain, vegetables, and fruit. On the sumptuous pastures, large herds of cattle and fine-fleeced sheep will graze. That is what the Stalin Plan for the Transformation of Nature will bring to the Soviet people.[2]

Lysenko took advantage of this opportunity to apply in practice his "discovery" that evolution took place without intraspecies competition, a discovery based on experiments on the "mutual assistance" among *kok-sagyz* plants in compact plantings. On the premise that plants of the same species not only do not impede each other's development when sown closely together but actually promote the growth of their fellow plants, Lysenko held that the traditional methods of forest planting, whereby trees are planted far enough apart so that they do not interfere with one another's growth, were incorrect. In his view, saplings help one another, and the weaker ones, in the interests of the well-being of their more successful fellow trees, die off, freeing space for the remaining trees. Proceeding from this theory of "self-immolation" (*samoizrezhivaniye*),[3] he insisted that the trees for the forest belts be planted by a "cluster method," in which six or seven acorns would be put into each of five holes that would be placed close together to form a cluster.

This notion had been sharply criticized soon after it had been put forth at the scientific conferences held November 4, 1947, and February 3–6, 1948, at Moscow State University.[4] Nonetheless, Stalin decreed that all the forest plantings be done according to Lysenko's method. The resolution authorizing the project specifically ordered VASKhNIL "to draw up instructions within two months for carrying out cluster plantings."

Two days after the plan was announced, on November 23, 1948, Lysenko convened a conference at VASKhNIL, at which he justified use of the cluster method in words such as these:

> Even without reference to biological theory, it can be proven in purely practical terms that, if one thing hinders two things, these two can always be united, even if temporarily, against their common enemy. For the time being, I will confine myself to this simple reference to substantiate the measures for cluster planting of erosion-control forest zones on old plowland in the steppe. . . .
>
> The scientific recognition of intraspecies competition is especially harmful in the practical business of forestry. . . . Wild vegetation, and particularly species of forest trees, possess the biologically useful attribute of self-immolation.[5]

Lysenko presented no scientific data showing that plants were capable of engaging in purposeful, "social" activity, sacrificing themselves so that the species would thrive, choosing independently which would die and which would continue to grow "on the shoulders of its dying fellow plants." The fact no biologist was prepared to make such an assertion did not deter him. (He admitted one exception: Cultivated plants would perish, without seeds, if planted too thickly together.)

Thus, the categories of political struggle—a temporary alliance against enemy weeds—were carried over into biology and became the core of Lysenko's concept of cluster planting. And to avoid repeat of the criticism that he failed to analyze and understand his own data, Lysenko did not cite figures from concrete experiments at all. Instead, he simply said, over and over again, "Our experiments irreproachably showed . . ." This phrase, in combination with such expressions as "genuine science does not tolerate chance," was supposed to give the illusion of scientific proof.

But "chance" dogged Lysenko. In the fall of 1949, the Chief Administration of Erosion-Control Forestation inspected the results on 38,700 hectares (i.e., 16 percent) of the 350,000 hectares that had been sown with acorns by the cluster method in the preceding spring. Given the Soviet practice of embellishing any figures, the inspection's data would hardly be expected to be objective, but even so, this verification painted a frightful picture. No mutual assistance between cluster-planted plants was found. Six months after the plantings of 1949, on 14,600 hectares (38 percent of the area inspected), only half of the acorns had produced saplings. On another 37 percent of the area, only 20 percent of the young trees survived; on another fifth, fewer than 10 percent of the plantings could be found; and the plants had perished completely on 3 percent of the area.[6]

This was a catastrophe. It appeared that the huge resources invested in the project had been wasted.

Lysenko reacted as if nothing untoward had happened. In the article in which he presented these figures, he supplied an optimistic conclusion:

The results of this large-scale production experiment, as the inspection showed, fully supported the vitality of the cluster method of planting acorns.... The main reason for the thinning suffered by the plantings ... was a failure to carry out the basic agrotechnological requirements stipulated in the instructions. Delays in planting in the arid zone turned out to be particularly harmful. Unfortunately, in these regions, as the inspection showed, 50 percent of the plantings were not carried out on time. [In other areas,] in place of 6–7 viable acorns, usually at most 1, 2, or 3 acorns capable of germinating were planted.[7]

History repeated itself the following year. Plantings over huge areas perished.[8] Yet the failure did not affect the authorities' determination to follow Lysenko's prescription. Three years later, the Chief Administration of Erosion-Control Forestation was still calling the cluster method the only "progressive" method.[9] Yet, although two and a half times more forest area was planted in the USSR between 1948 and 1958 than throughout the preceding 250 years, by 1956 only 4.8 percent of this remained in the form of viable trees—and those remained only because the kolkhoz workers violated Lysenko's instructions and planted and tended these plantings in the old manner.[10]

But while this "self-immolation" went on, Lysenko "clipped coupons": In 1949, he received his third Stalin Prize of 200,000 rubles. The reports of this award were accompanied by encomiums such as this:

When we say "Academician Lysenko," ... before our eyes a majestic panorama of the near future of our socialist agriculture opens up. We see vast fields of spreading wheat, vineyards in the central provinces, flowering fields in the polar regions, citrus plantations in the Ukraine, the North Caucasus, the Crimea, Central Asia. And in the torrid steppes of Stalingrad and many other areas, we see green expanses of broad-leafed oaks, as well as birch, whose beauty for some reason until now was associated only with the north. We see winter wheat that has found its new motherland in the steppes of Siberia, highly productive herds on collective and state farms, and much that it is still hard to foresee now but that will be a reality in the near future.[11]

In the end, the plantings—and the numerous replantings—failed to stop the dry winds and the drought and, of course, produced no change in the climate. Soon after Stalin's death in 1953, the newspapers stopped mentioning the reforestation scheme altogether. At a national conference on forestry in July 1954, the experts in attendance unanimously voted—in Lysenko's presence—against continuing the cluster method of planting.[12] It was officially estimated that the country had lost nearly a billion rubles by this gamble,[13] and that is probably an underestimate.

The "Law of Life of Biological Species": How Warblers Give Birth to Cuckoos

At the August 1948 session of VASKhNIL, Lysenko had taken issue with Darwinism on another question, the origin of species. "As a result of the development of our Soviet, Michurinist-oriented agrobiology, a number of questions of Darwinism arise differently. Darwinism is not only being cleared of mistakes, not only attaining a higher level, but in large measure is also changing a number of its propositions," he proclaimed. Specifically, he announced that he had discovered a new path of transition from one species to another. Whereas Darwinian theory described evolution as a gradual transformation of one species into another, Lysenko proposed an entirely different "theory": that "the transformation of one species into another occurs at a single leap," bypassing all intermediate stages. For example, he said, "By means of 'retraining' . . . after two, three, or four years of autumn plantings . . . *durum* [i.e., hard wheat] turns into *vulgare* [soft wheat], i.e., hard, 28-chromosome wheat [*Triticum durum*] turns into various forms of soft, 42-chromosome wheat [*T. vulgare*]; moreover, in this we do not find transitional forms between *durum* and *vulgare*." Lysenko offered no scientific data in support of this theory, but he tried to give it a philosophical grounding by referring to Stalin's beloved "law" of the transformation of quantitative into qualitative change:

> Darwin's theory comes from a recognition only of quantitative changes, only of an increase or decrease, and overlooks the fact that alterations, the transformations from one qualitative state into another, are obligatory and conform to natural laws. Yet, without the transformation of one qualitative state of organic forms into another qualitative state there would be no development, no transformation of species into species, only an increase or decrease in numbers, only what is commonly called growth.[14]

Back in 1941, M. G. Tumanyan had published an article had appeared in *Vernalization* claiming that hard wheat brought from Georgia turned into soft wheat after several years of cultivation in Armenia.[15] For seven years, this "discovery" remained neglected. But when Lysenko announced his new theory of evolution, Tumanyan's discovery was exhumed, and others like it began to appear in many Lysenkoist-controlled journals. V. K. Karapetyan and others found seeds of rye in wheat plantings and of barley in rye plantings; branched wheat had formed from soft wheat and *T. polonicum* from *T. turgidum*; cabbage had been generated from rutabaga and rape seeds. The parasitic plant broomrape (*Orobanche cumana*) had appeared on sunflower plants and hazel branches on hornbeam trees. Spruce trees had given birth to pine, and vice versa.[16] Again, no precise data or even scientific descriptions were given; the fact of such transformations was simply declared.

Lysenko himself topped them all. In several lectures and speeches, he announced that warblers had given birth to cuckoos! I heard him say this myself in a lecture at Moscow State University in the spring of 1955. He described how the lazy cuckoo placed its eggs in the nest of a warbler, and the warbler is then compelled by the "law of life of a biological species" to pay for letting the cuckoo take advantage of it by feeding on caterpillars, and as a result of the change in diet, it hatches cuckoos instead of warblers. The audience's reaction was not the Homeric laughter the proposition deserved. The majority of students seemed to believe it. Only a few of them (and possibly some among their teachers) attempted in timid notes to the lecturer to express their doubts.

In taking up the issue of the transformation of species, Lysenko evidently had a practical motive. The process of seed production was in a state of anarchy as a result of the application of Lysenko's notion of intravarietal cross-pollination, and as a result of the destruction of the well-organized system that Lisitsyn, Vavilov, and others had established to maintain pure seed production. Instead of the increase in harvests that had been promised, the crops were being inundated with weeds.[17] But if weeds arose in and of themselves, without external intervention, there would be no reason to fear an accusation of having spoiled the seed material. If wheat by itself gives rise to rye, and rye to oats, and oats, in turn, to wild oats, and so forth, no one could be blamed for breaking the rules of seed-growing and the testing of varieties.[18]

Lysenko did not attempt to explain why, throughout hundreds of years of careful observation, naturalists, biologists, agronomists, and selection specialists had not once encountered a scientifically irreproachable instance of generation of one species from another. Referring to his assertion about the generation of species as a firmly established phenomenon of nature, Lysenko wrote in 1949: "The theory of dialectics, of development, has given Soviet biologists the opportunity of disclosing how plant species are transformed into other species."[19]

This new doctrine of species alteration was quickly taken up by the microbiologists. Soon after the close of the August 1948 session of

VASKhNIL, an article appeared in a medical journal asserting that certain species of bacteria and viruses generated other species.[20] In 1949, the veterinarian Gevorg M. Boshyan announced that he had observed not merely the alteration of species or genera but the transformation of noncellular forms (viruses) into cellular forms (microorganisms) via a crystal stage.[21] And when Professor Andrei N. Belozersky of Moscow State University (later to be vice-president of the AN SSSR) claimed that DNA molecules disappear at some stages of development of cells and in their place appears a different type of nucleic acid, RNA,[22] Lysenko promptly claimed that this result provided further support for his theory (see chapter 13).

By raising his hand against Darwinism as an obsolete and essentially incorrect doctrine, Lysenko created immense confusion in the minds of those many specialists who had become accustomed to accepting any word issuing from official authorities, even if they did not believe it. Many hastened to declare that the evolutionary teaching of Darwin "at present holds merely historical interest" (Veselovsky, 1952), that the "evolutionary theory of the origin of new species by means of slow, gradual changes has been repudiated by Soviet science on the basis of the splendid research of Academician Lysenko, who has developed a new theory of species formation" (Ivanova, 1953), that "Lamarck and Darwin fundamentally erred" (Averintsev, 1953), that the mystery of the formation of species had been solved in the works of Lysenko (Dolgushin, 1953), that "there are no grounds for giving students this portion of Darwin's teaching; students should study the new theory of the formation of species" (Melnikov, 1953), and so forth.[23]

Another Pillar of Lysenkoism: V. S. Dmitriyev

Just as Lysenko had received the backing of a high official, Chekmenev, for the idea of cluster planting, now another came to his side for the idea of the generation of one species by another. This time the official was V. S. Dmitriyev, head of the agricultural planning division of the State Planning Committee (Gosplan), who had been associated with Lysenko for many years. His position at Gosplan meant he played a decisive role in the spread of Lysenkoist innovations: without his consent, it would have been impossible to plant a single hectare with new crops anywhere in the USSR.

At the August 1948 session, Dmitriyev had denounced all who took exception to any of Lysenko's ideas and had demanded that the AN SSSR "refresh the manifestly stagnant and reactionary atmosphere" that had formed in several of its institutes (a clear call for the kind of purges and mass terror that ensued in biology). And, in face of the terrible hunger of the war years, the postwar harvest failures, and his own knowledge (thanks to his position) of the most accurate figures available about the true state of affairs, Dmitriyev had proclaimed from the podium that Soviet agriculture had achieved "tremendous successes" in the postwar period and was "the most advanced and progressive system of any that the history of world agriculture has known at any time."[24] A year later, Dmitriyev was accepted as a part-time doctoral candidate at Lysenko's Genetics Institute (while retaining his Gosplan position). In the autumn of 1950, the staff at Lenin Hills laid out an experimental plot for his dissertation on the transformation of species. Because Lysenko had said that in unfavorable conditions of growth, one species would *have* to turn into another, the plot was laid out in "the lower portion of a slope adjoining a copse where subsoil waters came to the surface."[25] By 1952, the staff had completed the dissertation for him. In 1952, articles were published under his name describing the generation by rye of rye brome, "an inveterate weed of rye crops, causing great loss in agricultural production," and the generation of smooth-seeded vetch from lentils.[26] Dmitriyev's aim was to explain, without condemning the Lysenkoists' agricultural practices, why weeds spread on farm plots:

> The different species of weeds are similar to different species of cultivated plants (wild oats to oats, rye brome to rye, and so on); all species of weeds associated with the given species of cultivated plants (for example, special weeds of flax, buckwheat, or millet) are similar to corresponding cultivated plants, while one and the same weed (for example, wild oats), crowding out different species of cultivated plants, in many instances is similar to exactly those cultivated plants that it accompanies.

He described his methodology and his results in the following way:

> The experiment was laid out so as to sharply worsen the environmental conditions for rye. To this end, late sowing, excessive moisture, low soil fertility, close planting, sowing with undersized seeds, and so on, were employed. Under the conditions of the experiment, there was no tending of the crop. . . . In a sowing of nearly 15 [kilograms] of local large-meadow rye seed, individually selected, seed by seed, 12 plants of rye brome were obtained together with the rye. All these plants appeared on plots of land where excessive moisture was created."[27]

These phrases were the only evidence offered for the appearance of plants of a genus other than rye. There was no recognition that twelve tiny seeds of rye brome could have been carried in by wind, birds, or small animals. No definitions of method were reported, no statistical analyses or analyses of botanical, physiological, biochemical, or other properties. (On the fate of Dmitriyev's dissertation, see chapter 13.)

Dmitriyev was not the only one to become renowned in this way. A list of others, published in 1954 in the *Botanical Journal*, included D. A. Dolgushin, who "discovered" the formation of rye from oats; N. V. Myagkov (generation of rye by wheat); A. K. Feitsarenko (wheat from barley); Ye. I. Chirkova (rye from wheat); M. M. Kislik, who once more announced that oats "give birth to" wild oats; S. A. Kott discovered rye engendered from oats, vetch from peas, small-seeded vetch from smooth-seeded vetch, and so on and on.

The "Law of Transition from Nonliving to Living"

In explaining how cells of one species grew out of the cells of other species, Lysenko had help from Olga B. Lepeshinskaya, an Old Bolshevik who, together with Lenin, had lived for several years before the Revolution as an émigré in Geneva and whom Lenin knew very well. Returning after the Revolution, she managed—despite her lack of higher education—to enter the ranks of scientific workers. In 1931, she announced that she had discovered animal cell membranes that differed from those previously described,[28] and in 1934 she reported a still more sensational discovery: a process by which nonliving matter turned into living matter.[29] Up until then, it had been a fundamental postulate of biology—established by the German scientist and founder of pathological anatomy, Rudolf Virchow (1821–1902)—that a cell can arise only by division from another cell. As Lepeshinskaya later described her "discovery" that this was not uniformly true:

> This was in 1933. I was studying animal cell membranes. Wishing to study the changes in membranes with growth, I decided to follow this process at different stages of development of the frog, and I began with the tadpole. And what did I see? I saw yolk spheres of the most diverse forms. . . . After attentively studying several such preparations, it occurred to me that I had before me a picture of the development of some type of cell from yolk.
>
> The development of a cell—this was altogether new! Virchow, and after him the majority of modern biologists, believe that any cell comes only from a cell.
>
> But I recall that Engels said something quite different: "Noncellular forms begin their development from a simple albuminous lump, growing into one or another form of pseudopodium, from a monad."[30]

This hypothesis was criticized by a number of specialists, including Koltsov,[31] but Lepeshinskaya did not abandon her views or cease her experiments. She next ground hydras in a mortar, filtered the thin gruel through gauze and various sieves . . . and new live, dividing cells always appeared, she claimed, from this nonliving "cell-free material." Others maintained that several cells must have been preserved undamaged in this "cell-free material," which would provide a beginning for new cells. Lepeshinskaya was not strict about cleanliness in her experiments.

Nevertheless, Lepeshinskaya succeeded in making a scientific career. By using personal connections, she got her manuscript pushed through to Stalin: "In the spring of 1943, at the height of the war, Iosif Vissarionovich Stalin found time to familiarize himself with my works, still in manuscript form, and to tell me by telephone of his favorable attitude toward my work. These words supported my conviction that I was taking the right path."[32] That single conversation overruled all the scientists' objections. In 1945, the AN SSSR published the book by Lepeshinskaya in which she described her experiments in detail.[33]The foreword, drafted by Lepeshinskaya and Glushchenko but bearing Lysenko's signature, praised her work as "a major contribution to the theoretical foundation of our Soviet biology."[34] The book was submitted to the Stalin Prize Committee, but all of the committee members except Lysenko voted against it.

In 1946 or 1947, Lepeshinskaya had another book published, dealing with her old work on animal cell membranes and purporting to show its medical significance.[35] But her position was becoming as shaky as Lysenko's was at the same period, and the publication only stimulated further criticism. A group of thirteen well-known cytologists and histologists published an open letter in the newspaper *Medical Worker* (July 7, 1948) in which they said that Lepeshinskaya had "a very poor knowledge of biology in general and in particular of the objects studied by her. . . . Presenting utterly obsolete and thus scientifically reactionary views as advanced and revolutionary, Lepeshinskaya misleads the general reading public and disorients the young. . . . Lepeshinskaya's unscientific book is a sad blot on Soviet biological literature."[36] The letter was ill-timed. It appeared three weeks before the August 1948 session of VASKhNIL. At the meeting of the USSR Academy of Medical Sciences that followed soon after (see chapter 11), Lepeshinskaya denounced her critics, and her star rose again.

Lysenko now began to support her more energetically, for he realized that her idea placed a missing link in his hands. If cells of one species could turn into cells of a different species, it must mean that all intracellular structures, all molecules, also could change into something else. Lysenko surely realized the impossibility of such transformations.[37] But now he could circumvent this obstacle: Lepeshinskaya was showing that, in addition to cells, there was a special "cell-free" matter, nonliving but capable of becoming living under some as yet unclear conditions. Then new cells could arise from this living matter. So could one species perhaps turn into another species by passing through a stage of such "living matter"?

Drawing on his own experience, Lysenko knew that the way to establish Lepeshinskaya's authority was through the Party. He arranged for the Central Committee's science department to convene a meeting of the biology division of the AN SSSR, the Academy of Medical Sciences, and representatives of VASKhNIL to discuss Lepeshinskaya's ideas. This meeting, held from May 22 to May 24, 1950, followed the pattern of the August 1948 session and the subsequent meetings. Presiding over it was a compliant Lysenkoist, Aleksandr I. Oparin, head of the biology division of the AN SSSR. Lepeshinskaya, Lysenko, Glushchenko, and other speakers recited the struggles Lepeshinskaya had endured with her critics.[38] "Above all, she must be shown ideological-political help. We must acknowledge ourselves responsible for O. B. Lepeshinskaya's cause and lighten the burden now borne on the shoulders of our dear Olga Borisovna."[39] The book that had been rejected for the Stalin Prize five years earlier was now praised by the head of a medical research institute, Vladimir D. Timakov, as "saturated with the ideas of Marx, Engels, Lenin, and Stalin . . . a model of Party spirit in science."[40]

The reports read by Lepeshinskaya's supporters at the meeting claimed to offer further evidence of the transformations of nonliving substance into cells, or of one species or type of cell into another. M. M. Nevyadomsky asserted that lymphocyte-like cells form from the sarcoma virus: "Electron microscopy with magnification of 28,000 to 50,000 times," he said, "clearly shows that under great enlargement the virus becomes very similar to a tumor cell."[41] (Actually, the simply organized structure of a virus—a protein shell surrounding a strand of nucleic acid—and the highly complex animal cell, with its specialized organelles, look entirely different under an electron microscope.) Nikolai I. Nuzhdin, a corresponding member of the AN SSSR, said he had succeeded in discerning the living substance of which even Lepeshinskaya spoke rather vaguely. In his words, "a continual, incessant origination of the living from the nonliving" took place in nature.[42] Norair M. Sisakyan (who had spoken against the geneticists at the August 1948 session) peered still deeper. He purportedly was able "to reconstitute from fragments proteinaceous bodies possessing a number of vital functions." A special approach was necessary for such work, Sisakyan declared: "The problem of the artificial creation of protein molecules . . . is alien in its ideological orientation to scientists of the capitalist countries."[43] Lepeshinskaya cited all of this support, and the endorsement of the conference in general, in her later books.[44]

After the meeting, the presidium of the AN SSSR passed a resolution calling for revision of "the programs and textbooks in general biology, histology, cytology, and other disciplines with the aim of eliminating residues of idealistic conceptions in these fields" and "suggesting" that the editorial boards of its journals "criticize those who defend Virchovism."[45] The ministries of education, higher education, health, and agriculture issued similar instructions.[46] Once again there were mass dismissals of specialists who had somehow survived the purge of 1948. Lepeshinskaya strove to introduce her views into the educational system.[47] The USSR Academy of Medical Sciences, the State Agricultural Publishing House, the Young Guard publishing house, the State Cultural and Educational Publishing House, and even the Military Publishing House began to print her books (and pay her appropriate royalties), often repeating phrases, paragraphs, and whole pages. Other people dedicated their books and articles to her.[48] Movie theaters showed the film *Court of Honor*, which glorified Lepeshinskaya and stigmatized her "unprincipled persecutors," whose features were caricatures of well-known scientists. N. Pogodin's play, *Taking up the Cudgels* (Kogda lomayutsya kopya—literally, "When Lances Are Broken"), treating the same theme, was put on the stage.

In October 1950, Lepeshinskaya was awarded a Stalin Prize—by Stalin's personal decree, she and her daughter always claimed.[49] In the same year, a Stalin Prize was conferred on one of her supporters, Zhukov-Verezhnikov, as well as on Glushchenko. Her eightieth birthday, in 1951, was marked by many celebrations. She became a deputy of the Supreme Soviet of the

Russian Republic, and she was appointed to many important commissions and scientific councils.

In the spring of 1952, a second national conference on living matter was held, at which Lepeshinskaya boasted of her victory: "All of Virchow's followers, blindly defending his idealistic theory, have now for the most part realized their mistakes and honestly stated this in the press, as well as in their speeches at meetings of scientists. Now they are working under the guidance of the new cellular theory."[50] Others presented new evidence for her theory. Konstantin M. Zavadsky of Leningrad University reported that the young dividing cells of plants (meristem cells) arose from "living matter," unseen by the author but postulated nevertheless; Professor Lev S. Sutulov of Ryazan had found this same unseen substance turning into lymphatic cells and thence into connective tissue; Professor V. V. Averburg of Odessa reported that tuberculosis bacilli promoted the transformation of cells in the presence of living matter; N. I. Zazybin of the Dnepropetrovsk Medical Institute claimed new growth of nerve fibers from living matter.[51]

Mikhail S. Navashin, a Leningrad cytologist who was the most prominent remaining scientist in his field after the arrest and death of Levitsky and Karpechenko, had failed to support Lepeshinskaya when she first began propounding her theory. Now he repeated her words verbatim:

> According to the metaphysical conceptions prevailing until recently, the ability of reproductive cells to serve as the basis for new ontogenesis was explained by the presence in them of eternally young and immutable "germ plasm" which was not subject to the influence of the "perishable body" of the organism. . . . No less mistaken was the conception of . . . "reductive" division [meiosis]. This conception does not require criticism, since numerous plant species are known that have completely lost the property of reductive division.[52]

Despite this, and despite Navashin's later evidence in support of Lepeshinskaya's theory,[53] she continued to attack him both orally and in writing, accusing him of half-hearted conversion to her ideas.[54] One session at the conference was devoted to discussion of the transformation of living substance into cancer cells. A number of oncologists affirmed that "tumors originated from noncellular living matter."[55]

Lepeshinskaya and others were quick to assert that the living substance had direct medical applications: it facilitated the healing of wounds, the treatment of burns, and so on. N. N. Kuznetsov of the Kishinev Medical Institute reported some sensational results: He said he had stitched pieces of specially treated peritoneum taken from the cecum of cattle into the abdominal cavities of dogs and cats. The transplant material was first "killed" by soaking it in a water-formalin solution (70 percent alcohol), then sterilizing it in an autoclave, and, finally, drying it. These procedures, fatal to living tissue, did not affect the living matter, the author contended, and so allowed the peritoneum to revive.[56] At the suggestion of Zhukov-Verezhnikov, a paragraph was added to the meeting's concluding resolution saying that Kuznetsov's work established "the importance of biological stabilization of foreign tissues in an organism of a different species."[57]

Lepeshinskaya's ideas were so stunningly simple, were presented to readers in so categorical a fashion, and were praised so highly that they persuaded many, especially the young. Among them was Zhores Medvedev, who was studying at the Timiryazev Agricultural Academy at the time. In a long survey article published in 1953, he declared that "the outstanding works of O. B. Lepeshinskaya have enriched Soviet biological science concerning the development of cells and fully refuted the metaphysical views that formerly prevailed in cytology."[58] (Several years later, however, Medvedev reconsidered his position and wrote fervently about the fallacies of both Lysenko and Lepeshinskaya.)[59]

Another of Lepeshinskaya's admirers, Professor G. A. Melkonyan of Yerevan, reported in the Lysenkoist journal *Successes of Contemporary Biology* that he had extracted an *Echinococcus* tapeworm from a bone that had been preserved in a jar of formalin for several years and found that, in conformity with Lepeshinskaya's theory, a new, living, growing bone developed from the dead worms. "Facts are stubborn things," he wrote, repeating one of Stalin's favorite phrases,

> and they must be reckoned with and cannot be ignored, otherwise there can be no progress in science. . . . We, too, nearly gave in to this temptation to deny and ignore . . . when, noticing that bone tissue formed in the jar in place of the museum preparation that was preserved in it, we at first thought this must be a joke played by a patient who had replaced the preparation with bones. . . . Only more sober discussion . . . kept us from resolving to throw out the jar of bones and search for the perpetrator of the "joke." . . . Soon, after all the bones had been taken out, more and more new bones began to form in the same jar and liquid, which gave us the right to believe completely in the authenticity of the observed fact.[60]

Similarly, V. G. Shipachev, a biologist in Irkutsk, informed readers of his book that if they sewed cereal grains into the abdominal cavity of animals and then, after a while, made an incision in their stomachs and studied the purulent inflammations rising around the foreign bodies, one could "without difficulty" observe that the plant cells had decomposed, forming "Lepeshinskaya's living matter," and that normal animal (not plant) cells had formed from it.[61]

Lepeshinskaya's theory also inspired numerous degree dissertations. For her dissertation at Rostov University, F. N. Kucherova, who headed the department of histology and embryology, ground up pearl buttons, injected the powder into animals, and observed that living matter arose from the powder. She explained that there was nothing "special" about this, since "mother-of-pearl is made from shell, and shell, you know, was once alive!!!"[62] The attestation committee—which included Zhukov-Verezhnikov, Stoletov, Oparin, and other Lysenkoists—promptly awarded her the degree of kandidat, the equivalent of a Ph.D. Another such was one by Rem V. Petrov, at the Voronezh Medical Institute. Petrov, who later became vice president of the AN SSSR and now holds the same position at the Russian Academy of Sciences (see biographical sketches), argued that typhoid and dysentery bacteria are capable of arising from Lepeshinskaya's "living matter."[63]

Lysenko enthusiastically incorporated living matter into Michurinist doctrine in the abstruse language he used for theoretical issues:

> After primary living matter has appeared from nonliving matter, in appropriate conditions, living matter proceeded to arise from the nonliving by the very same laws, but now through the medium of the living. Living matter creates only the condition for the transformation of the nonliving into the living. Therefore, a most general law exists and operates by which nonliving nature is connected with living [nature], and according to which the potential characteristic of nonliving material to turn into living matter is realized.[64]

Thus, Lepeshinskaya's notion was elevated to a new law of nature: the law of "the transformation of the nonliving into the living."

The "Law of Life of a Species" and Cows Giving High-Fat Milk

In the late 1930s, Lysenko regarded himself as exclusively a plant scientist. In 1938, he wrote in a *Pravda* article, "Personally I, for example, can consider myself a consultant on vernalization and production of the best grain seeds. But what sort of consultant would I make on animal husbandry or mechanization?"[65] However, as times changed, he began venturing into animal husbandry and other areas of agricultural science about which he knew little. In 1952, he conceived the idea of creating a national herd of cows that would produce high-fat milk.

The Lenin Hills farm had its own herd of purebred East Frisian cows and bulls that had been brought there long ago to provide dairy products to the farm workers. Until 1947, the herd was cared for in traditional ways, but then one of the workers, Suren Ioannisyan, striving to distinguish himself, proposed that Lysenkoist theory could be applied to this task. If, as Lysenko maintained, the environment determined heredity, then it would follow that, if the cows were fed better, their progeny would produce milk of "higher quality"—i.e., milk with a higher fat content.[66] Lenin Hills had not shared in the severe feed shortage that afflicted other farms after the war. Consequently, its herd's annual consumption per cow tripled between 1947 and 1954, and the average weight of the cows went up from 416 to 675 kilograms.[67] But, as geneticists would have predicted, the fat content of the herd's milk remained stubbornly at 3.4–3.5 percent, for it was largely determined by hereditary characteristics, not by environmental factors.

Meanwhile, as Ioannisyan admitted, "Difficult calvings became frequent on the farm; often the calf or the cow was lost, sometimes both the cow and the calf."[68] This was probably the problem that drew Lysenko's attention, though in addition the shortage of animal fat had become a serious problem. The most likely cause of the problem was the increased weight of the cows. However, rather than change the feed (and thus admit that this environmental change had not changed heredity), Lysenko ascribed both the difficult calvings *and* the failure of fat content to rise to the use of purebred cattle. In 1948, Lysenko and Ioannisyan had begun breeding the East Frisian cows with Kostroma bulls:[69] They assumed that the fat content of milk from the cross-breed would be no less than the 3.9–4.4 percent of the Kostroma breed, although, according to the laws of genetics, the fat content is determined by the combination of many genes; as a result, milk-fat content from the progeny should be the average of that of the two parents. In this case, the cross-breed would give milk with a fat content in the range of 3.6 to 3.9 percent, and that is what happened.

Lysenko explained this "deficiency" by what he called the "law of life of a biological species." The fat content, he said, depended on how the first cell, the zygote, the start of the organism, develops. He suggested that the zygote will always select the path of development that will most facilitate the progress of its species.

A higher organism begins its life when the chromosomes of the spermatozoon (the paternal reproductive cell) and the chromosomes of the egg (the maternal reproductive cell) join. In Lysenko's opinion, the fertilized egg (the zygote) could itself select its path of development while still within the womb. "The zygote is no fool," he exclaimed in lectures. He believed that, in accordance with the "law of life of a biological species," organisms constructed their bodies so as to assure that their species would thrive, or, more precisely, so that the mass of the species would increase to the maximum degree.[70]

So, first of all they replaced the stud bulls. If the zygote was capable of selecting a path of development, it needed a father who was small in weight but would have progeny with high-fat milk. In 1952, a Jersey bull was bought for the farm in Denmark, with hard currency, and named "Bogatyr 60," in honor of the medieval warriors. The Jersey breed, pure-bred for over 200 years, was distinguished for the high fat content of its milk (around 6 percent), but its productivity was low. Therefore, according to the laws of genetics, the fat content of the milk of offspring from crosses with Jerseys would increase, but the total milk yield would decrease.

The first calves resulting from these crosses began to lactate at the end of 1955. And indeed, the fat content of the milk increased while the milk yield dropped, from 6,785 kilograms in 1954 and 6,670 in 1955 to 4,554 in 1956. Between 1954 and 1964, the milk yield per cow declined by 2,332 kilograms, or more than one-third, and as a result, even the total output of milk fat decreased, because the higher fat content could not compensate for the decrease in volume.[71] On the other hand, the problem of difficult births had apparently been overcome by the smaller-sized progeny; there were numerous calvings of the cross-breed, and the farm began to sell the calves to other farms. The only saving grace was that Lysenko, evidently because of peasant suspicion of anything "unnatural," rejected the use of artificial insemination; otherwise, many more cows would have been spoiled during this period.

But the facts about the failure of this breeding experiment were not disclosed until ten years later. In the meantime, Lysenko continued to claim that the data corroborated his "theories."[72] The USSR Ministry of Agriculture and ministries of several republics supported him. In January 1961 and again in June 1963, the USSR Ministry of Agriculture ordered an expansion of his experiment.[73] In return, Lysenko and his followers declared at meetings of various Party bodies that the USSR was overtaking the United States in the production of milk and butter.[74]

Prompted by Lysenko, Khrushchev, who had by then become general secretary of the Party, told the January 1961 plenary session of the Party Central Committee that an increase of only 0.1 percent in the fat content of milk (not of the 1 or 2 percent that Lysenko had promised to achieve), would "give the country an additional 30,000 tons of milk fat, or 36,000 tons of creamery butter, i.e., as much fat as 300,000 cows would give at an average milk yield of 2,600 kilograms."[75] Actually, however, the average milk yield was only about 1,500 kilograms, even according to the official data, so that, even if the fat content of milk were 3 percent (as, again, the official data reported it to be), and even if all milk-giving animals in the country were counted (sheep and goats as well as cows), the most that could be expected from the Lysenko program was 3,400 tons of milk fat.[76]

In addition to the campaigns on behalf of forest belts, Lepeshinskaya's living matter, and high-fat milk, Lysenko and his students and supporters were making claims that they had transformed varieties of winter crops into spring crops, and vice versa, through exposure to the special qualities of spring or autumn light. "Assimilation of spring light," wrote Lysenko, "produces a living body of grains having the properties of 'vernalness.' ... In the case of assimilation of autumn light, the living body of grains acquires properties of 'winterness.' ... Every agronomist and collective farmer can now within a two-year period transform any spring variety into a winter one that will winter well in a given region."[77] He also continued to extol the virtues of Williams's grassland crop rotation.[78] As we shall see in the next chapter, Khrushchev in 1955 finally revealed the damage that had been inflicted on agriculture by Williams's schemes, but Lysenko never changed his views. Until his death, he defended the validity of the "law of life of a biological species."

Lysenko's Collected Works

Ever since 1929, when the report he and Dolgushin had delivered at the genetics congress had been rejected by the referees of scientific journals, Lysenko had avoided the usual avenues of scientific publication. Instead, his works appeared in newspapers, popular magazines, and his own journal, *Vernalization* (renamed *Agrobiology* after the war). In this way, his articles could reach a much larger audience and did not have to run the gauntlet of rigorous review before publication. Then, by reprinting these pieces in large volumes, in expensive bindings with gold stamping, Lysenko sought to give the appearance of scientific respectability and authority to his work. These collections came out in many editions. The volumes *Agrobiology* and *The Stage Development of Plants*, both of them published by the State Agricultural Publishing House and each containing more than seven hundred pages, give a good idea of what these works were like.

The Stage Development of Plants contained fifty-nine articles, beginning with Lysenko's first publication in 1929 (see chapter 1). Nine of these were condensed reports or forewords to other works. Five were production instructions (how and when to vernalize wheat, potatoes, beets, and cotton; how to prune the tops of cotton stalks; how to cut potato tubers so as to use part for food and preserve the tops or eyes for later planting). Seven were popular articles, with titles like "With the Power of Mankind, We Will Seize the Key to Variability of Plant Forms from Nature." Almost half the articles originally appeared in *Pravda, Izvestia, Socialist Agriculture*, or *Bolshevik Banner* (Bolshevistskoye znamya), a newspaper of the Odessa region, or *Worker's Gazette* (Rabochaya gazeta), a newspaper of the Moscow region. Although the collection was published in 1952, it included not a single work written after 1939, and only five written between 1937 and 1939. Neither the table of contents nor the articles themselves mentioned the places of original publication.

Agrobiology, the *sixth* edition of which appeared in 1952, reveals a similar picture. This volume devoted more than 120 pages to reproducing three works on vernalization that were also included in *The Stage Development of Plants*. Twenty pieces were reprints of newspaper articles (including "J. Stalin and Michurinist Biology"). Other items were the foreword to a collection of Michurin's works, speeches at VASKhNIL sessions, and lectures delivered at Leningrad University, the public lecture hall of the Polytechnic Museum in Moscow, and the Scientists' Club, and to a gathering of kolkhoz chairmen. Eleven pages were devoted to the brochure *What's New in the Science of Biological Species*, which many of his supporters had criticized (see chapter 13). Finally, there were "Kolkhoz Cottage-Laboratories and Agroscience" (whose original title had been "Kolkhoz Cottage-Laboratories, Creators of Agroscience"), "The Michurinist Doctrine at the All-Union Agricultural Exhibition," two popular articles for an encyclopedia, and "Instructions for Planting Erosion-Control Belts in 1951." As in the other volume, prewar works filled 400 pages, and pieces published between 1941 and 1950 occupied another 163 pages. Only six short articles had been written at a later date. Despite the scientific tone of the subtitle, *Works in Genetics, Selection, and Seed Production*, the pieces contained none of the descriptions of methods and materials and none of the data and analysis that are obligatory in scientific papers. They referred instead to the "proofs" obtained by "peasant experimenters" in the field and in the cottage-laboratories, and to Lysenkoist theory.

Both volumes reproduced Lysenko's praise of Stalin, collectivization, and Marxist-Leninist dialectic. They repeated his claims of "epochal" advances in biology, medicine, and agriculture. And they preserved his accusations against his critics and his abuse of "bourgeois" and foreign science. A few minor changes were made from the way in which the original articles had been printed, and these were indicative of his sensitivity to changing political currents. There was, for example, no mention of his early ally, Yakovlev (see chapter 5). Yakovlev had been shot on July 29, 1938, as an enemy of the people. And of course, nowhere in either volume was there any indication of the destruction of Soviet science and the irreparable losses to Soviet agriculture that were the consequences of Lysenkoism.

I have only touched on a handful of the deceptions that Lysenko advocated during this period. Over and over again, he tossed out ideas and schemes as sound as the ones discussed here—and we will never know how many farmers, agronomists, scientists, and officials wasted their time and work in trying to put them into practice.

13

The First Fall

Our primitive thinking is a specter that frightens;
Though paper mislead, information enlightens.
—O. Mandelshtam, untitled poem

What suddenly turns people of limited talents from being modest
paper-pushers, not into genuine leaders of society but into its
systematic befuddlers of reason? Whence this sudden demand for
narrow minds that surrounds them with a halo of authority and
prestige? The opinion exists that there is an organic link between
the domination of limited people and periods of so-called social
reaction.
—M. Ye. Saltykov-Shchedrin, *Our Complacent Times*

The Lepeshinskaya Theories Discredited

At a conference in May 1950, Lysenko proclaimed that "there is no doubt
that the scientific conclusions reached by O. B. Lepeshinskaya are recognized and have joined other scientific discoveries in the solid foundation
of our developing Michurinist biology."[1] But when he pronounced these
words with such deep feeling, he could hardly have foreseen how quickly
that foundation would crumble and the entire structure of "Michurinist
biology," erected with such effort on the bones of so many great scientists,
would begin to settle and collapse.

The "Lepeshinskaya doctrine," with its claims for the existence of a
special "living matter" and the transformation of inanimate matter into
animate and vice versa, was the first to go. By 1953, challenges to these
ideas were being heard at scientific conferences and seen in Soviet publications. Indeed, in subsequent reprintings of this speech of Lysenko's, his
enthusiasm for Lepeshinskaya's conclusions was shifted from the past to
the future tense: instead of "have joined," he was reported to have said the
conclusions "will join" other scientific discoveries.[2]

Perhaps the decisive factor in this change was one of Lepeshinskaya's
own proposals. Beginning early in 1953, she began discussing the problem
of longevity, emphasizing the differences between the Soviet Union and
capitalist countries. "The deleterious social and living conditions in capitalist countries," she told an audience at the Moscow Polytechnical Museum,
"hasten premature aging of the working people, who labor to exhaustion,
become overtired, eat poorly, and are poisoned by every conceivable pol-
lutant on the job." In the USSR, however, longevity was enhanced by such

factors as prenatal care, child care, guaranteed vacations, opportunities for sports, occupational safety, health education, and "laughter and gaiety, constantly present in the lives of Soviet people and contributing to the health of the organism." "In our country, scientists, relying on the direct support of the Soviet government, the Communist Party, and its inspired leader, Stalin, have boundless scope for creativity," and so, she concluded, "The time will come when the age limit for Soviet citizens will exceed 150 years."[3]

But Lepeshinskaya announced that she had also discovered a specific substance that promoted longevity: ordinary baking soda, sodium bicarbonate.[4] Experiments with frogs and chickens, she said, proved that it was possible to prolong life by injections of solutions of baking soda, and she claimed that the experiments had reached a point where the method could be tested upon humans:

> I decided to conduct the first trial experiment on myself. The experiment consisted of taking soda baths. I dissolved 50–70 grams of sodium bicarbonate in bath water and bathed for 15–20 minutes.
>
> I took the baths twice a week, a total of fifteen baths. What changes occurred in my organism as a result? First of all, urine acidity was found to decline to a neutral level. This showed that the organism absorbed the soda through the skin and affected the chemistry of the urine. A small weight loss of the entire organism began quite soon, with a reduction of the excess fat so common with age, particularly midriff fat. This process was unquestionably related to heightened metabolism. It is important to point out that I felt better after the baths, and muscular fatigue declined and even disappeared.[5]

Moreover, she contended that baking soda could be used to treat a variety of ailments:

> It turned out that a soda ointment helped wounds to heal faster. Soda baths proved effective in treating some forms of such a grave and difficult ailment as thrombophlebitis (the presence of a blood clot in the vein, accompanied by irritation of the walls of the blood vessel). In cases of sepsis (bacterial infection of the blood), some physicians obtained good results by using a one-percent soda solution. It is to be assumed that the sphere of application of soda as a prophylactic and curative will increase with time.[6]

This "medication" had its attractions. Instead of subjecting themselves to complicated medical procedures, patients could merely take a pinch of soda in a glass of water. Lepeshinskaya's status as a prominent scientist and full member of the Academy of Medical Sciences persuaded people to trust her advice. As a result, in the words of Zhores Medvedev, "Soda temporarily disappeared from stores and pharmacies, and polyclinics had to cope with a stream of the rejuvenated suffering from the naive faith in the healing powers of this beaming grandmother."[7]

Lepeshinskaya extended her discovery to agriculture as well and declared that a one-percent soda solution even made field plants grow better.[8] But by venturing into the area of human medicine, Lepeshinskaya made herself vulnerable in a way that Lysenko had avoided. Following Stalin's death on March 5, 1953, she began to suffer setbacks. At a meeting of the Leningrad section of the Society of Anatomists, Histologists, and Embryologists on December 23 and 24, 1953, she and her doctrines were bluntly criticized by a number of speakers. Concluding the discussion, the chairman, Professor N. N. Gerbilsky, on the one hand welcomed "the strong, sharp challenge to the theoretical principles of histology" that Lepeshinskaya's work had delivered, but on the other hand observed that "the desire to supply the new theory with factual evidence, a desire fed by various motivations, caused the pollution of histological literature with many low-quality works."[9]

In response, the Lepeshinskaya forces called a national meeting of the society. It was also held in Leningrad, from June 22 to 24, 1954, and it was attended by about six hundred scientists and educators. Aleksandr N. Studitsky, a long-time supporter of Lepeshinskaya and Lysenko, presented the main report, illustrated with slides prepared by Yury S. Chentsov, Vladimir P. Gilev, and other of his students. Studitsky insisted that "the new materialist cell theory has been generally recognized" and that the preparations of Chentsov and Gilev showed incontrovertibly that "entire muscle structure was newly constituted from skeletal-muscular tissue grafted in ground-up form."[10] But V. G. Kasyanenko of Kiev gave a paper in which he said that he had tried to replicate Studitsky's experiments on rabbits but had found that "the only result was to dissolve tissue; the muscle was not restored."[11] Criticism of Lepeshinskaya was again heard at a conference of embryologists in January 1955.[12]

Meanwhile, articles opposing the Lepeshinskaya doctrines began appearing in a number of journals.[13] Within a few years after Stalin's death (and before Lepeshinskaya's own death in 1963), all mention of "living matter," the emergence of cells from unstructured elements, the regeneration of bone tissue, the curative and prophylactic properties of sodium bicarbonate, and the name of Lepeshinskaya herself quietly disappeared from textbooks and treatises. The 1972 edition of the *Great Soviet Encyclopedia* said that "Lepeshinskaya's concept of the noncellular structure of living matter has been rejected as unsubstantiated."[14]

The Criticism of "Birth" of Species

Meantime, not all was going well for Lysenko. Smoldering dissatisfaction with his ever more far-fetched ideas and proposals was spreading, even though he seemed to have strengthened his hold to a point where he no longer needed to fear criticism. His people controlled most of the biology journals and publishing houses. Journalists could not even entertain the thought of departing from the accepted dogmas, and if they did, the pervasive censorship would not have allowed a word that contradicted the official viewpoint.

For this reason, the general shock was all the stronger when the December 1952 issue of *Botanical Journal* carried two articles that openly and severely criticized Lysenko's cherished "new theory of biological species." One was by Professor N. V. Turbin, head of the Leningrad University Department of Genetics and Selection—and the same Turbin who had *supported* Lysenko so vigorously at VASKhNIL's August 1948 session (see chapter 11). The other was by an unknown in biology: N. D. Ivanov.

Proceeding from widely known biological facts, Turbin rejected Lysenko's attempt to revise the theory of species formation. He declared that "experiments" in the generating of species were unsubstantiated and those who sought to implant the new theory in biologists' minds were ignoramuses. There could be no theory without facts; they were as essential to theory as air to a bird's flight. Lysenko's new theory, he concluded was like the flapping of wings in a vacuum.[15] Turbin told me later that this comparison to describe the new "theory" infuriated Lysenko, who repeatedly spoke of it bitterly in conversations with close associates. Ivanov's article was mainly concerned with the specious use of quotations from the classics of Marxism-Leninism.[16]

The fact that articles critical of Lysenko appeared in print was immensely significant. Appearing while Stalin was still alive, they were widely interpreted as a Kremlin-sanctioned offensive against Lysenko. Rumors spread among biologists that Stalin, in conversation with some of his retinue, was supposed to have said, in the curt verdict that bespoke the greatest danger to its object, "Apparently Comrade Lysenko is getting a swelled head. We ought to set him right!"

Yu. A. Zhdanov, remembering his embarrassment in 1948, may also have encouraged publication of the articles and may have told Stalin about Lysenko's mistakes. A staff member of the *Botanical Journal,* D. V. Lebedev, told me that early in the 1950s the journal's editor in chief, V. N. Sukachev, and his circle of friends also constantly discussed how to bring criticism of Lysenko into the open. These ideas were helped along by the occasional rumors that Stalin was becoming dissatisfied with his old friend Lysenko. It was at this time that people began to say that Stalin had scrawled the notation "We ought to make Lysenko enjoy criticism" on a report received from some agronomist. It should also be emphasized that, at the beginning of the species discussion, the editors of the *Botanical Journal* were in direct contact with Alexander M. Smirnov, the inspecting office of the Party Central Committee's science department, a pupil of Pryanishnikov, and an adversary of Lysenko.[17]

But, as often happens, the actions of one group in the leadership ran counter to those of another: that same year saw a *Pravda* editorial sharply critical of the editors of *Soil Science* magazine (Pochvovedeniye) for publishing anti-Lysenko material (without mentioning him by name).[18] The presidium of the AN SSSR obediently adopted a resolution calling for an editorial retraction by the magazine.[19]

That Stalin had indeed acquired a sense of dissatisfaction with Lysenko's actions had become clear late in May or early in June 1952. Yu. A. Zhdanov told me that Party Central Committee Secretary A. I. Kozlov had urgently sent for Zhdanov and told him he had just come from G. M. Malenkov, who had given him Stalin's instructions to end the Lysenko monopoly in biology.[20] The first step, Kozlov told Zhdanov, was to reestablish a presidium of the Lenin Agricultural Academy (which Lysenko had ruled singlehanded, dispensing with a board), which should include Zhebrak, Lysenko's scientific adversary, as well as N. V. Tsitsin, whose attitude toward Lysenko shifted with the political winds. Kozlov and Zhdanov immediately chose a commission of six or seven persons to prepare these changes. Kozlov served as chairman. The members included A. N. Nesmeyanov, of the AN SSSR. Later they added Lysenko himself. At the commission's two meetings in the autumn of 1952, Lysenko fumed, stewed, spoke on every point raised, and defended his opinions at great length. But then preparations for the Nineteenth Party Congress began, and no one had time for the Lysenko question.

It was symptomatic that the first public blow against Lysenko was struck by a person from his own camp: Turbin. Turbin had compiled the Lysenkoist genetics textbook that had long been required in higher educational institutions and technical colleges: extracts from the basic writings of "the great masters of materialist biology, chiefly Lysenko and Michurin.[21] Thanks to this text, Turbin's name had become firmly linked with the leaders of the Michurinist school.

It was symptomatic that this blow was struck at the central Lysenkoist thesis of the day, a question with more than theoretical significance. Everyone understood that if the new "theory of the creation of species" were now to be held false, then a flawed concept underlay the state's plan for transforming nature. Michurinist biologists could not fail to see that such an accusation undercut the Lysenkoist constructs as a whole. Copies of the issue of *Botanical Journal* containing the Turbin and Ivanov articles were passed from hand to hand and read until they were in tatters.

The Lysenkoists felt compelled to counterattack. The first issue of the Lysenkoist journal *Successes of Contemporary Biology* for 1953 was late in appearing. Its first pages displayed a black-bordered portrait of Stalin, the announcement of his death, and the text of the appeal for "calm" from the Central Committee, the Council of Ministers, and the Supreme Soviet. These were followed by an article by Studitsky, assailing "renegades" for their "impertinence."[22] The *Journal of General Biology* carried articles in each of its issues in 1953 attacking the critics of Lysenko's theory of species. The first issue contained two such articles by Nuzhdin, the journal's assistant editor in chief and Lysenko's longtime deputy at the Genetics Institute. He heaped abuse upon Turbin and Ivanov, calling their criticism of

Lysenko "a relapse into Weismannism-Morganism" and referring to "the bankruptcy of bourgeois pseudo-science."[23] The next issue carried an article by Oparin, the journal's editor in chief, in which he wrote:

> The Central Committee of the Communist Party has read and approved Academician T. D. Lysenko's report [at the August 1948 session of VASKhNIL]. For all Soviet biologists, this document, personally reviewed by J. V. Stalin, is a precious program for the creative development of biology, one that defines its course and goals. Soviet creative Darwinism constitutes the granite foundation, the solid base on which all branches of biology are tempestuously developing.[24]

But this time the opposition was not intimidated, perhaps because of the suspicion that Lysenko was losing his hold on the Party leadership. Early in 1953, the *Botanical Journal* began a well-prepared attack on Lysenko's "theory of species." The editorial board had invited Lysenko to submit an article defending his theory. Lysenko accepted, and his article appeared in the first issue for 1953; it repeated his by-then familiar views on the subject.[25] An introductory note from the editors said they "will be happy to publish further statements by T. D. Lysenko in the future on the problems of species and species formation."[26] But the issue also carried an article by the journal's editor, Vladimir N. Sukachev, in which he demonstrated the weaknesses of the Lysenkoist arguments on the basis of factual material and without any irrelevant quotations.[27] From then on, Sukachev took on the role of leader of the anti-Lysenko movement. Although he was 73 years old by this time, he was a vigorous and spirited man, strong, somewhat heavy-set, with short gray hair and a penetrating gaze. A pupil of the botanist Ivan P. Borodin and of the forestry specialist Georgy F. Morozov, he had become a world-famous scientist. He was elected a corresponding member of the AN SSSR in 1920 and a full academician in 1943, was a member of several foreign academies, and had been president of the USSR Botanical Society since 1948. He was the first to formulate the goals and tasks of the new discipline dealing with the interrelated and interacting complexes of living and inanimate nature—the discipline that has since come to be known as ecosystem ecology. Together with Vladimir I. Vernadsky, Sukachev began to devise an approach to investigation of changes in the plant world in accordance with changes in the animal world and in human activity. From this approach came his important research in estimating the productivity of the plant world and the limits of human ability to ensure optimum conditions for the survival of forests, meadows, and pasturelands (and the biosphere as a whole). He founded the AN SSSR's Forest Institute in Moscow in 1944 (Khrushchev later ordered it moved to Krasnoyarsk, where it bears Sukachev's name) and was head of an ecological research group at the Botanical Institute in Leningrad. In the early 1950s, he began to grow deaf and took to wearing a hearing aid. Legend had it that he never missed a word he wanted to hear but kept silent when it was better to pretend not to have heard.

The second issue of the *Botanical Journal* for 1953 contained two articles analyzing Lysenko's errors on questions of species formation, and successive issues carried still more.[28] Issue no. 3 also carried an irate letter from Lepeshinskaya about the Turbin and Ivanov critiques, in which she responded only on the ideological level: "Lysenko treats the question of species formation as a dialectical materialist and in full accord with J. V. Stalin. . . . In the 36th year of Soviet rule, it is time to reject the defense of metaphysical views and stop using the guise of criticism to protect an erroneous, pseudoscientific stand."[29] Her agitation was understandable. Lysenko's "theory of species formation" and her own ideas about the emergence of cells from noncellular matter had now merged into a single theory applicable to all nature, "the law of transition from nonliving to living matter." Consequently, if Lysenko's conjectures about a transformation of warblers into cuckoos or wheat into rye were refuted, it followed that Lepeshinskaya's doctrines would be repudiated as well.

Two of the *Botanical Journal* articles were particularly revealing. One of them concerned the supposed appearance of a spruce branch on a pine tree, which we have noted before (see chapter 12). The claim to have observed this phenomenon, in a forest near Riga, was made in 1951, by one K. Ya. Avotin-Pavlov, who declared that it was an example of the "genesis" of one species from another and hence of the operation of the "new law of species."[30] The Lysenkoists were delighted with this finding and began to describe the pine tree in poetic fashion as having "sweated forth" a spruce branch. In 1952, under Avotin-Pavlov's guidance, a student, B. Rokyanis, wrote a Ph.D. thesis in which he interpreted the incident from the standpoint of the "new theory."

The facts, however, were quite different, as an article written by L. A. Smirnov showed. What had happened was that a pine and a spruce had been growing side by side; their branches had intermingled and had grown into each other's trunks. The spruce had been cut down in 1896, but the spruce branch went on growing on the pine trunk. The local foresters were quite familiar with the incident; one of them had described it at a meeting of the Riga Naturalists' Society in 1925, and an account had appeared in a German forestry journal in 1928.[31] It is clear that Avotin-Pavlov knew this—indeed, he mentioned the German article in his own article[32] —but he had simply falsified the account to serve his own interests.[33]

The other instance (also alluded to in chapter 12) concerned the claim of Suren K. Karapetyan that a hazel tree had grown from a hornbeam.[34] Lysenko himself repeatedly cited Karapetyan's claim and became greatly disturbed upon hearing that his follower might be exposed. When he was unable to suppress the story, when telephone calls form Moscow to the *Botanical Journal* in Leningrad were of no avail, Lysenko sent the following letter to the journal:

I have learned that Academician V. N. Sukachev, editor in chief of the *Botanical Journal*, has announced that No. 5 of your magazine will carry an article not only allegedly disproving S. K. Karapetyan's statements about a hornbeam producing a hazelnut tree, but accusing Comrade Karapetyan of dishonesty. Comrade Karapetyan's article appeared in the magazine *Agrobiology*.

Being acquainted in detail with a great deal of material concerning this matter and being confident that the editors of the *Botanical Journal* are unfamiliar with the material, I have decided to inform you of the following.

The assumptions expressed in S. K. Karapetyan's article about a hornbeam engendering a hazelnut tree are unassailable in light of the appearance of new hazel offspring on this same tree. In other words, the article by S. K. Karapetyan was and remains scientifically accurate.

It seems to me that, given my statement, the *Botanical Journal* should check more thoroughly all the materials concerning this question in order to avoid errors that could result in harm to our science and so as not to defame an honest person.[35]

And, indeed, the *Botanical Journal* editors kept the article out of No. 5 of the magazine, even though it was already in type. But not because they agreed with or feared Lysenko. Two months later, the article, refuting not only Karapetyan's "unassailable" and "scientifically accurate" assumptions, but the statement of Lysenko himself, saw the light. The editors delayed the article in order to print Lysenko's letter along with the article.

The article reported that Karapetyan had described the appearance of hazel branches on a hornbeam tree near Yerevan. Karapetyan insisted that these branches could not possibly be the result of a natural or artificial graft. He claimed there were no hazelnut trees near the hornbeam (which now, for greater effect, was called a hornbeamhazel).

However, this claim was studied by Ashot A. Rukhkyan, an Armenian specialist in animal husbandry who had developed an interest in general problems of biology and decided to study the tree described by Karapetyan. He not only found indisputable evidence of an ordinary artificial graft but he even tracked down the identity of the person who had made the graft, many years before: one R. Yesayan, a former employee of the forestry station.

More incriminating details came to the surface as the investigation proceeded. Not only had the traces of grafting been "overlooked," but the photograph of the grafted branch had been retouched to conceal the place where the graft was made. Another photograph of the "hornbeamhazel," which had been published to show that there were no hazel trees near the hornbeam, so that the phenomenon could not have been the result of a "natural" graft, had been retouched as well. A photo printed with the *Botanical Journal* article showed a thick growth of hazel around the hornbeam.[36] The exposure of Karapetyan's and Avotin-Pavlov's forgeries discredited all the data about the "sweating out of new species." Other Lysenkoist frauds were also disclosed by the journal.[37] The editors, unable to print all the letters received on these subjects, printed instead two lengthy reviews of them.[38]

Political Opposition Comes into the Open

But matters did not end with scientific articles and letters. Lysenko's opponents were now able to block the advancement of his favorites, as the case of V. S. Dmitriyev shows. We have seen before (chapter 12) that Dmitriyev's doctoral dissertation had been ghost-written by Nuzhdin and Lysenko's staff, and in 1952 it was presented for defense at the Genetics Institute. The title page listed Academician Lysenko as scientific advisor. The learned council of the Genetics Institute of the AN SSSR accepted the dissertation for defense, which went ahead successfully. (No one in his own institute would have challenged Lysenko.) The Higher Attestation Commission was to have approved the decision of the learned council and issued Dmitriyev's diploma of doctor of science. Up to this time, confirmations of Lysenko's supporters had gone through the Higher Attestation Commission without a hitch.

Under the accepted procedure, the dissertation was first sent to a so-called "black opponent," whose identity was not disclosed to the author of the dissertation. The "black opponent" chosen for the Dmitriyev dissertation was Turbin, and his evaluation was unfavorable.[39] Under pressure from Lysenko, the dissertation was submitted to another opponent, Professor Sergei S. Stankov, who had recently become chair of the department of geobotany at Moscow State University. Stankov also concluded that the dissertation did not merit the award of a doctoral degree. To complicate the situation, Sukachev attacked both the dissertation's data and the attempts to Nuzhdin and Dmitriyev to deflect criticism about it. He scathingly described their mode of scientific discussion as "not a discussion that advances science, but a pounding of water in a mortar."[40] Other articles criticizing Dmitriyev's work appeared in the press.[41]

A plenum of the attestation commission was called for February 20, 1954, to make a final decision on Dmitriyev's dissertation. Lysenko rarely attended these meetings, but on this occasion he came to defend his candidate. He seemed to have succeeded: The plenum voted to confer the degree of doctor of biology on Dmitriyev.

But barely a month later, the commission suddenly reversed its decision. *Pravda* reported that the reversal was the result of the "receipt of additional materials" concerning the dissertation, and together with the announcement of the action it printed a letter from Stankov, in which he characterized the dissertation as a "mockery of Soviet science" and described how Lysenko and his supporters had pressured the commission into awarding the degree.[42] *Pravda* did not say when or how Dmitriyev's doctoral degree happened to be revoked. Many years later, Stankov told me that he had sent his letter not to *Pravda* but to the science department of the Party Central Committee. Its officials had called Stankov in for a talk, trying to persuade him not to make an issue of "such a trifling matter," but Stankov stood his ground. The matter was referred even higher, to Stalin's successor. It turned out that Khrushchev liked Stankov's stand and disliked Dmitriyev, for reasons of his own; it was Khrushchev who had ordered *Pravda* to publish the letter and the Higher Attestation Commission to cancel Dmitriyev's degree.[43]

Khrushchev again implied criticism of Lysenko at a meeting of the Party Central Committee held in February and March 1954. At this meeting, for the first time, there was a frank discussion of the grain shortage, the low crop yields, the poor state of animal husbandry, and the exhaustion of the soil. This meeting marked the beginning of the endless agricultural reforms of Party Central Committee First Secretary Nikita S. Khrushchev, who hoped to solve the farming problems by sending Party functionaries into the villages, abolishing the machine and tractor stations, establishing rural Party agencies independent of other Party committees, etc. It was at this plenary session that he proposed to embark on planting vast idle lands in the so-called "virgin lands" in Western Siberia, the Altai, Kazakhstan, and the Volga region. In this connection, he announced that the Party no longer regarded the grass crop rotation system as the only correct farming method. This system had been promoted by Williams, and since Williams was now dead, it was widely believed that Khrushchev was making an indirect attack on Lysenko.

At the following year's Central Committee meeting in January–February 1955, Khrushchev accused the leadership of agricultural science of impeding the use of hybrid corn.[44] Though again he did not mention Lysenko by name, he could hardly be referring to anyone else. The resolution adopted at the meeting called for turning to hybrid seed everywhere. But that was easier said than done. There were no hybrid varieties in the country and no geneticists left to develop them. To correct matters quickly, it was decided to import large amounts of seed stocks from the United States (and to pay for them in gold). But the imported seed did not suffice for the area which was to be planted to corn, and in the spring of 1955, 17,200,000 hectares had to be planted with ordinary, low-yield varieties.[45] It took almost a decade to establish organizations for the production of hybrid seed and to develop the necessary lines—some of which appeared thanks to so-called "pocket selection," the practice whereby breeders who were sent abroad secretly pocketed foreign seeds that caught their fancy.

Criticism from Other Scientific Disciplines

In 1954, the *Bulletin of the Moscow Naturalists' Society, Biology Section*, also began to carry articles critical of Lysenko.[46] This journal, like the *Botanical Journal*, was edited by Sukachev, and he was assisted by Venyamin I. Tsalkin, a leading zoologist. The *Botanical Journal* was run by a team of friends and close colleagues of Sukachev's from the Botany Institute of the AN SSSR in Leningrad, Daniil V. Lebedev, Pavel A. Baranov, and Yevgeny M.

Lavrenko. While dealing primarily with questions of species formation, the critiques also struck at dogmatism in science generally.

In addition, the Moscow Naturalists' Society (of which Sukachev was president) initiated a genetics section in 1955, and every other week several hundred people gathered in the Great Zoology Auditorium of Moscow State University at 3 Herzen Street to listen to scientists whose names only a year or two ago seemed to have been erased from memory. The audience ranged from elderly geneticists who had survived Stalin's purges to young students, including myself. A remarkable spirit reigned at these sessions; there was none of the dogmatism, toadying, and fear that characterized Lysenkoist meetings. We students, in particular, were amazed to witness the mutual respect and at the same time the strictly critical tone with which these scientists addressed one another, the rigor of the technical discussions, and the sense of humor that invariably manifested itself. The speakers' demeanor presented a striking contrast to the pomposity, the ostentatious solemnity and self-importance, and the primitive arguments of the Lysenkoists.

Physicists and chemists, too, played a major part in clearing the air in biology. (The physicists had acquired considerable weight with the opening of the world's first atomic-power plant in June 1954.) Academician Igor Ye. Tamm, the world-renowned theoretical physicist (Nobel Prize winner in physics in 1958), organized a seminar in 1957 at the Lebedev Physics Institute of the AN SSSR to discuss problems of biology. Among the physicists, mathematicians, chemists, geneticists, and biologists who participated in the seminar were Lev A. Tumerman, who had just been released from years in prison camps;[47] Lev A. Blyumenfeld, who shortly afterward organized the biophysics department at Moscow State University; and the physicists Mikhail L. Tsetlin and Mikhail M. Bongard.

Academician Ivan L. Knunyants also joined in the struggle against Lysenko. Knunyants was a well-known chemist, a three-time winner of the Stalin Prize. His special field was fluoroorganic chemistry. He also was involved in the development and military applications of chemical weapons; he held the rank of major general, was on the faculty of the Military Academy of Chemical Defense, and was often to be seen at the biologists' seminars and lectures clad in his general's uniform. It was common knowledge that he disliked Lysenko, but his particular concern was to go beyond the individual errors in Lysenkoism and to consider the dogmatism characteristic of Lysenkoism as a whole. He and a journalist, Lev Zubkov, published an article in the *Literary Gazette* in 1955 that drew wide attention as evidence of the turn away from Lysenkoism. They wrote:

> The situation in such sciences as genetics and agronomy cannot be considered normal. With all due respect to the services of T. D. Lysenko, it would hardly be right to regard his school as the only possible direction . . . The Lysenko school . . . simply ignores many firmly established scientific facts and many timely tasks in this sphere. . . . It would be wrong to allow the Lysenko school . . . a kind of

monopoly, the "final say" as the ultimate judge on all the basic questions of a scientific discipline.[48]

In the socialist-bloc countries, the first critiques of Lysenkoism appeared in 1954. Helmut Böhme, who became president of the East German agricultural academy, spent more than two years of painstaking work to determine whether vegetative hybridization was indeed possible in the form in which Lysenko and Glushchenko espoused it. In a series of elegant experiments, he demonstrated beyond question that it was not possible.[49]

Special mention must be made of a lengthy and very well-written essay published in 1954 by the writer Oleg N. Pisarzhevsky. Entitled "Friendship among the Sciences and Its Violations," it made a tremendous impression: For the first time in all the years of Lysenkoism, someone was speaking out openly about the chief mistakes of this "doctrine."[50] Pisarzhevsky began by saying he had heard Lysenko speak at the VASKhNIL session in September 1953. Ordinary people, he wrote, saw Lysenko as "commander of the army of the fields, victoriously leading a handful of scientist-followers and an army of kolkhoz experimenters who held sacred their faith that the noble goal they ardently proclaimed—unlimited multiplication of the fruits of the earth—was attainable." But now, listening to the VASKhNIL president, the writer felt torn: "His speech, captivating me with its vivid imagery, at the same time left a certain sense of dissatisfaction."

Patiently and carefully, Pisarzhevsky laid out the source of his dissatisfaction. Originally, he had shared the respect of ordinary people for Lysenko and believed that "the dark strongholds of Weismannism-Morganism were being assaulted by a whole battery of irreproachable experimental data and generalizations of great boldness that sounded like revelations to many!" But as he became better acquainted with the Lysenkoists' actions and with the "antediluvian technology" that they used in their experiments, confidence in their data weakened. He cited example after example to show that the data presented by Lysenko and his "scientist-followers" were far from irreproachable; on the contrary, they revealed a desire on the part of the Lysenkoists to crush opponents by any means, to persecute them, with politically cunning tricks or crude ones, in the single-minded pursuit of attaining a monopoly in science. Pisarzhevsky drew a vivid picture of Lysenkoist deceit. Lysenko's idea that microbes feed plants (see chapter 14) proved false when checked. The polyploids that the Lysenkoists had condemned proved to be valuable plants, and the USSR, where varieties of polyploid crops, such as the latex-yielding *kok-sagyz* and buckwheat, had been first developed, had lost both the varieties and the lead in this work. Growth hormones were not an obsolete concept like "phlogiston" or "vital force," but a real biochemical substance that regulated growth in plants. Pisarzhevsky told in detail about the men and women who spent years of their lives studying genes and chromosomes and discovering laws of biology only to have the Lysenkoists reject and denounce them—and then it turned out that these geneticists, agronomists, and plant physiologists were not enemies of science and progress, much less enemies of the people, but true heroes of science and personally attractive individuals, unjustly defamed and expelled from science by the clique of Lysenko's myrmidons. They had worked more competently than Lysenko's adherents and they spoke truth to Lysenko's face, not out of a desire to humiliate him personally, but out of their devotion to the truth.

Pisarzhevsky concluded that the exaggerated claims of the Lysenkoists about the practical value of their "theories" were only empty boasts, and that the branches of science that Lysenko scorned and that he probably did not understand—biochemistry, biophysics, physiology, and agrochemistry—now had to be developed if progress were to be achieved.

Scientists also took heart from an editorial that appeared that year in *Kommunist*, the theoretical journal of the Party Central Committee.[51] It spoke about "the struggle against the despotic regime that has been established in some scientific institutions by scientists who were trying to create a kind of monopoly in science." It referred to Lysenko by name and said that VASKhNIL was an example of such an institution, where "monopolization of science leads to a situation in which administrative fiat replaces creative discussion of problems, the independent-minded are silenced, and scientific life is stifled." The essay—undoubtedly published with the prior approval of the Party Central Committee—singled out the controversy over Turbin's *Botanical Journal* article:

> Monopolization of science leads to a situation in which administrative fiat replaces creative discussion of problems, the independent-minded are silenced, and scientific life is stifled. This happened, for example, in the V. I. Lenin All-Union Academy of Agricultural Sciences. . . . The magazines *Successes of Modern Biology* and *Journal of General Biology* carried articles by A. N. Studitsky and N. I. Nuzhdin which, instead of serious consideration of the questions raised by Comrade Turbin, labeled him a Weismannist-Morganist, a vulgarizer of Marxism-Leninism, etc., etc.

Moreover, the article added, Turbin's replies "did not see the light of day," and it concluded, "Those who suppress criticism in science wreak tremendous harm upon science and should be promptly rebuffed."

The next year, an article critical of the Lysenkoist methods appeared in an agronomical journal. It was written by Yevgeny V. Bobko, a former student of Pryanishnikov's.[52] It pointed out that "standards for the methodology of agricultural field experiments" had been drawn up and published in 1946, but that, at the demand of the VASKhNIL leadership, "which held that these standards violated freedom of research," the entire press run of the publication containing the standards had been destroyed. Bobko asked: "Do science journals have the right to report the content and conclusions of research based on [faulty methodology], and do they not mislead readers thereby?"

The Lysenkoists did not remain passive in face of these attacks. When, for example, a memorandum by Dubinin urged the presidium of the AN SSSR to act to end the reign of pseudo-science in biology and to rebuild the Soviet genetics establishment, Lobashev responded (on December 2, 1954) to the presidium that

> every Soviet biologist experiences a natural feeling of protest against Professor Dubinin's sweeping defamation of the mighty progressive school that has developed in biology and genetics in our country since the 1948 session of VASKhNIL ... The impression arises that Professor N. P. Dubinin has not understood all that has happened in the development of science since that session. . . . There is no need to establish a new institute or an individual laboratory with the status of an institute. The academy system already includes the Genetics Institute.[53]

Lobashev was not alone. Thanks to such responses, Oparin, as the academician-secretary of the AN SSSR's biology section, was able to sit tight and do nothing about reviving the institutional base of Soviet genetics.

Nevertheless, the pressure from biologists, chemists, and physicists on the Party Central Committee to undo the work of Lysenkoism continued. To quell the dissatisfaction, the Central Committee ordered a special commission to study the situation in biology. On January 26, 1955, a rumor (apparently deliberately instigated) spread through Moscow that the new commission had recommended letting the geneticists work on a par with the Michurinists.[54]

In January 1955, the presidium of the AN SSSR set up, among other related commissions, a commission to draft measures to correct the hybrid corn situation (clearly in response to the Central Committee's resolution that month). Notably, not a single Lysenkoist was named to the commission.[55] The academy also established "brigades" to study the country's lag in specialized branches of biology: heredity, cytology, and polyploids (a strong field in Soviet science until 1948, thanks to Karpechenko, Zhebrak, Sakharov, and others). Again, not one Lysenko supporter was appointed.

Although pro-Lysenko articles continued to appear in the popular press,[56] and Lysenkoists continued to defend dissertations, occupy their positions, and hold power, the apparent changes in attitude at the top toward genetics could not fail to alarm the leader of the "Michurinists."

The Celebration of Michurin's Hundredth Birthday

In anticipation of the hundredth anniversary of the birth of Michurin in 1955, the government decreed an elaborate celebration of the event, and the Lysenkoists seized upon the occasion to advance their cause. Collections of Michurin's articles, with forewords and introductory articles by Lysenko, Prezent, and their supporters, were prepared for publication. Triumphant accounts of achievements under "the banner of Michurin" flooded the newspapers. The State Agricultural Publishing House issued a three-volume work, *The Michurinist Doctrine in the Service of the People*, whose editors included such well-known Lysenkoists as Varuntsyan, Glushchenko, Olshansky, Prezent, and Perov. It opened with a call by Lysenko to "compare the theoretical level of our Michurinist biology with the level of theory of the recent past, when Mendelism-Weismannism still dominated our biology. . . . It has always been a fault of innovators in our Soviet conditions that they have been unable to convince others and thereby remove the barriers and overcome the conservatism hindering progress."[57]

What was especially noteworthy about this work was that more than half of the first volume was taken up with articles by authors from a number of different countries, presented as the voices of all of progressive world science. The nations of the socialist bloc were represented, of course, but so also were France, Italy, Belgium, Switzerland, Japan, India, and Syria. The Lysenkoists attached great importance to Western scientists' support of Michurinism, or at least the appearance of such support. Taking advantage of the sympathy of many of them for the socialist ideology, Lysenko invited foreign visitors to come to the USSR to conduct "research" at Soviet expense. He even took the step of transmitting drafts of papers to them through emissaries such as Glushchenko, who went abroad frequently as a member of the World Peace Council and of various peace or scientific delegations. These papers then turned up in the form of mimeographed journals and pamphlets of a "Society of Friends of Michurin" (which listed no office address) and then again in the Michurin anniversary volume. After Lysenko's downfall, these pamphlets, and the society along with them, vanished.

Lysenko's adversaries could not ignore his propagandizing use of the Michurin anniversary. But how to resist Lysenko's pressure? They could not issue their own collections. Party agencies strictly controlled every publishing house in the country. It was equally impossible to organize their own meetings of scientific councils or scientific societies, academy sessions, etc., for the Lysenkoists had seized the controlling positions in virtually all the organizations. They countered with about the only means available to them: writing letters. Thus, Baranov, a corresponding member of the AN SSSR and director of its Botanical Institute, whose attitude toward Lysenko had changed from favorable to sharply negative, drew up a letter to Khrushchev, arguing that Lysenko should not be the speaker at the anniversary meeting. Baranov asked A. L. Kursanov, director of the Plant Physiology Institute, and Tsitsin, head of the Main Botanical Garden, to sign the letter as well, but they declined. Baranov sent it to Khrushchev over his own signature alone. and succeeded only in arousing the ire of the Party's general secretary.[58]

Another letter, to be sent to the Central Committee (but originally unrelated to the anniversary celebration), was written by Lebedev and his fellow Leningrad biologists Vladimir Ya. Aleksandrov and Yury M. Olenov. It was twenty-one pages long and was filled with details of Lysenko's scientific errors and the damage he had wrought as head of Soviet agricultural

science. It began by declaring that what the Lysenkoists had been presenting had nothing in common with Michurinist biology and expressing the
fear that the anniversary celebration would be used by them to conceal
their falsification of Michurin's scientific views and the abandonment of
the foundations of Darwinism. It continued:

> Modern genetics is one of the foundation stones of the doctrine of evolution,
> and Darwinism is inconceivable without it. As a result of T. D. Lysenko's activity,
> which constitutes a historically unprecedented deception of the state, genetics
> was in effect forbidden and Darwinism falsified. Modern genetics was replaced
> with T. D. Lysenko's "theories" in the genetics study programs and textbooks. . . .
> The system of awarding Stalin Prizes in 1948–1952, the elections to the USSR
> Academy of Sciences in biology, the approval of doctoral and candidates' disser-
> tations that were on a low level but conformed to the reigning dogmas, scien-
> tific appointments made on the basis of "loyalty" to T. D. Lysenko, the distortion
> of the teaching of biology—all this has led to a profound moral decline among
> many who are active in Soviet science and it has powerfully perverted young
> scientists and created this grave situation, requiring serious measures to liqui-
> date it.

The writers of the letter emphasized the political costs of Lysenkoism:

> T. D. Lysenko's activity exerted a sharply negative influence on some important
> sectors of ideological work, particularly philosophy. T. D. Lysenko's false theo-
> retical positions over the course of many years were palmed off as a new stage in
> the development of the dialectical-materialist interpretation of biological phe-
> nomena.

The letter called for a "public declaration by leading organizations" that
Lysenko's views were "his personal views, not Party directives." It demanded
the restoration of modern Darwinism, cytology, and genetics to research,
teaching, and the practice of agricultural breeding programs; large numbers
of people needed to be trained, it noted, in contemporary biological research methods. Boldly, it insisted on the replacement of the leadership of
VASKhNIL, the biology division of the AN SSSR, and the academy's Genetics Institute, the editorial boards of most of the biology and agricultural
journals, and the biology editors of the *Great Soviet Encyclopedia*.
    Above all, it asserted, Lysenko must be personally held to account:

> The ideologists of imperialism make extensive use of the present condition of
> our biology. . . . An example of this propaganda in the U.S.A. is the translation,
> without commentary, of works of T. D. Lysenko himself (such as his book
> *Heredity and Its Variability*), as well as works of his supporters (translation of A. N.
> Studitsky's article "Fly-Lovers and Man-Haters," with all the caricatures of the
> original).

The conclusion drawn from the above was that

condemnation of Lysenko as a person who caused tremendous harm to the science and national economy of the USSR is not only a most important requirement for an upswing in Soviet biology and agronomy, it is tremendously important internationally. And further measures manifestly should be directed toward liquidating the damage caused our country by T. D. Lysenko's activities.

The letter concluded:

> It is with a feeling of pain and bitterness that we sign this document about the state of Soviet biology. Even greater, however, are the sense of our responsibility to the people and the Communist Party, to whom we are obliged to speak the whole truth, and the deep faith that the Party and the government will help Soviet biology to emerge from the existing situation and, like other branches of natural science, make a full contribution to the great cause of building communist society.[59]

Baranov was the first to sign this letter, and sixty-five other biologists followed suit. Moreover, another 183 biologists sent a separate letter in which they expressed regret that they had been unable to sign the letter before it was sent but declared that they were "in agreement with all its basic points" and even believed that the letter "by no means fully set forth the moral and material harm that the activity of T. D. Lysenko has wrought upon our country in recent years."[60]

Other groups of biologists sent letters, too, as did a number of individuals. Among the latter was the naturalist Aleksandr P. Lyubishchev, who sent an open letter to *Pravda*, the *Literary Gazette*, and the magazines *Kommunist* and *Health*. All of them, of course, refused to publish it. This letter, which was widely circulated among scientists, said in part:

> Many of those who are celebrating the Michurin anniversary are unaware that we have essentially not one but two Michurins. The first is the true Michurin, an amateur selection specialist, a man of touching enthusiasm and indomitable optimism, self-critical, talented, honest, and industrious. . . . But his prickly character and insufficiently scientific discipline of mind led to a heritage that was a thicket of disjointed ideas and observations. . . .
>
> But there is another, mythical Michurin: founder not only of a field of science but of an entire "Michurinist biology," a person whose name stands for a whole epoch of reform of Darwinism, freeing it of accumulated encrustations deposited by the capitalist system, a fighter for materialist biology against reactionary currents, a name to be entered in the history of science alongside the names of Lamarck, Darwin, Kovalevsky, Sechenev, I. P. Pavlov, and even Pasteur . . .
>
> This second Michurin does not exist. He is simply a myth, a mask fabricated by Lysenko for purposes of monstrous deception and the seizure of power in science.[61]

In addition, twenty-four physicists, mathematicians, and chemists submitted a statement to the Central Committee, pointing out Lysenko's ruinous role in branches of science related to their fields and in "the general level of science as a whole." The signers of this statement included the signatures of three future Nobel Prize winners in physics—Igor Ye. Tamm, Lev D. Landau, and Pyotr L. Kapitsa—and the future Nobel Peace Prize winner Andrei D. Sakharov. It is noteworthy that the signers included the principal members of the team that worked in the secret town near Gorky, Arzamas 16, to create the Soviet atomic and hydrogen bombs: not just Tamm and Sakharov but also their colleagues Yakov B. Zeldovich, Yuly B. Khariton, and David A. Frank-Kamenetskii. In addition, several other famous physicists, chemists, and mathematicians joined the group. A. N. Nesmeyanov (president of the AN SSSR) and Igor V. Kurchatov, the head of the atomic project, were themselves members of the Party Central Committee and so refrained from signing, but they promised to talk personally with Khrushchev in support of the statement. They did, but Khrushchev called it and the other letters an outrage.[62] With his reaction on record, all of the petitions met with similar hostility within the Central Committee headquarters.

Nevertheless, for the first time in twenty-five years, many biologists nursed some hope that Lysenko had been dealt a palpable blow. They saw promising signs in the posthumous rehabilitation of Nikolai Vavilov in the summer of 1955.[63] The biologists anxiously followed the press as the barometer of the supreme Party leadership. The fact that, for more than a month preceding the date of the Michurin anniversary, *Pravda* did not mention Lysenko, (although it published articles about Michurin and T. Maltsev)[64] seemed a hopeful sign as well.

However, on the day of the Michurin anniversary, *Pravda* printed an article by Lysenko, with the usual abuse of idealists, mechanists, Weismannists, and neo-Darwinists.[65] Moreover, despite the scientists' protests, the Party leadership accepted the Lysenko program for the celebration. When the presidium of the anniversary meeting filed onto the stage of the Bolshoi Theater on October 27, 1955, amid applause, the spectators saw Lysenko take a seat in the place of honor, alongside Nikolai A. Bulganin, chairman of the USSR Council of Ministers; Kliment Ye. Voroshilov, chairman of the presidium of the USSR Supreme Soviet; Georgy M. Malenkov, recent head of the government, and Party leaders such as Kaganovich, M. G. Pervukhin, and Shepilov. Khrushchev was absent because he was out of Moscow.

The meeting was opened by Nesmeyanov, who on such an occasion had to speak warmly of Michurin's heirs, and the floor was then given to Lysenko to present the chief report. Lysenko insisted upon the correctness of his ideas about heredity, species formation, and so on, and in a lengthy account of the meeting, accompanied by a huge photo of the presidium, showing Lysenko at the rostrum, *Pravda* also treated these ideas as unshakeable scientific propositions.[66] As a climax, the I. V. Michurin gold medal was awarded to Lysenko.

At that time, many saw that the authorities realized they could not ignore the scientists' collective opinion, and they took an ambiguous position. On the one hand, they bowed to Lysenko by giving him the Bolshoi Theater stage and the Michurin medal. But, on the other hand, they began moving to correct the defects listed in "the letter of the 249." It was most symptomatic that none of the signers of the anti-Lysenko letters suffered for having spoken out. In addition, to the surprise of many, the *Botanical Journal*, the chief organ of Lysenko's critics, was doubled in size at the end of 1955. The physicists were promised a new scientific center for radiation genetics, to be staffed by real geneticists.

Meanwhile, the subject of genes had become a center of attention of scientists throughout the world in 1953, when the British journal *Nature* printed the first results of the work of James Watson and Francis Crick on the molecular structure of deoxyribonucleic acid (DNA)—the famous double helix. It was not only the biologists who were attracted by the double-helix hypothesis. For example, the physicist George A. Gamow (who was born in Odessa and had graduated from Leningrad University but lived in the United States from 1934 until his death in 1968; see biographical sketch) made important contributions to the understanding of the genetic code contained in DNA.

Soviet physicists were equally fascinated, and their interest triggered a remarkable incident in Moscow early in 1956. For some years, Kapitsa had been organizing seminars at the Theoretical Physics Institute; they were open to the public, were well attended, and became known as "Kapishniks." For the Kapishnik of February 7, 1956, Tamm was scheduled to talk on the study of DNA and the genetic code, and the geneticist Nikolai V. Timofeyev-Ressovsky on radiation genetics.[67] Word of the seminar spread through Moscow and surely reached Lysenko. He could not but realize the danger of such a public discussion. Again Lysenko resorted to a favorite ploy. Kapitsa's institute was informed that, in the Kremlin's opinion, it would be a political mistake to present these reports. According to the recollections of Timofeyev-Ressovsky:

Three days before [the scheduled date of the seminar], someone telephoned the Theoretical Physics Institute and recommended that the announcements of the genetics reports be taken down as conflicting with the resolution of the 1948 session of VASKhNIL. . . . Kapitsa ordered that the recommendation be ignored. The telephone call was repeated next day, with mention of a high official as the source of the recommendation. Then Kapitsa telephoned this high official and received an assurance that the official knew nothing about it, and that the seminar program was for the director alone to decide. So the seminar went off successfully.[68]

By 7 P.M. on the day of the seminar, a crowd thronged even the street outside the institute.

The auditorium, the wide corridor, and the stairs were crammed to bursting. Employees of the institute, overwhelmed by this flood of listeners, hastened to set up loudspeakers. . . . The seminar proved to be a momentous precedent, greatly easing and hastening the process of the development of biology in the years to come.[69]

Tamm subsequently gave many more talks on DNA and the genetic code, in Moscow, Leningrad, and Gorky. At every lecture, he was asked about Lysenko's role in Soviet genetics, and he invariably answered in blunt terms.[70]

The culmination of this process came as a surprise to many and a long-awaited event to just as many others. In April 1956, the newspapers announced, tersely and abruptly, that Lysenko had been released from the presidency of VASKhNIL "at his personal request."[71] He was replaced by Pavel P. Lobanov, who had presided at the August 1948 session of VASKhNIL but nevertheless disliked Lysenko personally. (Lobanov, a specialist in agricultural economics, had made his mark in Stalin's eyes by never taking off Sundays or vacations; Stalin made the young Lobanov Russian Republic Commissar of Agriculture and later USSR Commissar of Sovkhozes from 1938 to 1946.) Oparin also lost his post as academician-secretary of the biology division. The biochemist Vladimir A. Engelgardt replaced him in 1955.

Many scientists thought that Lysenko's fall was complete and that it would be followed by a lifting of the ban on genetic research, by a change in the teaching of biology, and by many other changes. But that time had not yet come.

14

President Once More

No times are more opaque than these,
   yet none are more transparent.
No plant is rooted out more often than weeds,
   yet none is more resilient.
   —Inna Lisnyanskaya, "What Shall I See in the Hours of Loneliness?"

He raised his fist triumphantly, waved it awesomely above his head,
and suddenly brought it down fiercely, as if smashing an opponent.
A great shout rose on all sides, amid deafening applause. Almost half
the hall applauded; they were innocently carried away: was Russia
disgraced openly, publicly, and how could one keep from shouting
with joy?
                                                    —F. M. Dostoyevsky, *Devils*

Khrushchev Addresses the Breakdown of Soviet Agriculture

The May Day holiday of 1956 was a grim one for Lysenko. For the first
time in many years, he did not receive an invitation to attend the traditional ceremonial May Day meeting in the Bolshoi Theater. And his personally assigned telephone line to the Kremlin (one of only 9,999 in the
entire USSR) had been cut off, so he could not offer his direct May Day
greetings to the Party leaders.[1] There was further unpleasantness a week
later, when he was severely criticized by the speakers at a meeting of the
aktiv of the AN SSSR. Corresponding member of the academy Vitaly L.
Ryzhkov, a virologist and botanist, said frankly that Michurinist biology
had set back Soviet science by a century, and a corresponding member,
Ezras A. Asratyan, who had been a Lysenkoist, now assailed Lysenko's
"Arakcheyev-like despotism in biology" (referring to Aleksei A. Arakcheyev,
minister of war under Tsar Alexander I, whose name had become synonymous with police despotism).

Glushchenko defended the Michurinists. He stressed Lenin's principle
of Party loyalty in science: All scientific activity was either loyal or hostile
to the Party. Hence, it was the duty of any Soviet scientist to respond to
threats to the Party. Ryzhkov's and Asratyan's comments were, he declared, "utter nonsense." There had been no repudiation of vernalization;
what's more, Lysenko's "theory of stage development had come to be
accepted by all scientists throughout the world." If vernalization had failed,
it was only because "the misfortunes of war carried off the old cadres of

vernalizers and no one trained new ones. The Ministry of Agriculture was to blame for this, and perhaps also the author of vernalization himself."[2]

But such statements were of little use in the face of the desperate situation in agriculture. Many already understood that vernalization and other Lysenkoist recommendations had been wrong from the start and that the war had nothing to do with it.

The country's leaders, for their part, were trying desperately to relieve the agricultural situation. In his address to the Twenty-first Party Congress on January 17, 1959, Khrushchev himself (after the fact, of course) described how bad things had been:

> Many kolkhozes had remained economically weak for many years, the growth of agricultural output came to a halt, and its level did not meet the country's increased demand for food and agricultural raw materials. Our agriculture was then in grave condition, fraught with dangerous consequences that could have held back the Soviet advance toward communism.[3]

Although Khrushchev undoubtedly understood that there were several ways to correct the situation, all were unacceptable. He could not but realize that the organizational structure of agriculture was at fault, but neither he nor anyone else could do anything much about it. To disband the collective farms would be to admit the failure of the socialist "reconstruction of the countryside." Khrushchev the Communist could not allow himself to harbor such a thought, and no one would let him disband the collectives, anyway. Nor could he grant the collective farms economic independence; that would have meant denying the nature of economic relations under socialism. It was essential to increase the use of chemical and organic fertilizers to compensate for the exhausted soil. But where were the fertilizers to come from? The chemical industry was in as bad shape as agriculture itself. The machinery on the farms was broken down, for the war had wrecked the limited equipment. Most of iron and steel output was going into military hardware.

Each need posed a separate dilemma, and Khrushchev began to thrash about from one solution to another. He banned all private livestock and allowed only communal herds. Instead of increasing the stock of farm machinery, he dissolved the machine and tractor stations serving the countryside. Instead of easing life for the peasants who could at least support themselves, if not feed the country, he added to their difficulties.

Meantime, the soil continued to deteriorate: because the number of cows and horses had declined, there was less manure. Rather than providing organic and chemical fertilizer for the lands that had been farmed from time immemorial, Khrushchev ordered new, virgin land to be plowed.

And now Lysenko brought forth a new proposal. With the help of A. S. Shevchenko, Khrushchev's powerful aide for agriculture, and other old friends in the Ministry of Agriculture, the State Planning Committee, and the agriculture departments of the Party Central Committee and Council of Ministers, he persuaded Khrushchev that agriculture could be saved if only the soil could be improved with much less fertilizer than the agrochemists called for. Lysenko's friends argued that Lysenko's personality and managerial skills were beside the point; what mattered was that he had a sensible idea, refined in experiments for five years, when the agrochemists had nothing to offer. Their steady refrain and Khrushchev's taste for large-scale schemes that promised quick and easy solutions to complex problems, gradually led Khrushchev into accepting Lysenko's plan by the autumn of 1956.

Khrushchev delighted in proclaiming the dawn of an era of unprecedented achievements ("we shall soon overtake America in production of meat and milk—in three or four years"; "every Soviet family will soon have its own apartment or house"; "we shall achieve prosperity in 1975–1980"; "the party solemnly declares that the present generation of Soviet people will live under communism"). Lysenko's promises fitted in perfectly with Khrushchev's style. For historians the only enigma remaining—to which no one today can provide an answer—is whether either of them actually believed in their promises or whether both knew the deception they were proposing in the name of the nation.

Organo-Mineral Mixtures: A New Panacea

In the months following the war, Lysenko had taken up the question of the best fertilizer. In 1946, he announced in *Izvestia*[4] that he had made a discovery: "All the fertilizers that we introduce into the soil, even in assimilable form, are first absorbed by the microflora, and it is the products of the microflora's life activity that provide nourishment to agricultural plants." He simply dismissed a century of scientific work showing that plants were nourished by the minerals and organic molecules dissolved in water. Instead, he said, "Plants . . . are fed by the products of the life activity of microorganisms."

In 1946, he had not used his new interpretation of the role of microbes in plant nutrition as the basis for sweeping recommendations to collective farmers and scientists, but confined himself to localized advice to Siberian peasants:

> The Siberian soil freezes so hard that the microflora is extremely sterile, and since plants obtain nutrition only from the products of the microflora's vital activity, the plants are starved until the microflora revives and its activity resumes.[5]

He provided no data of a study of "microflora sterilization" by frost (in fact, bacteria survive perfectly well at low temperatures and the best way to preserve them for decades is to keep them in dried form at a temperature of –20 degrees C.). He advised that it is necessary . . . to spread on each hectare . . . two to three centners of well-heated soil in which the microflora have revived. Upon receiving this "leaven," the entire soil quickly revives, and one can assume that early plantings will then flourish.[6]

Like his plan to have hundreds of thousands of collective farmers turn over heaps of vernalized wheat, or dig trenches to store potato tubers till summer, or to castrate individual ears of wheat with scissors, or plant thousands of oak saplings, this theory demanded enormous amounts of manual labor to make it succeed. The soil had to be dug up, heated, carried to the fields, and spread across millions of hectares. And this was proposed in 1946, when not just the cattle but even the horses had likely been slaughtered for meat and there were practically no trucks or tractors, and a shortage of farm workers.

No one followed the academician's recommendations, and he never reverted to them.

Three years later, in 1949–1950, Lysenko came up with another idea. He had "heard" that it would be better to produce superphosphate and potash fertilizers in the form of granules rather than in the customary powdered form (which made them easier to spread on the fields).[7] Small granules would dissolve more slowly over the course of a summer, providing nourishment throughout the growing period. He also contended that "the less the superphosphate or potash fertilizers come into contact with the soil, the less they will form chemical compounds that the plants cannot assimilate."[8] In the early 1950s, he combined this notion with new "discoveries" about soil microorganisms. At the VASKhNIL session on September 15, 1953, he claimed a major discovery. "Without the life activity of the appropriate soil microorganisms the soil does not contain the nutrition required by plants," he said, and added, "Specific types of soil microorganisms exist . . . for each type . . . of plant."[9] "Now the tactics of mineral nutrition are also clear to us: We must feed the microorganisms, not try to feed the plant directly. Then the norms of required fertilizer will be lower, the choice of fertilizers simpler, and the effect greater," he declared.[10] The way to feed microorganisms was to plow into the soil a mixture of three centners of superphosphate (preferably granulated) and one or two tons of manure, sometimes with the addition of lime and powdered phosphorite or dolomite, whichever was available. The thirty or forty tons of manure per hectare that the peasants had been spreading on the soil were no longer necessary. "The norms of required fertilizer will be lower, the choice of fertilizers simpler, and the effect greater," he declared.[11]

Lysenko's new ideas about soil microbes and fertilizers were sharply criticized by specialists in agrochemistry and plant nutrition. In 1955, Andrei V. Sokolov, a leading authority on mineral fertilizer, itemized the various methods of fertilization that Lysenko had advocated over the past several years and then said flatly, "Each recommendation was accompanied by claims of the extraordinary effectiveness of this latest proposal, but not one was confirmed in the experimental trials."[12]

In the fall of 1952, the staff at Lenin Hills, under the leadership of Artavasd A. Avakyan, began conducting field experiments with a mixture of superphosphate, manure, and lime, which they called "triplex" (*troichatka*). Just as Lysenko had predicted, there seemed to be a splendid harvest. The results were apparently confirmed the following year. A triumphant article immediately appeared, heralding triplex as the newest fruit of the Michurinist doctrine,[13] and Lysenko delivered one speech after another to advertise his latest proposal: at a conference of machine-and-tractor-station officials (January 26, 1954), a conference of sovkhoz officials (February 4, 1954), a meeting of the scientific council of the Timiryazev Academy (early March 1954), a conference of agricultural officials of the southwestern regions (March 18, 1955) and another of agricultural officials of the Central Black Earth zone (March 30, 1955), a conference of officials of the regions and autonomous republics of the non-black earth zone and a conference of agricultural officials of the northwest (April 6, 1955), and a seminar of students of agricultural educational institutions.[14] This frenzy of activity was probably a result of the fact that this was the time when Lysenko's theory of species was coming under heavy fire.

It wasn't long, however, before scientists were voicing their skepticism about Lysenko's latest idea. For example, at a conference of soil specialists held in April 1954, convincing facts were presented by the prominent agrochemist Fyodor V. Turchin (see biographical sketch).[15] D. L. Ashkinazi of the Dokuchayev Soil Institute pointed out discrepancies in the reports of the experiments at Lenin Hills:

> According to Lysenko's formula, three centners of lime were to be used, but when the experimental plots were being shown to a large excursion of the biology section of the AN SSSR, Comrade Avakyan told us that they had indeed used three centners of lime on the soil in 1952, but in 1951 . . . they had applied an additional three tons. In later discussions of the same experiment, at the September [1953] session of VASKhNIL, Comrade Avakyan "clarified" this point, saying that in this experiment they had applied not three tons of lime beforehand, but two (?) . . . As you see, the matter is completely confused [by Lysenko and Avakyan], but their articles nevertheless speak of three centners of lime.[16]

The presidium of VASKhNIL in 1954–1955 was ordered to perform some special experiments to determine the effectiveness of organo-mineral mixtures on various crops in specific conditions. Field tests began in 1954 at forty-three research institutes and experimental stations across the country. Specialists at the Fertilizer Research Institute, where many of Pryanishnikov's pupils were working, designed and carried out the experiments, too. The data analyses were published in 1955, and they did not confirm the results that had been obtained at Lenin Hills. There was no increase in the harvest where the soil was insufficiently fertile; where increases did occur, they were found to be due to the superphosphates and the humus.

"However," the report noted, "humus in small doses is dangerous, because it leads to a reduction of the effect in subsequent years."[17] In other words, one could hold out for a year or two on good soil with the Lysenko fertilizer method, but after that the soil would unavoidably become exhausted. As for lime, it was outright harmful in most regions (wherever soil acidity was not excessive). The report noted the high expenditure of labor on preparing the mixtures.

The authors of the report presented the results very cautiously. They refrained from denouncing triplex, contenting themselves instead with giving the figures and tactfully describing the organo-mineral mixtures in terms of "not always" and "not everywhere" effective, although a reader could draw far stronger conclusions from their data. However they phrased it, the meaning was plain: to get results, a farm had to use heavy doses of fertilizer.

Why it was that triplex seemed to have increased the yields so much at Lenin Hills was inadvertently revealed in an article by its director, Fyodor V. Kallistratov. As he described the experiments there, the plantings were made each season on a field that had received an especially heavy application of fertilizers in the preceding year—and not just those fertilizers that were included in the triplex. Sometimes the field had received two centners of nitrogen fertilizer (ammonium nitrate) and a centner of calcium chloride per hectare.[18] Under such conditions, the addition of a small amount of triplex would not have made any difference. This did not prevent Kallistratov from making absurd claims for the effectiveness of the nostrum.

It must also be noted that the Lenin Hills farm kept extremely poor records. Lysenko himself, for example, reported that the yields on the control plots for the triplex experiments ranged from 4.9 to 16 centners of wheat grain per hectare.[19] Such a range rendered the controls useless. Compared with the lower figure, the yield on the experimental field would represent a huge increase; compared with the higher figure, the increase would be minimal. The likely explanation for this wide range was the poor record-keeping; some control plots had probably been generously fertilized a year before, while others had not.

Much of this came to light once again at a plenary session of VASKhNIL that was held in 1956 and was devoted to a discussion of the new "theory of plant nutrition." It took place in the Hall of Tsars on the second floor of the former Yusupov palace and it was a memorable occasion for me. For the first time, I heard Lysenko speak not at a lecture to students at the Timiryazev Agriculture Academy, but before leading scientists, who not only packed the hall but overflowed into the adjoining small Chinese Hall and onto the staircases, where loudspeakers had been set up. In the stuffy, dimly lit hall, with its vaulted ceiling in the ancient Russian style, its walls painted with patterned ornamentation, its columns decorated with gold leaf trim, the portraits of the tsars looking down, Lysenko spat out the sentences of his address. The peasant style of his oratory was sprinkled with ornate figures of speech taken "from life." He wheezed as he strained for breath, and his voice grated, leaving the impression that an evil fiend had climbed up into the seat of the tsars. After Lysenko spoke, academy president Lobanov delivered the customary statement that practice was the best way to test any theory; he said this with no particular sympathy and even, I thought, with a barely discernible tinge of irony.

The next speaker was Andrei V. Sokolov, head of the phosphorus laboratory of the Research Institute on Fertilizers and Insectofungicides and of the agrochemistry department of the Dokuchayev Soil Institute. His speech—austere, objective, and elegantly reasoned—was in sharp contrast to Lysenko's. Sokolov described the way experimental work was conducted at Lenin Hills and showed how the Lysenkoists falsified the results. Lysenko then attacked Sokolov fiercely, declaring that he had failed to deal with his, Lysenko's, theory of plant nutrition.

At the agrochemistry section the next day, Sokolov answered this charge and went on to criticize the methods of Lysenko and his followers in blunt terms:

In my speech, I could not say anything about T. D. Lysenko's works, not because I wanted to ignore or scorn them. Not at all. I did so because . . . there are no works of his on these questions. They do not exist. No theory exists. . . .

[Lysenko] said his theory of plant nutrition rests on the facts of one species generating other species. I consider that a theory resting on facts that no one has ever established in biological science . . . cannot be considered a scientific theory. . . .

All the experiments at Lenin Hills were conducted in complete violation of all rules of scientific method . . . No conclusions at all can be deduced from them about the effect of fertilizers . . . about the benefit of the mixtures or their harm. . . .

Where does this lead? It leads to the conclusion that such [experimental] data absolutely cannot be used either to prove or to disprove; its only use is to illustrate the state of experimental work at Lenin Hills. And that sometimes leads to curiosities.

I participated in the excursion that inspected the Lenin Hills experiments. We were shown the fine effect of organo-mineral mixtures. Very well, but we wanted to see the plot alongside, where fertilizers had been applied according to a different method, in order to compare the two. It turned out to be impossible. When we asked to see replications, we were not shown them, and it was apparent that there were none. Finally, while inspecting the plantings, I discovered plots where the growth was exceptionally poor and yet they bore labels of the triplex recommended by T. D. Lysenko. I pointed out that in these experiments there were plots where plants under triplex grew well and others under triplex that did badly. And what happened? We left, and three days later Academician Avakyan entered this hall, carrying a heap of paper-wrapped plants. He dumped them on the table before Pavel Pavlovich [Lobanov] and explained: Last time it was found that triplex did not work on some plots. We went to the fields, dug up the plants, and discovered that the technician had made a mistake: he had left the triplex label but had not applied triplex to the soil.

If experiments are conducted only once, the results depend on the work of the technician. Need one characterize these experiments more plainly? All this happened right in this hall and on the Lenin Hills fields.

I consider that such experiments should not be conducted at all, they are useless.[20]

The transcript of this session was passed from hand to hand afterward and was widely discussed. It appeared to be the end of the new doctrine of plant nutrition.

Opposition Grows

The removal of Lysenko from the presidency of VASKhNIL in April 1956 gave his critics new courage. For instance, at a conference of personnel of agricultural science on June 19, 1956, USSR Minister of Agriculture V. V. Matskevich referred sarcastically to Lysenkoist theories about the inevitability of weeds and the transformation of one species into another: "lulled by the 'profound research'" of the Lysenkoists, "we ... expected the weeds ... to turn into ... pineapples."[21] Also, the first organizational measures of a clearly anti-Lysenkoist nature appeared.

On June 22, 1956, the presidium of the AN SSSR ordered that a Laboratory of Radiation Genetics be established as part of the academy's Institute of Biological Physics. Dubinin was appointed director, and the best of the surviving geneticists quickly gathered here. Although the institute offered no suitable premises, the geneticists' enthusiasm was so great that they found a solution for themselves. Next to the quarantine nursery of the Main Botanical Garden of the AN SSSR, not far from Lenin Avenue, stood a strange, small, almost windowless one-story structure, completely surrounded by a fence. Each morning, the streetcars disgorged large numbers of people at the nearby stop, sometimes automobiles brought others, including well-known physicists, and so many people swarmed through the gate in the fence that the small building could not possibly hold them all. It was obvious that a huge underground center or factory was situated beneath the small structure. Each evening, the flow reversed itself. Next door stood a huge power plant, with a tall water-cooling tower, above which a column of smoke wreathed day and night. At that time, this area was almost at the edge of Moscow. The tram tracks had been laid to reach it, and the conductors announced the stop as "Experimental Field." In fact, beneath the botanical garden lay a secret nuclear physics research center.

In the spring of 1956, the botanical garden which was located on the field above this underground center of nuclear physics was moved. The trees and bushes were dug up, the field was laid bare, and only the ramshackle three-room shed remained. The plans were to tear it down, but the geneticists, convinced that they would not otherwise have any work space, obtained the consent of Tsitsin, the botanical garden director, to occupy the shed. It lacked water, gas, and central heating.[22] Nevertheless, within a month or two after the first staff members appeared in the shed in May, desks, chairs, microscopes, and incubators full of *Drosophila* cultures had arrived, and research was in full swing in the new radiation genetics laboratory.

Meanwhile, the Soviet press finally broke its silence about major international discoveries in molecular genetics. In 1956, a popular science magazine for young people published interviews with the physicist Tamm, the reputable Soviet biochemist Engelgardt, the geneticist Dubinin, and others;[23] a journal *Biophysics* carried an article by Dubinin entitled "The Physical and Chemical Bases of Heredity,"[24] and *Chemical Science and Industry* (with the blessing of its editor in chief, Knunyants) published the translation of an article by Francis Crick about the structure of DNA.[25]

Probably the widest attention, however, was attracted by the publication of the proceedings of a "round table" conducted under the auspices of a new monthly magazine, *Our Contemporary* (Nash sovremennik).[26] The subject of discussion was Pisarzhevsky's recently published article on the Lysenkoist deceptions (see chapter 13). Representing the Lysenkoists were, in addition to Lysenko himself, Avakyan, Glushchenko, and Prezent, along with the entomologist I. A. Khalifman; Ya. F. Kucheryaviy, chief agronomist of the Moscow Regional Agricultural Administration; and the writer Vadim Safonov.

The only representatives of Lysenko's critics on hand at the start of the discussion were Fyodor V. Turchin, an agrochemist at the Fertilizer Research Institute, and the geneticist Vladimir V. Sakharov. However, a short while afterward Pisarzhevsky and Dubinin arrived—whereupon Lysenko "jumped to his feet and left without saying a word."[27] It was a telling sign of how Lysenko had changed, for in the past he would not have missed an opportunity to cross swords with any of his adversaries.

The published account of the round table began with a lengthy article by Avakyan,[28] and this was followed by an abridged transcript of the discussion. The Lysenkoists' style was familiar: labeling opponents pejoratively, citing mass experiments by collective farmers, presenting themselves as principled lovers of science.[29] But the statements of Sakharov,[30] Turchin,[31] Dubinin,[32] and Pisarzhevsky were read with the greatest interest.

Turchin showed that Lysenko's theory of plant nutrition was a fiction without scientific basis. Dubinin and Sakharov noted the damage Lysenkoism—and Glushchenko personally—had done to Soviet research on polyploids and specifically to the development of improved varieties of kol-sagyz and buckwheat.

Sakharov struck hard at the Lysenkoists' scientific facade. It was not "Michurinist biology" that defined them, he said, but rather the cult of personality, the "unprecedented identification with the views of your scientific leader that defines the essential character of the group of scientific workers who . . . claim the name 'Michurinists.'" "Following your rules," he continued, "you should rightfully and properly call yourselves not Michurinists, but Lysenkoists. . . . I have no hesitation in saying that there can be no Michurinist biology."[33]

Most crucial of all, declared Sakharov, was the damage to scientific thought from Lysenkoism. "Science cannot develop without contradiction and criticism." Yet, under their regime, "unanimous support" was given "by the entire obedient environment, even when T. D. Lysenko was spouting utter nonsense." The damage, moreover, had spread beyond biology to other fields of thought: Soviet philosophers, in looking to Lysenkoist speculations for a solid ideological foundation to dialectical materialism, found themselves supporting propositions that blatantly contradicted true science."[34]

In reply, Avakyan, Khalifman, and Glushchenko claimed that their words and deeds were being misrepresented. Glushchenko rejected the charge that he and the Lysenkoists had suppressed polyploid research. "Michurinist genetics does not deny a single fact, but has its own interpretation of the facts. This is our civil right."[35] He also emphasized the ideological aspect of their work:

> O. Pisarzhevsky's essay . . . was written for the purpose of turning back the development of materialist biology. This is a fantastic, unreal task, and hence the article was, to put it mildly, useless. . . . Attempts at revenge on the part of some biologists are surely doomed to failure. The guarantee of this is our Soviet reality and the doctrine of Marxism-Leninism, which is the foundation of advanced Soviet science.[36]

Publication of this discussion had a great impact. For the first time, biologists saw that criticism of Lysenkoism—not just of its details but of its essence—no longer brought in its wake dismissal from work, or arrest, or other frightful consequences. For none of the participants in the round table suffered. Early in 1957, Dubinin was even invited to deliver a report at a meeting of the presidium of the AN SSSR. The very fact that a "Morganist" was given the floor at a meeting of the presidium was stunning to many. Lysenko, a member of the presidium, pled another engagement. But the meeting was held and well attended, with the presence of the directors of the country's scientific establishment and of a number of prominent scientists, including academicians I. Ye. Tamm, I. V. Kurchatov, I. L. Knunyants, and others.

Dubinin dealt with such topics as "DNA, the tasks of radiational and chemical genetics, human genetics, and the relationship of genetics to selection, medicine, and the defense of the country."[37] Dubinin says that the invitation to address the meeting was the work of I. V. Kurchatov, the founder of the Soviet atomic industry.

Another event that caused a stir was a report to the All-Union Botanical Society in 1957 by F. Kh. Bakhteyev, a student of Vavilov's, urging revision of the textbooks in botany. The report was published in the society's journal, and the society adopted a resolution in support.[38]

All this anti-Lysenkoist activity culminated in an act of tremendous importance: In May 1957, the USSR Council of Ministers decreed the formation of a Siberian branch of the AN SSSR. Two applied mathematicians, Mikhail A. Lavrentyev and Sergei L. Sobolev, had convinced Khrushchev that such a new center would greatly spur the progress of all Soviet science. They intended to include biology and particularly genetics in it, but they knew Lysenko and were hostile toward him and his work.[39] Thus, Lavrentyev, taking advantage of Khrushchev's carte blanche, took the bold step of inviting Dubinin to be the director of one of the two biology institutes to be included in the Siberian branch, the Institute of Cytology and Genetics. Within the AN SSSR, this was a powerful alternative to Lysenko's institute.

The new institute was set up very quickly. An outstanding staff was assembled, including the cytologists Vera V. Khvostova and Yuly Ya. Kerkis, the plant geneticists Aleksandr N. Lutkov and Yury P. Miryuta, the biochemist Rudolf I. Salganik, and the statistician N. A. Plokhinsky. Raisa L. Berg, population geneticist, played a particularly active role at the institute.

The energetic Dubinin found a way to participate in an emerging sector of Soviet science, space research. As soon as the USSR launched the world's first artificial satellite on October 4, 1957, Dubinin sent the presidium of the AN SSSR a memorandum proposing to include genetic research in the program of work in outer space, and his proposal was adopted.[40] This move was bound to strengthen the hand of the geneticists. Because of the strict secrecy surrounding the project, Lysenko did not even guess what was happening.

Khrushchev Supports Lysenko

During these years, it was common talk among scientists that Lysenko had been removed from the presidency of VASKhNIL not because of opposition among scientists but because the new first secretary of the Party, Khrushchev, harbored a personal dislike of him. Khrushchev's behavior during his first year or two in that office seemed to bear out that belief. It was rumored that his daughter Rada, a journalist specialized in covering biology, sided with Lysenko's opponents.

However, Khrushchev had visited the Lenin Hills farm in either 1954 or 1955 and had been favorably impressed. Lysenko boasted to Khrushchev about the miraculous properties of his triplex. The persistent refrain of Lysenko's friends may also have had a cumulative effect. In any case, the

Party leader told a conference of agricultural personnel on March 30, 1957: "There are scientists who still dispute Lysenko ... If I were asked which scientist I vote for, I would say without hesitation: for Lysenko. I know he would not let us down, because he doesn't put his hand to bad things. I think few scientists understand the soil as does Comrade Lysenko."[41]

> Three years ago I visited the experimental farm where T. D. Lysenko showed me plantings on fields fertilized by the new method. This method is now becoming well established in Moscow Province and other provinces.

What finally decided Khrushchev in favor of Lysenko, according to a widely circulated story, was an incident about this time where Khrushchev decided to test organic mineral mixtures for himself. He ordered Lysenko and another "miracle-working" academician, N. V. Tsitsin, then popular in Kremlin circles, to plant one hectare each near his dacha. For many years, Tsitsin had promised the country's leaders to bring forth a remarkable new hybrid of couch grass with domesticated wheat and rye. Tsitsin was to sow his wheat-couch grass hybrid on his hectare, while Lysenko was to apply the organo-mineral mixture as fertilizer on the hectare that he, Lysenko, was to plant. The comparison made no sense, for no control plantings were made; each simply planted one hectare. Lysenko's grain yield proved larger. Khrushchev later loved to tell how he had "tested" the two academicians and how Lysenko had "won out" over Tsitsin.

Within a week (April 5, 1957) of Khrushchev's expressions of enthusiasm for Lenin Hills, his strong support of Lysenko at another conference of agricultural personnel was underscored by Party propaganda organs: Lysenko's name led *Pravda*'s listing of the dignitaries seated at the presidium alongside the Party's First Secretary of the Central Committee.[42] *Pravda*'s lengthy communiqué closed with the statement that "Academician T. D. Lysenko's speech ... attracted great attention."[43]

Two days later, *Pravda* printed Khrushchev's speech in which, following Lenin and Stalin's model, the new Party leader appealed to ideology rather than scientific argument.[44] Lysenko's triplexes had—he said approvingly—been supported by Comrade Krynkov, the party secretary of a district in Arzamas Province, if not by VASKhNIL's soil scientists, who had called Lysenko's recommendations "Scientifically groundless." Khrushchev derided the scientists' incorrect "policeman's attitude" as well as the position of noninterference supposedly taken by USSR Minister of Agriculture Matskevich and USSR Minister of Sovkhozes Benediktov. "They folded their hands like saints and refrained from intervening in this dispute," he said. "Ministers must not stand on the sidelines. Why do you turn your backs on what the people say and recognize?"[45] On April 27, *Izvestia* published a long article by Lysenko himself under a headline that read like a directive: "Apply Organo-Mineral Mixtures More Widely in the Non-Black

Earth Belt." Lysenko was riding high once more. His position was further strengthened when, at the end of June, Khrushchev's opponents within the Party (Malenkov, Molotov, Kaganovich, and Shepilov) were ousted from power for having tried to carry out a "plot" against the Party and government.[46]

Khrushchev continued to harp on his favorite theme: "We will amaze the whole world with our achievements."[47] Lysenko's projects fit Khrushchev's program admirably. "There is no nobler task for a Soviet scientist," Lysenko said in an interview, "than to help the Communist Party and the Soviet people in their heroic work of bringing about a sharp upsurge in agriculture."[48]

Are Physics and Chemistry Needed in the Study of Life?

Even if in the eyes of the country's supreme leader Lysenko was already the victor in the biology dispute, the scientists refused to accept defeat. The fear of ideological accusations and persecution that in Stalin's time had forced silence had now abated, thanks to Khrushchev's own attacks on the Stalinist "cult of personality." Although he himself succumbed to the temptation of introducing his own cult, he could not become a second Stalin. People were now bolder; they told jokes about him and laughed openly at his slogan, "We shall overtake America in meat output."

Thus, articles continued to appear, even in the mass media, about DNA, the genetic code, and the progress of science in other parts of the world.[49] An editorial in the main philosophical journal *Problems of Philosophy* listed among examples of an incorrect and "nihilistic" attitude toward science "the fact that valuable achievements of the chromosome theory of development have been cast overboard."[50] And, after a fierce struggle, first with G. M. Boshyan and N. N. Zhukov-Verezhnikov (see biographical sketches), and then with Oparin, Studitsky, Nuzhdin, and the editors of the *Great Soviet Encyclopedia*, Professor Vladimir Ya. Aleksandrov managed to publish in the second edition of the encyclopedia a major article, "Cytology," setting forth the basics of genetics.

Lysenko, nevertheless, seized every opportunity to speak in behalf of his own cause. Late in 1957, he and Nuzhdin, who was becoming a leader in the Lysenkoist camp, delivered lectures at the Moscow Polytechnical Museum. I attended, with a group of students and faculty of the Timiryazev Academy. The auditorium was packed, and the atmosphere was tense. The Lysenkoists had taken to asserting (falsely) that the molecular geneticists had rejected the views of classical genetics and the proposition that the gene was part of the structure of chromosomes. On this occasion, Lysenko declared that the connection between DNA molecules and genes was nothing more than an idle invention:

Having denied the classical interpretation of the gene as a bit of chromosome, the representatives of Morganist genetics switched to new positions, advancing the DNA molecule as the gene. . . . But it is not a way out of the situation [to say]: There is no gene, and at the same time it exists in the form of the DNA molecule. . . . They fly off on wings of fantasy that sweep them up into a realm of groundless speculations.

He also rejected the conclusion that had been drawn in the *Problems of Philosophy* editorial, saying that the charge of "nihilism" should be aimed instead "at formal genetics, which has repudiated its former conceptions of the gene, calling those ideas naive and childish. The Michurinists correctly showed that science cannot retain the idea of the gene, which does not reflect objective scientific laws."

Lysenko then turned to a discussion of his own doctrines. There was a stir—not quite laughter, but something like it—when he declared that "under certain circumstances, any part, any matter of the living organism, including ordinary plant sap" (the "juices" drawn from the soil and residing in the pores of the plant) could be the carrier of hereditary information. Toward the end of his lecture, Lysenko touched on the issue of the support that the geneticists had received from physicists, chemists, and mathematicians. It would have been undiplomatic to say that these critics should not be heard. Instead, he asserted that biological phenomena

do not squeeze into and cannot be confined to chemical and physical laws. . . . the objects of biology—microorganisms, plants, and animals—live, feed, and develop in accordance with biological, not chemical, laws. . . . Chemical and physical laws are the same in biological phenomena as in inorganic nature, but in biological phenomena they are subordinate to biological laws.[51]

Lysenko's anxiety over the involvement of representatives of the exact sciences in the genetics discussion was entirely understandable. I had many long hours of discussions with him in 1957–1958 and I was convinced that for the first time in his life he began to recognize that he was losing support in the upper echelons of science and power, that his reputation as an innovator and as a popular favorite were evaporating, that rumors and hints about his incompetence and even downright ridicule were spreading, and that he was no longer being described as a worthy academician but as a creation of the criminal cult of Stalin. It was entirely reasonable for him to associate this change with the intrigues of scientists who, he believed, knew nothing of biology but were increasingly gathering the reins of power over Soviet science.

He learned, for example, that Vladimir A. Kirillin, the head of the science department of the Party Central Committee, paid great heed to the physicists, chemists, and mathematicians, although Kirillin, fearing Khrushchev, did not display his hostility openly, but favored the opposed camp whenever he could.

A. N. Nesmeyanov, president of the USSR Academy of Sciences (see chapter 13) took a more unconcealed stand. His speeches often dealt with the need for research in the physics and chemistry of living matter. One of the laboratories in Nesmeyanov's institute was headed by Academician Ivan L. Knunyants. It was common knowledge that Knunyants could not stand Lysenko. At the slightest opportunity he spoke passionately and convincingly of Lysenko's mistakes. Knunyants's meeting the academy president in the institute corridors almost daily could not fail to influence him. Nikolai N. Semyonov, another leading chemist and science administrator, also gained great power. In 1956 he won the Nobel Prize in chemistry for his work on chain reactions. Semyonov and Knunyants maintained close contact and often visited one another socially, especially at their country cottages. The prominent geneticist Rapoport, who had so boldly challenged the Lysenkoists at the VASKhNIL session of 1948, impressed Semyonov. In 1957 Semyonov became academic secretary of the chemistry section of the USSR Academy of Sciences and strove to promote research in biochemistry, biophysics, and genetics. He appointed Rapoport as a head of the large Laboratory of Mutagenesis at his Institute of Chemical Physics of the AN SSSR.

Mention has already been made of the anti-Lysenkoist views of such prominent scientists as Kapitsa, Kurchatov, Engelgardt, Tamm, and A. D. Sakharov. The mathematicians A. A. Lyapunov and A. D. Aleksandrov were outspoken in their disagreement with Lysenko, Kolmogorov and Sobolev perhaps less loudly so. This is far from a complete list of these scientists who were establishing and directing new branches of science of the utmost importance to the state—atomic physics, nuclear power, space science, polymer chemistry. The military-industrial complex would have withered without them, so they had powerful positions from which to oppose Lysenko.

The combined efforts of these scientists caused a point to be included in a report written for Khrushchev in 1958 on the control figures for the coming seven-year economic plan, a point that must have seemed calculated to provoke Lysenko, for it suggested the expansion of the exact sciences into spheres of biology that he had regarded up until then as his personal fiefdom. The point read:

The complex of biological sciences will particularly grow in importance to the extent that the achievements of physics and chemistry are utilized in biology. Such branches of science as biochemistry, agrochemistry, biophysics, microbiology, virology, selection, and genetics will play a large role in this.[52]

Later that year, Nesmeyanov, treating this declaration as if it were already a Party directive, wrote in *Pravda*: "To the extent that biology is penetrated by chemistry and physics ... the complex of biological sciences will rapidly grow in importance, and physico-chemical biology is likely to become the future leader in the natural sciences." He urged the speedy construction of science centers in Novosibirsk, Irkutsk, and Pushchino (a science city for biological research that was planned on the Oka River

near Serpukhov, 86 miles from Moscow).[53] It was clear to all that the research conducted in these centers would not be guided by Lysenkoist
doctrines. (Construction of the center at Pushchino did not begin, however, until the middle 1960s.)

It infuriated Lysenko that other scientists were interfering in biological
work, "corrupting" young scholars and organizing "mob meetings" that he
considered not scientific but provocational gatherings. "What kind of science could go on there?" he protested during one of our conversations.
"None! And what kind of scientists are Academician Tamm and the
Morganist Dubinin? All they want to do is to fight me and stick close to
the scientific feeding trough. I'll sue them for slander!"

Nonetheless, the Lysenko lines of defense were being breached at one
point after another: at a conference on the application of mathematical
methods in biology held at Leningrad State University in May 1958;[54] at a
conference the next month on polyploids in plants at the biology department of Moscow State University under the aegis of the Moscow Naturalists Society;[55] and in a steady flow of anti-Lysenkoist articles in the *Botanical
Journal* and the *Bulletin* of the biology section of the Moscow Naturalists
Society. By this time, Lysenko must have realized that, if science in the
USSR were free and the scientists themselves determined the direction of
scientific research, he would long since have lost all his power. But it was
not the scientists who made such decisions; it was the political leaders.
Thus, it was the politicians to whom Lysenko turned, once again, to seek
protection for himself and to settle accounts with his critics. The Party
Central Committee was preparing to hold another session devoted to agriculture; and, when Lysenko was drawn into the preparation of material for
the meeting, he found it an opportune occasion on which to strike.

Party Criticism of the *Botanical Journal*

In 1957, Lysenko published a long two-part article, entitled "For Materialism in Biology!" The article was a response to the critics of the "Michurinist
doctrine."[56] The critics, however, pushed back. The August 1958 issue of
the *Botanical Journal* carried an article written by a Leningrad scientist,
Daniil Lebedev, who gathered all available information about the great
errors in Soviet biology that were attributable to Lysenko's domination.
Lebedev examined the consequences of prohibiting research on growth
substances, mutations (including polyploidy), inbreeding, hybrid corn, and
the breakdown in plant breeding and seed production. He compiled the
pronouncements of Party leaders and science officials referring to these
failures; and explained in clear form in each case that the responsibility
was Lysenko's. The result was extremely convincing, and the article gained
particular authority by virtue of the fact that it was published in the name
of the journal's editorial board.[57] It also had symbolic significance, since it
was published ten years after the August 1948 session of VASKhNIL.

The reply came in two forms. First, Lysenko was decorated again. On

September 27, 1958, the USSR Supreme Soviet gave Lysenko a present for his sixtieth birthday: his seventh Order of Lenin, "in consideration of his great services to agriculture and his practical assistance to production."[58] Second, and even more directly, *Pravda* printed on December 14, 1958, an editorial specifically and very sharply condemning the *Botanical Journal* article and giving Lysenko unqualified support.

> Filthy streams of disinformation continue to pour forth against materialist biology. . . .
>
> The fact that in our country people can still be found who continue to blacken and discredit materialist agrobiology provokes amazement and legitimate indignation.
>
> The works of Academician T. D. Lysenko have been made the chief target of these attacks. Some have gone so far in slandering the Michurinist scientist that they stoop to any means.

The editorial proclaimed Lysenko's successes: intravarietal crossing was a very fruitful idea; organo-mineral mixtures were adding thousands of tons to the harvests; the work on increasing milk fat was promising. And *Pravda* concluded that "the so-called discussion that has been going on for a number of years in the *Botanical Journal* does not help the development of materialist biology. On the contrary, it is detrimental to science [and] hinders the mobilization of all efforts to solve the very important tasks advanced by the Party."[59]

Lysenko had long craved to suppress the criticisms that were appearing in the pages of the *Botanical Journal.* I heard him refer frequently to the journal's "pernicious role" and to enemies "who found a comfortable hideout on its editorial board," describing them as unprincipled pseudoscientists who understood nothing of science. A year earlier, when Lysenko had made such accusations in *Izvestia*,[60] the AN SSSR had appointed a commission to look into the work of the *Botanical Journal.*[61] The commission proceeded to study every issue of the journal for the past two and a half years, and it concluded in September 1958 that the *Botanical Journal* is a "qualified, progressive journal" and that the editorial board had done work of high quality and that "the journal strives to elucidate as fully as possible questions within its scope and enjoys well-deserved authority both within the USSR and abroad." It pointedly observed that it had sent two letters to Lysenko asking him "to substantiate in greater detail" the accusations he had made and that Lysenko had not responded, "thereby expressing a disinclination to argue the grave charges he had made publicly against a journal that publishes the results of the work of a large body of Soviet botanists."[62]

The bureau of the biology division of the AN SSSR heard the commission's conclusion at a special meeting and confirmed it, emphasizing two points:

1. To approve the commission's conclusion . . .

2. To consider it appropriate to publish the commission's conclusion . . . in the news item section in the Biology Series of the Herald of the AN SSSR.[63]

The subsequent attack on the *Botanical Journal* in *Pravda* in mid-December of 1958 may have been designed to deflect attention from the commission's report. In any case, the editorial was merely a prelude to Khrushchev's speech to the Central Committee the following day. Although Khrushchev severely criticized many scientists, he praised Lysenko's work, saying that it had won "universal recognition."[64] In the discussion of Khrushchev's report, I. D. Mustafayev, a member of the Azerbaidzhan Academy of Sciences and an official of the Genetics and Selection Institute of that republic's Ministry of Agricultural Production and Procurements, played the part of a "representative of the masses." He had read horrifying things in the newspapers, he said, and they greatly disturbed him. The following dialogue ensued between him and Khrushchev:

Mustafayev. The situation in biology is particularly bad, as *Pravda* indicated on December 14, when it spoke of the incomprehensible conduct of the *Botanical Journal* and some of our scientists. Instead of engaging in businesslike, scientific mutual criticism and the identification of shortcomings, they have turned to an offensive tone and insult.

Khrushchev. We ought to take a look at the editors. Apparently they are opponents of Michurinist science. Nothing will change as long as they are there. They ought to be replaced by genuine Michurinists. That is the fundamental solution.

Mustafayev. Nikita Sergeyevich, such a tone is not confined to this journal. Sometimes Communist scientists don't think about how they ought to conduct themselves. Rumors recently reached me that our delegation in China, which included biologists, said Comrade Lysenko was done for, not only in matters of theory, but also of practice.

Khrushchev. Tsitsin said it.

Mustafayev. This is bad. Even if they have poor personal relationships, this does not give anyone the right to criticize the achievements of our science.

Khrushchev. He should have been asked at a Party meeting why he said this, should have been required to answer as a Party member.

Voices. Right.[65]

The next speaker was Lysenko, who did not deign to hide the low reputation of Lysenkoism in world scientific opinion:

We know that a so-called "discussion" is going on throughout the world in scientific journals and not infrequently in newspapers as well about Michurinist biology, which reactionaries of the capitalist countries call "Lysenkoism." . . . reactionaries in science and the journalists of the bourgeois world—especially the U.S.A., Britain, and other capitalist countries—ascribe all kinds of sins to me. They proclaim all my scientific work in biology and agronomical practice to be charlatanry and deception.

In the American journal *Heredity*, vol. 49, no. 1, 1958, the biologist Dobzhansky, an obvious enemy of the USSR, claimed that "the shameful situation in which Lysenko has placed materialist science will not soon be forgotten." . . .

[Dobzhansky] would like biology journals in the USSR to come out against dialectical materialism, against Marxism-Leninism. . . .

It seems to me that Academician A. N. Nesmeyanov, president of the Academy of Sciences, and Academician V. A. Engelgardt, secretary of the academy's biology division, do not consider our theoretical and biological positions, which form the basis for various practices in agriculture and animal husbandry, to be scientific. To this day, a thesis from which no practical conclusions can be derived is considered more scientific. (*Laughter, stir in the hall.*)

Lysenko went on to put forth what was probably intended as a suggestion for a new purge in biology—"It would be desirable to subject the work of the biological institutions to the criteria of practice, at least to some degree"—and he warned against "replacing biology with chemistry and physics." He offered no new practical proposals, beyond increasing the herd of cows at Lenin Hills, "every one of them producers of high-fat milk, so that soon the nation would have ample supplies of milk, butter, and "excellent meat." His concluding sentences were phrased clumsily but delivered with passion:

In general, comrades, there is no end to how much it is possible to solve practical agrotechnical and zootechnical questions in our kolkhoz and sovkhoz conditions as one gets to know more and more deeply the laws of the life and development of plants, animals, and microorganisms. For us biologists, this is the joy and happiness of creative work. Heartfelt thanks to the Soviet people, the Communist Party, and the Soviet government, and to Nikita Sergeyevich Khrushchev personally for the great concern and attention to science and the workers of science.[66]

The audience rewarded him with applause.[67]

To cap things off for Lysenko, the Central Committee made a remarkable gesture. A. B. Aristov, who was presiding at the meeting, moved the election of an editorial committee to draw up a resolution based on Khrushchev's speech; he read out the names of the people proposed for the committee and declared the motion had passed. Normally, no changes were allowed once a motion had been adopted. But suddenly a voice was heard from the presidium, proposing the addition of Lysenko's name to the list. The voice belonged to someone with such great influence in the Party—apparently, Khrushchev—that Aristov, the Central Committee secretary, had to alter the list already accepted, and Lysenko was included on the committee.[68] Thus, Lysenko, who was not even a Party member, was made a member of a committee entrusted with the editing of an important Party document. Even Stalin had never given such authority to Lysenko.[69]

In January, the presidiums of the AN SSSR and of its biology division, together with the division's aktiv, met to consider its response to the

Central Committee resolution, which called for, among other things, a change in the editorial board of the *Botanical Journal*. The tone of the resolution embodying this response differed fundamentally from similar resolutions passed in Stalinist times. It began with long, dense talk of "indubitable successes" and "solutions to problems." Only after tiresomely long paragraphs, filled with vague formulations, came the requisite point: "In the course of the past several years, the *Botanical Journal* has set itself the task of criticizing individual points of Michurinist doctrine and in particular the achievements of Academician T. D. Lysenko and his followers. This attitude on the part of the editorial board was wrong and hindered the development of Soviet biology." And then came something very different from what might have been expected—a comment that could almost have been an ironic rebuke to Lysenko and his followers: "Scientific criticism must be imbued with a spirit of good will and mutual assistance." Only after all this did the participants in the meeting say that they "acknowledged as correct the *Pravda* criticism of the erroneous position taken by the editorial board of the *Botanical Journal*." Even here, it was striking that the Central Committee's condemnation was not mentioned at all. An auto-da-fé in the spirit of 1948 did not come off.

What came next was still more remarkable. The resolution proposed immediate implementation of a measure that Lysenko had been fighting since 1956: "It is necessary to carry out the 1957 presidium decree about establishing an institute of radiation and physico-chemical biology and ensure the participation of physicists and chemists in its work."[70] Lysenko's efforts to keep physicists and chemists out of biology and to hinder Engelgardt from establishing his institute had collapsed.

The decision on the composition of the new editorial board for the *Botanical Journal* was announced (with, at last, mention of the Central Committee meeting, but only in passing) was tucked away in the back pages of the academy's journal.[71] Sukachev and his appointees were replaced, but Nesmeyanov was not, and none of the members of the old editorial board suffered either administratively or by Party action—an indication of how conditions had changed under Khrushchev.[72] True, the Lysenkoists soon managed to remove Engelgardt from the position of academician-secretary of the biology division and put one of their own, Sisakyan, in his place—but only with the title of acting secretary.

Khrushchev Interferes with the Siberian Institute of Cytology and Genetics

The scientists who gathered in Akademgorodok, the new science center near the Siberian city of Novosibirsk, plunged into research even before they got suitable premises. This was especially true of the staff of the Institute of Cytology and Genetics. Many of them had been cut off from science since 1948; some had engaged in work utterly unrelated to genetics. In recent years, a few lucky ones had begun to work in the radiation genetics laboratory at the old shed of the botanical gardens in Moscow. For all of them, the raw new place was a paradise.

Lysenko, on the other hand, was deeply troubled. He warned Khrushchev, in every way he could, that those people in Siberia were producing not science but nonsense of no use to the country, pouring funds down a bottomless pit out of which nothing would come.

The machinery of obstruction in such circumstances had been highly developed over the years. Committees are appointed to evaluate activities; the committees submit their reports, and appropriate conclusions are drawn.

Lysenko had no difficulty in finding suitable candidates for inclusion on such committees. One, for example, was A. G. Utekhin, who was head of the science sector of the agricultural department of the Central Committee. He had been an agronomist or perhaps a farm-machine operator in the Kuibyshev region; early in the 1930s, he had delivered a report in Moscow about the great success of vernalization. His data were considered by Academician Konstantinov as falsified, but, in spite of that, he was decorated with an order and quickly rose to the top, first as Party secretary at Lysenko's establishment in Odessa and then the Party secretary of the staff of the presidium of VASKhNIL. Another was Mikhail A. Olshansky, an old colleague of Lysenko's from Odessa days who had since become a full member of VASKhNIL. Nuzhdin, who was currently deputy scientific director at Lysenko's institute in Moscow and a corresponding member of the AN SSSR, also served as a committee member.

All the committees that visited Akademgorodok found what Lysenko expected. The work plans of the new institute were characterized by precisely those traits that had been condemned back in 1948: idealism, metaphysics, Morganism, Mendelism, Weismannism, vitalism, Virchowism, oversimplification, decadence, reaction, kowtowing to the West, an unhealthy penchant for harebrained schemes, theorizing, a lack of incentives for the kolkhoz peasantry, impracticality. Institute director Dubinin paid no attention to these reports, nor did the chairman of the Siberian branch of the academy, Lavrentyev.

Khrushchev, however, was not content. At the next Central Committee plenary session, on June 29, 1959, he criticized the appointment of Dubinin as director of the new institute.

The works of this scientist have brought very little benefit to science and practical work. If Dubinin is known for anything, it is for his articles and speeches against the theory, positions, and practical recommendations of Academician Lysenko.

I do not want to be a judge between the directions of the work of these scientists. Practice, life, as we know, is the judge. But practice speaks in favor of the biological school of Michurin and of Academician Lysenko, who carries on his work. Take the Lenin Prizes, for example. Who won the Lenin Prizes for plant breeding? The scientists of the materialist direction in biology, that is to say, the school of Timiryazev, the school of Michurin, which is the school of

Lysenko. But where are the outstanding works of the biologist Dubinin, who is one of the chief organizers of the struggle against Lysenko's Michurinist views? If he did not bring substantial benefit when he worked in Moscow, he is hardly likely to bring it in Novosibirsk or Vladivostok.[73]

Still, the months went by and the Siberian science executive were quietly ignoring the pronouncements of the Party leader.

Lysenko then tried another tactic: He offered some of the cows from his Lenin Hills herd to the Siberian division. Lavrentyev recalls:

Considering the strong support that Lysenko had, refusal of his offer had to be made with caution. We debated this in the presidium and decided not to respond to the proposal at all.

Our willfulness quickly became known in Moscow, which sent a high commission to check on the work of our biologists. The demand was made that we liquidate the Institute of Cytology and Genetics and establish a "Michurinist" institute, with a promise of staff and funds. I spoke somewhat incoherently about the unity of science, about the competition between scientific schools, about how we were all for Soviet science, but against mysticism. . . . A week later, I was informed that N. S. Khrushchev was very angry with me and was inclined to change the leadership of the Siberian division of the AN SSSR.[74]

But Lavrentyev had some organizational and political skills of his own. Because his story so clearly shows how "managed science" worked in real life, it is worth quoting at length:

I learned that Khrushchev was flying to Peking for the celebration of the tenth anniversary of the People's Republic of China and then intended to visit Novosibirsk, where the reorganization of the Siberian branch of the AN would be carried out, with the liquidation of "cytology and genetics" and the possible replacement of the leadership of the branch.

It was imperative at all costs to intercept Khrushchev before his arrival in Novosibirsk. Through Moscow friends I was included in one of the delegations to Peking, where I counted on meeting with Khrushchev and convincing him of the rightness of the position of the Siberian branch of the academy. . . .

By enormous efforts, I managed to arrive at the airport at the moment when the Soviet government delegation was to depart. I made my way through the crowd to Khrushchev, and to the question, "And what are you here for?" I replied: "Nikita Sergeyevich, take me with you." Thus, I ended up in Khrushchev's plane . . . The plane was going to Vladivostok. I tried to occupy Khrushchev with stories of science and the life of scientists since the times of Lomonosov.

After we took off from Vladivostok, I asked Khrushchev what he would like to look at in Akademgorodok. "Well, what do you suggest?" At first, I named geology, mechanics, and chemistry . . . The plan for the visit was received cordially, but when I mentioned the Institute of Cytology and Genetics, the mood changed abruptly. Khrushchev began to speak with great irritation about Dubinin and his colleagues, referred to the attempt to provide them with good practical workers, and said I specifically had hindered it. Khrushchev said outright that, in view of this situation, he would sharply reduce the funding and other provisions for the Siberian branch. My attempts to object only irritated him all the more. He stood up, walked to the opposite end of the plane compartment, and began to ruffle papers and sign them there. Watching the superb panoramas unfolding beneath us as we flew over the mountains of eastern Siberia, I could think of no way to get out of the situation. Two or three hours passed in this manner.

The mood lifted a bit during dinner. I said that although I was ignorant of agriculture and genetics, I was sure Lysenko was an obscurantist. I recalled the case of N. M. Sityi, my colleague at the Ukrainian Academy of Sciences, who created the canals to drain the Irpen floodlands at fabulously low cost by using wet dynamite as an explosive. When this achievement was submitted for a state prize, Lysenko objected that the use of explosions was unacceptable, because "soil is living matter, it will be frightened and will cease to be fruitful." The dinner ended in a relaxed atmosphere.

Khrushchev's visit to the Siberian science center at Akademgorodok went off well. All our scientific programs won approval, and the Institute of Cytology and Genetics was saved, together with its personnel and themes of research. But we were advised to change the director. After consultation with a small group of people, including Dubinin, Dmitry K. Belyayev, who held then the degree of candidate of biology, was chosen director.

Two years later, when Khrushchev visited Akademgorodok again, the question of the genetics institute ended with a jest. Entering the exhibit room, accompanied by the local officialdom, he turned to me with the question, "Where are your Weismannist-Morganists?" "I'm a mathematician," I replied, "and who can figure out which one is a Weismannist and which one a Morganist?" To which Khrushchev reacted with a joke. "It seems that a Ukrainian was walking along the Georgian Highway. He came upon a Georgian and an Ossetian in heated argument. They demanded that he resolve their dispute over whether the moon was a new moon or an old moon. The Ukrainian looked at the Georgian's dagger and then at the Ossetian, who also sported a dagger. The Ukrainian thought for a minute and finally said, 'I don't know, I'm a stranger here myself.'" There was general laughter, and they all proceeded to view the exhibits in a cheerful mood.[75]

As for Dubinin, he returned to Moscow, where he retained his position as director of the radiation and genetics laboratory and was even able to increase the size of his staff.

Andrei Sakharov Joins the Battle against Lysenkoism

Interest in genetic research on the part of nuclear physicists arose out of intensely personal experiences. Those who studied radioactive substances were often victims of radiation damage, and some of the trailblazers of nuclear physics paid the price of agonizing deaths for ignorance of the laws governing damage to hereditary structures by radiation.

But the geneticists began to understand the effects of irradiation on chromosomes, and, together with the physicists, they made intensive studies of those effects. The field of radiation genetics developed rapidly. Funds, laboratory equipment, and personnel were forthcoming, and the biologists' arsenal was enriched with methods previously used by the physicists. However, this work was going on abroad, outside the Soviet scientific establishment—in the United States, Britain, Japan, and West Germany—and much of it was classified as secret.

Soviet physicists were coming to realize what Lysenkoism and the rejection of genetics had cost them, and they became a force that helped revive genetic research in the Soviet Union. The establishment of a laboratory of radiation genetics has already been mentioned. In addition, a radiobiology section was organized at the Atomic Energy Institute in Moscow at Tamm's initiative, with the support of Kurchatov. Kurchatov's closest colleague, Stalin Prize winner Viktor Yu. Gavrilov, who participated in the Soviet atom bomb project, became head of this section. Experienced physicists such as Yury S. Lazurkin, Semyon Yu. Lukyanov, and Boris V. Rybakov transferred to the section. Leading theoretical physicists (notably D. A. Frank-Kamenetskii) consulted with biologists (Roman B. Khesin, Solomon M. Ardashnikov, Sos I. Alikhanyan, and others) at seminars, conducted at first by Kurchatov personally. Such geneticists as Boris L. Astaurov and Aleksandra A. Prokofyeva-Belgovskaya came to deliver lectures. A great many young scientists were hired as well, and soon a departmentwide seminar was meeting weekly under the leadership of Gavrilov, at which the biologists and the physicists learned more about each other's disciplines. Tamm's theoretical seminars on biology at the Lebedev Physics Institute of the AN SSSR were also of great importance.

At the same time, two higher educational institutions established special divisions within departments to train physicists to work on biological problems. With Tamm's help, Lev A. Blyumenfeld organized a division of biophysics in the physics department of Moscow State University in 1957, and in 1959 Lazurkin became head of a division of radiation effects, later renamed the division of molecular biophysics, at the Moscow Physicotechnical Institute.

At this stage, Andrei Sakharov became engaged in the physicists' work for a rebirth of radiation genetics research, and he plunged into the struggle against Lysenko with characteristic conviction and thoroughness. He carried tremendous weight among scientists and even more in the eyes of administrators. As a leading participant in the project to create the Soviet hydrogen bomb, he had received a second award of Hero of Socialist Labor in 1956 (and he had previously won Stalin and Lenin prizes). Now, while working on the problems of the effects of nuclear bomb tests on the genetic apparatus of living creatures, he set out to help break Lysenko's grip on Soviet biology.

Much of the history of that struggle has been lost. Many important speeches and other landmarks on the path to the rebirth of genetics in the USSR were not transcribed or recorded, and much has been done deliberately to suppress the traces. The number of surviving participants is of course steadily dwindling. Nevertheless, there is much that can be said.

In January 1958, Sakharov, using his position among the elite of Soviet science, obtained access to the Central Committee secretary and ideology chief Suslov, who was well known to be a patron of Lysenko. Sakharov bluntly described to him the sorry state of affairs in Soviet biology, the Lysenkoists' sway, and the urgent need to correct matters.[76] Although the conversation yielded no immediate change, it could not have failed to make an impact on Suslov.

It was in this period that Sakharov demonstrated that, contrary to the assertions of American experts, the testing of nuclear weapons in the atmosphere was far from harmless, that it had an effect upon the heredity of every living thing. Sakharov published these conclusions in October 1957. In 1959, he published another article on the same topic, the main article in a collection of several devoted to the same subject.[77]

The damage to genes from high levels of radiation was well established, but the effect of small amounts of radioactive substances that were carried through the earth's atmosphere and water and that only slightly increased background radiation was an open question. Many nuclear physicists denied that they had any harmful effects. For example, Edward Teller, the father of the American hydrogen bomb, declared that the damage from nuclear weapons testing was "the equivalent of smoking a cigarette twice a month."[78] Sakharov's research and mathematical calculations, however, showed convincingly the powerful damaging effect on hereditary structures of both the radiation at the moment of the explosion and the residual radiation, chiefly in the form of the long-lived radioactive carbon isotope, carbon-14; the role of mutations in the appearance of hereditary disease; and the possibilities of an increase in cancers, a decrease in the immunological response of organisms, an increase in the mutability of microbes and viruses, and periodic epidemics of new forms of pathogenic viruses and bacteria. It was the breadth of consideration of biological laws, combined with mathematical precision in calculating the doses, allowing even for the growth in world population, that made Sakharov's paper so important. At that time, scientists had not yet explored the capacity of living cells to "repair" themselves, and hence Sakharov could not take that consideration into account; but when allowance for that is made, his calculations remain valid to this day. Synthesizing the data of physics and biology, he demonstrated the damage caused by testing a type of weapon that was largely his own creation. It was an act of remarkable moral strength. While Teller was complacently saying that "mutations (hereditary diseases) should be welcomed as a necessary sacrifice to the biological progress of the human race,"[79] Sakharov declared: "I am inclined to regard uncontrollable mutations as an evil, as an additional cause of the death of tens and hundreds of thousands of people as a result of experiments with nuclear weapons." And he drew the precise, incontrovertible conclusion:

"Continued testing and any attempts to legitimize the nuclear weapon and its tests fly in the face of humanism and international law. The existence of radioactive danger from the so-called clean bomb bars any grounds for propaganda claiming that this kind of mass-destruction weapon is different in kind."[80]

By investigating the effect of radiation upon heredity, Sakharov was able to make clear the harm of Lysenkoism in obstructing the study of genetics, and he threw himself into the struggle along two lines: for banning nuclear testing and for eliminating the control of Lysenko and his followers over biology.

Both struggles bore fruit. After several unsuccessful appeals to Khrushchev,[81] Sakharov, taking advantage of the warming of relations between the Soviet Union and the United States, received the Party leader's approval to draft a treaty to forbid the testing of nuclear weapons in the atmosphere, under water, and in outer space (though not underground). The negotiations about the details of the treaty were completed in remarkably short time, and in 1963, Khrushchev and President John F. Kennedy signed the treaty. Most of the governments of the world joined it.[82]

On the other front, the Atomic Energy Committee of the USSR Council of Ministers and the Ministry of Foreign Affairs agreed that Soviet geneticists would participate in the work of the radiation committee of the United Nations, beginning in 1958,[83] and cytogeneticists Prokofyeva-Belgovskaya and Militsa A. Arsenyeva-Geptner went to Geneva to take part in the committee's work. Soviet geneticists participated in the Second International Conference on the Peaceful Use of Atomic Energy, also in Geneva, in September 1958.[84] Soviet data on the minimal radiation doses affecting human beings were made available to the world scientific community. In 1958, too, Astaurov was elected a corresponding member of the AN SSSR, which was the occasion for a celebration at the genetics section of the Moscow Naturalists Society.

Soviet Scientists Are Awarded the Leopoldina Gold Medals

In 1958 and 1959, preparations were going on throughout the world to celebrate the hundredth anniversary of the publication of Darwin's *Origin of Species*. In the USSR, the geneticists, evolutionists, and ecologists made such preparations, as did the Michurinists, who counted themselves as supporters of Darwinism—"creative" supporters, as they liked to say.

Soon after the end of World War II, Lysenko realized that the country's leaders were allocating substantial funds in support of the Soviet-led world "peace movement." He himself was not reluctant to talk about peace,[85] and he placed his people in the leadership of the movement. In 1950, Glushchenko became a member of the Soviet Peace Committee, then of its presidium, and finally of the World Peace Council. Lysenko himself almost never traveled abroad (perhaps the fact that his brother had fled to the West barred him from foreign travel), but Glushchenko did so frequently, with his wife, an interpreter, and ample funds.

Societies of "Amateur Michurinist Experimenters" and "Friends of Michurin" sprang up in the countries he visited. These societies published small bulletins and journals, mostly hectographed or mimeographed, using the same vocabulary, facts, and themes as the articles in the Lysenkoist journal *Agrobiology*. Glushchenko also cultivated foreign biologists and geneticists, many of whom received invitations from the Genetics Institute to visit the Soviet Union at the institute's expense, although the lack of a common language prevented serious professional discussion.

As the time approached for the hundredth anniversary of the *Origin of Species*, Lysenko and Varuntsyan, his assistant editor at *Agrobiology*, decided to dedicate a special issue of this magazine to articles by foreign authors. Because of his foreign contacts, Glushchenko was given the assignment of soliciting articles from these authors,[86] and he was able to obtain eighteen contributors, among them such well-known scientists as C. H. Waddington, Arne Müntsing, and K. Lindegren. Indeed, the journal filled not one but two issues (1959, nos. 5 and 6) with articles by foreigners—proof, to the Lysenkoists, of the international recognition of the "Michurinist doctrine."[87]

The satisfaction of the Lysenkoists, however, was dampened by another event. As part of its celebration, the German Leopoldina Academy of Sciences, one of the oldest academies in the world, which brought together scientists of both East Germany and West Germany, presented gold medals to a group of living scientists deemed to have made the greatest contribution to Darwinism. The Soviet recipients were Chetverikov, Timofeyev-Ressovsky, Dubinin, Shmalgauzen, and Sukachev—none of them Lysenkoists, and indeed opponents of Lysenko.

The award to Chetverikov was particularly significant, for he was entirely excluded from scientific life at the time. He had been exiled to the Urals for five years in 1929 without trial or investigation, then forbidden to return to Moscow and obliged to work instead as a mathematics teacher in a technical school in Vladimir. Later (again barred from Moscow), he had to settle in Gorky, where he became dean of the biology department and organized a department of genetics at the Gorky State University and a silkworm selection laboratory—only to be dismissed from this post in 1948 and to have his laboratory shut down.

Lysenko Again Becomes President of VASKhNIL

That Lysenko had not completely lost influence at home was shown at the Twenty-first Party Congress, held early in 1959. Though still not a Party member, he was given the floor at the congress and delivered an impassioned speech about the beneficial work of the Michurinists and their contribution to the accomplishment of the task of overtaking the United States in the production of meat, milk, and butter. At the same time, however, Nesmeyanov and Semyonov were able to call for developing research in biophysics and biochemistry. The congress resolutions were as contradictory as the speeches. On the one hand, they contained phrases about the advantages of "Michurinist biology"; on the other, they said that further development of the biological sciences was impossible without deeper study of the physical and chemical laws of living matter.

Lysenko persisted in seeking Khrushchev's favor. Khrushchev began taking Lysenko with him more and more often as he traveled about the country, and he displayed increasing irritation with the scientists who, he thought, failed to comprehend the value of Lysenko's proposals. Little by little, the ambivalence turned to clear support.

Lysenko pursued his advantage. As he had done with Stalin, he did not spare expressions of his love for the leader of all the peoples. Speaking in Khrushchev's presence at the Moscow Conference of Pace-Setters of Socialist Agriculture of the Non-Black Earth Zone on February 22, 1961, Lysenko, besides declaring that "Michurinist biology is creative Darwinism, the offspring of socialist agriculture," emphasized the continuity between Lenin and the current head of the Party and insisted that Khrushchev supported Lysenko's theories:

> Vladimir Ilyich Lenin, the Party Central Committee, and Nikita Sergeyevich Khrushchev have emphasized over and over that practice is the chief, the leading element in the unity of theory and practice. . . . Let me remind you of Nikita Sergeyevich Khrushchev's observation on this score at the January plenum. He said that one cannot conduct socialist agriculture without science. Those words expressed the concern of the Party and government for science, they defined the obligations of scientists to help the kolkhozes and sovkhozes directly or indirectly in all their scientific work.[88]

After speaking once again of microbes feeding plants and "manure-soil compost on the fields," he returned to the subject of Khrushchev and ascribed to him the idea that one can do with less fertilizer by resorting to triplex and composts. He wound up with a loyal subject's toast to Nikita Sergeyevich.[89]

The strategy worked. In August 1961, Lysenko was appointed (without election procedure) again president of VASKhNIL.

15

The Second Downfall

> Riffraff of every kind invariably emerges in troubled times of
> wavering or transition everywhere. . . . I am speaking just of scoun-
> drels. This scum that exists in every society rises to the surface in any
> period of change. . . . Without realizing it, this riffraff succumbs to
> the command of a small handful of "leaders" who pursue a definite
> aim and direct the riffraff in any direction they choose—unless they
> themselves are utter idiots (which, incidentally, also happens).
> —F. M. Dostoyevsky, *Devils*

> Not without reason is world history strewn with the names of rulers,
> leaders, commanders, and adventurers who all, with the rarest
> exceptions, began splendidly but ended very badly; who all, at least
> in words, sought power for the sake of good but then, obsessed with
> power and intoxicated by it, came to love it for its own sake.
> —Hermann Hesse, *The Bead Game*

A Struggle for Supremacy

In September 1961, the Committee on Inventions and Discoveries granted
a USSR state patent to Astaurov, a student of Chetverikov's, for a discovery. This was the first biological discovery ever registered for a patent.
Astaurov was awarded it for his discovery of a process for regulating the
sex of silkworms by irradiation and otherwise influencing their cell nuclei,
chromosomes, and genes. Of course, "patent" as understood in the West is
an exclusive grant of rights to *a person* to use an invention for private profit.
In the Soviet Union, *the state* retained all rights for use of the invention
without asking the permission of the author. But the honor of a patent, as
recognition of the importance of a discovery, was substantial.

How did Astaurov come to this outstanding result? Astaurov's silkworm
laboratory had been shut down after the August 1948 session of VASKhNIL.
But working at the Institute of Animal Histology, Embryology, and Morphology, he was able to restore to 1955–1956 his pure genetic lines of
silkworms and returned to the actual genetic investigations but used for
their description, the term "biology of development." He developed the
methods of killing nuclei of egg cells with irradiation figured out how to
replace the killed nucleus of the female cell with the nucleus of the male
generative cell (spermatozoid) and how to induce the female cells to
divide and form the adult organism without fertilization by male cell.
Using these techniques, he developed the method of obtaining silkworms

of either sex, male or female, at will. Moreover, Astaurov now was able to obtain male silkworms exclusively, and these inherited "all the characteristics of the male parent." In those days, such a patent for any scientific discovery was an extraordinary event. But after all, no one in the world had ever achieved such a thing. The process made it possible to increase silk output by almost one fourth, since "cocoons of males yield 25–30 percent more silk than those of female silkworms." Astaurov's discovery held forth the hope of further miracles when similar kinds of manipulations might be made on other animals.

Early in September, *Pravda* printed a long article by Astaurov; it stretched across two pages of the newspaper, with his photo.[1] In an editorial, the newspaper called for Astaurov's work "outstanding" and asserted that it "opens up tremendous prospects for raising the productivity of agricultural production and increases human mastery over the forces of nature."[2]

Lysenko was no doubt disturbed by this achievement of genetic science, but he could draw comfort from the fact that Khrushchev continued to hold him in high regard. Khrushchev was prepared to shield his favorite even in a matter such as the grass-field crop rotation system. In 1954, when he had just launched upon his career as Party boss, he put the blame for failures in agriculture on Williams's scheme for rotating field crops with grasses, and deep tillage. It was generally assumed that he considered Lysenko the ringleader in establishing this system. In 1961, however, although Khrushchev condemned the Williams system and called for "the swiftest liquidation of the effects of its use," he excluded Lysenko from the ranks of its advocates. Rather, he contrasted Lysenko with those who "dishonored" science—those who "ought to be dragged out of the swamp by their ears, hauled off to the bathhouse, and given a scrubbing"—and listed him first among "genuine" scientists who could be heeded with benefit to the cause.[3] Khrushchev blamed other scientists, and turned to the subject of those whom it was harmful to heed and to whom, in his words,

one wants to say: Don't disgrace your learned title, don't dishonor science! (Applause.) ... Excuse my language, but how can I not say: What the hell do the people need such "science" for? (Stir in the hall. Applause.)

For Khrushchev, to be useful, science had first to accord with "the outlook of our party" (Marxism-Leninism) and, second, to be practical:

Many scientific research establishments ... do not light the way for practice, they have lagged behind life, and some scientists ought to be dragged out of the swamp by their ears, hauled off to the bathhouse, and given a scrubbing. (Stir in the hall. Applause.) We'll help drag you out, comrade scientists (stir in the hall), but get out of the grass-fields swamp yourselves. (Stir in the hall.)[4]

But Khrushchev's support was by then a shaky reed. By exposing the

Stalinist "cult of personality," Khrushchev had made possible open discussion of the consequences of the cult; indeed, he himself called for their eradication. Yet Lysenko was one of the most conspicuous followers of Stalinism. By opening the gates to criticism, Khrushchev placed his favorite under the hammer in spite of himself.

The chorus of voices condemning this "little Stalin in biology" grew in volume, and in April 1962, Khrushchev had to consent to Lysenko's dismissal, once again, from the post of president of VASKhNIL. Now we know that many outstanding scientists, including physicists A. Sakharov and I. Kurchatov, chemists A. Nesmeyanov and N. Semyonov, and others, used every appropriate occasion to try to explain to the country's boss how dangerous it was to keep Lysenko as VASKhNIL's president. Khrushchev's action was tempered, however, by his offer to let Lysenko choose his own successor. Olshansky, Lysenko's deputy for many years at the Odessa institute and a man of unquestioning loyalty, became the new president.

Celebrations and Everyday Reality

In the summer of 1962, the Lysenkoists found an occasion to demonstrate to the whole country that, Lysenko's dismissal notwithstanding, they were monolithic, successful, and optimistic. In other words, they decided to congratulate themselves on the fiftieth anniversary of the Institute of Genetics and Plant Breeding. (They were reckoning from the first experimental field at Odessa, and they ignored the fact that Lysenkoists had run the institute for only about thirty of the fifty years.) The figure "50," framed in a laurel wreath, adorned the facade of the main building of what was now the T. D. Lysenko Institute. Numerous interviews were given to the newspapers, and the parquet floor of the conference hall was polished in anticipation of the arrival of foreign guests. Glushchenko sent notice of the anniversary to the many foreign "Friends of Michurin" societies, with accounts of the institute's chief accomplishments, so that greetings began to arrive from abroad, echoing these accounts. From the French society, for example:

> Here in the capitalist world, plant breeding is falling more and more into the hands of cosmopolitan monopolists who subordinate the work to their self-serving purposes. The monopolies have made it their rule to distribute only hybrid seed and hybrid animals, the quality of which is shamelessly limited to the first generation.
>
> ...The Morganists' reactionary ideology is not merely an ideological argument for them, a means of justifying the policy of the imperialists even in their most frightful racist crimes. This theory has become... the basic means of defending profits.[5]

Many foreign scientists were sent invitations, with their travel, their stay in Odessa, and excursions around the country paid for; not a few accepted.

The celebration itself was boring. Lysenko himself, his students and followers had no new data or anything that could engage the enthusiasm of the listeners: the lectures to conference participants repeated the same phrases that everybody heard already many times.

But when the celebrations were over, unpleasantness awaited the Lysenkoists back in Moscow. In 1961, Nesmeyanov had been replaced as president of the AN SSSR by Mstislav V. Keldysh, a well-known researcher in aerodynamics and outer space.[6] Keldysh decided to investigate personally, without the help of "officially recognized" advisors, what the geneticists and the Lysenkoists had actually accomplished. He read intensively, spoke with dozens of leading scientists, and visited a number of institutes.[7] In October 1962, he went to Lysenko's institute and to Lenin Hills. Lysenko showed Keldysh the fields and the cows, but Keldysh was not impressed, and an altercation between Lysenko and his colleagues further spoiled the visit. Lysenko called his assistant Kushner an "ignoramus" and went on to insult Sisakyan and Glushchenko as well. Kushner and Sisakyan swallowed the insults, but Glushchenko exploded and began to justify himself to Keldysh. It was a distasteful scene.[8]

But the worst blow against Lysenko was inflicted by Zhores A. Medvedev's book, copies of the manuscript of which began to circulate early in 1962. Its calm, detailed recital of the facts about Lysenko's rise and fall was enormously convincing and compelling. A commission of the AN SSSR, which included Engelgardt, Astaurov, and Khadzhinov, among others, recommended that it be published, and a copy of the manuscript was sent to the publishing house of the AN SSSR called "Nauka" (Science), but the authorities could not bring themselves to issue it. Nevertheless, it became widely known among scientists. Medvedev himself was subsequently expelled from the USSR and deprived of his Soviet citizenship.

Defense on Two Fronts

Toward the end of 1962, Lysenko was confronted with attack from both the biologists and the representatives of other basic sciences. In an effort to protect himself, he sought support among Party apparatchiks. The resolutions adopted by the Party Central Committee and the government during this period were marked by ambivalence. Typically, they contained two paired sections on the same subject. First came mention of the achievements of Michurinist biology and the need to proceed further along this path; then, after a paragraph or two referring to physics, chemistry, or mathematics, came a section about the value of employing the methods of those sciences to develop the new biology. Thus, for example, a decree adopted in January 1963 said:

Soviet biologists of the Michurin school have achieved great successes and hold a leading position in genetics, selection, and seed-growing, particularly in questions of controlling heredity and its variability; they have made a substantial contribution to the theory and practice of agricultural production.

The decree went on to stress the necessity of "even more widely and deeply developing the Michurinist direction in biology, which proceeds from the fact that life conditions are the leading factor in the development of the organic world." But then, returning to a discussion of the biological sciences, it proclaimed that "elucidation of the essence of life phenomena, discovery of the laws of development of the organic world, and study of the physics and chemistry of living matter are to be regarded as the chief tasks of these sciences."[9]

In an effort to bolster his position, Lysenko assembled a great conference at VASKhNIL in December 1962. It heard more than seventy reports on "methods" of directing heredity. ("Methods" was always used in the plural, but actually only one method was discussed: transfer of the plant into alien environmental conditions.) The emphasis at the conference was on changing spring varieties into winter crops by sowing them for two or three years in the fall. Some of the conferees discussed the reverse, the transformation of winter into spring varieties, but in each case, they reported, it was the external environment that created the desired qualities.[10]

At the close of the conference on December 3, 1962, and in a *Pravda* piece two months later, Lysenko asked rhetorically: "Who now ... seriously doubts the possibility of literally molding, literally creating, winter-hardy winter plants out of entirely non-winter-hardy plants, such as spring wheat or barley, by utilizing the conditions of the nonliving external environment?" He listed this discovery among the outstanding achievements of Soviet science and rejoiced that "*priority in this important theoretical discovery in biology belongs to the Soviet Union and to Michurinist biology.*" He also sought to belittle the significance of the work of Watson and Crick on the structure of DNA. These molecules, he said, could in no way be considered the bearers of heredity. He was even willing to accept some elements of Weismann's ideas, as long as the principle that the DNA molecules could be the home of the genes was rejected:

> Weismann and his followers are right in saying that the embryos of new generations do not arise, do not take their beginning, from the soma of the parents. . . . But it is wrong to assert that a special, mythical substance of heredity exists apart from the living body (the soma). . . . It is likewise impossible to ascribe an attribute of life, i.e., heredity, to a nonviable substance, deoxyribonucleic acid, for example.

He touched on another sore subject, the role of chemistry and physics in biological research, and again beat a small retreat in one direction while attacking in another. "It is very important to study the physics and chemistry of living matter, not only for purposes of medical and agricultural practice, but also for theoretical biology," he said. But the offensive followed immediately: "This is particularly important for learning the law of the transformation of inorganic into living matter through the medium of living matter. . . . No chemical or physical cognizance of living matter gives a conception of the biological laws by which the organic world lives and develops."[11] Lysenko's repeated claim to be a staunch materialist was belied by this quasi-mystical view of living matter.

The Party Again Assails Lysenko's Critics

When Medvedev's samizdat manuscript began to circulate and prominent scientists in various disciplines joined Lysenkoism's critics, the scientific and moral failures of Lysenko became plainly visible to many of the country's intelligentsia. Although a "new type" of intelligentsia had arisen from the efforts of the Communist Party, although the overwhelming majority of the graduates of Soviet higher educational institutions came from worker and peasant backgrounds, their introduction to culture, art, and science prevented them from obediently responding to manipulation by the machinery of the state.

It was against this background that Lysenko was caught in the public spotlight now, and a great many people disliked what they saw. Such characteristics as his peculiarities of speech and his down-to-earth slogans that had engendered general liking for him in the 1930s and 1940s, when he could be seen as a simple peasant lad who had risen to the crest of the wave, now aroused antipathy. The fact that he had only a smattering of education no longer attracted sympathy; the crudeness of his ideas began to grate. His desire for power was seen as criminal, for it had brought gifted scientists to their deaths in the camps and prisons. The harm he had done was indisputable, and his promises had lost their allure.

But the Kremlin leader still regarded Lysenko, with all his mistakes and crimes, as a correct and consistent fighter for the approved ideals; his critics were held guilty of bourgeois distortions and departures from Leninism.

Although early in the 1960s, Medvedev had moved from the Timiryazev Agricultural Academy to the Institute of Medical Radiology in Obninsk, far from Moscow, he was the target of criticism from Nikolai G. Yegorychev, first secretary of the Moscow city Party and a member of the Central Committee. He accused Medvedev of "deviation from Lenin's instructions" and said he "incorrectly treats fundamental questions of the development of Soviet biology, besmirches Michurinist science, and heaps praise on bourgeois research." Yegorychev mentioned that Medvedev "wrote a monograph entitled 'Biology and the Personality Cult.' This work incorrectly treats fundamental questions of the development of Soviet biology, besmirches Michurinist science, and heaps praise on bourgeois research that is not consistently materialist."[12]

Yegorychev also criticized another book, *The Biosynthesis of Proteins and Problems of Ontogenesis*, which Medvedev had written while at Obninsk.[13] In an introductory chapter of this book, Medvedev had briefly recounted the difficulties in developing genetic research in the USSR as a result of Lysenko's activities. As required by Soviet authorities, the first ten copies of the book printed were sent to the Party Central Committee, the Central Book Repository, and the Lenin Library to obtain formal permission for printing the rest of the run. Suddenly orders came from the Central Committee, from the very top, to hold up the entire edition. One of Suslov's aides had brought him a copy with the several dozen sentences about Lysenko and genetics underlined in red pencil. Orders followed to change them. The offending pages were removed and were replaced by a "neutral" section. Even with this revision, Medvedev's book did not satisfy Yegorychev, who continued his denunciation to Suslov (and Khrushchev):

> Medvedev did not lay down his arms. He found a new base in the Kaluga region and wrote (and the State Medical Publishing House issued) the book *Biosynthesis of Proteins and Problems of Ontogenesis*, containing the same mistakes. A scientific guise sometimes serves as a cover to hide ideological contortions! . . . In the battle with bourgeois ideology we must attack, always attack—this is what the Party teaches us![14]

Nevertheless, early in 1963 an article co-authored by Medvedev and Kirpichnikov appeared in the general-interest magazine *Neva*. The article declared openly for the first time that the August 1948 session of VASKhNIL was the consequence of Stalin's authoritarian rule and that any reference to it as an infallible event in the history of Soviet science benefited only Lysenkoist enemies of Soviet science.[15] This brought an outburst of indignation from Olshansky, who in the Party Central Committee's newspaper, *Rural Life* (Selskaya zhizn), on August 18, 1963, denounced both the two authors and the magazine for "slander of Michurinist science" and "kowtowing to foreign science based on Weismannist-Morganist teachings." He declared that hybrid corn had come about by accident, not through genetic research, and that those who discovered it (among whom he named only G. H. Shull) had given a "non-Mendelian" explanation.[16]

This condemnation of genetics was supported by a *Pravda* editorial, which recapitulated what Olshansky had said and went beyond it, denouncing not only the views expressed in Medvedev's and Kirpichnikov's article but their entire scientific activity and labeling them "misanthropes," "idealists," "mechanists," and "slanderers."

> It seems that the authors . . . of the *Neva* article see the future of Michurinist materialist genetics to lie in a merger with the idealistic conception of "classical genetics." Such compromise in biology is impermissible. . . .

The *Pravda* editors reaffirmed that the Party considered the Lysenkoist concepts an inseparable part of the ideological doctrine that was unraveling in the USSR.

Michurinist biology stands in the front lines of the struggle for communism. Based firmly on the granite foundations of Marxism-Leninism and on dialectical materialism, Michurinist biology is boldly penetrating life and delving deeper and deeper into the mysteries of nature.

In sum, the article was considered as "incorrect and harmful to our science."[17]

The editors of *Neva* printed an admission that they had made a "gross error" by publishing Medvedev's and Kirpichnikov's article,[18] but—unlike what would have happened only a few years before—neither author was arrested or tried. They were not even dismissed from their jobs. Lysenko did not succeed in strengthening his position in the AN SSSR. Its president, Keldysh, did not change the direction of research in the AN SSSR. In short, Lysenko's pressure on Khrushchev had little effect.

Another struggle took place soon afterward over the nomination of Nuzhdin to be a full member (academician) of the AN SSSR. In 1963 the Central Committee had given its consent to a reorganization of the academy's structure.[19] It was to be divided into three sections: physico-technical sciences and mathematics, chemico-technical sciences and biology, and social sciences.[20] Academician Nikolai S. Semyonov, a Nobel Prize winner who was openly favorable to the geneticists, became head of the chemico-technical and biology section. Lysenko resolved to enhance the position of biology in the section by packing the academy with his supporters.

Elections to fill seats left vacant by the deaths of academicians were scheduled for June 1964. But in addition, the Central Committee ordered that funds be allocated for three additional seats, to be assigned to the general biology division and occupied by specialists in genetics. Although the word "Michurinist" was not used, it was taken for granted that only "Michurinist geneticists" could be elected. Khrushchev personally took part in the discussion of nominees, and the Party Central Committee decided that the new seats were to be filled by specialists in plant breeding who adhered to Lysenkoist views, such as Lukyanenko or Remeslo but above all Nuzhdin, who had become Lysenko's closest colleague. Khrushchev gave Nuzhdin a strong endorsement, and the Central Committee adopted a resolution supporting his candidacy. Moreover, Nuzhdin's candidacy was taken up at a meeting of the secretariat of the Party Central Committee. After Khrushchev gave him the highest endorsement, a special resolution supporting his candidacy was adopted and a representative of the Party in the academy delivered this decision to the presidium of the academy. Khrushchev summoned Keldysh and in the strongest terms (evidently knowing the president's dislike of Lysenko) demanded assurance of the election of Lysenko's protégés and of Nuzhdin above all. He threatened to take administrative measures against the academy, even to disband it and transfer its institutes, laboratories, and other organizations to the State Committee on Science and Technology, if his wishes were not carried out.

The elections were held in two stages, with secret balloting in both. First, the candidates were put up for election in the respective divisions of the academy. Thanks to the docile majority Lysenko had assembled in biology over the course of a decade and a half, two of his candidates, Lukyanenko and Nuzhdin, won recommendation. Normally, confirmation at the second stage, a general meeting of the academy, was automatic for candidates recommended by their division. But in this case things turned out differently.

In the debate at the general session, Engelgardt gave a detailed account of Nuzhdin's pseudoscientific activity. Tamm passionately condemned the efforts of Nuzhdin and other Lysenkoists to brand genetics a false science and described the tremendous harm they had done to Soviet science. Andrei Sakharov spoke coolly and therefore especially convincingly about the repressions suffered by outstanding scientists, in particular charging that Lysenko and his supporters were responsible for the imprisonment and death of Vavilov.[21] For Nuzhdin, who begun his career as a student of Vavilov and who had later betrayed his teacher, Sakharov's speech was especially influential: 23 for Nuzhdin, 120 against. Lukyanenko was elected.

By this time, Tamm and Sakharov had become legendary figures not only among physicists but in biological circles, too. They knew about Khrushchev's warnings to Keldysh, and it took a good deal of courage in their part to speak out against the personal protégé of the Party boss. For Sakharov, the struggle turned out to be personally important. It brought forth his unique courage and moral strength. This was perhaps the first time that Sakharov showed his capacity for public action and his fearlessness on behalf of humanistic ideals—the trait that later brought him worldwide recognition.[22]

The Kremlin's wrath was aroused. Khrushchev seriously turned to the plan to disband the AN SSSR. A commission was formed to look into various aspects of the academy's work, and there were discussions of the plan to merge the academy with the State Committee on Science and Technology.

The Lysenkoists also went into battle. Olshansky wrote that the supposed successes of genetics were "harebrained schemes, cheap sensations devoid of proof"; that the *Neva* article by Medvedev and Kirpichnikov was slanderous; and that Medvedev's book *Biology and the Personality Cult* contained nothing but fabrications, including the "monstrous assertions that scientists of the Michurin school are guilty of the repressions that some workers of science have experienced." "It is clear to all that this is no longer just a farce but a dirty political game."

His main target, however, was Sakharov. (Because Tamm had won the Nobel Prize in physics, the Lysenkoists preferred not to mention him.)

Zh. Medvedev's political game apparently made an impression on some ill-informed and extremely naive persons. How else can one explain the fact that Academician A. D. Sakharov, an engineer by specialty, delivered a public speech at a meeting of the AN SSSR in which he indulged in an insulting attack against the Michurinists, in the style of the throwaway leaflet circulated by Zh. Medvedev and quite far removed from science?

And he made a clear threat:

Isn't it time to tell Zh. Medvedev and other slanderers of his ilk that they must either back up their perfidious accusations with facts or answer for their slanders before the courts? . . . Obviously they cannot back up their accusations with facts because *there are no such facts.*[23]

On October 2, the Leningrad journalist P. Shelest made similar accusations in the same newspaper.[24] Ominous clouds were gathering in the skies over genetics, even over all science.

The "Little October Revolution"

On September 30, after setting in motion the machinery for breaking up the AN SSSR, Khrushchev left for a vacation in the south, intending to finish the job upon his return. But on October 14, 1964, the Party leaders assembled the Central Committee, expelled Khrushchev, and retired him on pension. Leonid Brezhnev took power. The public called this bloodless coup "the Little October Revolution."

The news spread that Khrushchev's support of Lysenko was among the chief reasons for his ouster. On October 15, the day before the decision of the Party Central Committee on Khrushchev's dismissal was made public, Moscow newspaper editors called in leading geneticists Efroimson and Rapoport and writers known for their critical attitude toward Lysenko, notably Oleg Pisarzhevsky, asking them to write articles about Lysenko's mistakes. A spate of such articles soon appeared.[25] Perhaps the broadest and most vivid of these was one by Pisarzhevsky, who had written about the Lysenkoist frauds before (see chapter 13). Now he told of the genuine achievements of the geneticists and contrasted them with the insignificance of the Lysenkoists' "theories," the baseness of their deeds, the unattractiveness of their comrades-in-arms, such as Lepeshinskaya and Boshyan, and the unprincipled behavior of their cheerleaders, such as the playwrights Pogodin and the Tur brothers. His article was published in the *Literary Gazette.*[26]

Pisarzhevsky was determined to complete Lysenko's downfall. He attended an intensive series of meetings in one editorial office after another. But two days after his article had appeared, he suffered a heart attack on his way to one of these meetings, and he died before help could reach him.

Shortly after Pisarzhevsky's death, the editors of the *Literary Gazette* received a letter from the chief zootechnician at Lenin Hills, Dmitry M. Moskalenko, defending Lysenko and his followers. The editors turned it over to another journalist who was a friend and neighbor of Pisarzhevsky's, Anatoly A. Agranovsky. He decided to take Pisarzhevsky's place in answering Moskalenko. He visited Lenin Hills twice, spoke with Moskalenko at length, and produced a revealing essay.[27] In it, for example, he described a visit to the cow barn:

> I saw a barn that was a model in every respect. It was roomy, very clean, with plenty of light and air. The cows were well fed, beautiful, almost haughty. Dmitry Mikhailovich Moskalenko conducted me along white-tiled walls, reading from the milking records hanging at each stall. His talk was strewn with figures of fat content of the milk. Everything bespoke his pride in the farm and his confidence that the evidence was incontrovertible.
>
> "Facts are stubborn things," Moskalenko said. "These are cows, not some kind of chromosomes!"
>
> "What do you know about chromosomes?" I asked.
>
> "We don't need to know."
>
> "Have you even read about them?"
>
> "What for?" he said. "It's a dead issue. Those chromosomes don't do anything for livestock."
>
> "Well, all right," I said, "but tell me, do they exist in nature or not?"
>
> The chief zootechnician didn't answer.

He also wrote that the people at the farm

> tried to fatten the cows by feeding them sour cream. . . . The cows grew fat but produced watery milk. . . . They tried yeast. . . . It had no effect. They got 400 kilograms of cocoa husks, the waste of cocoa-bean processing, from a confectionery factory, and fed it to the cows; the milk yield declined, and the fat content still did not increase.

Nor did the quality of the breed improve, in spite of the claims that the environment shapes heredity.

Huge expenditures for supplies had been made. For example, the chickens had been fed so much, in the hope of increasing egg production, that it was calculated that they had been consuming an average of two kilograms of grain per egg—and they still were laying only seventy eggs a year. Financial records were in disarray; a given purchase could be entered at different prices in different places. "Once they wrote off 1,170 kilograms of fish meal, costing 772 rubles, as feed for the calves," but it turned out that the records were falsified, no fish meal reached the calves, and "they never did explain where the fish meal went." "If fish are silent, you can imagine how silent fish meal is," the journalist wrote. Yet the people at Lenin Hills were surprised at the criticism that was being directed at them and they remained confident that they would be protected from it. As Moskalenko said to Agranovsky:

Where did this epidemic of criticism come from? Everything was going fine, everybody praised us, and suddenly, out of a blue sky: "Hide, Vanka, there is no god!" Never mind. They'll teach those scribblers a lesson. They'll call them in and warn them. And that will be the end of it. They write such prejudiced stuff!

In some ways, he proved to be right. Although criticisms of Lysenko from both scientists and journalists continued to appear for a while,[28] they died down around the beginning of 1965, and Moskalenko and most of the other Lysenkoists retained their positions.

An article by Andrei L. Kursanov is a good illustration of the maneuvering that was going on as the ideological winds shifted. Together with A. A. Imshenetsky, A. I. Oparin, and N. M. Sisakyan, he had regarded Lysenko favorably for many years, voted for his candidacy, and came forward with "proofs" of Lepeshinskaya's theories as well. In this article, which appeared at the end of 1964, he praised the geneticists' successes and expressed admiration for Rapoport and Nadson, but he also spoke about the achievements of the Michurinists. He made no condemnation of Lysenkoism, but merely said:

Against the background of the general progress of biology that now gives rise to an atmosphere of optimism and confidence in further great successes, it seems inexplicable that some researchers strive persistently to ignore the progress in biology and artificially to confine the scope of the permissible approach within the bounds of primitive experiments and arguments lacking proof.[29]

It was an artful straddling of the fence.

I myself was a victim of the silence that came to be enforced at about this time. I was invited to contribute to a book, *The Microworld of Life*, which was to appear at the end of 1965. In response to this invitation, I wrote an essay about the discoveries of genetics, containing a section about Lysenko and his errors. Despite arguments from me and the book's editor, David M. Goldfarb, the publishing house refused to include that section. When the book appeared, the section had been deleted.[30]

Meanwhile, Lysenko received a curious and ambiguous kind of support from abroad. John Haldane, the well-known British biologist, died on December 1, 1964. Haldane had been a member of the British Communist Party and of its Central Committee, and he had retained his faith in Marxism even after leaving the party. Knowing that he was suffering from an incurable illness, Haldane had written his own obituary, in which he devoted considerable space to Lysenko, describing him as a self-made scientist who had been given too much power. Haldane wrote:

I consider Lysenko a very good biologist, and some of his ideas were right. . . . And I believe Soviet agriculture and Soviet biology were very unfortunate in that he was given so much power under Stalin. . . . I . . . am deeply convinced that if I had been made dictator over British genetics or English philosophy I would have played just as catastrophic a role.

The entire obituary was published in a Soviet weekly that specialized in news about foreign countries.[31]

Nevertheless, Lysenko suffered a significant organizational blow in February 1965. At a meeting of the members of VASKhNIL, neither he nor Olshansky was reelected to the academy's presidium. He may well have had reason to fear the loss of his other positions as well, such as his leadership of the Lenin Hills farm.

The Commission to Investigate Lenin Hills

Soon after Agranovsky's article appeared, the AN SSSR formed a commission to investigate affairs at the Lenin Hills farm.[32] The members of the commission had no history of unpleasant relations with Lysenko, and had never spoken out against him. Among them were A. I. Tulupnikov, a corresponding member of VASKhNIL, who served as chairman; E. K. Guneyeva and Yu. M. Krinkin, senior zootechnicians at the Main Breeding Administration of the USSR Ministry of Agriculture; N. A. Kravchenko, a professor at the Ukrainian Academy of Agricultural Sciences; D. S. Lesik, deputy chief of the Main Seed-Growing Administration of the USSR Ministry of Agriculture; and I. L. Popok, deputy head accountant of the Central Accounting Office of the presidium of the AN SSSR.[33] The commission did not include any members of the AN SSSR itself, or any other prominent scientists, because its focus was on the management of the farm rather than on the validity of Lysenko's theories.

Even within this narrow scope, the commission's findings were astonishing.[34] Pisarzhevsky's and Agranovsky's articles paled by comparison. The laboratories of the experiment station alone employed 98 staff members, as well as many more field workers, in 1964. Expenditures on research between 1954 and 1964 amounted to the equivalent of 2.4 million new rubles (the ruble had recently been revalued, and the new ruble represented ten old rubles), of which salaries accounted for 1.3 million rubles, and yet, the commission said, "The laboratories are presently outfitted with primitive scientific equipment (optical microscopes, scales, thermostats, etc.)." It was interesting that the main propagandist of socialistic agriculture did not manage his own enterprise on socialist principles: Lenin Hills—unlike other kolkhozes and sovkhozes—did not send all its grain yield to the government agencies. "During the 1960–1964 five-year period, they obtained 11,400 centners of wheat, of which they turned over only about 700 (6.1%) to the state." Experiments were being conducted on warm-climate crops like tea, grapes, and walnuts, even though winter temperatures in the latitude of Moscow stay below –20 degrees Celsius (or -4 degrees Fahrenheit) for at least two months.

The commission also found that far larger doses of fertilizers had been used than had been reported, and that fertilizers other than Lysenko's organo-mineral mixtures had been added to the soil. No comprehensive studies of the farm's soils had been made; even the simplest analysis, that for soil acidity, had been made only twice, in 1948 and 1955. (It will be recalled that soil maps had been proclaimed "antiscientific" in the 1930s, and so none had been prepared since the experiment station was founded.) And contrary to the Lysenkoists' claims, the farm had not done well at all with its field crops. "The yield of winter wheat has remained practically unchanged, while the yield of vegetables, potatoes, root fodder, and sugar beets has substantially declined," said the commission. These failures had been concealed by reporting only selective data, comparing the highest yields from the experimental plots with the lowest yields from the control plots.

Conditions with respect to the farm's livestock were no better. There was "no plan of thoroughbred breeding or methodology for conducting experiments. Scientific information on the results of breeding have not been published." The commission did not find any scientific results which could confirm Lysenko's theories:

> According to his [Lysenko's] "law of the life of biological species" the offspring should have developed along the lines of the small Jersey breed. . . . Study of the dairy farm records . . . did not confirm these propositions. A direct relationship was not found between the fat content of the milk of mixed breeds and their live weight at birth. . . .
> There was also no confirmation . . . of the hypothesis that the fat content of milk from the offspring is unrelated to the fat content of milk from the maternal parent.
> Thus, contrary to Academician T. D. Lysenko's assertions, analysis of the data . . . does not refute, but confirms the well-known scientific fact that the fat content of milk from mixed breeds reveals intermediate inheritance.[35]

All of this was systematically concealed by slaughtering the animals that did not fit Lysenko's theories; the commission learned about it by studying the farm's financial records, in which the slaughter of "below-standard animals" was noted.[36] The commission requested a staff veterinarian to prepare a memorandum about the outcomes of matings and calvings and the procedures for determining the disposition of animals; the veterinarian "said he prepared the information for the commission and turned it over to the management," but "despite repeated requests," the commission never received it.

One of the most serious charges was that Lysenko had lied in a speech he had made at a plenary meeting of the Party Central Committee in February 1964, when he stated with conviction that all the calvings at the dairy farm invariably followed his protocols and that not a single cow born at the farm was ever slaughtered because it produced low-fat milk.[37] Because the farm was modifying embryos in a desired direction, he asserted, all the cows that grew from these embryos would have the desired attributes; consequently, cows yielding low-fat milk could not appear in the farm's herd and it was thus unnecessary to dispose of any animals. But it now appeared that the farm did dispose of animals, and did so quite often.

Lysenko Tries to Answer the Commission's Report

When the commission concluded its work, it sent a first draft of its report to Lysenko, who wrote a long reply, which was included in the final report. His response was a curious mixture of childish hurt feelings and fierce attacks. He accused the commission members of distorting the words and deeds of himself and his staff, and his answer bristled with such expressions as "malicious slander," "slanderous fabrications," "deliberate deception," "a crooked mirror." He flatly denied having lied to the Central Committee, insisting—without offering any proof—that there had not been a single instance when an animal had been slaughtered only because it yielded low-fat milk.

The commission, in turn, included in its final report a number of "clarifications" concerning Lysenko's comments, pointing out, for instance, that it and its subgroups had met "several times" with him. Its final meeting with him, after he had read the draft report, "lasted more than six hours."[38]

The accusation that Lysenko had deliberately misled the party leadership was especially dangerous. Therefore, at the very beginning of his comments on the commission report, he exclaimed: "So it would appear that I lied to the plenum of the Party Central Committee? Let the commission name at least one cow of the new mixed-breed, high-fat dairy herd that was disposed of at our farm specifically because it yielded low-fat milk.. There has been no such instance on our farm. Not one to this day."[39] He offered no proof; appendix tables in the commission report showed that mixed-breed calves were disposed of chiefly because of low-fat milk.[40] Over the course of ten years, 68 percent of the entire herd (54 cows or calves out of 79 mixed-breed), had been slaughtered or sold or died. But Lysenko asserted that "all these tables have nothing to do with the question under discussion."[41] The commission then had to supply a "Clarifications Concerning the Comments of Academician T. D. Lysenko," listing several of the more revealing instances of disposal of cattle.[42]

While all this was going on, a major shift in the organization of VASKhNIL was taking place. The February 10, 1965, general meeting of VASKhNIL had elected its new presidium—but neither Lysenko nor Olshansky had been reelected. Lysenko had good reason to fear the loss of his other positions, including his directorship of Lenin Hills.

The Public Discussion of the Commission's Report

Meantime, President Keldysh of the AN SSSR was trying to bring matters to a conclusion. The commission was given a deadline for reporting what it had done. On April 22, 1965, it discussed its report with Lysenko. He stood pat, denouncing the commission's work, but offered no concrete objections.

In the April issue of the popular, nationally circulated magazine *Science and Life*, N. N. Semyonov listed Lysenko's scientific mistakes and said plainly that he and his supporters had moved "scientific discussion onto the plane of demagogy and political indictments." Almost half of the April issue of the most import magazine for teachers, *Biology in the School*, also was devoted to criticism of Lysenkoism. But matters ground to a halt over the summer.

Finally, Keldysh got impatient with Lysenko's footdragging and set September 2, 1965, for a joint meeting of the presidium of the AN SSSR, the board of the Ministry of Agriculture, and the presidium of VASKhNIL to discuss the report that the commission had submitted. On the day preceding the meeting, Lysenko sent a letter to Keldysh saying he would not attend:

> I do not see the sense of a joint meeting to discuss all the . . . matters presented in the report of a commission that not only committed numerous distortions but also maliciously slandered me. And since, despite my requests, the leadership of the joint meeting is not taking steps to test the truth of the grave charge that has been made against me, I cannot take part in this meeting.[43]

The meeting went ahead without Lysenko, though a number of his supporters did attend. Keldysh served as chairman, and alongside him sat Minister of Agriculture Matskevich, Minister of Sovkhozes I. P. Volovchenko, and Lobanov, the president of VASKhNIL. Observers from the science and agriculture departments of the Central Committee were in the audience. Keldysh began by reading Lysenko's letter, adding that he had told Lysenko that "he would be behaving wrongly if he did not attend the joint meeting," since the Lenin Hills farm was under the jurisdiction of the AN SSSR.[44] The chairman's motion to discuss the report in the absence of Lysenko was carried unanimously.

The meeting heard reports refuting several of Lysenko's theories.[45] One of the most interesting of these was delivered by Ye. M. Bodrova, a researcher at the Institute of Fertilizers and Soil Science, who described a ten-year study of the effects of triplex. More than five hundred experiments, conducted "by all the zonal and branch institutes and the largest regional experimental stations in both non-black-earth and black-earth zones of the Soviet Union" showed that "the effect of triplex . . . was almost one and a half times less than that of manure" and that "the aftereffect of the organo-mineral mixture on the second and subsequent crops was considerably weaker than that of ordinary applications of manure." At the close of the meeting, Keldysh expressed surprise that no one had spoken up in Lysenko's behalf. Kallistratov, director of the experimental section at Lenin Hills, said, "I was prepared to speak and wanted to put my name down on the list of speakers, but after you said the discussion was ended . . ." There followed this exchange:

Keldysh: If you had said you wanted to speak, we would have given you the floor.
Kallistratov: You said debate was finished. In any event I did not dodge speaking.

Keldysh: If you wish to speak, we shall give you the floor.
Kallistratov: If you insist, I shall speak.

Keldysh then exploded: "What do you mean, 'insist'?"[46] Kallistratov had no choice but to start speaking:

Everything said here has created the impression that our farm is no good. That is not so at all. In 37 years of my working on that farm, together with the collective, there has not been a day when our collective failed to achieve the highest fulfillment of the decisions of the Party and government for the improvement of agriculture.

He said that the farm had been misrepresented, that the commission's report was "not objective," and that—though he had "respect" for the commission's members—either "they were misled or they closed their eyes."[47] He was then subjected to angry questioning from Matskevich, Volovchenko, and others:

Matskevich: Do you confirm that the milk yield at Lenin Hills dropped from 6,785 to 4,453 kilograms? The drop in milk yield—is it a fact or not?
Kallistratov: It's a fact.
Matskevich: Was all the fodder home-grown or did you get some from outside the farm?
Kallistratov: Some was brought in from elsewhere.
Matskevich: Why do you credit total livestock output to home-grown fodder?
Kallistratov: I never spoke anywhere of livestock products from our own fodder. Milk output was attributed to our own fodder, but I did not speak of meat.
Voice from the audience: Then why do you calculate in terms of output per 100 hectares of plowland?
Kallistratov: I was always speaking merely of volume of output.
N. F. Rostovtsev [a member of VASKhNIL]: How do you explain the high expenditure of fodder—nine kilograms in standard feed units—per kilogram of weight gained by calves?
Kallistratov: That's difficult for me to answer. I was not prepared for that question.
Volovchenko: What was the productivity of your hens?
Kallistratov: We closed down the poultry farm, and rightly so, because a poultry farm with only a thousand chickens is no poultry farm.
Volovchenko: You didn't answer the question. I asked about the hens' productivity.
Kallistratov: It was low: 67–68 eggs per hen [per year].[48]

The resolution passed at the end of the meeting approved the commission's report, saying it had "given a completely objective appraisal of the work" of the Lenin Hills farm and had disclosed many gross violations of scientific research methods and management of the experimental farm. It recommended revocation of two decrees of the agriculture ministry that had supported the farm's work in increasing the fat content of milk; it declared the use of breeding bulls from the Lenin Hills herd "impermissible"; and, perhaps most significantly, it said it was "advisable to consider the question of strengthening the leadership of the scientific experimental station and the Lenin Hills auxiliary research and production farm"—in effect, a call to replace the farm's executives.[49]

A Tenuous Ban on Criticism

It is noteworthy that the meeting had been carefully confined to questions of the management of Lenin Hills; the wider questions of Lysenko's theories and their destructive impact on Soviet science were completely ignored, almost as if it would not be tactful or prudent to mention them. It is equally striking that no one at the meeting ever alluded to an investigation of the Lenin Hills Experiment Station that the presidium of the AN SSSR itself had ordered almost a year earlier, immediately after Khrushchev's fall. That earlier investigating commission had included Engelgardt and other anti-Lysenkoist academicians, as well as auditors from USSR Ministry of Finance. Its report called attention to scientific mistakes, falsified records, and outright forgeries. These findings were transmitted to V. S. Konoplyov, a responsible officer of the party central staff, who in turn reported them to Andrei Ya. Pelshe, a member of the Politburo and chairman of the Party Control Committee. Pelshe ordered the commission to cease its work and not to make public the information it had gathered. So shocked was Konoplyov that he died a few days later. In the academy presidium it was believed that the orders came from the main ideologist of the Party, M. A. Suslov.[50]

Perhaps it is not surprising, then, that Lysenko, Kallistratov, Ioannisyan, and their colleagues kept their jobs at Lenin Hills, and that the research there continued to use the methods of the past four decades. Furthermore, Lysenko retained his memberships in the AN SSSR, the Ukrainian Academy of Sciences, and VASKhNIL, and his positions as director of the AN SSSR's Genetics Institute in Moscow and scientific director of the Plant Breeding and Genetics Institute in Odessa, part of the VASKhNIL network. Even when, in the middle of the following year, the members of the general biology section of the AN SSSR refused to reelect him as director of the Genetics Institute, practically all of Lysenko's colleagues there kept their positions.[51]

Lysenko also remained the scientific director of Gorki-Leninskiye, the Lenin Hills Experiment Station, where more than 100 researchers with faculty rank and about 100 other employees worked under his guidance. He continued to participate in the sessions and general assemblies of three academies, invariably sitting in the front rows at each meeting, and not hesitating to speak out in discussions and debates.

At the close of each year, as was required of academicians, he sent the academies a fat folder of his reports. These, too, showed no change. They continued to assert that genes did not exist and that DNA consisted of molecules that possessed no specific hereditary material. Once in 1973 or 1974, Lobanov gave me the most recent of these reports and asked me to review them: "Take a look," he said, "maybe they contain something new; after all, he has two hundred idlers on his rolls at Lenin Hills." But I found nothing new. It was clear that Lysenko considered all critical comments on his work to be attempts by his enemies to do him harm and that as soon as the Party and government leaders were replaced, he would be reinstated and the "Michurin approach" would prevail again.

Anyone who ate in the dining room of the AN SSSR on Lenin Prospekt in the late 1960s and early 1970s regularly encountered Lysenko there. His appearance had not changed, except that perhaps he stooped a bit, but there was a noticeable change in his behavior: he made efforts to befriend those academy members who were being persecuted. For example, one day he encountered Venyamin G. Levich, a corresponding member of the academy, in the cloakroom. Levich had submitted an application to emigrate to Israel and was being denounced for it. Lysenko had never been close to him, but now he suddenly strode toward him, shook his hand, and asked: "How are things, Venyamin Grigoryevich? Tough? Things are hard for me, too!"[52]

Andrei Sakharov and his wife, Yelena G. Bonner, told me of a similar incident, which occurred around 1973. As we were talking soon after their return from seven years of illegal exile in Gorky in December 1986, the conversation turned to Lysenko. Suddenly, Bonner asked: "Andrei, do you remember that as we entered the academy dining room, I was delayed at the entrance for a moment, and you went to the center of the dining hall, when suddenly Lysenko jumped up from a corner table, rushed up to you, made a big gesture of holding out his hand, and shook your hand meaningfully?" "Yes," replied Sakharov, "that was just at the time when the academicians' letter accusing me of betraying the motherland had been published, and Lysenko apparently wanted to show that we were both being persecuted, he and I."[53]

A Fresh Party Ban on Criticism

However, Lysenko had not only kept most of his positions by summer of 1966, he also got a reprieve from attacks in the press; evidently, he was still regarded as useful to the political leaders. Several directives to stop criticizing him were handed down from the press and mass media department of the Party Central Committee.[54] Any writer who wanted to give full publicity to anti-Lysenko material was given the official formula: we cannot allow passions to be inflamed, emotion would not be helpful, and in general we are against revanchism—the term that became a standard piece of ideological vocabulary.

Who ordered the suppression of criticism? Who made it possible for Lysenko to keep his footing? The answer remains something of a mystery.

Many assumed that Lysenko was being protected by Suslov, who, as ideological boss, could be blamed for anything. Suslov did indeed play a big role. Everyone who tried to publish anti-Lysenko materials knew it well. I obtained real confirmation of the ban later when a related document came into my possession. It was a letter to the Party Central Committee of February 1967, signed by V. Stepakov, head of the ideology department of the Central Committee; S. Trapeznikov, head of the science department; and V. Karlov, head of the agriculture department. It disclosed that the Party had forbidden publishing anti-Lysenkoist materials and had orally delivered this ban to the publishing house directors and the editors in chief of national newspapers and magazines at a specially organized conference. This letter reveals so much about the hold that Lysenko still had on the Party leadership, and about the way in which science and the press continued to be managed in the Soviet Union, more than a dozen years after Stalin's death, that it is worth quoting at length:[55]

> During the past two years, newspapers and popular-science and literary magazines have published many useful statements of prominent scientists and specialists in various branches of biology and agricultural science. At the same time, however, articles have begun to appear whose authors incorrectly inform readers about the present state of biology, specifically genetics and plant breeding; indulge in unjustified attacks upon some Soviet scientists; and analyze the development of biology over the past thirty years without a sufficiently deep scientific basis. . . .
>
> In December 1964, the ideological and agricultural departments of the Party Central Committee held a conference of newspaper and magazine editors, at which desires were expressed concerning the need for skilled, truthful treatment of contemporary problems of science and practice. The flood of one-sided, nonobjective articles receded after this conference, but subjectivist articles harmful to the interests of the development of science and the upbringing of scientific cadres and specialists have begun to appear again recently.
>
> The editorial boards of some newspapers (*Komsomol Pravda* and *Literary Gazette*) and magazines (*Problems of Philosophy, Genetics*, and *Bulletin of the Moscow Naturalists Society*) wrongfully adopt the role of arbiters in scientific disputes, opening their pages to a group of writers who treat the situation in biology one-sidedly.
>
> *Scope* [Prostor], the magazine of the Kazakhstan Writers' Union (nos. 7 and 8, 1966), published Mark Popovsky's "documentary novel," *The Thousand Days of Academician Vavilov*. It turned out to be an abridgment of the concluding part of the book *Man atop the Globe*, which the publishing house Sovetskaya Rossiya was preparing to release. The novel does not give a true portrait of the famous scientist N. I. Vavilov. Treating historical facts selectively, the author undertook to idealize and canonize N. I. Vavilov. At the same time he portrays another, no less famous scientist, I. V. Michurin, as a gardener "more used to wielding pruning shears and shovel than the pen."
>
> M. Popovsky dwells in detail and quite unambiguously on the causes and circumstances of Vavilov's downfall and death. Essentially, he concludes that the blame for the demise of N. I. Vavilov and other prominent scientists belongs to

the entire national political situation that surrounded them, as well as to Lysenko and his comrades-in-arms. The author exaggerates, creating a picture of terrible repressions, terror, and illegality reigning in the period he describes.

". . . Commissars of agriculture and heads of the Party Central Committee agriculture department are removed, one after another. 'Enemies of the people' are found everywhere, including of course in agriculture. They are sought out and found, identified, and blamed for all the failures, miscalculations, mistakes, and outright stupidity."

"Each arrest shook Nikolai Ivanovich [Vavilov]; people were disappearing whom he had known for many years and whom he trusted. . . . The institute director vouched for the loyalty of arrested and exiled persons and pleaded that they be returned to Leningrad. . . .

"But he did not succeed in saving anyone."

This Popovsky novel repeats in greatly softened form the substance of lectures he delivered before large numbers of scientists, students, and teachers in many Moscow and Leningrad institutes. In lectures about the causes and circumstances of Vavilov's tragic death, he said the USSR prosecutor had granted him access to the record of the Vavilov investigation and permission to publish documents from it. During a lecture at the Institute of the Plant Industry in Leningrad, he read out the records of confrontations and Vavilov's testimony, allegedly extracted from him by torture; the Vavilov death certificate; and informers' reports against Vavilov written by scientists, some still living, some now dead. The lecturer, appropriating the functions of investigator, prosecutor, and judge, accused many persons and in effect called for vengeance upon them.

Such lecturers by writer M. Popovsky appear all the more strange because in the past he glorified "the people's scientist" Lysenko no less passionately, calling him "a remarkable scientist and patriot." . . .

In this connection, there can be no justification for the stand taken by the editorial board of the journal *Problems of Philosophy* in undertaking systematic publication of material presenting the situation in biology one-sidedly and opening the pages of the journal to L. [sic] P. Efroimson, whose articles are marked by particular harshness bordering on vilification. Many of this writer's newspaper and magazine articles deny wholesale and without proof all the achievements of our country's biology and agricultural science of the past three decades. Such "criticism," casting doubt upon the labors of many honest Soviet scientists, evokes bewilderment not only among our specialists, but also in the scientific community of the fraternal socialist countries.

The publication, by certain organs of the press, of discussion articles unsupported by experimental data and pursuing basically revanchist, "exposé" goals, could create uncertainty among readers, especially young readers, and cause nihilism and disbelief in scientists and scientific ideals and principles. The practice of publishing such articles inflames passions, creates tensions in relations among biologists, diverts them into undesirable disputes, and does not promote a normal creative atmosphere.

All this has become possible because Party committees and persons in charge of newspapers and magazines have become less demanding of skilled treatment of modern problems of science and practice.

The Party Central Committee departments of propaganda, science and educational institutions, and agriculture deem it necessary to call the attention of the union-republic central committees, territory committees, and regional committees of the Party, persons in charge of newspapers and magazines, and the presidiums of the AN SSSR, VASKhNIL, the USSR Academy of Medical Sciences, and the academies of science of the union republics to the necessity of heightening the responsibility of officials for the quality and ideological line of published material.

We wish to request that Comrade P. N. Demichev [a candidate member of the Politburo who was responsible for mass media] be assigned to address directors of print media, radio, television, and motion pictures on this question.

Although public criticism of Lysenko was thus quelled in the late 1960s, the anti-Lysenko forces did succeed in advancing their cause in other respects. Lysenko's journal, *Agrobiology*, was closed down, and in its place a somewhat larger and genuinely scientific journal, *Agricultural Biology*, began to appear. It became harder to publish overtly Lysenkoist articles and books (although works containing the same ideas, without aggressively calling attention to them, were printed). Textbooks began to omit Michurinist biology and the once-obligatory attacks on Mendelism-Morganism-Weismannism and Virchowism.

Thus, Lysenko personally and his "theories" were disgraced. However, Lysenkoists were still legion in the academies, institutes, and ministries; almost all the full members of VASKhNIL were ardent followers, as were several full members of the AN SSSR. They were not ready to give up their power. In January 1970, with the active support of V. F. Krasota, the head of the department of higher education of the USSR Ministry of Agriculture, Glushchenko and the philosopher G. V. Platonov drafted a letter to Leonid Brezhnev, who had succeeded Khrushchev as head of the Party, and circulated it among their colleagues. They obtained twenty-two other signatures, mostly members of VASKhNIL or professors or lecturers at various agricultural and other institutes. Lysenko himself and his closest collaborators kept aloof from the project. One of the reasons was to avoid shadowing of their activity and to show that they considered themselves as independent scientists, another reason was personal: Ever since 1962, when Lysenko had ridiculed Glushchenko during Keldysh's visit to Lenin Hills, the two had virtually broken off contact.

The letter did not defend Lysenkoism as such but rather Michurinism (though it also sought to link Michurin's name with that of Darwin, as, indeed, Lysenko had done). It conceded that "research in molecular biology, genetics, biophysics, and biochemistry" had achieved "positive results." Nevertheless, it emphasized the support that Lenin, the Communist Party, and the Soviet government had always given Michurin and the Michurinists, and it complained that "in recent years, under the flag of combating mistaken positions of T. D. Lysenko, many biologists and press organs have been opposing the ideas of Darwin and Michurin."

Publishing houses and scientific and popular magazines have ceased to print works written from the point of view of the Darwinist-Michurinist school in biology. Textbooks and teaching aids do not present the doctrine of Michurin and his followers. . . . Many scientists and journalists seek to portray the Michurin trend as old-fashioned . . . and as if it had been pushed aside by the tempestuous development of molecular biology and genetics. . . . Some Soviet geneticists are publishing their books and articles abroad, where they try in every way to discredit the Michurinist teaching.

To counter this "wave of slander" and to make "vital corrections," the letter recommended that steps be taken:

1. To restore the Michurinist problematics of research in scientific institutions and higher education and to cease the discrediting of supporters of the Michurinist teaching.
2. To grant the representatives of the Michurinist school equal rights with the supporters of classical genetics in publishing the results of scientific research.
3. To eliminate the presently observed one-sidedness in the presentation of biological problems in study programs, textbooks, and teaching aids.
4. To advise editors of philosophy and biology journals to intensify the struggle against ideological and metaphysical conceptions in biology and against biological conceptions in sociology.[56]

As a result of the letter, a number of the signers were invited to meet with Matskevich and Lobanov. Matskevich evidently tried to be even-handed, saying that it had been "wrong" to suppress the geneticists but that they had made no "great discoveries" and that "instances of suppression of biologists and selection specialists of the Michurinist school, who have done great service to our science and practice," were not be tolerated, either.[57] Later, Matskevich gave appointment to geneticists B. Astaurov, D. Belyayev, and others. Matskevich tried to quiet them and said that Lysenkoists' demand will not lead to changes Party's policy.[58] Otherwise, except perhaps for preventing the dismissal of a few minor figures, the appeal came to naught. It was the last attempt of the Michurinists to restore the status quo.

Denouement

The Michurinists now began to make some accommodations to the new world of science. The heads of institutes and departments began to recruit one or two young staff members to represent the disciplines of molecular biology and genetics. At Odessa, for example, the son of a local boss was appointed as a junior scientist at the laboratory of the director of the institute, A. S. Musiiko. Soon, Musiiko sent this young protégé for a year to the United States to learn about the fashionable new branches of science. Two of the most prominent signers of the letter, Remeslo and Lukyanenko, acquired their own "molecularists." Gradually and without fanfare, molecular biology, genetics, biophysics, and biochemistry began to supplant "Michurinist biology" in the schools, textbooks, and laboratories. I myself became a part of this process when, in 1970, I was invited to head a new laboratory of molecular biology and genetics in VASKhNIL and was promised funds, staff, and eventually an institute. At my initiative, a scientific council on molecular biology and genetics was formed in VASKhNIL, and I became its academic secretary. The council was granted some authority, but I soon became convinced that undertakings of this kind were doomed without a change in the general situation.

But such change was difficult to make. Of the many examples of this, one came to my attention. In 1970, a memorandum was drawn up for the government, explaining that progress in plant breeding required new kinds of equipment that were not being produced in the Soviet Union. The USSR Council of Ministers approved the memorandum, and we were requested to submit promptly a list of the devices needed, the names of firms producing them and the countries in which they were located, and an estimate of the cost. The Council of Ministers adopted a program for setting up almost fifty selection centers outfitted with the new equipment. Foreign currency was allocated, and the Ministry of Foreign Trade was told to place large orders, including entire laboratories.

Four years later, of more than a hundred automated climatic chambers that had been imported from the Netherlands, fewer than a third had been erected, and metal parts of the rest were rusting away, and most of the American ultracentrifuges, Japanese spectrophotometers, Swedish equipment for separating substances, and similar devices were not being used. No one really wanted them, and no one had trained personnel to use them. Lysenkoists were not loath to display the equipment to visiting committees as a sign that they had turned over a new leaf and were operating at the level of the highest world standards, but it was only for show.

Thus, Lysenko had fallen, but the restoration of biology was a slow, ill-managed, and halting process. Lysenko remained scientific director of Lenin Hills until his death in 1976. Kallistratov then took over, but he retired after three years and died soon thereafter. As of 1983 (the last year of which I have knowledge), Ioannisyan was still working at Lenin Hills and proudly recalling his years of association with Lysenko.

When Lysenko died, the press kept silence. The close associates and Lysenko children informed their relatives by phone. Several dozen people gathered at the cemetery to show the last honors to the former famous person. His children tried to obtain permission to bury Lysenko at the most prestigious Russian national cemetery at the Novo-Devichi convent, but the request was denied. Lysenko found his eternal peace at the Kuntsevo cemetery, nominally a branch of Novo-Devichi on the outskirts of Moscow.

Conclusion

"No!" I exclaimed. "Education is a serious business, boys have to have Latin grammar walloped into them."
—A. A. Fet, letter to L. N. Tolstoy

It is pleasant and even tempting to rule over people, to shine before others, but there is also something demonic and dangerous in this.
—Hermann Hesse, *The Bead Game*

During the years in which I was gathering the material on the history of Lysenkoism—reading the speeches, articles, and books and seeking out witnesses to the drama, both in the Lysenko camp and among the scientists who opposed him—I sometimes saw Trofim Denisovich before me as I remembered him from my student days: a dry, stringy figure, dressed in a gray, loose raincoat, wrinkled jacket, and grease-stained trousers, baggy at the knees. His cracked voice resounded from the lines of articles and reports. His dry, stringy figure seemed about to appear in the doorway. I wanted to see him once again, to sit once again at the long desk in his office at the Timiryazev Academy, small and cramped, so out of keeping with his high position but so befitting his homely appearance. In those years, I myself went about in a patched and threadbare coat, I was constantly undernourished, and it did not occur to me to wonder why a wealthy academician, let alone an academy president, sported such attire, whether it was a pose, a flaunting of his prestigious proletarian-peasant origins, or represented an inner credo, reflecting the consistent nature of a strong individual, utterly and completely devoted to work and entirely uninterested in outward appearance, fashionable tailoring, and fine clothing.

Nor did it ever enter my head as a young student, shy with girls, to ask myself how his wife and children viewed his plain living, or whether there were any women whom he wanted to attract. Did he go to the theater, attend concerts, read romantic novels, visit friends? Did he have any close friends? Not the lackeys, the cluster of hangers-on who always attach themselves to prominent figures, but real friends? Did he meet with them in home settings, and, if he did, did he drink the customary Russian glass of vodka, or perhaps four or five? Or didn't he drink at all when he acquired the position of the president? And how did he feel about money? Was he a skinflint or generous?

At the beginning of my work on the book, it seemed crystal clear to me that Lysenko was not simply a mediocrity, but a scoundrel, a monster. Over time, however, I was able to become more patient, and even began to respect his methodical, precisely calculated actions, his extraordinary boldness, his ability to concentrate forces and parry his enemies' blows, to speak compellingly in public, to resolve psychological problems, and to escape traps and scramble back on his feet after a fall.

The bloody jaws of the Stalinist machine ground up giants, including many in agricultural science as well as three commissars of agriculture, Yakovlev, Eikhe, and Chernov. Meanwhile, Lysenko dodged and weaved and escaped unscathed. His scientific adversaries directed their blows against him, and some of them doubtless used all means to denounce and destroy him, as tens of millions of others were destroyed in that terrible time. Yet he survived every nasty scrape. It would be a mistake to underestimate the cunning and self-possession of this man.

As I talked to people who had known him, his personality became a little clearer, although his actions were not always simple nor did they lend themselves to easy interpretation. He was indeed something of an ascetic. He did not care how he dressed; he could wear one coat for years on end, and tie the same worn shoelaces long after they broke and were knotted together in many places, and not be in the least embarrassed. He read little, and no one could remember his going to the theater or a concert on his own initiative. Glushchenko told me that he and his wife once invited Lysenko to see *King Lear* at the Central Jewish Theater, and the great Jewish actor Solomon Mikhoels (whose death Stalin later ordered) played so well that it moved Lysenko to ask Berta Abramovna Glushchenko to take him to the theater again.

As for women in general, he was apparently indifferent to them. Colleagues who knew him well recalled a few incidents involving women in which something may have happened at one time or another, but here too the initiative seems to have come from the women, and any relationships that may have developed were brief. "Who would hold back with a wife like his Aleksandra Alekseyevna?" one academician remarked to me. "She didn't wash his clothes, didn't give him dinner, didn't look after him at all, I think." Nevertheless, it appeared that he did hold back, on the whole. He lived for other goals.

In the post-Stalin period, he developed an undeviating daily routine, working from morning to 6:00 P.M., at which time he went off in the same direction each day—to the top Soviet officials' dining room on Granovsky Street. There he dined, obtained food in the special store for his family, and went home. Glushchenko told me that, while Lysenko dined and received food there, his chauffeur used the time to buy one or two bottles of the beer Lysenko liked. Several times a month, Lysenko bought a bottle of dry wine, though, as far as is known, no vodka. (I heard a different story from someone in the geneticists' camp, who learned from an acquaintance, the daughter of a prominent linguist and a corresponding member of the AN SSSR, that her father was a friend of Lysenko and sometimes got beastly drunk with him and at such times they cursed the Soviet regime together. But was it true?!)

Upon returning home, he slept an hour or two, then generally telephoned Prezent or Glushchenko (who lived close by) to come over. They would talk about their science until two or three in the morning.

Lysenko never wrote his articles in his own hand, but dictated to a stenographer. Then his more literate colleagues (most often Prezent or Glushchenko) would correct the draft and return it to Lysenko, who dictated revisions if he considered it necessary. He did not know the rules of grammar and never used punctuation. Once I saw a dedication written on the flyleaf of a book in Lysenko's hand in 1937:

> Dear . . . I give you my first work think and believe your first work will be much better truer [the words "much better truer" were repeated and crossed out, then the dedication continued:] hope your work will be continued and chiefly more true as you will do
>
> T. D. Lysenko

At that time, and long afterward, his handwriting resembled chicken tracks. By the 1950s, he was writing in a more legible, if childlike, hand, but still without punctuation. (Oddly enough, this was a trait he and Dubinin had in common. I worked with Dubinin for several years and tried on a number of occasions to correct his punctuation, until, after perhaps my tenth reminder, he shouted: "Remember, I'm an academician and I don't have to keep worrying about commas! I can always find smart people like you to insert them wherever they're needed.")

It was widely known that Lysenko was not parsimonious. If he heard of someone in need, he gave money, sometimes large sums, freely and unostentatiously; he knew how to give without offending. Unscrupulous individuals cozened him more than once, but their greed and guile did not extinguish his readiness to help others. In Odessa, his deputy director for administration and management, A. Rodionov, benefited in no small way from his kindness. This ordinary worker—whose job application, in the blank for "education," declared: "Incomplete secondary self-education"—had been elevated to that position by Lysenko. For some reason, Lysenko came to believe that the Rodionov family was in straitened circumstances, and for several years he regularly provided funds to him, passing along the supplementary income received as scientific advisor to graduate students who were writing theses. He continued this practice until by accident he learned that Rodionov had built a handsome summer cottage for himself. Thereupon, Lysenko put an immediate stop to his beneficence and refused to talk to Rodionov for a long time.

He quarreled frequently with his sister's husband, who lived in the Lysenko family home in Karlovka but came to Moscow often to speculate in goods that he sold in the capital. When there, he stayed in Lysenko's apartment. The quarrels began when Lysenko discovered the purpose of his brother-in-law's visits to Moscow. The brother-in-law neither changed his behavior nor ceased to impose upon Lysenko's hospitality, but Lysenko never ejected him. This is all the more remarkable when one recalls how others at the upper levels in Stalin's time treated relatives of whom they disapproved.

His behavior toward his father was also specific. Denis Lysenko worked as chief of a field crew at Lenin Hills. But his son ordered the farm not to pay the father the wages due him, on the grounds that Lysenko supported him completely. Denis was sociable with all of Lysenko's circle and loved to invite them to his cottage. There, he always offered them the same fare: a slab of Ukrainian salt pork and a slug of vodka. To refuse the refreshments was to offend the old man, and in such cases he always declared that that had been his diet all his life and he was healthy as a bull. Four months before his death, the colorful old fellow told Trofim he felt the end coming on and asked to be sent home to Karlovka. His wish was obeyed, and he died in his home there, seated at a table, his head in his hands.

These details add touches of color to the portrait, but they should not be allowed to obscure the fundamental traits that came to dominate Lysenko's professional life: an extreme drabness of personality, narrowness of interests, and poverty of knowledge. Fate was kind to him early in life. It put the talented scientist Derevitsky in his path at Gandzha. It afforded him contact with such influential figures as Tulaikov and enabled him to breathe the atmosphere of scientific enthusiasm at Vavilov's Institute of the Plant Industry. Conceivably, Lysenko could have become a genuine scientist. But the state was bestowing its favors upon those who followed the ways of Leninism and Stalinism, and that gave him his second stroke of fortune. The Moscow journalist Fyodorovich lauded Lysenko in the central Party newspaper, and thereafter the young agronomist rolled on like a pebble, gaining momentum but always rolling away from education, science, and scientists. Like the Antichrist in Vladimir Solovyov's legend, whose every effort came to naught after he concluded a pact with the devil, Lysenko's entire subsequent life became a spiritual wasteland: Everything he put his hand to ended in failure. Leaping from one conjecture to the next and unable to deal seriously with any of them as a genuine scientist should, he debased himself without realizing it. A thirst for fame and power overcame him, and he used all his exceptional natural ability to satisfy it. During the years of his rise, he probably felt happy, but he failed to see that he was losing more and more, despite his outward success. The aides and students who surrounded him, less talented than he but no less malicious, hastened the process of disintegration of the personality, impoverishment of the mind, and dulling of the conscience.

He did not go to church; he apparently no longer believed in God and had no spiritual advisor, no one to whom to confess his sins and perhaps no inclination to do so. The worst sin, the sin of arrogance, gripped his soul. He seemed to fear even to remain alone with his thoughts, and that may be why he invited his minions to stay with him and sought peace in their company. Lysenko remained what he had begun: essentially the same person throughout his life: a semiliterate "expert," a self-taught amateur. His very first work was based on deceit and was not at all the "discovery" that the newspapers trumpeted and that many naively assume to be the case even today.[1] He did not grow in knowledge later, either, but instead found that he could rise on the ladder of power without it. The political and social system opened the gates to the undistinguished, as long as they were "our kind," while blocking all paths for those who "didn't belong," however educated and productive they might be.

His personal ambition, his capacity for hard work, his native wit, and his staying power might have helped him to grow, but, caught up as he was in false pride that turned more and more into a morbid vanity, these qualities were reduced to a banal stubbornness and a dislike of anyone who undertook to instruct him. He lost the capacity for self-criticism and surrounded himself with flatterers. They called him a genius, when he was merely an inspired mediocrity. But he lived in a world where mediocrities had seized power and ruled every sphere of life. The Soviet system had not created mediocrities, but it provided them with opportunities for power. It invited them into the ranks of scientists and gave them preference in appointments in the institutes and academies, so the entire phenomenon of Lysenkoism was a Soviet phenomenon.

But it was not only in science that Lysenko remained forever mediocre. He never overcame his drabness in everyday life. His private life, like that of Stalin, was empty. Art, music, books, the joys of friendship, flights of the spirit, even the passionate love of a woman—all of that remained outside his world and never touched him. His wife was as dreary as he. Their three children—Yury, a marine physicist at Moscow State University; Lyudmila, who had both a medical degree and a Ph.D. and worked as a cardiologist at the Institute of Cardiology; and Oleg, who had a candidate degree in agricultural sciences and was an agronomist at Lenin Hills—inherited his vanity and bitter hardness. Now they speak up wherever they can about the greatness of their misunderstood father, and they dash off protests and objections whenever they hear public mention of Lysenko's mistakes.

Neither Lysenko himself nor Stalin and Khrushchev understood that his victory feast, celebrating his heroic crushing of the foes of his "doctrine" and the enemies of socialism, was a Barmecide feast. The entire society governed by the "victors" was hopelessly ill, and the symptoms of Lysenkoism alone were sufficient to disclose the root causes of the disease. Outwardly, the body still seemed strong, and few recognized how serious was the calamity that was brewing; even as the Communists rejoiced at their domination of a third of Europe, of Mongolia and China, of Vietnam and

North Korea, the Lysenko canker showed how far advanced was the gangrene of the entire system.

In any society, there are charlatans and people who are simply mistaken. They may try to deceive their fellows, either by design or out of ignorance. But in a healthy society, others will call attention to their errors, test their assumptions, and make objective appraisals. Shams are exposed, and no one punishes those who do the exposing; members of the government or secret police do not hurl political accusations against seekers of scientific truth. But that is what happened when an alliance of the Lysenkos, the Stalins, and the Berias was part of the onrushing, bloody chariot of socialism.

Of course, there have been moments in the life of civilized societies also, even in recent history, when obscurantists temporarily acquired weight in society: Darwin's works have been removed from school libraries in the United States, for example, but such fevers quickly pass when the social organism is strong. Yet even at the height of the illness, scientists have not been seized and humiliated, imprisoned, or executed, and the development of science was not brought to a halt.

There also have been instances in which individual thinkers have proposed ideas that less farsighted colleagues took ten or twenty years to appreciate. Such instances occur to this day. But these pioneers achieved their successes not by arbitrarily rejecting all past science at one fell swoop but by proposing new ideas that built on the work of their predecessors. In the 1950s, for example, Barbara McClintock discovered the existence of mobile elements on chromosomes and worked out the theory of their operations. It took twenty years for genetic engineers to take up her ideas and for her to receive the Nobel Prize she merited. Such a sad (after all, twenty years were lost) and happy (after all, her work was not in vain) case demonstrates the health of the system that Lenin, Stalin, Khrushchev, and Lysenko accused of every conceivable sin. They did not understand (or perhaps did not want to understand) the suicidal nature of their strivings. Neither did the thousands of Lysenkoists.

It would be unjustifiable to blame Lysenko alone for the failure to understand the principles of scientific research and for shutting himself up in so narrow an existence. He lived in a society that was created by its ideological leaders, though it must also be said that he himself liked that society, as he so often affirmed at length. Myth-making, in combination with bluster and a rejection of the values of genuine science, set the spirit of the times, and Lysenko fell in with these currents. He was then sucked into a maelstrom of vast social changes, whirled about, and swallowed, as a whirlpool swallows wood chips and great logs alike.

It would be equally unjustifiable, however, to blame all the horrors of the Soviet system on Stalin, and especially naive to hold him guilty of everything in the case of Lysenko. Lysenko came to the fore thanks to his considerable natural abilities. He fought for a position atop the pyramid of power and won it not by chance or by a whim of Stalin's but by his skill in waging the kind of battle that was necessary. It was a system that rated imitations above genuine gems, and, even by its standards, he broke all records. He outfoxed even Stalin and was able to pull the wool over his eyes when other Party leaders already had seen through Lysenko. Thanks to his courtier's intuition and his shrewdness, thanks to his ability to divine Stalin's secret designs, he always struck the right chord with "the great helmsman," never arousing his irritation.

And no one could compare with Lysenko in the ability to rub shoulders with the common people and talk their language. So, while he rose high, he retained the gift of communication with those at the bottom, even if he appealed to their prejudices rather than to their reason.

The opinion is widespread that his assistants, the lackeys who gathered around him, served him ill. One cannot but agree with that judgment. They applauded his every word and hastened to present him with the proofs he wanted. The fakery of his aides proved to be a curse of Lysenkoism and in the end brought down the whole "doctrine." Lysenko ought to have disowned his supporters. But to do that he would have had to rise above himself, and that is beyond anyone's power.

On the other hand, the Lysenko school was not composed solely of cynical knaves. There were also many ordinary people, perhaps not highly educated, but in their own way not altogether incompetent, either. Nevertheless, all of them adored their leader, idolized him, could not tolerate the thought that he could have been wrong in anything or failed to understand anything. I met such people more than once, and each time came up against their granite-like conviction in the universal correctness of their leader's ideas.

I encountered this faith once during a visit to Lenin Hills after Lysenko's death. Glushchenko had persuaded me to examine his experiments in turning winter into spring wheat. He asked a long-time staff member, a woman who had worked many years with Lysenko and now had entered Glushchenko's service, to join us. We spent the whole day in the fields and experimental plots. I inquired into every detail of their work and tried to probe their data and identify the genetic cause of the transformations. It was elusive. I saw that this staff member wanted very much to convince me of some things and dissuade me from others. She bore herself well, was restrained, patient, and tolerant, listened with interest to my objections and sought to answer them gently. But suddenly, perhaps out of fatigue, I said something, evidently too sharply, about the naiveté of Lysenko's attempts to dismiss the reality of genes. This brought a response from her, the gist of which was that Trofim Denisovich knew everything on earth, while we were truly naive to imagine that our limited minds could reach his level. I was surprised and asked her, "Surely you don't believe that Lysenko was always right?" To which she replied firmly, without affectation and somewhat wearily: "Trofim Denisovich was a genius. All his ideas were brilliant and will be adopted in the future." It would have been tactless to laugh at her words and probably hopeless to try to disabuse her. I kept my peace, choosing silence as the only way to express disagreement, and soon after took my leave.

I have often recalled that conversation, and the image of that woman who had preserved a deep admiration for Lysenko has stayed in my memory. I was amazed and even somewhat angry that she and other Lysenkoists regarded their former patron as an unrecognized genius who was simply ahead of his time and therefore had been unjustly humiliated at the end of his life. They regretted that time had dimmed the halo of his glory. It made me think of the stories of Napoleon's soldiers, who forgot the hardships of army service, the harshness of the tyrant, and the bitterness of defeat and retained only a sacred feeling of veneration for their commander. Lysenko had personally insulted many of his followers, had treated many of them arrogantly, had slighted them, ill-treated them, and thwarted their education and careers, while openly favoring rogues and frauds like Ioannisyan and Karapetyan. Sometimes, they spoke freely about this, and it would seem that they had only to shake their head and the rose-colored glasses would fall from their eyes and show them another aspect of Lysenko—his scientific ignorance and intellectual bankruptcy. But that never happened. No matter how badly they spoke of him as a person, dredging up—with an effort, it is true—all kinds of unpleasant incidents, one had only to dig deeper, to tap their scientific credo, and the categorical declaration would burst forth: "Lysenko was a genius!"

Only when I ceased to look upon these people as more or less attractive or repulsive individuals, articulate or semiliterate, and thought of them as *scientists*, that is, as specialists in their work, did I understand what lay at the heart of it. All these people, the whole school of Lysenko's followers, bore the mark of scientific ignorance. Each knew only some small craft, some narrow theme, and had never studied the scientific arguments of their opponents. The logical effect of such selection of staff was that they could only accept Lysenko's ideas uncritically. What would grate upon any well-trained biologist's ear sent the Lysenkoists into raptures. Lysenko's ideas were demagogic and recklessly unscientific, but they impressed these people as both practical and revolutionary. Scientific authorities were being pulled down off their pedestals, their abstruse ideas and laws dismissed out of hand. The sense of participating in what Lenin called "the great task of cleansing science of the reactionary, bourgeois rubbish left to us as a heritage of the old world" swelled the Lysenkoists' self-importance. This righteousness and conviction of a lofty mission engendered the worship of their leader and his brilliant ideas. They rejected any suggestion that Lysenko had collaborated in repression. They ascribed the arrests and deaths of scientific adversaries to Stalin alone. Sometimes, in passing, they said there was no scientific progress without a drama of ideas, but they never asked whether that drama always had to cost human lives.

One evening, someone who had been very close to Lysenko told me how Lysenko had saved people who were unjustly arrested. He gave me two examples. In one, his very first graduate students had written a letter to *Socialist Agriculture* in 1937 about what they considered unpardonable carelessness, bordering on sabotage, on the part of two members of the Odessa institute staff, Kuksenko and Garkavy. When the newspaper published this letter, Kuksenko and Garkavy were immediately arrested. But Lysenko wrote to the NKVD, and after some time Kuksenko and Garkavy were released. The other instance involved F. I. Filatov, the editor of the first issues of *Vernalization*, who was arrested merely because a portrait of the poet Sergei Yesenin (whom Stalin did not like) hung above his desk. Lysenko intervened on his behalf and achieved his release. (Filatov later worked in Saratov as a loyal Lysenkoist.)

But I knew of a different sort of incident. A. K. Zaporozhets, a pupil of Pryanishnikov's and an agrochemist and director of an institute, had been arrested, also in 1937. His wife, the sculptor Olga V. Kvinikhidze-Zaporozhets, managed to get an audience with Lysenko and appealed to him to help her husband. Lysenko was rushing off somewhere. She walked to his car with him, still pleading her husband's case. When Lysenko entered his car alongside the driver, the sculptor gathered her courage and entered also, taking the back seat and continuing her entreaty. Lysenko remained sternly silent and brushed aside the petition for pardon that she repeatedly sought to give him. As he left the car, he slammed the door. (Zaporozhets never returned; supposedly he was executed.) In Odessa, it had been a matter of his own people; when he was being asked to save someone in the other camp, his goodness of heart seemed to evaporate.

Thus faded the pastoral scene, to be replaced by a different kind of picture altogether; the good-hearted genius turned into an evil sorcerer.

Finally, the Lysenkoists and those who nurtured him failed to realize how great a harm Lysenko did to the country that put its trust in him. When a leader's first orders lead to success, his authority grows and people begin to believe in his strength. Their individual enthusiasms, insignificant by themselves, snowball into one tremendous will that they believe can accomplish wonders. The greatness of their collective achievement reflects back on the leader who gave the first impulse and endows him with the aura of genius. But when the leader issues orders that cannot be carried out, everyone loses. The leader himself comes to be seen not as a genius, but as a charlatan. Moreover, the whole basis of his commands, the ideology that spurred them, becomes suspect as well. A thread leads inexorably back from the unachieved goals to the impossible orders, from the one who gave the orders to the inefficacy of the doctrine that directed him. It is not simply that the sum total of the leader's life proves lamentable: his story highlights the sins of the whole society.

As I conclude this book, I am put in mind of the poignant words in "The Silver Prince," Aleksei Tolstoy's tale of the reign of Ivan the Terrible, for they express the thought that has been central in my retelling of Lysenko's story:

> May God help us to erase from our hearts the last traces of that terrible time . . . ! We forgive the sinful shade of Tsar Ivan, for not he alone bears the responsibility for his reign; not he alone created his abuse of power. . . . but let us honor the memory of those who, though dependent upon him, still maintained their virtue, for it is difficult not to fall at a time when all concepts are reversed, when baseness is called virtue, when betrayal becomes the law, and honor itself and human dignity are considered a criminal violation of duty![2]

> Moscow, 1979–1986
> Columbus, Ohio, and Oakton, Virginia, 1988–1993

Biographical Sketches

Gaister, Aron I. (1899–1937). Attended a gymnasium before the Revolution, despite the severe restrictions on the admission of Jews, but was expelled in his last year for revolutionary activity. Graduated from the Institute of Red Professors in 1921 and remained there to teach economics. Worked in the State Planning Committee (1921–1931) and the Commission for Soviet Control (1933–?). From 1935 until his death, he was simultaneously deputy commissar of agriculture and vice-president of VASKhNIL. In June 1937, Gaister presented a report at a meeting of the Council on Labor and Defense, for which Stalin praised him so immoderately that Gaister suspected something was amiss; on returning home, he said to his wife, Rachel, "My fate is sealed." He was arrested three days later, while in the office of the commissar of agriculture, and was charged with participating in an attempt on the life of Politburo member Valerian V. Kuibyshev, seeking to exterminate all sheep in the USSR, and undermining the economy. He was shot on October 30. His wife was arrested as well, and at the beginning of the 1950s their two daughters were arrested, the arrest warrants stating that they were "sufficiently convicted under Article 7–35 of being daughters of enemies of the people." The daughters served prison terms in a northern camp. After Stalin's death, they were rehabilitated, completed their studies, and became staff members of scientific institutes.

Gamow, George A. (1904–1968). Born in Odessa and graduated from Leningrad University. Worked in Göttingen, Copenhagen, and London, 1928–1931; lived in France and England in 1933 and in the United States from 1934 until his death. He was a prominent theoretical physicist, who discovered the quantum mechanical explanation of alpha decay and, in collaboration with Edward Teller, later the father of the American hydrogen bomb, formulated the theory of beta decay. He was a recognized authority in astrophysics, who had hypothesized the expanding universe. In 1954, he studied the general laws of the genetic code and showed how various combinations of three nucleotides could code for various amino acids. His success led many outstanding Western physicists to interest themselves in the problems of the new science of molecular genetics.

Glushchenko, Ivan Ye. (1907–1987). Graduated from the Kharkov Agro-Economics Institute in 1930. Named an academician of VASKhNIL; awarded the Stalin Prize (1943 and 1950), the A. N. Bakh Prize (1950), and the I. V. Michurin gold medal. Author of a biography of Lysenko: "A Brief Sketch of the Scientific-Research and Production Activity of T. D. Lysenko" (Kratky ocherk nauchno-issledovatelskoi i proizvodstvennoi deyatelnosti T. D. Lysenko), which served as the introduction to *Trofim Denisovich Lysenko.*

Gorbunov, Nikolai P. (1892–1937). Graduated from the Petersburg Technological Institute in 1917. In the same year, he became director of the Information Bureau of Central Executive Committee and then secretary of the Council of People's Commissars and personal secretary to Lenin. He was a political worker in the Red Army (1919–1920); executive director of the Russian Republic Council of People's Commissars (1920–) and of the USSR Council of People's Commissars (1922–); rector of the Bauman Moscow Higher Technical School (1923–1929); and deputy director of the Karpov Chemistry Institute (1931–1933). In 1935, he was appointed an academician and the permanent secretary of the AN SSSR and an academician of VASKhNIL. He was arrested and shot in 1937.

Kostov, Doncho S. (1897–1949). Born in Bulgaria; graduated from the university in Halle, Germany, in 1924, and became known as a specialist in plant genetics. In 1932, attracted by the ideas of communism, he emigrated to the Soviet Union and became a research fellow at the Genetics Institute of the AN SSSR (1932–1939) and a professor at Leningrad University (1934–1936). In 1939, he returned to Bulgaria, where he became director of the Central Agricultural Research Institute in Sofia and, in subsequent years, a professor at Sofia University; director of the Institute of Applied Biology and Development of Organisms, a unit of the Bulgarian Academy of Sciences; and a member of the Yugoslavian Academy of Arts and Sciences. However, after the August 1948 session of VASKhNIL, he became a victim of political persecution, and in August 1949 he died of a heart attack.

Lukyanenko, Pavel P. (1901–1973). Rose to high administrative position in agricultural science by toadying to Lysenko, but then left administrative work to take up wheat selection in earnest. Developed several high-quality varieties, including Bezostaya-1, which was sown on millions of acres in the USSR and many East European countries. He could well be placed in the category of people who laid the foundations of the "green revolution," which so greatly increased crop yields. Nevertheless, even when, much later, Lysenko had lost the support of the Party hierarchy, Lukyanenko still defended him and sought to revive "Michurinist theory." Lukyanenko's death was a peculiar tragedy. In the early 1970s, vast acreage was planted to two new varieties he had developed, Aurora and Kavkaz. Smut infected them badly during a year of heavy rains. Lukyanenko visited one of the infected fields, saw the terrible crop loss, and suffered a fatal heart attack on the spot. (O. Pavlov, "A Spike under a New Program," *Izvestia,* January 19, 1985, p. 2.)

Petrov, Rem V. (b. 1930). Completed Voronezh Medical Institute (1953); received degree of doctor of medical sciences (1961); elected full member of the Academy of Medical Sciences (1978). Director of a laboratory of the Institute of Biophysics of the Ministry of Health (1962–1983); head of the department of immunology at the Second Moscow Medical Institute (1974–1983); director of the Institute of Immunology of the Ministry of Health (1983–); president of the All-Union Society of Immunologists (1983–). Elected full member of the AN SSSR (1985) and later became its vice president. Joined Communist Party in 1956.

Pryanishnikov, Dmitry Nikolayevich (1865–1948). Russian agronomy chemist, biochemist, and plant physiologist, member of the U.S.S.R. Academy of Sciences and VASKhNIL, the Hero of Socialist Labor. He was graduated from Moscow University (1887) and Petrovskaya Agricultural and Forest Academy (1889; now the Moscow Timiryazev Agricultural Academy). From 1895 he was the chairman of the Department of Agrochemistry at this academy. He founded the Scientific Research Institute of Fertilizers and Insecto-Fungicides and All-Union Institute of Fertilizers, Agrotechnics, and Soil Studies, now named after him. His basic works were devoted to the study of plant nutrition and the role of fertilizers in agronomy. He formulated in 1916 the theory of nitrogen nutrition of plants; he developed the principle of transformation of nitrogenous compounds in plants, discovered the role of asparagin in plant metabolism. He was awarded two orders of Lenin, several other decorations, and the Lenin Prize.

Sisakyan, Norair M. (1907–1966). Received a candidate's degree in biochemistry in 1938, when he was hailed as typical of those who had risen from the ranks; see O. Pisarzhevsky, "Candidate of Agricultural Sciences Sisakyan," *Knowledge Is Power* (Znaniye—Sila), 1938, no. 10:10–13. Indeed, as late as 1924 he had been utterly illiterate, but that year he entered the Komsomol and came under the guidance of another colorful person risen from the ranks, who took pride in describing himself as "a former homeless waif"—Ezras A. Asratyan (who later became a member of the Armenian Academy of Sciences and was active in the 1950 purge of neurophysiologists). Asratyan taught Sisakyan the Armenian alphabet, and a year later Sisakyan, without attending classes, obtained a certificate stating that he had passed the examinations for completion of elementary school. He next enrolled in the Timiryazev Academy, and—though he still only barely understood Russian—completed it in 1932. He went to work at Pryanishnikov's institute but, when he proved incapable of the work there, was transferred to the Biochemistry Institute in 1935. Two years later, he joined the Party and soon headed that institute's Party unit. Afterward, he became a professor in the animal biochemistry department of Moscow State University, a corresponding member (1955) and then full member (1960) of the AN SSSR, secretary of the academy's biology division (1959), and chief scientific secretary of the academy's presidium (1960). Received Stalin Prize (1952). He developed an interest in the biology of outer space, and in 1956 was elected vice president of the International Astronautical Academy and had a crater on the moon named after him.

Shlikhter, Aleksandr G. (1868–1940). Studied at Kharkov University and later at the University of Bern, Switzerland, but did not complete a higher education. From 1891 on, devoted himself to revolutionary activity in Russia. In October 1917, became commissar of supplies of the Moscow Revolutionary Military Committee. Commissar of agriculture, 1917–1920. Chairman of the executive committee in Tambov Province, 1920–1921, during which time more than 11,000 peasants were killed or wounded during the suppression of a peasant rebellion (*Great Soviet Encyclopedia,* 3rd ed., s.v. "Antonovshchina"). After several years in diplomatic work, was named commissar of agriculture for the Ukraine in 1927. Also served as director of the Ukrainian Institute of Marxism-Leninism, president of the Ukrainian Association of Institutes of Marxism-Leninism, vice-president of the Ukrainian Academy of Sciences, and candidate member of the Politburo in the Ukraine (1926–1927). In 1928, was named an academician of the Ukrainian Academy of Sciences, and in 1936 was awarded a doctoral degree in economics, without writing a dissertation.

Turchin, Fyodor V. (1908–1965). A pupil of Pryanishnikov's, he worked in the Ya. M. Samoilov Research Institute of Fertilizers and Insectofungicides in Moscow and became head of the nitrogen fertilizers laboratory there. Defended his doctoral dissertation and managed to obtain accreditation shortly before the August 1948 session of VASKhNIL. Became one of the most respected specialists in plant nutrition and a convincing opponent of Lysenko. One of his sons, Valentin F. Turchin, a well-known theoretical physicist in the 1970s, became a leading civil-rights champion, a collaborator of Andrei Sakharov, and an organizer of the Moscow group of Amnesty International. The authorities forced him to emigrate in 1978. He is now a professor of computer science in the United States.

Vyshinsky, Andrei Ya. (1883–1954). At first a Menshevik, he switched to the Bolsheviks after their seizure of power. Gained prominence in 1928 as prosecutor at the first Moscow show trial, the case of fifty-five engineers and alleged foreign spies accused of sabotaging the Shakhty mines in the Donets coal basin. He later served as chief prosecutor at all the major political show trials of the 1930s. He was considered a leading specialist in criminal law and was notorious for extracting "confessions" by any means. He was professor of law and rector of Moscow State University. In 1949, he was appointed foreign minister and became widely known in the West as a Soviet spokesman in the United Nations. At the Nineteenth Party Congress in 1952, he was named to alternate membership in the Party presidium, but was dropped a few months later in the reorganization that took place after Stalin's death. He committed suicide.

Williams, Vasily R. (1863–1939). Son of a construction engineer who had emigrated from the United States in the mid-nineteenth century to escape, he claimed, rumors that he had American Indian forebears. After his father's death, the family was left impoverished. Nevertheless, he managed to graduate from the Petrovskaya Agricultural and Forestry Academy (later the Timiryazev Agricultural Academy) in Moscow in 1887. Subsequently taught there and became chair of the department of soil science. From 1922 to 1925, was the first "Red Rector" of the academy, and joined the Communist Party in 1928. Elected member of Belorussian Academy of Sciences in 1929, full member of the AN SSSR in 1931, and member of VASKhNIL in 1935. Served as deputy to the Supreme Soviet of the USSR and was twice awarded the Lenin Prize.

Yakovlev, Yakov A. (1896–1938). Pseudonym of Yakov A. Epshtein. Born into the family of a Grodno schoolteacher. Studied at Petrograd Polytechnical Institute. Involved in Party work in Petrograd and Yekaterinoslav (later Dnepropetrovsk) from 1917. Member of the Central Committee of the Communist Party of the Ukraine, 1919–1920; deputy commissar of the Workers' and Peasants' Inspection, 1926; commissar of agriculture for the USSR, 1929–1934, and later a member of the Central Committee of the CPSU. In photographs taken during those years, he is shown standing with the Party and government leaders around Stalin.

Yudin, Pavel. F. (1899–1968). Graduated from the Institute of Red Professors and was immediately appointed director of the Philosophy Institute of the AN SSSR. Later worked on the staff of the Party Central Committee, served as deputy supreme commissar in the Soviet occupation zone in Germany (1953–?), and was ambassador to the People's Republic of China (?–1959). Elected a member of the AN SSSR (1953).

Zhukov-Verezhnikov, Nikolai N. (1908–1981). Graduated from Moscow State University in 1930. In 1948, became full member of the Academy of Medical Sciences. Director of Institute of Experimental Biology (1948–1950); editor in chief at State Medical Publishing House (Medgiz) (1949–1953); deputy minister of health and head of laboratory of experimental immunobiology of the Institute of Experimental Biology (1952–1954). He was responsible for the gathering of the "evidence" that U. S. troops had used bacteriological weapons during the Korean War. He regarded himself as an expert on plague; in 1954, he reported to the Soviet government that he had ended an outbreak of plague in Siberia, but it later turned out that it had not been plague but tularemia. The error cost him his position as deputy minister of health. In the last years of his life, he joined the leadership of the Soviet Peace Fund and the Soviet Peace Committee.

Notes

Introduction

Epigraph sources: N. Eidelman, *Lunin* (Moscow: Molodaya gvardiya, 1970), 274; L. Tolstoy, quoted in P. I. Biryukov, *Conversations with Tolstoy* (1922), 3–4:48.

1. Loren R. Graham, *Science, Philosophy, and Human Behavior in the Soviet Union* (New York: Columbia University Press, 1987), 69.

2. Among the earlier works are J.P.S. Hudson and R. H. Richens, *The New Genetics in the Soviet Union* (Cambridge: Cambridge University Press, 1946), and Julian Huxley, *Heredity East and West: Lysenko and World Science* (London: Schuman, 1949). Later and more detailed studies include four by David Joravsky: *Soviet Marxism and Natural Science, 1917–1932* (New York: Columbia University Press, 1961); *The Lysenko Affair* (Cambridge: Harvard University Press, 1970); "The First Stage of Michurinism," in *Essays in Russian and Soviet History*, ed. J. S. Curtiss (New York: Columbia University Press, 1963), 120–132; and "The Vavilov Brothers," *Slavic Review* 24, no. 3 (September 1965): 381–394. Other important books published in the West are Dominique Lecourt, *Lyssenko: Histoire réelle d'une "science prolétarienne"* (Paris: François Maspero, 1976); Dominique Lecourt, *Proletarian Science: The Case of Lysenko* (London: New Left Books, 1977); Mark Popovsky, *Academician Vavilov's Trial* (in Russian) (Ann Arbor, Mich.: Hermitage, 1983) (published only in the West); Semyon Reznik, *The Road to the Scaffold* (in Russian) (Paris and New York: Tretaya volna, 1983) (published only in the West); Loren Graham, *Science and Philosophy in the Soviet Union* (New York: Alfred A. Knopf, 1972), esp. pp. 195–256; and Alexander Vucinich, *Empire of Knowledge: The Academy of Sciences of the USSR (1917–1970)* (Berkeley and Los Angeles: University of California Press, 1984). See also the following articles: Mark B. Adams, "The Founding of Population Genetics: Contributions of the Chetverikov School, 1924–1934," *Journal of the History of Biology* 1 (Spring 1968): 23–29, and "Biology after Stalin: A Case Study," *Survey* 23 (Winter 1977–1978): 53–80; Nils Roll-Hansen, "A New Perspective on Lysenko?" *Annals of Science* 42 (1985): 261–278; and Richard Lewontin and Richard Levings, "The Problem of Lysenkoism," in *The Radicalization of Science*, ed. H. Rose and S. Ross, (London: Macmillan, 1976), 32–64. A personal account by a Soviet geneticist is Raisa L. Berg, *Dust Storm* (in Russian) (New York: Chalidze, 1983).

3. The pioneer in this respect was Zhores A. Medvedev, whose samizdat manuscript on the subject was circulated in the 1960s. An abridged and revised version was later published in English: *The Rise and Fall of T. D. Lysenko* (New York: Columbia University Press, 1969). See also Roy A. Medvedev and Zhores A. Medvedev, *Khrushchev: The Years in Power*, trans. I. Michael Lerner (New York: Columbia University Press, 1976. A relevant work that was published in the Soviet Union is Semyon Reznik, *Nikolai Vavilov* (Moscow: Molodaya gvardiya, 1968).

4. Nils Roll-Hansen, "Genetics under Stalin" (book review), *Science* 227 (1985): 1329.

5. See, for example, Hannah Arendt, *The Origins of Totalitarianism* (New York: Harcourt, Brace & World, 1968), esp. part 3, "Totalitarianism."

1. "We All Came from the People"

Epigraph sources: 1 John, 2:19; T. D. Lysenko, "My Path into Science," *Pravda*, October 1, 1937.

1. Trofim Denisovich Lysenko, *Materials for the Bibliography of Scientists of the USSR*, Biology Series, Agrobiology, 1st ed. (Moscow: USSR Academy of Sciences, 1953), 3.

2. *Short Encyclopedic Dictionary* (Maly entsiklopedichesky slovar) (St. Petersburg: Brokhauz-Efron, 1902), 3:1591, s.v. "Uman."

3. Tikhon Kholodny, "Academician T. D. Lysenko," *NW*, 1938, no. 7:192.

4. Trofim Denisovich Lysenko, 3, 6.

5. T. D. Lysenko, "Technique and Methodology for Selection of Tomatoes at the Belaya Tserkov Selection Station," *Bulletin of the Selection and Seed-Growing Administration* (Byulleten Sorto-semenovodcheskogo upravlenia), 1923, no. 4:72–76; T. D. Lysenko and A. S. Okonenko, "Grafting of Sugar Beets," ibid., 77–80.

6. Personal communication from I. Ye. Glushchenko.

7. T. D. Lysenko, "My Path into Science," *Pravda*, October 1, 1937, 4.

8. T. D. Lysenko, "The Effect of the Thermal Factor on the Length of the Phases of Development of Plants: An Experiment with Cereals and Cotton," *Transactions of the Ordzhonikidze Azerbaidzhan Central Experimental Selection Station* (Trudy Azerbaidzhanskoi tsentralnoi opytno-selektsionnoi stantsii im. tov. Ordzhonikidze), no. 3 (Baku, 1928). This work was reprinted in a collection of Lysenko's writings, *The Stage Development of Plants* (Stadiinoye razvitiye rastenii) (Moscow: Selkhozgiz, 1952), 5–189 (see p. 15).

9. Vit. Fyodorovich, "The Winter Fields," *Pravda*, August 7, 1927, 5.

10. Lysenko, "Effect of the Thermal Factor."

11. Lysenko, *Stage Development of Plants*, 188.

12. In Soviet literature, especially after 1948, the "pioneering" work of Lysenko was described thousands of times. In Western literature, see Medvedev, *Rise and Fall of T. D. Lysenko*, and Joravsky, *The Lysenko Affair*. See also Roll-Hansen, "Genetics under Stalin," 1329.

13. G. Gassner, "Beobachtungen und Versuche Über den Anbau die Entwicklung von Getreidepflanzen im Subtropischen Klimat," *Jahresbuch Vereinigung für Angewandte Botanik* 8 (1920): 95–163; G. Gassner, "Beitrage zur physiologischen Charakteristik Sommer und Winterannular Gewächse, ins besondere der Getreidepflanzen," *Zeitschrift für Botanik* 10 (1918): 417–430; W. W. Garner and H. A. Allard, "Effect of the Relative Length of Day and Night and Other Factors on Growth and Reproduction in Plants," *Journal of Agricultural Research* 18 (1920): 553–606.

14. Ye. I. Grachev, in *Farming Gazette* (Zemledelcheskaya gazeta), no. 12, October 10, 1874; A. D. Murinov, "Spike Formation in Winter Rye and Wheat after a Spring Planting," *Journal of Experimental Agrochemistry* (Zhurnal opytnoi agrokhimii) 14 (1913): 238–254; A. D. Murinov, "Biology of Winter Cereals: Spike Formation of Winter Rye and Wheat after a Spring Planting," in *Results of Vegetative Experiments and Laboratory Work of the Moscow Agricultural Institute* (Iz rezultatov vegetatsionnykh opytov i laboratornykh rabot Moskovskogo s.kh. instituta) 9 (1914): 167–252.

15. N. A. Maksimov and A. T. Poyarkova, "On the Physiological Nature of the Differences between Spring and Winter Races of Cereals," *Transactions in Applied Botany, Genetics, and Selection* (Trudy po prikladnoi botanike, genetike, i selektsii) 14, no. 1 (1924–1925): 211–234; B. A. Vakar, "On the Effect of Temperature on Spike Formation of Winter Rye and Wheat," *Journal of Scientific Agronomy* (Nauchno-agronomichesky zhurnal) 12 (1925): 776–785. See also the discussion of Grachev's work in Ya. Sukhanov, "Plant Designer," *Izvestia*, January 21, 1982, 6; and the survey of research in I. Vasilyev, "Vernalization of Grain and Leguminous Cultures," *SRA*, 1936, no. 12:128–150.

16. In 1858, the American plant physiologist J. H. Klippart wrote: "To convert winter wheat into spring wheat, nothing more is necessary than that the winter wheat should be allowed to germinate slightly in the fall or winter, but kept from vegetation by a low temperature or freezing, until it can be sown in the spring. This is usually done by soaking and sprouting the seed, and freezing it while in this state and keeping it frozen until the season for spring sowing has arrived." "An Essay on the Origin, Growth, Diseases, Varieties, etc., of the Wheat Plant," *Twelfth Annual Report of Ohio State Board of Agriculture, 1857* (Columbus, 1858), 757, as quoted in Medvedev, *T. D. Lysenko*, 154.

17. Vasilyev said flatly, in 1936, "All the facts established by Lysenko were previously known." "Vernalization of Grain and Leguminous Cultures," 133.

18. G. S. Zaitsev, *The Influence of Temperature on the Development of Cotton* (Vliyaniye temperatury na razvitiye khlopchatnika), Transactions of the Turkestan Selection Station, no. 7 (Moscow and Leningrad: Promizdat, 1926). This work was reprinted in the series *Library of Cotton Growing* (Biblioteka khlopkovogo dela), 1927, no. 7:5–68. See also G. S. Zaitsev, *Toward a Method of Evaluating Cotton Plantings* (K metodike otsenki khlopkovykh posevov), in his *Selected Works* (Moscow: Selkhozizdat, 1963).

19. Lysenko, *Stage Development of Plants*, 11.

20. Ibid., 16, 136, 142.

21. V. T. Batyrenko, "Expand More Broadly Confirming Experiments according to Lysenko's Method," *AG*, November 19, 1929, 3–4.

22. I. Vasilyev, "The Vernalization of Grain-Legume Crops," *SRA*, 1936, no. 12:133.

23. N. M. Tulaikov, "Vernalization of Winter Forms," *AG*, November 13, 1929, no. 212, 3.

24. T. D. Lysenko, "What Is the Essence of the Hypothesis of the 'Winter Nature' of Plants?" *AG*, December 7, 1929, 3. In this article, Lysenko made a point of noting that he was simultaneously a staff member of the Gandzha station and of the Odessa institute.

25. "The Influence of the Thermal Factor on the Phases of Plant Development and a Program of Research on This Question with Beets," *Transactions of the All-Union Conference on Problems of Scientific Agronomical Research in the Sugar Industry* (Materialy Vsesoyuznogo soveshchaniya po voprosam nauchno-issledovatelskoi agronomicheskoi raboty v sakharnoi promyshlennosti) (Moscow: Scientific and Technical Administration of the Supreme Council of the National Economy, 1929), 34–36.

26. *New Generation* (Smena), January 11, 1929, 3.

27. T. D. Lysenko and D. A. Dolgushin, "On the Essence of the Winter Crop," in *List of Reports and Theses of the National Congress on Genetics, Selection, Seed Growing, and Animal Husbandry, Leningrad, January 10–16, 1929* (Spisok dokladov i tezisy Vsesoyuznogo syezda po genetike, selektsii, semenovodstvu, i plemennomu zhivotnovodstvu v Leningrade, 10–16 yanvarya 1929 g.) (Leningrad: Organizational Bureau of the Conference, 1929), 131–132. The complete report appeared under the same title in the *Transactions* of the congress, vol. 3 (Leningrad: Printing House of the Naval Forces of the Workers' and Peasants' Red Army, 1929), 189–199, and it was reprinted in Lysenko, *Stage Development of Plants*, 193–201.

28. [T. D.] Lysenko, "What Is the Essence of the Hypothesis of the 'Winter Nature' of Plants?" *AG*, December 7, 1929, 3, reprinted in Lysenko, *Stage Development of Plants*, 205.

29. *Leningrad Pravda*, January 16, 1929, 3.

30. A. F. Maurer, "In Memory of Gavriil Semyonovich Zaitsev (1887–1929)," *BJ* 43 (1958): 1771–1774.

31. *"Every cereal under certain conditions can be turned into a spring cereal. This has already been achieved in laboratory conditions.* Of course, these experiments cannot be transferred to field conditions. But undoubtedly extensive manipulation of greenhouse plants will be possible." *Leningrad Pravda*, January 16, 1929, p. 3 (emphasis in the original). The statement that "every cereal . . . can be turned into a spring cereal" is an exaggeration of what Maksimov had said; perhaps the reporters had been influenced by what Lysenko and Dolgushin had said, but the limited applicability of the method still reflected Maksimov's views.

32. V. L. Grigoryev, "Agronomist Lysenko's Discovery: Lysenko's Method Will Be Applied in Practice on the Sovkhozes and Kolkhozes of the Ukraine," *Pravda*, July 21, 1929, 4. Karlovka was actually only 1,400 kilometers from Gandzha, and to the northwest rather than to the north. See also "Agronomist Lysenko's Discovery," *EG*, August 4, 1929.

33. A. Shlikhter, "On Spring Planting of Winter Crops: Agronomist Lysenko's Discovery," *Pravda*, October 8, 1929, p. 3.

34. Lysenko's own account, published six years afterward, is utterly ambiguous on these points: "During the spring and summer of 1929 we continued our researches . . . at the selection station in Azerbaidzhan. . . . In the summer of that year our press (the newspapers) informed the Soviet public of a large-scale, complete maturation of spring-sown winter wheat under the practical agricultural conditions of the Ukraine. (This sowing was not accidental. It was conducted at my suggestion by my father, D. N. Lysenko, at his farm.)" He makes no mention of verification by the Commissariat of Agriculture but says merely: "This practical sowing confirmed the main conclusions of our research. . . . The Soviet public came to the support of our interpretation of the length of the vegetative period of plants." *The Theoretical Bases of Vernalization* (Teoreticheskiye osnovy yarovizatsii) (Moscow and Leningrad: State Publisher of Kolkhoz and Sovkhoz Literature, 1935), as reprinted in *Stage Development of Plants*, 343.

35. T. D. Lysenko, "A New Phase in Plant Physiology," *SA*, November 12, 1932, reprinted in *Stage Development of Plants*, 250; T. D. Lysenko, "Basic Results of Vernalization of Agricultural Plants," *BV*, 1932, no. 4:3. In 1938, on the occasion of Lysenko's election as a deputy to the Supreme Soviet, a biographical article about him put the sown area at one hectare: Kholodny, "Academician T. D. Lysenko," 193.

36. Lysenko, *Stage Development of Plants*, 336.

37. V. M. Molotov, "The Tasks of the Second Five-Year Plan," in *Seventeenth Congress of the All-Union Communist Party (b): Stenographic Report* (XVII syezd Vsesoyuznoi kommunisticheskoi partii (b): Stenograficheskey otchet) (Moscow: Partizdat, 1934), 360.

38. *Trofim Denisovich Lysenko*, 7.

39. T. D. Lysenko, "Vernalization Combined with Superior Agricultural Technology," *SA*, March 21, 1935, 3.

40. *Vern.*, 1936, no. 1 (4): 127.

41. T. D. Lysenko, "Do Not Distort the Theory of Vernalization," *SA*, December 26, 1934, reprinted in Lysenko, *Stage Development of Plants*, 327–329.

2. The Unrecognized Threat

Epigraph sources: I. I. Puzanov, *Shattering the Idols* (samizdat, 1960s); Anton Chekhov, letter to Aleksei Suvorin, August 1 (o.s.), 1892, from *Letters of Anton Chekhov*, trans. Michael H. Heim in collaboration with Simon Karlinsky (New York: Harper & Row, 1973).

1. T. D. Lysenko, "On the Matter of Regulation of the Vegetative Period of Agricultural Plants," *SA*, June 2, 1930, 2.

2. "Vernalization of Winter Varieties," *AG*, November 13, 1929, 3.

3. *AG*, November 19, 1929, 3–4.

4. Lysenko, "The 'Winter Nature' of Plants"; emphasis in the original.

5. As he wrote later, "Hundreds of kolkhoz experimenters were enlisted in the cause of managing the development of agricultural plants, and their projects were the basis for creating the technique of vernalization of winter and spring grains." T. D. Lysenko, "Vernalization," *Agricultural Encyclopedia* (Selskokhozyaistvennaya entsiklopedia), as reprinted in Lysenko, *Stage Development of Plants*, 455.

6. "A Preliminary Report about Vernalization of Wheat Sowings on Sovkhozes and Kolkhozes in 1932," *BV*, 1932, no. 2–3:3.

7. Lysenko must have known about these negative aspects. The journal *Bulletin of Vernalization*, which he edited, carried a number of articles about them; see, for example, E. E. Geshele, "The Fight against Fungal Diseases in Vernalization," and F. Nemliyenko, "Concerning the Fight against Blight in Vernalization of Wheat," 1932, no. 2–3:69–80 and 81–86. Lysenko himself said, in a speech at a meeting of the Scientific and Technical Council of the Combined Seed Growing Association in 1934, "More

than once we observed that 100 percent of plants that were altered by vernalization were infected by fungal diseases, while the controls, right next to them in the same field, were infection-free." "Physiology of Plant Development in Selection," *Seed-Growing* (Semenovodstvo), 1934, no. 2:20–31, as reprinted in *Stage Development of Plants*, 304. Characteristically, however, he claimed at the same time that in many other cases vernalized crops were *more* resistant to fungal diseases.

8. Lysenko, "What Is the Essence of the Hypothesis of the 'Winter Nature' of Plants?" *AG*, December 7, 1939, 3. No initials were given with the author's name.

9. J. V. Stalin, "On the Rightist Deviation in the Party," *Works* (Sochinenia), vol. 12 (Moscow: Gosudarstvennoye izdatelstvo politicheskoi literatury, 1949), 83.

10. *SA*, February 24, 1931, 3.

11. Lysenko, "Vernalization of Wheat Sowings," 3.

12. Ibid. The name of the journal was changed to *Vernalization* in 1935.

13. Vernalization of fruit trees was proposed at a conference of experimental fruit growers held in Michurinsk (formerly Kozlov) in 1934; see T. D. Lysenko, "Vernalization and Fruit Growing," *Fruit and Vegetable Growing* (Plodoovoshchnoye khozyaistvo), 1934, no. 11:50–51. During his visit to Michurinsk, Lysenko tried to establish a friendship with Michurin, who was much in favor with the country's political leaders (see chapter 5). However, according to a personal communication from the geneticist N. N. Sokolov, who at one time worked with Michurin, the latter disliked Lysenko and slammed the door in his face when Lysenko came to pay him a visit.

14. N. I. Vavilov, "New Directions in Research on Plant Breeding," *SA*, September 13, 1931, 2; emphasis in the original.

15. *SA*, September 13, 1931, 2.

16. Ibid., 3.

17. Ibid. The story of Narkom Yakovlev's support of Lysenko was described by Yury Dolgushin in his articles on Lysenko in the popular science journal *Znanie-Sila* [Knowledge is Power], 1938, no. 17: 12; 1938, no. 11: 7–9. See also his book *Lysenko* (Kiiv-Kharkiv, 1935), and an article by V. Safonov, "The Secret of Academician Lysenko," *Pioneer*, 1938, no. 8: 24–35.

18. Ibid.; emphasis in the original.

19. Ibid.

20. Ibid.

21. *BV*, 1932, no. 1:71–72.

22. T. D. Lysenko, "Warm-Climate Plants Can Be Vernalized as Well as Wheat," *SA*, November 1, 1931, 3.

23. T. D. Lysenko, "Vernalization and the Fight against Drought," *Izvestia*, October 29, 1931, 3.

24. Editorials in *Pravda*, October 30, 1931, 2, and *Izvestia*, October 29, 1931, 3. The words in capital letters were printed in boldface type as well.

25. Personal communication from N. V. Turbin, who was a participant in the conference.

26. A. I. Vorobyov, "Vernalization As a Method of Accelerating Grape Selection, *BV*, 1931, no. 2–3:65.

27. *Izvestia*, November 1, 1931, 2, and November 22, 1931, 3.

28. *Trofim Denisovich Lysenko*, 3.

3. Bluff after Bluff

Epigraph sources: Vladimir Solovyov, 1885; T. D. Lysenko, "Vernalization: A Powerful Means of Increasing the Harvest" (speech at a meeting in the Kremlin), *Pravda*, February 15, 1935, p. 2.

1. See, for example, *SA*, February 24, 1931, and September 13, 1932. Lysenko repeatedly presented these estimates at meetings of the collegium of the USSR Commissariat of Agriculture and of the Academy of Agricultural Sciences.

2. I. V. Stalin, "Report on the Work of the CC [Central Committee] of the ACP (B) [All-Union Communist Party (Bolshevik)] to the Seventeenth Party Congress," in *Stenographic Report on the Work of the Seventeenth Congress of the ACP (B), January 26–February 10, 1934* (Moscow: Partizdat, 1934), 19.

3. V. M. Molotov, "Report on the Second Five-Year Plan for the Development of the Economy of the USSR," in ibid., 360.

4. Ibid.

5. L. M. Kaganovich, "Speech at the Sixteenth Congress of the ACP (B)," in *Stenographic Report on the Sixteenth Congress of the ACP (b)* (Moscow and Leningrad: Moskovsky rabochii, 1931), 68.

6. Stalin, "Report . . . to the Seventeenth Party Congress," 23.

7. *Great Soviet Encyclopedia* (Bolshaya sovetskaya entsiklopedia), 3rd ed. (Moscow, 1976), 23:231.

8. *SA*, December 18, 1933, 3.

9. *Pravda*, July 9, 1929, 5.

10. *Pravda*, August 3, 1931, 3. Stalin himself was head of the Workers' and Peasants' Inspection for several years, and he effectively controlled the organ later as well, assigning to it the functions of a supragovernmental monitor (the Central Control Commission eventually was combined with the Workers' and Peasants' Inspection into one controlling organ). "Vitreousness" refers to a translucent, brittle appearance of the seed if the protein content in the endosperm is high; it is thus a visual indicator of food quality.

11. A. A. Sapegin, "The Use of X-Rays for Selection Purposes," *SA*, August 30, 1931, 3.

12. Personal communications, independently, from V. Sakharov, V. Efroimson, and A. Zhebrak.

13. Lysenko, "My Path into Science," 4.

14. D. A. Dolgushin, "The History of a Variety," *Vern.*, 1935, no. 3:13. The account of the work of this "team of researchers" that follows is drawn from Dolgushin's article, 13–48. It should be pointed out that Lysenko was not an academician at the time of these events.

15. Ibid., 23.

16. Ibid.

17. Ibid., 23–24.

18. Ibid., 25–26.

19. Ibid., 26.

20. Ibid., 35.

21. Ibid., 41–42.

22. Ibid., 42.

23. Ibid., 46.

24. *Vern.*, 1935, no. 1:3–4.

25. Ibid.

26. P. N. Konstantinov, "Making Vernalization More Precise," *Plant Breeding and Seed Growing*, 1937, no. 4:12–17; P. N. Konstantinov, P. I. Lisitsyn, and D. Kostov, "A Few Words about the Work of the Odessa Institute of Plant Breeding and Genetics," *Socialist Reconstruction of Agriculture*, 1936, no. 10; A. Sapegin, "On Chromosomes, Division, and Hybrid Vigor," ibid., 69–77; G. K. Meister, "Some Critical Remarks," in *Collection of Discussion Articles on Questions of Genetics and Plant Breeding* (Moscow: VASKhNIL, 1936), 48–54.

27. T. D. Lysenko, "The Organism and the Environment. Transcript of a Lecture Delivered at the Polytechnical Museum in Moscow, January 11, 1941" (Moscow: Selkhozgiz, 1941), 12.

28. Ibid., 13.

29. Ibid., 14, 18; T. D. Lysenko, "Potatoes in the Southern Districts of the USSR.

Discussion of Problems of the Third Five-Year Plan," *Pravda*, April 27, 1937. See also Lysenko, *Stage Development of Plants*, 602.

30. T. D. Lysenko, "The Kolkhoz Cottage-Laboratories: Creators of the New Agroscience," *Vern.*, 1937, no. 5, as reprinted in T. D. Lysenko, *Agrobiology*, 6th ed. (Moscow: Selkhozgiz, 1952), 204.

31. *Kommunist* (Ukraine), March 21, 1935; *SA*, March 26, April 28, July 8, July 30, October 9, and November 7, 1935; *Pravda*, June 25 and October 27, 1935; *Izvestia*, July 15 and September 15, 1935. See also *Kolkhoz Experimentation* (Kolkhoznoe opytnichestvo), 1935, no. 8:13–16, and *Kolkhoz Brigadier* (Kolkhozny brigadir), 1935, no. 22:3–6.

32. *BVASKhNIL*, 1935, no. 7:1–3, as quoted in Lysenko, *Stage Development of Plants*, 657.

33. Lysenko, "Potatoes in the Southern Districts of the USSR," as reprinted in *Stage Development of Plants*, 587.

34. Lysenko, "The Organism and the Environment," 6. The lecture was originally published as an article, "Theory of Vernalization of Plants and Degeneration of the Potato in the South," *Vern.*, 1935, no. 2:3–22.

4. Vavilov and Lysenko

Epigraph sources: Inna Lisnyanskaya, "Rains and Mirrors," *Poems* (Paris: YMCA Press, 1983); Lysenko, "My Path into Science," *Pravda*, October 1, 1937.

1. His father's surname was originally Ilyin but, for unknown reasons, he later changed it to Vavilov. This and other information about Vavilov's father is drawn from V. Keler, *Sergei Vavilov* (Moscow: Molodaya gvardiya, 1961), 15, 19, and F. Kh. Bakhteyev, *Nikolai Ivanovich Vavilov, 1887–1943* (Novosibirsk: Nauka, 1987), 22–23. Keler may have drawn some of his information from L. B. Levshin, *Sergei Ivanovich Vavilov* (Moscow: Nauka, 1977), 9–13.

2. Quoted in Keler, *Sergei Vavilov*, 15, 19.

3. N. Vavilov, "On the Origin of Cultivated Rye," *Transactions of the Bureau of Applied Botany* 10 , no. 7–10 (1917): 561–590.

4. T. I. Korotkova, *N. I. Vavilov in Saratov (1917–1921): Documentary Outlines* (Saratov: Privolzhskoye knizhnoye izdatelstvo, 1978), 12–14.

5. The idea of a homologous series of mutations was first described by the German geneticist E. Baur, whose work was translated into Russian as *Vvedeniye v eksperiment-alnoye ucheniye o nasledstvennosti* (Introduction to the Experimental Study of Heredity) (Moscow, 1911).

6. An English translation can be found in *Journal of Genetics* 12 (1922): 47–89.

7. Korotkova, *N. I. Vavilov in Saratov*, 89. Barulina was Vavilov's second wife, whom he married after divorcing his first wife, Yekaterina N. Sakharova, an agronomist.

8. *Pravda*, July 22, 1925, 6.

9. Ibid.

10. M. A. Popovsky, *We Must Hurry* (Nado speshit) (Moscow: Detskaya literatura, 1968), 97.

11. Ibid., 119–120.

12. Ibid., 139–141.

13. Ibid., 100.

14. T. Yakovleva, "A Taste of Charity," *Komsomol Pravda*, March 29, 1986, 4.

15. *Leningrad Pravda*, January 13, 1929, 2.

16. Geography and travel became—perhaps even more than botany—Vavilov's life passion. His son Yury has recounted (personal communication) that an enormous globe stood on the floor at their home and his father often sat in an armchair before it and tested Yury—who was not ten years old—by pointing to a country, sea, mountain range, or river and asking him to name it.

17. P. L. Kapitsa, *Experiment, Theory, and Practice* (Eksperiment, teoria, praktika) (Moscow: Nauka, 1987), 135.

18. N. I. Vavilov, *Theoretical Foundations of Plant Breeding* (Teoreticheskiye osnovy selektsii), 3 vols. (Moscow and Leningrad: Gosudarstvennoye izdatelstvo selskokhozyiastvennoi i kolkhoznoi literatury, 1935).

19. *Pravda*, May 1, 1929, 4; emphasis in the original.

20. Theodosius Dobzhansky, "N. I. Vavilov: A Martyr of Genetics, 1887–1942," *Journal of Heredity* 38 (August 1947): 229–230.

21. Popovsky, *We Must Hurry*, 182. Later, Popovsky gave a somewhat different assessment of Vavilov's conduct. He wrote: "Vavilov was also taken in by the mythology of his time. Soviet propaganda was full of the idea of the advantages of socialist agriculture, kolkhozes, and so forth, and [Vavilov], who was thoroughly familiar with world agriculture, easily gave in to the myth. In his works and speeches, even in completely intimate conversations, there is not the slightest opposition to the idea of the socialization of man in agriculture. At the beginning of the thirties, Vavilov became a kind of Ehrenburg of science, winning over Western public opinion to the Stalinist regime." M. A. Popovsky, "The Vavilov Affair (Chapters from a Book)," *Pamyat* (*Istorichesky Sbornik*), no. 2 (Moscow, 1974; Paris, 1979), 26. The comparison of Vavilov and Ehrenburg is unjustified, for it is far more likely that Vavilov's position was genuine.

22. *From the History of Biology* (Iz istorii biologii), vol. 2 (Moscow: Nauka, 1970), 180.

23. N. I. Vavilov, "Wheat in the USSR and Abroad," *Pravda*, October 28, 1935, 3.

24. Popovsky, *We Must Hurry*, 119–120.

25. Personal communication from Nikolai P. Dubinin, who was a speaker at the congress.

26. *New Generation*, January 22, 1929.

27. Mark A. Popovsky, "The One Thousand Days of Academician Vavilov," *Scope* (Prostor) (Alma-Ata), 1966, no. 7:4–27 and no. 8:98–118.

28. Zh. A. Medvedev, "At the Sources of the Genetics Discussion," *NW*, 1967, no. 4:226–234.

29. Popovsky, *The Affair of Academician Lysenko.*

30. Archives of VASKhNIL, 141, *svyazka* 17, *delo* 35, *list* 18, p. 16.

31. Vavilov to Eikhfeld, November 11, 1931, Leningrad State Archives of the October Revolution and Socialist Construction, *fond* of VIR, no. 9708, *delo* 409, *list* 155, p. 16 (hereafter cited as Archives of the October Revolution).

32. Vavilov to Lysenko, ibid.

33. Vavilov to Kovalev, Archives of the October Revolution, *fond* of the VIR, *delo* 469, *list* 24225.

34. *Scientific Monthly* (July 1949): 367.

35. O. Munerati, "Il pre-tratiamento della sementi secondo in metodo del dott. Lyssenko," *Giornale di agricultura della domenica* 43 (1933): 263.

36. N. I. Vavilov, "In North and South America (From a Report on an Overseas Trip)," *Izvestia*, March 29, 1933, 2.

37. Vavilov to A. A. Bogomolets, president of the Ukrainian Academy of Sciences, Archives of the October Revolution, *fond* of the VIR, *delo* 673, *list* 3.

38. P. Yakhtenfeld, "On the Road to Vernalized Cotton," *SA*, December 20, 1933, 3.

39. A. Savchenko-Belsky, "Move Vernalization Forward to the Masses," *SA*, December 10, 1933, 2.

40. Ibid.

41. Ibid.; emphasis in the original.

42. Quoted in A. P. Basova et al., "The Problem of the Vegetative Period in Plant Breeding," in Vavilov, *Theoretical Foundations of Plant Breeding*, 1:865.

43. Lysenko, "Physiology of Plant Development in Plant Breeding," 20–21 (also in Lysenko, *Stage Development of Plants*, 304). See also Lysenko, "Vernalization of Agricultural Plants," 3–5 (*Stage Development of Plants*, 27–271).

44. Basova et al., "Vegetative Period in Plant Breeding."

45. Archives of the Academy of Sciences of the USSR (Leningrad branch), *fond* 803, *opis* 1, *delo* 73.

46. Archives of VASKhNIL, *opis* 450, *list* 192, *delo* 3.

47. Archives of the October Revolution, *fond* of the VIR, no. 9708, *delo* 520, *list* 12. See also N. P. Dubinin, *Perpetual Motion* (Vechnoye dvizheniye) (Moscow: Gospolitizdat, 1973), 163.

48. Ibid., *list* 28.

49. Archives of VASKhNIL, *opis* 450, *svyazka* 196, *delo* 43, *list* 21.

50. The debate over the degree of Vavilov's help to Lysenko has a curious behind-the-scenes dimension. In 1967 I wrote a letter to *Novy Mir*, pointing out that Popovsky's views were much better substantiated than Medvedev's. The editors refused to publish it. I had asked Dubinin—with whom I was then working—to cosign the letter, in the hope that the name of an academician would carry some weight. Dubinin agreed at first, but then kept the letter a long time and in the end did not sign. But several years later, I was startled to see the text of the letter published verbatim in his memoirs, as his own! Dubinin, *Perpetual Motion*, 163–164.

51. *Stenographic Report on the Work of the Seventeenth Congress of the ACP (b)*, 155.

52. It is noteworthy that, under Sapegin, the institute had been called the Institute of Genetics and Plant Breeding, but when Lysenko was in charge, the word "genetics" was for a time omitted. Later, with the introduction of "Michurinist" genetics (see chapter 4), the institute began to call itself the Plant-Breeding-Genetics Institute.

53. *Vernalization of Agricultural Plants* (in Ukrainian) (Kharkov: Derzhsilgospvidav, 1932); *Vernalization and the Budding of Potatoes* (Yarovizatsia i glazkovaniye kartofelya) (Kharkov: Derzhsilgospvidav, 1933); "Instructions for the Vernalization of Spring Durum Wheats," *Vernalization Bulletin*, 1932, no. 1:62–70; *A Brief Instruction for the Vernalization of Cotton* (Odessa: Lenin Typography, 1933); "Physiology of the Development of Plants in the Work of Plant Breeding," *Semenovodstvo*, 1934, no. 2:20–31; speech in *Plant Breeding in the Service of the Socialist State. Transactions of the All-Ukrainian Conference on Plant Breeding (September 17–20, 1931)* (in Ukrainian) (Kharkov: Derzhsilgospvidav, 1932), 54–55.

54. A. Shaikhet, "The Ukrainian Institute of Plant Breeding," *Construction of Machine-Tractor Stations and State Farms* (Na stroike MTS i sovkhozov), 1934, no. 4:10–24.

5. 1935: The Year of Triumph

Epigraph sources: Goethe, *Faust*, Part One; K. Popper, *Logic and the Growth of Scientific Knowledge*.

1. The speech, and the audience's and Stalin's reactions to it, are in T. D. Lysenko, "Vernalization: A Powerful Method for Increasing Yields. Discussion of the Report of Comrade Ya. A. Yakovlev at the Second All-Union Congress of Kolkhoz Shock Workers," *Pravda*, February 15, 1935, 2.

2. The complete speech was published in a brochure: *T. D. Lysenko et al., Agricultural Science and Kolkhoz Experimentation. The Second All-Union Congress of Kolkhoz Shock Workers* (Selskokhozyaistvennaya nauka i kolkhoznoye opytnichestvo. Vtoroi Vsesoyuzny syezd kolkhoznikov-udarnikov) (Moscow: Ogiz-Selkhozgiz, 1935), 14–15.

3. See, for example, Loren Graham, *Science and Philosophy in the Soviet Union* (New York: Knopf, 1972), 209.

4. Ye. V. Ryzhkova, "Academician Isai Izrailevich Prezent," *LSUH*, 1948, no. 10:90–101. See also *The Scientific Staff of Leningrad*, vol. 5 of *Science and the Scientific Staff of the USSR* (USSR Academy of Sciences, 1934), 995.

5. *Scientific Workers of Leningrad* (Nauchnye rabotniki Leningrada), part 5 of *Science and Scientific Workers of the USSR*, part 5, ed. Oldenburg (Leningrad: AN SSSR, 1934), 295. The Communist Academy had been founded in 1918 as the Socialist Academy of the Social Sciences. In 1919, its name was changed to Socialist Academy and in 1924 to

Communist Academy. In 1936, it was incorporated into the AN SSSR and ceased to exist as a separate unit.

6. I. I. Prezent, *The Theory of Darwinism in the Light of Dialectical Materialism* (Leningrad: Leningrad Branch of the Communist Academy, 1932); "Against the Extremely Harmful 'Philosophy of Agronomy,'" *UBM*, 1934, no. 3:202. Several speeches of Prezent's were also published.

7. D. R. Weiner, "Community Ecology in Stalin's Russia: 'Socialist' and 'Bourgeois' Science," *Isis* 75 (December 1984): 684–696.

8. *I. I. Prezent, The Class Struggle on the Natural-Science Front* (Klassovaya borba na yestestvenno-nauchnom fronte) (Moscow and Leningrad: Gosuchpedgiz, 1932), 63.

9. Personal communication from N. V. Turbin, full member (academician) of VASKhNIL and the Belorussian Academy of Sciences.

10. *Pravda,* January 2, 1936, 3.

11. "We need . . . not simply to speak of mutations and the laws of heredity, but, in studying these laws, to clarify how they serve or should serve our construction." Prezent, "Class Struggle," 70. In an article published in 1935, though written earlier, Prezent referred to Weismann, Mendel, and Morgan as scientific geniuses; see Dubinin, *Perpetual Motion*, 159.

12. See, for example, I. I. Prezent, "Statement in the Discussion 'The Basic Aims and the Path of Development of Soviet Ecology,'" *SB*, 1934, no. 3:52–63.

13. Personal communication from Vladimir Efroimson.

14. A. N. Bakharev, ed., *I. V. Michurin: Collected Works*, 4 vols., 2d ed. (Moscow: Selkhozgiz, 1948), 1:1–108.

15. Personal communication from D. V. Lebedev. Lebedev was a colleague of Baranov's at the Botanical Institute of the AN SSSR; he had worked with Vavilov and Karpechenko as a postdoctoral student in plant genetics and later became an editor of the *Botanical Journal.* He was a strong critic of Lysenko. He once explained to me that he survived both World War II (as an army officer) and the Lysenko years only because of his "hybrid vigor as the offspring of a Russian father and a Jewish mother!" He is now a scholar at the St. Petersburg branch of the Institute of the History of Natural Sciences and Technology.

16. A. I. Revenkova, *Nikolai Ivanovich Vavilov, 1887–1943* (Moscow: Izdatelstvo selskokhozyaistvennoi literatury, 1962). Like his mother and his brother Sergei, N. I. Vavilov generally slept only four or five hours a night, and Stalin's invitation could hardly have disturbed him, especially since everyone in the country knew that Stalin worked at night. Commissariats, regional Party committees, and other organizations adjusted to this schedule of work, and hardly anyone, even Vavilov, could turn down an invitation to visit the all-powerful leader. These details do cast doubt on the accuracy of Revenkova's account.

17. *Decree of the Council of People's Commissars,* June 4, 1935, no. 1114.

18. T. D. Lysenko, "On the Reconstruction of Seed-Growing," *Vern.*, 1935, no. 1:51. For other examples of Lysenko's misuse of scientific terms, see his "First Results," *Vern.*, 1936, no. 5 (2): 3–14; "On Two Trends in Genetics," *Vern.*, 1937, no. 1 (10): 29–75.

19. "Resolution of the Concluding Session on Grain Cultivation of the Lenin All-Union Academy of Agricultural Sciences (June 1935, Odessa)," *BVASKhNIL*, 1935, no. 8:15–16.

20. *Vern.*, 1936, no. 2–3:96.

21. See *Pravda,* September 8 and 9 and October 3–8 and 12, 1935.

22. "Speech of the President of the Academy Comrade A. I. Muralov at the Opening Session of ALAAS," *SA*, October 29, 1935, 1–2.

23. "Statement of the President of the Lenin Academy of Agricultural Sciences A. I. Muralov, 'Closer to Practice, to Production!'" *SA*, November 1, 1935, 2.

24. T. D. Lysenko, "From the Materials of the First Session of the All-Union Lenin

Academy of Agricultural Sciences," *BVASKhNIL*, 1935, no. 7:1–3. See also Lysenko, *Stage Development of Plants*, 657.

25. Lysenko, "From the Materials of the First Session," 1.

26. Ibid., 3.

27. Dolgushin, "History of a Variety," 3.

28. Editorial, "Reception of Workers in the Agricultural Sciences at the Sovnarkom of the USSR," *SA*, December 9, 1935, 1.

29. Editorial, "Make Closer the Tie between Agricultural Science and Practice!" *SA*, December 18, 1935, 1.

30. Vavilov, *Theoretical Foundations of Plant Breeding*, 1:xv.

31. N. I. Vavilov, "Plant Breeding as a Science," in ibid., 10, 12.

32. N. I. Vavilov, "The Botanico-Geographical Bases of Plant Breeding," in ibid., 72. Sapegin devoted his chapter entirely to vernalization: "The Significance of Vernalization for Plant Breeding," in ibid., 807–814. Other contributors also wrote about Lysenko's work; see V. S. Fyodorov and I. M. Yeremeyeva, "Intraspecific Hybridization," 388–389, and L. I. Govorov, "A Plant-Breeding Program for Drought Resistance," 837–838. Basova and her colleagues, in their contribution, "The Problem of the Vegetative Period in Plant Breeding," wrote (865), "Only T. D. Lysenko, in his theory of plant development by stages (vernalization), has essentially found the most correct way to resolve the problem of the vegetative period." In all, Lysenko's name was mentioned 29 times in this first volume, competing with Darwin (27 citations) and Vavilov (55).

33. N. I. Vavilov, "Speech at the Meeting of Outstanding Grain-Yield Achievers, Tractor Drivers, and Threshing-Machine Workers with Leaders of the Party and Government, Delivered on December 29, 1935," *Pravda*, January 2, 1936, p. 2. Despite what Vavilov said, the crossing of "dissimilar, geographically distant, seemingly not very suitable varieties" had long been common practice in hybridization.

34. By contrast, when Pryanishnikov spoke, he did not utter any of the stock phrases or offer toasts to Stalin or the Communist Party.

35. Lysenko, "Vernalization."

36. Quoted here from the speech as reproduced in Lysenko, *Stage Development of Plants*, 699.

37. Ibid.

38. Ibid., 700.

39. Ya. A. Yakovlev, "In the Battle for a Stalinist 7–8 Billion Poods of Grain!" *Pravda*, January 4, 1936, p. 3.

40. *Pravda*, January 4, 1936, p. 3.

41. *Pravda*, January 3, 1936, p. 1.

6. Confrontation with the Geneticists

Epigraph sources: Semyon Lipkin, *A Nomadic Fire*; Claude-Adrien Helvetius, *On the Mind*.

1. See, for example, his speech of December 1935, in Lysenko, *Stage Development of Plants*, 645–650.

2. Lysenko himself made some uncharacteristically cautious interpretations of the data; see his "Vernalization of Wheat Sowings." Actually, the tables of data accompanying this article—all of them based on scattered questionnaire returns—show that even these cautious interpretations were exaggerations; taking into account the nature of the data, it is clear that vernalization had produced no net increase of yields.

3. Ibid., 3.

4. Ibid., 3–4.

5. Sapegin, "The Significance of Vernalization for Phytoselection," 812.

6. P. N. Konstantinov, P. I. Lisitsyn, and D. Kostov, "Some Remarks about the Work of the Odessa Institute of Plant Breeding and Genetics," *SRA*, 1936, no. 10, reprinted in

Vern., 1936, no. 5:15–29. See also P. N. Konstantinov, "Making Vernalization More Precise," *Plant Breeding and Seed Production*, 1937, no. 4:12–17.

7. *Vern.*, 1936, no. 1(4): 118.

8. Lysenko, "Vernalization of Wheat Sowings," 5–6.

9. Konstantinov, Lisitsyn, and Kostov, "The Work of the Odessa Institute," 16, 18, 29.

10. *Vern.*, 1936, no. 1 (4): 121. The resolution also pointed out that in the Donetsk region a mere 4.3 percent of the land had been sown with vernalized seed.

11. Lysenko, "Speech at the Meeting of Outstanding Grain-Yield Achievers," 3.

12. T. D. Lysenko, "On the Level of the Epoch," *Cottage-Laboratory*, 1936, no. 2:7–11; Science Collective of the Odessa Institute of Plant Breeding and Genetics, "Competition among the Workers in Agricultural Science," *Pravda*, April 26, 1936, p. 3; T. D. Lysenko, "Five Central Questions: On the Unity of Science and Practice and the Work of the Hut-Laboratories," *SA*, March 6, 1936.

13. Science Collective of the Odessa Institute, "Competition among the Workers in Agricultural Science."

14. T. D. Lysenko, "First Results," *Izvestia*, October 12, 1936, p. 3; also in *Vern.*, 1935, no. 5 (8): 5.

15. Ibid.; emphasis in the original.

16. T. D. Lysenko, "The Role of Agricultural Science in the Solution of the Yield Problem," *Science and Technology Front* (Front nauki i tekhniki), 1936, no. 2:60–61.

17. Lysenko, "Speech at the Meeting of Outstanding Grain-Yield Achievers," 3.

18. T. D. Lysenko, "On the Intravarietal Crossing of Plants by Self-Pollination," *Plant Breeding and Seed Production*, 1936, no. 11:13.

19. Ibid.

20. Personal communication from Yakov M. Varshavsky. A similar instance of Lysenko's tactics has been told to me by the writer F. F. Shakhmagonov. Stalin and the well-known author and Nobel Prize winner Mikhail M. Sholokhov, for whom Shakhmagonov worked as secretary, were taking a walk at Stalin's dacha in Kuntsevo, outside Moscow, when Stalin said: "What a fine fellow Lysenko is, and how well he knows nature. He and I were walking along this same road in the autumn when before our eyes a tomato fell from a bush. 'Look, Comrade Stalin,' Lysenko said to me, 'if this tomato is left untouched, then throughout the entire autumn and winter its pulp will nourish its seed, stored inside the fruit, and then in the spring this seed, having fed off the fruit, will come forth and a new tomato plant will grow up.' I ordered that this fallen tomato not be touched, and in the spring the seed sprouted, and a plant grew up. There are not many who understand nature so well," Stalin concluded. Sholokhov, who was of peasant origin himself and still lived in the countryside, said he was disgusted by this primitive "understanding" of nature, familiar to any peasant, that so amazed Stalin.

21. Konstantinov, Lisitsyn, and Kostov, "The Work of the Odessa Institute," 128.

22. Lysenko, "Five Central Questions," 3.

23. Lysenko, *Stage Development of Plants*, 704.

24. Lysenko, "Kolkhoz Cottage-Laboratories," 18.

25. T. D. Lysenko, "The Cultivation of Seed Potatoes in the Conditions of the Southern USSR," in Lysenko, *Stage Development of Plants*, 599.

26. *Izvestia*, February 3, 1937. The resolution was entitled "On Summer Plantings of Potatoes According to the Method of Academician T. D. Lysenko."

27. T. D. Lysenko, "On Summer Planting of Potatoes," *SA*, April 6, 1938, p. 3; see also Lysenko, *Stage Development of Plants*, 606.

28. Ibid.

29. T. D. Lysenko, *Agrobiology*, 6th ed. (Moscow: Selkhozgiz, 1952), 529.

30. Ibid., 528–529.

31. The practice of summer planting of potatoes was subjected to severe criticism by

G. N. Linnik, "On the Reasons for the Degeneration of Potatoes," *BJ*, 40 (1955): 528–541. The article concluded that "the effort to mindlessly increase summer plantings in the entire southern Ukraine without regard to moisture conditions has brought only harm." Linnik was on the staff of the Dokuchayev Agricultural Institute in Kharkov.

32. T. D. Lysenko and I. I. Prezent, "The Stakhanovite Movement and the Tasks of Soviet Agrobiology," *Vern.*, 1935, no. 3:3–12.

33. *Pravda*, October 13, 1935, p. 1.

34. Personal communication from I. E. Glushchenko.

35. T. D. Lysenko, "On the Intravarietal Crossing of Plants by Self-Pollination," *SRA*, 1936, no. 10, as reprinted in T. D. Lysenko, *The Biology of Plant Development* (Kiev and Kharkov: Gosudarstvennoye izdatelstvo kolkhoznoi i sovkhoznoi literatury, 1940), 107, 105. Lysenko's allusion to Vavilov's "example of flax" is not clear. I have been unable to find evidence of any experiment of Vavilov's to which this accusation of a fabricated result might apply.

36. See the following articles in *SRA* for 1936: A. Sapegin, "On Chromosomes, Division, and Hybrid Vigor," no 10:69–77; A. Zhebrak, "The Categories of Genetics in the Light of Dialectical Materialism," no. 12:78–88; B. Vakar, "On the Degeneration of Varieties as a Function of Self-Pollination," no. 12:113–127; L. Delone, "Does 'Formal Genetics' Do Anything for Practice in the Study of New Varieties?" no. 12:59–68; and P. Yakovlev, "On the Theories of the 'Real' Geneticists," no. 12:47–58. Also among these articles was Konstantinov, Lisitsyn, and Kostov, "The Work of the Odessa Institute."

37. Archives of the *VASKhNIL, opis* 450, *delo* 59, session of December 25, 1936.

38. *Pravda*, December 26, 1936, p. 2.

39. Konstantinov, Lisitsyn, and Kostov, "The Work of the Odessa Institute." Konstantinov's opponent at this meeting was one of his former students, Andrei G. Utekhin, who subsequently attacked his teacher in a number of other forums.

40. G. K. Meister, "Some Critical Notes," in *Collected Discussion Articles on Problems of Genetics and Plant Breeding* (Moscow: VASKhNIL, 1936), 48, 53. Lysenko's article, "Revival of Varieties," appeared in *SA*, 1935, June 25, no. 173:2–3.

41. M. M. Zavadovsky, "Genetics, Its Achievements and Wanderings" and "Against Exaggerations in Attacks on Genetics," in *Collected Discussion Articles on Problems of Genetics and Plant Breeding*, 93, 109.

42. N. I. Vavilov, "Concluding Word," in *Controversial Problems of Genetics and Plant Breeding: The Work of the IV Session of the VASKhNIL, December 19–24, 1936* (Moscow and Leningrad: Selkhozgiz, 1936), 473.

43. B. M. Zavadovsky, "For Reconstruction of Genetic Science," *UBM*, 1937, no. 2:119–133.

44. N. P. Dubinin, "Address at the IV Session of the *VASKhNIL*," in *Controversial Problems of Genetics and Plant Breeding*, 335.

45. Dubinin, *Perpetual Motion*, 167.

46. Ibid.

47. I. I Prezent, "Against Formalism and Metaphysics in Genetic Science: Report at the IV Session of the *VASKhNIL*," *Vern.*, 1937, no. 1:86, 102.

48. D. A. Dolgushin, "Address at the IV Session of *VASKhNIL*," in *Controversial Problems of Genetics and Plant Breeding*, 264–265.

49. T. D. Lysenko, "On the Two Tendencies in Genetics: Report at the IV Session of the *VASKhNIL*, December 23, 1936," *Vern.*, 30, 41–42, 63–64.

50. T. D. Lysenko, "Concerning Academician G. K. Meister's Article 'Some Critical Notes,'" in *Collected Discussion Articles on Problems of Genetics and Plant Breeding*, 55–68.

51. Lysenko, "On the Two Tendencies in Genetics, 71.

52. Ibid., 104. Lysenko claimed to have changed spring barley into a winter form at his institute, but this claim was later persuasively discredited; see F. Kh. Bakhteyev, "The Documentary History of One 'Transformation,'" *BJ* 42 (1957): 133–135.

53. Lysenko, "On the Two Tendencies of Genetics," 74.

54. From a speech by Aleksandra Prokofyeva-Belgovskaya at a meeting of the USSR Society of Geneticists and Breeders.

55. Quoted in Dubinin, *Perpetual Motion*, 167.

56. Lysenko, "On the Two Tendencies of Genetics," 71–72.

57. T. D. Lysenko, "Concluding Remarks," *Vern.*, 1937, no. 1:66.

58. *Pravda*, December 29, 1936, p. 3; also in G. K. Meister, "Concluding Remarks," in *Controversial Problems of Genetics and Plant Breeding.*

59. *Izvestia*, December 24, 1936; *Sovkhoz Gazette* (Sovkhoznaya gazeta), December 24, 1936; *SA*, December 24, 1936. See also *Pravda*, December 26, 1936.

60. *From the History of Biology* 2:187.

7. Agricultural Science by Terror

Epigraph sources: Maximilian Voloshin, *Magic*, 1923; Robert Conquest, *The Great Terror* (New York: Macmillan, 1973).

1. "On the Contingents and Plans of Study of Graduate Students at the *VASKhNIL*," *SA*, December 5, 1933, p. 3.

2. *Vern.*, 1937, no. 5.

3. A. Musiiko, "Artificial Pollination," *Kolkhoz Experimentation* (Kolkhoznoye opytnichestvo), 1938, no. 4:24.

4. T. M. Belyayev, "Talents and Gifted People," *Vern.*, 1937, no. 5:54.

5. As quoted in ibid., 55.

6. T. S. Maltsev, "To Science through Experience," *Vern.*, 1937, no. 5:43.

7. Ibid., 42–43.

8. Belyayev, "Talents and Gifted People," 56. See also the enthusiastic report by V. Ippolitov, "The Path to Science: The Results of the Ukrainian Gathering of Directors of Cottage-Laboratories," *SA*, November 17, 1937, p. 3.

9. T. Maltsev, "A Dream and a True Story," in the brochure *The Great Happiness of Living in the Stalinist Epoch* (Moscow: Profizdat, 1950), 64, 66.

10. N. M. Tulaikov, *On Soils: Conversations about Agriculture* (O pochvakh: Selskokhozyaistvennye besedy), 6th ed. (Moscow, 1922); *Problems of Fallow Fields and Crop Rotation in Wheat Farming* (Problemy zalezhi i sevooborota v pshenichnom khozyaistve) (Moscow and Leningrad: Selkhozgiz, 1930); *The Struggle with Drought in Grain Farming* (Borba s zasukhoi v zernovom khozyaistve) (Moscow: Academy of Sciences, 1933); *Grain Farming by Irrigation in the Transvolga* (Oroshayemoye zernovoye khozyaistvo Zavolzhya) (Leningrad, 1934); and *Principles of Construction in the Agrotechnology of Socialist Agriculture* (Osnovy postroyenia agrotekhniki sotsialisticheskogo zemledelia) (Moscow: Selkhozgiz, 1936). See also *Rural Life* (Selskaya zhizn), January 6, 1962, and Tulaikov's *Selected Works* (Izbrannye proizvedenia), published posthumously after his rehabilitation (Moscow: Selkhozgiz, 1963).

11. For example, in October 1931 alone, *Pravda* published an article by him (October 27, p. 2) and two excerpts from his speeches (October 28 and 30).

12. Lysenko, "Academician Konstantinov."

13. V. N. Stoletov, "Against Alien Theories in Agronomy," *Pravda*, April 11, 1937, p. 2.

14. "Destroy Completely the Alien Trend in Agronomy," *Communist* (Saratov), April 18, 1937, p. 2.

15. M. Larionov, "The Saratov Hotbed of Alien Theories," *BVASKhNIL*, 1937, no. 6:53–59.

16. N. Dmitriyev, V. Minayev, and D. Krinitsky, "Clarity Is Needed in the Position of the Academy of Agricultural Sciences (On the Mistakes of Academician Tulaikov)," *SA*, July 4, 1937, p. 2; M. Abrosimov, "The Erroneous 'Theories' of Agrotechnology and Sabotage on the State Grain Farms," *SRA*, 1937, no. 7:80–93.

17. Personal communication from D. V. Lebedev.

18. *Plenary Session of the CC of the CPSU, December 15–19, 1958: Stenographic Report* (Moscow: Gospolitizdat, 1958), 323. Brezhnev acknowledged the value of Tulaikov's ideas—without mentioning his name—at the 1981 Plenary Session of the Central Committee and at the Twenty-fifth Party Congress.

19. All of these accounts are in Pavel Penezhko, "A Shaft of Memory," *Soviet Russia,* September 21, 1986, p. 4.

20. *Pravda,* April 28, 1936, p. 3.

21. Ya. A. Yakovlev, *Deputies of the Extraordinary VIII Congress of the USSR: Report of the Chairman of the Mandate Commission* (Moscow: Partizdat, 1936), p. 22; *Pravda,* December 2, 1936, p. 1.

22. *SA,* October 29, 1937, p. 1.

23. *Pravda,* January 13, 1938, p. 1.

24. *Pravda,* August 3, 1940, p. 1.

25. *Izvestia,* December 31, 1935, p. 1.

26. Konstantin Fedin, "Happiness Is Being Young," *Pravda,* January 27, 1938, p. 4.

8. Lysenko Singles Out Vavilov and Koltsov

Epigraph sources: O. Mandelshtam, *Collected Works,* 2nd ed., ed. G. P. Struve and B. A. Filippov (Washington: Inter-Language Associates, 1967), 1:286; L. N. Tolstoy, *War and Peace.*

1. I learned of the existence of this card file from Lysenko's former personal secretary in 1966. She had just come to Dubinin's Institute of General Genetics, which had been recently created to replace Lysenko's Genetics Institute after his downfall. Dubinin had been required to take her on along with Lysenko's other former staff members. When, on her first day at work, she came by my laboratory to introduce herself, she asked if I was the Soyfer who had published articles in the 1950s and 1960s in scientific journals. I asked her how she knew about this, and she told me that, at Lysenko's request, she had systematically scanned the scientific literature and recorded the names and any anti-Lysenko views of the authors. The file had, she said, two or three thousand names in it.

2. Ya. A. Yakovlev, "On Several Tasks of the Agricultural Publishing House," *Vern.,* 1937, no. 2:11.

3. See especially V. I. Lenin, *Materialism and Empiriocriticism* (Moscow: Zveno, 1909), in *Collected Works,* vol. 14, Politizdat, 1947, 5–357.. I have discussed the effect that Lenin's categorization of disciplines had on Soviet science in "'They were experts in everything. And in chemical valency, too,'" *Rossiyskaya Gazeta,* July 29, 1992, p. 2.

4. Yakovlev, "Tasks of the Agricultural Publishing House," 13, 14, 16.

5. I. I. Prezent, "Soviet Agrobiology Is on the Level of the Method of Dialectical Materialism," *Vern.,* 1937, no. 3:49–66; quotations from 63–64. The Stalin speech published in this issue (3–36) was entitled "On the Shortcomings of Party Work and Measures for the Liquidation of Trotskyites and Other Double-Dealers." Prezent's use of the "Trotskyite" label echoed Stalin's use of it in this speech. The Uranovsky whom Prezent mentioned had been a colleague of Prezent's at Leningrad University and had publicly charged him with sexual misconduct with women students (personal communication from Professor Lobashev, who was on the university's faculty at that time).

6. N. Koltsov, "The Physico-Chemical Bases of Morphology," *Achievements of Experimental Biology,* series B, vol. 7, no. 1 (1928): 3–31. "[Kolstoff was] brilliant . . . the best Russian zoologist of the last generation, and an amiable, unbelievably cultured and clear thinking scholar, admired by everybody who knew him" (Richard B. Goldschmidt, *The Golden Age of Zoology: Portraits from Memory,* Seattle: University of Washington Press, 1956, 106).

On Koltsov see also M. B. Adams, "Science, Ideology, and Structure: The Kol'tzov Institute, 1900–1970," in *The Social Context of Soviet Science,* ed. Linda Lubrano and Susan

Solomon (Boulder, Colo.: Westview, 1980), 173–204; M. B. Adams, "Sergei Chetverikov, the Kol'tsov Institute and the Evolutionary Synthesis," in *The Evolutionary Synthesis*, ed. Ernst Mayr and William Provine (Cambridge, Mass.: Harvard University Press, 1980), 242–278.

7. B. L. Astaurov and P. F. Rokitsky, *Nikolai Konstantinovich Koltsov* (Moscow: Nauka, 1975), 132.

8. This account was given to me by Chetverikov himself. In 1926 Sergei S. Chetverikov had laid the foundations for the new discipline of population genetics in his genetics laboratory in Koltsov's institute. His students, N. V. Timofeyev-Ressovsky, B. L. Astaurov, P. F. Rokitsky, D. D. Romashov, S. M. Gershenzon, and others, obtained the first experimental proofs of their teacher's theories and presented them at the Fifth International Congress of Genetics in Berlin in 1927. After his arrest and exile to the Urals on a false, politically motivated charge, population genetics in the USSR declined noticeably. American geneticists, recognizing the importance of the work Chetverikov had launched, soon outstripped the Russians in this field.

9. Dubinin, *Perpetual Motion*, 60.

10. N. K. Koltsov, "The Improvement of the Human Species: Speech at the Annual Meeting of the Russian Eugenics Society, October 20, 1921," *Russian Eugenics Journal* (Russky evgenichesky zhurnal) 1 (1923): 1–27; "The Genealogies of Our Leading Individuals," ibid. 4 (1926): 103–143; "On the Descendants of Great People," ibid. 6 (1928): 164–177.

11. Personal communications from A. R. Zhebrak and V. V. Sakharov.

12. A. Nurinov, "On an Excessively Tolerant Note," *SA*, April 3, 1937, p. 2.

13. The account of this meeting which follows is drawn from the editorial, "In the Light of Criticism and Self-Criticism: Condensed Stenographic Record of the Discussions in the Aktiv of the Academy," *BVASKhNIL*, 1937, no. 4:19–29.

14. The brochure referred to was probably Koltsov's "Improvement of the Human Species," which had been printed separately in 1923 (Petrograd: Vremya).

15. Nurinov, "On an Excessively Tolerant Note." Nurinov had published political notes before; see, for example, his "Greater Class Vigilance in Science," *Transactions of the State Scientific Institute for the Agricultural Hybridization and Acclimatization of Animals* (Trudy Gosudarstvennogo instituta selskokhozyaistvennoi gibridizatsii i akklimatizatsii zhivotnykh), vol. 2 (Askania-Nova, 1935), 8.

16. Ya. A. Yakovlev, "On Darwinism and Some Anti-Darwinists," *Pravda*, April 12, 1937, and *SA*, April 14, 1937, pp. 2–3.

17. I. Prezent and A. Nurinov, "On N. K. Koltsov, the Prophet from Eugenics, and His Eugenics Collaborators," *SA*, April 12, 1937, pp. 2–3.

18. G. Yermakov and K. Krasnov, "The Reactionary Exercises of Certain Biologists," *SRA*, 1937, no. 7:108–116 (quotation on 108–109).

19. I. Fortunatov, M. Zaitseva, and others recounted this in 1987, during several memorial meetings held in Moscow.

20. "Lenin Academy of Agricultural Sciences on Intravarietal Cross-Fertilization" and "On Intravarietal Crossing of Self-Pollinated Plants by Academician Lysenko's Method," *SA*, April 28, 1937, p. 1; emphasis in the original.

21. Vavilov to Muller, May 8, 1937, Archives of the October Revolution, *fond* of the VIR, no. 9708, *delo* 1436, *list* 104.

22. "On the Darwinist Path," *SA*, April 29, 1937, p. 1.

23. T. D. Lysenko, "Develop Intravarietal Crossing of Wheat More Widely," *SA*, May 4, 1937, p. 2, and "Principles of Intravarietal Crossing," *SA*, May 21, 1937, 2–3.

24. V. R. Williams, "On the Tasks of Agriculture in the Third Five-Year Plan"; N. I. Vavilov, "Plant-Breeding in the USSR in the Third Five-Year Plan"; and "From the Editorial Board (On N. I. Vavilov's Article 'Plant-Breeding in the USSR in the Third Five-Year Plan')," *SA*, 1937, no. 7.

25. *Great Soviet Encyclopedia* (Bolshaya sovetskaya entsiklopedia), 3rd ed. (Moscow,

1979), s.v. "Muralov." In 1986, the newspaper *Evening Moscow* (Vechernyaya Moskva) published an article that in effect rehabilitated Muralov: N. Rodionova, "A Life Dedicated to Struggle: The Hundredth Anniversary of the Birth of A. I. Muralov," June 23, 1986. The article described Muralov as having lived a happy life as a professional revolutionary, an organizer of Soviet rule, commissar of agriculture of the Russian Republic, and president of VASKhNIL. Not a word was said of the circumstances of his death.

26. N. Korsunsky, "The Vicious Work of the Flax Institute," *SA*, November 27, 1937, p. 2; editorial, "It's Bad at the Institute of Mechanization and Electrification of Agriculture," *SA*, November 28, 1937, p. 3; letter to the editor by M. F. Neznayev and others, "A Plan Cut Off from Life," *SA*, December 28, 1937, p. 2.

27. I. Shman, "The 'Scientific' Activity of the Cotton Institute's New Districts," *SA*, December 28, 1937, p. 2.

28. Editorial, "Bring Order to the Breeding of Seed Potatoes," *SA*, December 3, 1937, p. 2.

29. Editorial, "An Anniversary of the Masters of Selection," *SRA*, 1936, no. 6:3.

30. Mark Popovsky's first published account of Vavilov's downfall came in a long article called "The One Thousand Days of Academician Vavilov," which appeared in the journal *Scope* (Prostor), 1966, no. 7, 4–27, and 1966, no. 8, 98–118. This journal was published in Alma-Ata by the Central Committee of the Communist Party, Kazakhstan, 19XX). In 1968 Popovsky published the children's book *We Must Hurry: From the Journeys of Academician Vavilov* (Nado speshit: Puteshestviya Akademika Vavilova) (Moscow: Detskaya Literatura, 1968). Later, Popovsky gave more details in a book entitled *Academician Vavilov's Trial* (Delo Akademika Vavilova), which was published in Russian by Hermitage Press (Ann Arbor, 1983). Selected chapters of this book were published as "The Vavilov Affair" in the journal *Memory: A Historical Almanac* (Pamyat), issued in Moscow in samizdat form in 1977 and printed in Paris in 1979, vol. 2:25–207 and 301–325. The English translation of the book was published as Mark Popovsky, *The Vavilov Affair*, with a foreword by Andrei Sakharov (Hamden, Conn.: Archon Book, 1984).

31. The case number is given in Popovsky, *Academician Vavilov's Trial*, 272.

32. According to the statistical survey of the USSR, which was published only in 1962, in 1959 the total number of employees in the country was 78,811,000 persons. Among them the number of prison and labor camp chief wardens was 2,126,000. The total number of miners was 589,000 and of railroaders 939,000. The results of the *All-Union General Census of the Population of 1959*, vol. 1, Moscow, 1962, 161–164. See also Conquest, *The Great Terror*, 561.

33. Popovsky, "The Vavilov Affair" and *Academician Vavilov's Trial.*

34. Popovsky, "The Vavilov Affair," 290.

35. Ibid.

36. A. K. Kol, "Applied Botany, or the Leninist Renewal of the Land," *Economic Gazette,* January 29, 1931, p. 3.

37. A. K. Kol, "The Reconstruction of Plant-Breeding in the USSR," in *Collection of Discussion Articles on Problems of Genetics and Selection* (Moscow: VASKhNIL, 1936), 134, 138, 151; *SRA*, 1936, no. 10.

38. G. N. Shlykov, "Introduction of New Plants and Genetics," *SRA*, 1936, no. 9, and *The Introduction of Plants* (Moscow and Leningrad: Selkhozgiz, 1936), 504.

39. N. Vavilov, "The Paths of Soviet Plant-Breeding Science (A Response to the Critics)," *SRA*, 1936, no. 12:38, 39–40.

40. A. K. Kol, "Against Morphological Abstractness in the Study of World Resources," *Vern.*, 1937, no. 3;67, 79.

41. O. N. Pisarzhevsky, *Pryanishnikov* (Moscow: Molodaya gvardiya, 1963), 220.

42. Popovsky, *Academician Vavilov's Trial*, 178.

43. Popovsky, "The Vavilov Affair," 306.

44. Popovsky, *Academician Vavilov's Trial*, 166.

45. Ibid.

46. Popovsky first disclosed this story in a talk at the VIR in 1966. Sidorov was in the audience; he "rushed from the hall as if scalded. Soon afterward, as if he were an indispensable administrator, he was transferred to another institute, with the same rank of deputy director." Popovsky, *Academician Vavilov's Trial* (chapters excerpted from the book), in *Memory, Almanac on History*, vol. 2 (Moscow, 1977; Paris 1979), 268, 292.

47. Archives of the October Revolution, Archives of the All-Union Institute of the Plant Industry, *fond* 9708, *yedinitsa khranenia* 1377, *list* 15–16.

48. Ibid.

49. "Clean Up the Academy of Agricultural Sciences—Mercilessly Root Out Enemies and Their Lackeys from Scientific Institutions," *SRA,* January 11, 1938, p. 2; Popovsky, *Academician Vavilov's Trial,* 131.

50. T. D. Lysenko, "On New Paths," *Pravda,* April 9, 1938, p. 3.

51. Popovsky, *Academician Vavilov's Trial,* 280–299.

52. Ibid., 287.

53. *Pravda,* May 11, 1938, p. 3.

54. B. Keller, "Genetics and Evolution," *SRA,* 1936, no. 12:23–32 (quotation from 24).

55. B. A. Keller, "Great Plans and Small Deeds," *Pravda,* April 6, 1938, p. 3.

56. I. V. Stalin, *Speech at the Reception in the Kremlin for Workers in Higher Education, May 17, 1938* (Moscow: Gospolitizdat, 1938).

57. *Pravda,* May 26, 1938, p. 6.

58. *Pravda,* May 28, 1938, p. 6.

59. Editorial, "The Struggle for Leading Science," *Herald of the Academy of Sciences of the USSR* (Vestnik AN SSSR), 1938, no. 6:6.

60. Personal communication from I. A. Rapoport.

61. Editorial, "A Chronicle," *Herald of the Academy of Sciences of the USSR,* 1938, no. 6:75–77.

62. *Pravda,* July 27, 1938, p. 2.

63. Prezent and Nurinov, "On N. K. Koltsov"; Yermakov and Krasnov, "Reactionary Exercises of Certain Biologists."

64. Quoted in B. L. Astaurov and P. F. Rokitsky, *Nikolai Konstantinovich Koltsov* (Moscow: Nauka, 1975), 152–153.

65. A. N. Bakh, B. A. Keller, Kh. S. Koshtoyants, N. I. Nuzhdin, and others, "Pseudo-Scientists Do Not Belong in the Academy of Sciences of the USSR," *Pravda,* January 1939.

66. *Herald of the AN SSSR,* 1939, no. 2.

67. Dubinin, *Perpetual Motion* 3rd ed. (Moscow: Politizdat, 1989), 124–135.

68. N. K. Koltsov, "The Molecules of Heredity," *Science and Life,* 1935, no. 5:4(388)–14(397).

69. Quoted in V. Polynin, *A Prophet in His Own Land* (Moscow: Sovetskaya Rossia, 1969), 113.

70. I am grateful to V. S. Kirpichnikov for providing me with a copy of this letter.

71. I. Prezent, "On the Pseudo-Scientific Views of Professor N. K. Koltsov," *UBM,* 1939, no. 5:146–153 (quotation from 153).

72. N. I. Vavilov, "How to Structure the Course in Genetics, Selection, and Seed Production," *SA,* February 1, 1939, as reprinted in *Selected Works of N. I. Vavilov,* vol. 1 (Moscow and Leningrad: Nauka, 1965), 384–386 (quotation from 385).

73. T. D. Lysenko, "Concerning the Article of Academician N. I. Vavilov," *SA,* February 1, 1939, 3. *The Short Course in the History of the Communist Party* was the textbook written under Stalin's direction (and allegedly in part by him) that was obligatory reading for everyone at the time.

74. Personal communications from N. I. Shapiro, A. A. Prokofyeva-Belgovskaya, and P. F. Rokitsky.

75. This information came in a lecture by A. A. Prokofyeva-Belgovskaya on the occasion of her eightieth birthday. I taped the proceedings secretly—the official tape recording was confiscated by the KGB immediately after the meeting.

76. D. Krinitsky, "Survey of Letters to the Editor," *SA*, September 8, 1939.

77. Once again, I would like to express my gratitude to V. S. Kirpichnikov for providing me with a copy of this letter.

78. Pukhalsky (b. 1909), soon after this speech, became a collaborator of Lysenko's. I was able to observe Pukhalsky closely for three years, when we shared an office during my tenure as scientific secretary of the VASKhNIL presidium's Council for Molecular Biology and Genetics. Pukhalsky, though not really a scientist, was at that time an acting member of VASKhNIL and of its presidium. In November 1987, he presided over the meetings marking Vavilov's hundredth birthday. At the final session of these meetings, I asked him whether he regretted having taken a wrong position in 1939 and thus having hastened Vavilov's downfall. In reply, he calmly declared that my question was based on a misunderstanding, that he had never caused Vavilov any harm, and that he had merely believed in Lysenko's ideas "just like everyone else at that time." As of 1990, Pukhalsky was still directing Russia's scientific research in agriculture from his position on the presidium.

79. K. M. Dmitriyev, "Under the Banner of Darwinism: At the All-Union Conference on Selection and Seed Production," *Vern.*, 1939, no. 2 (23): 119.

80. Ibid., 121.

81. Ibid.

82. Popovsky, "The Vavilov Affair," 296.

83. Transcribed from my tape recording.

84. Quoted from Zhores A. Medvedev, "The Biological Sciences and the Cult of Personality," 133–135. This is a samizdat manuscript, and it differs somewhat from the subsequently published version, Medvedev, *Rise and Fall of T. D. Lysenko*, in which the corresponding passage appears on 61–64.

85. Decree No. 7 of the Presidium of the VASKhNIL, May 23, 1939, cited in Popovsky, *Academician Vavilov's Trial*, 297–298.

86. Popovsky, *Academician Vavilov's Trial*, 297–298.

87. G. N. Shlykov, "In Bondage to Pseudo-Science," *Soviet Subtropics* (Sovetskiye subtropiki), 1939, no. 6:57–61; I. Prezent, *Vern.*, no. 2.

88. Personal communication from Professor V. P. Efroimson, who said that it was Stalin himself who gave the instructions to Mitin.

89. *UBM*, 1939, no. 11:89, 92.

90. Ibid., 92.

91. Ibid., 90–91.

92. Ibid., 89.

93. Ibid., 95.

94. Ibid., 93–94.

95. Ibid., 139–140.

96. Ibid., 147, 159, and T. D. Lysenko, "True Genetics Is a Michurinist Theory," in *Agrobiology*, 282 (reprinted from Lysenko's speech at the discussion, in *UBM*, October 7, 1939).

97. *Agrobiology*, 274.

98. Ibid., 192, 280.

99. Vavilov wrote in 1936 ("The Paths of Soviet Plant-Breeding Science"): "I became acquainted with Michurin in 1920 and visited him repeatedly thereafter. In 1923, I wrote a memorandum about him and sent it to the Russian Republic Commissariat of Agriculture, and in 1924 I prepared the first book about Michurin." The book referred to was V. V. Pashkevich, ed., *I. V. Michurin: Results of His Work in the Hybridization of Fruits* (Moscow: Novaya Derevnya, 1924), to which Vavilov had written a foreword.

100. M. Mitin, "For a Leading Soviet Genetic Science," *Pravda*, December 7, 1939, p. 3.

101. Ibid.
102. *UBM*, 1929, no. 11:99, 125.
103. This was an account by Yefrem S. Yakushevsky, who worked at the VIR for many years and who spoke to Vavilov on November 28, 1939, eight days after the meeting with Stalin. The recollection was recorded by D. V. Lebedev, who told it to me in 1987.
104. *From the History of Biology* 2:189.
105. Quoted in Medvedev, *Rise and Fall of T. D. Lysenko*, 59.
106. Quoted in ibid., 67.
107. From a tape-recording made by me at the meeting.
108. Tape-recorded by me at the same meeting.
109. I have in my possession a typed carbon copy of the table of contents of this volume, which was kindly given to me by Professor Vladimir V. Sakharov in 1965.
110. Also tape-recorded by me at the same meeting.

9. Koltsov and Vavilov Perish

Epigraph sources: Konstantin Balmont, "To Alexander Herzen," 1920; Friedrich Nietzsche, *Thus Spake Zarathustra*, 1883.

1. Personal communication from A. R. Zhebrak. See also Popovsky, *Academician Vavilov's Trial*, 153.
2. "Expedition of Leningrad Scientists," *Leningrad Pravda*, July 26, 1940, p. 2.
3. Popovsky, *Academician Vavilov's Trial*, 155–157.
4. F. Kh. Bakhteyev, "Nikolai Ivanovich Vavilov, 1887–1943," *Sibirskoye Otdelenie Izdatelstva "Nauka"* (Novosibirsk, 1987), 218–219.
5. *Leningrad Pravda*, August 27, 1940.
6. Quoted in Popovsky, "The Vavilov Affair," 299.
7. I. Ye. Glushchenko, "Memoirs" (Vospominaniye) (unpublished).
8. This story was told to me by a number of people.
9. Popovsky, *Academician Vavilov's Trial*, 178–179.
10. The story was printed in the "wall newspaper" of the Institute of Cytology and Genetics of the Siberian division of the Academy of Sciences at Akademgorod. Dr. M. Golubovsky kindly gave me the copy of this imprint.
11. Popovsky, *Academician Vavilov's Trial*, 183.
12. S. Gurev and V. Kostin, "Against the Conservative Tendency in Biological Science," *Leningrad Pravda*, August 28, 1940, pp. 2–3.
13. Evgenia Albats, "Genius and Villainy," *Moscow News* (Moskovskiye novosti), November 15, 1987, p. 10.
14. Yu. Polyansky, "Develop a Leading Soviet Genetic Science at Leningrad University," *Leningrad University*, October 15, 1940, p. 2.
15. T. D. Lysenko, "What Is Michurinist Genetics?" *Agrobiology*, 373 (reprinted from *Leningrad University*, November 23, 1940).
16. The foregoing information is from Anatoly Shvarts, "This Lucky Man Karpechenko," *Novoye russkoye slovo* (The New Russian Word) (New York), December 8, 1985, p. 5. See also the other articles in this series, December 5, 1985, p. 5, and December 6, 1985, p. 5.
17. Popovsky, "The Vavilov Affair," 314, citing the Archives of the October Revolution, *fond* of the VIR, *delo* 1833, *list* 110. Eikhfeld remained director of the institute until 1951, when he was succeeded by another member of the commission, Sizov. Later, Eikhfeld became a vice-chairman of the Supreme Soviet, a member and president of the Estonian Academy of Science, a member of VASKhNIL, and a corresponding member of the AN SSSR, as well as a Hero of Socialist Labor. On his ninetieth birthday (January 25, 1983), he was awarded his seventh Order of Lenin "for services in the development of Soviet science." *The Great Soviet Encyclopedia*, 3rd ed., says that he was a pupil of Vavilov's, but that is not true.
18. Popovsky, "The Vavilov Affair," 284. Vavilov's interrogator was NKVD Senior

Lieutenant A. G. Khvat, who eventually rose to the rank of colonel and retired on a "personal pension," the special pension granted to individuals who had held high office or had performed distinctive service to the state. In 1987, he told an interviewer, Yevgenia Albats, that he had been expelled from the Party in 1962 "in connection with the Vavilov affair" (Albats, "Genius and Villainy"). But Popovsky relates that "in April 1965, USSR Deputy General-Prosecutor Malyarov told me, with distress in his voice, that it was impossible, alas, to bring investigator Khvat to trial for having tortured Vavilov and fabricated the case against him, because the time elapsed was covered under the statute of limitations applying to the crimes he had committed." Popovsky, *Academician Vavilov's Trial,* 264.

19. Popovsky, "The Vavilov Affair," 285.

20. Ibid., 303. During the interrogation, Khvat showed Vavilov thirty-eight declarations by various people that could be used as testimony against him. Fifteen years later, when the case was reviewed, it was revealed that most of these had been fabrications. (Popovsky, *Academician Vavilov's Trial,* 284). Albats, "Genius and Villainy," reports that when she asked Khvat whether he believed that Vavilov was guilty, Khvat replied, "I didn't believe in the espionage, of course. There was no evidence to support it. [The indictment that Khvat drew up nevertheless included an espionage charge.] As for sabotage—well, there were some things in science that he led in the wrong direction, and I formed a commission of experts under the leadership of an academician of VASKhNIL . . . and I talked to Lysenko." Asked how Vavilov had behaved under interrogation and whether he had tried to implicate others, Khvat replied: "No. He wasn't that kind of person, I think. . . . He remained calm. He answered questions, and afterward inserted additional statements in the record [which prisoners had to read and sign after each day's interrogation]. . . . When he had nothing to do, he asked me for paper and pencil and wrote something about his specialty. He wrote a lot. I put his writings in the file." And when Albats asked, "Weren't you sorry for Vavilov? He was facing the firing squad," Khvat said, "Ah, how many of them there were!"

21. Lev Sidorovsky, "Vavilov: The Great Scientist through the Eyes of His Relatives and Colleagues and the Lines of His Letters," *New Generation,* August 13, 1987, p. 2.

22. Popovsky, "The Vavilov Affair," 308.

23. Ibid., 305.

24. Ibid., 304.

25. Thirty years later, I. S. Shatilov, vice-president of VASKhNIL and Yakushkin's closest pupil, published a long and admiring article about him: "Academician I. V. Yakushkin," *Herald of Agricultural Science* (Vestnik selskokhozyaistvennoi nauki), 1985, no. 11.

26. Sidorovsky, "Vavilov," 2.

27. Popovsky, *The Vavilov Affair,* 179.

28. Sidorovsky, "Vavilov," 2.

29. Transcribed from a tape-recording made by me.

30. Sidorovsky, "Vavilov."

31. Popovsky, "The Vavilov Affair," 305.

32. Glushchenko, "Memoirs."

33. Quoted in Pisarzhevsky, *Pryanishnikov,* 157.

34. Zaporozhets's successor, I. I. Usachev, later accused a group of Pryanishnikov's students of fostering Trotskyism: *Bulletin of VASKhNIL,* 1937, no. 4:23.

35. Ye. Lyashenko, "Agrochemical Maps and the Struggle for the Harvest," *Pravda,* September 4, 1937, p. 2.

36. G. Pavlov, "Taking Cover under the Flag of 'Scientific Work,'" *SA,* September 21, 1937, p. 3.

37. Ye. Lyashenko, "Once More on Agrochemical Maps," *SA,* November 13, 1937, p. 3.

38. S. B., "In the All-Union Lenin Academy of Agricultural Sciences: Plenary Session of the Section on Agronomical Chemistry," *SA,* November 15, 1937, p. 3.

39. S. B., "The Plenary Session of the Section on Agronomical Chemistry Has Ended," *SA*, November 20, 1937, p. 3.

40. *SA*, January 11, 1938, p. 2.

41. I am grateful to Pryanishnikov's daughter, Lidia Pryanishnikova, professor of botany at the Timiryazev Agricultural Academy, for these recollections.

42. Pisarzhevsky, *Pryanishnikov*, 219.

43. Popovsky, *Academician Vavilov's Trial*, 193.

44. T. D. Lysenko, "On Heredity and Its Variability," *SRA*, 1943, no. 1–2:47–69.

45. Lidia Pryanishnikova has provided me with a copy of this telegram.

46. A copy of this memorandum was kindly provided to me by I. Ye. Glushchenko. The memorandum included a proposal for a study of nitrogen fixation by microorganisms, a proposal that was decades ahead of the times; this has now become one of the central problems of biology.

47. *Pravda*, December 26, 1936, p. 2. For more on Boris Zavadovsky, see chapter 6.

48. B. M. Zavadovsky, "Speech at the August 1948 Session of VASKhNIL," in *On the Situation in Biological Science: Stenographic Report on the Session of VASKhNIL, July 31–August 7, 1948* (Moscow: OGIZ-Selkhozgiz, 1948), 292. On the other hand, it was after this same session of the academy that Nikolai I. Shapiro "discovered" that the cause of genetics was doomed and became transformed into a Lysenkoist. In 1977, he (together with Academicians Belyayev and Dubinin) blocked the nomination of Melvin Green, a professor at the University of California and president of the American Genetics Society, to be president of the Fourteenth International Genetics Congress, which was to be held in Moscow. Shapiro charged that Green, who had frequently visited Soviet scientific centers and knew many of the Soviet geneticists personally, was "anti-Soviet."

49. M. Ye. Lobashev, *Essays in the History of Russian Livestock Breeding* (Ocherki po istorii russkogo zhivotnovodstva) (Moscow and Leningrad: Akademika nauk, 1954), 3, 6, 325.

50. Edmund W. Sinnott and L. C. Dunn, *Principles of Genetics* (New York, 1932), translated into Russian by S. Gershenzon and A. Gaisinovich as *Genetics: Theory and Practice* (Moscow and Leningrad: Gosizdat biologicheskoi i meditsinskoi literatury, 1934).

51. A. O. Gaisinovich, "Observations on the Works of I. I. Mechnikov," in I. I. Mechnikov, *Selected Biological Works* (Izbrannye biologicheskiye proizvedenii), Classics of Science Series (Moscow: Akademia nauk, 1950), 757, 715.

52. A. S. Krivisky, "The Biological Nature of Bacteriophage," *Nature* (Priroda), 1952, no. 10:49, 53–54.

53. A. S. Krivisky, "Transforming the Nature of Microbes: Results of the All-Union Conference on Directing the Mutation and Selection of Microorganisms," *Nature* (Priroda), 1952, no. 2:70, 71; G. A. Nadson and G. S. Filippov, "On Influence of X-rays on Sexual Reproductivity and the Formation of Mutants in Imperfect Fungi (Mucoraceae)" (in Russian), *Herald of Roentgenology and Radiology* 3 (1925): 305–311; M. N. Meissel, "Influence of Chloroform on Development of Yeasts" (in Russian), *Microbiology Journal*, 1928, no. 4.

54. Ibid., 66–67, 73.

55. Popovsky, "The Vavilov Affair," says that Shlykov was convicted of a misdemeanor. However, Efroimson was serving a sentence at that time in the labor camp near Dzhezkazgan, in Kazakhstan, and he reports seeing Shlykov there. This camp held only persons sentenced under Article 58 of the criminal code—nominally covering subversion and counterrevolutionary activity, but actually a catch-all law used by the secret police tribunals—and Efroimson therefore believes that Shlykov was caught in the same net that he had used to entrap others.

56. A sixty-page abstract of the dissertation may be found in the Lenin Library in Moscow.

57. See the abstract referred to in n. 55, 14–15, 59, 58.

10. Lysenko's Support Falters

Epigraph sources: Boris Pasternak, "Spektorsky," in *Poems, Short and Long* (Leningrad, 1977), 503; J. V. Stalin, speech at the Red Army Academy graduation, *SA*, May 6, 1935, 1.

1. Its Russian name was Gorki. The Russian word for a hill is *gorka*, the plural of which is *gorki*. The word thus has nothing to do with the name of the famous writer Maxim Gorky (Aleksei Peshkov), who took his nom de plume from the Russian adjective that means "bitter."

2. *Herald of the Academy of Sciences of the USSR*, 1965, no. 11:5, 6.

3. Personal communication from Petrenko's daughter, Maria G. Podyapolskaya-Petrenko.

4. T. D. Lysenko, "On Several Basic Tasks of Agricultural Science: Revised Stenographic Report at the General Meeting of Academicians and Corresponding Members of the Academy of Sciences of the USSR at Sverdlovsk, May 6, 1942," in Lysenko, *Agrobiology*, 405.

5. T. D. Lysenko, "What the All-Union Genetics Institute Will Be Working On in 1939," *Vern.*, 1938, no. 6:21–26, and "Ways of Discovering Winter-Hardy Varieties of Winter Crops in the East," *Vern.*, 1939, no. 3:15–26.

6. T. D. Lysenko, *The Next Tasks of Soviet Agricultural Science* (Moscow: OGIZ-Selkhozgiz, 1943), 10, and "What Is the Essence of Our Proposal for Sowing Winter Crops in the Siberian Steppe on the Stubble?" *Sovkhoz Production* (Sovkhoznoye proizvodstvo), 1944, no. 4:16–23.

7. "On Matters of Principle in Scientific Work," *Party Life* (Partiinaya zhizn), 1956, no. 9:27–35.

8. Personal communications from Professor V. P. Efroimson and Dr. A. Karavanov.

9. After the war, he disappeared from the Soviet Union and, it was said by some, turned up in the United States. Soviet citizens who listened to foreign broadcasts have said they heard him on some Western radio programs, giving disparaging talks on Soviet life.

10. A. R. Zhebrak, "Soviet Biology," *Science* 102 (1945): 357–358. Zhebrak concluded on this hopeful note: "Together with American scientists, we who are working in this field in Russia are building up a common, worldwide biology. . . . In the future, the scientists of the two countries will progress together in an atmosphere of mutual understanding and comradeship."

11. Personal communication from Zhebrak's son Eduard.

12. Dubinin, *Perpetual Motion*, 267–268.

13. I. Benediktov, "For a High Culture in Soviet Agriculture," *Izvestia*, March 27, 1946, p. 2.

14. See T. D. Lysenko, "The Tasks of the All-Union Lenin Academy of Agricultural Sciences in Light of the Resolution of the Plenum of the CC of the ACP(B) 'On Measures for the Advancement of Agriculture in the Postwar Period,'" *Agrobiology*, 1947, no. 2:3.

15. Lysenko, *Agrobiology*, 539. This speech has been published in English: "The Tasks of VASKhNIL," in *Stenographic Transcript of an Open Party Meeting of VASKhNIL, 1947, on Tasks of the Academy in Light of the Plan of the CPSU Central Committee on Measures of Increasing Agriculture after the War*.

16. T. D. Lysenko, "Natural Selection and Intraspecies Competition," speech reprinted in Lysenko, *Agrobiology*, 489, 492, 498. Incidentally, Marx and Engels had challenged the Malthusian hypothesis long before.

17. As a student between 1952 and 1954, I spent much time with students and faculty at Gorky State University and then at the Timiryazev Agricultural Academy and often heard biologists discuss their past and current opinions of Lysenko.

18. N. I. Yermolayeva, "The Propagation of Peas after Sowing and Crossing Them at Various Intervals," *Vern.*, 1938, no. 1–2:127–134.

332 Notes to Pages 164–169

19. I heard Lysenko make these statements in lectures at the Timiryazev Academy.

20. A. N. Kolmogorov, "On a New Confirmation of Mendel's Laws," *Annals of the AN SSSR* (Doklady AN SSSR) 27 (1940): 38–42.

21. T. D. Lysenko, "Natural Selection and Intraspecies Competition," *SA*, 1946, nos. 5, 6, 8, 10, and 12; reprinted in *Agrobiology*, 1946, no. 2, 3–27.

22. P. M. Zhukovsky, "Darwinism in a Distorting Mirror," *Selection and Seed-Growing*, 1946.

23. In 1946, it was published in *Agrobiology*, no. 2, and in *Sovkhoz Production*, no. 1; in 1947, in *Transactions of the Genetics Institute of the Academy of Sciences of the USSR* (Trudy Instituta genetiki AN SSSR), no. 14; and afterward, in successive editions of the collection of Lysenko's works entitled *Agrobiology*.

24. T. D. Lysenko, "Cobbler, Stick to Your Last," *Pravda*, June 23, 1946, p. 5. See also T. D. Lysenko, "On a 'Distorting' Mirror and Certain Anti-Darwinists," *Agrobiology*, 1946, no. 3:151–153.

25. Zhdanov's "pogrom" speeches have been published in English under the deceptively mild title of *Essays on Literature, Philosophy, and Music* (New York: International Publishers, 1950).

26. Zhebrak, "Soviet Biology," 357.

27. I. Prezent, "The Struggle of Ideologies in Biological Science," *Leningrad Pravda*, March 6, 1947, p. 2.

28. A. Surkov, A. Tvardovsky, and G. Fish, "Before the Court of Society," *Literary Gazette* (Literaturnaya gazeta), August 30, 1947, p. 1.

29. I. D. Laptev, "An Antipatriotic Act under the Flag of 'Scientific' Criticism," *Pravda*, September 2, 1947, p. 2. As a reward for this article, Laptev was appointed a member of VASKhNIL by Stalin in 1948. In 1969, when Lysenko's authority was in decline, P. P. Lobanov, then president of the academy, expelled Laptev, along with Prezent and another Lysenkoist, S. F. Demidov. A few days after the expulsion order was issued, Prezent died of blood poisoning; he was buried with an academician's honors.

30. S. V. Kuleshov et al., *USSR/SSSR. Our Motherland: The Attempt to Write Political History* (Moscow: Terra, 1991), 434.

31. I learned these facts about the trial from interviews with most of the people involved.

32. Personal communication from Zhebrak's son Eduard.

33. "Scientific Discussions," *Literary Gazette*, November 29, 1947, p. 4.

34. A. (*sic*) Shmalgauzen, A. Formozov, A. Sabinin, and S. Yudintsev, "Our Objections to Academician T. D. Lysenko," ibid., November 29, 1947, p. 4; A. A. Avakyan, D. Dolgushin, N. Belenky, I. Glushchenko, and F. Dvoryankin, "For Creative Darwinism, Against Malthusianism," ibid.

35. T. D. Lysenko, "Why Does Bourgeois Science Rise Up against the Work of Soviet Scientists?" ibid., October 18, 1947, p. 4; reprinted in Lysenko, *Agrobiology*, 544–545.

36. N. Turbin, "My Opinion about Academician T. D. Lysenko's Theoretical Views," ibid., December 10, 1947, p. 4.

37. M. B. Mitin, "For the Flourishing of Soviet Agrobiological Science," ibid., December 27, 1947, p. 4. The roundup of letters and the story about the meeting of the philosophy department also appeared on this page.

38. A decade later, Efroimson continued to document Lysenko's errors. In 1958, he gave me a memorandum on Lysenko's responsibility for mistakes related to the use of genetics for military purposes and asked me to send it to the son of Deputy Minister of Defense Marshal M. V. Zakharov. The son and I had studied together in the physics department of Moscow State University. Young Zakharov sent the memorandum to his father, and the marshal studied it carefully, a fact he asked us to relay to Efroimson.

39. Medvedev, *Rise and Fall of T. D. Lysenko*, 111.

40. Svetlana Alliluyeva, *Only One Year*, trans. P. Chavchavadze (New York and Evanston, Ill.: Harper and Row, 1969).

41. Graham, *Science and Philosophy*, 443–450. Graham cites Leonard Shapiro, *The Communist Party of the Soviet Union* (New York, 1960), 508; Georg von Rausch, *A History of Soviet Russia* (New York, 1962), 403; and Donald W. Treadgold, *Twentieth Century Russia* (Chicago, 1964), 452.

42. Graham, *Science and Philosophy*, 443. In 1991, the Central Committee archives were opened to investigators to a limited extent.

43. These and the following excerpts from Zhdanov's lecture, entitled "Controversial Questions of Contemporary Darwinism," were taken from a transcript that was kindly furnished to me by Yury Zhdanov in December 1987 at my home in Moscow, during a lengthy discussion of these matters. Although Zhdanov convinced me that the copy he gave me was an exact transcript of the lecture, it is clear from the age of the paper that the typescript was made recently.

44. As we shall see shortly, Lysenko later claimed that he had been "refused an invitation to the seminar" and thus had to resort to this means of hearing Zhdanov. It is, however, very unlikely that anyone would have dared reject such a request for an invitation from the president of VASKhNIL, deputy chairman of the Supreme Soviet, an academician three times over, and a Hero of Socialist Labor. We must assume, then, that this was another false accusation of Lysenko's.

45. The letter, dated April 17, 1948, was found in the archives of VASKhNIL. I published it in *The Lantern* (Ogonyok), 1988, nos. 1 and 2, and in "New Light on the Lysenko Era" in *Nature* 339 (1989): 415–420.

46. Ibid., no. 1.

47. Once, in a public lecture that I attended at Moscow State University, Lysenko said: "This is what I am like: Everything that I say proves true, and everything turns out to be a discovery. I said that interspecies competition does not exist; it proved to be a discovery. Not long ago, I said soil microbes play a role in nourishing plants—again a discovery. That's how it always is!"

48. M. Yakubintser, "The Muslinka Wheat," *Kolkhoz Experimentation*, 1938, no. 7, 51–57.

49. *Preliminary Indications of Kakhetian Branched Wheat* (16 pages, in Georgian) (Tbilisi: Kommunist, 1946).

50. E. Mar, *A Heroic Wheat* (Bogatirskaya pshenitsa) (Moscow: Detgiz, 1949), 17–20.

51. Ibid., and Gennady Fish, "The Wheat of the Future," *The Young Collective Farmer* (Molodoi kolkhoznik), 1949, no. 1: 19.

52. See, for example, V. Severgin, *Elementary Principles of Natural History, Including the Animal, Vegetable, and Mineral Kingdoms* (Nachalnye osnovania yestyestvennoi istorii, soderzhashchie tsarstva zhivotnykh, proizrastanii, i iskopayemykh), part 1, *The Vegetable Kingdom* (St. Petersburg, 1794), 122–123; Bronevsky, "On the Sowing of a Different Type of Grain in Omsk," *Agricultural Journal* (Zemledelchesky zhurnal), 1834, no. 6; A. M. Bazhanov, *On the Cultivation of Wheat, with a Description of Varieties Bred in Russia* (O vozdelyvanii pshenitsy s opisaniyem porod, razvodimykh v Rossii) (Moscow: Moscow Imperial University, 1856); Baikov, comp., *Review of Agriculture on Independent Estates in 1832 and 1833* (Obozreniye selskogo khozyaistva udelnykh imenii v 1832 i 1833 godakh) (St. Petersburg, 1836), 85; "Egyptian Mummy Wheat," *Transactions of the Free Economic Society* (Trudy Volnogo Ekonomicheskogo Obshchestva) (St. Petersburg) 3 (1851), no. 1:1; I. I. Solntsev, "A Test of Chinese Winter Wheat," *Herald of Russian Agriculture* (Vestnik russkogo selskogo khoyaistva), 1893, no. 23:794.

53. *SA*, 1937, no. 156:3.

54. F. M. Kuperman, "Branched Forms of Winter Wheat, Rye, and Barley," *Vern.*, 1940, no. 2:101–105.

55. See, for example, Bazhanov, *Cultivation of Wheat*, 38, 40; N. Shcheglov, *Economic*

Botany, including Descriptions and Illustrations of Plants That Are Useful and Harmful to Man (Khozyaistvennaya botanika, zaklyuchayushchaya v sebe opisanie i izobrazhenia poleznykh i vrednykh dlya cheloveka rastenii), vol. 1 (St. Petersburg, 1828); M. V. Spafaryev, "The Question of 'Paradise' Wheat," *Agricultural Gazette*, 1837, no. 42:334–335; O. Shimansky, "Response to the Question about 'Paradise' Wheat," ibid., 1837, no. 68:542; A. Yablonsky, "Information on the Yield of Mummy Wheat," *Transactions of the Free Economic Society* (Trudy volnogo economicheskogo obshchestva) 1 (1852): 69; M. Zenzinov, "Letter to the Free Economic Society from Nerchinsk on the Cultivation of Wheat in That Area," *Economic Notes* (Ekonomicheskiye zapiski), 1860, no. 30:240; A. Fonton, "Experience with Seeds of Egyptian Wheat," *Experience in the Agriculture of Southern Russia* (Opyt selskogo khozyaistva yuzhnoi Rossii) (Odessa), 1850, no. 7:448–450; N. Vasilyev, "Botanical Varieties and Types of Grain Plants in Russia," *Agriculture and Forestry* (Selskoye khozyaistvo i lesovodstvo), 1905, no. 1:43; V. K. Kobelev, "The Wheats of Afghanistan (Composition and Distribution)," *Transactions in Applied Botany, Genetics, and Selection* (Trudy po prikladnoi botanike, genetike i selekcii) 19 (1928), no. 1:21; M. Tumanyan, "Branching Soft Wheat," ibid., series 5 (1934), no. 2:141; G. V. Zabluda, "On the Branching of Ears in Short-Day Conditions," *Reports of the Academy of Sciences of the USSR* (Doklady AN SSSR) 30 (1941), no. 6:533–535. There was even an article about branched wheat in the newspaper in which Lysenko's articles frequently appeared: *SA*, September 15, 1938, p. 3.

56. Gennady Fish, "The Wheat of the Future," *Young Collective Farmer* (Molodoy kolkhoznik), the journal published by All-Union Komsomol Organization, January 1949, no. 1:19. Fish mentioned the discouraging history of branched wheat but transformed it into a triumph of Soviet science over foreign:

> Comrade Stalin, with his brilliant foresight, perceived the potential of this wheat and asked Academician Lysenko to develop it. . . . Trofim Denisovich has succeeded in large part in solving the riddle of branched wheat and, despite everything said or written about it in "world literature," has moved it out of the furrow, out of the small plots and cottage houses, and into the fields of the state farms. In only the second year of work on it, it has become the highest yielding of all varieties known to man.

The phrase "world literature" alluded—as any Soviet reader would have known—to the "struggle against cosmopolitanism" and all things foreign that gripped the USSR after World War II. Another journalist, Eugene Mar, wrote: "Foreign scientists" had, indeed, "taken an interest in branched wheat, but gave up quickly after a few failures" (*A Heroic Wheat*, 19). "After all, American and British landowners would have seen no advantage in the collection of higher yields because it would immediately lead to the lower prices (hence lower profits) that increased harvest would have brought about." But Fish and Mar ignored the reports that Russian farmers and scientists had published for years on their own futile attempts to grow branched wheat.

57. See, for example, the following articles in *SA*: N. Solovyov, "The Propagation of Branched Wheats," January 22, 1948, p. 4; editorial, "Experiences with Branched Wheat," May 23, 1948, p. 4; editorial, "Branched Wheat in the Ukraine," June 4, 1948, p. 3.

58. In an interview with Yury Zhdanov in 1987, I asked him what position his father took in all of this. He replied that his father repeatedly urged him to stay away from Lysenko and added, wryly, "Yury, don't tangle with Lysenko. He'll cross you with a cucumber!"

59. Right up to 1953, Lysenko and other "Michurinists" continued to claim that they had obtained high-yielding forms of branched wheat: see, for example, "The Advice of Academician T. D. Lysenko to Field-Team Leader M. I. Laptev," *SA*, March 25, 1949, p. 23; D. A. Dolgushin, *The Michurinist Principles of the Selection and Seed-Growing of Cultivated Plants* (Michurinskiye printsipy selektsii i semenovodstva kulturnykh rastenii), tran-

script of a public lecture delivered in the Central Lecture Hall of the All-Union Society for the Dissemination of Political and Scientific Knowledge (Moscow: Pravda, 1949), p. 23; V. N. Remeslo, "Selection of Spring Wheat," in *Scientific Report of the Mironov Selection Station for 1944–1949* (Nauchnyi otchet Mironovskoi selektsionnoi stantsii za 1944–1949 gody), no. 1 (Kiev and Kharkov, 1951), 51–57. Gennady Fish, reporting that Avakyan had supposedly raised six sacks of grain from a single glassful of seed in 1948, exclaimed, "It was as if communism had already been achieved on this farm field!" Fish, "The Wheat of the Future," 21. Articles in praise of branched wheat also appeared in *Komsomol Pravda*, August 13, 1948; *Literary Gazette*, March 19, 1949; and *Sovkhoz Gazette*, 1949, no. 156:3. Finally, however, one year after Stalin's death, V. Ya. Yuryev, an outstanding specialist in wheat selection, exposed the branched-wheat farce in his article, "From the Practice of Selection and Seed-Growing of Grain Crops," *Agriculture* (Selskoye khozyaistvo), August 5, 1954. As for the collective farmers, they recognized the futility of the venture quite early, and they never planted branched wheat at all, except on paper. Meanwhile, the Lysenkoists found branched wheat useful for another purpose: Many of them obtained advanced degrees by writing dissertations about it.

  60. I have no reason to doubt Shepilov's account, but there is probably no one who can confirm it. Yury Zhdanov attended the meeting and had described it to me earlier, but he said that he sat far from Stalin, whose voice did not carry, and therefore he did not hear what Stalin said. He told me he was asked to write an explanatory memorandum about the lecture incident, which he did a few days later. (*Pravda* subsequently printed the memorandum as Zhdanov's repentance letter; see chapter 11.) He learned that the Kremlin had instructed the Moscow city Party committee to punish him (it was in itself extraordinary that a lower-echelon Party committee would be ordered to discipline a top Party official like Zhdanov), but events moved so rapidly that the city committee did not get around to it. There was one curious detail in Zhdanov's account. He remarked that Shepilov had let him down by not admitting he had authorized the lecture. After my conversation with Shepilov, I telephoned Yury and told him I had interviewed Shepilov. Zhdanov became agitated and asked what Shepilov had told me. I refrained from discussing it further.

  61. Personal communication from I. Ye. Glushchenko.

  62. In point of fact, the academy did not have any charter at all. Not until the mid-seventies was one adopted, after extended debate in the Ministry of Agriculture and the agriculture department of the Central Committee.

  63. While I was a student at the Timiryazev Academy, between 1954 and 1957, I was working in the laboratory one evening with my scientific advisor, Ivan I. Gunar, shortly before the anniversary of the October Revolution. I told him of a very poor lecture by Bushinsky that I had recently heard, and I asked how he had become a member of the agricultural academy (as well as a corresponding member of the USSR Academy of Sciences). By way of answer, Gunar telephoned Bushinsky under the pretext of wishing him a happy holiday, and he then added, "By the way, I was working with a student here and we couldn't remember the chemical formula for carbonic acid. Can you recall it?" The formula is a simple one, known to every soil scientist. As Gunar expected, Bushinsky couldn't give the formula. Instead, he launched into a rambling account of his services in the Revolution and his part in the "storming" of the Winter Palace, and then hastily said goodbye.

  64. This is recounted in Zilber's memoirs, the manuscript of which is in the possession of his family, and Zdrodovsky told his friends the same sort of thing. After the war, Muromtsev, a longtime NKVD officer, became a doctor and director of the Institute of Epidemiology and Microbiology, where Zilber was head of a laboratory. He once tried to explain to Zilber that he "had to" beat him and Zdrodovsky because otherwise others would have beaten them more severely. Zilber was so infuriated by this act of "repentance" that he flew into a rage, struck Muromtsev, and smashed the furniture in his office. Muromtsev did not report the incident; Zilber's scientific authority was such that

it would only have reflected badly on himself. When Muromtsev died in 1960, his colleagues at the institute did not attend his funeral.

65. *Pravda,* July 28, 1948. The report listed the names of all the new appointees.

11. The Defeat of the Geneticists

Epigraph sources: Mikhail Lermontov, "Glory," 1830–1831; Mikhail Saltykov-Shchedrin, "The Mon Repos Refuge."

1. The typewritten manuscript of the report lay for many years on a table in Lysenko's office on Bolshaya Kaluzhskaya Street (now Lenin Prospekt), with Stalin's notes in colored pencil (mostly exclamation points alongside crossed-out words or phrases). Lysenko used to enjoy startling visitors by showing it to them. There were many rumors about these notes. I was told by Glushchenko that some of them were joking and funny, e.g., "Then is '2 X 2 = 4' also a bourgeois fabrication?—J. St."

2. T. D. Lysenko, "Report on the Situation in Biological Science," in *On the Situation in Biological Science: Transcript of the Session of the VASKhNIL, July 31–August 7, 1948* (O polozhenii v biologicheskoi nauke: Stenografichesky otchet o sessii VASKhNIL, 31 iyulya–7 avgusta 1948 g.) (Moscow: OGIZ-Selkhozgiz, 1948), 140.

3. V. Safronov, *The Land in Flower (History of the Development of Agrobiological Science and the Flourishing of the Michurinist Doctrine in the USSR)* (Moscow, 1952), 338–339. This book was awarded a Stalin Prize one year later.

4. Personal communication from Turbin, who was close to Lysenko at the time. Stoletov's performance as liaison pleased the leadership and enhanced Lysenko's standing. It also enabled Stoletov to build a good relationship with Yury Zhdanov, which was useful to Stoletov later as he embarked upon a dizzying career. Stoletov had been deputy director of the Institute of Genetics. Immediately after the August 1948 session, he became director of the Timiryazev Academy; in 1950, he was appointed deputy minister of agriculture for science, and a few months later, minister of higher education. After Stalin's death, however, he occupied a series of lesser posts. He was among the first to abandon Lysenko when he sensed the weakening of high-level support for him.

5. *On the Situation in Biological Science,* 40.

6. Ibid., 73.

7. Ibid., 121.

8. Ibid., 138.

9. Ibid., 166.

10. Ibid., 279.

11. Ibid., 411.

12. Talking to me about the session, Rapoport said, with a laugh: "The stenographers decided that they would help me. During one of the breaks, I walked past their table, and one of the stenographers, who knew me slightly, winked and said: 'Don't worry, we left out the sharpest parts of your speech and your retorts.'"

13. *On the Situation in Biological Science,* 134.

14. Ibid., 137.

15. Ibid.

16. Ibid., 471.

17. Ibid.

18. Ibid., 472–473, 475.

19. Mikhail Gorbachev paid respect to Nemchinov in a recent speech, "On the Tasks of the Party in the Radical Restructuring of the Administration of the Economy," in *Materials of the Plenum of the Central Committee of the CPSU, June 25–26, 1987* (Moscow: Gospolitizdat, 1987), 42.

20. *On the Situation in Biological Science,* 153.

21. Ibid., 488, 507.

22. Personal communication from Efroimson.

23. *Pravda*, August 7, 1948, p. 5. Yury Zhdanov has told me that this letter had been written to Stalin personally and he therefore regarded it as an internal Party document; he did not expect it to be published.

24. *On the Situation in Biological Science*, 523–525. Other portions of Zhukovsky's recantation are worth quoting at length:

Comrades, yesterday evening I decided to deliver the following statement. I deliberately say "late yesterday evening" because I did not know then that today *Pravda* would print Comrade Yu. Zhdanov's letter, and there is no connection between my present statement and Comrade Yu. Zhdanov's letter. I believe Deputy Minister of Agriculture Lobanov can confirm this fact, since I telephoned him yesterday to ask him to give me the floor today for this statement. . . .

My speech two days ago, before the Party Central Committee outlined the watershed that divides the two schools of biology, was unworthy of a Communist party member and Soviet scientist.

I admit I took a wrong stand . . .

I am a person of responsibility, for I work in the Stalin Prizes Committee and in the commission of experts for awarding high academic degrees. Therefore, I believe, I have a moral obligation to be an honest Michurinist, an honest Soviet biologist. . . .

I am sure that, knowing me, you will believe me now, too, when I say I speak not out of cowardice. An important trait of mine is that I have always been highly impressionable. Everyone knows I take everything deeply. Therefore you will believe me that this session indeed made a tremendous impression upon me. . . .

It has been said here—and it is a justified rebuke—that we have not been waging a struggle in our press against foreign reactionaries in biology. I say here that I will wage this struggle and give it political importance. I believe Soviet biologists should speak out at last in our scientific press about the fact that a great ideological chasm divides us, and only those foreign scientists who understand that a bridge must be extended toward us and not toward them can expect our consideration.

25. Ibid., 525–526. Alikhanyan's apologia is strikingly parallel to Zhukovsky's:

Comrades, I asked the chairman for the floor not because I read Yury Andreyevich Zhdanov's statement in *Pravda* today. I decided yesterday to present this declaration, and Deputy Minister of Agriculture P. P. Lobanov can confirm that I spoke of it with him by telephone yesterday, August 6. I have very carefully followed the proceedings here and experienced much in these days. . . . It is a matter of a struggle between two worlds and two world outlooks, and we should not cling to old ideas that our teachers handed down to us. . . .

We yielded to polemical passions that our teachers kindled in this discussion. Because of these polemics we failed to perceive the new, growing direction in genetics. . . . the Michurin doctrine. . . .

I cannot imagine my existence without active and useful work for the benefit of Soviet society and Soviet science. When I went into battle with my soldiers, I believed in our party, our ideology. And today I sincerely believe that I am behaving honestly and truthfully as a scientist and marching with the party, with my country; and, if you, Comrades, do not do the same, you will be left behind, you will lag behind the progressive development of science. Science cannot tolerate indecisiveness and lack of principle. . . .

It cannot be concealed that this will be an extremely difficult and painful process. Perhaps many will not understand this. Well, we can't help that; they're just not with us, meaning they will be unable correctly to appreciate the help our party has given us in the radical turn our science has taken, they will be unable to grasp that it is a matter of disagreement on fundamental and not individual questions.

Only in our country, the country of the most advanced Weltanschauung, could the buds of the new scientific movement flower, and our place is with this new, progressive movement.

26. Ibid., 512.
27. T. D. Lysenko, "The Coryphaeus of Science," *Pravda*, March 8, 1953.
28. *On the Results of the Work of the Session of the Lenin All-Union Academy of Agricultural Sciences and the Tasks of Further Development of Michurinist Agrobiology in the Ukraine* (in Ukrainian) (Kiev and Kharkov, 1948).
29. Ibid.
30. Ibid.
31. *Pravda*, August 15, 1948, p. 3.
32. Twenty-five years later, Rapoport was nominated to be a corresponding member of the Academy of Sciences. He told me at that time that a Party functionary had sought him out to urge him to withdraw his old rejection of Party membership and return to the Party. If he did so, he was told, his election to the academy would be assured, but not otherwise. "First let the Party issue a statement that it was wrong in supporting Lysenko's stand and his report to the August session of the VASKhNIL," was his reply, "and then I'll think about your proposition." Nevertheless, Rapoport was elected, and later he won a Lenin Prize for his scientific work. Afterward, he did return to membership in the Party.
33. Decree No. 1213, August 23, 1948.
34. In 1965, Zhebrak tried to return to the department of genetics and plant breeding at his alma mater, the Timiryazev Academy—a department which he had founded—but he was blocked by political-minded members of the council. He died soon afterward.
35. Popovsky, *Academician Vavilov's Trial.*
36. Efroimson was freed and rehabilitated in 1955, but he was prevented from returning to work in genetics by Dubinin, who harbored personal animosity toward him. After a period of existence on odd jobs, he eventually found work as a bibliographer in the Library of Foreign Literature. He wrote the following in the margin of a typewritten samizdat copy of the manuscript of this book: "May the name of Margarita Ivanovna Rudomino, director of the Library of Foreign Literature, be remembered with the greatest gratitude for having saved hundreds of Moscow intellectuals from the label of 'parasite' or worse during the hardest years when they returned to Moscow after having served their sentences."
37. Thirty years later, a memorial volume honoring Sabinin's memory was published: F. E. Reimers, ed., *D. A. Sabinin and His Creative Heritage: From the Recollections of Contemporaries* (D. A. Sabinin i yego tvorcheskoye naslediye: Iz vospominanii sovremennikov) (Novosibirsk: Nauka, Siberian Division, 1981). However, this work did not mention the manner of Sabinin's death or the circumstances that led up to it. Mikhail V. Volkenshtein, a corresponding member of the Academy of Sciences, has told me that Reimers, the editor of the volume, used to criticize Lysenko in private but deferred to him in public. On one occasion in the 1970s, Volkenshtein encountered Reimers shaking hands with Lysenko in the academy dining room on Lenin Avenue. The two men had been having a cordial conversation, but upon seeing Volkenshtein enter the dining room, Reimers beat a hasty retreat. That evening, he telephoned Volkenshtein at home and said, "But I washed my hands thoroughly afterward."
38. S. I. Vavilov, "Introductory Remarks at the Expanded Session of the Presidium of the Academy of Sciences of the USSR," *Herald of the Academy of Sciences of the USSR*, 1948, no. 9:25, 26.
39. Ibid., 47.
40. Ibid., 105. The reference to the elder Zhdanov is curious. At about this time, he had gone to the Dolgiye Borody Sanitarium in the Valdai Hills for a rest. While there,

he suddenly died—of a heart attack, according to the official announcement, though many people believe that secret police chief Beria was responsible for his death. Lysenko could not have been unaware of Zhdanov's unfavorable opinion, but he nevertheless shrewdly eulogized him in a tribute entitled "He Inspired Us to fight for the Further Flowering of Science": *Izvestia*, September 1, 1948, p. 1. Robert Conquest, in his book *The Great Terror* (Russian edition: Edizioni Aurora, Firenze, 1974), wrote , "Soviet biology was not completely destroyed until 1948—after the political defeat of Zhdanov and his death." (592).

41. Ibid., 52. In point of fact, neither Dobzhansky nor N. V. Timofeyev-Ressovsky was a "White émigré" in the formal sense of the term; they did not leave for the West until the mid-twenties and so in Soviet terminology were "non-returnees." Dobzhansky left the USSR for the United States in 1927 and never returned. Timofeyev-Ressovsky went not to the United States but to Germany in 1925, where he worked in a research institute near Berlin. When Soviet troops arrived toward the end of World War II, they arrested him, and he was sent first to a prison, then to a labor camp, and then to a sharashka.

42. Ibid., 162.

43. Ibid., 67.

44. Ibid., 197.

45. Ibid., 170.

46. Ibid., 173, 179.

47. Levshin, *Sergei Ivanovich Vavilov*, 33–34.

48. "In the Presidium of the Academy of Medical Sciences of the USSR: Problems of Medicine in the Light of the Decisions of the Session of the Academy of Agricultural Sciences," *Medical Worker* (Meditsinsky rabotnik), September 15, 1948, p. 2; "From the Participants in the Expanded Session of the Presidium of the Academy of Medical Sciences of the USSR . . . To Comrade Iosif Vissarionovich Stalin," ibid., 1; "For a Leading Biological Science, for the further Development of Soviet Medicine," ibid.

49. "In the Presidium of the Academy of Medical Sciences of the USSR: Problems of Medicine in the Light of the Decisions of the Session of the Academy of Agricultural Sciences," *Medical Worker* (Meditsinsky rabotnik), September 15, 1948, p. 2; "From the Participants in the Expanded Session of the Presidium of the Academy of Medical Sciences of the USSR . . . To Comrade Iosif Vissarionovich Stalin," ibid., 1; "For a Leading Biological Science, for the Further Development of Soviet Medicine," ibid.

50. "For a Leading Biological Science."

51. *Herald of the Academy of Sciences of the USSR*, 1948, no. 10:70.

52. E. A. Chudakov, "Toward the Reconstruction of Academic and Scientific Work in the Area of the Technical Sciences," ibid., 1948, no. 12:6.

53. B. V. Kukarkin, *Research on the Structure and Development of Stellar Systems on the Basis of the Study of Variable Stars* (Moscow: Gosudarstvennoye izdatelstvo tekhniko-teoreticheskoi literatury, 1949), 5.

54. "An Answer to Professor Muller," *Herald of the Academy of Sciences of the USSR*, 1948, no. 11:5. Another Nobel Prize winner, Barbara McClintock, told me in 1988 that she had met Vavilov when he was visiting the United States and that she had seriously considered his proposal that she go to the Soviet Union to work at the Genetics Institute. Laughing, she remarked that by turning down the invitation she may have saved herself from a death in Stalin's labor camps in Siberia.

55. V. M. Molotov, *The Thirty-first Anniversary of the Great October Socialist Revolution* (Moscow: Gospolitizdat, 1948), 20. Emphasis in the original.

56. Graham, *Science and Philosophy*, 214; Medvedev, *Rise and Fall of T. D. Lysenko*, 134.

57. I. V. Stalin, *Works*, vol. 1 (Moscow: Gospolitizdat, 1946), 301.

58. Ibid.; emphasis in the original.

59. This division of life processes into only two tendencies exemplifies Stalin's failure to recognize the wide spectrum of developmental processes and their complex

interdependence. This narrow attitude toward nature and natural resources was consistent with Michurin's slogan, "We cannot await nature's favors; our task is to seize them from her," and it led to ecological disaster.

60. Stalin, *Works*, 1:303, 307–309, 313–314; emphases in the original.

61. At one of the presidium meetings, in 1956 or 1957, Academician Ye. S. Varga asked Lysenko how he could justify accepting money for membership in the presidium while absenting himself year after year from its meetings. Lysenko turned crimson, snorted, but did not answer. Personal communication from Academician Ivan L. Knunyants.

62. The decree was printed in *Pravda*, June 30, 1937, p. 2.

12. The Period of Great Agronomical Deceptions

Epigraph sources: N. N. Semyonov, "Science Does Not Tolerate Subjectivism," *Science and Life* (Nauka i zhizn), 1965, no. 4:38; A. A. Zinovyev, *A Bright Future* (Svetloye budushcheye) (Lausanne: L'Age d'Homme, 1978), 198.

1. Ye. M. Chekmenev, "Speech at the August Session of VASKhNIL," in *On the Position in Biological Science*, 235–236.

2. Ye. M. Chekmenev, "Before the Great Offensive," *The Lantern* (Ogonyok), 1949, no. 10, as reprinted in K. N. Tarakanov, *Collected Articles on Questions of Michurinist Biology: An Aid to the Secondary-School Teacher* (Sbornik statei po voprosam michurinskoi biologii: V pomoshch uchitelyu srednei shkoly) (Moscow: Uchpedgiz, 1950), 38. In an article, "Soviet Fact and American Fiction," also in *The Lantern*, Valentin Zorin (who became in the 1970s–1980s one of the leading Communist journalist commentators) praised the Stalin plan, reporting that in the United States they did not fight against soil erosion, while in the USSR they would now put an end to it. (This article is summarized in *The Current Digest of the Soviet Press* 1, no. 19:17–18.)

3. Graham, *Science and Philosophy*, 238, uses the term "thinning out," but this does not convey the sense of volition and self-sacrifice in Lysenko's term.

4. See *The Intraspecies Struggle of Animals and Plants* (Vnutrividovaya borba zhivotnykh i rastenii) (Moscow: Moscow State University Press, 1947); S. D. Yudintsev and A. D. Zelikman, "Results of the Conference," *Herald of Moscow State University* (Vestnik Moskovskogo gosudarstvennogo universiteta), 1948, no. 4.

5. T. D. Lysenko, "Experimental Sowings of Forest Varieties by the Cluster Method: Report at the Meeting of the Scientific Workers of VASKhNIL, January 23, 1948," as reprinted in Tarakanov, *Collected Articles on Questions of Michurinist Biology*, 11; Lysenko, *Agrobiology*, 587, 588–589. Unlike "wild" vegetation, he added, "cultivated plants, such as wheat and a number of others, do not possess the biological property of self-culling.... Plantings of grains, for example, that are too thick, especially in the dry regions, perish completely without producing seeds." Lysenko, *Agrobiology*, 589.

6. T. D. Lysenko, "Results of the Experimental Sowings of the Forest Belts in 1949 and 1950," in Lysenko, *Agrobiology*, 677. It was later reported that, by 1956, "not more than 6 percent of the cluster plantings remained," and to preserve even those "urgent restoration work was required," which would have involved an expenditure of about 75 percent of what the original project had cost. This work was never done. See *Botanical Journal* 43 (1958): 714.

7. Ibid. At a conference of the Academy of Agricultural Sciences in 1949, Lysenko said that "rendering the utmost scientific aid to the kolkhozes and state farms in mastering and implementing the cluster method of forest planting is a responsibility and honorable duty of all workers of agricultural science, forestry specialists, and agronomists." T. D. Lysenko, "Results of the Work of the VASKhNIL and the Tasks of Agricultural Science: Report at the Anniversary Session of the VASKhNIL, 1949," in Lysenko, *Agrobiology*, 632.

8. Lysenko, "Results of the Experimental Sowings," 689.

9. Decree no. 38 of the Chief Administration for Erosion-Control Forestation, March 30, 1952.

10. See the report by V. N. Sukachev to the Academy of Sciences in *Herald of the AN SSSR* (Vestnik AN SSSR), 1965, no. 3.

11. "An Outstanding Contribution to Science," *Biochemistry* 14 (1949): 193–195.

12. "Conference on Erosion-Control Forestation," *Forest Economics* (Lesnoye khozyaistvo), 1955, no. 3:37–51.

13. V. Ya. Koldanov, "Some Results and Conclusions of Erosion-Control Forestation," *Forest Economics*, 1954, no. 3:10–18. Koldanov was the deputy minister of forestry.

14. Lysenko, *Agrobiology*, 621.

15. M. G. Tumanyan, "On the Experimental Acquirement of Soft Wheat from Hard," *Agrobiology*, 1941, no. 2:13–18.

16. M. G. Tumanyan, "The Problem of the Origin of Weed Rye," *Izvestia of the Armenian Academy of Sciences*, 1949, no. 2:35–44; T. D. Lysenko, "What Is New about the Biological View in Science," in Lysenko, *Agrobiology*, 669 (about the discovery by Karapetyan, Yakubintser, and Gromachevsky of rye grains in ears of wheat); N. D. Mukhin, "Changes in the Usual Forms of Soft and Spring Wheat into Branched Wheat," *Agrobiology*, 1952, no. 4; S. K. Karapetyan, "The Generation of Hazel from Hornbeam," *Agrobiology*, 1952, no. 5:23–29; and K. Ya. Avotin-Pavlov, "The Self-Grafting of Spruce to Pine," *Forest Economics*, 1951, no. 11:88–90, and "The Generation of Spruce by Pine," *Agrobiology*, 1952, no. 5:30–35. For a list of other instances, see *BJ*, 1954, no. 2:221–223.

17. V. Ya. Yuryev, "Isolation of Winter Rye and the Influence of Cross-Pollination on Different Varieties," *Selection and Seed-Growing*, 1948, no. 11.

18. This theory also had the benefit, from Lysenko's point of view, of offering an alternative to Vavilov's propositions about the centers of origin of cultivated plants: the idea that a given kind of cultivated plant gave birth to other kinds of cultivated plants.

19. Lysenko, "I. V. Stalin and Michurinist Biology," 641.

20. V. D. Timakov and M. N. Zhukov-Verezhnikov, "The Study of the Heredity of Microbes and Michurinist Doctrine," *Medical Worker*, 1948, no. 37:3.

21. G. M. Boshyan, *On the Nature of Viruses and Microbes* (Moscow: Medgiz, 1949).

22. A. N. Belozersky, "Bacterial Nucleoproteids and Polynucleotides," *Herald of Moscow University* (Vestnik Moskovskogo universiteta), 1949, no. 2:125–134.

23. See N. V. Turbin, "For Darwinism in the Theory of Species Formation," *Herald of Leningrad University* (Vestnik Leningradskogo universiteta), Biology, Geography, and Geology Series, 1954, no. 10:31–32.

24. *On the Situation in Biological Science*, 267, 261, 259.

25. V. S. Dmitriyev, "On the Primary Sources of Certain Weed Plants," *Journal of General Biology* (Zhurnal obshchei biologii) 14 (1952): 43.

26. Dmitriyev, "On the Primary Sources of Certain Weed Plants," 41–70, and V. S. Dmitriyev, "On the Primary Source of the Origin of Smooth-Seeded Vetch," *Agrobiology*, 1952, no. 1. In 1970–1971, Dr. Alexander Fyodorov, who worked at the Institute of Genetics, and a Dr. Koval, who worked in Gosplan, told me about Dmitriyev's ghostwritten dissertation and articles.

27. Dmitriyev, "On the Primary Sources of Certain Weed Plants," 53, 43–44.

28. O. B. Lepeshinskaya, *The Membrane of Red Blood Cells As a Colloidal System and Its Variability* (Obolochka krasnykh krovyanykh kletok kak kolloidnaya sistema i yeyo izmenchivost) (Moscow and Leningrad: Glavnauka and Glavizdat, 1931).

29. O. B. Lepeshinskaya, "The Problem of the Formation of Cells in a Living Organism. 1. The Formation of Cells and Blood Residuals from the Yolk Spheres of Chicken Embryos," *Biological Journal* (Biologichesky zhurnal) 3 (1934): 233–255. See also O. B. Lepeshinskaya, "Die Entstehung von Flussigkeit im Blastocoel aus Dotterkörnern (Beobachtungen an *Acipenser stellatus*)," *Cytologia* 6 (1935): 294–299.

30. O. B. Lepeshinskaya, *The Origin of Cells from Living Matter* (Moscow: Molodaya gvardiya, 1951), 9.

31. N. K. Koltsov, "Is Self-Conception of the Nucleus and the Cell Possible?" *BJ* 3 (1934): 255–260.

32. O. B. Lepeshinskaya, "The Development of Living Matter and the Origin of Cells," in *Pavlovian Doctrine in Theoretical and Practical Medicine* (Ucheniye Pavlova v teoreticheskoi i prakticheskoi meditsine), 2nd ed. (Moscow: Medgiz, 1953), 36.

33. O. B. Lepeshinskaya, *The Origin of Cells from Living Matter and the Role of Living Matter in the Organism* (Proiskhozhdeniye kletok iz zhivogo veshchestva i rol zhivogo veshchestva v organizme) (Moscow and Leningrad: Izdatelstvo Akademii nauk SSSR, 1945).

34. T. D. Lysenko, Foreword to ibid.

35. O. B. Lepeshinskaya, *The Membranes of Living Cells and Their Biological Significance* (Moscow: Medgiz, 1946/1947). The title page and the cover of the book give different dates of publication. From other evidence, it seems most likely that the book was published in 1947.

36. P. Makarov and others, "Concerning an Unscientific Conception," *Medical Worker*, July 7, 1948, p. 3. The signers included a number of academicians and corresponding members of both the AN SSSR and the Academy of Medical Sciences.

37. At the time I was studying at the Timiryazev Academy, I had a discussion with Lysenko about this idea of transformation. In order to overcome my skepticism, he stood up from his armchair, moved it away from the wall, and invited me look at a stand that stood behind the armchair. On this stand was a clump of dirt filled with interlaced roots, from which rose about ten stalks of wheat, ending in ears of clearly different varieties. "Here, you see," Lysenko said, "all these different varieties grew from one grain. Moreover, this was not done for show but for its own sake." "Did you do this yourself?" I asked. "No," he replied, "my pupils presented it to me." "Then how can one know that this grew from one wheat grain and that this is a single plant? The root system is so interlaced that you can't make out anything!" (I knew at that time that A. Sinyukhin, a biology student at Moscow State University who admired Lysenko, had distinguished himself by gluing together parts of two species. He had been caught and exposed.) "I told you," he said, "from one seed—that means that from one . . . " "Well, then, give me one grain from each ear," I suggested. "I will sow them in conditions that exclude cross-pollination, and we shall see what grows from them and whether it is really possible for just one grain to produce all these different species." Lysenko at once fell silent, moved the armchair back to the wall, and changed the subject as if the topic were entirely exhausted.

38. Lysenko's speech, lauding Lepeshinskaya's "discoveries," was published, more than a year later, in a general-circulation newspaper: "The Work of O. B. Lepeshinskaya and the Transformation of Species," *Literary Gazette*, September 13, 1951.

39. I. Ye. Glushchenko, in *Conference on the Problem of Living Matter and the Development of Cells, May 22–24, 1950: Stenographic Report* (Soveshchaniye po probleme zhivogo veshchestva i razvitia kletok) (Moscow: Izdatelstvo AN SSSR, 1951), 130.

40. V. D. Timakov, in ibid., 133.

41. Ibid., 163.

42. Ibid., 120.

43. Ibid., 124–125.

44. See, for example, O. B. Lepeshinskaya, *The Cell: Its Life and Origin* (Kletka: Yeyo zhizn i proiskhozhdeniye) (Moscow: Goskultprosvetizdat, 1952), 4–5.

45. *Izvestia of the Academy of Sciences of the USSR*, Biology series, 1950, no. 5.

46. For example, on August 13, 1952, the Ministry of Higher Education issued decree no. 1338, "On the Reconstruction of Scientific and Educational Work in Histology, Embryology, Microbiology, Cytology, and Biochemistry in the Light of the Theory of O. B. Lepeshinskaya on the Development of Cellular and Noncellular Forms of Living

Matter": *Bulletin of the Ministry of Higher Education of the USSR* (Byulleten Ministerstva vysshego obrazobania SSSR), 1952, no. 10:1–2. The minister at the time was V. N. Stoletov, one of the organizers of the August 1948 session.

47. O. B. Lepeshinskaya, "The Development of Cells from Noncellular Living Matter," *Nature Study in the School* (Yestyestvoznaniye v shkole), 1950, no. 4:101–110; reprinted in a teachers' guide, *Problems of Michurinist Biology* (Voprosy michurinskoi biologii), 2nd ed. (Moscow: Uchpedgiz, 1951).

48. See, for example, L. A. Kalinichenko, *New Achievements of Soviet Biology* (Novye dostizhenia sovetskoi biologii) (Moscow: Obshchestvo po rasprostraneniyu politicheskikh i nauchnykh znanii, 1950); L. V. Plyushch, *The Outstanding Work of the Soviet Scientist, Professor O. B. Lepeshinskaya, and Its Significance for the Development of Biological Science: Materials for Lectures* (Vydayushchiyesya raboty sovetskogo uchenogo, prof. O. B. Lepeshinskoi, i ikh zhacheniye dlya razvitia biologicheskoi nauki: Materialy dlya lektsii) (Moscow: Obshchestvo po rasprostraneniyu politicheskikh i nauchnykh znanii, 1951); K. Yu. Kostryukova, "A Great Contribution to Materialist Biology," in *Problems of Physiology* (Voprosy fiziologii), no. 2 (Kiev: Academy of Sciences of the Ukrainian SSR, Naukova dumka, 1951), 199–204.

49. Lectures, writings, and articles by Lepeshinskaya and her daughter.

50. O. B. Lepeshinskaya, "Cell Theory at a New Stage of Development," in I. N. Maisky and others, eds., *New Data on the Problem of the Development of Cellular and Noncellular Forms of Living Matter: Proceedings of the Conference on the Problem of the Development of Cellular and Noncellular Forms of Living Matter in Light of the Theory of O. B. Lepeshinskaya* (Novye dannye po probleme razvitia kletochnykh i nekletochnykh form zhivogo veschestva: Trudy konferentsii po probleme razvitia kletochnykh i nekletochnykh form zhivogo veschestva v svete teorii O. B. Lepeshinskoi) (Moscow: USSR Academy of Medicinal Sciences, 1954), 10.

51. I. N. Maisky and others, *Cellular and Noncellular Forms of Living Matter*, 37–48, 80–81, 100–107, 137–146.

52. M. S. Navashin, "On Living Matter in the Reproductive Process of Plants," in ibid., 49–50. Her assertion that many plants have lost the property of reductive division is completely false.

53. M. S. Navashin, Ye. N. Gerasimova-Navashina, and M. S. Yakovlev, "On the Role of Noncellular Living Matter in the Reproductive Process of Plants," *Izvestia of the Academy of Sciences of the USSR*, Biology Series, 1952, no. 5:8–32.

54. O. B. Lepeshinskaya, "Reply to M. S. Navashin," *UBM*, 1937, no. 2:134–140; O. B. Lepeshinskaya and V. G. Kryukov, "On Certain Mistakes in the Understanding of the Theory of the Development of Living Matter," *Izvestia of the Academy of Sciences of the USSR*, Biology Series, 1953, no. 3:16–24.

55. L. P. Lipchina, "On the Proliferation of Cancerous Cells," in Maisky and others, *Cellular and Noncellular Forms of Living Matter*, 196. See also, in the same work, the reports by F. M. Khaletskaya (Institute of Oncology), 174–181; L. I. Falin (Smolensk Medical Institute), 182–184; and L. M. Shabad (corresponding member of the Academy of Medicine), 185–190.

56. Ibid., 151–157.

57. Ibid., 271. In a collection of articles for biology teachers, Dr. A. A. Safronov described a new method of treating wounds, which consisted of placing blood on them, since blood, he said, contained a high concentration of living matter. "Not firing an 'antiseptic gun' at microbes but drawing living substance into the wound and creating the conditions necessary for its development" was the proper method of treatment. A. A. Safronov, "Treating Wounds in the Light of O. B. Lepeshinskaya's Teaching," in O. B. Lepeshinskaya, ed., *Extracellular Forms of Life: A Collection of Materials for Teachers* (Moscow: Academy of Pedagogical Sciences of the RSFSR, 1952), 187. See also O. B. Lepeshinskaya, "Successes of the New Theory of the Origin of Cells," *Nature* (Priroda), 1952, no. 1:85–87.

58. Zh. A. Medvedev, "Biochemical Regularities in the Growth, Ageing, and Renewal of the Cellular Forms of Living Material," *Successes of Contemporary Biology* (Uspekhi sovremennoi biologii) 35 (1953): 338. For other examples, see M. F. Nikitenko, review of *The Development of Vital Processes in the Precellular Period*, by O. B. Lepeshinskaya, *Successes of Contemporary Biology*, 35 (1953): 305–310, and the following articles by A. S. Krivisky: "The Biological Nature of the Bacteriophage," *Nature* (Priroda), 1952, no. 10:53–54; "On the Role of Filtered Forms in the Biology of Microorganisms," *Microbiology* (Mikrobiologiya), 21 (1952): 596–607; and "Noncellular Forms of Life," *Nature* (Priroda), 1953, no. 10:54–60.

59. Samizdat version of Medvedev, *Rise and Fall of Lysenko.*

60. G. A. Melkonyan, "On the Possibility of Osteogenesis outside an Organism after Anabiosis of Bone Cells," *Successes of Contemporary Biology* 30 (1948): 309. As a result of this and similar articles, this Lysenkoist journal came to be known among scientists as *Jokes (potekhi) of Contemporary Biology* instead of *Successes (uspekhi) of Contemporary Biology.*

61. V. G. Shipachev, *On the Historically Formed Evolutionary Path of Development of the Animal Cell in Light of the New Dialectico-Materialistic Cell Theory* (Ob istorichesky slozhivshemsya evolyutsionnom puti razvitia zhivotnoi kletki v svete novoi dialektiko-materialisticheskoi kletochnoi teorii) (Irkutsk: Irkutsk Regional Publishing House, 1954). (The foreword to this book was signed by Lepeshinskaya.) Shipachev's ignorance of the elementary details of cell structure was exposed two years later by V. Ya. Aleksandrov in a brilliant article, "Toward the Question of the Transformation of a Plant Cell into an Animal Cell and Vice Versa," *BJ* 40 (1955): 244–250. Prior to publication of this article, Aleksandrov sent a typewritten copy to Khrushchev, with a cover letter that said, "This . . . is one illustration of the intolerable state to which our biology has been brought." (A copy of this letter was kindly provided to me by the author.) Among other errors, Shipachev claimed to see a complex cellular structure in the root hairs of plant shoots, which in fact are merely elongated parts of single cells.

62. See the article by F. N. Kucherova, "Management of the Embryonic Development of Animals by Means of Influence Exerted through the Maternal Organism," *Successes of Contemporary Biology*, 1950, no. 1:145–160.

63. Rem Viktorovich Petrov, "Ontogenesis of Secondary Cultures of Bacteria of Typhoid Fever and Dysentery in the Process of Their Development from Living Matter," Dissertation of the Candidate of Medical Sciences, Voronezh Medical Institute, 1954.

64. As quoted in N. N. Semyonov, "Science Does Not Tolerate Subjectivism," *Science and Life* (Nauka i zhizn), 1965, no. 4:41.

65. T. D. Lysenko, "On New Paths," *Pravda*, April 8, 1938, p. 3.

66. S. L. Ioannisyan, *How the High-Producing, High-Fat-Milk Herd Was Created at Lenin Hills* (Kak bylo sozdano vysokoproduktivnoye zhirnomolochnoye stado v "Gorkakh Leninskikh") (Moscow: Znaniye, 1961), 5.

67. Ibid., 6.

68. Ibid., 7.

69. Ibid., 5.

70. Sergei N. Muromtsev, a microbiologist and KGB officer—with as much expertise in cows as Lysenko himself had—described Lysenko's ideas and plans in an article, "Toward a New Success in Socialist Animal Husbandry," *Nature* (Priroda), 1952, no. 10:58.

71. *Herald of the Academy of Sciences of the USSR*, 1965, no. 11:16. The same source—a commission appointed to investigate the activities at Lenin Hills—also noted that meat production fell by more than 40 percent during this ten-year period.

72. It is possible that Ioannisyan was responsible for this deception, since he supplied Lysenko with the figures. Ioannisyan, incidentally, was director of the Lenin Hills farm when these experiments began and remained so until at least 1988.

73. See the decree of January 5, 1961, "On the Experience of the Work at the Lenin Hills Experimental Farm in Raising the Fat Content of Milk," and the decree of June

26, 1963, "On Improving Work on the Creation of a Cattle Herd Producing High-Fat Milk on the Kolkhozes and Sovkhozes through the Use of Pedigreed Animals Originating at the Lenin Hills Experimental Farm and Their Offspring."

74. See Ioannisyan, *How the . . . Herd Was Created at Lenin Hills*, 3.

75. Quoted in ibid., 4.

76. Calculations made by the author from the figures in Khrushchev's speech.

77. T. D. Lysenko, "The Transformation of Nonwinterized Spring Varieties into Winter-Hardy Winter Varieties," in Lysenko, *Agrobiology*, 715, 718.`

78. T. D. Lysenko, "On the Agronomical Teaching of V. P. Williams," *Pravda*, July 15, 1950.

13. The First Fall

Epigraph sources: O. Mandelshtam, untitled poem (1934), in his *Poems* (Leningrad: Sovetsky pisatel, 1978), 172; M. Ye. Saltykov-Shchedrin, *Our Complacent Times*, in his *Collected Works* (Moscow: Khudozhestvennaya literatura, 1969), 7:153–154.

1. In *Conference on the Problem of Living Matter and the Development of Cells, May 22–24, 1950: Stenographic Report* (Moscow: Academy of Sciences of the USSR, 1951), 111–112.

2. Lysenko, *Agrobiology*, 702.

3. O. B. Lepeshinskaya, *On Life, Ageing, and Longevity* (Moscow: Znaniye, 1053), 46–48.

4. Ibid., 41.

5. Ibid., 40–41. See also O. B. Lepeshinskaya, "On the Principle of a Cure by Soda Baths," *Clinical Medicine* (Klinicheskaya meditsina) 31 (1953), no. 1:26–30.

6. Ibid., 42. Lepeshinskaya did not overlook the applications of her "discovery" to agronomical practice. She reported receiving letters in which "directors of experimental plots who treated beet seed with a 1% soda solution achieved a 37% increase in yield," and she cited an article in the magazine *Young Collective Farmer* in which a Komsomol member said that the same solution made plants grow better in general—and she offered to send a copy of the magazine "to those who were interested." Ibid.

7. Zhores Medvedev, *Rise and Fall of T. D. Lysenko*, 184.

8. Lepeshinskaya, *On Life, Ageing, and Longevity*, 42.

9. *Archives of Anatomy, Histology, and Embryology* (Arkhiv anatomii, gistologii, i embriologgii) 31 (1954), no. 2:70. This journal, and several others, carried full reports of the meeting.

10. "Report of the Plenary Session of the Administration of the All-Union Society of Anatomy, Histology, and Embryology," ibid., no. 4:92. Chentsov was later awarded a doctoral degree in biology and became professor and chair of the department of cytology and histology at Moscow State University. Gilev left the USSR and now lives in the West.

11. Ibid., 93.

12. See *Theses of the Reports at the Conference of Embryologists in Leningrad, January 25–31, 1955* (Leningrad: Leningrad University Press, 1955).

13. V. Ye. Kozlov and P. V. Makarov, "On the Nature of the Formative Processes in Matter Made from Hydra Cells," *Herald of Leningrad University*, Biology, Geography, and Geology Series, 1954, no. 7; A. G. Knorre, "Morphological Characteristics of the Elements of the Yolk of the Chicken Egg," *Proceedings of the Academy of Sciences of the USSR* (Doklady Akademii Nauk SSSR) 103 (1955), no. 1; G. I. Roskin, "Yolk Spheres: On the Question of Their Properties and Structure, and the Methods of Research," *Bulletin of the Academy of Sciences of the USSR*, Biology Series (Izvestia Akademii Nauk SSSR, seriya biologicheskaya), 1955, no. 4; L. N. Zhinkin and V. P. Mikhailov, "The 'New Cell Theory' and Its Factual Basis," *Achievements of Contemporary Biology* 39 (1955), no. 2:228–244.

14. *Great Soviet Encyclopedia*, 3rd ed., vol. 14, p. 345. Lepeshinskaya never responded to the repudiation of her theories. Indeed, in the final years of her life, which she spent

at the Biophysics Institute of the USSR Academy of Sciences, she became consumed with a "new" idea. Together with her daughter, Olga Panteleimonovna, she collected bird droppings, dried them on a tin sheet, burned them, poured the ashes into a retort containing boiled water, corked the retort, and left in it a warm place. Probably because the mixture had not been completely sterilized, a bacterial or fungal growth appeared in the retort within a few weeks. Mother and daughter contended that, in accordance with their "theory," the fungal or bacterial cells appeared after the nonliving matter of the heat-treated droppings had passed through a stage of "living matter." Reports of these "discoveries" never appeared in print, but Olga Panteleimonovna described them at a conference that I attended. When another speaker said that the time had passed when such "discoveries" were taken on faith, she cried out: "The forward movement of our science is like high waves. Today, it is you who ride the crest, tomorrow we shall rise to the top again!" During her speech, she had declared that even a temperature of minus 1,000 degrees Celsius could not destroy living matter. "But there is no such temperature," someone objected, "Minus 273 degrees Celsius is absolute zero." "You don't know the dialectic," she replied. "If plus 1,000 degrees exists, minus 1,000 must exist also."

15. N. V. Turbin, "Darwinism and the New Theory of Species," *BJ* 37 (1952), no. 6:798–818. Dmitry D. Brezhnev (no relation to Leonid Brezhnev), a close friend of Turbin's—they had studied together at the Voronezh Agricultural Institute—who held a high position in the Leningrad regional Party committee, has told me that it was he who, having learned of the formation of the Kozlov commission, encouraged Turbin to publish this article, promising him support in Party circles. (Brezhnev later became first vice-president of VASKhNIL.)

16. N. D. Ivanov, "On T. D. Lysenko's New Theory of Species," *BJ* 37 (1952), no. 6:819–842.

17. D. V. Lebedev, personal communication.

18. *Pravda*, November 17, 1952.

19. *Bulletin of the Academy of Sciences of the USSR,* Biology Series, 1953, no. 6:117–118.

20. Personal communication from Yury Zhdanov.

21. N. V. Turbin, "Khrestomatiya po genetike," in *Sovetskaya Nauka* (Moscow, 1949).

22. A. N. Studitsky, "For a Creative Amplification of the Problem of Species Formation," Successes of Contemporary Biology 34 (1953), no. 1:1–26.

23. N. I. Nuzhdin, "A Relapse into Weismannism under the Banner of a Defense of Darwinism" and "The Bankruptcy of False Morganist Science," *Journal of General Biology* 14 (1953), no. 1:3–22, 71–81.

24. A. I. Oparin, "J. V. Stalin, the Inspirer of the Leading Biological Science," *Journal of General Biology* 14 (1953), no. 2:90–95.

25. T. D. Lysenko, "A New Departure in the Science of the Biological Species," *BJ* 38 (1953), no. 1:44–54.

26. *BJ* 38 (1953), no. 1:44.

27. V. N. Sukachev, "On the Intraspecies and Interspecies Relationships among Plants, *BJ* 38 (1953), no. 1:55–96.

28. M. I. Ilyin, "The Process of Species Formation in Angiosperms," and M. P. Vinogradov and T. V. Vinogradova, "On the Criticism by N. V. Turbin and N. D. Ivanov of the New Concepts of Species Formation," *BJ* 38 (1953), no. 2:215–231 and 234–245. Among them were N. V. Pavlov, "On Species Formation by Means of Regeneration," no. 3:378–385; M. V. Kulikov, "Academician T. D. Lysenko's 'New Departure in the Science of the Biological Species' and Biostratigraphy," no. 3:389–393; E. V. Bobko, "Toward the Problem of Method in the Study of the Formation of New Species," no. 3:401–406; A. I. Tolmachev, "On Certain Problems in the Theory of Species Formation," no. 4:530–555; N. I. Kosets, "Has the Possibility of the Generation of Hazel from Hornbeam and of Spruce from Pine Been Proven?" no. 5:696–707; P. A. Baranov, "On Species Formation," no. 5:669–695; B. M. Kozo-Polyansky, "Problems in the New Theory of the

Species," no. 6:830–845; Ye. M. Lavrenko, "On the Study of the Process of Species Formation in Nature," no. 6:346–352; and D. F. Petrov, "Toward the Problem of the Origin of Species," no. 6:853–861.

29. O. B. Lepeshinskaya, "The Malignant Criticism by N. V. Turbin and N. D. Ivanov of T. D. Lysenko's Work on the Species," *BJ* 38 (1953), no. 3:386–388.

30. Avotin-Pavlov, "The Self-Grafting of Spruce on Pine."

31. K. P. Kupfer, "Adoption von Fischtensweigen durch Kiefernstamme," *Mitteilungen der Deutsche Dendrologischen Gesellschaft*, 1928.

32. Avotin-Pavlov, "The Self-Grafting of Spruce on Pine," 90.

33. L. A. Smirnov, "Toward the Question of the Interesting Case of the Self-Grafting of Spruce on Pine in the Vicinity of Riga," *BJ* 38 (1953), no. 3:418–421. Even the newspaper of the Latvian Communist Party Central Committee felt compelled to say that "Avotin-Pavlov faked the story to create a cheap sensation and satisfy his ambitions": Editorial, "On the Honesty of a Scientist," *Cina*, March 21, 1953.

34. Karapetyan, "The Generation of Hornbeam from Hazel."

35. T. D. Lysenko, letter to the editor, *BJ* 38 (1953), no. 6:891.

36. A. A. Rukhkyan, "On the Case of the Generation of a Hazel by a Hornbeam," *BJ* 38 (1953), no. 6:885–891. For further discussion of this case, see A. A. Yatsenko-Khmelevsky, "The Dilizhan Hornbeamhazel and the Problem of the Generation of Species," *BJ* 39 (1954), no. 5:882–889. (Dilizhan is the name of a village in Armenia.)

37. Z. T. Artyushenko, V. N. Zamyatin, and S. Ya. Sokolov, "The Alder-Forming Branch of Birch," *BJ* 38 (1953), no. 3; A. L. Takhtadzhan, "Some Problems in the Theory of the Species and the Systematics of Contemporary and Fossil Plants," *BJ* 40 (1955), no. 6:789–796.

38. "Review of Articles and Letters Received by the Editors of the *Botanical Journal* in Connection with the Discussion of the Problem of the Species and Species Formation," *BJ* 39 (1954), no. 1:76–89, and 40 (1955), no. 2:217–226. The editors who wrote these reviews also published important articles of their own, spelling out the viewpoints of the editorial board: L. A. Smirnov, "Some Results of the Discussion on the Problem of the Species and Species Formation and Its Further Tasks," *BJ* 39 (1954), no. 2:202–223, and D. V. Lebedev, "Broaden and Deepen the Theoretical Discussions on the Problem of the Species and Species Formation," *BJ* 40 (1955), no. 2:206–216.

39. In January 1954, at a conference held by the soil biology department of Leningrad University, Turbin, though again critical of Lysenko, also said: "I dare say . . . that, despite my criticism of T. D. Lysenko's views, I can more easily find common ground with him than with some of the present supporters and defenders of his views, for he is a genuine scientist, which unfortunately cannot be said of those supporters and defenders, whose behavior resembles a weathervane that turns with the wind." *Herald of Leningrad University*, Biology, Geography, and Geology Series, 1954, no. 10:87–88.

40. V. N. Sukachev, "On Intraspecies Competition and on Ecosystem Ecology (Some Notes on Articles by N. I. Nuzhdin and V. S. Dmitriyev)," *Journal of General Biology* 14 (1953), no. 4:326.

41. See, for example, A. M. Semyonova-Tyan-Shanskaya, "The Revival of Vegetation on the Steppe Fields in Connection with the Question of the 'Generation' of Species," *BJ* 38 (1953), no. 6:862–873.

42. S. Stankov, "About a Faulty Dissertation: Letter to the Editors," *Pravda*, March 26, 1954.

43. In a talk with Professor V. Ya. Aleksandrov in 1987, Professor A. M. Smirnov, who worked at the time of these events in the science department of the Party Central Committee, confirmed the fact that the order to publish Stankov's letter in *Pravda* came from Khrushchev.

44. N. S. Khrushchev, *On Increasing the Output of Animal Products: Report at the Plenum of the CC of the CPSU, February 25, 1955* (Moscow: Gospolitizdat, 1955).

45. V. P. Efroimson, "On the Role of Experiment and Data in Agricultural Biology," *Bulletin of the Moscow Naturalists' Society, Biology Section* 61 (1956), no. 5:83–91.

46. B. M. Kozo-Polyansky, "On the Relationship of 'A New Departure in the Science of the Biological Species' to Darwinian Theory," *Bulletin of the Moscow Naturalists' Society, Biology Section* 59 (1954), no. 3:85–88; I. I. Puzanov, "Mutations by Leaps and Metamorphoses," ibid., no. 4:67–79.

47. After his release, Tumerman worked at the Institute of Radiation and Physico-Chemical Biology (later renamed the Institute of Molecular Biology). When his son emigrated to Israel, Tumerman reluctantly went with him and lived and worked there until his death in 1986.

48. I. Knunyants and L. Zubkov, "Schools in Science," *Literary Gazette*, January 11, 1955, p. 1.

49. Helmut Böhme, "Untersuchungen zum Problem der genetischen Bedeutung von Pfropfungen zwischen Pflanzen," *Zeitschr. Pflansenzuchtung* 33 (1954), no. 4: 37–418. At one time, Böhme had studied under Turbin at Leningrad University; he possessed a fluent command of Russian and was thoroughly familiar with the subject of vegetative hybridization, since Turbin had completely shared Lysenko's and Glushchenko's faith in the possibility of influencing heredity by ordinary grafting. Turbin even published an article to that effect in 1949: N. V. Turbin and A. N. Khabarova, "A New Method of Vegetative Hybridization," *BJ* 36 (1949), no. 6.

50. Oleg Pisarzhevsky, "Friendship among the Sciences and Its Violations," *Almanac: The Thirty-seventh Year* (Almanakh: God 37–i), 1954, book 3 (18): 193–254. ("The Thirty-seventh Year" in the title of this journal refers to the number of years since the Bolshevik Revolution. The name of the journal was later changed to *Our Contemporary* [Nash sovremennik].)

51. Editorial, "Science and Life," *Kommunist*, 1954, no. 5:1.

52. Ye. V. Bobko, "The Quality of Scientific Work in Agronomy Must Be Increased," *Soil Science*, 1955, no. 12:77–80.

53. As quoted in Dubinin, *Perpetual Motion*, 355.

54. Ibid., 356.

55. Its members included Dubinin; P. A. Baranov, a corresponding member of the AN SSSR; Professor M. I. Khadzhinov; and M. I. Kalinin, an official of the USSR Ministry of Agriculture.

56. See, for example, V. Safonov, "A Tale of Steep Heights," *Almanac: The Thirty-eighth Year*, 1955, book 20:193–229.

57. T. D. Lysenko, "For the Further Development of the Michurinist Doctrine," in *The Michurinist Doctrine in the Service of the People* (Michurinskoye ucheniye na sluzhbe narodu) (Moscow: Selkhozgiz, 1955), 1:6–7, 8–9.

58. Personal communication from D. V. Lebedev.

59. I am grateful to V. Ya. Aleksandrov for providing me with a copy of this letter and a list of the signers.

60. I am again grateful to V. Ya. Aleksandrov for providing me with a typewritten copy of this letter.

61. A copy of this letter was kindly provided to me by M. D. Golubovsky in 1979. Later, Dr. D. V. Lebedev provided me with a copy of the original of the letter with the complete list of signers.

62. Personal communication from D. V. Lebedev.

63. A year later, after Stalin's death, the office of the military prosecutor started reinvestigating Vavilov's trial, along with thousands of other trials. The report, signed by Justice-Major Kolesnikov on August 8, 1955, indicated that the "investigation of the Vavilov trial found that prejudice had been shown in the original trial by criminal processional court." Then Vavilov's wife, Yelena A. Barulina, received a curt notice from the prosecutor that Vavilov's sentence had been lifted because he had not committed the offense for which he had been charged (she circulated the notice)

(Popovsky, *Academician Vavilov's Trial* [Ann Arbor: Hermitage, 1983). Immediately after Vavilov's rehabilitation, the council of the All-Union Botanical Society decided to publish a collection of articles devoted to his memory, under Lebedev's editorship. I have been told by Lebedev that, after the book had gone to press, Sisakyan demanded the removal of the articles by Lebedev, Timofeyev-Ressovsky, Olenov, and Raisa L. Berg. Publication was held up, and it appeared only five years later—without their contributions. Sisakyan's demand had presumably been made with the agreement of the Party Central Committee. To commemorate what would have been Vavilov's seventieth birthday, seminars were held in Moscow and Leningrad and one of his book-length manuscripts was published: *The World's Resources in Varieties of Cereals, Grain Crops, Legumes, Flax, and Their Use in Plant Breeding* (Moscow-Leningrad: AN SSSR, 1957).

64. P. Yakovlev, "Make Fuller Use of the Heritage of I. V. Michurin," *Pravda*, October 7, 1955, p. 2; N. Sokolov, "A Valuable Contribution to Agronomical Science: On the Book by T. S. Maltsev, *Problems of Agriculture*," ibid., October 10, 1955, p. 2.

65. T. D. Lysenko, "A Feat of Science," *Pravda*, October 27, 1955, p. 2.

66. "The One-Hundredth Anniversary of the Birth of I. V. Michurin," *Pravda*, October 28, 1955, p. 1.

67. Timofeyev-Ressovsky (1900–1980) had lived in Germany from 1925 until 1945, when he returned to the Soviet Union. He had several discussions with Nils Bohr and so was well prepared to conduct a dialogue with physicists. The Lysenkoists spread a story that he had been a fascist sympathizer, but there was nothing to it; his own son had perished at the hands of the Gestapo. See D. A. Granin, *The Bison*, trans. from the Russian (New York: Doubleday, 1989); this book is a fictionalized biography of Timofeyev-Ressovsky.

68. N. V. Timofeyev-Ressovsky, "From the History of the Dialogue of the Biologists and the Physicists," in *Remembrances of I. Ye. Tamm* (Moscow: Nauka, 1981), 194–195. Tamm told me in 1957 that the call to the institute was made in the name of Suslov and that it was Suslov to whom Kapitsa had spoken. However, Granin, *The Bison*, 865, says, apparently on the basis of information from Timofeyev-Ressovsky, that Kapitsa's call was made to Khrushchev himself. This fact was confirmed to me in 1993 by the son of P. L. Kapitsa, Sergei, who was in his father's office at the moment of the telephone conversation with Khrushchev. According to Sergei Kapitsa, Khrushchev was aggressive at the beginning of the conversation but under the pressure of Kapitsa became calm.

69. Timofeyev-Ressovsky, "Dialogue of the Biologists and the Physicists," 194–195.

70. In 1956 and 1957, I often heard Lysenko berate Tamm. Once, he went so far as to say he was going to sue Tamm (as well as Dubinin) for slander. "Tamm is a good-for-nothing physicist," he shouted. "I know that for sure. All the prominent physicists participated in the creation of the Obninsk nuclear power plant, their names appeared in the newspapers, and Tamm's was not among them. His reputation is inflated and now he is gaining a cheap popularity merely by criticizing me."

71. *Pravda*, April 10, 1956, p. 2.

14. President Once More

Epigraph sources: Inna Lisnyanskaya, "What Shall I See in the Hours of Loneliness?" (1980), in her Rain and Mirrors: Verses (Paris: YMCA Press, 1983), 213; F. M. Dostoyevsky, *Devils*.

1. Personal communication in a conversation with Lysenko.

2. Unpublished memoirs of Glushchenko (typescript), 198.

3. N. S. Khrushchev, *On the Planned Figures for the Development of the Economy of the USSR in 1959–1965: Report at the Special Twenty-first Congress of the CPSU, January 27, 1959* (Moscow: Gospolitizdat, 1959), 9.

4. T. D. Lysenko, "Agricultural Science in the Struggle for the Fulfillment of the Stalinist Program," *Izvestia*, March 6, 1946, p. 2.

5. T. D. Lysenko, *The Soil Nutrition of Plants: A Fundamental Problem in the Science of*

Agriculture (Pochvennoye pitaniye rastenii: Korennoi vopros nauki zemledelia) (Moscow: Selkhozgiz, 1955), 33.

6. Lysenko, *Soil Nutrition of Plants*, 33.

7. As a student, I heard Lysenko make precisely this vague assertion of the source of an idea—"I hear from someone"—in one of his lectures at the Timiryazev Academy.

8. T. D. Lysenko, *Toward New Successes in the Realization of the Stalinist Plan for the Reformation of Nature* (K novym uspekham v osushestvlenii stalinskogo plana preobrazovania prirody) (Moscow: Selkhozgiz, 1950), 15.

9. T. D. Lysenko, *On the Soil Nutrition of Plants and an Increase in the Yield of Agricultural Crops* (O pochvennom pitaniye rastenii i povysheniye urozhainosti selskokhozyaistvennykh kultur) (Moscow: Selkhozgiz, 1954), 9, 11. This brochure contains Lysenko's report to a session of VASKhNIL, September 15, 1953.

10. Lysenko, *The Soil Nutrition of Plants* (1955), 33. Lysenko's claim that "the norms of required fertilizer will be lower" may have been shrewdly chosen, because Soviet reserves of phosphorous compounds, one of the chief components of agricultural fertilizers, were close to exhaustion.

11. Lysenko, *The Soil Nutrition of Plants* (1955), 33.

12. A. V. Sokolov, review of Lysenko, *The Soil Nutrition of Plants* (1955), *Soil Science*, 1955, no. 11:99.

13. T. D. Lysenko, "The Task of the Science of Soil Nourishment in Increasing the Yield of Agricultural Crops," *Achievements of Science and of Leading Experience in Agriculture* (Dostizhenia nauki i peredovogo opyta v selskom khozyaistve), 1953, no. 11.

14. This list was compiled by me from information in Lysenko, *Soil Nutrition of Plants*.

15. F. V. Turchin, "The Feeding of Plants and the Application of Fertilizers," *Soil Science*, 1954, no. 6.

16. D. L. Ashkinazi, "Speech Concerning the Reports of A. V. Sokolov, F. V. Turchin, and O. K. Kedrov-Zikhman at the Conference of Soil Scientists, April 20–26, 1954," ibid.

17. P. G. Naidin and A. K. Selavri, "On the Effectiveness of Mixtures of Organic and Phosphoric Fertilizers and Lime," *Soil Sciences*, 1955, no. 10:23–35 (quotation on 28).

18. F. V. Kallistratov, "An Experiment in the Application of Organo-Mineral Mixtures on Winter Wheat," *Agriculture* (Zemledeliye), 1955, no. 7:52–55.

19. Lysenko, *Soil Nutrition of Plants*, 113. Lysenko wrote about this 1946 recommendation to the Siberian collective farmers and cited his old phrases (ibid.).

20. These remarks are quoted from the samizdat manuscript by Medvedev, "Biological Sciences and the Personality Cult" (1962). They are reproduced in part in Medvedev, *Rise and Fall of T. D. Lysenko*, 175.

21. V. V. Matskevich, "On the Tasks of Agricultural Science in Carrying Out the Decisions of the Twentieth Congress of the CPSU," *Herald of Agricultural Science*, 1956, no. 1:34.

22. Dubinin, *Perpetual Motion*, 365.

23. *Tekhnika-Molodyozhi* (Technology for Young People), 1956.

24. N. P. Dubinin, "The Physical and Chemical Bases of Heredity," *Biophysics* (Biofizika), 1956.

25. F. Crick, "The Structure of Hereditary Matter," *Chemical Science and Industry* (Khimicheskaya nauka i promyshlennost) 1 (1956), no. 4:472–477. See also James Watson and Francis Crick, "The Structure of DNA," in *Problems of Cytophysiology* (Problemy tsitofiziologii) (Moscow: Izdatelstvo inostrannoi literatury, 1957), 58–70.

26. *Our Contemporary*, 1956, book 3.

27. Dubinin, *Perpetual Motion*, 368.

28. A. A. Avakyan, "On Friendship among the Sciences and Its Violations: Response to an Opponent (on the Occasion of an Article)," ibid., 130–131.

29. Speech by I. A. Khalifman, ibid., 145.

30. Speech by V. V. Sakharov, ibid., 158–162.
31. Speech by F. V. Turchin, ibid., 153–158.
32. Speech by N. P. Dubinin, ibid., 168–173.
33. Speech by Sakharov, ibid., 159.
34. Ibid., 153–158.
35. Speech by Glushchenko, 165.
36. Ibid., 162, 168.
37. Dubinin, *Perpetual Motion*, 374.
38. F. Kh. Bakhteyev, "On the State of the Teaching of Botany in the Secondary School," *BJ* 43 (1958), no. 1:145–153. For the text of the resolution, see ibid., 153–154. See chapter 9 for Bakhteyev's recollections of Vavilov's abduction by the NKVD.
39. See M. A. Lavrentyev, "Experiences of Life: 50 Years of Science (Memoirs)," *Economics and the Organization of Industrial Production* (Ekonomika i organizatsia promyshlennogo proizvodstva), 1980, no. 1:146. Lavrentyev (ibid., 146–147) tells the following interesting story, illustrative of Lysenko's methods: The science department of the Central Committee had formed in the end of 1950s a commission not to investigate Lysenkoist frauds, but "to rectify contacts with Lysenko and his group." Lavrentyev was appointed a member of the commission, along with Engelgardt, Sukachev, and Kapitsa. One day, they visited the Lenin Hills farm, where "Lysenko expounded his scientific ideas (the soil needn't be fertilized, it need only be 'awakened'—it is living and will give birth itself...") At one end of the fields, Lysenko showed them a row of shrubs and "declared that all the shrubs had a single, unified root system. Sukachev protested that this was ridiculous. 'Let's dig up a few shrubs, and you yourself will be convinced that your theory of intergrowth of the roots is silly.' Lysenko: 'If you don't believe it, plant bushes of your own and dig them up as much as you like, but I won't let you dig up these. I don't need to. I know without digging that they have a single root system. Besides, I tell you I'm going to file a complaint against you for your slanderous journal article.' What followed was quite funny. The problem was that Lysenko wheezed heavily, and Sukachev, who was hard of hearing, thought that Lysenko was still insisting on the interknit roots. This dialogue went on for ten minutes. Sukachev: 'It's all nonsense, they aren't intergrown.' Lysenko: 'I'll file a complaint against you...'" The commission never accomplished its task of "rectifying" contacts. Lavrentyev had seen the consequences of Lysenko's activities in the Ukraine and, in the 1950s, had seen many letters and statements from scientists to the Party Central Committee protesting about Lysenko's dismissal of leading scientists and suppression of genetics research. Ibid., 146.
40. Dubinin, *Perpetual Motion*, 378.
41. N. S. Khrushchev, "For a Sharp Increase in the Production of Meat and Milk in the Districts of the Central Black-Earth Zone," *Pravda*, April 1, 1957, p. 2.
42. V. Polyakov and K. Pogodin, "Meeting of the Agricultural Workers of the Arzamas, Gorky, and Kirov Regions, Mari, Mordovian, and Chuvash ASSR," *Pravda*, April 8, 1957, p. 2.
43. Ibid.
44. *Pravda*, April 10, 1957, p. 2.
45. "Comrade Lysenko's Speech," *Pravda*, April 10, 1957, p. 2.
46. *Pravda*, July 4, 1957, pp. 1–2.
47. Khrushchev, "For a Sharp Increase in the Production of Meat and Milk."
48. Editorial, "The Interesting Work on Livestock-Breeding at Lenin Hills: A Conversation with Academician T. D. Lysenko," *Pravda*, July 17, 1957, p. 5.
49. See, for example, the article by V. A. Engelgardt in *Komsomol Pravda*, June 9, 1957.
50. Editorial, "On the Elucidation of the Philosophical Problems of Natural Science," *Problems of Philosophy* (Voprosy filosofii), 1957, no. 3:3–18.
51. T. D. Lysenko and N. I. Nuzhdin, "For Materialism in Biology" (mimeographed

copy available at the Lenin State Library, shelf number B 59–11/112), 22, 13, 10, 38, 60, 50; emphasis in the original.

52. N. S. Khrushchev, *Theses of the Report "Control Figures for the Development of the Economy of the USSR for 1959–1965"* (Moscow: Politizdat, 1958).

53. A. S. Nesmeyanov, "The Tasks of Soviet Science in the Light of the Seven-Year Plan for the Development of the Economy of the USSR," *Pravda,* December 1, 1958, pp. 2–3.

54. See *Materials on the Conference on the Application of Mathematical Methods in Biology, May 12–17, 1958* (Leningrad: Leningrad State University, 1958).

55. See *Theses of the Reports at the Conference on Polyploids in Plants, June 25–28, 1958* (Moscow: Moscow Naturalists Society, 1958).

56. T. D. Lysenko, "For Materialism in Biology!" *Agrobiology,* 1957, no. 5:4–12 and no. 6:3–17. Both parts of the article were reprinted in *Problems of Philosophy,* 1958, no. 2:102–111.

57. "Discussions: On Certain Problems of Soviet Biology," *BJ,* 1958, no. 8:1135–1145. The article was actually written by D. V. Lebedev of the Botany Institute.

58. *Pravda,* September 29, 1958, p. 1.

59. Editorial, "On Agrobiological Science and the False Positions of the *Botanical Journal,*" *Pravda,* December 14, 1958, pp. 3–4.

60. T. D. Lysenko, "Theoretical Successes of Agronomical Biology," *Izvestia,* December 8, 1957.

61. The commission members were Ezras A. Asratyan, Andrei L. Kursanov, Yevgeny N. Mishustin, Ivan I. Tumanov, and Pyotr I. Lapin.

62. "Conclusion of the Commission of the Biology Division of the AN SSSR on the Activity of the *Botanical Journal,*" appendix to the resolution of the Bureau of the Biology Division of the AN SSSR of September 23, 1958, no. 210–130/277, protocol no. 28, paragraph 5. In the resolution itself, the bureau gave its approval to the commission's conclusions.

63. Resolution of the Bureau of the Biology Division of the AN SSSR of September 23, 2958, no. 210–130/277, protocol no. 28, paragraph 5.

64. *Plenum of the Central Committee of the CPSU, December 15–19, 1958: Stenographic Record* (Moscow: Politizdat, 1958), 83.

65. Ibid., 233–234. After Khrushchev was dismissed as first secretary of the Party, Mustafayev switched to the role of a fighter for genetics, becoming a member of the presidium of the All-Union Society of Geneticists and president of the Azerbaidzhan Society of Geneticists and Breeders.

66. Ibid., 235–238, 240.

67. It is worth nothing that Lobanov, president of VASKhNIL, did not mention Lysenko once during his speech or offer any praise for the Michurinists. He did say, rather ambiguously, that "by better feeding and maintenance of the dairy livestock . . . it is possible to increase the fat content of milk by 0.1 percent . . . which is fully within the capacity of every kolkhoz and sovkhoz" (ibid., 375)—i.e., Lobanov was convinced that it is possible to reach the same result without application of Lysenko innovations but simply with better supply of kolkhozes and sovkhozes with feed and tools.

68. Ibid., 355.

69. On December 18, *Pravda* ran Mustafeyev's speech condemning the *Botanical Journal* on the front page, and Lysenko's on page three.

70. Editorial, "For a Strengthening of Biology's Connection with Practice," *Herald of the AN SSSR,* 1959, no. 3:5–7.

71. Ibid., 112.

72. Actually, the new editorial board had been named the day after the Central Committee meeting, in a phone call to the journal from the office of the presidium of the AN SSSR (according to a personal communication from D. Lebedev). This was

probably done deliberately, to head off a Party investigation of the journal and of the individuals who might be held to blame for the journal's stand. In the course of such an investigation, the "accused" might have been vindicated.

73. *Pravda,* July 2, 1959.

74. Lavrentyev, *Experiences of a Life,* 146–147.

75. Lavrentyev, ibid., 147–150. This account was originally published in the journal *Economics and Organization of Industrial Production,* thanks to the persistence of its editor in chief, A. G. Aganbegyan (later well known as an economic adviser to Gorbachev), who refused to give in to the objections of one of Lysenko's sons, saying, "Lavrentyev is also an important person and I cannot correct him."

76. *A Sakharov Collection* (Sakharovsky sbornik) (New York: Khronika, 1981), 249.

77. A. D. Sakharov, "The Radioactive Carbon of Nuclear Explosions and Nonthreshold Biological Effects," in A. V. Lebedinsky, ed., *Soviet Scientists on the Danger of Nuclear Weapons Testing* (Sovetskiye ucheniye ob opasnosti ispytany yadernogo oruzhia) (Moscow: Glavnoye upravleniye po ispolzovaniyu atomnoi energii, 1959), 36–44.

78. E. Teller and A. Latter, *Our Nuclear Future: Facts, Dangers, and Opportunities* (New York: Criterion, 1958), 124.

79. Teller and Latter, *Our Nuclear Future,* 124.

80. Sakharov, "Radioactive Carbon of Nuclear Explosions," 41, 37.

81. See *A Sakharov Collection,* 249.

82. Ibid., 250.

83. Dubinin, *Perpetual Motion,* 370.

84. A. A. Prokofyeva-Belgovskaya and S. I. Alikhanyan, "Important Problems of Genetics," *Herald of the AN SSSR,* 1959, no. 1:98–100.

85. See, for example, the excerpts from speeches in "The Work of Peace Will Triumph," *Herald of the AN SSSR,* 1951, no. 9:3.

86. Unpublished memoirs of Glushchenko, 281.

87. Many years later, I asked Müntsing, a Swedish geneticist who was editor of the journal *Hereditas,* why he had contributed an article, and he replied: "I always respected Russia, I remembered Vavilov, and I believed that by sending strictly genetic articles to the USSR, I was helping, as much as I could, to restore genetics in the USSR." Glushchenko, in recounting his foreign successes, ignored the report in the *Tokyo Shimbun* that "the scientists did not have to read the comics today; a Russian blabbermouth was the speaker" and "a cutting refutation" (Efroimson's words) in *Hereditas* after his article. Levan and Müntsing wrote in 1950 about his Danish visit: "Most of the audience at this session [at which Glushchenko spoke] came less in hope of hearing fresh facts or theories than to observe and hear persons who deny the most elementary facts about heredity. Chemists who denied the existence of molecules or atoms would have drawn just as large an audience if they began to express such views at an international chemistry congress." Cited in an article by V. P. Efroimson.

88. T. D. Lysenko, *The Nutrition of Plants and the Fertilization of the Fields* (Pitaniye rasteny i udobreniye polei) (Moscow: Selkhozgiz, 1961), 4.

89. Ibid., 3–4.

15. The Second Downfall

Epigraph sources: F. M. Dostoyevsky, *The Devils;* Hermann Hesse, Der Glasperlensspiel.

1. B. Astaurov, "On the Threshold of Great Discoveries," *Pravda,* October 8, 1961, pp. 2–3.

2. Editorial note, ibid., 2.

3. N. S. Khrushchev, "Proper Utilization of the Land: The Most Important Condition for a Rapid Increase in the Production of Grain, Meat, Milk, and Other Agricultural Products," *Izvestia,* December 16, 1961, pp. 1, 2. For another speech by Khrushchev containing praise of Lysenko, see *Pravda,* August 3, 1962, pp. 1–2.

4. N. S. Khrushchev, "Proper Utilization of the Land: The Most Important Condition for a Rapid Increase in the Production of Grain, Meat, Milk, and Other Agricultural Products," *Izvestia*, December 16, 1961, pp. 1–3.

5. "Information Note on the Conference of Selection Scientists," *Rural Life*, June 22, 1962, p. 4.

6. Associates of Nesmeyanov say that he resigned his post because of his objection to the transfer of academy institutes to the jurisdiction of ministries and administrative bodies. He feared that the transfer would destroy basic science because practical interests would dictate all research. Although the transfer did not happen, people were very concerned and considered the plan another example of political intrusion. Adams, "Biology after Stalin," 76, says that Nesmeyanov's resignation was engineered by Lysenko.

7. He visited the Institute of Cytology and Genetics in Novosibirsk, Minsk Laboratory of N. Turbin, and other laboratories.

8. The incident is described in Glushchenko's memoirs, 282–284.

9. *Pravda*, .

10. Vasily N. Remeslo was particularly active at this conference. He had developed a high-yield variety of soft spring wheat, "Mironovskaya 264" (a 42–chromosome variety), and declared that he obtained it "by training it" from 28–chromosome hard wheat. *Pravda*, January 25, 1963, p. 1, mentioned this.

11. T. D. Lysenko, "Theoretical Principles of Directed Change in the Heredity of Agricultural Plants," *Pravda*, January 29, 1963, pp. 3–4.

12. N. G. Yegorychev, "Speech at the Plenum of the CC of the CPSU," *Evening Moscow* (Vechernyaya Moskva), June 19, 1963, p. 4.

13. Zh. Medvedev, *The Biosynthesis of Proteins and Problems of Ontogenesis* (Biosintez belkov i problemy ontogeneza) (Moscow: Medgiz.)

14. Yegorychev, "Speech at the Plenum."

15. Zh. Medvedev and V. Kirpichnikov, "The Prospects for Soviet Genetics," *Neva*, 1963, no. 3:165–178.

16. M. A. Olshansky, "Against Falsification in Biological Science," *Rural Life*, August 18, 1963, pp. 2–3.

17. Editorial, "Against Falsification in Biological Science," *Pravda*, August 21, 1963, p. 6.

18. *Neva*, 1963, no. 9:162.

19. M. V. Keldysh, "On Measures for the Improvement of the Activity of the Academy of Sciences of the USSR and the Academies of Science of the Union Republics," *Herald of the AN SSSR*, 1963, no. 6:3–22.

20. Ibid.

21. Many years later, Sakharov told me that when he had concluded his remarks and was returning to his seat, he heard Lysenko whispering angrily, over and over: "Slanderers like that ought to be jailed, ought to be jailed . . ." Then—according to Tatiana N. Shcherbinovskaya—Lysenko jumped up and strode swiftly from the hall, muttering loudly enough to be heard in the gallery, "I am not guilty of Vavilov's death, not guilty, not guilty!"

22. In a conversation I had with Tamm some time later, he recalled the impression that the young Sakharov had made on him at their first encounter. Tamm felt that Sakharov did not have the makings of a good physicist. Rather, he told Sakharov, "You have a kind of humanitarian cast of mind. But," he went on, "three years later, Sakharov and I made the hydrogen bomb. How wrong I was!" Time showed, however, that Tamm was not wrong, after all: Sakharov was not only a great physicist, but he became one of the great humanists of our time as well.

23. M. Olshansky, "Against Disinformation and Slander," *Rural Life*, August 29, 1964, p. 5; emphasis in the original. Most likely, Olshansky referred to Sakharov as an "engi-

neer" rather than as a theoretical physicist in order to belittle him; the general public was unaware of Sakharov's research because it was classified. In this same article, Olshansky also impugned Efroimson's patriotism; Efroimson sent a reply to *Rural Life*, with copies to the Central Committee and other bodies, but it was not published.

24. P. Shelest, "A Long Way from Production: On the Serious Mistakes in the Work of the Botanical Institute of the Academy of Sciences of the USSR," *Rural Life*, October 2, 1965, p. 3.

25. I. Rapoport, "Chemical Mutagenesis," *Rural Life*, October 22, 1964, p. 3; V. Dudintsev, "No, the Truth Is Inviolable!" *Komsomol Pravda*, October 23, 1964, pp. 2–3; V. Kozhevnikov, "Preserve Your Honesty from Childhood," *Komsomol Pravda*, November 2, 1964, pp. 2–3; V. Gubarev, "When There Isn't Enough Tact," *Komsomol Pravda*, November 10, 1964, p. 4; N. Vorontsov, "Life Is Pressing Us: Modern Textbooks in Biology Are Needed," *Komsomol Pravda*, November 11, 1964, p. 3; V. Efroimson and R. Medvedev, "Practice Is the Criterion" (letter to the editor), *Komsomol Pravda*, November 17, 1964.

26. Oleg Pisarzhevsky, "Let the Scientists Debate," *Literary Gazette*, November 17, 1964, pp. 1–2.

27. Anatoly Agranovsky, "Science Takes Nothing on Faith," *Literary Gazette*, January 23, 1965, p. 2.

28. Two of the most forthright of these were N. N. Semyonov, "Science Does Not Tolerate Subjectivism," *Science and Life*, 1965, no. 4:38–43, 132, and M. D. Golubovsky, "On the Development of Genetics in Our Country and Scientific Truth (On the Pages of Newspapers and Magazines)," *Biology in the School* (Biologia v shkole), 1965, no. 4:86–90. But see also N. P. Dubinin, "To Conquer a Living Fortress," *Komsomol Pravda*, November 21, 1964, p. 4; D. Belyayev, "On the Basis of the Laws of Genetics," *Pravda*, November 22, 1964, p. 3; Yu. Kerkis, "What Vegetative Hybridization Is," *Literary Gazette*, March 4, 1965, and "Once More on Vegetative Hybridization," *Literary Gazette*, July 17, 1965; M. Khadzhinov, "Genetics and the Problem of Hybrid Plants," *Rural Life*, December 1, 1964; V. Mamontova, "A Good Variety Is the Basis of the Harvest," *Pravda*, January 8, 1965, p. 2; P. Zhukovsky, "On Some New Methods of Applied Genetics," *Rural Life*, November 19, 1964; B. Sokolovskaya, "What Is Not Said in the Textbook," *Teachers' Gazette* (Uchitelskaya gazeta), December 22, 1964; V. Zhdanov, "The Aim Is to Control Hereditary Variability," *Medical Gazette* (Meditsinskaya gazeta), February 2, 1965; V. Gubarev, "The Two Poles of Life," *Komsomol Pravda*, February 27, 1965; M. Popovsky, "The Right to the Truth," *Komsomol Pravda*, November 27, 1964, and "About the Honor of a Scientist," *Soviet Russia*, February 4, 1965; V. Voronov, "Concerning the Question of the Fat Content of Milk," *Rural Life*, November 25, 1964. (It is worth noting that Voronov was himself on the staff of Lysenko's Genetics Institute.)

29. A. L. Kursanov, "From Molecular Biology to Selection," *Pravda*, December 19, 1964, p. 2.

30. V. N. Soyfer, "Man Apprehends the Laws of Heredity," in D. M. Goldfarb, ed., *The Microworld of Life* (Mikromir zhizni) (Moscow: Znaniye, 1965), 124–162.

31. John Haldane, "A Scientist Departs from Life," *Overseas* (Za rubezhom), December 26, 1964, p. 22.

32. The resolution was adopted on January 19, 1965, five days after the article appeared. The membership, chosen by agreement with the USSR Ministry of Agriculture and the president of VASKhNIL, and its agenda were approved on February 18. Resolutions of the presidium of the AN SSSR no. 37–171, January 29, 2965, and no. 33–260, February 13, 1965.

33. Resolution of the presidium of the AN SSSR no. 33–260, February 13, 1965.

34. The commission's report is in *Herald of the AN SSSR*, 1965, no. 11.

35. Ibid., 21–22.

36. Ibid., 22.

37. See the materials of the February plenum of the Party Central Committee, 1964.
38. *Herald of the AN SSSR,* 1965, no. 11:73.
39. Ibid., 56.
40. Ibid., 52–53.
41. Ibid., 57.
42. Ibid., 58.
43. Ibid., 79–80.
44. Ibid., 81–82.
45. Ibid., 110–113.
46. Ibid., 121.
47. Ibid., 121–123.
48. Ibid., 124.
49. Ibid., 128.
50. The stenographic transcript of the commission's report was preserved by the presidium. Personal communication from Tatyana Shcherbinovskaya, then scientific secretary of the biology division of the AN SSSR.
51. Early in the 1970s, Lysenko was replaced as director of the Odessa institute by A. A. Sozinov. One of Sozinov's first acts was to take down the sign that showed the institute's name as the T. D. Lysenko All-Union Order of Lenin and Order of the Red Banner Plant Breeding and Genetics Institute—even though the name had not been officially changed.
52. Personal communication from a friend of Levich's, Mikhail V. Volkenshtein, a corresponding member of the AN SSSR. Many Jewish scientists began to apply for emigration permits to Israel to escape both the ordinary anti-Semitism they encountered in everyday life and the official anti-Semitism of the state, which restricted the promotion of scientists of the "Jewish nationality." To his credit, Lysenko never revealed any ethnic prejudices or personal anti-Semitism. Among his close associates were both many Jews (notably Prezent) and Armenians (Avakyan, Babadzhanyan, Varuntsyan, and others).
53. The first article to assail Sakharov appeared in 1973: Yu. Kornilov, "Provider of Slander" (Postavshik Klevety), in *Literary Gazette,* August 18, 1973. It was quickly followed by the letter that Sakharov alluded to, a letter published in *Pravda* on August 29, 1973, and signed by party members of the USSR Academy of Sciences. The signers included the Nobel Prize winners N. Basov, A. Prokhorov, N. Semyonov, I. Frank, P. Cherenkov; as well as Chief Scientist Y. Khariton, Sakharov's colleague from the secret town of "Arzamas 16"; the geneticist N. Dubinin; mathematicians M. Keldysh and A. Tikhonov; biochemists A. Braunshtein, Y. Ochinnikov, V. Engelgardt, and others. Sakharov told me in 1987 that this letter gave him great pain.
54. The other side of this coin was the reappearance of articles assailing genetics. See, for example, P. Shelest, "Remote from Production: On the Serious Shortcomings in the Work of the Botanical Institute of the Academy of Sciences of the USSR," *Rural Life,* October 2, 1965, p. 3, in which the author refers to genetics in abusive terms and casts slurs on the work of Vavilov and other scientists.
55. The copy that I have contains only four pages, though it was evidently a five-page document.
56. Quoted from Glushchenko's memoirs.
57. This information comes from a report of the meeting that was prepared by "a group of participants." A copy of this report is in my possession.
58. Personal communication from D. K. Belyayev.

Conclusion

Epigraph sources: A. A. Fet, letter to L. N. Tolstoy, in *The Works of A. Fet* (Sochinenia A. Feta) (Moscow: Izdatelstvo khudozhestvennoi literatury, 1982), 2:215; Hermann Hesse, *The Bead Game.*

1. In addition to the references in the Introduction, see Nils Roll-Hansen, "Genetics under Stalin," *Science* 227 (1985): 1329.

2. A. K. Tolstoy, "The Silver Prince: A Tale of the Times of Ivan the Terrible," in his *Collected Works in Four Volumes* (Sobraniye sochinenii v chetyryokh tomakh) (Moscow: Pravda, 1969), 2:497–498.

Note to chapter 9, p. 144ff, added in proof, February 10, 1994: I am grateful to Daniil V. Lebedev for permission to quote from his January 23, 1994, letter to me summarizing the case file of Vavilov's close colleague G. D. Karpechenko in the KGB archives (examined in October–December 1993; the archive prohibits copying the documents).

Vavilov's file—as Mark Popovsky confirmed to me by telephone on February 6, 1994—shows that on November 5, 1940, after three months of interrogation, the NKVD forced Vavilov to name additional accomplices in his "anti-Soviet activities." Employing the interrogator's stock phrases, Vavilov testified that Karpechenko was among those scientists who had pursued theoretical studies and not the practical goal of selecting new varieties of crops. Mark Popovsky and others had always assumed that Lysenko's program to exterminate genetics had brought about the arrests of Karpechenko and Govorov (on February 15, 1941) and Levitsky, Flyaksberger, Kovalev, and Maltsev (on June 28, 1941). From Karpechenko's file, however, it now appears that the investigators construed Vavilov's use of these apparently innocent phrases as evidence that Karpechenko had taken part in the larger conspiracy, "the anti-Soviet Delegation of Rightists," that Vavilov had originally "confessed" to joining. This gives greater plausibility to the hypothesis that Stalin was fabricating evidence for a show trial of a conspiracy to sabotage agriculture comparable to the Trotskyite or Bukharinite plots. The two explanations do not exclude each other, of course.

Vavilov's testimony that "earlier he had not accused Karpechenko of participating in the anti-Soviet plot, but he must now do so [because Karpechenko] had supported his program of wrecking which had diverted institutes [VIR] from the practical tasks of Soviet agriculture" gave the NKVD grounds to reopen a 1937 case against Karpechenko for anti-Soviet activities and wrecking. The arrest warrant stated that Karpechenko "had been exposed as a participant of an anti-Soviet plot" and "under the leadership of N. I. Vavilov [he] had conducted an open struggle against the vanguard methods [of scientific work] and the treasured achievements of Academician Lysenko in obtaining high crop yields." Karpechenko categorically refused to confess to any wrecking. But, apparently learning of Vavilov's testimony against him, he "at first confessed, then denied . . . participation in an anti-Soviet organization. . . . Beginning on March 7, [he] consistently held to one line: he explains his studies (goals, results), and [the interrogators] embellishes with the words—my wrecking lay in that I did not implement the new varieties." On June 25, 1941, Vavilov and Karpechenko were brought face-to-face before an interrogator. "During this personal meeting, disagreement was revealed relating to only one question: when had [Vavilov] recruited [Karpechenko] to his anti-Soviet ring?" Karpechenko insisted on 1937; Vavilov asserted it was much earlier, in 1931–1932.

The court found Karpechenko, Vavilov, Govorov, and Bondarenko guilty on July 7, 1941. Karpechenko's final declaration to the court implies that he had been tortured: "The bill of indictment submitted to me is understandable, but I cannot confess my guilt. During the preliminary deposition, I did confess to all the charges brought against me. But I made this confession under duress of the methods used during the deposition." Karpechenko's plea for mercy was denied. He was shot on July 28, 1941. (In 1955, the official notification of Karpechenko's posthumous rehabilitation falsely informed his wife that he had simply died in prison on September 17, 1942.)

Levitsky's firm denial of any participation in "the Trotskyite-Kamenevite plot" and his assertion of the practical benefits of his cytological work forced his trial to be postponed for lack of evidence; he died in the Zlatoust prison on May 20, 1942 [see N. G. Levitskaya and T. K. Lassan, "Grigorii Andreevich Levitskii: Materials for His Biography." *Cytology*, 1992, no. 8:102–125]. On September 13, 1942, Flyaksberger died in the same prison; Maltsev and Kovalev survived and were released in the mid-1950s [see D. V. Lebedev, "From the Memoirs of an Anti-Lysenkoist with a Pre-War Length of Service," in *Repressed Science* (Leningrad: Nauka Publishing House, 1991), 264–282]. In 1955, when the military prosecutor required Lysenko to explain his earlier statements against Vavilov and the other geneticists who had perished, Lysenko—clearly seeking to evade any responsibility for their arrests or deaths—argued that he and Vavilov had merely disagreed over theoretical biology–which had, he said, nothing to do with legal investigations, judicial bodies, or treasonous views.

Name Index

Subject Index

ABOUT THE AUTHOR

Valery N. Soyfer is Distinguished University Professor and Director of the Laboratory of Molecular Genetics at George Mason University. As a biology student in Moscow in the 1950s, he became friends with the geneticists who were just beginning to challenge Lysenko's sway over Soviet science. Soyfer also attended Lysenko's lectures and had many long conversations with him—a remarkable opportunity to observe Lysenko's power and charismatic charm firsthand. In the 1960s and 1970s Soyfer studied molecular mechanisms of mutagenesis and repair and discovered repair enzymes in higher plants. He has published fifteen books in Russian, English, and German. In 1980, after publicly supporting Academician Andrei Sakharov, Dr. Soyfer was stripped of his Doctor of Science degree and his post as scientific director of a scientific institute. As a jobless *refusenik* in Moscow, he used his time to interview Lysenkoists and their opponents and gained access to personal and official archives long inaccessible to scholars. The original Russian manuscript of this unique biography circulated underground in *samizdat* form and was smuggled to the West for publication. When Dr. Soyfer was unexpectedly allowed to leave the USSR in 1988, Rutgers University Press greeted him with a contract for the work. He worked closely with the press and the translators to prepare this edition in English. Dr. Soyfer's research today concentrates on molecular genetics and on the long-term consequences of environmental contamination; he is also active as a consultant on Russian scientific affairs.

About the Translators

Leo Gruliow is editor emeritus of the *Current Digest of the Post–Soviet Press*. In the course of a long career as journalist and translator, he has also been Moscow correspondent of the *Christian Science Monitor* and has translated Solzhenitsyn's *Cancer Ward* (under the pseudonym Rebecca Frank). Rebecca Gruliow is an editor and Russian translator. She studied Russian as an American high school student living in Moscow and at Bryn Mawr College.